KU-541-780

Social Work Law

Second edition

Alison Brammer

School of Law, Keele University

PEARSON
Longman

Harlow, England • London • New York • Boston • San Francisco • Toronto
Sydney • Tokyo • Singapore • Hong Kong • Seoul • Taipei • New Delhi
Cape Town • Madrid • Mexico City • Amsterdam • Munich • Paris • Milan

Pearson Education Limited

Edinburgh Gate
Harlow
Essex CM20 2JE
England

and Associated Companies throughout the world

Visit us on the World Wide Web at:
www.pearsoned.co.uk

First published 2003
Second edition published 2007

© Pearson Education Limited 2003, 2007

The right of Alison Brammer to be identified as author of this work has been
asserted by her in accordance with the Copyright, Designs and Patents Act 1988.

All rights reserved. No part of this publication may be reproduced, stored in a
retrieval system, or transmitted in any form or by any means, electronic, mechanical,
photocopying, recording or otherwise, without either the prior written permission of
the publisher or a licence permitting restricted copying in the United Kingdom issued
by the Copyright Licensing Agency Ltd, 90 Tottenham Court Road, London W1T 4LP.

All trademarks used herein are the property of their respective owners. The use of
any trademark in this text does not vest in the author or publisher any trademark
ownership rights in such trademarks, nor does the use of such trademarks imply
any affiliation with or endorsement of this book by such owners.

ISBN-13 978-1-4058-1205-4
ISBN-10 1-405-81205-2

British Library Cataloguing-in-Publication Data
A catalogue record for this book is available from the British Library

10 9 8 7 6 5 4 3 2 1
09 08 07

Typeset in 10/12.5 pt Sabon
Printed and bound in Great Britain by Ashford Colour Press, Hampshire

The publisher's policy is to use paper manufactured from sustainable forests.

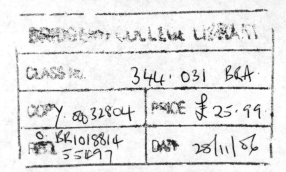

BRISTOL COLLEGE LIBRARY

CLASS No.	344.031 BRA
COPY. 0032804	PRICE £25.99
o. BR1018814 55697	DATE 28/11/06

Social Work Law

BRIDGEND COLLEGE LIBRARY
COWBRIDGE ROAD
BRIDGEND
CF31 3DF
Tel: 01656 302312
Return on or before the last date stamped below.

STATIC COPY
NOT FOR LOAN

k Law, second edition Companion Website
co.uk/brammer to find valuable **student**
cluding:

tions to help you test your understanding
uestions and answer hints to practice
nowledge
e resources on the web
ncards that allow you to check definitions
ns during revision
ary to explain legal terms
on major legal changes affecting the book

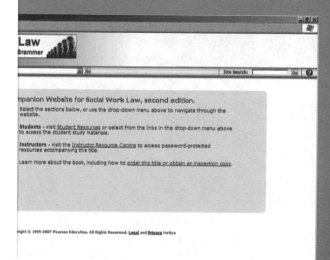

Law
Brammer

Site Search:

mpanion Website for Social Work Law, second edition.

Select the sections below, or use the drop-down menu above to navigate through the website.

Students - visit Student Resources or select from the links in the drop-down menu above to access the student study materials.

Instructors - visit the Instructor Resource Centre to access password-protected resources accompanying this title.

Learn more about the book, including how to order this title or obtain an inspection copy.

ight © 1995-2007 Pearson Education. All Rights Reserved. Legal and Privacy Notice

We work with leading authors to develop the strongest
educational materials in law, bringing cutting-edge
thinking and best learning practice to a global market.

Under a range of well-known imprints, including
Longman, we craft high quality print and electronic
publications which help readers to understand and apply
their content, whether studying or at work.

To find out more about the complete range of our
publishing, please visit us on the World Wide Web at:
www.pearsoned.co.uk

Brief contents

Contents

Part 1 Legal context of social work practice — 1

1 Introduction to law and social work practice — 3

2 Sources of law 31

3 Courts and law officers 55

4 Social workers' role in law   88

5 The Human Rights Act 1998 and social work practice   123

6 Discrimination 150

9 Child protection 245

12 Education   362

13 Youth justice   379

15 Mental health   462

16 Mental capacity   505

Supporting resources

Visit **www.pearsoned.co.uk/brammer** to find valuable online resources

Companion Website for students

- Interactive questions to help you test your understanding
- Seminar style questions and answer hints to practice applying your knowledge
- Links to valuable resources on the web
- Interactive flashcards that allow you to check definitions against key terms during revision
- An online glossary to explain legal terms
- Regular updates on major legal changes affecting the book

For instructors

- PowerPoint slides that can be downloaded and used for presentations

Also: The regularly maintained Companion Website provides the following features:

- Search tool to help locate specific items of content
- E-mail results and profile tools to send results of quizzes to instructors
- Online help and support to assist with website usage and troubleshooting

For more information please contact your local Pearson Education sales representative or visit **www.pearsoned.co.uk/brammer**

Guided tour of the book

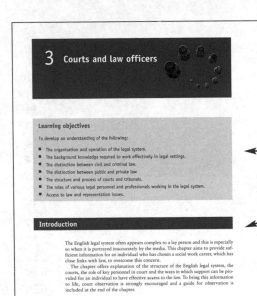

3 Courts and law officers

Learning objectives

To develop an understanding of the following:

- The organisation and operation of the legal system.
- The background knowledge required to work effectively in legal settings.
- The distinction between civil and criminal law.
- The distinction between public and private law.
- The structure and process of courts and tribunals.
- The roles of various legal personnel and professionals working in the legal system.
- Access to law and representation issues.

Introduction

The English legal system often appears complex to a lay person and this is especially so when it is portrayed inaccurately by the media. This chapter aims to provide sufficient information for an individual who has chosen a social work career, which has close links with law, to overcome this concern.

The chapter offers explanation of the structure of the English legal system, the courts, the role of key personnel in court and the ways in which support can be provided for an individual to have effective access to the law. To bring this information to life, court observation is strongly encouraged and a guide for observation is included at the end of the chapter.

55

Learning objectives at the start of each chapter identify the key points within each topic.

Chapter **introductions** concisely outline the main themes and issues, allowing you to clearly identify the most important areas.

Real **forms** are used to bring the subject to life, highlighting how the law operates in practice.

Diagrams are used to clearly explain complex legal processes.

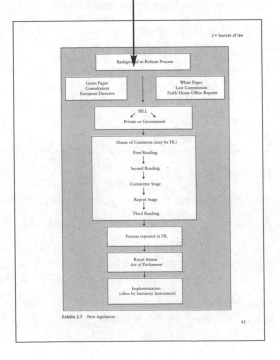

Exhibit 4.1   Sample social worker witness statement in child care case

Exhibit 2.3   New legislation

Chapter summaries provide you with an outline of the key topics to ensure that you have understood all of the essential points.

Websites listed at the end of each chapter direct you to interesting further reading on the internet.

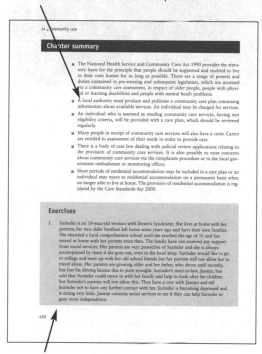

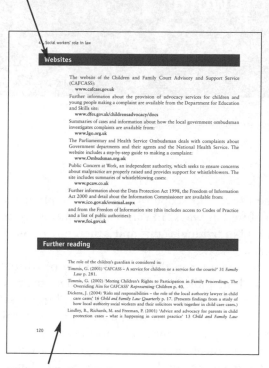

End-of-chapter **exercises** provide you with an opportunity to test your knowledge and ensure that you have understood the chapter.

Further reading sections at the end of each chapter encourage independent study, enabling you to expand and develop your knowledge.

A companion website, **www.pearsoned.co.uk/brammer**, includes regular updates on major legal changes affecting the book, links to valuable web resources, an online glossary and flashcards to test your knowledge of key terms, interactive questions, examination style questions and answer hints, chapter objectives, and PowerPoint slides for lecturers.

Visit the *Social Work Law, second edition* Companion Website at **www.pearsoned.co.uk/brammer** to find valuable **student** learning material including:

- Interactive questions to help you test your understanding
- Seminar style questions and answer hints to practice applying your knowledge
- Links to valuable resources on the web
- Interactive flashcards that allow you to check definitions against key terms during revision
- An online glossary to explain legal terms
- Regular updates on major legal changes affecting the book

Foreword

As the range and scope of this book amply demonstrates, social workers engage with the law in many different ways. In certain fundamental respects, the law provides a framework for the protection of individual rights and is therefore of huge importance in underpinning the activity of social workers.

At the time when the second edition of Alison Brammer's book is being prepared, the government and the judiciary are in conflict over the proper balance between the security of the state and the rights of certain individuals, believed to be a threat to that security. But this is only an illustration of a wider issue. In such matters, most social workers will respect and value legal provisions, seeing in them a safeguard against the abuse of power. They will also recognise that their own powers and responsibilities are, to a significant extent, derived from the law and that they cannot be immune from the checks and balances that come with it.

However these are somewhat abstract considerations and for many who are engaged in child welfare work, especially with child protection, the application of family law to their day-to-day work is far from abstract. Within this sphere, law has developed and changed quite dramatically since the principle of legalised state intervention into family life was accepted about a hundred years ago.

At the heart of such work usually lie family tensions, either between the interests of different parties within the family or between the family and external agencies, including those which employ social workers. Very often in difficult cases the social worker must engage with the law in the process of resolving these dilemmas. This is the point when anxious managers, anxious social workers and (probably anxious) local authority lawyers must debate the best course of action to recommend to the courts.

Recent research (Dickens 2006) has illustrated the complexities of these relationships. It serves to remind us that behind the actual case, lie issues of status and confidence between social workers and those involved in the judicial process. If the social worker feels 'disrespected' - why is this so? If the social worker believes that the courts are not well attuned to problems of child maltreatment of an emotional or neglectful kind – why is this so? The 'why' is not only about the facts but also about perceptions. Thus there are very important questions about relationships at the level of practice which urgently need addressing. Although at present, they most often arise in child welfare, demography and (slowly) emerging law in relation to vulnerable adults will surely throw up similar tensions. (The operation of the Mental Capacity Act 2005 will be an example).

Alison Brammer has provided for social workers, managers, students and family lawyers an invaluable resource to facilitate constructive dialogue.

This book is not for bedside reading nor for comprehensive study at 'one go'. It may be described as comprehensive reference book with an unusually reflective content.

It is beautifully organised; there are excellent indices of cases, specific laws and concise useful bibliographies and information about web sites. The reflective content enables the reader to get well behind the dry pages of the legislation itself. Each particular law is put in context and then examined by themes and issues. For some of today's students and workers the discussion of the Human Rights Act and the Mental Capacity Act 2005 will be of particular interest. These detailed discussions are preceded by chapters which examine the settings involved and also, importantly, the relationship of social work to the law.

This is the kind of material which enables the practitioners to clarify their position vis-à-vis the legal framework within which most of them operate. In this way the fear and anxiety which many experience in this sphere of work can be better managed. The book is an important contribution to the literature as a factual resource but also a balanced clarification of the complex issues involved.

Olive Stevenson
Professor Emeritus
University of Nottingham

Further Reading

Dickens J. (2006) 'Care Control and Change in Child Care Proceedings: dilemmas for social workers, managers and lawyers', *Child and Family Social Work* 11(1) 2006.

Preface

Aims

The aims of this book are to:

- Improve knowledge of law and its application to social work practice.
- Clarify legal terminology, conventions and practice and introduce basic legal skills.
- Identify the statutory responsibilities of social workers.
- Establish links between law and social work values.
- Demonstrate how law can promote good practice and empower service users whilst acknowledging the converse.
- Provide a comprehensive account of 'service user law'.
- Engage with professional and contextual issues surrounding law and social work.

The law covered in this text is specifically that which applies in England and Wales. The law applicable in Scotland and Northern Ireland is not included other than on occasion by way of comparison. Social work practice in statutory Social Services Departments forms the main focus of discussion although it is recognised that an increasing number of people in the social work profession are employed in the private and voluntary sector and where possible relevant issues relating to those areas are addressed.

Terminology

It is important to add a note on terminology at this stage. Language in law and social work practice is always changing – though not necessarily at the same pace. At times a choice had to be made between various terms and styles and a brief explanation for those choices follows.

Throughout the text the term 'service user' is employed rather than 'client'. In practice this term is now more commonly accepted as the appropriate term. The reasoning behind this preference is that reference to 'service user' is less discriminatory as it implies a more active and equal position with the social worker and emphasises that social work practice and the law deals significantly with provision of services and support and is not confined to issues of protection and control. It is the term used in current TOPSS (The Training Organisation for the Personal Social Services) documentation. It is recognised that in some particular circumstances the term may not seem appropriate to all or some of the players. For example, in child protection where a parent emphatically denies the existence of 'significant harm' yet action is taken to remove the child, that parent may not perceive herself as a service user or a client and may relate more closely to terms such as victim or adversary.

He is used throughout the text rather than s/he or they, which can appear clumsy, though more acceptable in terms of anti-discriminatory practice. The main reason for use of he is that legislation is framed in these terms, though application of the Statutory Interpretation Act 1978 means that he should be taken to refer to she also. This usage is adopted therefore for reasons of clarity and consistency.

The glossary includes explanation of a range of terms used throughout the book. Some are technical legal terms which are unavoidable and in rare cases may still be expressed in Latin. Other terms are more recent in origin and an explanation is provided of their meaning in the context of social work law. Terms included in the glossary are highlighted in bold italics the first time they appear in the text. The same applies to abbreviations used.

Approach

A few thoughts about learning the law will further explain the approach of this text.

Learning social work law is most effective as part of an approach which conforms to what Biggs (1994)[1] describes as 'the qualitative outlook'. Under this premise, students learn in a cumulative fashion through interpretation of new materials with existing knowledge and understanding. The task for teachers of social work law is thus to encourage understanding, not simply to transmit vast amounts of content which can be reproduced in a test situation without any real understanding of the subject matter or its interrelationship with other areas (the quantative outlook). The qualitative approach involves use of activities to help understanding. Elements typically present in this approach include: a positive motivational context; a high degree of learner activity, both task-related and reflective; interaction with others, at peer level and hierarchically; a well-structured knowledge base, that provides depth and breadth for conceptual development and enrichment (Biggs, 1994).

To learn a new subject it is necessary to be aware of expectations, motivation and attitudes. It is possible that some social work students feel that the study of law is imposed on them if they wish to pursue a career in social work, rather than it being a genuine choice. A few students may still consider that law has no relevance to social work and therefore have little commitment to its study. Others may grasp the aspects of law that might be interpreted as oppressive or discriminatory and see their role as fighting against law rather than embracing it as a tool to improve practice.

For some students, reluctance to study law is founded in a preconception that law is dry and boring. A response to such concerns is to encourage students to take some ownership of the study of law by incorporating it fully into their professional development as a social work practitioner. Guiding this approach, is Rogers' (1969)[2] view that significant learning takes place when the subject matter is perceived as having relevance to your own purpose.

To learn law it is necessary to spend some time on basic skills of legal research, 'the ability to find, use and apply legal source material; the ability to read cases and statutes and apply them to new or complex situations' (Kenny, 1994, p. 47)[3]. The introduction of these skills should be set against a context of an understanding of the respective roles of social workers and solicitors. In practice social workers should have access to legal advice for complex cases. The aims of studying law as a social worker should not include a desire to turn into quasi-lawyers, but having an appropriate knowledge of law and awareness of how to access the law that supports professional practice.

Before embarking on the study of law as part of a social work course, it is apposite to develop an awareness of the sensitive nature of some areas of study. It is important to acknowledge the possible existence of personal and professional experience of certain issues e.g. domestic violence, and the need to foster a 'safe' working environment.

One way to achieve this is through the development of 'ground rules' which can if necessary be revisited throughout a course of study. Ground rules might include issues such as: respect for each other's beliefs and opinions, confidentiality within the group, sharing resources, appropriate use of language, time out if appropriate, and full participation. From my experience of following this approach with groups of mature students I would support the view of Egan (1974),[4] that, 'an adult way of learning is best established when a group agrees to and respects and values each other, and that this is best achieved through a contract that establishes ground rules' (in Rowland, 2000, p. 65).

The approach taken in this text is to provide the opportunity to learn law in a way which is relevant to social work practice and develops critical analysis. Chapters therefore include, learning objectives, discussion points, signals to evaluate law, including deficiencies in current law and commentary on proposals for reform, case analysis and exercises in the form of case study discussion, as a facet of problem-based learning (Savin-Baden, 2000).[5] A limitation of case studies is that it is not usually possible to provide the amount of detail that would be available in a real situation. This can be a positive feature, however, in that it can encourage questioning and provide for a greater range of options to be considered e.g. a reference in a case study to a 'child in need' as defined by the Children Act 1989, s. 17 might prompt thought or discussion about gate-keeping, prioritisation of services, concepts of need versus protection, ethnocentric interpretations of need, medical versus social need – all issues hidden behind a seemingly straightforward legal term. The companion website will include answers to case studies and exercises.

Keeping ahead of the game – further reading, website addresses and accompanying website

Professionals working in all of the areas covered in this book need to be alert to changes in policy, legislation and case law, all of which impact on practice. Reading a textbook on social work law, however comprehensive, is unlikely to equip the social practitioner fully for the diverse situations which will be encountered. In part this is an inevitable result of the speed of changes and developments in law.

Some sections of this text have had to consider both existing law and future, as yet unimplemented, legislation or proposals for reform. In addition, the potential for challenge of existing law via the Human Rights Act 1998 should not be overlooked and its impact is considered throughout. The approach adopted therefore is to encourage and enable the reader to consider the study of law as a career-long aspect of professional development, and to achieve this to develop the skills necessary to access up to date materials and indications of future direction. Three principal features of the book support this aim.

■ Further reading

Space dictates that certain important publications, such as government policy and consultation documents, can only be referred to in brief. References are provided in further reading to encourage the reader to access the original documents and to expand and develop on the knowledge gained in the text. Certain key documents e.g. 'Framework for Assessment of Children in Need', will become an essential part of the social work 'toolkit'. The text aims to encourage a critical and reflective approach to the role of law. Published research and academic articles included in further reading support this notion and the requirement for research-based practice. This is a generic text but it is recognised that on qualification most social workers will choose an area of specialism and may wish to research that area in greater depth.

■ Website addresses

In addition to the more traditional library-based sources of information, there is a wealth of information which can be accessed via the internet. Website addresses are included at the end of each chapter. Sites are included through which significant documents such as government publications can be accessed. In addition, for each topic there are websites listed reflecting the particular issues, e.g. charitable or research-based organisations, which can provide further insight into an area.

■ Accompanying website

This text has its own accompanying website available at www.booksites.net/brammer. It will include an outline of developments since publication with references to key publications, new cases, statute implementation dates etc, which keep the reader up to date beyond the date of publication. Further discussion points are also included to build on ideas introduced in the exercises. Points arising from the case studies and answers to exercises are included and a new test bank of questions will accompany this second edition.

Outline of content

The remainder of this text is divided into three parts: the legal context of social work practice; children and families; and vulnerable adults. Criminal justice issues are dealt with in Chapter 13 regarding juvenile offenders and Chapter 18 for adults. Two additional chapters at the end of the text cover asylum law and welfare. Both areas are relevant to each of the three parts of the text but have been positioned at the close of vulnerable adults as it is arguable that asylum seekers and people who are homeless have a vulnerability. There have been significant changes within social work law since publication of the first edition and these are reflected in the updated second edition. Some particular points deserve a mention. Chapter 1 commences with an overview of the new framework for qualification for social workers and expectations as to legal competence. The importance of the Human Rights Act 1998 is signified by fuller discussion of this area in a chapter of its own. The chapter on discrimination has moved to the first section, 'Legal Context of Social Work Practice, as issues of discrimination and oppression are relevant to areas addressed in all the subsequent chapters. Major new pieces of legislation have prompted new chapters on Adoption and Mental Capacity and the growing significance of education law for social workers is addressed in a separate chapter. Finally, as matters which many service users experience, a new chapter on Welfare and Homelessness is included.

Whilst I hope the views in this chapter are persuasive and coherent, ultimately they are expressed by a lawyer. Accordingly, a summary of feedback follows from two exercises carried out with Social Work students.

■ Why study law?

- relevant to ALL areas of practice
- avoid litigation
- social workers operate within tight guidelines which are dictated by law
- know powers within law and limitations
- understand nature of state's role in protection
- understand clients/service-users' rights and lack of rights – enables empowerment
- advocacy
- defines boundaries of how citizens should behave – controlling side of care and control
- law protects client group and social workers

- social workers need a good working knowledge of the legal system, e.g. access to services
- to fulfil obligations to service users/clients
- to challenge unfair discrimination
- to influence and shape legal systems
- to guard against personal litigation
- social workers work in partnership with other professionals and agencies which are dominated by the legal framework – to know professional boundaries
- because it's interesting!

What are the barriers to use and understanding of the law?

- rigidity
- jargon, language and terminology
- format
- continuous change in some areas, lack of change in others
- contradictory content
- not accessible
- inconsiderate to victim
- subject to interpretation
- discriminatory
- elitist
- tradition, e.g. dress etc. in court setting
- time – adjournments etc.
- too generic
- lack of time and resources to learn
- politics influences changes in law.

The author has endeavoured to explain the law as at 1 April 2006 and some developments thereafter are included. Updates on the many areas of Social Work Law which are the subject of reform proposals and developing case law will feature on the accompanying website at www.booksites.net/brammer.

Notes

1. J.Biggs (1994) 'Student Learning Research and Theory: where Do We currently Stand?', in J, Gibbs (ed.) *Improving Student Learning*. Oxford: The Oxford centre for staff Development.

2. C. Rogers (1969) *Freedom To Learn*. Merrill.

3. P. Kenny (1994) *Studying Law*. London. Butterworths,

4. Egan, cited in S. Rowland (2000) *The Enquiring University Teacher*. The Society for Research into Higher Education / Open University Press, p. 65.

5. M. Savln-Baden (2000) *Problem - based Learning in Higher Education, Untold Stories*. Oxford: Oxford University Press.

Acknowledgements

On a personal note, thanks are due to the many people whose support made this second edition possible.

I am grateful to all at Pearson for their efficiency, guidance and good-natured support.

The experience of teaching law to non-law students prompted this text originally. I continue to be indebted to students (past and present) of the Keele University MA in Social Work, the new Social Work Degree and the MA Child Care Law and Practice, together with the practitioners I meet at training events around the country, for their enthusiasm, commitment and insight and experience of the practical application of law. I'd like to thank colleagues at Keele for their encouragement and to Jane Boylan, Andrew Dunning and Rita Langton who read chapters and provided helpful comments. Kelvin Johnstone revised and updated the section on education from the first edition into a chapter of its own. Thank you Kelvin for that contribution and for your continuing support.

My greatest thanks must go to friends and family, especially my parents and Marcie, for their support, tolerance and encouragement throughout the writing process.

Finally, special thanks and dedication to my wonderful family: Lawrence, a star on and off the pitch; Faith, for those Einaudi moments, Eliot, keep on strumming and Dave and Rosa, keep on running.

■ Publisher's acknowledgements

We are grateful to the following for permission to reproduce copyright material:

Exhibit 2.2 from *Children Act 1989, Chapter 41,* is reproduced under the terms of Crown Copyright Policy Guidance issued by HMSO; Exhibit 3.3 copyright of and reproduced by kind permission of the Legal Services Commission, London, UK – www.legalservices.gov.uk; Exhibit 7.1 from *Adoption: a new approach, Cm 5017,* Secretary of State for Health, 2000. Crown copyright material is reproduced under Class Licence Number C01W0000039 with the permission of the Controller of HMSO and the Queen's Printer for Scotland; Exhibit 7.3 from *The Framework for*

Assessment of Children in Need and their Families; © HMSO, Crown copyright material is reproduced with the permission of the Controller of HMSO and the Queen's Printer for Scotland; Exhibit 9.1 from *NSPCC Policy Practice Research Series: Assessing Risk in Child Protection,* © NSPCC 1998, reproduced with permission of NSPCC (Cleaver, H., Wattam, C. and Cawson, P. 1998); Exhibits 18.1 reproduced with permission of West Mercia Police Authority; Exhibit 18.3 reproduced with permission of The Magistrates' Association, © The Magistrates' Association. In some instances we have been unable to trace the owners of copyright material, and we would appreciate any information that would enable us to do so.

Table of cases

Table of legislation

Table of Statutory Instruments

List of abbreviations

AA	Adoption Act 1976
ACA	Adoption and Children Act 2004
ACPC	Area Child Protection Committee
AIA	Asylum and Immigration Act 2004
ASBO	Anti Social Behaviour Order
ASW	Approved Social Worker
CA 1989	Children Act 1989
CA 2004	Children Act 2004
CAF	Common Assessment Framework
CAFCASS	Children and Family Court Advisory and Support Service
CAMHS	Child and Adult Mental Health Services
CAO	Child Assessment Order
CCRC	Criminal Cases Review Commission
CDA	Crime and Disorder Act 1998
CDCA	Carers and Disabled Children Act 2000
CDS	Criminal Defence Service
CEOA	Carers (Equal Opportunities) Act 2004
CHAI	Commission for Healthcare Audit
C(LC)A	Children (Leaving Care) Act 2000
CPS	Crown Prosecution Service
CRE	Commission for Racial Equality
CRO	Community Responsible Officer
CRS	Complaints Review Service
C(RS)A	Carers (Recognition and Services) Act 1995
CSA	Care Standards Act 2000
CSCI	Commission for Social Care Inspection
CSDPA	Chronically Sick and Disabled Persons Act 1970
DDA	Disability Discrimination Act 1995
DES	Department for Education and Skills
DfES	Department for Education and Skills
DPA	Data Protection Act 1998
DPP	Director of Public Prosecutions
DP(SCR)A	Disabled Persons (Services, Consultation and Representation Act) 1986

DRC	Disability Rights Commission
DVCVA	Domestic Violence Crime and Victims Act 2004
DWP	Department for Work and Pensions
EA	Education Act 1996
ECHR	European Court of Human Rights
ECHR	European Convention on Human Rights
ECT	Electro Convulsive Therapy
EOC	Equal Opportunities Commission
EPA	Enduring Power of Attorney
EPO	Emergency Protection Order
ERA	Employment Rights Act 1996
EWO	Education Welfare Officer
GSCC	General Social Care Council
FLA	Family Law Act 1996
HA	Housing Act 1996
HASSASSAA	Health and Social Services and Social Security Adjudications Act 1983
HRA	Human Rights Act 1998
HSPHA	Health Service and Public Health Act 1968
IAA	Immigration and Asylum Act 1999
IEP	Individual Education Plan
IMCA	Independent Medical Capacity Advocate
ISSP	Intensive supervision and surveillance programme
LASSA	Local Authority Social Services Act 1970
LEA	Local Education Authority
LPA	Lasting Power of Attorney
LSCB	Local Safeguarding Children Boards
MCA	Mental Capacity Act 2005
MHA	Mental Health Act 1983
MHRT	Mental Health Review Tribunal
NAA	National Assistance Act 1948
NASS	National Asylum Support Service
NHSA	National Health Service Act 1977
NHSCCA	National Health Service and Community Care Act 1990
NIAA	Nationality, Immigration and Asylum Act 2002
NR	Nearest Relative
NSF	National Service Framework
PACE	Police and Criminal Evidence Act 1984
PCA	Protection of Children Act 1999
PCCA	Protection of Children Act index
PCC(S)A	Powers of Criminal Courts (Sentencing) Act 2000
POVA	Protection of Vulnerable Adults
PSPD	People with Severe Personality Disorders

RMO	Responsible Medical Officer
RRA	Race Relations Act 1976
RR(A)A	Race Relations (Amendments) Act 2000
SAO	School Attendance Order
SEN	Special Educational Needs
SENCO	Special Educational Needs Coordinator
SENDA	Special Educational Needs and Disability Act 2001
SI	Statutory Instrument
SOA	Sexual Offences Act 2003
SSFA	School Standards and Framework Act 1998
YJCEA	Youth Justice and Criminal Evidence Act 1999
YOP	Youth Offending Panel
YOT	Youth Offending Team

Law Reports

AC	Appeal cases
All ER	All England Law Reports
CCLR	Community Care Law Reports
Ch	Chancery Division
ECHR	European Court of Human Rights
Fam	Family Division
FCR	Family Court Reporter
FLR	Family Law Reports
QB	Queen's Bench Division
TLR	Times Law Reports
WLR	Weekly Law Reports

Journals

BJSW	British Journal of Social Work
CC	Community Care
CFLQ	Child and Family Law Quarterly
Crim LR	Criminal Law Review
DCLD	Discrimination Case Law Digest
Fam Law	Family Law
JCL	Journal of Child Law
JSWFL	Journal of Social Welfare and Family Law
LAG	Legal Action Group Bulletin
LS	Legal Studies
MLR	Modern Law Review
NLJ	New Law Journal
SJ	Solicitors Journal

Legal context of social work practice

Chapters:

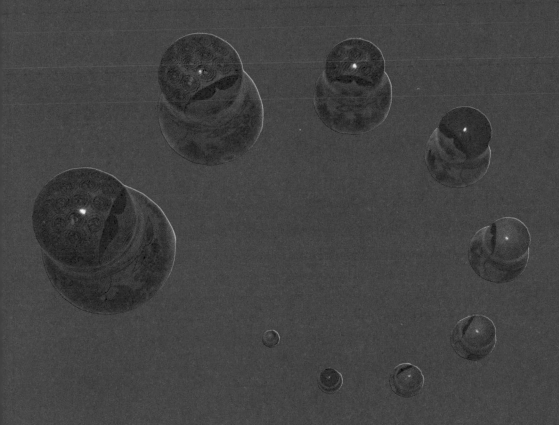

1 Introduction to law and social work practice

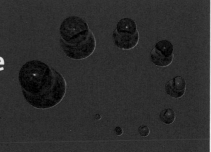

Learning objectives

To develop an understanding of the following:

- The legal framework that regulates social work.
- The framework for qualification as a social worker.
- Regulation of social work.
- The role of law in countering discrimination.
- Incorporating an anti-oppressive and anti-discriminatory practice perspective into the study of law.
- The relationship between law and social work practice.
- The skills and knowledge required to work effectively with the law.
- An appreciation of the limitations of law.
- Values which influence social work practice and their link to the law.

Introduction

In this introductory chapter the relationship between law and social work practice and reasons for the study of law are examined. The discussion begins with consideration of why law has become more prominent in social work education and practice, supported by reference to the new framework for social work education. Relevant sections of the Local Authority and Social Services Act 1970 are outlined as the major legal framework that establishes Social Services Departments, with relevant additions from the Children Act 2004. A summary of key legislation relevant to social work practice demonstrates further the dominance of law. The chapter continues with explanation of some of the key legal concepts for social work practice: confidentiality; accountability; rights, duties and powers; and the introduction of key values – partnership, choice, empowerment, anti-discriminatory and anti-oppressive practice – and the extent to which these values are supported by the law.

Relationship between law and practice

The relationship between law and social work practice and the place of law as an element in taught social work programmes continues to be the subject of ongoing debate. Polarised views have developed. Both positions on the relationship between law and social work practice are encapsulated in the following quote:

> Deciding when to invoke the law is not a simple matter. Both Blom-Cooper's (1998) view that the law is the beginning and the finish of any action, and Stevenson's belief that an ethical duty of care is the mainspring of social work action, distort by over-simplification the reality of practice. Competence in practice, requires both an acknowledgement of the relevance and applicability of the law and also assessment skills inspired by social work values, theoretical knowledge and practice wisdom.[1]

Law clearly plays an important role in social work practice today. Substantial legislation has been passed in recent years, which has a profound effect on social work practice, notably the Children Acts of 1989 and 2004, the National Health Service and Community Care Act 1990, the Crime and Disorder Act 1998 and the Adoption and Children Act 2002. The understanding of law underpins and provides duties and powers for social work and understanding the statutory and legal requirements is essential for effective and fair social work practice. Nevertheless, research has found that social workers were uneasy about acting as statutory agents.[2] Furthermore, Jones *et al.* found that social workers became stressed when their work brought them into the sphere of law, believing they were considered as having limited credence and status in that field.[3] Recent evidence in a SCIE review suggests continuing unease, '. . . social work students and practitioners experience contact with the law and legal system as stressful'.[4]

Clearly it is not sufficient for instruction concerning pieces of legislation relevant to social work practice, such as the Children Act 1989, to be delivered without reference to contemporary social work practice and the incorporation of social work values relating to oppression, service users' rights and discrimination. Good social work practice is of much greater complexity than simply executing prescribed duties under legislation. Questions of interpretation and application of legislation are not confined to lawyers. The law attempts to balance apparently conflicting principles and practices which must be applied by social workers and key legal judgments have dealt with the relationship between the law and social work practice. For example, in R v. *Gloucestershire County Council, ex parte Barry* [1997] 2 All ER 1, a rather confused picture emerged over the extent to which social workers, in exercising a duty to assess disabled people for support services, can take a local authority's resources into account. Another decision made it clear that where legal remedies are available they must be applied proportionately, as in where a supervision order was made, as a proportionate response to the circumstances of the case rather than the care order applied for: *Re O (A Child) (Supervision Order: Future Harm)* [2001] EWCA Civ 16. Inappropriate use of legal powers is potentially dangerous and has proved damaging to the social work profession in the past.

Preston-Shoot *et al.* (1998) argue that the role of law now has a 'centrality, pre-eminence . . . within social work practice'.[5] Even so, it is also true that neither child abuse nor delinquency or other social problems that social workers encounter can simply be legislated away. The effective teaching and learning of social work law must acknowledge the relevance and application of law but that needs to be set against a context of social work values and practice skills. Taking this approach, it is argued that a new academic discipline has emerged, that of 'social work law'.[6]

In the mid-1980s there was significant media interest in social work, with particular emphasis on social workers' apparent lack of knowledge of law and legal procedures arising from a number of significant child abuse inquiry reports. Following these tragedies, research emerged which critically confirmed a deficiency within practitioners to identify and observe legal duties and positively to use available legal powers.[7] Rules and Requirements for the DipSW were published in 1995 (replaced by the new framework – see below) and stated that: 'Students must be required to demonstrate through formal written assessment their understanding and application of the legislation relating to social work in the country in which they train' (para. 3.4.2). CCETSW[8] produced Rules and Requirements relating to legal knowledge (set out as background information at note 9).[9] It is clear then that there has been an expectation for some time that, to be legally competent, a social worker must be able to apply relevant law to factual situations and not simply regurgitate its provisions in the abstract. Knowing which action a social worker might take in response to an emergency, or how a social worker might present materials to a court, requires understanding of the relationship between law and social work practice. Understanding and application of law in social work practice is now addressed within the new framework for social work qualification.

■ The qualifying framework

The current social work qualification, a degree in social work, was introduced in September 2003 as an aspect of the Department of Health's objectives to raise the profile and status of the profession. It replaced the Diploma in Social Work. Masters level qualifications in social work are also available at many academic institutions. The degree incorporates an emphasis on practical application of skills and knowledge, including legally based skills and knowledge. To support this, students spend a minimum of 200 days in practice and, where possible, the expertise of service users and carers are actively involved in shaping and delivering degree programmes.

The teaching, learning and assessment curriculum for the new degree (incorporating law teaching) is provided through three key sources:

∎ The Requirements for Social Work Training (DH).[10]
∎ Topss National Occupational Standards for Social Work.[11]
∎ Quality Assurance Agency Subject Benchmark Statement.[12]

It will be necessary to become familiar with these requirements in their entirety during the qualification process and to be continually aware of the requirements as they inform practice. Here, the focus is on how these requirements impact on social work and the law, and on identifying those requirements of most obvious application.

∎ The Requirements for Social Work Training (DH, 2002)

As part of the social work degree, the DH requirements stipulate that students must have experience: in at least two practice settings; of statutory social work tasks involving legal interventions; of providing services to at least two user groups (e.g. child care and mental health). Programme providers are also required to demonstrate that students undertake specific learning and assessment in key areas, such as: assessment planning intervention and review; partnership working and information sharing across professional disciplines and agencies; and law.

∎ National Occupational Standards

Topss, the Social care workforce strategy body (England), which produced National Occupational Standards for Social Work, became *Skills for Care* in April 2005. The focus of Skills for Care is primarily concerned with adult social care, and the new Children's Workforce Development Council will focus on the strategy for the children's services workforce. The National Occupational Standards for Social Work are organised around areas of competence, or key roles of social workers. For each of the key roles, there is a requirement to 'understand, critically analyse, evaluate, and apply . . . knowledge' of the legal, social, economic and ecological context of social work practice, country, UK, EU legislation, statutory codes, standards, frameworks and guidance relevant to social work practice and related fields, including multi-disciplinary and multi-organisational practice, data protection and confidentiality of information.

The key roles are:

Key role 1: Prepare for, and work with individuals, families, carers, groups and communities to assess their needs and circumstances

Key Role 2: Plan, carry out, review and evaluate social work practice, with individuals, families, carers, groups, communities and other professionals

Key Role 3: Support individuals to represent their needs, views and circumstances

Key Role 4: Manage risk to individuals, families, carers, groups, communities, self and colleagues

Key Role 5: Manage and be accountable, with supervision and support, for your own social work practice within your organisation

Key Role 6: Demonstrate professional competence in social work practice.

■ QAA benchmarks

Students will be expected to demonstrate knowledge before award of a degree, which is to include:

The significance of legislative and legal frameworks and service delivery statements (including the nature of legal authority, the application of legislation in practice, statutory accountability and tensions between statute, policy and practice). The current range and appropriateness of statutory, voluntary and private agencies providing community-based, day-care, residential and other services and the organizational systems inherent within these. The significance of interrelationships with other social services, especially education, housing, health, income maintenance and criminal justice.

The complex relationships between justice, care and control in social welfare and the practical and ethical implications of these, including roles as statutory agents and in upholding the law in respect of discrimination.

In summary, the study of law as part of a social work programme can be broken down into three component parts:

1. As a structure within which social workers must practise, in many cases giving evidence in court or providing reports for court. Awareness of court procedures and the roles of others within the justice system may help to ease the anxiety and unease which often accompanies this area of practice and make contact with legal advisers and others in the legal process more effective. Working knowledge of the court system will also enable a social worker to advise and provide support to a service user facing court proceedings.

2. Law as the instrument which gives social workers licence to practise through legal powers, duties and limitations, e.g. the duty to investigate suspicion of abuse, the power to provide support services. An understanding of how law develops and the various sources of law, policy and procedure, and accountability.

3. The need to have an understanding of legal issues which service users may face even though there may not be a direct social work responsibility involved in the issue, e.g. legal remedies for domestic violence.

■ Regulation of social work

Under the Care Standards Act 2000 (CSA), responsibility for training and regulation of social workers has been vested in the General Social Care Council (GSCC). (The GSCC took over the function of professional social work education and training from CCETSW.)

The role of the GSCC is described as 'the guardian of standards for the social care workforce', its aim being to increase protection of service users, their carers and the general public. A key role for the Council is regulation of qualifying and post-qualifying training in social work. Codes of practice for social care workers and their employers have been developed by the Council. The CSA 2000 provides a registration requirement for social workers (included in the term 'social care workers' under the Act) to register with the GSCC (s. 56). The ultimate aim of the Council is for all individuals engaged in social care work (currently approximately 1 million) to be registered. In practical terms, registration requirements are being phased in over a period of time and linked to the provision of training programmes which enable individuals engaged in social care to acquire relevant qualifications (as approximately 80 per cent of the workforce has no relevant qualification). The first category to be required to register are qualified and student social workers. Social workers make up around 14 per cent of the social care workforce. The requirement for registration under the CSA 2000 applies to: anyone engaged in relevant social work; a person who is employed in or manages a children's home, care home or residential family centre; a domiciliary care agency; fostering agency or voluntary adoption agency; a person from a domiciliary care agency who provides personal care in an individual's own home (s. 55).[13]

It is possible for a person to be removed from the register under s.59, and there is a right of appeal against removal under s.68 to the Care Standards Tribunal. This process and its relation to the Protection of Children Act list (see further in Chapter 9) was considered by the Care Standards Tribunal in *Arthurworrey* v. *Secretary of State for Education and Skills* [2004] EWCST 268 (PC). The applicant, Lisa Arthurworrey, was employed as a social worker by Haringey Council and was allocated the case of Victoria Climbié in 1999. She subsequently gave evidence at the public inquiry into Victoria's death. Following an internal review panel Part 8 inquiry at Haringey, she was suspended from duty and the Council referred her to the Protection of Children Act list. She successfully appealed against inclusion on the list and her name was removed from the list. The tribunal had to consider whether, under the Protection of Children Act 1999, she was, guilty of misconduct that harmed a child or placed a child at risk of harm, and unsuitable to work with children (s.4(3) **PCA** 1999). Misconduct can include omissions. The 11 particulars of misconduct presented to the tribunal included: failure to conduct a proper interview with Ms Kouao (Victoria's aunt); failure to complete all the tasks required of her and identified at a strategy meeting; and failure to make contact or to take adequate steps to make contact with Victoria.

The tribunal considered the definition of misconduct and noted the need to consider the context in which the individual was working, including levels of support and supervision. In considering whether her actions amounted to misconduct, the tribunal considered five factors which were relevant to all of the allegations: experience, training, the complexity of the case, the question of supervision, and the office environment.

The tribunal found no misconduct and whilst as a result it did not have to decide on suitability to work with children, it commented that Ms Arthurworrey was a suitable person to work with children, describing her as a 'straightforward and caring individual who has fully acknowledged the mistakes she made in connection with this case'.

As to the use of **POCA**, the tribunal made it clear that to list an individual for 'professional mistakes should be an unusual occurrence, to be used only in the most clear cut cases'. It suggested that the procedure to remove an individual from the General Social Care Council register is the preferable route in cases of mistakes and poor professional practice. The concluding comments of the tribunal were: 'The message that we wish to make beyond the particular case that we have been considering is that Government must ensure that social workers are better trained, better resourced, and better supervised. In this way, it is hoped that the tragedy of Victoria will not be repeated.'

Protection of title

It is an offence for a person to use the title 'social worker' or imply that he is a qualified social worker if he is not registered with the General Social Care Council (s. 61 CSA).

▪ Legal framework of social work

The statutory context of social work is provided by the Local Authority Social Services Act 1970 (**LASSA**) (as amended) and a summary of the main provisions is a useful reference point.

Section 1 establishes the authorities which have social services functions as county councils, metropolitan and London Boroughs and unitary authorities, but not district councils.

Sections 2–5 of the LASSA are repealed by the Children Act 2004 to give effect to the organisational changes introduced following recommendations in the Climbié report.

Personnel requirements specified by the LASSA are amended by the Children Act 2004. The duty to appoint a Director of Social Services is removed and replaced by a requirement to appoint a Director of Children's Services for each children's services authority, and a Director of Adult Social Services. The Director of Children's Services is appointed for the purpose of prescribed functions including those exercisable by the LEA: social services that relate to children; children leaving local authority care; the Children's services authority for cooperation, safeguarding and promoting the welfare of children and information databases; any health services for children that are transferred to the local authority. Guidance has been published on the 'Role and Responsibilities of the Director of Children's Services'.

Adequacy of staffing levels is a matter for debate in the current climate of under-resourced local authorities, increasing responsibilities of social services and heavy caseloads carried by individual social workers. It would not be surprising to see this issue raised via judicial review proceedings or as an aspect of a human rights challenge. Whilst 'adequacy' is a difficult term to define, extreme staff shortages, excessive caseloads and unallocated cases would be difficult to defend. *R. v. Hereford and Worcester County Council, ex parte Chandler* (1992) (unreported) was a case where leave for judicial review was granted, one of the grounds being that C had not received the one-to-one service he required because the authority had inadequate staff in breach of its s. 6 duty. The case was settled before hearing by providing the service and compensation.[14]

Section 7 of LASSA 1970 contains a number of important provisions. It provides for the Secretary of State to produce directions for the exercise of social services functions (discussed further in Chapter 2); establishes complaints procedures (discussed further in Chapter 4); contains the power for the Secretary of State to require an inquiry into social services functions (discussed in Chapter 9); and provides for the default powers of the Secretary of State (see Chapter 4). The LASSA 1970 also contains a list in Sch. 1 (updated regularly) of the permitted actions or functions of social services authorities.

▪ Summary of key legislation impacting on social work practice and defining service user groups

General

> Equal Pay Act 1970
>
> Local Authority Social Services Act 1970
>
> Local Government Act 1972
>
> Sex Discrimination Act 1975
>
> Race Relations Act 1976
>
> Interpretation Act 1978
>
> Disability Discrimination Act 1995
>
> Housing Act 1996
>
> Data Protection Act 1998
>
> Human Rights Act 1998
>
> Access to Justice Act 1999
>
> Immigration and Asylum Act 1999
>
> Public Interest Disclosure Act 1999
>
> Freedom of Information Act 2000
>
> Race Relations (Amendment) Act 2000
>
> Nationality, Immigration and Asylum Act 2002
>
> Homelessness Act 2002
>
> Housing Act 2004
>
> Civil Partnership Act 2004
>
> Gender Recognition Act 2004
>
> Domestic Violence Crime and Victims Act 2004

Legislation relating to children and young persons

> Children and Young Persons Acts 1963 and 1969
>
> Family Law Reform Act 1969

Child Abduction Act 1984

Children Act 1989

Human Fertilisation and Embryology Act 1990

Child Support Act 1991

Education Act 1996

Family Law Act 1996

Protection of Children Act 1999

Children (Leaving Care) Act 2000

Special Educational Needs and Disability Act 2001

Adoption and Children Act 2002

Children Act 2004

Legislation relating to adults' services

National Assistance Act 1948

National Assistance (Amendment) Act 1951

Health Services and Public Health Act 1968

Chronically Sick and Disabled Persons Act 1970

National Health Service Act 1977

Mental Health Act 1983

Enduring Powers of Attorney Act 1985

Disabled Persons (Services, Consultation and Representation) Act 1986

National Health Service and Community Care Act 1990

Carers (Recognition and Services) Act 1995

Disability Discrimination Act 1995

Community Care (Direct Payments) Act 1996

Care Standards Act 2000

Carers and Disabled Children Act 2000

Carers (Equal Opportunities) Act 2004

Mental Capacity Act 2005

Criminal justice legislation

Bail Act 1976

Police and Criminal Evidence Act 1984

Public Order Act 1986

Criminal Justice Act 1991

Probation Service Act 1993

Criminal Justice and Public Order Act 1994

Sex Offenders Act 1997

Protection from Harassment Act 1997

Crime and Disorder Act 1998

Youth Justice and Criminal Evidence Act 1999

Criminal Justice and Court Services Act 2000

Powers of Criminal Courts (Sentencing) Act 2000

Sexual Offences Act 2003

Anti-social Behaviour Act 2003

The above summary does not include *all* legislation which a social worker may encounter in everyday practice. It is, however, a selection of some of the more important pieces of legislation that directly impact on social work practice. There are also areas of overlap as some pieces of legislation could apply, for example, to children and adults, e.g. the Chronically Sick and Disabled Persons Act 1970, though it tends to be associated more with adult service users. The Local Authority Social Services Act 1970, Sch. 1 contains a comprehensive list of enactments conferring functions assigned to social services committees.

▪ Limitations of law

Whilst accepting that law shapes social work practice and provides social workers with powers and duties, it is also necessary to appreciate the limitations of the law.

- ▪ Law will not always provide clear direction – rather it sets boundaries for practice, and there is often a huge discretion on ways to practise within those limits (this may also be seen as an advantage).
- ▪ Particular provisions are often open to interpretation and may appear unclear. Sometimes it is necessary to 'wait and see' until case law clarification is produced, e.g. case law on meaning of 'significant harm'.
- ▪ Discrete laws may appear to be in conflict with each other.
- ▪ Law may not keep pace with practice developments, e.g. greater openness in adoption was not anticipated in the Adoption Act 1976, but the need to consider contact has been incorporated into the Adoption and Children Act 2002
- ▪ Legal language may not be updated to reflect terms adopted in practice.
- ▪ There are gaps in the law. An example of this is the lack of a legislative duty to investigate and powers to intervene in adult protection.
- ▪ Law may not help a social worker decide when to act; that may be a matter of risk assessment.
- ▪ Law may appear to be discriminatory itself, e.g. restriction on voting rights for detained patients under the Mental Health Act 1983, or may be applied in a discriminatory fashion, e.g. police discretion to stop and search exercised disproportionately to include high numbers of young black men.[15]

- Law is reactive rather than proactive – with the exception perhaps of the Human Rights Act 1998, English law tends to react to situations that have occurred, by punishing or providing a remedy, rather than setting out codes of behaviour.

- The law can seem to be a bureaucratic machine, concerned more with processing forms accurately and following procedures than dealing with the central issue in a case. This approach is partly due to the need to follow principles of natural justice and for justice to be seen to be done.

Key legal concepts

▪ Confidentiality

An important source for social workers faced with ethical dilemmas is the 'Code of Ethics for Social Work' adopted by the British Association of Social Workers.[16] In the principles of practice, the Code provides the following guidance on sharing information:

> The social worker recognises that information clearly entrusted for one purpose should not be used for another purpose without sanction. The social worker respects the privacy of clients . . . and confidential information about clients gained in relationship with them or others. The social worker will divulge such information only with the consent of the client (or informant) except where there is clear evidence of serious danger to the client, worker, other persons or the community, or in other circumstances, judged exceptional, on the basis of professional consideration and consultation.

Confidentiality is also addressed in the GSCC Code of Practice as an aspect of the requirement for social care workers to 'strive to establish and maintain the trust and confidence of service users and carers'. In particular, this includes: 'Respecting confidential information and clearly explaining agency policies about confidentiality to service users and carers.'

As a starting point in any discussion on confidentiality the social worker can draw guidance from the above statements. It is clear that a presumption of confidentiality of information surrounds much of the work of a social worker but also that there are exceptions which will displace the presumption. Without any principle of confidentiality the extent to which individuals would be prepared to share sensitive and private information would be limited, frustrating the objectives of many areas of social work. An absolute guarantee of confidentiality should never be given to a service user, however, as there are circumstances where the law and good practice require information to be shared. A further qualification is necessary here in that, where it becomes apparent that information of a confidential nature needs to be shared, this should be carried out with sensitivity and limited to the minimum number of people/agencies necessary. In many situations, if information needs to be shared, the first step will be to ask for permission from the service user or other person who provided the information. As any duty of confidentiality is owed to that person, then once consent is obtained, assuming the individual has the capacity to consent, there should be no concerns about breach of confidentiality provided the information is disclosed in an appropriate way. For example, permission to disclose information to another professional would not justify disclosure to the press. The legal basis which supports confidentiality and is relied upon to justify non disclosure is 'public interest immunity'. For example, in an early case, *D v. NSPCC* [1978] AC 171, the House of Lords ruled that the identity of someone who had alleged a child had suffered abuse could not be revealed to the child's parents. The information was immune from disclosure.

It may not be possible to maintain confidentiality in the following circumstances.

Statutory duty

Under a limited number of pieces of legislation there is a statutory duty to disclose information. Currently, relevant statutes are the Prevention of Terrorism Act 2005, the Public Health Acts, the Road Traffic Acts, the Misuse of Drugs Act 1971 and the Police and Criminal Evidence Act 1984 (**PACE**). The relevant legislation applies to very specific circumstances and it would be appropriate to obtain legal advice before disclosing on this basis.

Crime and Disorder Act 1998

This legislation is dealt with separately because it contains a section which gives permission for disclosure but does not contain a duty to disclose. Section 115 provides that:

s. 115

(1) Any person who, apart from this subsection, would not have power to disclose information–
   (a) to a relevant authority; or
   (b) to a person acting on behalf of such an authority,
   shall have power to do so in any case where the disclosure is necessary or expedient for the purposes of any provision of this Act.

(CDA 1998)

Relevant authority includes the police, health authorities, probation and other local authorities.

Interest of the subject

Professionals will often have to share information about an individual in the best interests of that person. This is at the heart of multi-disciplinary work and is supported by a number of official documents. For example, 'Working Together' (1999)[17] states in the section on sharing information: 'Where there are concerns that a child is, or may be at risk of significant harm, however, the needs of that child must come first. In these circumstances the overriding objective must be to safeguard the child' (para. 7.28). 'Professionals can only work together to safeguard children if there is an exchange of relevant information between them' (para. 7.29) (see also *Re G (a minor)* [1996] 2 All ER 65). The emphasis must be on sharing relevant information with appropriate professionals who are likely to work with or have an interest in, for example, the protection of a child. The same principle can be applied to the conduct of a child protection conference. 'Working Together' also advises that 'Effective collaboration requires organisations and people to be clear about . . . the protocols and procedures to be followed, including the way in which information will be shared across professional boundaries and within agencies, and be recorded' (para 5.2).

Information sharing under the Children Act 2004

The Children Act 2004 provides some clarification on information sharing between professionals working with children. Information databases are being established under s. 12 in order to support professionals carrying out their duties to cooperate and safeguard and promote the welfare of children. The information that will be held on the database is prescribed by the Act and includes basic identifying information about the child, an identification number, names and contact details for parents/carers, and contact information about providers of key services, e.g. health and education and the lead professional for the child (if appointed). The database will not include case information or assessment details. It is intended to provide a speedy mechanism for professionals involved with a child to locate each other and share relevant information. Information sharing trials are ongoing (by authorities referred to as Information sharing and assessment trailblazers) and all areas are expected to have developed Information Sharing Indexes by 2008.

Cross-government guidance, 'Information Sharing: Practitioner's Guide' has been published (2006) and aims to provide some clarification of this difficult area. The guidance will include: principles of information sharing; core guidance on sharing information including a checklist and flowchart, good practice illustrations and further guidance on legal issues.

Public interest

There may be occasions where the public interest outweighs the subject's interest in maintaining confidentiality, especially where there is a real threat of harm to others. It is a balancing exercise. In *W* v. *Egdell* [1989] 1 All ER 1089, a psychiatric report was disclosed to the Home Secretary on the basis that the public interest in the appropriate authorities being made aware of the 'dangerousness' of a patient outweighed the duty of confidence to the patient.

Court order

The need for justice in every case that reaches court provides the public interest to justify disclosure of confidential material in court proceedings. There is a duty to provide all relevant information to the court (whether or not it supports the social worker's argument). Rules of disclosure also mean that most relevant information, including statements, will be exchanged by the parties prior to the hearing. Information which becomes part of the court proceedings in this way cannot be disclosed to anyone beyond the parties to the case without the court's permission. For example, in child protection proceedings the court may authorise disclosure of material which is necessary to enable an expert to conduct an assessment of the child; or for use in criminal proceedings if prosecution of an alleged perpetrator is being considered. The court will order disclosure in other circumstances, for example to a professional body, if it is in the public interest to protect the public from a member of the profession upon a question as to suitability or misconduct.

Further specific guidance on confidentiality in relation to Social Services Departments is contained in circular LAC (88) 17, which should be read in the light of developing case law.

The provisions of the Data Protection Act 1998 and the Freedom of Information Act 2000 are discussed in detail in Chapter 4.

■ Accountability

Accountability in social work practice is an increasingly significant yet complex area. A social worker may be accountable on a number of levels. At the very least, accountability lies to the Social Services Authority in its role as employer and also as holder of the social services functions that are delegated to social workers acting as agents of the authority. Correspondingly, the local authority is liable for the actions of its employees. Only when acting as an Approved Social Worker does a social worker acquire individual liability for action. In addition, a social worker must be accountable to the service user, in that it is possible to explain and justify why particular decisions are made. This accountability may be tested via the Local Authority Complaints System if a service user is dissatisfied, by complaint to the Local Government Ombudsman and ultimately by invoking judicial review procedures or action against a public authority under the Human Rights Act 1998. Other formal processes, including the functions of registration and inspection, support the notion of accountability, and in specified areas there is a duty to consult with service users (**NHSCCA** 1990). In cases involving statutory responsibilities toward children, accountability is to the child who is the subject of the case. There are circumstances where the social worker effectively works as an officer of the court and is accountable to the court, e.g. when directed to prepare and present a report or to comply with an undertaking or to follow the court's directions as to supervision of contact. Beyond those clear instances, accountability may also lie to team managers, section heads, practice teachers, the university or other institution during prequalification placements.[18]

The issue of local authority liability in tort is discussed in the context of challenging decisions in Chapter 4.

Inspection and regulation

Performance of public services, including social services, is increasingly being monitored through inspection and audit systems as a means of ensuring greater accountability.

The role of the GSCC in relation to social work as a profession has been discussed above. The Care Standards Act 2000, which established the GSCC, also set up a new regulation and inspection body, known as the Care Standards Commission. After the first year of operation its role was taken over by the Commission for Social Care Inspection, which also brought together into one regulatory body, the work of the Social Services Inspectorate (SSI) and the Audit Commission.

At the same time, a second independent inspectorate with a remit covering health services was established, known as the Commission for Healthcare Audit and Inspection (CHAI). In both cases the Government objective was to strengthen accountability of those responsible for the commissioning and delivery of health and social services and the two inspectorates are expected to work closely together.

The Commission for Social Care Inspection (**CSCI**) role includes: inspection of all public, private and voluntary social care organisations, and of local social service authorities; registration of services that meet national minimum standards; publishing an annual report to Parliament on national progress on social care and an analysis of where resources have been spent;[19] publishing star ratings for social services authorities.

Reflecting the 'Every Child Matters: Change for Children' policy, the CSCI functions in relation to children's social care have been merged with Ofsted to create a single children's services inspectorate, cutting across education and social care. The framework for the new inspections, known as joint area reviews, was introduced as part of the Children Act 2004 reforms. It is intended to reduce duplication of inspection and will have the 'five outcomes' for children as its focus (see further in Chapter 7).

▪ Duties and powers

Most social work areas of responsibility defined by legislation may be categorised as either duties or powers.

Duties

Where a duty is imposed by law, social services are obliged to carry it out; it is a mandatory obligation to carry out a particular function. There is no discretion or allowance for shortfall of resources. Breach of a duty could found an action for judicial review. An example is the duty to carry out an assessment for community care services under s. 47 of the National Health Service and Community Care Act 1990. The section reads:

s. 47

> (1) where it appears to a local authority that any person for whom they may provide or arrange for the provision of community care services may be in need of any such services, the authority–
> (a) shall carry out an assessment of his needs for those services; . . .
>
> (NHSCCA 1990)

The important word is *shall,* which suggests an imperative. As a general rule, where 'shall' appears, a duty is imposed.

Powers

Where a power is provided, there is an element of discretion. Power provides the authority to act in a particular way but there is scope to decide how to act. An example is the power in para. 16 of Sch. 2 to the Children Act 1989 in respect of children looked after by a local authority.

Sch. 2 ▶

> (2) The authority may –
>   (a) make payments to –
>   (i) a parent of the child; . . .
> in respect of travelling, subsistence or other expenses incurred by that person in visiting the child;
>
>   (CA 1989)

The important word is *may.* The authority may act in a particular way; they have a discretion but are not under an obligation. Guidance may be issued, which assists the interpretation of powers.

In some provisions what appears to be a duty is in effect softened by adding an element of discretion or choice. To return to the National Health Service and Community Care Act 1990, s. 47, the provision continues with para. (b): having regard to the results of that assessment, the local authority shall then decide whether his needs call for the provision by them of any such services. The duty is to carry out an assessment, but the authority then has a discretion: it can *decide* whether to provide any services. Another way in which duties are softened is by use of terms such as 'as far as is reasonably practicable', again introducing some leeway into the obligation. The word 'responsibility' is sometimes used loosely to refer to duties and powers and in so doing suggests a rather fuzzy position. If there is a duty or power contained in legislation it is preferable to talk in those terms and to be clear about the distinction between the two and the consequences.

The circumstances where it would be appropriate to refer to responsibilities are in respect of a professional's ethical code, or in relation to agency policies which cover matters other than those set out in legislation.

▪ Rights

The term 'rights' is open to wide interpretation, ranging from moral rights in the widest sense, through civil, political and cultural rights to a rather more restrictive interpretation of rights as something that an individual is legally entitled to. Unlike other countries which have a formal written constitution, often based on a Bill of Rights, UK law tends not to be expressed in positive rights. Rather it takes a more negative and reactive stance so that it is fair to assume that a person has the right to act in a particular way unless the law expressly prohibits it. This position may change over the years: it has been suggested that the introduction of the Human Rights Act 1998 will result in a rights-based culture and accessible avenues in which challenges can be brought if rights are infringed.

In social work, rights which have already been clearly incorporated into law include:

- The right to an assessment for services under the National Health Service and Community Care Act 1990.
- The right of a carer for an assessment of their needs to provide care under the Carers and Disabled Children Act 2000.
- The right not to be discriminated against in specified circumstances, e.g. provision of goods and services on specified grounds, including race, sex and disability.
- The right of a child (if of sufficient understanding to make an informed decision) to refuse a medical or psychiatric examination under the Children Act 1989.
- The right of access to information held about you under the Data Protection Act 1998.

Chapters 7 and 16 include discussion of children's rights and the rights of vulnerable adults, particularly in cases where capacity is limited.

Values

It is crucial to recognise that the law does not exist in a vacuum. Each day social workers make numerous difficult decisions relating to the lives of service users. Law is one of many factors that will be balanced in arriving at an appropriate decision reflecting good social-work practice. A value system is an essential prerequisite for making such decisions. It is also appropriate for use of law to be informed by a framework of values. Values may influence which route to follow if there are a range of legal options available, e.g. the choice between removing a child or an adult from home if child abuse is suspected, or even whether it is appropriate to have recourse to law at all, recognising that the law itself has deficiencies.

The GSCC sets out core values for social work in its Code of Practice.

Core Values for Social Work Practice

- Protect the rights and promote the interests of service users and carers.
- Strive to establish and maintain the trust and confidence of service users and carers.
- Respect the rights of service users whilst seeking to ensure that their behaviour does not harm themselves or other people.

> - Uphold public trust and confidence in social care services.
> - Be accountable for the quality of their work and take responsibility for maintaining and improving their knowledge and skills.
>
> GSCC

In addition, it has already been noted that the British Association of Social Workers has developed a Code of Ethics (2002).

It may be argued that some social work values directly conflict with the objectives of available law. For example, it is difficult to reconcile the values of anti-discriminatory and anti-oppressive practice with some of the terminology utilised in the Mental Health Act 1983 and its tendency to define and categorise individuals by reference to one characteristic, their medical diagnosis of mental health. Conversely, there will be cases where the law can be used directly to support values. For example, it may be empowering for an individual who has been abused to have direct recourse to the Family Law Act 1996 and to obtain an injunction removing the abuser from the household. It may also be argued that certain values that are often closely associated with social work are actually enshrined within legislation. For example, Art. 14 of the European Convention on Human Rights, the right not to be discriminated against, supports the social work value encapsulated in the Code of Ethics, i.e. recognising 'the value and dignity of every human being irrespective of origin, race, status, sex, sexual orientation, age, disability, belief or contribution to society'.[20]

The effect of personal values should also be acknowledged. It is important constantly to question individual values and consider the effect they have on practice. The position taken on a particular issue will probably be arrived at by the application of a combination of personal values, social work values and legal values, as demonstrated by, for example, the issue of whether an old person with Alzheimers disease should be able to live independently, be cared for by family members or move to residential accommodation. Factors which influence the position taken will include: personal views on whether you would be willing and able to care for a parent in such circumstances or would want to be cared for by your children; the values of empowerment, autonomy and choice; and the extent to which a person whose capacity is reduced should enjoy the same rights of autonomy, in the context of risk factors associated with living alone. The legal position includes a duty to provide community care support, and a duty to provide residential accommodation, direct payments, issues of substitute decision-making and management of financial affairs.

This example illustrates the complexity of everyday situations social workers will face. An approach based exclusively on either social work values or legal values provides an incomplete picture.

▪ Partnership

Partnership may operate at a number of levels.[21] On at least two levels it is integral to good social work practice.

Service users

Partnership with service users may include working to involve them fully in decision-making processes, whether by provision of appropriate literature and information, advocacy services, etc., or active involvement in, for example, conferences and reviews. The concept of partnership is integral to the philosophy and practice of the Children Act 1989. Yet there is no specific mention of partnership within the Act itself. It features in the Guidance which supports the Act, e.g. Volumes 2 and 3 of the *Children Act 1989 Guidance and Regulations*,[22] and may be read in to certain provisions, notably, under s. 17, the duty to promote the upbringing of children in need by their families so far as that is consistent with promoting welfare. Whether a true, meaningful partnership can exist between a professional social worker and a service user has been questioned in view of the obvious power imbalance. It may be an objective which is easier to realise in a case where Social Services are providing support to a child in need than in a contested child protection scenario. In the latter case, where the views of the social worker and the parents may be in direct conflict, it is still important that the social worker applies elements of a partnership approach, particularly by keeping lines of communication open, sharing and explaining information and any decisions that have been taken and not adopting an inflexible or adversarial stance. Aldgate (2001) suggests further that some of the key features of partnership with parents are:

- A shared commitment to negotiation and actions concerning how best to safeguard and promote children's welfare.
- A mutual respect for the other's point of view.
- Recognising the unequal nature of power between parents and professionals.
- Recognising that parents have their own needs which should be addressed.
- Good communication skills on the part of professionals.
- The establishment of trust between all parties.
- Integrity and accountability on the part of both parents and professionals.
- Shared decision-making.
- A joint recognition of constraints on the services offered.
- A recognition that partnership is not an end in itself.[23]

Professionals

Another application of partnership may be evident in working relations between different professional groups in an inter-disciplinary framework. The need to work together gained explicit recognition in guidance such as 'Working Together to Safeguard Children' (2006) and 'No Secrets' (2000) and the consequences of failure to work together and share information is well documented in a number of Child Abuse Inquiry Reports.[24] The Youth Offending Teams (**YOTs**) established under the Crime and Disorder Act 1998[25] present a formal template for multi-disciplinary work to prevent youth crime. The Children Act 2004 develops partnership between professionals further. A statutory duty to cooperate with a view to improving children's well being is imposed on children's services authorities and their relevant partners (s. 10). Relevant partners include district councils, police, probation boards, youth offending teams, health authorities and Connexions (see further discussion in Chapter 7).

▪ Choice

Promoting choice has been recognised as an important value for some time, particularly in the context of adults whose decision-making capacity may be limited.[26] The GSCC Code of Practice identifies that promoting the interests of service users and carers includes: 'Supporting users' rights to control their lives and make informed choices about the services they receive.' The reality of choice, however, is firmly located in a resources debate. Against a context of community care policy which purports to enable people to live independently in their own homes for as long as possible, across the country individuals whose care needs reach a level that costs more to meet in the community than by residential care may feel they have little real choice. Equally, if local authorities cannot recruit sufficient foster carers or prospective adoptive parents then a young person in a care home may struggle to see how he or she can make a positive choice about his or her home.

▪ Empowerment

Social workers may be able to provide support to an individual and empower that person to take action for him or herself to improve circumstances. Working in a very paternalistic manner might be seen as restricting opportunities for empowerment. Promoting empowerment is closely linked to anti-oppressive and anti-discriminatory practice and to recognition of rights.[27]

▪ Anti-discriminatory, anti-oppressive practice

The legal context to anti-discriminatory and anti-oppressive practice can be found in anti-discrimination legislation and various references in other pieces of legislation (see Chapter 6). Good practice in social work has, however, developed beyond these legal minimum standards for anti-discrimination. Anti-discriminatory, anti-oppressive practice is integral to social work and the GSCC Code of Practice stresses the importance of 'Promoting equal opportunities for service users and carers' (1.4) and 'Respecting diversity and different cultures and values' (1.5). This is an area where the role of law has been questioned, in particular because although the aim of early anti-discriminatory legislation was to alter entrenched attitudes and promote change, is it possible for the law, with its focus on dealing with individual problems, and which itself has been charged with discriminatory practice, to be an instrument of social change? A simple evaluation of the effectiveness of the legislation would suggest that whilst the legislation and the work of the Equal Opportunities Commission (**EOC**), Commission for Racial Equality (**CRE**) and Disability Rights Commission

(DRC), has broken down some barriers, much systematic discrimination still continues. It is important, however, for social workers to have a basic understanding of anti-discrimination legislation as there may be circumstances where clients encounter discrimination and may seek their social worker's advice.

In addition, social workers have a legal obligation to comply with the law and social-work actions themselves may be covered by anti-discriminatory legislation. The scope of existing anti-discrimination legislation is covered in detail in Chapter 6. At this stage, it is important to be aware of the following provisions, which support the need to promote anti-discriminatory and anti-oppressive practice.

The Race Relations (Amendment) Act 2000 includes a positive duty on local authorities to promote race equality and includes within the remit of the Act certain previously excluded bodies, such as the police. A new s. 71 is inserted into the Race Relations Act 1976, which states that:

s. 71

(1) Every body or other person specified in Schedule 1A[28] . . . shall, in carrying out its functions, have due regard to the need –
  (a) to eliminate unlawful racial discrimination; and
  (b) to promote equality of opportunity and good relations between persons of different racial groups.

(RRA 1976)

This is supported by a power for the Secretary of State to impose duties to ensure better performance of the above duties.

The 2000 Act also inserts a new s. 19B into the Race Relations Act 1976, which states that it is unlawful for a public authority, in carrying out any of its functions, to do any act that constitutes discrimination. This provision has clearly been introduced in response to the introduction of the Human Rights Act 1998. Section 6 of the 1998 Act imposes a duty on public authorities to act in compliance with the articles of the European Convention, including Art. 14, which reads:

Art. 14

The enjoyment of the rights and freedoms in this Convention shall be secured without discrimination on any ground such as sex, race, colour, religion, political or other opinion, national or social origin, association with a national minority, property, birth or other status.

(ECHR)

This article clearly envisages discrimination on a wider range of grounds than covered by our existing legislation. Although it is currently limited to discrimination in the enjoyment of rights set out under the Convention, the introduction of a free-standing discrimination article is possible in the future.

Other specific provisions in legislation direct anti-discriminatory practice. For example, s. 22(5) of the Children Act 1989 requires that, in making placement decisions, due consideration be given to a child's religious persuasion, racial origin, and cultural and linguistic background.

The structures and provisions of the English legal system can themselves be viewed as disempowering and discriminatory. It is thus essential to deal proactively with issues of equal opportunities. All legislation employs the male pronoun, though under the Interpretation Act 1978 'he' is intended to include 'she'. Unless directly quoting from legislation, it is important to avoid talking in a way which might be construed as sexist and explain the above reasoning if it is necessary for the sake of accuracy. Other 'discriminatory' language which is present in legislation such as the National Assistance Act 1948 has been referred to earlier.

It is important in acknowledging the limitations of law to recognise that law will not always provide the answers: e.g. in discrimination issues, practice developments have progressed more rapidly than law. Such an approach encourages critical awareness and may reassure those who feel that legal solutions are being imposed on their practice at the expense of other interventions more traditionally associated with social work, which are therapeutically based. The following equal opportunities statement was prepared for a child care law course but could equally apply to other areas of social work practice:

> Child Care education, policy and practice needs to recognise the prevailing social, economic, political and cultural context in which we all live. In recognising the powerful links between personal and professional issues, we assert the need to challenge inequalities and oppression wherever they may arise. Thus we seek to promote a form of child care practice which is opposed to inequality and oppression which is based on race, language, age, gender, disability, class, sexual orientation and religious belief.
>
> The task of child care professionals is to enable, facilitate and empower, individuals, groups and communities who may use, or provide, a child care service in a given locality to gain, retain and maintain control of their own affairs, in so far as this is compatible with their/others' personal safety. Child care education should be compatible with the task identified.[29]

■ Formal guidance on values and principles

There are examples of value frameworks, sometimes expressed as principles in both legislation and policy guidance. 'No Secrets: Guidance on developing and implementing multi-agency policies and procedures to protect vulnerable adults from abuse',[30] includes a statement that agencies should adhere to the following guiding principles:

1. actively work together within an inter-agency framework;
2. actively promote the empowerment and well-being of vulnerable adults;
3. act in a way which supports the rights of the individual to lead an independent life based on self-determination and personal choice;
4. recognise people who are unable to make their own decisions;

5. recognise that the right to self-determination can involve risk and ensure that such risk is recognised and understood by all concerned and minimised wherever possible;

6. ensure the safety of vulnerable adults.

A second example can be found in the Mental Capacity Act 2005, which includes in s. 1 general principles to be followed in relation to individual capacity. The inclusion of principles in a piece of legislation is significant and the principles referred to support good practice.

---

s. 1

The principles

(1) The following principles apply for the purposes of this Act.

(2) A person must be assumed to have capacity unless it is established that he lacks capacity.

(3) A person is not to be treated as unable to make a decision unless all practicable steps to help him to do so have been taken without success.

(4) A person is not to be treated as unable to make a decision merely because he makes an unwise decision.

(5) An act done, or decision made, under this Act for or on behalf of a person who lacks capacity must be done, or made, in his best interests.

(6) Before the act is done, or the decision is made, regard must be had to whether the purpose for which it is needed can be as effectively achieved in a way that is less restrictive of the person's rights and freedom of action.

(MCA 2005)

▪ A framework for decision-making

The application of a framework for decision-making provides a logical format in which to balance social work and legal values in order to reach a decision. This approach has been advocated by Braye and Preston-Shoot (1997), and the following simplified version (adapted from the above) can be adopted and applied to the majority of decisions a social worker will face. Given the approach of the media to social work crisis, which focuses on scapegoating, it is essential that processes of decision-making are clear. Further imperatives for openness and transparency in decision-making are provided by the Data Protection Act 1998 and the Human Rights Act 1998. Thus, 'a decision-making framework is both a safety device and a moral imperative'.[31] The framework suggested here is divided into stages of background work and taking action, but it is acknowledged that in practice there may not be a clear dividing line between the two.

Background

▪ Identify the problem requiring social work intervention, source of referral, background information, previous involvement in the case. How is information to be recorded?

■ Obtain further information if necessary, making use of inter-agency contacts.

■ Identify the level of risk in the situation – there may be different levels of risk to different people.

■ Consider the purpose of intervention – in the long and short term – what do you want to achieve and why?

■ Are there competing interests among the individuals concerned (e.g. different assertions of 'rights', safety of professionals may be an issue)?

■ Does the legal framework mandate or permit types of action, duties or powers?

■ Is it appropriate to seek legal advice at this stage, relevant, e.g., to collection of evidence, immediate protection?

Taking action

■ Is an emergency response required, possibly requiring police involvement?

■ Is there a level of agreement or is it necessary to invoke formal powers (not mutually exclusive concepts)?

■ What guidance exists as to how a decision to intervene is reached – e.g. is a formal meeting such as a planning meeting or case conference required, who holds the decision-making power in the authority (team manager, Director)? Has adequate supervision been present?

■ Have consultation responsibilities been complied with?

■ Is everybody involved who needs to be – within the agency and in partnership with other agencies, e.g. health, education?

■ What mechanisms will achieve the desired outcomes? Is it necessary to go to court; are resources available?

■ What review requirements exist after action has been taken?

Chapter summary

■ Law provides for the structure of Social Services Departments and the mandate to practise.

■ Law sets parameters within which discretion may be exercised in reaching decisions.

■ Law does not exist in a vacuum as a discrete entity but should be incorporated into social work practice.

■ A value framework should inform use of law and selected values – partnership, empowerment, anti-oppressive and anti-discriminatory practice find some support in the law but may also be interpreted as contradictory in places.

■ The concept of accountability is complex and may lie to various bodies, including your employer and the courts.

- The confidentiality of information and records may be protected by public interest immunity. Confidentiality of information and records cannot be guaranteed, however, and it may be necessary to disclose information where it is in the interest of a child, in the public interest, ordered by a court, or as part of multi-disciplinary work.

- A framework for decision-making, incorporating analysis of legal options and values can support good practice and guard against defensive practice.

Websites

General Social Care Council: this body replaced CCETSW and has responsibility for regulation of the social care workforce, including social workers:
www.gscc.org.uk

British Association of Social Workers: including the Code of Ethics:
www.basw.co.uk

Directgov – the entry point for Government information and services online, this website incorporates an open.gov section, which has an alphabetical listing of central Government departments, agencies and bodies and of local councils (a really useful bookmark):
www.uk.online.gov.uk

Further reading

A number of articles explore the relationship between law and social work practice:

Braye, S. and Preston-Shoot, M. (1992) 'Honourable intentions: partnership and written agreements in welfare legislation' 6 *Journal of Social Welfare and Family Law* pp. 511–28.

Braye, S. and Preston-Shoot, M. (1994) 'Partners in community care? Rethinking the relationship between the law and social work practice' 2 *Journal of Social Welfare and Family Law* pp. 163–84.

Braye, S. and Preston-Shoot, M. (1999) 'Accountability, administrative law and social work practice: redressing or reinforcing the power imbalance?' 21(3) *Journal of Social Welfare and Family Law* pp. 235–56.

Braye, S. and Preston-Shoot, M. (2001) 'Social Work Practice and Accountability' in Cull, L.-A. and Roche, J. *The Law and Social Work.* Basingstoke: Palgrave.

Preston-Shoot, M., Roberts, G. and Vernon, S. (1998) 'Social Work law: from interaction to integration' 20(1) *Journal of Social Welfare and Family Law* pp. 65–80.

Preston-Shoot, M. (2000) 'What if? Using the law to uphold practice values and standards' 12(4) *Practice* p. 49.

Preston-Shoot, M., Roberts, G. and Vernon, S. (2001) 'Values in social work law: strained relations or sustaining relationships?' 23(1) *Journal of Social Welfare and Family Law* pp. 1–22.

CSCI (2005) *The State of Social Care in England 2004–5*. London: CSCI (a comprehensive overview of social care across public, private and voluntary sectors which found some improvements but much further work to be done.

Useful reference sources include:

Encyclopedia of Social Services and Child Care Law. London: Sweet & Maxwell (4 volumes, updated regularly).

French, D. (1996) *How to Cite Legal Authorities*. London: Blackstone Press.

Hardy, S. (1997) *Butterworths Student Statutes: Social Work Law*. London: Butterworths.

Kenny, P. (2005) *Studying Law*. London: (5th edn)/OUP.

The documents that provide the framework for the social work degree:

Department of Health (2002) *Requirements for Social Work Training*. London: Department of Health.

GSCC (2002) *Codes of Practice for Social Care Workers and Employers*. London: General Social Care Council.

TOPSS (2002) *The National Occupational Standards for Social Work*. Leeds: Training Organisation for the Personal Social Services.

Notes

[1] S. Braye and M. Preston-Shoot (1990) 'On teaching and applying the law in social work: it is not that simple', 20(4) *British Journal of Social Work* pp. 333–53, p. 343.

[2] C. Ball, R. Harris, G. Roberts and S. Vernon (1988) 'The Law Report: Teaching and Assessment of Law in Social Work Education', CCETSW.

[3] F. Jones, B. Fletcher and K. Ibbetson (1991) 'Stressors and strains amongst social workers: demands, supports, constraints and psychological health' 21(5) *British Journal of Social Work* pp. 443–69.

[4] S. Braye, and M. Preston-Shoot (2005) *Teaching, learning and assessment of law in social work education*. London: Social Care Institute for Excellence.

[5] M. Preston-Shoot, G. Roberts and S. Vernon (1998) 'Social Work law: from interaction to integration' 20(1) *Journal of Social Welfare and Family Law* pp. 65–80.

[6] Ibid., p 65.

[7] DHSS (1991) 'Working Together: Guidelines for Inter-agency Co-operation for the Protection of Children'. London: HMSO.

[8] CCETSW ceased to exist from 2002 upon implementation of the Care Standards Act 2000, which introduced the General Social Care Council (s. 54).

9 C. Ball, M. Preston-Shoot, G. Roberts and S. Vernon (1995) *Law for Social Workers in England and Wales,* CCETSW: 'Students need to understand:

i. that the law gives social workers their mandate to practise:

(a) as employees of the statutory bodies (when, for example, employed as a local authority social worker); or officers of the court (when employed, for example, as a probation officer),

(b) by defining the various groups of people in respect of whom social workers have duties and powers,

(c) by defining a social worker's legal functions in relation to each client group;

ii. that legally accountable powers, when appropriately used, can promote and encourage good social-work practice: e.g. by emphasising the importance of prevention and rehabilitation; by setting out the conditions upon which compulsory intervention is permissible; by ensuring that compulsory intervention with a person's rights takes place in accordance with proper legal safeguards, such as due process of law and adherence to principles of natural justice;

iii. that the exercise of legal powers may be oppressive or discriminatory if not used in ways that avoid discrimination and respect clients' rights; and that social and legal institutions and processes, such as the court system, to which social work practice must often relate, are frequently identified as discriminatory and racist in operation and practice.

Students need to know:

i. the substantive law which is relevant to social work practice, and its nature and sources;

ii. the relationship between local authority and probation policy and the law;

iii. the structures and processes of the relevant court and tribunal systems.

10 DH (2002) 'Requirements for Social Work Training'. London: DH.

11 Training Organisation for the Personal Social Services (TOPSS) (2002) The National Occupational Standards for Social Work. Leeds: TOPSS.

12 Quality Assurance Agency (QAA) (2000) Subject benchmark statements: Social policy and administration and social work. Gloucester: QAA for Higher Education.

13 See the GSCC website www.doh.gov.uk/gscc/ for further information.

14 Cited in L. Clements (1996) *Community Care and the Law.* London: Legal Action Group Books.

15 W. Macpherson (1999) 'The Stephen Lawrence Inquiry: Report of an Inquiry by Sir William Macpherson of Cluny et al.'. London: The Stationery Office.

16 The Code referred to may be accessed via the BASW website at www.basw.co.uk.

17 HM Government (2006)*Working Together to Safeguard Children.* London: The Stationery Office.

18 For a full discussion, see S. Braye and M. Preston-Shoot (2001) 'Social work practice and accountability' in L.-A. Cull and J. Roche (eds) *The Law and Social Work: Contemporary Issues for Practice.* Basingstoke: Palgrave.

19 See CSCI (2005) *The state of social care in England 2004–5.* London: CSCI (a comprehensive overview of social care across public, private and voluntary sectors which found some improvements but much further work to be done).

20 BASW (1996) 'The Code of Ethics for Social Work', point 6.

[21] See discussion in relation to the use of written agreements in S. Braye and M. Preston-Shoot (1992) 'Honourable intentions: partnership and written agreements in welfare legislation' 21(6) *Journal of Social Welfare and Family Law* pp. 511–28.

[22] Department of Health (1991).

[23] J. Aldgate (2001) 'Safeguarding and Promoting the Welfare of Children in Need Living with their Families' in L.-A. Cull and J. Roche (eds) *The Law and Social Work: Contemporary Issues for Practice*. Basingstoke: Palgrave.

[24] See Department of Health (1991) *Child Abuse: A Study of Inquiry Reports*. London: HMSO; and P. Reder, S. Duncan and M. Gray (1993) *Beyond Blame: child abuse tragedies revisited*. London: Routledge.

[25] Section 39.

[26] Department of Health/SSI (1989) *Homes are for Living In*. London: HMSO.

[27] See S. Braye and M. Preston-Shoot (1995) *Empowering Practice in Social Care*. Buckingham: Open University Press.

[28] Schedule 1A includes government departments, armed forces, NHS, local government, educational bodies, housing bodies and police.

[29] Keele University (2001) 'MA Child Care Law and Practice Handbook' p. 2.

[30] Department of Health (2000).

[31] S. Braye and M. Preston-Shoot (1997) *Practising Social Work Law*. Basingstoke: Macmillan Press.

2 Sources of law

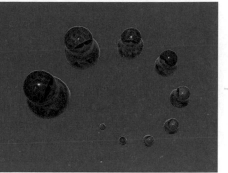

Learning objectives

To develop an understanding of the following:

- The language, terminology and conventions of law and to become fluent in the use of appropriate legal terminology.
- The substantive content and sources of law that give social workers powers and duties.
- The status of legislation, case law, policy and guidance.
- The process of making legislation.
- The application of case law and the doctrine of precedent.
- Legal research skills and to begin to develop a critical approach to law.
- The process of law reform and in particular the role of the Law Commission.
- The influence of European and international law and Conventions.

Introduction

What appears clear . . . is that social work students and practitioners experience contact with the law and legal system as stressful. They are concerned about their lack of familiarity with legal settings, languages and procedures, and about the frequency with which the legal rules change. They express uncertainty about how the law interfaces with social work values and organizational procedures. Furthermore, legal accountability, which might benefit service users, can be unsettling for social work practitioners. They conceptualise the law as intimidating, conflictual, and more likely to be obstructive than empowering.

(Braye and Preston-Shoot, 2005[1])

31

Given the above statement, it is essential at an early stage to gain an understanding of law and to develop confidence and enthusiasm in using law. The first step is knowing what law is and where it comes from. That is the focus of this chapter. Sources of law, including case law and legislation, are written and cited in accordance with recognised conventions that can make them appear unduly complicated to a lay person.[2] It is worth spending some time unravelling these conventions so as to become comfortable with direct sources.

Law which is relevant for social work practice is contained in a variety of forms. Much of it is fairly recent and can be linked to Government initiatives, such as the 'modernisation agenda' and efforts to tackle social exclusion. The process of introducing new law which impacts on social work practice shows no sign of slowing down. For effective practice, it is essential to have an understanding of existing law and also to be aware of likely areas of reform. There will be occasions when it is necessary for a social worker to refer directly to a source of law. To return briefly to the qualification framework discussed in Chapter 1, understanding law is clearly specified as a requirement for qualification and effective practice. National Occupational Standards require that for each area of competence, a student must 'understand, critically analyse, evaluate and apply . . . knowledge' of '[t]he legal, social, economic, and ecological context of social work practice . . . UK, EU legislation, statutory codes, standards, frameworks and guidance relevant to social work practice . . .' This is reinforced by the Quality Assurance Benchmarks, which require subject specific knowledge to include 'the significance of legislative and legal frameworks and service delivery standards (including the nature of legal authority, the application of legislation in practice, statutory accountability and tensions between statute policy and practice)'. For all of these reasons it is important, at an early stage in a career in social work, to gain familiarity with direct sources of law.

This chapter explains the range of sources of law and the relative importance or status of different types of law, in relation to social work practice. Legislation, as the primary source of law, is considered first, including an explanation of the development of new legislation. This is followed by consideration of rules, regulations, directions, guidance or policy and codes of practice, which supplement primary legislation. The law of the United Kingdom is contained, not only in statutes, but also in the form of case law, which collectively is known as the common law. The extent to which a legal decision has an influence on subsequent cases through the operation of precedent is considered, and an exercise is offered to provide insight into the way that decisions of the courts are reported.

One of the exciting aspects of the study of social work law is the speed at which it changes and develops. Keeping track of those developments is also one of its most challenging demands. New laws may be driven from a number of directions, some overtly political in nature. A significant amount of law, however, has been introduced following the work of the Law Commission, an independent body, whose role is considered in some detail below. Perhaps the greatest influence on the future development of law in this country is likely to be the Human Rights Act 1998, which is the subject of Chapter 5. This chapter concludes with reference to the influence of other European and international law Conventions.

As a preliminary issue, which has a bearing on all the subsequent sections, the chapter commences with a discussion of the language of law.

Language of law

The use of complicated, sometimes almost unintelligible, legal language has often been cited (by students and others) as a real barrier to understanding law. There are a number of possible responses to this complaint and comments to be made about legal language.

First, to agree! Most lawyers could cite at least one legal provision which they have read and re-read and still not understood, or which they consider they could have drafted in a more satisfactory manner. An example of a provision which seeks to introduce a fairly straightforward point, but does so in a convoluted way, is the 'no order' principle of the Children Act 1989. This states:

s. 1

> (5) Where a court is considering whether or not to make one or more orders with respect to a child, it shall not make the order or any of the orders unless it considers that doing so would be better for the child than making no order at all.
>
> (CA 1989)

In other words, any order made by a court should result in a positive benefit for the child! In practical terms, to use the example of care proceedings, it will be for the local authority to convince the court that, through making the order, the application of the terms of the care plan will be positively better for the child than making no order at all. Secondly, legal language is used to ensure precision and thoroughness in legislation. Certain terms are employed because they have a precise legal meaning, for example, negligence and recklessness. It may sometimes be helpful to turn to a law dictionary for help in deciphering difficult terminology. The glossary included in this text explains legal terms which a social worker is likely to encounter.

Thirdly, all professions develop their own special language or jargon and lawyers are no exception. Neither are social workers. An occasion comes to mind when a magistrate asked a social worker, when giving evidence, to talk about brothers and sisters rather than siblings! Increased interagency working may lead to development of more shared language in the longer term. Fourthly, legislation does not change at a comparable pace to practice developments. There are numerous examples of use of language in legislation (and case law) which it would be considered unacceptable to use in practice. This is most obvious where legislation made many decades ago is still in common usage. One example is the National Assistance Act 1948, s. 29, which refers to:

s. 29

. . . welfare of persons who are blind, deaf, dumb or otherwise handicapped, or are suffering from mental disorder of any description, or who are substantially and permanently handicapped by illness, injury, or congenital deformity or such other disabilities as may be prescribed.

(NAA 1948)

Aside from any concerns about labelling individuals, it is clear that many of the terms used in this section would now be considered inappropriate or even offensive. Although different views are held, reference to an individual being hearing impaired or without speech is suggested as preferable to referring to an individual as deaf or dumb. It has also become accepted practice now to refer to disability rather than handicap.

Fifthly, in an attempt to leave categories open and broad for interpretation in practice, the law can appear vague and imprecise. In the checklist to the welfare principle of the Children Act 1989, s. 1(3)(d) refers to the child's 'age, sex, background and any characteristics of his which the court considers relevant'. Later in the Act, at s. 22(5)(c), when making decisions local authorities are required to give due consideration to a child's religious persuasion, racial origin and cultural and linguistic background. It is likely that in the welfare checklist 'any characteristics of his' is intended to include religious persuasion, racial origin and cultural and linguistic background; however, it is unfortunate that in the first section of the Act such reference is implicit rather than explicit.

Sixthly, there is a clear movement to introduce greater use of simpler, far clearer language into the legal system. This was clearly recognised in 1975, when the Report of the Committee on the Preparation of Legislation made a number of recommendations, including issue of explanatory notes with new Bills and an emphasis on preparing legislation for users, noting that legislation that cannot be understood by people whose interests it serves is likely only to bring the law into disrepute. Since then, all Bills and new legislation have been accompanied by detailed explanatory notes. Both the legislation and the explanatory notes are available from the Office of Public Sector Information.[3] One of the central aims of the reforms[4] of civil justice was to simplify the process of litigation and encourage the use of clearer and simpler language. Many terms commonly used by lawyers might be described as 'legalese' and could be substituted by plain language without affecting their meaning: e.g. 'people' instead of 'persons'; 'under' instead of 'pursuant to'; and 'end' instead of 'expiration'.[5]

There may be cases where legal language conflicts with the principles and practice of anti-discriminatory and anti-oppressive values. In those circumstances it is appropriate to use the preferred terms adopted in practice, unless quoting directly from the particular legal provision.

Legislation

Legislation applicable in England and Wales is introduced by Parliament and the process involves scrutiny and amendment by both the House of Commons and House of Lords. Up to the stage where Royal Assent is given, draft legislation is referred to as a Bill. During the parliamentary process, the content of the legislation may be altered significantly, as a result of debate and amendments; for example, the Children Act 1989 almost doubled in size.

Most new legislation is introduced by the Government, and is preceded by a *white paper* that outlines the proposals and background to the need for reform. A white paper is a command paper presented to Government (usually by a Government minister) as a statement of Government policy. Elements of new laws may be traced back to election manifestos or reflect particular events or circumstances prevailing in society, e.g. greater fear of crime. There may have been a detailed consultation period prior to this, in some cases coordinated by the Law Commission, or other bodies such as the Department of Health or Home Office. As part of the consultation process, a *green paper* may have been published which puts forward proposals for consultation. A recent example is the 'Every Child Matters' green paper published in September 2003 which preceded the Children Act 2004. Most Government proposals for legislation in the forthcoming year of office are announced in the Queen's Speech (prepared by the Cabinet) at the State Opening of Parliament in November each year.

Legislation may also commence as a Private Member's Bill; however, it is now fairly unusual for a Private Member's Bill to become law, because parliamentary time is short and is mainly taken up with Government matters. A well-known example of a Private Member's Bill is the Abortion Act 1967, which was introduced by David Steel MP. In some cases a Bill may start life as a Private Member's Bill then, as the issue gains the Government's support, a Government Bill on the subject is introduced. Such was the case with the Disability Discrimination Act 1995, and the Civil Partnership Act 2004, though in each case some pressure groups were disappointed by what they felt was ultimately a watered-down version of their proposals.

■ Process of new legislation

The process can be understood as a series of steps beginning with the first reading.

First reading

A Bill can be introduced for first reading in either the House of Commons or the House of Lords. In practice it is more common for Bills to be introduced in the House of Commons, particularly where there are financial implications. There is no debate about the Bill at first reading, the clerk simply reads the title of the Bill and it is then formally printed ready for debate at subsequent stages.

Second reading

Debate on the main principles of the Bill starts at this stage. A vote can be taken on the Bill as a whole at the end of second reading.

Committee stage

Following second reading, all Bills move to a standing committee for further consideration.[6] There are between 16 and 50 members on a committee, which includes a cross-section of political party representation with a majority of members from the Government. The committee can hear evidence from experts, and works through the Bill clause by clause, making amendments, which are drafted by parliamentary counsel, where necessary.

Report stage

The outcome of the committee stage is reported to the House. Further debate takes place and more changes can be made at report stage. Often this will include attempts to restore provisions lost or amended in committee stage, or to remove committee additions.

Third reading

At third reading, debate becomes more focused and is confined to the contents of the Bill. At the earlier second reading the debate will usually have been more wide ranging, involving a review of the Bill in the context of the subject to which it relates. Most issues have been determined by third reading stage and it may proceed without debate unless at least six MPs table a motion. A vote can be taken but it would be unusual for a Bill to fail at this stage. The Bill then moves to the House of Lords.

House of Lords

In the House of Lords a similar process takes place. First reading starts the process, followed by second reading, committee stage, report stage and third reading, following which a motion is put forward. The Bill returns to the House of Commons with the Lords' amendments to it, which must then be considered by the Commons. Amendments may be made to the Bill through the whole process, even at a very late stage, as was seen in the instance of the Adoption and Children Act 2002. A much called-for but controversial late amendment in the House of Commons extended eligibility to adopt to couples, not limited to married couples. It is essential for the two Houses finally to reach agreement on the changes made by each other if the Bill is to succeed, though in limited circumstances it is possible for the Government to use its House of Commons majority to overrule House of Lords opposition.

Royal Assent

The short titles of Bills which have received *Royal Assent* are read out in each House. Obtaining Royal Assent, the signature of the Queen, converts the Bill into

House	Stage	Date
Commons	First Reading	17 June 2004
Commons	Second Reading	11 October 2004
Commons	Committee – 12 sittings	19 October – 4 November 2004
Commons	Report	14 December 2004
Commons	Third Reading	14 December 2004
Lords	First Reading	15 December 2004
Lords	Second Reading	10 January 2005
Lords	Committee – 5 sittings	25 January – 8 February
Lords	Report (day 1)	15 March 2005
Lords	Report (day 2)	17 March 2005
Lords	Third Reading	24 March 2005
Commons	Consideration of Lords Amendments	5 April 2005
Commons	Royal Assent	7 April 2005

Exhibit 2.1   Legislative passage of the Mental Capacity Act 2005

an Act of Parliament. It is possible to track the progress of a Bill through Parliament by reference to Hansard, the daily official report of each House.[7] To illustrate the timescale legislative passage may involve, the Mental Capacity Act 2005 developed as shown in Exhibit 2.1.

To complete the picture it is worth remembering that the Law Commssion started their consultation process around mental capacity in 1989, and the Government white paper 'Making Decisions' was published in 1999.

Commencement

Legislation is not automatically implemented on receipt of the Royal Assent. Often the Act will be brought into force at a later date by a commencement order, e.g. the Criminal Justice and Court Services Act 2000 (Commencement No. 4) Order 2001, or there may be a commencement section at the end of the statute, which specifies the date. Implementation may be delayed for a number of reasons. A delay of two years took place before the Human Rights Act 1998 came into force on 2 October 2000. One reason for this delay was the need for a major training programme to be conducted at all levels of the judiciary. Longer delays may occur: e.g. parts of the Family Law Reform Act 1986 were not implemented until 2001.[8]

Acts may come into force in sections over a period of time and some parts of legislation are never implemented. The Lord Chancellor announced in 2001 that the part of the Family Law Act 1996 relating to reform of divorce laws would not be implemented, following pilot programmes throughout the country, which trialled mediation and compulsory meetings for divorcing couples, and suggested this part of the

Act would be unworkable. A further example of a section of legislation which has never been implemented – in this case despite a broad level of support – is the provision in the Disabled Persons (Services, Consultation and Representation) Act 1986 containing the right to advocacy services. It may be suggested that it is the financial resource implications of certain provisions that may delay or even scupper implementation.

Amendment

Legislation may continue to be amended after it receives Royal Assent and has been implemented. Amendments are introduced by new legislation in related areas. This provides an opportunity to fine-tune the earlier legislation, update it and ensure consistency without having to repeal the Act and replace it in full. The Children Act 1989 has been amended on a number of occasions, most recently by the Adoption and Children Act 2002. Amongst other things (further detail in Part 2), the definition of 'harm' as part of the threshold criteria for care proceedings was amended to include 'impairment suffered from seeing or hearing the ill-treatment of another'. This reflects growing understanding of the impact of domestic violence on children. The disadvantage of this process is that it becomes more difficult to keep track of the terms of the original Act as amended. Major amendments to sections can be identified by their use of capital letters, e.g. the new s. 14A of the Children Act 1989 establishes the special guardianship order as introduced by the Adoption and Children Act 2002.

Presentation of legislation

Legislation is presented in a standardised format, see Exhibit 2.2. The title of the Act and its year are printed on the front page, with a Chapter number. This indicates the stage in the parliamentary sitting when the Act is passed, i.e. the Children Act was the 41st Act passed during that parliamentary year. It is followed by 'Arrangement of Sections', a contents list, then a description of the objects of the Act (the preamble), which, in relation to the Children Act 1989, is:

> An Act to reform the law relating to children; to provide for local authority services for children in need and others; to amend the law with respect to children's homes, community homes, voluntary homes and voluntary organisations; to make provision with respect to fostering, childminding and day care for young children and adoption; and for connected purposes.

The language used to refer to parts of a Bill changes after it receives Royal Assent. A Bill is divided into clauses, subclauses and paragraphs. An Act of Parliament, or statute, contains headed sections, subsections and paragraphs which may be organised into parts (e.g. Children Act 1989, Part II – Orders with respect to children in family proceedings; Part III – Local Authority support for children and families). The provisions in an Act are cited according to convention. Section 17(1)(a) of the Children Act 1989, refers to section 17, subsection (1), paragraph (a), of the Children Act 1989 (loosely referred to as the duty to children in need). If not familiar with

Children Act 1989

CHAPTER 41

LONDON
HER MAJESTY'S STATIONERY OFFICE
£13·40 net

Exhibit 2.2   Front cover of Children Act 1989
Source: HMSO, Crown Copyright

this section, it would be useful for the reader to take the opportunity to find that section in the Act and see exactly what it says. Schedules at the end of an Act carry the same force of law as the main body of the Act, but often include more detailed or supplemental matters, such as procedural requirements or formalities, transitional arrangements, repeal of earlier legislation and minor amendments.

In practice, to find out if a statute is implemented in part or in full, Butterworths *Is it in Force?*[9] should provide the answer. Exhibit 2.3 illustrates the parliamentary process of introducing legislation.

■ Delegated legislation

Delegated legislation, sometimes referred to as secondary legislation, has the same force of law as Acts of Parliament or primary legislation, but is not made by Parliament in the process described above. Examples of delegated legislation are the Children (Leaving Care) (England) Regulations 2001 (SI 2000/2874) and the Mental Health Review Tribunal Rules 1983 (SI 1983/942).

Most delegated legislation is made by ministers by *statutory instrument* (**SI**) and is in the form of regulations, orders, rules and byelaws. The preamble to a statutory instrument usually makes clear the authority for its issue, e.g. 'In exercise of the powers conferred by section X of the Y Act, the Secretary of State for (Z department) makes the following regulations . . .' A vast body of law is produced this way and often serves to provide the detail to an associated Act of Parliament. The lack of parliamentary scrutiny means that delegated legislation can be introduced fairly quickly. Regulations often deal primarily with process and procedures, such as the Protection of Children and Vulnerable Adults and Care Standards Tribunal Regulations 2002 (SI 2002/816), but can also deal with substantive issues. In exceptional cases delegated legislation may be declared void by the courts if the minister exceeded his powers by introducing the particular delegated legislation. In doing so, the minister would have been acting *ultra vires* or outside his powers. In addition to ministers, local authorities may also make secondary legislation in the form of byelaws, and can thus respond to particular issues in their area. This power to make a byelaw will have its source in an Act such as the Local Government Act 1972 or the Public Health Act 1936.

Since devolution, the National Assembly for Wales can make delegated legislation and guidance where the power to do so is provided by Act of Parliament. This provides the opportunity to more closely reflect priorities set by the Assembly, but it will often share similarities with equivalent provision in England. As an example, it would be useful to compare the guidance prepared in England and Wales on establishing adult protection procedures, 'No Secrets' (England)[10] and 'In Safe Hands' (Wales).[11]

The range of different types of official advice and guidance documents can be confusing, particularly in relation to the question of legal responsibility to comply with their contents. As a general rule, it must be considered professional good practice to comply with any level of official advice. In some cases, however, a difficulty can arise where advice is ambiguous or where each local authority has some scope to interpret advice differently and may actually implement it through a local authority policy. The question must then be asked, to what extent can regional variations be justified or in the public interest?

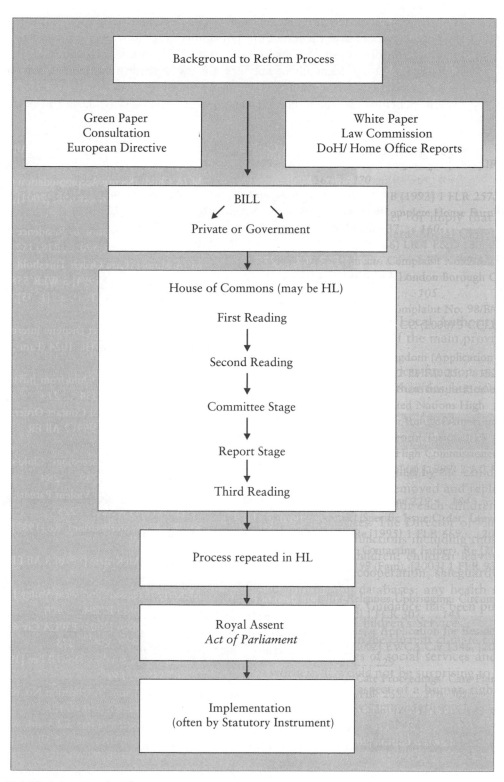

Exhibit 2.3 New legislation

An outline of the different types of advice documents and their status follows. If there is a doubt over the level of responsibility created by documents, this is an area where (if only to avoid judicial review) it would be prudent to obtain legal opinion. Recognising that legal advice may not always be readily available, a starting point is to refer to Sch. 1 to the Local Authority Social Services Act 1970 (LASSA 1970). This Schedule lists the permitted functions of Social Services Departments.

▪ Regulations

As stated above, regulations carry the force of law. Usually regulations provide the detail, which supplements a duty or power contained in primary legislation. For example, the Community Care, Services for Carers and Children's Services (Direct Payments) (England) Regulations 2003 (SI 2003/762).

▪ Guidance documents

There are a variety of types of guidance documents which, as the term suggests, provide guidance on putting legislation into practice. Guidance relating to social services matters is frequently contained in a circular, issued by the Department of Health. Local authority circulars are automatically issued to every local authority that will be affected by their contents. Circulars can be obtained direct from the Department of Health (or from its website).[12] Circulars are also issued by other departments, such as the Home Office. Within the general term 'guidance', documents are issued of differing status, commonly referred to as formal policy guidance and general practice guidance. Local authorities are under a stronger obligation to follow the former.

Formal policy guidance

It is often clear that guidance is in fact formal policy guidance because it will be identified as issued under the Local Authority Social Services Act 1970, s. 7(1), which states that local authorities shall 'act under the general guidance of the Secretary of State'. Examples of this type of policy guidance include 'No Secrets: Guidance on developing and implementing multi-agency policies and procedures to protect vulnerable adults from abuse' (HM Government, 2006) and 'Working Together to Safeguard Children' (Department of Health, 1999). Guidance may be issued by more than one department. The 'Framework for the Assessment of Children in Need and their Families' (2000) was issued by the Department of Health, the Department for Education and Employment, and the Home Office. The status of this type of guidance was explained in the case of *R* v. *Islington London Borough Council, ex parte Rixon* [1997] ELR 66:

> If this statutory guidance is to be departed from it must be with good reason, articulated in the course of some identifiable decision-making process . . . In the absence of any such considered decision, the deviation from statutory guidance is in my judgment a breach of law.

From this statement, the consequences of not following this type of guidance are clear.

General practice guidance

Guidance that is not issued under LASSA 1970, s. 7(1) can be regarded as general guidance and of a lower legal status. Again, this type of guidance may be issued as a local authority circular or it may be written as a letter and referred to as a local authority social services letter. It can be described as advice from the Department of Health rather than as a directive. Practice guidance can be quite detailed and give particular examples of ways in which a local authority might demonstrate good practice in implementing its responsibilities. For example, the Department of Health published 'Practice Guidance on Assessing Children in Need and their Families' (2000). Whilst this type of guidance does not carry s. 7 status, it would nevertheless be unwise for a local authority to ignore it. A decision of a local authority which did not have regard to relevant practice advice would clearly be judicially reviewable as one that did not take into account all relevant factors.

■ Directions

In addition to the duty to exercise functions under guidance, LASSA 1970, s. 7 also refers to the duty to act in accordance with directions.

s. 7

> (1) Without prejudice to section 7 of this Act, every local authority shall exercise their social services functions in accordance with such directions as may be given to them under this section by the Secretary of State.
> (2) Directions under this section –
>   (a) shall be given in writing; and
>   (b) may be given to a particular authority, or to authorities of a particular class, or to authorities generally.
>
> (LASSA 1970)

Directions have the force of law and must always be complied with (LASSA 1970), e.g. the Complaints Procedure Directions 1990.

■ Codes of practice

In some pieces of legislation the relevant minister is authorised to make a code of practice. A code of practice, though made further to an Act of Parliament, has a slightly different status to delegated legislation, and does not of itself carry the force of law. Nevertheless, it is clear in many cases that breach of a code will have serious implications. Perhaps the best example of this is in relation to police powers. Codes of practice have been made by the Home Secretary under the Police and Criminal

Evidence Act 1984 (**PACE**). Code C deals with the detention, treatment and questioning of people in the police station. If there is a breach of the code, evidence obtained by the breach may be excluded.[13]

Codes of practice carry the advantage that they can be updated regularly, to reflect changes in practice and changes in society, even if the primary legislation does not change. For example, Code C to PACE 1984 was most recently updated in 2004. A Code of Practice has been prepared to accompany the Mental Capacity Act 2005. Section 42 of the Act confirms that a code or codes of practice will be issued to accompany the Act for guidance of people acting in connection with the Act, for example in assessing whether a person has capacity. The Act also imposes a duty to have regard to the Code on a variety of people, including independent mental capacity advocates and a donee of a lasting power of attorney. This gives an indication of the significance of this particular Code.

The common law: case law and precedent

The common law is comprised of decisions of the courts on matters brought before them, known collectively as case law and 'weighted' according to the doctrine of precedent.

■ Precedent

The doctrine of *precedent* can be explained as the principle that decisions of cases made at the higher level of the court hierarchy are binding on other (lower) courts contemplating a decision (illustrated in Exhibit 2.4). The highest UK court is the House of Lords and its decisions are binding on inferior courts. Application of the doctrine of precedent promotes certainty and consistency and has been described as a 'convenient time saving device',[14] which avoids 're-inventing the wheel' each time an issue requiring a decision comes before a court. It provides an opportunity for the courts to develop, interpret and expand the law, adding detail that it would be impracticable to include in legislation. Disadvantages of precedent are that it can seem unnecessarily restrictive and inflexible and that a 'poor' decision can stand for a long time. The courts are also limited to determination of the issues that people choose to litigate. Huge areas of ambiguous law may remain on the statute book awaiting clarification until an aggrieved individual decides to bring the issue to the attention of the court. Precedent as a term can be used to describe the process outlined, of inferior courts following the decisions of superior courts. It can also be used to describe a particular case, e.g. the *Gloucestershire* decision is a precedent on the issue of resources and assessments,[15] (*R v Gloucestershire County Council, ex p Barry* [1997] 2 All ER 1).

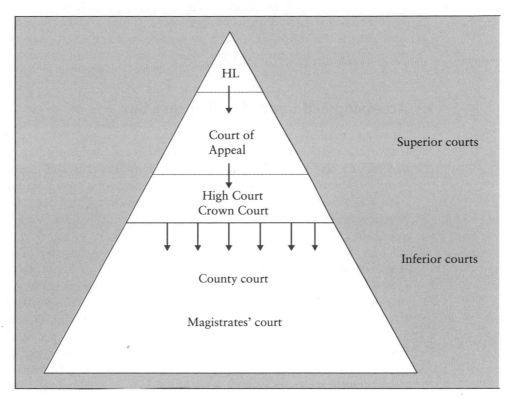

Exhibit 2.4   Precedent

What exactly is binding?

Decisions reached by the higher courts are often incredibly complex and include a range of arguments, which may at times appear to contradict and conflict, either between different judgments or even within one judgment. Not all of the detail included in a judgment is binding on subsequent decisions; only the part of the judgment that is referred to as the *ratio decidendi*. This roughly translates as the reason for the decision or the central core of reasoning. In some cases it is not always readily apparent and the search for the *ratio decidendi* can become the subject of further legal argument and debate in subsequent cases. Much of the detail of the judgment is classified as *obiter dicta,* or statements made in passing, which are not crucial to the case but may be considered persuasive in subsequent decisions.

The key question in many cases will turn on whether a particular line of precedent has to be followed. In order to avoid a precedent that is unfavourable to the outcome sought, it is necessary to be able to distinguish the case from the case which set the precedent. Cases may be distinguished in a number of ways. It may be possible to distinguish on the facts: i.e. there is a material difference in the facts between the current case and the precedent, which justifies a different decision. Cases may be distinguished on the issues, or on the basis that there is an unclear *ratio* in the case, which it is argued forms the precedent. It may also be argued that the precedent need not be followed because, when that case was heard, key cases that would have influenced the outcome were either omitted or misinterpreted.

■ Accessing and understanding case law

Case law decisions are published in law reports. Law reports can actually be traced back around 700 years. In fact it is unlikely that, as a social worker, you would need to look at a case from before the 1950s given the structure and formation of Social Services Departments and the legislation affecting social work responsibilities. It is most likely that access will be to new cases, which may have an effect on existing practices. Law reports contain the full text of a legal judgment and further details about the case.

Older collections of law reports tend to be known by the name of the reporter, e.g. Barnewall and Alderson. The Incorporated Council of Law Reporting introduced 'The Law Reports' in 1865 as a series divided according to the court which heard a particular case. The divisions that can be found today are Appeal Cases (**AC**) for cases in the Court of Appeal and House of Lords, Chancery Division (**Ch**), Queen's Bench (**QB**), and Family Division (**Fam**), for cases heard in each of the respective divisions of the High Court. There are also two 'general' series, which include major cases covering a wide range of issues, known as the All England Law Reports (**All ER**) and the Weekly Law Reports (**WLR**). In addition to these sources, useful reference can be made to the Family Law Reports (**FLR**), the Family Court Reporter (**FCR**) and the Community Care Law Reports (**CCLR**), two specialist series that concentrate on a particular area of law, as their names suggest. With the increasing influence of European law sometimes it may also be necessary to find a decision of the European Court. These decisions are contained in the European Human Rights Reports (**EHRR**).

Ombudsmens' decisions are highly relevant to social work practice and, although not binding in the same way as case law from the courts, they may be persuasive. These decisions can be accessed from the Local Government Ombudsman website[16] and a selection have also been reported in the Community Care Law Reports.

Where a short summary of a case is required, it is useful to look in *The Times* newspaper, which provides up-to-date reports of cases decided sometimes as recently as the previous day. A further option is to look at case note sections in certain journals, which have the advantage of incorporating some commentary on the implications of a decision as well as a summary of the facts and judgment. Journals including the *New Law Journal, LAG Bulletin, Solicitors Journal* and *Family Law* have case law sections. Major cases will also be reported more widely and may be subject to media scrutiny on television and in the broadsheet and tabloid press.

Case names are written according to convention and follow a logical pattern. For example, in the case *X (Minors)* v. *Bedfordshire County Council* [1995] 3 All ER 353, an action is brought by 'X' (the letter is used to anonymise the party and '(Minors)' tells us it is a case concerning children), 'v.' means against, followed by the name of the other party, Bedfordshire County Council. The date in square brackets refers to the year in which the case is reported, '3' refers to the volume of the law report for that year, 'All ER' is an abbreviation for the series of law report, here the All England Law Reports, and 353 is the page. Sometimes the title of the case will also include a reference to the level of court where it was heard, e.g. HL refers to the House of Lords. There is an exercise at the end of this chapter designed to develop understanding of case law.

Neutral citation

It is now possible to access many case reports on the internet. In recognition of this, a citation system particular to reports available on the web has been developed, known as 'neutral citation', because it is not linked to any particular law report. The citation begins with the year then follows with UKHL; EWCA Civ or Crim; or EWHC Admin or Fam, and refers respectively to a decision made by the House of Lords or in England and Wales made by the Court of Appeal Civil or Criminal Division or the High Court Administrative or Family Court. The number following gives the case position for that court, i.e. whether it was the first or thirty-first case heard by the court in that year.

For example: *Re O and N (Children) (Non-accidental Injury: Burden of Proof), Re B (Children)* [2003] UKHL 18.

- ■ [2003] – this case was heard in 2003.
- ■ UKHL – a decision of the House of Lords.
- ■ 18 – the eighteenth case heard by the House of Lords in that year.
- ■ *Re O and N, Re B* – we can also see that two appeals (concerning the same key issue) were joined together for the House of Lords' consideration.
- ■ (*Children*) – the cases concerned children.
- ■ (*Non-accidental Injury: Burden of Proof*) – the substantial issues for the court to consider.

■ Judge-made law

The volume of law being introduced in the form of primary and delegated legislation has increased dramatically in recent years. It might be suggested that, as a result, the significance of the common law has correspondingly reduced. In fact, as case law often deals with ambiguity and matters of interpretation in legislation, it remains a key element of English law. This highlights an issue which is discussed in detail by Griffith (1991),[17] namely the extent to which the judiciary have a creative function in developing the common law and interpreting statutes. Whilst their suitability for this task continues to be questioned, it seems commonly accepted that judges do create law, and are not confined simply to applying parliamentary legislation. What limits are there on this creative process? Rules of statutory interpretation have developed over the years to assist the judiciary where a statute is unclear, where it does not specifically provide for the situation before the court, or where a complex case appears to relate to apparently conflicting provisions (known as the literal, mischief and golden rules). The judiciary can sometimes be quite creative in making and adapting the common law in the absence of statute. This was clearly illustrated in the development of case law on High Court declarations, in the absence of a clear statutory framework for making decisions where an individual lacks mental capacity (discussed further in Chapter 16).

■ Practice Directions

As well as giving judgments in decided cases, the courts also issue Practice Directions from time to time. These directions are intended to give guidance on how to conduct particular cases. As an example, in February 2000, the Lord Chief Justice of England and Wales gave a Practice Direction entitled *Trial of Children and Young Persons in the Crown Court*. Its objective was to ensure that the trial process 'should not expose the young defendant to avoidable intimidation, humiliation or distress'. It included the following directions (amongst others):

- ■ The trial should, if practicable, be held in a courtroom in which all participants are on the same or almost the same level.
- ■ The trial should be conducted according to a timetable which takes full account of a young defendant's inability to concentrate for long periods. Frequent and regular breaks will often be appropriate.

■ Judicial review

A significant body of case law has developed through the process of judicial review, an aspect of administrative law, which is of great importance for public authorities and has produced cases including the *Gloucestershire* decision referred to above. In a judicial review case the central issue is a review of the way a particular decision was taken. It should not normally be seen as an appeal against an unfavourable decision, nor an opportunity for the court to substitute a different decision. Applications for judicial review are brought in the administrative court office of the High Court Queen's Bench Division, which is staffed by nominated, experienced judges. A judicial review may be brought against any body that performs a public function. Local authorities are clearly within that category, as are police authorities, Government ministers, inferior courts and tribunals, and disciplinary bodies such as the General Medical Council.

Judicial review is available to anyone who has a sufficient interest in the matter in question. This is wider than the victim test under the Human Rights Act 1998 (explained further in Chapter 5). The category is intended to exclude vexatious litigants. The grounds for judicial review have developed through a series of cases and include illegality, procedural impropriety and irrationality. A public body acts illegally when it goes beyond its jurisdiction or powers or is said to be *ultra vires*. This can include a failure to follow a specified procedure, or taking into account irrelevant matters when reaching a decision. The grounds for judicial review also extend to cases where a breach of the rules of *natural justice* is argued, such as not being informed of the case against you, or not having the opportunity to present your case: e.g. *R.* v. *Harrow London Borough Council, ex parte D* [1990] 3 All ER 12 related to a mother's complaint that she did not know the allegations against her which were discussed at a case conference.

The orders that can be made in a judicial review case include: mandatory orders formerly called 'mandamus', requiring a public authority to carry out its duty; quashing orders, previously known as 'certiorari', which quash a decision; and prohibitory orders, restraining a public body from acting in a particular way. The court can make a declaration on a question of law or rights, or an injunction which regulates behaviour. It is possible for an award of damages to be made in conjunction with any of the above orders. As a preliminary, it is necessary to obtain leave to proceed with an application for judicial review. Normally it will be necessary for the individual to have exhausted any other appropriate remedies before bringing the claim for judicial review. For example, this might include initial reference to the local authority's complaints process and complaint to the *local government ombudsman.*

Law reform

The impetus for law reform may be provided by a variety of sources. Overwhelming public pressure on an issue will be difficult for Government to ignore and may prompt new legislation or speed the process of reform. In many cases new legislation is borne out of a process of research and consultation, which may be led by a particular Government department or an independent body, and influenced by lobbying by interested groups. The work of probably the most significant independent body, the Law Commission, is discussed below. The Children Act 1989 provides a useful illustration as it developed through a combination of the above. Reports recommending reform of areas of child law had been produced by both the Department of Health and the Law Commission. Simultaneously, events in Cleveland heightened public awareness of child abuse and proved a catalyst to the subsequent, and relatively quickly introduced, Act.

∎ The Law Commission

The Law Commission is an independent body comprising five commissioners and various support staff. It was established by Parliament in 1965 to review the law of England and Wales and make proposals for reform when appropriate. The reform process includes stages of research, which may involve comparative analysis with other systems of law, and consultation with interested bodies, lawyers, the general public, academics and experts. Proposals are often accompanied by draft Bills. The Law Commission works on a number of different projects at any given time, usually directed by the Lord Chancellor or the Government in terms of the specific area. The Commission publishes an annual report, which provides details of ongoing work, consultation papers and any resulting legislation. Currently the Commission is examining the law as it applies to unmarried couples on termination of their relationship, including whether contracts between cohabitants setting out how they will share their property in the event of the relationship ending should be legally enforceable.

In addition to reform, the Commission also consider *consolidation, codification* and *revision* of statutes. Consolidation involves drawing together fragmented legislation on a particular area into one statute. Fragmentation most often occurs where legislation has been repeatedly amended. Revision of statutes ensures that obsolete provisions are repealed. (When the Children Act 1989 was introduced, eight pieces of legislation relating to children were repealed in their entirety and others limited.) A major ongoing project is the codification of the criminal law. The Commission published a draft Criminal Code in 1989 and from that a number of draft Bills have been produced, which collectively will form a criminal code when enacted. The significance of this objective should not be underestimated. This chapter has shown that English law is contained in two distinct sources, statute and case law. In contrast, most other countries with a more modern constitution have a single code for an area of law. To develop English law similarly should lead to a clearer and more accessible system, which can be understood by lawyers and lay people.

Unfortunately, not all of the Law Commission's recommendations are adopted by Parliament and translated into legislation. In fact, only about two-thirds of their proposals for law reform have become legislation. This is so even in areas where antiquated, inappropriate legislation exists and there is widespread support for reform. It can also take many years for recommendations that are adopted to become law. An obvious example is the Law Commission's work on mental capacity and public powers of protection for vulnerable adults. The Law Commission worked on this area from 1991 to 1995, publishing four consultation documents, a final report and a draft Bill. This was followed by a consultation paper, 'Who Decides?' (1997) and 'Making Decisions' (1999), which contained Government proposals. In the final document the Lord Chancellor gave a commitment to introduce legislation 'when Parliamentary time allows'. That time proved to be in 2005 when the Mental Capacity Act received Royal Assent. The final legislation contains many, but not all, of the Law Commission recommendations.

Chapter summary

- There is a vast range of law and official guidance relevant to social work practice and it is located in a number of different sources, including: primary and secondary legislation; policy and practice guidance; directions; codes of practice and case law.

- New legislation is created by Parliament. Starting as a Bill, proposed legislation goes through a process of scrutiny in the House of Commons and the House of Lords until it receives Royal Assent and becomes an Act of Parliament. Most new legislation actually comes into force some time after it receives Royal Assent, by a separate commencement order.

■ In addition to primary legislation, social workers should be aware of the range of rules, regulations and guidance frequently issued to supplement the Act, which may be regularly updated. These documents vary in status and, although they may not have the full force of law, failure to comply with the guidance they contain may have severe consequences for an authority.

■ The other major source of law in the United Kingdom is case law decided by judges, also known as the common law.

■ The significance of a particular case depends in part on the doctrine of precedent, through which decisions of superior courts form precedents which the inferior courts are bound to follow when faced with similar cases.

■ Case law can be found in a range of law reports, and is reported in a standardised way which provides a summary of the facts of the case, the judgments of judges who hear the case, the date and the level of court.

■ Law is regularly updated, consolidated and reformed and the Law Commission is an important independent body whose task it is to review and offer proposals for reform of the law.

Exercises

The best way to understand case law and legislation is to read some.

Choose one of the cases listed below, all of which will be referred to in this text and are significant cases in social work law:

R v. Gloucestershire County Council, ex parte Barry [1997] 2 All ER 1

Gillick v. West Norfolk and Wisbech Area Health Authority and Another [1986] AC 112

Re F (Adult: Court's Jurisdiction) [2000] WLR 1740

Re O and N (Children) (Non-accidental Injury:Burden of Proof), Re B (Children) [2002] 3 FCR 418

1. Locate the case in a law library.

2. Read the case fully, including all the judgments.

3. Identify the following from your case:

   (a) names of parties

   (b) court/venue

   (c) name(s) of judge(s)

   (d) date and length of hearing

   (e) full reference case reported under – which law report

(f) headnote

(g) catchwords

(h) decision

(i) judgment

(j) cases referred to in judgment

(k) points of law

(l) legal representatives.

4. Search on the internet for an electronic version of the case and note the neutral citation.

5. Identify the implications of the decision for social work practice.

Access the Adoption and Children Act 2002 and research the following points:

■ What is the short title of the Act?

■ How many Chapters and how many Schedules does the Act contain?

■ Who is eligible to adopt?

■ Which part of the Act contains amendments to the Children Act 1989 and how many are there?

■ When can local authority foster parents apply to adopt a child they have fostered?

■ How long does a child have to live with adopters before an application for adoption can be made?

■ How is suitability of adopters to be assessed?

■ How many adoption registers are there and what do they cover?

■ What are the grounds for dispensing with parental consent to adoption?

■ Is the Act fully in force?

■ Did any provision come into force earlier than the bulk of the Act – if so, which?

You will also need to have sight of the Children Act 1989 to answer the final two points.

■ Identify three differences between the special guardianship order introduced by this legislation and the residence order established under the Children Act 1989.

■ Compare and contrast the welfare test and checklist under the ACA 2002 and the Children Act 1989. Are there any significant differences?

For each of the following – identify its source and status, e.g. the Children Act 1989 is primary legislation produced by Parliament.

■ The Children Act 1989.

■ The definition of murder.

■ Code C Detention Treatment and Questioning 2004.

■ 'In Safe Hands' (2000).

■ *Mabon* v. *Mabon and others* [2005] EWCA Civ 634.

■ President's Direction: HIV Testing of Children [2003] 1 FLR 1299.

∎ The Special Guardianship Regulations 2005.

∎ *Achieving Best Evidence in Criminal Proceedings: Guidance for Vulnerable or Intimidated Witnesses including Children* (2001).

Websites

The Law Commission website, which includes details of law reform programmes:
www.lawcom.gov.uk

For legislation and explanatory notes to new legislation:
www.opsi.gov.uk

The official website for Parliament provides information about Parliament, gives access to Hansard (the report of parliamentary debates) and judgments of the House of Lords, and tracks progress of Bills before Parliament:
www.parliament.uk

Department of Health site for a complete listing of local authority circulars (LACs) and local authority social services letters (LASSLs):
www.doh.gov.uk/publicationsandstatistics/fs/en

The Home Office site provides information on the progress of law reform in the criminal law arena:
www.homeoffice.gov.uk

Case law reports are available from a number of websites, some of which are subscription only (e.g. Westlaw). The list below are all generally accessible:

www.bailii.org
Provides access to British and Irish legal information including cases and legislation. There is a useful keyword search facility and it is possible to view cases from each of the different courts (and tribunals) and in 'most recent order'.

www.hmcourts-service.gov.uk
This database includes selected decisions from the High Court and the Court of Appeal. Judgments from the House of Lords are available on the Parliament website (above).

www.timesonline.co.uk/law
The site of *The Times* newspaper includes its case report section and is often the first to publish (abbreviated) law reports.

Further reading

Thomas, P.A. (2001) (4th edn) *How to use a Law Library; An Introduction to Legal Skills*. London: Sweet & Maxwell. (An accessible, detailed guide to finding and understanding legal materials.)

Golding, J. (ed) (2005) *Is it in Force? 2005. A guide to commencement of statutes passed since 1st January, 1980 (incorporating statutes not yet in force)*. London: LexisNexis. (Use this text to check whether an Act or any of its provisions have been implemented – usually available for reference in any law library.)

Encyclopaedia of Social Services and Child Care Law. London: Sweet & Maxwell. (A loose-leaf encyclopaedia which is updated regularly and contains legislation, regulations and rules, relevant circulars alongside explanatory text.)

Notes

1. S. Braye and M. Preston-Shoot (2005) *Teaching, Learning and Assessment of Law in Social Work Education*. London: Social Care Institute for Excellence.

2. See: D. French (1996) *How to Cite Legal Authorities*. London: Blackstone Press.

3. www.opsi.gov.uk.

4. The 'Woolf Reforms; so called after Lord Woolf CJ, who led the reform of civil procedure.

5. For further information and examples, visit the Plain Language Commission website at www.clearest.co.uk.

6. Occasionally an MP may move for the Bill to go to a special standing committee or a committee of the whole House.

7. Available online at www.hansard-westminster.co.uk.

8. By SI 2001/777.

9. J. Gold (ed.) (2005) *Is it in Force? 2005*. London: Lexis Nexis. A guide to the commencement of statutes passed since 1 January 1980 (incorporating statutes not yet in force).

10. DH (2000) 'No Secrets: Guidance on developing and implementing multi-agency policies and procedures to protect vulnerable adults from abuse'. London: DH.

11. National Assembly for Wales (2000) *In Safe Hands: Implementing Adult Protection Procedures in Wales*. Cardiff: National Assembly for Wales.

12. www.doh.gov.uk/publications/coinh.html.

13. See further discussion of police powers in Chapter 12.

14. T. Ingram (2000) *The English Legal Process* (8th edn). London: Blackstone Press.

15. For a full discussion of precedent, see T. Ingram (2000) *The English Legal Process* (8th edn). London: Blackstone Press.

16. www.lgo.org.uk/digest.htm.

17. J.A.G. Griffith (1991) *The Politics of the Judiciary* (4th edn). London: Fontana Press.

3 Courts and law officers

Learning objectives

To develop an understanding of the following:

- The organisation and operation of the legal system.
- The background knowledge required to work effectively in legal settings.
- The distinction between civil and criminal law.
- The distinction between public and private law
- The structure and process of courts and tribunals.
- The roles of various legal personnel and professionals working in the legal system.
- Access to law and representation issues.

Introduction

The English legal system often appears complex to a lay person and this is especially so when it is portrayed inaccurately by the media. This chapter aims to provide sufficient information for an individual who has chosen a social work career, which has close links with law, to overcome this concern.

The chapter offers explanation of the structure of the English legal system, the courts, the role of key personnel in court and the ways in which support can be provided for an individual to have effective access to the law. To bring this information to life, court observation is strongly encouraged and a guide for observation is included at the end of the chapter.

Courts and the English legal system

The hierarchy of the court structure is inextricably bound up with the doctrine of precedent, explained in the previous chapter. It may be helpful to visualise the structure as a staircase climbing from the magistrates up to the House of Lords. Alternatively, a pyramid shape, again with the House of Lords as the pinnacle and the magistrates' court at ground level, captures both the hierarchy of the system and also roughly reflects the relative workload at each level. To a certain extent, courts can be distinguished according to whether they deal with civil or criminal cases (though there are overlaps).

■ Distinguishing between civil and criminal law

There are a number of ways in which the distinction between civil and criminal law can be drawn.

Parties

In a criminal case the dispute is between the state and an individual or 'body'. The parties are referred to as the prosecution and the defence or the accused. The substance of the case is an allegation of behaviour, which falls within the definition of a criminal offence (in statute or common law, e.g. theft or murder). It will be a matter over which society as a whole is taken to have an interest in expressing at least its disapproval and ultimately, if proved, may consider it necessary to sentence the perpetrator of the offence.

In a civil case the dispute is between individuals, referred to as the claimant or applicant (previously the term plaintiff was used) and the defendant, or in divorce cases, the petitioner and the respondent.

In criminal or civil cases an 'individual' as described above may, in fact, be something other than a single person, as the term would suggest. It could include a company or corporation, a charity, health authority or local authority.

Civil disputes may be further classified as *private* or *public* matters. In a public matter a body may act on behalf of the state in a civil case. An obvious example of this is where a local authority issues care proceedings in respect of a child in its area. This is a civil matter, but could also be described as an aspect of public rather than private law because it involves a public body exercising a public function. A civil matter, which is private as opposed to public, would include a divorce between two individuals, or could be a *contract* dispute between an individual and a company or public body, the nature of the dispute in these matters, e.g. contract, being the defining issue. It is notable that the Children Act 1989 covers aspects of both the public and private law relating to children.

Remedies

The outcome or *remedy* in a case will differ according to whether it is a civil or criminal matter. In a criminal case the object is to determine the question of guilt and then to make an appropriate disposal. According to different perspectives, this penalty may be framed in terms of punishment, rehabilitation or retribution and includes imprisonment, community orders, fines and compensation orders.

In civil cases an order will be made giving judgment to either party (crudely speaking, the winner). This can include an element of paying the other side's costs. The order that can be made will depend on the type of case and may include injunctions, which order a person to carry out a particular action or order them to refrain from particular action, e.g. a non-molestation order. The most frequent order in civil cases is for compensation or damages to be paid by one party to the other to compensate for loss or damage and special rules and conventions are used to arrive at the level of damages. It will be noted that there is another overlap here, in that compensation orders can also be made in criminal cases. This order is discussed in more detail in Chapter 18. Also, breach of a civil order may be a criminal offence, e.g the anti-social behaviour order discussed in Chapter 13.

Standard of proof

In a civil case the standard of proof is known as *balance of probabilities*. This means that the point to be proven has to be more probable than not. In percentage terms this might be understood as a 49:51 per cent balance, i.e. the scales only just have to tip. In a criminal case the standard of proof is higher and is known as *beyond reasonable doubt.* Again, to conceptualise this in percentage terms, it might equate to approximately 97 per cent, a high level but still allowing for a slight degree of doubt. The statue of the Scales of Justice outside the Old Bailey in London serve to remind us of this analogy. As with the other areas of distinction between civil and criminal justice discussed here, however, there are exceptions to these principles. The civil courts have in certain cases innovated the concept of a standard of proof which is higher than balance of probability yet falls short of beyond reasonable doubt.

In the case of *Re H and R (Child Sexual Abuse: Standard of Proof)* [1996] AC 563, the House of Lords delivered a majority judgment in a case where a care order was sought for a 15-year-old girl who alleged sexual abuse over a period of time by her mother's cohabitant. He had been acquitted of rape in the criminal court. Lord Nicholls stated that stronger evidence was required for serious allegations because it was less likely that they would have occurred. In a dissenting judgment in *Re H*, Lord Lloyd commented that 'it would be a bizarre result if the more serious the anticipated injury, whether physical or sexual, the more difficult it became for the authority to . . . secure protection for the child'. Lord Nicholls' position has been confirmed in *Re ET (Serious Injuries: Standard of Proof)* [2003] 2 FLR 1205. Whatever the justification, the development of a sliding-scale standard of proof, even if linked to the 'seriousness' of the case, serves to introduce confusion and uncertainty.

The same circumstances may lead to criminal and civil cases and illustrate the application of the different standards of proof; for example, harm caused to a child may constitute a criminal offence and may give rise to care proceedings. In the criminal case the evidence focuses on whether the court is satisfied 'beyond reasonable doubt' that the defendant caused the harm and should be convicted. In care proceedings the court must be satisfied on a balance of probabilities that the threshold of 'significant harm' is reached and that the child should be made subject of a care order; it is less concerned with precisely attributing blame for injuries caused. A statement from *Re U (A Child) (Serious Injury: Standard of Proof)* [2004] EWCA Civ 567 reminds us that 'it by no means follows that an acquittal on a criminal charge or a successful appeal would lead to the absolution of the parent or carer in family or civil proceedings'.

The criminal law has been amended recently following a number of cases where injuries to children have been caused and care proceedings have been taken, but it has not been possible to convict the perpetrator due to evidential difficulties and the higher standard of proof. The case of *Re O and N (Children) (Non-accidental Injury: Burden of Proof); Re B (Children)* [2003] UKHL 18 is discussed fully in Chapter 9. The new criminal law is contained in the Domestic Violence, Crime and Victims Act 2004 (**DVCVA 2004**), which introduced the new offence of 'familial homicide' in s. 5. The offence applies where a child (or vulnerable adult) dies as a result of an unlawful act of a person of the same household, who either caused the death or, aware of the risk, failed to protect the child. In such a case more than one adult can be charged with the offence and it is not necessary to precisely establish who caused the death and who failed to protect.[1]

The standard of proof should not be confused with the ***burden of proof***. The burden of proof rests on the party asserting a particular point – 'he who alleges must prove'. In criminal cases it is for the prosecution to prove guilt to a standard beyond reasonable doubt rather than for the defence to prove innocence.

Very occasionally the burden of proof in a criminal case may switch to the defence. For instance, in attempts by the defence to show good cause why the defendant was carrying what was alleged to be an offensive weapon, the burden would be on the defence to prove this and the standard of proof would then be the civil one of balance of probabilities. In a civil case the burden may switch between the parties, particularly if there are counterclaims.

Each of the criteria can be seen to have a number of qualifications or exceptions. Very little in the law is absolutely clear-cut, though there is often an expectation from the public that precision is the very essence of the law. This may also explain why lawyers rarely give advice in terms of absolute 'yes' or 'no' answers; rather, the tendency is to talk along the lines of likelihood and alternative pathways. To draw an accurate distinction between criminal and civil matters or confidently to categorise a case as civil or criminal it is necessary to look at the features of the case in entirety. Exhibit 3.1 summarises the differences between a civil and criminal case and identifies the courts with civil and criminal jurisdiction.

■ Courts exercising civil jurisdiction

Civil cases may be heard in the House of Lords, the Court of Appeal (Civil Division), the High Court Family Division, Chancery Division and the Queen's Bench Division, known as the superior courts. The inferior courts dealing with civil cases are the county court, which has a jurisdiction over the majority of civil cases,

	CIVIL	CRIMINAL
Parties	Claimant/Applicant and Defendant Petitioner and Respondent	State/Prosecution versus Defendant/Accused
Remedies	Compensation Injunctions (Costs)	Sentence 'Punishment' Deterrence/retribution
Standard of Proof	Balance of probabilities	Beyond reasonable doubt

Courts   Magistrates

County   Crown

Tribunals
High Court   Queen's Bench
Family
Chancery

Court of Appeal

(Civil Division)   (Criminal Division)

House of Lords
European Court of Justice

NB: Courts listed on central line have both civil and criminal jurisdiction

Exhibit 3.1   Distinguishing features of civil and criminal cases

including cases concerning family and child issues and personal injury cases, and the magistrates' court, which, although dealing mainly with criminal matters, hears civil claims relating to family and child matters. The majority of civil disputes fall into three categories: personal injury action seeking compensation following an injury; actions for breach of contract; and debt. Some civil cases also involve circumstances where the permission of the courts is required before a particular action can be taken, e.g. a High Court declaration authorising sterilisation of a woman with a learning disability, or approval to remove a child from the jurisdiction. The Government has indicated that it supports reform of the courts dealing with first instance (i.e. not appeals) civil and family cases (High Court, County Court and Family Proceedings Court) into a single civil and family court and has adopted this as a long-term Government objective requiring legislation at some time in the future.[2] Tribunals also exercise civil jurisdiction.

■ Outline of a civil case

For every potential civil litigant there are a number of risks to be evaluated. These risks range from the most obvious one of losing the case, through to the effects of delays in the proceedings and the cost of the proceedings. Litigation is unpredictable and can be a very stressful and demanding experience.

There will usually be a period of negotiation and exchange of correspondence before a civil action formally begins. If, through this informal process, it is not possible to settle the dispute, court proceedings may be commenced. The detail of the civil system is contained in the Civil Procedure Rules 1998.

Imagine a scenario where a person, John, when visiting his mother in a residential home, is injured by slipping on a pool of water left after a member of staff had been mopping the floor. Despite an initial letter from John to the manager of the home and a further letter from a solicitor to the head office of the company which runs this and a series of other homes, the home has not acknowledged liability or offered any compensation, and John now feels he has no alternative other than to commence proceedings. The process would begin with John filling out a claim form and paying a fee to the court office, which stamps the claim form with the court's official seal. At this stage proceedings are formally issued. Next, within four months, John must serve the claim form, with a response pack, to the home. *Service* is the technical term for delivery of a legal document (usually by first class post). On receipt of the claim form, the home should return an acknowledgement of service and also indicate whether it intends to admit, defend or counterclaim in response to John's claim form. Next, statements of case are produced by both parties, the factual contention of the party bringing the case (John) and (from the care home company) a response to allegations made by John and particular defences that are available. In this example the home might deny that there was water on the floor or argue that, even if there was, it was adequately signposted with an appropriate warning. The court will make an early assessment of the likely complexity of the claim and allocate the claim to one of three case management tracks:

1. *Small claims track:* limited to claims involving less than £5,000 or £1,000 in a personal injury case. It is intended to be both inexpensive and quick.

2. *Fast track:* appropriate for cases which are considered more important and have a value of £5,000–£15,000 or, for personal injury cases, £1,000–£15,000. In fast track cases it would be usual for the matter to be capable of hearing at a one-day trial with a maximum of two experts for each party. In some fast track cases oral evidence may be excluded.

3. *Multi-track:* all other cases will be allocated to multi-track. These are the cases which typically involve more than £15,000 and are more complex.

A judge will then give some directions for the steps that the parties need to take to progress the claim to final hearing. These directions might include producing photographs. Each party will inspect the other's documents, a process known as *disclosure,* and exchange other types of evidence, including reports of experts and witness statements. Through disclosing these documents in advance some cases will be settled without the need for a full hearing. It should also enable the parties to consider the strength of their claim in the context of all the evidence and should mean that there are no significant surprises at the trial. Cases will be listed for trial as soon as is possible and procedures emphasise the need to reduce any unnecessary delays.

If the case reaches trial, witnesses will be called to give oral evidence, relating to the facts in contention, and other evidence including documents will be considered by the judge. At the conclusion of the trial, judgment will be given in favour of one of the parties. In the example, if the home was found to have been negligent in allowing the pool of water, which caused the injury to John, to be on that floor, it is likely to have to pay John the costs incurred in bringing his claim, including legal advice and representation in court. As part of the judgment an award of damages may also be awarded to John to compensate for his loss, including pain and suffering, loss of earnings, loss of amenity, costs of medical treatment, etc. The risk of having a judgment awarded against you is the real incentive to settle a case!

■ Courts exercising criminal jurisdiction

Courts that deal with criminal cases are: the magistrates' court, which has both an adult and a youth crime jurisdiction; the Crown Court; the Queen's Bench Division of the High Court; the Criminal Division of the Court of Appeal; and the House of Lords. The starting point in a consideration of a criminal case is the classification of the crime. There are three groups of offences recognised by the criminal law:

1. *Summary offences:* the less serious criminal offences, including numerous motoring and traffic offences, drunkenness offences, threatening behaviour, taking and driving away (TWOC) and are tried by magistrates.

2. *Indictable offences:* the most serious offences, which are tried 'on indictment' in the Crown Court, including murder, rape, arson and robbery.

3. *Either way offences:* as the name suggests, may be tried in the magistrates' court or the Crown Court depending on the seriousness of the offence and the preference of the defendant. Either way offences include criminal acts where there is a possible range of seriousness, such as theft, which may be charged in a petty shoplifting case or a major theft of property worth millions of pounds.[3]

Offences may also be classified according to the type of harm done. This is often reflected in the legislation which establishes particular offences, e.g. the Theft Act 1968 or the Sexual Offences Act 2003. Crimes may be committed: against property, e.g. burglary; physical integrity of the person, e.g. rape or assaults; or general public rights of citizenship, e.g. public order offences.

■ Brief outline of the criminal process

The first stage in the criminal process is arrest. An individual may be arrested on a warrant issued by a magistrate, or, more commonly, by a police officer. On arrest, the suspect must be given a caution, and told what he is being arrested for. Following arrest, a decision will be taken on whether the individual is to be charged with an offence. Following charge the issue of remand must be considered. There is a presumption in favour of bail, which should be refused only in specified circumstances, such as there being substantial grounds to believe that the accused person would abscond, commit a further offence, interfere with witnesses, or otherwise obstruct the course of justice.[4] Conditions may be attached to bail addressing a particular risk, e.g. regular reporting to the police station to ensure attendance at court.

Following charge (a decision that the CPS are increasingly involved with), full control of progress of the case is taken by the Crown Prosecution Service (**CPS**). The CPS will review the evidence that the police have gathered and independently make the decision whether to prosecute, based on likelihood of success and whether prosecution is considered to be in the public interest.

The next stage will depend on the nature of the offence. All offences which are ultimately tried in the Crown Court must be committed to that court by the magistrates. A preliminary hearing, known as committal, determines whether there is a *prima facie* case, to go to trial in the Crown Court. In an either way case, the clerk will explain the right of election, i.e. that the accused has the right to choose whether the case is heard by magistrates or in the Crown Court before a jury. If the accused chooses trial before the magistrates, it is still possible for the case to be committed to Crown Court for sentence if the magistrates consider their sentencing powers are insufficient. Various factors influence the defendant's choice between the magistrates and the Crown Court, including delay and the type of offence. Following committal, the case is usually adjourned to allow both the prosecution and the defence to prepare fully for trial.

At trial, the charge will be read and the defendant enters a plea of guilty or not guilty. In some minor cases in the magistrates' court it is possible for the defendant to enter a guilty plea by post. If a guilty plea is entered, the prosecution provides an outline of the facts of the case and details of the defendant's *antecedents*, then the case moves to sentencing. If the defendant pleads not guilty, in the Crown Court the jury will be sworn in. There then follows a standard procedure for introducing the evidence upon which the case is decided:

■ The prosecution opening speech – usually includes a summary of the evidence which the prosecution intends to call.

■ The prosecution will then introduce its evidence, including witnesses, who must take the oath or affirm before giving their evidence. The prosecution asks questions of the witness, known as *examination-in-chief*. The witness must then face questions from the defence, known as a *cross-examination*, the objective of which is to discredit and disprove the truth of the witness's evidence. Following cross-examination the prosecution may *re-examine*, or ask further questions, but that is limited to any new issues which have arisen out of cross-examination, rather than going over and trying to reinforce the evidence already given.

■ At the close of the prosecution case, i.e. when the prosecution has provided all the evidence on which it intends to rely, the defence has the opportunity to submit a plea that there is *no case to answer*. If this is accepted the defendant is acquitted.

■ Assuming that submission is not successful, the case then proceeds with defence evidence, including, in many cases, the evidence of the accused.

- When all the evidence has been produced, a closing speech is made by the defence.
- In the Crown Court, the judge will sum up for the benefit of a jury. In summing up, the judge deals with points of law and summarises the evidence.
- The foreman of the jury will deliver its verdict, and either the accused will be acquitted, if found not guilty, or, if found guilty, the case moves to sentence. Only if the jury are unable to reach a unanimous decision, will the judge accept a majority verdict.[5] The Chair of the Bench in the magistrates' court delivers the verdict and pronounces sentence.

For cases where there is a possibility of a prison sentence, a pre-sentence report is provided to the court (discussed in Chapter 18). The final stage in the process before sentence is announced is the plea in mitigation, presented by the defence. The range of sentences that may be ordered depends on the offence for which the defendant is convicted. Sentencing options range from absolute discharge, through to fines, *community orders* (replacement for probation and community service), compensation orders, suspended sentence of imprisonment and imprisonment for any period up to life sentence. These sentencing options are discussed in Chapter 18.

For a young person charged with a criminal offence, the basic procedure is very similar to that outlined above but the case will usually proceed in the youth court. A range of different sentencing or disposal options is available to the court and these are dealt with in detail in Chapter 13.

The court structure

The courts are now managed by the Court Service, an executive agency of the Department of Constitutional Affairs, in place of direct responsibility to the Lord Chancellor.[6]

Magistrates' court

The magistrates' court is the inferior criminal court, dealing with between 95 and 96 per cent of all criminal cases and a significant civil jurisdiction. It is one of the oldest courts and, despite a number of changes over the years, it has retained the basic principle that lay members of the community form this tier of the judiciary. Reform under the Courts Act 2003 altered the organisation of magistrates' courts. Instead of a separate commission of the peace for each region in England and Wales, administered by Magistrates' Courts Committees, there is now a single commission of the peace and magistrates have a national jurisdiction. Magistrates' courts are administered by the Court's Service. The criminal jurisdiction of the magistrates' court comprises: trial of summary offences; acting as examining justices to determine whether a *prima facie* case exists for offences triable on indictment to be committed to the Crown Court; and conducting mode of trial examination for either way offences. Appeals lie from the magistrates' court to the Crown Court against sentence and conviction, and to the Queen's Bench Division of the High Court on a point of law or application for judicial review.

Youth court

The youth court is a specialist branch of the magistrates' court (Criminal Justice Act 1991), which deals with defendants aged between 10 and 17. The court will consist of three magistrates (at least one male and one female) who are drawn from the youth court panel, and the procedure is intended to be less formal than in the adult court. Parents are also expected to attend court where the young person is under 16. Observation and reporting by the press is limited. Terminology also differs, with 'finding of guilt' and 'order made upon finding of guilt' used in preference to conviction and sentence. A limited category of criminal proceedings against juveniles are dealt with in the adult magistrates' court or Crown Court, including very serious offences and cases where a juvenile is charged jointly with an adult.

Magistrates' court civil jurisdiction

In addition, the magistrates' court has a significant civil jurisdiction. In exercising a significant part of this jurisdiction the court is known as a *family proceedings court* and deals with cases brought under the Children Act 1989 and also the Family Law Act 1996. The types of cases heard include: care proceedings; applications for residence and contact orders; emergency proceeding orders; child assessment orders; and injunctions for domestic violence. Due to the special nature of these cases, magistrates sitting in the family proceedings court are required to be members of the family panel and receive special training.

Other aspects of the civil jurisdiction of magistrates' courts include dealing with recovery of council tax, and functions which might be described as administrative.

■ County courts

There are 218 county courts in England and Wales, exercising a civil jurisdiction. The county court is classified as an inferior court and has tended to deal with less serious civil matters (small claims track and the fast track), work being divided between it and the High Court. Cases in the county courts are heard by circuit judges and district judges (formerly registrars), and are usually listed in the county court for the district where the defendant lives. The county court also includes the small claims court. Partly as a result of the small claims jurisdiction of the county court, it is not unusual for individuals to be unrepresented in the county court. The county court office will offer a certain amount of assistance to a litigant in person and can be a useful source of information, providing a variety of leaflets, etc.

For family law matters there is a distinction between county courts which are designated as family hearing centres, and those which are designated care centres and adoption centres. There are few more serious cases than care applications heard in the county court care centres and in these cases the parties will usually be represented in order to deal with the complex issues that arise. Family hearing centres deal with divorce and related matters including *s. 8 orders.* Judges in the county court dealing with Children Act cases have to be specially nominated.

County court jurisdiction is wide and includes: actions for contract or *tort;* trust and probation; housing matters; cases under the Consumer Credit Act 1974; divorce; child care issues under the Children Act 1989, including residence and contact orders; injunctions under the Family Law Act 1996 for non-molestation or excluding a party from the matrimonial home. The county court deals with discrimination claims on the grounds of race, sex or disability in cases not related to employment, e.g. provision of goods and services. Appeals lie to the Court of Appeal (Civil Division). Though it is a civil court, a judge in the county court may commit a person to prison for contempt of court.

■ Crown Court

The Crown Court is a superior court and deals with indictable criminal offences and those either way offences referred by the magistrates' court. There are 78 branches of the Crown Court in England and Wales, including the Old Bailey in London. Each court centre may actually contain several court rooms. Where the defendant pleads not guilty, a jury will normally sit with the judge. In those cases it is for the jury to determine whether or not the defendant is guilty, and the judge's role is to deal with matters of law, provide a summing up to the jury and pronounce sentence. The Criminal Justice Act 2003 permits cases to be tried by judge alone where there is a real risk of jury tampering, and in certain complex fraud cases. The Crown Court also hears appeals against sentence and conviction by magistrates. In appeal cases a jury is not involved, but the judge will sit with up to four lay magistrates. Circuit judges and recorders hear cases in the Crown Court. Appeals (about 8,000 per year) from the Crown Court lie to the Court of Appeal, Criminal Division, then to the House of Lords. The Criminal Justice Act 1988 introduced a power for the prosecution to appeal against an over-lenient sentence imposed by the Crown Court as, e.g., in *Attorney-General's Reference (No. 24 of 2001); sub nom R. v. David Graham Jenkins* (2001) CA C9500543. In that case a sentence of six months' imprisonment for an offence of gross indecency with a 4-year-old child (the defendant's stepdaughter) was unduly lenient and was substituted with a total sentence of 18 months' imprisonment.

The jury

A jury in the Crown Court will have been chosen at random from people in the community aged between 18 and 70 and on the register of electors. The object is to produce a jury that represents the community at large. Some individuals are not eligible to sit on a jury. Included in this category are: the police; lawyers and judges; probation officers and children's guardians; people with a mental illness; members of the clergy; and people with criminal convictions. If called to jury service, it may be possible to be excused if you have already provided jury service in the last two years or if you are aged over 65, an MP, a member of the armed services or a member of the medical profession. In addition, the court has a general discretion and can excuse a person from jury service for a good reason, e.g. exceptional work commitments, caring responsibilities, but probably not holidays. There are limited powers for the prosecution and the defence to object to particular individuals sitting on the jury. In addition, a juror should not take part in a case where he or she has a personal interest or is closely connected to a party or a witness.

▪ The High Court

The High Court deals with civil and criminal cases, including cases which originate in the High Court and appeals from lower courts. Its jurisdiction is so wide that it has been described as a 'hotchpotch'.[7] There are three divisions of the High Court: Family Division, Chancery Division and Queen's Bench Division. Judges in the High Court are referred to as Mr/Mrs Justice Smith, or Smith J. The Constitutional Reform Act 2005 provides for the creation of new posts of Head of Family Justice (to be held by the President of the Family Division) and a new post of President of the Queen's Bench Division.

The Family Division

The Family Division deals with matrimonial issues, any issues relating to children (and their property), adoption, and exercises the inherent jurisdiction and wardship. The High Court tends to deal with the more complex child care cases, perhaps involving a number of different applications, difficult evidence or cases with an international element. As the Children Act 1989 created concurrent jurisdiction for the magistrates' family proceedings court, the county court and the High Court regarding children, the Children (Allocation of Proceedings) Order 1991 (SI 1991/1677) deals with the transfer of cases between the three levels. Cases under the Human Fertilisation and Embryology Act 1990 are allocated to the Family Division.

A developing area of law in the High Court Family Division is the use of declaratory relief. This is an order which the court makes to declare that a particular course of action or treatment would not be considered unlawful and so could not therefore form the basis of a civil action in tort (e.g. a doctor who performs a sterilisation after a declaration has been made authorising the operation could not be sued for battery). Declaratory relief has been used in a range of cases where a person has not been able to give consent to particular medical treatment because of mental incapacity. The basis of the order is the common law doctrine of necessity, guided by application of the best interests of the incapacitated person. A well-known case is *Airedale National Health Service Trust* v. *Bland* [1993] 1 All ER 821, where a declaration was made stating that it would not be unlawful to withhold medical treatment, nutrition and hydration from a patient in a persistent vegetative state. A more recent stream of cases suggests that the courts are prepared to make declarations that deal with wider welfare issues as well as medical issues. This presents an important exercise of the law-making role of the judiciary. Chapter 17 deals with these cases in more detail.

Queen's Bench Division

The Queen's Bench Division is the largest division of the High Court and has the widest ranging jurisdiction. Most of the work of this division comprises civil issues which are considered too complex for the county court to deal with or involve larger amounts of money than the county court limit for compensation, for example serious injuries arising out of traffic accidents. The Queen's Bench Division also includes a commercial court and the Court of Protection. The Court of Protection is increasingly significant for vulnerable adults, as it offers a number of options for dealing with an incapacitated person's financial and property affairs. These issues are considered in more detail in Chapter 16. The Queen's Bench Division plays an important role in relation to civil liberties. It is the court that can issue the writ of *habeas corpus,* which authorises the release of a detained person.

The majority of judicial review cases commence in the Queen's Bench Division. Judicial review is the process whereby administrative decisions taken by a range of bodies, importantly, including local authorities, can be challenged. An example of a judicial review decision of particular significance for Social Services Departments was the *Gloucestershire* case,[8] which was followed by a series of other cases dealing with the extent to which a local authority's resources can be taken into account in carrying out assessments of individual needs for services. Judicial review plays an important role in ensuring that local authorities and other public bodies do not exceed their powers (*ultra vires*). The basis for intervention by the court is often referred to as *Wednesbury* reasonableness after the case of *Associated Provincial Picture Houses Ltd* v. *Wednesbury Corporation* [1948] 1 KB 223. In essence, a decision may be subject to review if it is so unreasonable that no reasonable authority would have made it. In addition, the authority must have considered all relevant factors and disregarded irrelevant factors.

The Queen's Bench Division also hears appeals on a point of law, from the magistrates' and Crown Courts. The head of the Division is the Lord Chief Justice.

The Chancery Division

The Chancery Division deals with a range of specialised work, including bankruptcy, mortgages, land charges, probate (including challenges to wills and administration of estates), revenue law, patents and company law.

▪ Court of Appeal

The Court of Appeal is housed with the High Court in the Royal Courts of Justice in the Strand, London. The courts have their own Citizens' Advice Bureau to help litigants in person. Usually, three senior judges will sit together to hear cases in the Court of Appeal: they can include the Lord Chancellor, Master of the Rolls, Lord Chief Justice, President of the Family Division, Lords of Appeal in Ordinary and Lords Justices of Appeal, and any High Court judge. Whilst one might expect this court to be very formal, in fact hearings in the Court of Appeal are quite different from hearings in the High Court or Crown Court: it is unusual for witnesses to give evidence; the hearing consists of legal argument from barristers, often including Queen's Counsel; the judges themselves are often interactive and will question counsel about specific points and ask to hear argument relating to particular aspects of the case. Judges are referred to as Lord Justice of Appeal, or Smith LJ. The Court of Appeal hears significantly more cases than the House of Lords.

Civil Division

The civil arm of the Court of Appeal hears appeals on a variety of civil matters from the High Court, county court and tribunals. The Master of the Rolls presides over the Civil Division of the Court of Appeal.

Criminal Division

The Criminal Division of the Court of Appeal hears appeals against sentence from the Crown Court (the majority of its work); appeals against conviction; cases may be referred by the Attorney-General to deal with a point of law or where a sentence imposed is considered unduly lenient. The Criminal Cases Review Commission can refer cases to the Court of Appeal.

■ The House of Lords

The House of Lords is the highest UK appeal court. It hears civil appeals from the Court of Appeal, with leave (permission) from the Court of Appeal, or if the House of Lords has itself given leave. It is possible in certain circumstances to 'leapfrog' the Court of Appeal and appeal direct from the trial court to the House of Lords, if the trial court and the House of Lords agree and there is a point of general public importance at stake. For a criminal case to reach the House of Lords the ground of appeal must be a point of law.

Five judges sit in Committee rooms in the Houses of Parliament to hear appeals and decide whether an appeal should be allowed or disallowed. It is not uncommon for different views to be taken by the judges; reading case reports can give real insight into the complexities of judicial decision-making and the difficulty of arriving at a consensus over some of the issues that are litigated. In some circumstances a majority judgment will be given. This can lead to a rather perverse outcome in some cases. For example, in *Gillick,* both the Court of Appeal and the House of Lords delivered majority judgments. The judges in the Court of Appeal and the House of Lords are of a similar level of expertise. In the final analysis, adding together the judges in the Court of Appeal and the House of Lords, it must have been somewhat dissatisfying for Mrs Gillick to find that, although the final judgment of the House of Lords was against her, and is taken to have established the mature minor principle, in fact more judges supported her view than not! Perhaps this sort of outcome is one of the reasons why it is argued that it is unnecessary to have two senior Appeal Courts. Judges in the House of Lords are Lords of Appeal in Ordinary (Law Lords) and are referred to as, e.g., 'Lord Smith of Greenshire'.[9]

▪ European Court of Justice

The European Court of Justice, which sits in Luxembourg, is the supreme authority for matters affecting the European Union. Its judgments are binding on all UK courts including the House of Lords. European Community law is drawn from European Community treaties and legislation adopted by the Council of the European Union, usually in the form of regulations and directives. As Britain is a member of the European Union, UK law automatically includes European regulations. Each member state has some discretion with directives, which are binding but include some flexibility for the member state as to the manner in which the obligations are translated into national legislation. A recent example of the effect of a European Union directive can be seen in the Government's announcement that it intends to introduce legislation to prohibit age discrimination in employment. The European Equal Treatment Directive 2000 requires all member states to introduce anti-discrimination legislation dealing with ageism (among other things) by 2006. Following publication of a 'Code of Practice on Ageing in Employment' (2001),[10] which contained guidelines for employers, the Employment Equality (Age) Regulations have been drafted and are due to be fully implemented by October 2006.

▪ European Court of Human Rights

The European Court of Human Rights sits in Strasbourg and is the supreme authority on the European Convention on Human Rights (ECHR) 1950. The United Kingdom 'incorporated' the ECHR into domestic law via the Human Rights Act 1998 (discussed in Chapter 5) but members of the United Kingdom retain a final right of appeal to the European Court of Human Rights.

▪ Coroners' court

> The role of Her Majesty's coroner and the coroner's inquest is under unprecedented scrutiny in the aftermath of the Shipman case, the inquiry into the Bristol heart babies and the Alder Hey Hospital organs scandal. Each has thrown the work of coroners into sharp focus. Yet little is known about what they do and their wide-ranging powers.[11]

In the light of the above quote, it is not surprising that the Department of Constitutional Affairs (which assumed responsibility for coroners' courts, from the Home Office, in 2005), is leading a programme of reform of coroners' courts. The review found a number of weaknesses in the system, including the lack of 'a clear and reliable process for clarifying the relationship between the inquest and other formal processes for investigating death' (para 2.4k). A Coroner Reform Bill (2006) has been published.[12]

There are 157 coroners' courts in England and Wales in which coroners sit and determine the facts surrounding the circumstances of a death. Evidence is focused on questions of who the deceased was, the medical cause of death, and to enquire about the cause of death if it was due to violence or otherwise appears to be unnatural. It is not part of the process to determine any issues of criminal liability. The coroner, an independent judicial officer, determines in each case whether there will be an inquest, to which witnesses will be called to give evidence. The coroner has an inquisitorial role and a wide discretion to decide what witnesses will be called and the type of evidence and questioning. The bereaved family do not automatically have any support and are not entitled to legal aid. The verdicts which a coroner can pronounce are limited to death by misadventure or natural causes, accidental death, suicide or an open verdict. The inquest will normally be adjourned until after the trial of any person charged with causing the death. Coroners are usually lawyers (of at least five years' standing) but they can be doctors who are also legally qualified. Coroners receive approaching 200,000 reports of deaths each year, mainly from doctors and the police, and around one-eighth lead to an inquest. In a small proportion of cases a jury will sit with the coroner, including where the death occurred in prison.

■ Tribunals

The court structure outlined so far has been supplemented by a system of tribunals commonly associated with the rise of the welfare state and exercising administrative and judicial functions. There are now around 80 different types of tribunals, supervised by the Council on Tribunals. Some of the more important tribunals in social work terms include: the Care Standards Tribunal; Employment Tribunal; Mental Health Review Tribunal; Asylum and Immigration Tribunal; Criminal Injuries Compensation Appeals Panel; and Social Security Tribunal. The Care Standards Tribunal has a wide jurisdiction and hears cases relating to regulation of residential homes for adults and children, registration of childminders and inclusion on the Protection of Children and Protection of Vulnerable Adults lists. The Care Standards Tribunal website provides access to case reports and a guide to its procedures.[13]

The tribunal system was originally intended to provide a quicker and more informal mechanism for dealing with certain specific areas of law than the traditional court system. Membership varies between tribunals. Often there will be a panel chair who is legally qualified, assisted by two 'wing members' who are representatives of bodies with relevant expertise, combining the advantages of lay decision-making with legal competence. For example, the Care Standards Tribunal may be comprised of a barrister as chair, with someone who has experience with the social services, and perhaps someone who has experience of running a private residential home.

A major disadvantage of the tribunal system is that generally legal representation under the Community Legal Service is not available to assist individuals to bring their case. This effectively deters some individuals from bringing a claim and may disadvantage others who find themselves arguing against experienced lawyers. Despite the lack of financial support, in many areas, because of the issues at stake, it has become commonplace for lawyers to be involved. This may be one reason why tribunals have become increasingly legalistic in their format. Rules of procedure for each tribunal are usually prescribed alongside the principal legislation affecting matters to be heard by the tribunal. Tribunals must give reasons for their decisions[14] and if it makes a decision which is mistaken in its application of law a claim for judicial review or appeal to the High Court will lie. The Employment Appeal Tribunal is a specialised venue for appeals from the Employment Tribunal.

A comprehensive review of the tribunal system in 2001 called for a new culture within the system and reforms which will make it 'independent, coherent, professional, cost-effective and user-friendly'.[15] This has been followed by a white paper, 'Transforming Public Services: Complaints, Redress and Tribunals' (2004). It proposed a new Tribunals Service, accountable to the Department of Constitutional Affairs (due to be launched in 2006) and creation of a new Administrative Appeals Tribunal. A concern as to the independence of tribunal members has been addressed in the Constitutional Reform Act 2005, which provides that in future a Judicial Appointments Commission will select tribunal members.

■ Public and private hearings

As a general principle, court proceedings should normally be held in public, in open court. In a number of circumstances, however, the public and the press will be excluded and a case will be heard privately, or *in camera*. Cases heard in camera may still take place in a court room, or, commonly, the case may be heard in chambers (smaller rooms in court buildings). In these circumstances the only people present will be the parties to the dispute and their legal advisers. The majority of cases relating to children are heard in camera.

Article 6 of the European Convention on Human Rights is relevant to the public or private nature of hearings. The Article states that:

Art. 6

> Everyone is entitled to a fair and public hearing.
>
> (ECHR)

It is unlikely that the effect of this Article will be to require that all cases which have been heard in camera, e.g. relating to domestic violence injunctions, will need to be heard in public in future. It is arguable that, if that were the case, Art. 8, respect for private and family life, might be violated. The more likely effect of Art. 6 will be for cases to continue to be heard in private, but for the judgment or decision to be given in public. The European Court of Human Rights ruled on this point in *B* v. *United Kingdom, P* v. *United Kingdom* (Application Nos 36337/97 and 35974/97) (2002) 34 EHRR 19. The court found that denial of a hearing and pronouncement of judgment in public in child custody proceedings did not violate the right to a fair trial. The proceedings were described as prime examples of cases where the exclusion of the press and public might be justified in order to protect the privacy of the child. Witnesses should be able to express themselves candidly on highly personal issues without fear of public curiosity or comment. Pronouncing judgment in public would frustrate those aims.

■ Taking the courts into the twenty-first century

The court service is taking seriously the need to speed up justice and improve communications. Information technology developments which have been piloted include: use of e-mail to notify agencies such as the police and prisons of the outcome of cases; electronic screens outside courts giving details of the progress of cases; electronic presentation of evidence such as photographs, maps and witness statements, and video links to prisons. All Crown Courts now have video link facilities.

■ Social-work involvement in the courts

There is the potential for social workers to be involved professionally with cases at all levels of the court structure. Involvement may be as applicant to the court, or witness, or in giving support to a service user. Exhibit 3.2 outlines the main areas of social work involvement.

■ Rules of evidence

It should not be necessary for social workers to have an in-depth understanding of the rules of evidence – a complex area of law. A broad understanding of some principles of evidence, however, is an aid to understanding court procedures and will help ensure that information is recorded in a way that enables its use in court. It will also be helpful if a social worker has to give direct evidence or prepare statements for the court. Chapter 4 deals with techniques of giving evidence, sometimes referred to as 'courtcraft', and provides a summary of the main rules of evidence.

Law officers

The legal profession in England and Wales is divided into two main branches: *solicitors* and *barristers.* This contrasts with many other countries where there is simply one type of lawyer or advocate. Justification for continuation of the division is a constant source of debate. Traditionally, the solicitor's role has been to deal with legal work unrelated to court proceedings, such as conveyancing and preparation of cases for court, whereas barristers have presented cases. Increasingly, the divide between these roles is becoming blurred, with solicitors' rights of audience to present cases extended to a wider range of courts.

■ Solicitors

There are almost 100,000 practising solicitors in England and Wales, of whom about 80 per cent work in private practice; the remainder are employed in companies or by

Magistrates' court Civil	Family proceedings	Emergency Protection Orders, Child Assessment Orders, Care and Supervision Orders, Exclusion Orders, ASBO, Curfew Orders, Provision of reports
Magistrates' court Criminal court	Youth	Crime and Disorder Act Cases Provision of reports
	Adult	Reports to court [Probation Officer's role]
County court	Adoption and Placement Orders	
	Special Guardianship	
	Contact and residence	
	Section 37 Investigation Children Act 1989	
	Exclusion Order – Family Law Act 1996	
	Race, sex, disability discrimination cases	
	Displacement of nearest relative – Mental Health Act 1983	
Crown Court	Provision of reports in adult criminal cases for juveniles charged with adults	
High Court Family Division	Family proceedings jurisdiction as for magistrates' and county court – more complex cases Wardship Declaratory relief	
Queen's Bench	Court of protection – receivership New orders under the Mental Capacity Act 2005 Judicial review	
Chancery		
Court of Appeal	Appeals on point of law	
House of Lords	Appeals on point of law	
At each level the social work involvement may vary between applicant, report writer, witness, litigation friend, or may be general support to client.		

Exhibit 3.2 Areas of social work involvement at each level in the court structure

local or central government and the Crown Prosecution Service. Once a male domi-nated profession, women now represent just over 40 per cent of the profession and 8.3 per cent of the profession are from minority ethnic groups. Greater balance can be expected in the future, as new admissions comprise 56 per cent women and 17 per cent with known ethnicity.[16] Rules of conduct are set down by the professional body for solicitors, the Law Society. Self-regulation operates via the Law Society's Consumer Complaints Service (which replaced the Office for the Supervision of Solicitors in 2004), which deals with complaints made where the solicitor has broken the rules of professional conduct. The outcomes of complaints are published in the *Law Society's Gazette* and include examples ranging from unbefitting conduct to misuse of client funds. If dissatisfied with the outcome of complaints, the Legal Services Ombudsman may become involved.

Solicitors can offer advice on all areas of law and can represent a client's interests in litigation, including advocacy, and draw up legal documents such as wills and trusts. There is a growing trend towards solicitors developing large firms and associated practices with international offices, as law becomes more complex and solicitors choose to work in specialised areas of law. The analogy of the solicitor to the medical general practitioner still holds true, however, particularly in smaller firms where solicitors will deal with wide-ranging areas of law. Solicitors' dealings with their clients are protected by privilege and generally remain confidential unless the client gives authority to disclose. So, even if a client confesses to his solicitor that he has committed a murder, the solicitor cannot tell anyone.

Since 1994, solicitors with significant experience of advocacy have been able to obtain rights of audience to appear in the higher courts, including the Crown Court and High Court.[17] Solicitor-advocates will still be distinguishable from barristers, as they do not wear wigs and must address the judge from further back in the court. It is possible for solicitors to apply to become Queen's Counsel; however, as yet only five appointments have been made. Solicitors may be paid directly by the client, via the Community Legal Service, or through the contingency fee scheme (no win no fee arrangements)[18] and may undertake a certain amount of pro bono (free) work.

Local authorities have a wide range of legal responsibilities, in social services matters and other areas, and usually employ solicitors to conduct this work. It is important for social workers to know which solicitors in the local authority legal section deal with legal issues arising from social services responsibilities and to build good working relations with them.

■ Barristers

Barristers, also known as *counsel,* are the smaller of the two branches of the legal profession in England and Wales; there were around 14,000 practising barristers in 2004. Of those barristers, about 68 per cent are male and just over 10 per cent are from an ethnic minority. Senior, more experienced barristers may be appointed Queen's Counsel (QC) and in complex cases a QC and junior barrister will conduct the case. Barristers are regulated by the Bar Council. The majority of barristers are self-employed and operate from offices known as 'chambers', which are managed by a barristers' clerk, effectively the barristers' agent. Chambers tend to be situated near major courts. Barristers are usually instructed or briefed by solicitors, but it has become possible for them to accept instructions direct from lay clients. Barristers have rights of audience in the higher courts and their training focuses on advocacy and evidence. Barristers may also be consulted by solicitors where specialist legal advice, in the form of an opinion, is required. As with solicitors, barristers may take on some cases without charging a fee; a Bar Council survey in 2000 found that the Bar carries out pro bono work each year worth between £7–38 million.[19] Complaints against barristers are dealt with by the Complaints Commission of the Bar Council.

■ Crown Prosecution Service

The Crown Prosecution Service (CPS), headed by the Director of Public Prosecutions, was set up in 1986. From that date the dual role of the police as investigator and prosecutor was separated,[20] with the Crown Prosecution Service taking on responsibility for all prosecutions. The CPS employs solicitors and barristers and works independently of the police, taking the decision whether to bring a prosecution in a particular case, based on the evidence accumulated by the police. Recent guidance from the Director of Public Prosecutions, which is being implemented incrementally, requires Crown Prosecutors to determine whether a person is to be charged in all indictable only, either way or summary offences, where the custody officer is satisfied that in all the circumstances of the case there is at least a reasonable suspicion against the person of having committed an offence (in accordance with Art. 5 of the European Convention on Human Rights) and that at that stage it is in the public interest to proceed. There are some exceptions which the police may continue to charge, including most road traffic offences, absconding and some public order offences, and, during the transitional period, all cases where a guilty plea is likely and the case is considered suitable for sentence in the magistrates' court.

Crown Prosecutors will be deployed as Duty Prosecutors for such hours as shall be agreed locally to provide guidance and make charging decisions.

Guidance is provided by a Code for Crown Prosecutors. A key element of the code is the two-part test for prosecution:

1. examination of the evidence;
2. whether prosecution is in the public interest.

Factors in favour of prosecution include whether the offence was motivated by any form of discrimination or the victim is particularly vulnerable. The most recent edition of the Code (5th edition, 2004) recognises that the CPS is a public authority within the meaning of the HRA 1998, and must therefore comply with the terms of the European Convention on Human Rights.

■ Criminal Defence Service

The new Criminal Defence Service (**CDS**) is modelled on a form similar to the Crown Prosecution Service.[21] A defendant will apply to the court for a right to representation where he wishes to be represented at public expense, and must satisfy the interests of justice test before the request can be granted. The order is known as a Representation Order and the defendant's acting solicitor must have in place a contract (a franchise) with the Legal Services Commission.

▪ Magistrates/Justices of the Peace (JPs)

It is difficult not to have preconceived ideas and stereotypes about different professions, and the law is no exception. Being a highly popular choice for media attention, whether in the tabloids, broadsheet press or on television as the subject of documentaries or, increasingly, in popular entertainment, there are many influences on how we see members of the legal profession. Sadly, the impressions given are not always too close to reality, either in terms of procedural accuracy, or glamour and style! This was illustrated most clearly in a role play exercise carried out with students some years ago. Each member of the group was assigned a part in a courtroom scenario and given guidance on the role to be taken and evidence they could give, but otherwise was free to develop the character as they wished. Three students played the bench of magistrates and came dressed in 'suitable attire'. This consisted of a lounge suit and old school tie for the male magistrate. One female magistrate wore a twinset and pearls and glasses dangling from a long gold chain were perched at the end of her nose. The second female 'magistrate' wore a huge hat covered in artificial flowers and fruit!

It would be difficult to design a better prompt for a discussion on the principles of the magistracy offering justice by one's peers. The example above might suggest that there is a stereotypical view of a magistrate as a judgmental member of the middle class with little in common with many of the individuals who appear in the magistrates' court. Research carried out by Parker *et al.* on magistrates' sentencing practices and ideology in the late 1980s appears to support that view and found a level of mistrust of social workers.[22] The magistracy has received criticism at a number of levels, including inconsistency in sentencing, prejudice and resistance to change.

It is useful to consider some statistics which give an indication of the current make-up of the magistracy. There are 28,029 magistrates in England and Wales (2004). This figure is composed of nearly as many women (13,846) as men (14,183). The current percentage of magistrates from ethnic minority groups is 6.3 per cent, and recruitment drives aim to increase this further.

All magistrates are appointed by the Lord Chancellor, following recommendation by a local advisory committee. Membership of advisory committees, once a fairly closely guarded secret, is now a public matter. New magistrates may have put themselves forward to the committee, possibly in response to advertising campaigns of the advisory committee, or may be recommended by others, including existing magistrates. Prospective magistrates are interviewed by the advisory committee, which has the task of ensuring that the composition of the bench broadly reflects the community it serves. It is difficult precisely to identify the qualities required in a magistrate but, broadly speaking, magistrates should be of good character, have a good local knowledge and understanding of the local community, be able to work as a member of the team, be able to reach reasoned decisions and be aged between 27 and 65 years. The following will not be appointed to the magistracy: anyone not of good character and personal standing; an undischarged bankrupt; a serving member of the police or armed forces; a person from an occupation which might conflict with the role of a magistrate; or a close relative of an existing magistrate on the same bench. Magistrates must retire at 70.

In response to criticism that magistrates were untrained and unprepared for the task, the level of training provided has increased in order that magistrates should deliver more consistent and reasoned decisions whilst still retaining the qualities of the laity. Magistrates receive training before they sit in courts and continue to receive training throughout their service. The training provided places considerable emphasis on the need for consistency in decision-making against the context of current developments. Magistrates' court sentencing guidelines are issued to all magistrates and provide a structure which aims to guide magistrates' decisions on establishing the seriousness of each individual case and the most appropriate disposal (see example in Chapter 18). Training topics include basic rules of court procedure, the implications of the Human Rights Act 1998, sentencing powers and options, and communication skills. Specialist training is provided for work in the family or youth court and for magistrates who will sit as chair in court. Magistrates are unpaid volunteers, but may receive expense allowances. This remains a barrier to the objective of widening recruitment of the magistracy because the issue remains as to who can afford to be a magistrate, and this is likely to distort the representativeness of the bench.

Apart from lay magistrates, there are 130 district judges (magistrates' courts) who are paid professional lawyers. Until recently, they were referred to as stipendiary magistrates. Unlike lay magistrates, they can sit alone and are found mainly in London and in large cities where there is a high volume of work.[23]

■ Justices' clerk

An important figure in the magistrates' court is the justices' clerk. The clerk has overall responsibility for administration, organisation and finance, but is best known for his or her role in court of giving advice to the magistrates on law and procedure and having overall control of the conduct of the proceedings. The clerk usually reads out the charge and takes the plea in criminal cases, identifies the parties in civil cases and administers the oath. The particular style and demeanour of the clerk can have an enormous impact on the tone of the proceedings, including the level of formality, sympathy toward applications for adjournments, etc. The first question from many advocates arriving at court will be which clerk they have. A justices' clerk will normally be a barrister or solicitor qualified for at least five years. The responsibilities of the justices' clerk have gradually increased beyond keeping a record of the proceedings, and there are a range of decisions which the clerk will take independently of the magistrates, including: allocation of cases to higher courts; appointment of children's guardians; fixing dates of directions and main hearing; serving reports; issuing a witness summons and warrant for arrest; extending bail periods; requesting a pre-sentence report or welfare report, etc. In contrast, the role of the clerk in higher courts is mainly administrative because the judiciary are legally qualified.

■ Judges

Judges are appointed by the Lord Chancellor and are drawn from barristers and, more recently, solicitors. There are no career judges in the United Kingdom. Judges are appointed to a particular level in the court system ranging from 12 Lords of

Appeal in Ordinary, who sit in the House of Lords, through to 35 Lord Justices of Appeal, 106 High Court judges, 624 circuit judges, 1,417 recorders, 434 district judges and 797 deputy district judges. Given that most judges are appointed from the Bar, it is not surprising that there are few women and a small percentage of judges are from an ethnic minority. There is only one female judge in the House of Lords, two in the Court of Appeal and ten in the High Court. The House of Lords and Court of Appeal do not have any judges from an ethnic minority, and only one High Court judge by self-classification came from an ethnic minority. In the lower courts roughly 4 per cent of recorders, 2 per cent of district judges and 3 per cent of deputy district judges are drawn from an ethnic minority.[24] This inevitably raises questions as to diversity and impact on decision-making.

■ Attorney-General

The Attorney-General is a member of the Cabinet and hence the post is a political appointment. He answers questions in Parliament, advises and represents the Crown (or Government) in any proceedings in our domestic courts of the High Court or above, or in disputes before the European Court of Human Rights. The Attorney-General has to give consent before certain prosecutions can be brought, e.g. incitement to racial hatred under the Public Order Act 1986. The Solicitor General is deputy to the Attorney-General.

■ Director of Public Prosecutions

The Director of Public Prosecutions (**DPP**) is head of the Crown Prosecution Service. The duties of the DPP are laid out in the Prosecution of Offences Act 1985. The DPP can represent the Crown when appeals are brought in the Court of Appeal or House of Lords.

■ Official Solicitor

The post of Official Solicitor carries a wide remit, including representation of wards of court, conducting litigation for children and for people with a disability, acting as 'friend of the court' (*amicus curiae*) to assist the court, and responsibility for bail and *habeas corpus*. The work of the Official Solicitor relating to children has now been amalgamated into one service with that of children and family reporters (previously known as court welfare officers) and children's guardians (previously known as guardians *ad litem*) under the Criminal Justice and Court Services Act 2000. The service is known as the Children and Family Court Advisory and Support Service (**CAFCASS**), and operates as a non-departmental public body subject to National Standards.[25] In relation to work with children, the Official Solicitor is referred to as CAFCASS Legal Services and Special Casework. The Official Solicitor has a continuing role to play in cases involving adults who lack mental capacity.[26]

∎ Children's guardian and children and family reporter

As the children's guardian is usually a qualified social worker, and the children and family reporter will often have trained as a probation officer, these roles are dealt with in more detail in Chapter 4.

∎ Probation service

Probation and after-care service is the responsibility of the Home Office. Duties include after care of offenders released from custody, and provision of Social Inquiry reports to assist courts to determine the most suitable method of disposal. The role of the Probation Service is covered in more detail in Chapter 18.

∎ Lord Chancellor and the Department for Constitutional Affairs

The Lord Chancellor has a number of significant roles, though the post has experienced some changes since the creation of the Department for Constitutional Affairs, which replaced the Lord Chancellor's Department, and he no longer sits as a judge in the House of Lords.

The new department is headed by a Lord Chancellor, Lord Falconer, who also holds the title, Secretary of State for Constitutional Affairs. This would appear to be another aspect of the Government's drive to modernise public services.

The Department for Constitutional Affairs incorporates most of the responsibilities previously held by the Lord Chancellor's Department. It is, however, a department which will lead through a number of significant constitutional reforms. These reforms include:

- ∎ A new Supreme Court to replace the Appellate Committee of the House of Lords and associated reform of the House of Lords.
- ∎ A Judicial Appointments Commission.
- ∎ Abolition of the role of Lord Chancellor as judge and speaker of the House of Lords.
- ∎ Consideration of the role of Queen's Counsel (QC), in particular whether there are benefits to retaining this rank.

Access to law and representation issues

It is a reality that in some situations the only advice available to a service user is that of the social worker. For this reason alone, a basic knowledge of the range of law likely to be encountered by a service user is desirable. Even when legal advice has been obtained, a social worker may still have a role in 'interpreting' and explaining that advice. This section considers various avenues for obtaining advice on legal issues and representation if necessary, focusing on the new Community Legal Service. It is also worth noting that lawyers are not the only source of legal advice. Social workers working in different specialities can be a useful resource to each other: e.g. education social workers, social workers in hospital settings and approved social workers can all provide information relating to legal aspects of their area of work.

Trade unions have obvious expertise in employment law and usually provide advice to members in connection with employment matters, and sometimes representation. Examples of areas of likely expertise include unfair dismissal, discrimination at work and whistleblowing.

Voluntary agencies can often provide specialist help to social workers and clients within their area of expertise. Many have legal advisers and helplines and publish useful factsheets, e.g. Action on Elder Abuse, Disabled Parents Network, Counsel and Care, VOICE and the Children's Legal Centre. Support may also be specifically focused to the needs of professionals, e.g. the Association of Child Abuse Lawyers (ACAL) provides practical support for lawyers and other professionals working for adults and children who have been abused.

For many individuals, and for particular types of cases, effective access to the legal system and presentation of a case will be possible only if legal representation is available. The provision of free legal aid and assistance was established after the Second World War and most recently was covered by the Legal Aid Act 1988. It provided for assistance via the green form scheme, civil legal aid, criminal legal aid, assistance by way of representation (ABWOR) and the duty solicitor scheme. There were various difficulties with this system, including escalating costs and scattered provision.[27] This system has undergone a process of reform, the details of which are contained in the Access to Justice Act 1999.

The Community Legal Service has a useful website at www.clsdirect.org.uk. According to this, the Community Legal Service aims to be:

- accessible
- positive
- transparent
- reliable
- impartial.

The Community Legal Service is organised into partnerships, including organisations offering legal and advice services such as solicitors, Citizens' Advice Bureaux, law centres and community centres. The Community Legal Service Quality Mark (Exhibit 3.3) is awarded to organisations that reach certain quality standards and aims to make providers instantly recognisable to the public.

Under the new Legal Services Commission, there are effectively two ways in which an individual can obtain support in a legal action. In criminal matters the Criminal Defence Service funds those areas covered by s. 13 of the Access to Justice Act 1999. In civil matters assistance may be available through Community Legal Services incorporating solicitors, law centres and Citizens' Advice Bureaux (Access

Community Legal Service

Exhibit 3.3   CLS Quality Mark
(*Source*: Copyright of and reproduced by kind permission of the Legal Services
Commission, London, UK – www.legalservices.gov.uk)

to Justice Act 1999, s. 8(2)). Eligibility depends on the application of funding criteria rather than the old 'means and merit' test.

The Community Legal Service is intended to be an inclusive service addressing, at a local, regional and national level, the legal needs of the whole community. In this sense it goes further than the Legal Aid Board, which had responsibility only for services provided to those individuals who qualified financially. The Community Legal Service is comprised of quality assured organisations which carry a quality mark and can provide information, general help and specialist help. Providers are organised in partnerships likely to include solicitors, law centres and advice agencies, local authorities and other funders of legal services, and information providers such as libraries and post offices. All civil legal help, including representation at court, will be made available through contracts with quality assured suppliers, probably those solicitors who would previously have acted under legal aid. Potentially, the Community Legal Service can be more innovative in providing advice and assistance services and is currently piloting different ways of delivering services including: telephone advice lines, outreach services and support services (including training) for solicitors.

Different levels of service are available:

■ *Legal help*: Advice and assistance with any problem.

■ *Help at court*: A solicitor or adviser is able to speak on your behalf at certain court hearings without formally acting in the entire proceedings.

■ *Approved family help*: This includes assistance through negotiation and issue of proceedings and representation. It is split into mediation and general family help.

■ *Legal representation*: This equates to the service previously known as civil legal aid. It takes two forms:

>   *Investigative help:* Funding for the investigation of the strength of a claim;
>   *Full representation:* Funding is provided for representation in legal proceedings.

■ *Support funding for conditional fee agreements*: Investigative support funding may be available to investigate the strength of a claim with a view to a conditional fee agreement. In addition, partial funding of high-cost proceedings under conditional fee agreements may be available.

Financial eligibility of an individual claimant is assessed based on gross income during the month preceding the application (including income of the applicant's partner). If this is less than the current limit (which is varied each year), the Commission goes on to assess disposable income and capital, by offsetting various allowances (e.g. tax, national insurance, childcare expenses, dependants) against gross income. The scheme recognises that there will be circumstances when a person is ineligible under the scheme but representation is required to ensure a fair hearing, and has scope to make one-off grants of exceptional funding. A solicitor or advice worker at a Citizen's Advice Bureau or law centre can advise on whether there is a reasonable cause of action and eligibility for funding. The Community Legal Services Directory maintains a list of solicitors and advisors who undertake publicly funded work.

The Lord Chancellor will set specific budgets for specific aspects of the Commission's work. Priority is given to child protection cases, cases where a client is at risk of loss of life or liberty, other cases concerning child welfare, domestic violence cases, cases alleging breach of human rights by public bodies, and other 'social welfare' cases, including housing proceedings.

■ Criminal Defence Service

The Criminal Defence Service replaces criminal legal aid. The object is to provide quality assured defence services to anyone who is accused of a criminal offence. In addition to the many solicitors who already undertake criminal legal aid work, it is intended that there will be some salaried defenders working as a counterpart to the Crown Prosecution Service. Whether it is appropriate for the state both to prosecute and to defend is an issue of concern to some. Advice and assistance in the police station is provided free of charge where a person is arrested or will be interviewed or taking part in identity procedures.

Chapter summary

- In order to understand the court structure in England and Wales it is useful to be able to distinguish between a civil and a criminal case. That distinction is reflected in the way the parties to a case are referred to, the outcome or remedies, and the standard of proof.

- The standard of proof in a civil case is 'balance of probabilities' and in a criminal case it is 'beyond reasonable doubt'.

- The courts exercising civil jurisdiction are the House of Lords, the Court of Appeal (Civil Division), the High Court, county court and magistrates' court. Within the magistrates' court, the magistrates' family proceedings court hears matters related to children. Cases are allocated to the appropriate level by case management tracks.

■ The courts exercising criminal jurisdiction are the House of Lords, the Court of Appeal (Criminal Division), Queen's Bench Division of the High Court, Crown Court and magistrates' court. The magistrates' court divides into an adult court and a youth court. The level at which a case is tried depends partly on classification of the offence as a summary, either way or indictable offence.

■ The courts are organised in a hierarchy, with the House of Lords as the most senior court and the magistrates' court as the most inferior court. This hierarchy is inextricably bound to the doctrine of precedent.

■ A growing body of law is dealt with by tribunals, which are intended to deal with specific areas, e.g. employment law, in a less formal environment.

■ In addition to the domestic courts, the European Court of Justice is the most senior court in matters affecting European Community law. The European Court of Human Rights hears cases related to the European Convention on Human Rights.

■ The legal profession divides into solicitors and barristers (counsel). Solicitors have tended to deal with preparation of cases whilst barristers appear in court, but that division of work is becoming increasingly blurred. The Crown Prosecution Service is responsible for prosecution of criminal offences and a Criminal Defence Service has recently been introduced.

■ A case will be decided either by magistrates, lay members of the public, in the magistrates' court or by judges in the higher courts. Other significant personnel in the legal system include the Attorney-General, Director of Public Prosecutions, Official Solicitor and Lord Chancellor.

■ The Legal Services Commission has responsibility for provision of legal support via the Community Legal Service. This scheme replaced Legal Aid.

Exercises

Which court?

Identify the court where the following matters are likely to be heard (there may be more than one option in each scenario) and where appropriate advice might be sought in relation to the issues at stake:

■ An application for possession of a council house due to rent arrears.

■ A claim of unfair dismissal after Jack was 'forced' to resign following racial harassment and name calling on the factory floor and consistent refusals in response to requests for overtime which his contemporaries all enjoyed.

■ An uncontested adoption of James, an 18-month-old boy with Down's Syndrome.

■ A criminal charge of burglary against brothers, Phil (16) and Greg (20).

- An application for an injunction to remove Peter from the home he shares with his girl-friend, Julie, who came to Social Services asking for help after he pushed her down the stairs during an argument.

- A claim for compensation for a broken leg and whiplash caused in a car accident.

- A claim for breach of contract, arising from cancellation of a marquee and catering for 100 people, when Robert and Rachel called off their wedding the night before it was due to take place.

- An application for care proceedings in respect of six children, of three different fathers, two of whom are cared for by maternal grandparents. The father of one child is threatening to take him out of the country to live with his parents in Greece.

- A challenge to the refusal by a pub landlord to serve a group of five adults with learning disabilities, the reason given that one of the group was a wheelchair user and it would not be possible to get him out quickly if there was a fire.

Court observation guide

Through observation, students should be able to identify aspects of the roles of personnel in court, the procedure and legal issues. Aim to spend at least a couple of hours in court.

The following questions – some factual matters and others asking for your impression of the proceedings – should help you to get more from your visit. The exercise will be most valuable if you visit a variety of courts and draw comparisons between them.

- What type of court are you in? Is it superior or inferior or is it a tribunal?

- Does the court deal with civil or criminal matters or a combination of these?

- Who is adjudicating – if a judge, what level, and, if magistrates, how many are sitting?

- What are the roles of the clerk and the usher?

- How many parties are represented in court and how many lawyers represent each party, e.g. solicitors only, solicitors and barristers, junior barristers and Queen's Counsel?

- Does the court deal with a number of separate cases or is the case before it scheduled for a long hearing?

- Are there representatives of the press, probation, social services, etc. in court?

- Are there many members of the public watching the proceedings?

- Who is in charge?

- How formal are the proceedings?

- How do the advocates refer to each other?

- How is the judge/magistrate addressed?

- What is the 'dress code' in court?

- What conclusions can you draw from 'body language' in court?

- Are there any 'expert'/'professional' witnesses?

■ What types of evidence are adduced, e.g. oral testimony, documents, reports, weapons, plans, photographs?

■ Who keeps a record of the proceedings and how?

■ Is the courtroom in a modern or traditional court? Sketch the layout.

■ Comment on the 'facilities' at the court – are there places to wait comfortably, a tea room, somewhere for children?

■ Did the cases raise any issues in relation to social work values?

Websites

The Department for Constitutional Affairs, for information on magistrates, judges and QCs:
www.dca.gov.uk

The Court Service–an executive agency of the Department of Constitutional Affairs, for information on courts, procedures and forms:
www.hmcourts-service.gov.uk

The Law Society, the professional body for solicitors:
www.lawsociety.org.uk

The Bar Council, the professional body for barristers:
www.barcouncil.org.uk

The Crown Prosecution Service – website provides information about the service responsible for prosecuting criminal cases investigated by the police and provides access to the Code of Practice:
www.cps.gov.uk

The Children and Family Court Advisory Service (CAFCASS):
www.cafcass.gov.uk

The Lay Magistrates Association:
www.magistrates-association.org.uk

The website of the Legal Services Commission. Forms available from the website provide details of eligibility for income and capital for different levels of Community Legal Services, plus leaflets explaining rights in a range of circumstances:
www.legalservices.gov.uk

A useful starting point if you are seeking legal help and advice:
www.clsdirect.org.uk

Citizens' Advice Bureau:
www.nacab.org.uk

The public information site of the Citizens' Advice Bureau:
www.adviceguide.org.uk

Further reading

Textbooks providing a clear overview of the legal system include:

Partington, M. (2006) *Introduction to the English Legal System*. (3rd edn) Oxford: Oxford University Press.

White, R.C.A. (1999) *The English Legal System in Action* (3rd edn). Oxford: Oxford University Press.

Genn, H. (2006) *Tribunals for Diverse Users*. London: Department of Constitutional Affairs. (Interesting research into three tribunals: the Appeals Service, Criminal Injuries Compensation Appeals Panel and the Special Educational Needs and Disability Tribunal which found that '. . . with rare exceptions tribunals treated users from all ethnic backgrounds with courtesy and respect'. The report also highlights need for the judiciary to have the skills to enable unrepresented parties to present their cases.)

Critical examination of the senior judiciary and magistracy is provided by:

Griffith, J.A.G. (1991) *The Politics of the Judiciary* (4th edn). London: Fontana Press.

Parker, H., Sumner, M. and Jarvis, G. (1989) *Unmasking the Magistrates*. Milton Keynes: Open University Press.

Francis, A. (2000) 'Lawyers, CABx and the Community Legal Service: A new dawn for social welfare provision?' 22(1) *Journal of Social Welfare and Family Law* pp. 59–75. (Considers provision of legal advice.)

Notes

1 The new offence is discussed in more detail in Chapters 9 and 17.

2 This follows the consultation paper, 'A single civil court?', published by the CDA in February 2005.

3 Either way offences are listed in Schedule 1 to the Magistrates' Courts Act 1980.

4 Bail Act 1976.

5 Juries Act 1974, s.17.

6 The court service website includes useful information about the way courts operate: see www.courtservice.gov.uk/info_home.htm.

7 M. Berlins and C. Dyer (1990) *The Law Machine*. London: Penguin.

8 *R* v. *Gloucestershire County Council, ex parte Barry* [1997] 2 AU ER I, discussed further in Chapter 9.

9 The membership (names of judges) is included at the front of the All England Law Reports.

10 Eurolink Age, 2001.

11 R. Rhodes-Kemp (2001) 'Is it time for an inquest into the coroner's role?' *The Times* 13 February 2001.

[12] Fundamental review of death certification and coroner services: report, Reforming the coroner and death certification service: position paper, DCA – The Shipman Inquiry: www.the-shipman-inquiry.org.uk.

[13] www.carestandardstribunal.gov.uk.

[14] Tribunals and Inquiries Act 1971, s. 12.

[15] 'Tribunals for users – one system, one service' (2001) London: The Stationery Office, available from the Lord Chancellor's Department website at www.lcd.gov.uk.

[16] Bi.earch Unit.

[17] Courts and Legal Services Act 1990, s. 27.

[18] Conditional Fee Agreements Order 1998 (SI 1998/1860).

[19] G. Slapper (2001) 'English and European Law, the legal professions, the Salaried Defence Service, judges, conditional fees, freedom of information, and the criminal justice system' 32(1) *Student Law Review* pp. 29–33.

[20] Guidance to Police Officers and Crown Prosecutors issued by the Director of Public Prosecutions under s. 37A of the Police and Criminal Evidence Act 1984.

[21] It came into being in 2001 when, in matters concerning representation in criminal proceedings, the Access to Justice Act 1999 replaced the Legal Aid Act 1988.

[22] H. Parker, M. Sumner and G. Jarvis (1989) *Unmasking the Magistrates*. Milton Keynes: Open University Press.

[23] The Magistrates Association is a good source of information about the magistracy: www.magistrates–association.org.uk.

[24] DCA Judicial Statistics as at 1 October 2005.

[25] Consequential amendments have been made to the Adoption Rules, Family Proceedings Rules, Family Proceedings Courts Rules and Magistrates' Courts (Adoption) Rules.

[26] For more information, visit the CAFCASS website at www.cafcass.gov.uk/index.htm.

[27] See M. Cousins (1994) 'The politics of legal aid: a solution in search of a problem' 13 *Civil Justice Quarterly* p. 111.

4 Social workers' role in law

Learning objectives

To develop an understanding of the following:

- The various roles of a social worker when working with the law.
- The skills employed as a witness.
- The relationship between lawyers and social workers.
- Basic rules of evidence.
- Advocacy.
- The various ways social work decisions may be challenged.
- The concept of whistleblowing and application of the Public Interest Disclosure Act 1998.
- Statutory regulation of record keeping, confidentiality and access to information, the Data Protection Act 1998 and the Freedom of Information Act 2000

Introduction

Previous chapters have described essential features of the English legal system. In this chapter the focus moves to two key areas: consideration of the various roles of the social worker in the legal system and ways in which social work practice can be challenged. Roles include acting as the applicant in proceedings, as McKenzie friend, witness, report writer, member of CAFCASS, appropriate adult and advocate. The chapter continues with an introduction to the concept of 'courtcraft', focusing on the role of the social worker in court, and rules of evidence.

Increasingly, social work practice is being challenged by service users and the legal options for challenge are outlined, followed by consideration of 'whistleblowing' as a mechanism for highlighting and challenging undesirable practices in relation to social work services.

Appropriate record keeping is an essential aspect of the social worker's role and, it may be argued, an increasing burden to the practitioner. Guidance on record keeping and the legal framework for access to records concludes the chapter.

Social work roles in the legal system

■ Applicant

As representative of the local authority, a social worker may be in the role of applicant in court in a range of proceedings. Usually a solicitor or barrister will conduct the case and the social worker then becomes the key witness in the application. Examples of such cases include: Emergency Protection Orders; Child Assessment Orders; Care and Supervision Orders (and their variation or revocation); application to displace the nearest relative under the Mental Health Act 1983; placement orders in adoption cases, applications for High Court Declarations in relation to vulnerable adults who lack capacity.[1] For many types of proceedings, a report from the social worker will be required by the court. Some principles of report writing are discussed later. The actual application process usually involves completion of standard forms for the court, and these are generally dealt with by the local authority solicitor.

■ McKenzie friend

The case of *McKenzie* v. *McKenzie* [1970] 3 All ER 1034, established the principle that where a person is not legally represented (and is therefore known as a *litigant in person*), he can nevertheless bring someone along to help in court. This person is known as a McKenzie friend. The majority of courts will permit a McKenzie friend to give advice to the individual in court as long as they conduct themselves reasonably. The McKenzie friend cannot directly address the court, as he does not by this status have rights of audience. The involvement of a McKenzie friend is particularly useful in tribunals, where Legal Aid is not usually available, and it is a role that a social worker may take on.

It is also important to be aware that a service user may be supported by a McKenzie friend who is not a social worker. The role of the McKenzie friend in family proceedings was the subject of a recent case, *Re O (Children)*; *Re W-R (A Child)*; *Re W (Children)* [2005] EWCA Civ 759. In the first two of the three appeals heard together, litigants in person (individuals who appear in court without legal representation) had been denied the assistance of a McKenzie friend in contact and residence proceedings. In the third, a McKenzie friend had been permitted but severe restrictions were placed on the documentation he was allowed to see. The Court of

Appeal allowed the appeals. It noted that Art. 6 ECHR was engaged in any application by a litigant in person for assistance of a McKenzie friend and that there was a presumption in favour of allowing this and ensuring a fair hearing. There was no reason why the McKenzie friend should not have access to court papers, provided they were used solely for the purpose of assisting the litigant in person with his case. This is a particularly important decision given the reduction in public funding for representation.[2]

■ Witness

The role of the social worker as a witness is considered fully at the end of this chapter. At this stage it is important to note that the witness owes a duty to the court to tell the truth, even if in exceptional circumstances this may mean expressing a personal view which conflicts with the agency stance.

■ Report writer

In the majority of cases where a social worker is involved in court proceedings he will provide a report for the court. The type of report varies between civil and criminal cases and cases involving young people. In some cases the content is prescribed by regulations or national standards, e.g. pre-sentence reports, permanence reports in adoption cases. In other cases reports provided to court will vary in style according to the author, though certain conventions may be followed.

Reports may be requested by the court exercising a general discretion or by a specific power such as under s. 7 of the Children Act 1989:

s. 7

(1)   A Court considering any question with respect to a child under this Act may –
   (a) ask an officer of the service; or
   (b) ask a local authority to arrange for –
      (i)   an officer of the authority; or
      (ii) such other person (other than a probation officer) as the authority considers appropriate, to report to the Court on such matters relating to the welfare of that child as are required to be dealt with in the report.

. . .

(5) It shall be the duty of the authority or an officer of the service[3] to comply with any request for a report under this section.

(CA 1989)

It is clear from the wording of the section and reference to 'that' child that the court can ask specific questions pertinent to the particular circumstances of the child concerned, e.g. relating to levels of contact with an estranged parent.

The probation service has a major role in providing reports to the criminal courts. These reports provide information to the court and an element of assessment to assist with sentencing. National standards[4] dictate the content and structure of such reports. When a report is being prepared, the nature and purpose of the inquiry should be made clear to the subject of the report, and their consent should be obtained. Reports will normally be shared with the subject.

■ Children's guardian

Guardians tend to be experienced social workers. Local authorities were, until the introduction of the Children and Family Court Advisory and Support Services (**CAFCASS**) in 2001, required to ensure an adequate number of suitably qualified guardians *ad litem* were available for work in their area. The term 'guardian *ad litem*' has been replaced by 'children's guardian' since the creation of CAFCASS.

The role of the guardian *ad litem* was created to provide an independent voice for the child in cases concerning the child's welfare, following the Maria Colwell Report.[5] The role of the guardian was considerably extended by the Children Act 1989 – s. 41 identifies specified proceedings in which a guardian must be appointed by the court.[6] The principal role of the guardian is to prepare a report for the court, following their inquiries, and to safeguard and protect the interests of the child. The guardian will usually conduct interviews with professionals who have had dealings with the case, the parents and other significant adults, as well as the child. The guardian must ascertain the views of the child, but is not bound to follow those views in the final recommendation. If the court does not follow the final recommendation of the guardian, it is required to give reasons for not doing so (*Devon County Council* v. C [1985] FLR 1159). Where the views of the child conflict with those of the guardian and the child is of sufficient maturity, the child may be separately represented by their own solicitor. The child needs to have sufficient understanding to participate in the proceedings, giving instructions as the case develops, and the courts have shown some reluctance to permit children to participate directly in adversarial litigation without the protection of a guardian (*Re N (Contact: Minor Seeking Leave to Defend and Removal of Guardian* [2003] FLR 652). The guardian is usually involved in public law proceedings but increasingly also has a role in some private law proceedings.[7]

In order to carry out the role, guardians are authorised by the Children Act 1989, s. 42 to examine and take copies of all relevant material relating to the child held by the local authority. Increasingly, the guardian is asked to comment on the local authority's care plan for the child, as well as the order that is recommended to the court. Amendments introduced by the Adoption and Children Act 2002 have made it possible to extend the role of the guardian beyond the final care order in some cases. An Independent Reviewing Officer will monitor the care plan and may refer the case to CAFCASS if appropriate and the guardian may then take the case back to court. This reform can be traced back to *Re S (Children: Care Plan); Re W (Children: Care Plan)* [2002] UKHL 10. The role of the Independent Reviewing Officer is considered further in Chapter 10.

Under the Criminal Justice and Court Services Act 2000, a major reorganisation of the way reports are presented to courts has taken place. The Court Welfare Service, guardian *ad litem* panels and the children's division of the Official Solicitor's office have been amalgamated into a Children and Family Court Advisory and Support Service (CAFCASS). This body is independent of the local authority and responsible to the Department for Education and Skills.[8] The functions of CAFCASS are set out in s. 12 of the Criminal Justice and Court Services Act 2000. To:

- Safeguard and promote the welfare of the child.
- Give advice to the court about any application made to it in such proceedings.
- Make provision for children to be represented in such proceedings.
- Provide information, advice and support for children and their families.

■ General principles of report writing

In most circumstances, there are some general principles that can be followed in preparing a report for court. These include the following:

- Basic information should be included on the front page, including the name of the court and the case number; the name and date of birth of the subject; the type of application; and the author's name and professional address.
- Clarity and concision of language will always help the reader.
- Avoid dense pages of text and use bullet points (though sparingly – the other risk is to overdo the abruptness).
- Remember who the report is for – and make appropriate adjustments to style and vocabulary.
- Consider the structure and length of the report – there may be guidance to follow.
- Include a chronology of events.
- A genogram may be useful if there is a complex family make-up.
- Avoid jargon (ask a non-interested person to check this out and you may be surprised by how much jargon slips in!).
- Be non-discriminatory in the language used.
- Distinguish between facts and opinion.
- Avoid unnecessary repetition within the report of material available to the court in other documents.
- Remember that it is the business of the court to make findings of fact.
- Conclusions should flow logically from the body of the report.
- Where more than one option is available to the court, set out and discuss each in turn, and make a realistic recommendation.
- Objectivity is all; avoid over-personalising your report, although it is inevitable that you will be drawing upon your experience.[9]

■ Increasingly, there are strict timetables for filing of evidence, including reports. Failure to adhere to timetables invites criticism; if unavoidable, it is important to seek court approval.

Reports in care proceedings are dealt with in more detail in Chapter 9.

■ Appropriate adult

Under the Police and Criminal Evidence Act 1984 (**PACE**) and associated codes of practice, a social worker may be required to act as an appropriate adult in connection with certain vulnerable adults and juveniles who are detained in police custody. For a juvenile, three categories of people may act as appropriate adult: the parent or guardian (or care authority for a child who is looked after); a social worker; or any other responsible adult who is not a police officer or employed by the police. In this capacity, social workers have a positive role to play in safeguarding the rights and civil liberties of the person who is detained.[10] First preference is for the parent, although it is arguable that there are advantages for the police in using a social worker as an appropriate adult in place of a parent or guardian. Social workers are certainly more likely to have an understanding of the process; there is a professional relationship between the agencies and a social worker is less likely to be emotionally involved.

Code C on the detention, treatment and questioning of suspects (updated 2004) outlines the role of the appropriate adult. The role includes more than simple observation, and encompasses advising the person being questioned, observing whether or not the interview is being conducted properly and fairly, and facilitating communication with the person being interviewed. In order to carry out this role, the social worker needs to have some understanding of police powers and procedures at the police station, including the role of the custody officer. The appropriate adult may also exercise certain rights of the individual being detained, including the right to legal advice. In most cases, therefore, both an appropriate adult and a solicitor should be present during questioning of a juvenile or a vulnerable adult. The role of the appropriate adult in PACE interviews is considered in more detail in Chapters 13 and 18.

■ Advocacy

At times it is appropriate or necessary for a child (or adult) to have the support of an advocate to speak on their behalf. The 'advocate' in this context is a skilled person, distinct from the legal advocate in court. Under existing law there is limited statutory recognition of the role and characteristics of advocacy, though the value of advocacy services is recognised in a number of official documents, e.g. Department of Health (1991) 'The Children Act 1989 Guidance and Regulations', vol. 3 'Family Placements'. In the absence of a statutory framework and allocated resources, advocacy schemes have developed piecemeal and are provided throughout the country by a number of major charities such as the Children's Society, VOICE and National Youth Advocacy Service. Providing support for children and young persons or vulnerable adults to make representations and complaints to social services about aspects of service provision is an important role for advocates. In such circumstances the role of the advocate has been described as follows:

> The role of the advocate is to ascertain the wishes and feelings of children and young people and ensure their voice is heard in all decision-making forums, both in and out of court. It also means being proactive in ensuring that children and young people receive their fair share of the resources that they may need in order to fulfil their full potential as adults and citizens of the future.[11]

The Adoption and Children Act 2002 introduces a statutory requirement to make advocacy services available for children and young people who are or wish to make a complaint. The Act amends the Children Act 1989 by introducing a new s. 26A and accompanying regulations and guidance provide further detail.[12]

A further role for advocacy is envisaged by the Mental Capacity Act 2005. This legislation introduces the role of the Independent Mental Capacity Advocate (**IMCA**), whose role is to represent and support people who are faced with a serious decision about medical treatment or accommodation; lack capacity to make the decision for themselves; and do not have any family or friends. This role is explored further in Chapter 16.

Working in court

■ Courtcraft skills

The English legal system is largely based on the adversarial model (as opposed to the inquisitorial model adopted in some other countries).[13] Under this model, evidence is tested and the court will decide on the merits of the application before it, but cannot guarantee to ascertain the 'truth'. Increasingly, it is recognised that the outcome of a case will depend not only on the relative merits of a case, and the skills of the advocates, but also on the 'performance' of witnesses. The study and development of appropriate skills in court is known as 'courtcraft' and the following section outlines some of the steps that can be taken to prepare to give evidence for the first time, or to improve performance as a witness. Training and practice in this area is vital. Even relatively small-scale role-play exercises can help to ease some of the anxiety that is experienced by most people (including solicitors) before entering court.

Use of the word 'performance' is deliberate. One of the best ways to understand the court experience and to demystify it is to think of it as a theatre, where everyone takes a part: some know their lines better than others, some wear costumes, there are props, the proceedings run according to ritual, with intervals, and the outcome may ultimately prove to be a mystery!

The key to a good court experience is preparation. This starts long before a court hearing is anticipated. In the majority of cases, evidence will be required relating to circumstances some time before the actual hearing. It is vital, therefore, that accurate records are kept from the first referral, and are sufficiently detailed. Records should be dated and recording should take place contemporaneously with events, or as soon as possible afterwards. Relevant information about resources should also be recorded, e.g. the availability of foster carers. Always distinguish between fact and opinion. Records should also include details of notifications to other agencies, their involvement, and any information that has been shared. It is possible that some of the detail that is kept on file may not be presented to the court, because of rules of evidence. These rules vary according to the type of case, in particular depending upon whether it is a civil or criminal matter. An outline of some of the key rules of evidence is provided at the end of this chapter; however, this is an area where guidance should normally be provided by the solicitor representing the local authority.

If the file may be taken into court, it is important to be familiar with the contents so as not to become flustered when searching for a key document. Rules on disclosure of evidence, however, should mean that there are very few surprises during court hearings, and new documentary evidence will not normally be produced at such a late stage. Thorough preparation includes having knowledge, not just of personal evidence and report, if one is to be submitted to the court, but also of any other reports that the court will receive, particularly if there are areas of inconsistency.

Part of the preparation stage should include having a pre-court conference with the lawyer presenting the case, to make sure that there have been no sudden last-minute changes to the case. This may be the local authority solicitor but may also include a 'conference with counsel' if a barrister is presenting the case. The professional relationship between the lawyer presenting the case and the social worker who instructs the lawyer should be seen as another aspect of multi-disciplinary working together where communication is essential. It is vital to remember that, while a social worker is likely to have in-depth knowledge of the case, the solicitor will normally know only what he has been told by the social worker and can present the case only on that basis. Studies of the social worker/lawyer relationship have found that unclear boundaries between the two roles can be a major source of tension and the simplified delineation of roles, i.e. the lawyer advising and the social worker instructing, are difficult to maintain in practice. Dickens (2004) concluded that improved communication and understanding of respective roles is essential here as for all inter-professional relationships.

Preparation also involves being aware of the various legal options available to the court. This is particularly important now that courts have a wide range of disposal options in youth justice cases, and are not limited to granting or refusing the order applied for in family proceedings but can draw on a range of powers. An integral part of the evidence is being able to show that all relevant alternatives have been considered and that the case has been considered on an individual basis rather than within a rigid policy framework.

Moving on from pre-court preparation to the actual hearing, there are further steps that can be taken to reduce stress. These include basic points like checking up on transport arrangements, getting to court in plenty of time, finding which court the case will be heard in if the court building has more than one room, and if possible having a look inside the court and becoming familiar with the layout. The court usher will usually be helpful if approached. Before entering the courtroom, any mobile phones or pagers should be switched off. Dress may be a contentious issue, although it may be argued that it should not be necessary to compromise individual dress sense because you are in a court of law. The counterargument is that appearance of witnesses is likely to influence the court, at least at a subconscious level, and nothing should detract from the focus of the case, i.e. your clients, the child, or the accused. Once professionals become regular court attenders, it is easy to forget that for the individual concerned the issue at stake may be life-changing, and it is important to show some respect for that situation. Dress should therefore be sufficiently formal to demonstrate respect for the occasion without being uncomfortable.

Once the proceedings begin, the social worker's role may be to instruct the solicitor throughout the case or it may be to appear as one of several witnesses.

■ Giving evidence

When a witness enters the court and is directed to the witness box, he is required to take the oath or affirmation, before giving oral evidence to the court. A Christian will hold the New Testament (a Jew will hold the Old Testament) and say, 'I swear by Almighty God that the evidence I shall give shall be the truth, the whole truth and nothing but the truth.' Members of other religions and sects take an oath in a manner and with such ceremony as they declare to be binding: for instance, a Hindu will hold the Gita and state, 'I swear by the Gita that the evidence . . .' etc.; a Moslem or follower of Islam will swear on the Koran and state, 'I swear by Allah . . .', etc.

Anyone who does not wish to swear an oath can affirm by saying: 'I do solemnly, sincerely and truly declare and affirm that the evidence I shall give, shall be the truth, the whole truth and nothing but the truth.' Where youths are concerned, the procedure follows that for adults except that the oath reads: 'I promise before . . . to tell the truth', etc. Where a child under the age of 14 gives evidence, he does so unsworn.

Taking the oath provides a useful opportunity to test voice level, take a few deep breaths and start to focus the mind. It also presents the opportunity to find a position where eye contact with the judge or magistrates is possible. Although the majority of questions will come from the solicitors or barristers, answers should be addressed to the bench or judge. Magistrates should normally be referred to as 'your worship(s)' and judges as 'your honour'. Evidence normally begins with introductions and this is an opportunity to establish expertise as a prerequisite to giving opinion evidence. The case of *F* v. *Suffolk County Council* (1981) 2 FLR 208 stated that the courts will presume that a qualified social worker is an expert for general issues of child care.

The process of giving evidence is divided into three parts. First, the solicitor representing your case conducts examination-in-chief. In many civil proceedings, where a witness statement has been submitted, the witness will simply be asked to confirm the contents of their statement, or may go straight to cross-examination. Where examination-in-chief does take place, evidence should normally be presented as a logical narrative and is the opportunity to present your arguments persuasively. Remember that in examination-in-chief the solicitor cannot ask leading questions. A leading question is one that suggests the answer. For example, 'Did you draw the conclusion that this child had been sexually abused?' would be a leading question, whereas, 'Did you draw a conclusion about this child?', followed by 'What was that conclusion?' would not. Examination-in-chief will usually follow the format and content of the witness statement. Exhibit 4.1 illustrates how a statement of a social worker in a child care case might be presented.

Case No. ....

In The .... (High) (County) (Magistrates') Court
Application under Children Act 1989, Section ....
RE [*Name and date of birth of child*]
BETWEEN
.... Applicant
and
.... Respondent
STATEMENT OF EVIDENCE OF
I, ... of [professional address]
WILL SAY:

1. I am a social worker employed by the [*authority*]. I have been the social worker for [*child*] since ...... I hold the [*qualifications and outline of experience*]. I make this statement from facts within my own knowledge and also from interviews with .... and from social work records which are true to the best of my knowledge and belief.
2. [*Description of family whom the case concerns.*]
3. [*Brief outline of presenting problems, which resulted in application being made*].
4. [*History and previous involvement (if any) of family with social services or other professional services*].
5. [*Detailed account of involvement and current evidence. All relevant factual detail and important interviews. Dates and recommendations of any case conferences. If reference is made to matters told to the witness by another person, this should be clear; as should the person's name and professional capacity and circumstances in which the conversation took place*].
6. [*Professional opinions formed resulting from the facts.*]
7. [*Application of the welfare checklist of the Children Act 1989, s.1(3), providing conclusions on each point*].
8. [*Immediate and future plans for the child, including any further investigations*].

I would therefore respectfully recommend that this Honourable Court order that .....
....
I, ..., make this statement believing the contents to be true and I understand that it may be placed before the court.

Signed..........

Social Worker
Dated

Exhibit 4.1   Sample social worker witness statement in child care case

In civil cases the current rules encourage advance disclosure of evidence. A strict timetable for filing evidence will be created by the court following the 'Judicial Case Management in Public Law Children Act Cases' protocol (June 2003). The protocol is considered in detail in Chapter 9.

Next comes the (often dreaded) cross-examination. At this stage the most important advice is to keep calm. The objective of the opposing advocate is to discredit and challenge evidence and elicit evidence favourable to the opposition. It is necessary to remain assertive and convincing to counter this attack. This includes being aware of body language as well as oral answers and remembering to address answers to the bench. Taking a moment to turn away from the advocate and towards the bench can provide a vital few seconds of thinking time. The advocate may ask leading questions in cross-examination, but if inappropriate questions are directed to the witness, or the advocate makes statements which the witness is not invited to challenge or comment on, it is really the role of the solicitor to object, rather than the witness. It is acceptable to request that a question be repeated or clarified if it was not heard or understood.

Thirdly, in some cases the witness may be re-examined by his own solicitor on any new points that have arisen in cross-examination. This is the final opportunity to argue the case. Finally, the magistrates or judge may also ask some questions, after which the witness is released.

The following comments from a Registered Homes Tribunal decision give an indication of the qualities to aim for as a witness. It was stated that the registration and inspection officers 'gave their evidence in clear, cogent and convincing terms without any hint of embellishment or animosity towards the Appellants'.[14]

Understanding some basic principles of the English legal system and the types of language which will be used (as outlined in these early chapters) can soon make the court experience seem like an extension of everyday practice. The following list outlines three steps to becoming a good witness, in terms of preparation, familiarity and role.

Preparation: know the case

Accurate recording of all events.

Good working relationship with the solicitor.

Provide sufficient copies of all relevant documents.

Basic understanding of rules of evidence.

Knowledge of the range of relevant legal options.

Familiarity: know the court

Locate venue.

Acquaint self with layout of court or tribunal.

Knowledge of procedure of court or tribunal.

Knowledge of the various roles of court personnel.

Role: know yourself

Establish expertise, qualifications and experience.

Consider appropriate behaviour of a witness.

Aim for honest, clear and accurate presentation.

Dress appropriately.

Speak slowly, allowing sufficient time for the clerk to take notes.

Address answers to the bench, not the advocate.

Be aware of the effect of body language.

Avoid any personalised comments.

Keep calm.

▪ Rules of evidence

Lawyers will advise upon technical aspects of evidence. A basic understanding is an aid to the preparation of evidence and comprehending the procedures in court. There are three main types of evidence: testimony, to which most of the rules below apply; documents, including statements of truth (formerly called affidavits); and real evidence, which is produced to the court as exhibits, e.g. objects, photographs, and can include a witness's demeanour.

▪ Admissibility

Evidence must be admissible for it to be heard by the court. Admissibility turns on relevance and is a matter of law, for the magistrates or judge – not the jury – to decide. Broadly speaking, the relevance of an issue will be dictated by the relevant statute or body of case law. For example, the Children Act 1989, s. 31 outlines the criteria upon which evidence can be given in an application for care proceedings. The evidence will be relevant if it logically helps to prove or disprove a fact in issue, e.g. evidence to prove or disprove whether the cause of a bruise was non-accidental. The proof may be direct or circumstantial.

▪ Hearsay

There is a general presumption against the admissibility of hearsay evidence in criminal cases. The object of this hearsay rule is to ensure that the court hears the best, most direct evidence available. Hearsay can be explained as: 'Evidence of a fact given to the court in some way other than through the oral testimony of a witness who has first-hand knowledge of that fact, and given as evidence of the truth of that fact.'

Evidence which is given simply to prove that something was said, rather than to prove the truth of the statement, is accepted as an exception to the hearsay rule. This is important, as a social worker may frequently want to report to the court statements made by a service user or child without claiming that the statement is necessarily true. There are other significant exceptions to the rule against hearsay, which have been introduced by statute, e.g. under the Children (Admissibility of Hearsay Evidence) Order 1991 (S1 1991/1115). Hearsay evidence is now generally admissible in civil cases. Even where hearsay evidence is admissible, corroboration is likely to be required, and the witness is likely to be cross-examined as to the source and reliability of the hearsay evidence, with a view to undermining the evidence. There has also been some relaxation of the rule against hearsay in criminal proceedings under the Criminal Justice Act 2003.

A case concerning admissibility of hearsay evidence serves to remind us of the significance of the distinction between civil and criminal matters: *Clingham* v. *Kensington and Chelsea Rajal London Borough Council* [2001] EWHC Admin 1. The application, in civil proceedings, was for an anti-social behaviour order under s. 1 of the Crime and Disorder Act 1998. The evidence in question consisted of evidence of police officers that would refer to information received from other officers and allegations of anti-social behaviour from members of the public who were too frightened to give evidence or could not be identified. The High Court ruled that the evidence was hearsay but in a civil case it was admissible, though the court would consider what weight to attach to it depending on the full circumstances of the case. The defendants' argument that proceedings for an anti-social behaviour order were akin to criminal proceedings, and therefore criminal rules of evidence should be followed, did not succeed. Nor did the argument that, as some of the evidence was hearsay without the possibility of cross-examination, the trial was not fair as required by Art. 6(1) of the ECHR.

■ Opinion

Traditionally, as the courts seek facts, there is a preference against opinion evidence. In some cases, however, opinion evidence can be crucial to the outcome and is effectively required by statute, e.g. evidence as to whether a child is 'likely to suffer significant harm' (Children Act 1989, s. 31). In order for opinion evidence to be accepted by the court, it is necessary for the witness to be an expert in the fields about which the opinion is proffered. As a preliminary, therefore, it is necessary to establish the expertise of the witness.

Expert opinion evidence should contain information that goes beyond a level of general understanding which might be expected of a lay person. Expert evidence may need to be defended on the basis of relevant experience and research, and cross-examination on opinion should be anticipated. A social worker will frequently be in the position of an expert witness. Reference to relevant research and theory to support the stance taken in a case is therefore important and care should be taken not to express opinions beyond what can reasonably be supported.

■ Corroboration

Corroborating evidence is that which backs up evidence already provided. There used to be rules that required a judge to give the jury a 'corroboration warning' in respect of certain classes of witnesses, including complainants in sexual cases, but this has now been abolished.[15] A judge may still give a warning to the jury about accepting a particular piece of evidence, e.g. in *R* v. *Spencer* [1987] AC 128, a case involving the prosecution of members of staff in Rampton Special Hospital for alleged abuse of patients. The jury was warned of the danger of convicting on the unsupported evidence of special hospital patients who, in the words of the court, were of bad character, mentally unstable and may have a common grudge against staff.

The judge has a more general discretion to give a warning in any case where it appears the witness has 'a purpose of his own' to serve. Also, in criminal cases the Criminal Justice and Public Order Act 1994 allows the jury to draw an adverse inference from the accused's failure to answer questions in the police station or failure to give evidence. (This is sometimes incorrectly referred to as abolition of the right to silence.)

■ Competence

Competence depends on a witness being able to understand the duty to tell the truth and also the extra obligation and sanction involved in the oath or affirmation. Witnesses are generally both **competent** and **compellable,** meaning that they must give evidence, though it may be necessary to secure attendance by a witness summons. Under s. 80 of the Police and Criminal Evidence Act 1984, the spouse of the accused is now competent and compellable to give evidence in respect of an assault or sexual offence committed against her or a child. This provision was introduced due to concerns that women who had suffered domestic violence were frequently reluctant to give evidence against their assailant.

■ Evidence of children and vulnerable adults

In civil and criminal cases, children (under the age of 14) give evidence unsworn. There are special provisions for children and vulnerable adults to give evidence behind screens or using video link. Videotapes of evidence can be provided for the court. Relevant provisions of the Youth Justice and Criminal Evidence Act 1999 are discussed in more detail in Chapters 13 and 18. A social worker will often be in the position of supporting children and vulnerable adults who give evidence – and their families – and should be prepared for a range of possible outcomes, including withdrawal of a case by the CPS.

Evidence in child protection cases is considered in more detail in Chapter 9.

■ Relationship with lawyers

The importance of establishing good working relationships with a range of other professionals is now well established. 'Working Together to Safeguard Children' (1999) (2006), 'No Secrets: Guidance on developing and implementing multi-agency policies and procedures to protect vulnerable adults from abuse' (2000), and the Crime and Disorder Act 1998 formally recognise this principle. Although sometimes on the periphery of this network, it is important for social workers to establish good working relations with lawyers for the cases that ultimately reach court, but also for the provision of legal advice on a regular basis. Early contact between social workers and solicitors can lead to better final outcomes in the legal process.

In order to build good working relations it is important to be clear about the parameters of the respective roles as solicitor and social worker. In essence, social workers decide whether to become involved in a case and then instruct a solicitor; the solicitor then gives advice and represents the authority in court. A good working relationship will be more flexible than this strict demarcation suggests and will operate along the lines of partnership and cooperation. Sometimes, the solicitor will instruct a barrister for the court hearing. The solicitor will then liaise with the barrister and retain responsibility for day-to-day management of the case and provision of information and materials to the barrister. It is not possible for a social worker directly to instruct a barrister.

What are the barriers that may prevent a good working relationship? A practical barrier comes in the form of contractual arrangements in some authorities, which mean that social workers have less direct access to lawyers, and may have to obtain permission from managers to seek legal advice that the department will subsequently be charged for. Beyond that, some preconceptions held by both professions may militate against effective partnership. Solicitors may be perceived as entrenched in the adversarial tradition and focused on winning cases at all costs, an approach that might not be appropriate in, e.g., child care cases. On the other hand, social workers might be perceived as idealistic and unrealistic about what lawyers can actually achieve within the limits of the law – a quick fix is not always possible. Such preconceptions may actually be rooted in a tension between the values of solicitors and social workers, and concern that some actions of social workers are subject to legal scrutiny. The way forward can include joint training initiatives, formation of multi-disciplinary interest groups, dissemination of information, e.g. legal fact sheets providing summaries of case law developments. In terms of managing individual cases, it is useful to spend time at the initial point of contact demarcating tasks and respective responsibilities.

Social work and the law share certain features because of the professional nature of both jobs. The Royal Commission on Legal Services identified five characteristics of a profession: it has a governing body; it has a specialised field of knowledge acquired by training and experience; admission to the profession is dependent on a period of training, and competence is tested; there is an element of self-regulation; there is a professional ethic.

Lawyers and social workers actually share many skills. It is useful to break down the respective roles of lawyer and social worker and identify comparable skills, e.g. assessment, research, communication, negotiation, interviewing and presentation skills. Building on common ground can make the task of working together less daunting. Awareness of role boundaries also lays the foundations for establishing constructive ways for solicitors and social workers to work together.[16]

Challenging social work practice

Invariably there will be situations where aspects of social work decisions (not confined to decisions relating to court processes) will be challenged. As the social worker is normally employed as an agent of the Social Services Authority, whether or not the decision has been taken with the support of legal advice, a decision will be viewed as a decision of the agency. Whilst it is convenient to talk in terms of a decision, what is in fact being challenged may be a course of conduct over a particular case. It is not generally possible for any person to complain in the abstract about the actions of a Social Services Authority; they must normally be personally affected and/or have a personal interest in the case. That stance is certainly supported by the victim test under the Human Rights Act 1998. Other limitations are considered under each avenue for challenge.

Six potential avenues for challenging social work decisions exist:

- local authority's complaints procedure
- complaints to the local government ombudsman
- default power of the Secretary of State
- judicial review
- local authority monitoring officer
- action for damages
- complaints under the Human Rights Act 1998.

■ Local authority's complaints procedure

Complaints procedures in relation to both adults services and child care cases had their foundation in the Local Authority Social Services Act 1970, s. 7B, with specific directions covering the detail of the complaints procedure.[17]

The Department of Health and Department for Education and Skills are involved in reviewing the policy and procedure for complaining about social care services. A Department of Health consultation paper, 'Listening to people', identified key areas for improvement in handling complaints and a new complaints procedure has been proposed. The new procedure still shares a similar informal resolution stage, followed by investigation by the local authority, the third stage, however, allows for the complaint to be considered by a Complaints Review Service (**CRS**) operated by the Commission for Social Care Inspection.[18] At this 'review' stage, the CRS will decide whether to take no further action, or refer back to the local authority or it may itself conduct a review. The CRS review may actually be in the form of an independent complaints panel, an investigation by the CRS or a referral to the local government ombudsman. The new procedure was due to be implemented in October 2005 but has been deferred in the light of proposed inspection reforms. In the meantime local authorities will continue to operate the existing complaints procedure.[19] It is likely that the complaints process for children will be similarly reformed.[20]

■ Existing procedure

The principal features of the procedures are that: to make a complaint or representation a person must be a qualifying individual; the complaints procedure has an independent element; and there are three stages to the process – the informal stage, the formal stage and the review stage.

Informal stage

A person is a qualifying individual if social services have a power or a duty to provide a service to him/her, and the need for that service is known by the department. The person may already be in receipt of services. When a representation is received from a qualifying individual, the department should first attempt to resolve it informally, acting swiftly in response to representations that may simply be oral at this stage. This informal stage must not be used to dissuade an individual from making a formal complaint. The person can ask to go direct to the formal stage, omitting the informal stage.

Formal stage

If the complaint is not resolved at the informal stage, the Social Services Department must give the complainant an explanation of the formal and review stages of the complaints procedure and invite him/her to make written representations. It is good practice also to offer assistance and guidance on the use of the procedure, and appropriate accessible materials should be available, e.g. leaflets written for people whose first language is not English. All written representations received by the department must be registered. The local authority should consider the complaint and reply within 28 days if possible. If it is not possible to reply within 28 days an explanation for the delay should be given. After consideration of the complaint the complainant should be notified in writing of the decision.

Review stage

If not satisfied with the decision at the formal stage, the complainant can request a review by a panel. This request should be made within 28 days of notification of the outcome of the formal stage. The panel should then meet within 28 days of receipt of the request to hear the complaint. The panel consists of three people, and at least one must be an independent person, neither a member nor an employee of the authority. The complainant is entitled to make written and oral submissions to the panel and may be accompanied by a person who is able to speak on their behalf, e.g. an advocate or friend rather than formal legal representation. The meeting should be conducted as an informal hearing. The panel can make a recommendation to the local authority, which should be recorded in writing within 24 hours of the hearing. Due to the involvement of an independent person, the panel are not able to make decisions which are binding on the local authority; nevertheless, the local authority must have regard to the panel's recommendations and should depart from them only if there are very good reasons for doing so. The independence of panels and their compliance with Art. 6(1) ECHR was questioned in *R (Beeson)* v. *Dorset CC* [2002] EWCA Civ 1812. The court held that the procedure does not breach Art. 6 because of the availability of recourse to judicial review and, taken together, the panel with the addition of judicial review provides the necessary fairness.

From the time limits outlined, it is clear that from first making the complaint, the process will take a minimum of three months, assuming there is no informal stage. Practice suggests that in fact considerably longer delays are commonplace. There is also the risk that, even if the outcome of the review panel is in the complainant's favour, the local authority is not bound to follow it. Not surprisingly, some complainants may wish to take their complaint a stage further and may explore the additional options below.

The new Children's Commissioners for Wales and for England may also have a role in examining some cases and monitoring arrangements for complaints. The Commissioners' roles are discussed in more detail as part of the discussion on children's rights in Chapter 7.

■ Local government ombudsman

Also known as the Commissioner for Local Administration, the local government ombudsman can investigate a complaint against a local authority where there has been maladministration, which causes an injustice to the complainant. There are three local government ombudsmen in England dealing with complaints from different parts of the country. Maladministration for these purposes includes: unreasonable delay; bias; disregard of procedures; and incompetence. The complaint should normally have arisen no more than 12 months before the local government ombudsman is contacted. In practice, because the ombudsman will normally expect a complaint to have been considered first by the complaints procedure outlined above, this time may be exceeded.

A significant number of investigations by the ombudsman have concerned delays in processing assessments for services. *Investigation into Complaint No. 97/A/2959 against Hackney London Borough Council* (1998) CCLR 66 provides a useful illustration. The case concerned two brothers aged 41 and 39, both with learning difficulties. They had been attending a day centre for about ten years. In 1995, Hackney transferred management of the centre to a charity as part of reorganisation of services for people with learning difficulties and reorganisation of the community care division. The transfer took place on the understanding that Hackney and the charity would reassess the needs of all users of the centre within six months. Despite reminders from the charity and Edward and Robert's parents, Mr and Mrs Foster, the assessment did not commence until 1997. Mrs Foster lodged a complaint, which was upheld in January 1997 by the Social Services Complaints Review Panel concluding that Hackney had been negligent and recommending that the reassessment be carried out within three months. The Director of Social Services wrote explaining that the cause of the delay was lack of resources. By November 1998 Hackney had still not completed risk assessments or a care plan for Edward or Robert.

The local government ombudsman reached the following conclusions:

1. The delay in carrying out reassessments (about 22 months) amounted to maladministration.

2. Hackney had still not completed a risk assessment at the time of the investigation; record keeping was poor, as were communications with Mr and Mrs Foster,

to whom they had failed to explain the nature and purpose of the reassessment. These faults all amounted to maladministration.

3. Injustice had been caused by the maladministration. In particular, Mr and Mrs Foster had suffered anxiety and had been put to considerable time and trouble. Also, Edward and Robert had missed the opportunity of benefiting from earlier provision based on proper assessment.

It was recommended that Hackney should pay £1,500 compensation to Mr and Mrs Foster. Of general application, it was recommended that Hackney should review the needs of other people using the day centre; review provision of written information about the community care assessment process; review supervision arrangements for care managers; and implement a system to ensure that recommendations of review panels are implemented without unreasonable delay. As ombudsman decisions are often reported by the media, the 'embarrassment' factor for local authorities may have a greater impact than the relatively low compensation levels. This case provides a clear example of the damaging effect of delay relating to service provision for vulnerable adults. The full report is particularly interesting to read for the insight it gives into the extent and process of the detailed investigation carried out by the ombudsman.

A further ombudsman decision concerned services for children. In *Rochdale Metropolitan Borough Council* (03/C/18598) (2005) Mr Elliott complained that the Council failed to advise him of the implications of him taking care of a young child, 'Harry', who was not related to him but who was half-brother to his own children. He complained that: he was given no financial or other support during the first 15 months he cared for Harry; the financial implications of seeking a residence order were not explained; alternatives to that residence order were not discussed with him; the Council failed to provide the continuing support he needed to care properly for Harry; the Council excluded him from meetings held to discuss Harry's future; and the Council did not deal with his complaints properly.

The ombudsman found that the Council had left a 17-month-old baby with Mr Elliott without undertaking even the most cursory of checks upon either him or his ability to care for a young child. For the following 12 months, largely unsupported by the Council, Mr Elliott made legal decisions about Harry which he was simply not entitled to make. The ombudsman concluded that Mr Elliott was either not advised at all or advised badly concerning the options available to him. The ombudsman found that only when Mr Elliott complained to the Council that he could no longer care for Harry was it discovered that he had, all along, been entitled to receive some financial support from the Council. The ombudsman found that the Council failed to interpret letters from Mr Elliott as formal complaints.

Mr Elliott obtained a residence order for Harry but, had he been accepted as a foster parent, he would have received a great deal more in terms of financial and general support. Fortunately for Harry, Mr Elliott proved to be an appropriate carer who had done an excellent job in looking after him.

The ombudsman found maladministration causing injustice to Mr Elliott. The Council agreed to apologise to Mr Elliott and to pay him £8,000. This represented compensation plus the additional monies Mr Elliott would have received if he had been treated as a family and friends carer.

Complaints to the ombudsman should be made in writing and the ombudsman has a power to require access to relevant information held by the local authority. The complaint is sent to the Council's Chief Executive for consideration and response. The ombudsman will prepare a report and can make recommendations, including compensation awards, and, whilst the local authority is not strictly bound to follow these recommendations, in practice they usually do. Advantages of complaining to the ombudsman include that the process is free, there is a possibility of informal settlement, compensation may result and the investigation is independent.

Maladministration complaints in respect of the National Health Service, including social work in hospital settings, are dealt with by the Parliamentary and Health Service Ombudsman.

■ Default power of the Secretary of State

The Local Authority Social Services Act (LASSA) 1970, s. 7C authorises the Secretary of State to hold an inquiry into the exercise of social services functions by a local authority (excluding duties under the Children Act 1989). The default power is limited to statutory duties and does not extend to the exercise of discretionary powers. As yet, the Secretary of State has not exercised this default power. The type of situation where it might arise would be where a local authority completely failed to provide a statutory service, or did not have a complaints procedure, or disregarded a direction. In those cases, under LASSA 1970, s. 7D, the Secretary of State could declare that the local authority is in default of its social services functions and order the authority to comply with those duties within a specified timescale.

■ Judicial review

Judicial review is a legal process that allows the High Court to exercise a supervisory role over the decision-making of public bodies. It is a public law remedy. Judicial review cases are focused on the process of decision-making rather than the merit of the ultimate decision. Judicial review has proved to be a useful tool for checking the actions of local authorities, as illustrated by a series of cases that related to the relevance of resources of a local authority when carrying out community care assessments. Judicial review is discussed further in Chapter 2. Some of the advantages of using judicial review to challenge decisions are that groups and organisations can bring cases or support individuals to bring a case provided they have a sufficient interest in the matter, and that leave is required to bring an action but, once obtained, early settlement is common. For an individual applicant 'sufficient interest' in this context would include the service user affected by the decision as well as carers. An obvious disadvantage to judicial review is expense if the complainant does not qualify for legal assistance. Proceedings are generally lengthy, though it is sometimes possible to deal with cases on an urgency basis and also to make interim injunctions prior to the final hearing. In addition, it is normally necessary first to have exhausted alternative remedies, including the local authority complaints procedure, and there are fairly strict time limits for bringing an action (within three months of the action complained of).

■ Monitoring officer

Local authorities must appoint a monitoring officer under s. 5 of the Local Government and Housing Act 1989. The officer must report to the authority any matters, including proposals, decisions or omissions, where the local authority has or is likely to contravene the law or a Code of Practice; or concerning any maladministration or injustice that could be investigated by the local government ombudsman. This can present a useful opportunity for a local authority to put matters in order before a complaint progresses, perhaps to a judicial review.

■ Action for damages

As society becomes increasingly litigious, there will be circumstances when a service user decides that they are unhappy about a service or the actions of a social worker and wants to sue. In such circumstances, what is the position concerning liability? In the majority of cases where professional actions are challenged, the basis of the challenge is in negligence. An alternative route, less often relied upon, is breach of contract. The tort of negligence has three elements that must be satisfied before an action will succeed:

1. a duty of care was owed;
2. there was a breach of that duty; and
3. damage resulted as a consequence of the breach.

The first question to be addressed, then, is whether a social worker owes a duty of care to a client. A famous case, *Donoghue* v. *Stevenson* [1932] AC 562, established the principle that a general duty of care is owed to your neighbour, i.e. to any person closely affected by your conduct, and whom you should reasonably foresee might be injured by it. It is also established that if a person is considered to be a professional or expert, this duty or standard will be applied more rigorously. Vicarious liability is the principle whereby employers will be held responsible for the actions of their employees, provided they were acting in the course of their employment and not 'on a frolic of their own'.[21] For social workers it is also relevant to note that social work functions are vested in the authority rather than the individual who works as an agent of the authority. Effectively, then, an aggrieved individual will bring an action in negligence against the authority rather than the individual social worker. Certain bodies have traditionally been protected from negligence claims by 'public interest immunity', i.e. the principle that it would not be in the public interest for actions of the body to be subject to challenge because of the impact this would have on the work of the body.

A series of cases have produced contrasting decisions concerning local authority liability in tort but appear to signal a gradual erosion of the public interest immunity enjoyed by social workers (Preston-Shoot *et al.*, 2001).

X (Minors) v. *Bedfordshire County Council* [1995] 3 All ER 353: the court found the authority was immune from a claim in negligence on the basis that 'general policy decisions' are not justiciable and cannot provide a basis for civil liability in negligence.

Osman v. *United Kingdom* (1998) 5 BHRC 293: the practice of English courts deciding that as a matter of law it would not be fair, just and reasonable to impose liability in particular types of cases was declared to be in breach of Art. 6, the right to a fair trial, as it precludes an individual from having the balance struck between their hardship and the public interest on the facts of the particular case. This case concerned the claim that the police owed no duty of care to the public, at risk from criminal threats known to the police.

Barrett v. *Enfield London Borough Council* [1999] 3 All ER 193: this case effectively narrowed the basis for striking out claims against a local authority. Barrett brought an application alleging that Enfield had looked after him negligently whilst he was in care. He based this claim specifically on the fact that he had been moved to six different residential homes, he had been fostered twice without any plans for adoption being made, he had not been provided with properly trained social workers or appropriate psychiatric advice, and proper arrangements had not been made to reunite him with his mother. The authority's application to strike out the proceedings failed. It was decided that it was not appropriate to strike out proceedings unless it was possible to give a certain answer to the question of whether the action would succeed and this was increasingly difficult to do in the developing area of negligence law. A local authority is unlikely to be found negligent for injury caused in the exercise of their statutory discretionary powers where their exercise was not wholly unreasonable or involved balancing of competing interests. The question should, however, be decided in the light of individual facts and the extent to which actions were of an operational rather than a policy nature. In practice it is not always easy to distinguish between policy and operational matters, as each one affects the other.

Phelps v. *Hillingdon London Borough Council* [1999] 1All ER 421, CA; [2001] 2 AC 619, HL: this case signalled a significant change in approach. In an education setting, it was held that a local education authority can be liable in negligence for incompetent education, directly if it employs obviously incompetent staff, or vicariously for incompetent acts or omissions by education professionals, unless, exceptionally, it is able to establish that recognising liability would so interfere with the performance of its duties that it would be wrong to do so. The facts of the case included the failure of an educational psychologist to identify that a child was suffering from dyslexia.

W and Others v. *Essex County Council and Another* [2000] 2 All ER 237: claims were made by foster parents on behalf of their children, who were sexually abused by a foster child placed with them by the local authority. They claimed that the authority and their social worker knew that the boy was an abuser and had withheld that information. The court found that it was fair, just and reasonable to impose a duty of care in the circumstances.

S v. *Gloucestershire County Council; L* v. *Tower Hamlets London Borough Council* (2000) 3 CCLR 294, CA: actions in negligence were brought against the local authorities. The substance of each claim was that, when they were living in foster care as children, the foster father had sexually abused them and, in consequence, they had suffered physical and long-term psychological damage. The hearing of this case was delayed until the House of Lords gave its decision in *Barrett* v. *Enfield London Borough Council* [1999] 3 All ER 193.

The European Court of Human Rights has also played a part in this developing line of case law. The *Bedfordshire* case reached the European Court as *Z* v. *United Kingdom* (Application 29392/95) (2001) 34 EHRR 97. The House of Lords had struck out the negligence claims against the local authority. The European Court held unanimously that the United Kingdom had breached Art. 3, the right not to be subjected to inhuman or degrading treatment, by failing to protect the children from long-term abuse and neglect. The court further decided that the fact that a person, especially a child as in this case, was not able to pursue a remedy in damages against the local authority meant the United Kingdom also breached Art. 13. The children were not afforded an effective means of redress for their treatment by the council. The court awarded damages and costs. Further, in *E v United Kingdom (Application No. 33218/96)* [2003] 1 FLR 348, four applicants complained that the local authority had failed to adequately protect them from physical and sexual abuse by their mother's partner over several years, and were awarded compensation.

In contrast, the courts have ruled that in relation to investigation of child abuse, no duty of care is owed to parents. Thus, in *D* v. *East Berkshire Community NHS Trust; K* v. *Dewsbury Healthcare NHS Trust; K* v. *Oldham NHS Trust* [2003] EWCA Civ 1151, claims by parents who had been the subject of unfounded accusations were not allowed. In childcare cases the interests of the child and the parents were in potential conflict, priority had to be given to the duty to investigate and no duty should be owed to parents. Also, in *D* v. *Bury Metropolitan Borough Council* [2006] EWCA Civ 1, the Court of Apeal confirmed that a local authority did not owe a duty of care to parents in the conduct of care proceedings in respect of their child, and the fact that an interim care order was conducted by agreement did not mean that a duty had arisen. An interim care order was obtained in respect of a four-month-old baby who sustained fractured ribs thought to have been caused by non-accidental injury. The local authority then found that the child had brittle bone disease and he was returned to his parents and the care proceedings were discharged. The parents' claim for psychological harm caused by the alleged negligence of the authority was rejected.

Analysis of the above decisions suggests that it can no longer be said that local authorities enjoy an absolute immunity from liability in negligence. It probably remains easier to establish liability at operational level than policy level. In future, even if it is not possible to bring a claim in negligence against the local authority, the option remains of pursuing a claim under the Human Rights Act 1998.

■ Human Rights Act 1998

Provisions under the Human Rights Act 1998 allow victims to bring an action against a local authority if it has acted in a way which is incompatible with the terms of the Articles of the European Convention on Human Rights.[22] Some illustrations of this have been discussed above and Chapter 5 provides more detail on the new right of action against public authorities (including local authorities).

■ Employer's duty of care to staff

As employers, local authorities owe a duty of care to their staff and may be required to pay compensation if found to be negligent. This was argued in *Colclough v. Staffordshire County Council* [1994] CLY 2283, where a social worker suffered injury trying to lift a 15-stone service user who had fallen out of bed. She had not received any training or information about manual handling. Simlarly, in *Harvey v. Northumberland County Council* [2003] All ER (D) 347 (Feb), the Council was found liable to its employee, a residential social worker in secure accommodation, for failing to train him in restraint techniques.

Stress-related injury has also been the subject of negligence claims. In *Walker v Northumberland CC* [1995] 1 All ER 737, a social worker returned to work after suffering a nervous breakdown. He had been a team leader dealing with child protection cases. On his return it was foreseeable that, without further support, he could suffer a further breakdown. Appropriate support was not provided and, following a second breakdown, he took early retirement. The local authority, his employer, were found to be in breach of their duty of care and paid damages. Clearly for damages to be paid there must be foreseeable damage and the authority would be expected to take reasonable steps so as not to breach their duty. Where an authority does not respond once it is aware that an employee is suffering stress, it could be liable in negligence as above and might also have obligations under the Management of Health and Safety at Work Regulations 1999 (SI 1999/3242).

Whistleblowing

Whistleblowing may be defined as: 'The disclosure by an employee (or professional) of confidential information which relates to some danger, fraud, or other illegal or unethical conduct connected with the workplace, be it of the employer or of his fellow employees.'[23]

In the context of social work practice, whistleblowing can in some circumstances be an appropriate response to concerns about bad practice and is a legitimate aspect of the social work role. A feature of a number of inquiry reports such as Longcare (1998)[24] and the Waterhouse Report (2000)[25] has been the acknowledgement that abuse can go on undetected by outside agencies for a considerable period of time. Yet abuse cannot remain hidden from the people employed in or concerned with such establishments. Lack of employment and other protection for whistleblowers and their fear of recrimination may be partly to blame for those people not coming forward, or perhaps why, if concerns were raised, it was possible to ignore or suppress them. There were a number of unsuccessful attempts to introduce whistleblowing legislation as Private Member's Bills, but legislation is now in force in the Public Interest Disclosure Act 1998. The Act amends the Employment Rights Act 1996 (ERA 1996) and will protect workers who disclose certain information in the public interest from being dismissed or penalised in other ways by their employer.

The advantages of responsible whistleblowing are not limited to the immediate concern of the whistleblower. Whistleblowing can cultivate an open culture in the workplace, in which constructive criticism and suggestions for improving standards will be listened to with a welcome ear. Abuse inquiries provide some of the clearest examples of why whistleblowing is important. Speaking out about bad practice and abuse can prevent further suffering and may even be lifesaving. It can challenge environments which actually foster bad practice, promote proper lines of accountability, protect and enhance professional reputations by weeding out influential individuals such as Frank Beck in the Leicestershire child abuse scandal,[26] and lead to recommendations for improvements in practice which are of general application across the field. One of the recommendations of the Waterhouse report was that: 'Every local authority should establish and implement conscientiously clear whistleblowing procedures enabling members of staff to make complaints and raise matters of concern affecting the treatment or welfare of looked after children without threats or fear of reprisals in any form' (Recommendation 8).

These advantages may not be sufficient, however, to encourage an isolated worker to make a disclosure. The most obvious deterrent is fear of the reaction of the employer and possible sanctions, which might include victimisation or dismissal. An incident which causes concern to one worker may not be viewed collectively as a clear example of bad practice. Confusion about appropriate standards may act as a further deterrent and may be particularly influential where a senior member of staff advises a newly qualified professional that this is the way things are done 'in the real world'! Clear national standards could assist here. Peer group pressure may prevent a worker from speaking out against a colleague, as may fear of reprisals from work colleagues, e.g. being 'sent to Coventry'. Junior or less qualified staff may not have the confidence to complain about the practice of those who are more senior in the workplace hierarchy. This can be further exacerbated if there is a fear that management will not listen to or respond to concerns. The existence of complaints procedures will often assist a worker who wishes to raise a concern; however, if the procedure is unnecessarily complex, this may equally act as a further deterrent.

The Employment Rights Act 1996, as amended by the Public Interest Disclosure Act 1998, sets out a framework in which Dehn and Ells[27] suggest responsible whistleblowing is possible by:

- Reassuring workers that silence is not the only safe option.
- Providing strong protection for workers who raise concerns internally.
- Reinforcing and protecting the right to report concerns to key regulators.
- Protecting more public disclosures, provided there is a valid reason for going wider and that the particular disclosure is reasonable.
- Helping to ensure that organisations respond by addressing the message rather than the messenger and resist the temptation to cover up serious malpractice.

It is a requirement under ERA 1996 that, to qualify for protection, the worker must act 'in good faith' and must have reasonable grounds to believe the truth of the information disclosed. This requirement is clearly designed to deter malicious and false allegations. In *Street v Derbyshire Unemployed Workers' Centre* [2004] EWCA Civ 964, the Court of Appeal dismissed a claim where there was evidence of personal antagonism. For a statement to be made in good faith requires that the predominant motivation for making the report is public interest. One of the recommendations of the Shipman report is for the good faith test to be removed on the basis that it is sufficient to rely on the other requirements.

A qualifying disclosure is one relating to one or more of the following categories:

■ a criminal offence;

■ failure to comply with a legal obligation;

■ a miscarriage of justice;

■ danger to the health and safety of any individual;

■ damage to the environment; or

■ deliberate concealment of information that would show any of the previous categories.[28]

These categories would include most, if not all, malpractice within the social sector.

Wider disclosures will be protected if there is a specific reason for the whistle-blower to go wider, e.g. the whistleblower believes evidence would be concealed or destroyed, or where the worker has previously made a disclosure to his employer, which is substantially the same, and no action resulted. To be protected it must be reasonable for the disclosure to be made in the way it is made and factors determining reasonableness will include the seriousness of the issue, to whom the disclosure is made, whether the failure disclosed is likely to continue and whether it is in breach of any duty of confidentiality owed by the employee. Disclosures to the press are unlikely to be encouraged.

Section 43J of ERA 1996 presents an important development in employment rights. It makes void any provision in an agreement that purports to prevent a worker from making a protected disclosure. In other words, 'gagging clauses' are made illegal.

If a worker who has made a disclosure does suffer any detriment by his employer, there is a right of complaint to the Employment Tribunal and compensation is payable. Detriment includes acts and omissions, and examples of behaviour could include disciplinary proceedings, suspension, and denial of promotion, salary increases or other benefits normally enjoyed. Where a worker is dismissed or selected for redundancy because he made a protected disclosure, this will be treated as an unfair dismissal.

A limitation of ERA 1996 is that employers are not obliged to introduce whistle-blowing procedures; nor is there likely to be a great deal of consistency in the procedures that do exist. It is worthy of note that most Social Services Departments already have whistleblowing procedures in place. Legally, workers are under no obligation to raise concerns or draw attention to areas of malpractice, though professional codes of practice may encourage sensible whistleblowing. In contrast, in the United States there are many examples of 'mandatory' reporting laws. Ultimately, the legislation will have made a most significant impact if it can promote more open cultures in which whistleblowing is positively encouraged as a way of improving practice.

A report by Public Concern at Work ('Two years back, Three years forward, Ten years old' (2003)) is encouraging. Calls to their helpline suggest that people are now twice as likely to report wrongdoing in the workplace than they were five years ago. The principal issues reflected in calls were safety risks and financial misconduct, but the care sector generated 17 per cent of calls in 2002. A greater number of claims are being taken to the Employment Appeal Tribunal under the Act. In 2004/5, 869 applications were made compared with 157 in 1999/2000.

Record keeping

Accurate record keeping has always been an essential aspect of good social work practice and is vital in cases which reach court. Recent years have seen the development of much greater rights of access by the individual to official records. Absolute confidentiality of records is unlikely to be guaranteed. The relevant law on access to records is now contained in the Data Protection Act 1998 and Freedom of Information Act 2000.

■ The Data Protection Act 1998

The Data Protection Act 1998 (**DPA** 1998) came into force on 1 March 2000. It repeals its predecessor, the Data Protection Act 1984. The new Act was implemented to respond to an EC directive requiring the data protection laws of EC members to be harmonised. In effect it provides individuals with new rights of access to their personal data and imposes new obligations on data controllers, such as local authority social services departments to operate good data protection practices. The general principle is that people are entitled to access information held about themselves (subject to a few exception). The DPA 1998 applies to both electronic and manual records. There is accompanying guidance to the Act.[29] The scheme of the legislation is contained in eight basic principles, which define how personal data can be managed. The language of DPA 1998 is rather technical, and explanation of some of the key terms is necessary before consideration of the principles.

Personal data

The term 'personal data' includes any information held either manually or electronically, which relates to a living individual and from which it is possible to identify that individual. Personal data may include, e.g., National Insurance numbers or expressions of opinion about an individual. The individual is referred to as the data subject.

Data controller

The data controller is the body that manages the purposes for which information is processed. For example, the Department of Health will be the data controller for the protection of vulnerable adults register established under the Care Standards Act 2000.

Processing

The term 'processing' covers a wide range of activities or action involving personal data. It would include opening and reading a file about an individual, collecting, storing, destroying or altering personal information.

Exempt information

There are some important categories of exempt information to which the principle of access to personal information does not apply. Exemptions include information required for the purpose of safeguarding national security; personal data processed for the prevention or detection of crime, the apprehension or prosecution of offenders or the assessment or collection of any tax where disclosure would be prejudicial; references (except where access is given by the person who holds the reference and the author is not identified); and personal information about someone else.

Data protection principles

1. *Personal data shall be processed fairly and lawfully.* To comply with this provision, it is important that when information is obtained from an individual, the purpose for which that information is required is made clear. Before processing information, at least one of the following conditions should apply: the consent of the data subject has been obtained; processing is necessary under contract, law or for another legal obligation (e.g. an employee providing personal information to HM Revenue and Customs); processing is necessary to protect the interests of the data subject, or for the administration of justice, exercising a legal function or function of a government department. The final condition will apply to much of the data processing carried out by Social Services Departments, such as good practice under 'Working Together' or statutory duties under the Children Act 1989.

2. *Personal data shall only be obtained for specific lawful purposes and must not be processed in any way that is incompatible with that purpose.* Under this principle it will be necessary to have policies regarding the retention and disposal of data.

3. *Personal data shall be adequate, relevant and not excessive for the purpose for which it is collected.* Organisations should not hold irrelevant information.

4. *Personal data shall be accurate and kept up to date when necessary.* Systems for checking accuracy and updating need to be in place.

5. *Personal data must be kept no longer than necessary.* If the reason for keeping the information no longer exists, it should be destroyed.

6. *Personal data shall be processed in accordance with the rights of data subjects.* Individuals have the right to access a copy of personal data held about them. Although technically it is not necessary to respond to a request unless it is received in writing, it may be good practice to respond to oral requests in some circumstances. A request does not have to be framed in technical language: e.g. 'I would like to see the information you have got on me' should be accepted as a request. If satisfied that the request comes from the data subject and a fee of £10 has been paid, then the request must be complied with within 40 days. Care must be taken not to release personal data that may relate to another individual, and in some circumstances the request may be refused if a disclosure would cause damage or distress to the data subject. Schedules 2 and 3 provide more detail.

7. *Appropriate security measures should be taken against any unlawful processing of personal data or accidental loss, damage or destruction of personal data.* Clear systems for accessing data need to be established. This may range from password protected access to electronic data to who has the keys for the filing cabinet.

8. *Personal data should not be transferred outside the European Economic Area unless the country to which it is transferred has an equivalent type of data protection legislation.* This applies even if the subject of the information goes to live outside the area.

Implications of the DPA 1998

In the future, greater care must be taken over the way information about individuals is recorded, and the substance of the information that is recorded must be limited to that which is essential to the carrying out of social work responsibilities. Training on good data protection practice should be available. Social work records, whether held manually or electronically, are clearly covered by the Act.

An Information Commissioner has been introduced to regulate the Data Protection Act 1998 and may bring enforcement proceedings if there has been a breach of the Act. If there is a breach, e.g. if personal information about an individual is inappropriately made public, and the individual suffers harm, then compensation can be claimed and criminal action may be taken against the data controller. It is important to note that there may be personal liability under the DPA. If, for example, an individual disclosed personal information in an e-mail to another person in an unauthorised way, the individual could be held responsible and fined up to £5,000. Inappropriate disclosure of personal information could also constitute a breach of the individual's right to respect for private and family life contained in Art. 8 ECHR.

■ Freedom of Information Act 2000

Provisions of the Freedom of Information Act 2000, which came into force in January 2005, complement the Data Protection Act 1998.[30] Taken together, this 'right to know' legislation supports the movement for greater 'transparency' in organisations that hold information about the public, and should lead to greater care in handling and recording information, and greater accountability in public spending. The Act applies to approximately 100,000 public authorities. Between April and June 2005 there were 8,400 requests for information made to the Government. The Act is not limited to personal information held about an individual. In summary the 2000 Act introduces:

■ A general right of access to information that public authorities carrying out their public functions hold (subject to some exemptions). This will indirectly include organisations which contract with public authorities. Information may be requested about any aspect of the public authorities' remit.

■ If the information requested falls within one of the exemptions listed in the Act, it will generally not be provided, although there is a duty to disclose exempted information where it is 'in the public interest' to do so. The authority is also excused from replying to 'vexatious or repeated' requests.

■ Exempt information includes that relating to security measures; court records; personal information (this could be accessed via DPA 1998); information provided in confidence; legal privilege; personal information concerning a third party; and health and safety (see ss. 21–44 for the full list).

■ A new Information Tribunal to enforce rights under this Act and the DPA 1998.

■ A requirement for public authorities to adopt a publication scheme, dealing with manner of publication, types of information routinely published and whether a charge will be made. For example, the Department of Health Scheme lists information it makes available as including NHS annual accounts, statistics on health and healthcare, and advice for the public. Information should normally be made available within 20 days unless an exemption applies.

■ Each authority should have a designated senior member of staff responsible for records management.[31]

■ The Information Commissioner has powers to enforce the Act.

The issue of sharing information is also of great importance in the health service. Following the Caldicott review in 1997, 'guardians' of personal information were introduced into NHS organisations to ensure lawful and appropriate handling of patient information. This model was also adopted into local authorities with social services responsibilities from 2002. Guardians have the task of auditing existing systems of data handling and results will be fed into performance reviews.[32]

Chapter summary

■ Frequently, a social worker will represent the authority as the applicant for a particular order, e.g. care order, and may have to provide a report for the court.

■ The children's guardian, an experienced social worker, independent of the local authority and appointed by the court to represent the best interests of the child, provides reports to the court in many applications concerning children.

■ A social worker may act as an 'appropriate adult' in cases where a child or vulnerable adult is being interviewed by the police at a police station. The role is to 'advise, observe and facilitate communication'.

■ As social workers will often be required to give evidence in court, it is essential to develop skills for giving evidence. The study of this topic is known as 'courtcraft'. In essence, it involves good preparation, familiarity with court venues and procedures, and clear understanding of the role in court.

■ Knowledge of rules of evidence (which vary between civil and criminal matters) can be useful when preparing a case and giving evidence. Evidence must be admissible, i.e. relevant; hearsay should be avoided where possible; experts can give opinion evidence; a witness must be competent to give evidence (able to take the oath); and sometimes corroborating evidence will be required.

■ Social work decisions may be challenged in six different ways: local authority complaints procedure; local government ombudsman; default powers of the Secretary of State; judicial review; local authority monitoring officer; action for damages.

■ Law to protect people who whistleblow on bad practice is contained in the Public Interest Disclosure Act 1998.

■ The Data Protection Act 1998 and Freedom of Information Act 2000 govern access to personal information that is held manually or electronically.

Exercises

Consider what action should be taken in the following circumstances and whether the Public Interest Disclosure Act 1998 would offer employment protection:

1. John is a student social worker on placement in a day centre for adults with learning disabilities. He is concerned that one of the staff has made racist remarks about two of the adults who come to the centre. He is reluctant to raise this with the manager of the day centre because of the close friendship between the manager and the staff member. He mentions it to his practice teacher and then makes a formal report to regulation and inspection.

2. Jane has worked as a care assistant at a residential home for three weeks. She has had a row with the manager because he has refused Jane's request to have Saturday night off. The next day Jane contacts a reporter for the local newspaper and claims that residents in the home suffer from neglect. The reporter visits the home and attempts, unsuccessfully, to interview the manager, who tells Jane to leave the premises and not to bother coming back.

Courtcraft

Spend some time thinking about any court experiences you may have had, or anticipate what you think it would be like to give evidence. Consider the following questions:

■ What are my most important aims when giving evidence to the court?

■ What impression would I like to make at court?

■ Who am I accountable to when giving evidence?

■ What anxieties do I have about giving evidence?

■ What strategies can I adopt to ensure I say what I want to say?

■ How can I translate nerves into confidence?

■ What happens if we 'lose'?

Revisit the court observation guide in Chapter 3 and include in your analysis: consideration of rules of evidence; and courtcraft skills.

Access to information

Consider whether the following requests for information are likely to be granted and whether the Data Protection Act 1998 or the Freedom of Information Act 2000 provides the authority:

■ A wants to know how much the local parish council has spent on new 'dog fouling' signs.

■ B wants to know the location of CCTV cameras in the local hospital and in the area of the town railway station.

■ C wants to see the reference provided recently for a job he unsuccessfully applied for.

■ D wants to see the local authority contract with the domiciliary care agency providing a service to her mother.

■ E wants to know the ages of the prospective adopters of her child who was removed from her care.

■ F wants to know the home address of the Director of Social Services.

Consolidation

The following exercise is designed to consolidate some of the issues discussed in the first four chapters and to reinforce the principle that social work takes place within a legal framework.[33] It is particularly valuable when used to analyse a case, perhaps experienced during placement.

Relevant legislation: Isolate the legislation relevant to the case. Was it familiar? Did you need to carry out any research or seek legal advice? Was the legislation comprehensible and clear on the relevant issues?

Accountability: What bodies were you accountable to in working with this case? Were the lines of accountability clear?

Function and role: What was your function and role in this context?

Basis of involvement: Did you have a right or a duty to be involved with the client?

Client group: What characteristics of this person allowed or required you to be involved? NB use legal definitions.

Discrimination: Did you consider any aspects of discrimination arose in this case and were you equipped to deal with them?

Control of case: Once involved, what did you decide you could or ought to do and were you able to follow this through?

Client choice: What choices, if any, did your client have and what influenced that choice?

Appeals/complaints: What recourse did all the parties have to challenge any decisions?

Websites

The website of the Children and Family Court Advisory and Support Service (CAFCASS):

www.cafcass.gov.uk

Further information about the provision of advocacy services for children and young people making a complaint are available from the Department for Education and Skills site:

www.dfes.gov.uk/childrensadvocacy/docs

Summaries of cases and information about how the local government ombudsman investigates complaints are available from:

www.lgo.org.uk

The Parliamentary and Health Service Ombudsman deals with complaints about Government departments and their agents and the National Health Service. The website includes a step-by-step guide to making a complaint:

www.Ombudsman.org.uk

Public Concern at Work, an independent authority, which seeks to ensure concerns about malpractice are properly raised and provides support for whistleblowers. The site includes summaries of whistleblowing cases:

www.pcaw.co.uk

Further information about the Data Protection Act 1998, the Freedom of Information Act 2000 and detail about the Information Commissioner are available from:

www.ico.gov.uk/eventual.aspx

and from the Freedom of Information site (this includes access to Codes of Practice and a list of public authorities):

www.foi.gov.uk

Further reading

The role of the children's guardian is considered in:

Timmis, G. (2001) 'CAFCASS – A service for children or a service for the courts?' 31 *Family Law* p. 281.

Timmis, G. (2002) 'Meeting Children's Rights to Participation in Family Proceedings. The Overriding Aim for CAFCASS' *Representing Children* p. 40.

Dickens, J. (2004) 'Risks and responsibilities – the role of the local authority lawyer in child care cases' 16 *Child and Family Law Quarterly* p. 17. (Presents findings from a study of how local authority social workers and their solicitors work together in child care cases.)

Lindley, B., Richards, M. and Freeman, P. (2001) 'Advice and advocacy for parents in child protection cases – what is happening in current practice' 13 *Child and Family Law*

Quarterly p. 167. (Discussion of the particular need for advocacy of parents whose children are subject of child protection investigations.)

Both of these texts provide more detail on evidence:

McEwan, J. (1992) *Evidence and the Adversarial Process.* Oxford: Blackwell.

Spencer, J.R. and Flin, R. (1990) *The Evidence of Children: The law and psychology.* London: Blackstone Press.

Aspects of challenging social work are addressed in the following articles:

Bailey Harris, R. and Harris, M. (2002) 'Local Authorities and Child Protection – The Mosaic of Accountability' 14 *Child and Family Law Quarterly* p. 117.

Williams, C. (2002) 'The practical operation of the Children Act complaints procedure.' 14 *Child and Family Law Quarterly* p. 25.

Lindsay, M.J. (1991) 'Complaints procedures and their limitations in the light of the Pindown Enquiry' 6 *Journal of Social Welfare and Family Law* p. 432.

Hunt, G. (ed.) (1998) *Whistleblowing in the Social Services.* London: Edward Arnold. (Provides consideration of whislteblowing and examples in the specific context of social services.)

Notes

1 See further discussion of the term 'vulnerable adult' in Chapters 14 and 17.

2 See also *Guidance from the President's Office: McKenzie Friends* [2005] Fam Law 405; L. Reed (2005) 'McKenzie Friends in Family Proceedings' 35 *Family Law* p. 820.

3 The term 'officer of the service' is substituted for 'probation officer' by the Criminal Justice and Courts Service Act 2000, reflecting introduction of CAFCASS.

4 National Probation Service (2005) 'National Standards'.

5 DHSS (1974) 'Report of the Committee of Inquiry into the Care and Supervision Provided in Relation to Maria Colwell'. London: HMSO.

6 See also the Family Proceedings Rules 1991 (SI 1991/1247) Pt IV and the Family Proceedings Courts (Children Act 1989) Rules 1991 (SI 1991/1395).

7 CAFCASS *Guidance on Representation of Children in Private Law Proceedings Pursuant to Rule 9.5 Family Proceedings Rules* (April 2005); s. 122 of the Adoption and Children Act 2002.

8 Aspects of the role of CAFCASS are discussed further in Chapters 7 and 9.

9 Department of Health (2000) *Reporting to Court under the Children Act: A Handbook for Social Services.* London: The Stationery Office.

10 M. Haley and A. Swift (1985) 'P.A.C.E. and the Social Worker: A step in the right direction?' 6 *Journal of Social Welfare Law* pp. 355–73.

11 J. Timms (2001) 'Advocacy Services for Children and Young People' in L.-A. Cull, and J. Roche (eds) *The Law and Social Work: Contemporary Issues for Practice.* Basingstoke: Palgrave.

[12] The Advocacy Services and Representations Procedure (Children) (Amendment) Regulations 2004 (SI 2004/719); Providing Effective Advocacy Services for Children and Young People Making a Complaint under the Children Act 1989: Get it Sorted. (DFES) www.dfes.gov.uk/childrensadvocacy/docs.

[13] See critique in J. Lane and C. Walsh (2002) 'Court Proceedings', in K. Wilson and A. James (eds)(2nd edn) *The Child Protection Handbook*. Edinburgh: Bailliere Tindall.

[14] *Fallon* v. *Lancashire County Council* (1992) Decision 208.

[15] Criminal Justice and Public Order Act 1994.

[16] M. Bell and R. Daly (1992) 'Social workers and solicitors working together?' 22 *Family Law* pp. 257–61.

[17] Provided for by Children Act 1989, s. 26 and National Health Service and Community Care Act 1990, s. 50.

[18] The body established by the Health and Social Care (Community Health and Standards) Act 2003, to replace the National Care Standards Commission.

[19] Draft regulations have been subject to further consultation in ' Learning from Complaints: consultation on changes to social services complaints procedures for adults' (2004).

[20] This is suggested in a DES consultation document, 'Getting the best from complaints: consultation on the changes to the social services complaints procedures for children, young people and other people making a complaint' (2004).

[21] A phrase used to describe actions outside the course of employment, originates from *Joel* v. *Morrison* (1834) 6 C & P 501, p. 503.

[22] Human Rights Act 1998, s. 7.

[23] Lord Borrie, QC (1996) *Four Windows on Whistleblowing*. London: Public Concern at Work.

[24] T. Burgner *et al.* (1998) *Independent Longcare Inquiry*. Buckinghamshire County Council.

[25] Department of Health (2000) *Lost in Care*. London: HMSO.

[26] Leicestershire Social Services (1993) *The Kirkwood Report*.

[27] P. Ells and G. Dehn (2001) 'Whistleblowing: Public Concern at Work' in L.-A. Cull and J. Roche (ed.) *The Law and Social Work: Contemporary Issues for Practice*. Basingstoke: Palgrave.

[28] Employment Rights Act 1996, s. 43B.

[29] Department of Health (2000) *Data Protection Act: Guidance to Social Services*. London: Stationery Office.

[30] See further: P. Birkinshaw (2001) *Freedom of Information: The Law, the Practice and the Ideal*. London: Butterworths.

[31] Further information and a Code of Practice to the Act can be found at www.homeoffice.gov.uk/foi.

[32] See LAC (2002) 2.

[33] Adapted from 'A checklist of legal issues in cases' in 'Teaching, Learning and Assessing Social Work Law. Report of the Law Improvements Project Group' (1991).

5 The Human Rights Act 1998 and social work practice

Learning objectives

To develop an understanding of the following:

- The context in which the Human Rights Act 1998 was introduced.
- How the Articles of the European Convention are incorporated into domestic law.
- The meaning of 'public authority'.
- The terms of the Articles and their case law interpretation.
- The concepts of proportionality and margin of appreciation.
- The impact of the Act on social work practice.
- The influence of European and international law and Conventions.

Introduction

The Human Rights Act 1998 (HRA 1998) is having a real influence on the development of law in the United Kingdom. Areas of social work law and practice have already been subject to challenge via the Act. It continues to provide an additional scrutiny of practice and its influence is apparent in official documents. For example, the working definition of adult abuse in 'No Secrets' reads: 'Abuse is a violation of an individual's human and civil rights by any other person or persons.' It is therefore essential to have a working knowledge of the principles under the Act that are likely to be asserted. Human rights will permeate all areas discussed in this book, so while the opportunity is taken here to introduce a framework of the Act, there will be further reference throughout the text to its implications in specific areas. Inevitably, some of those references will be necessarily speculative, given the relatively recent introduction of the Act and the pace of litigation. The potential long-term impact of the HRA 1998 should not be underestimated. Jack Straw, Home Secretary at the time the Act was introduced, claimed: 'The Human Rights Act 1998 is the most significant statement of human rights since the 1689 Bill of Rights'.[1]

In social work terms, the Act is at least an opportunity to promote best practice. At best it may also promote a real culture of rights, which is empowering for service users. This had been explained as follows:

> A culture of respect for human rights would exist when there was a widely-shared sense of entitlement to these rights, of personal responsibility and of respect for the rights of others, and where this influenced all our institutional policies and practices. This would help create a more human society, a more responsive government and better public services, and could help to deepen and widen democracy by increasing the sense amongst individual men and women that they have a stake in the way in which they are governed.[2]

It presents opportunities to reinterpret, amend and update legislation and lessen the impact of established case law and may provide the catalyst for reform of antiquated and discriminatory laws.

The actual impact of the Act will not be apparent until it has been in force for some time. Many have made their own predictions; however, Lord Justice Sedley has commented: '. . . neither those idealists who hoped to see a new era of respect for individual rights and freedoms, nor those who, like the Scottish judge Lord McCluskey, foresaw "a field day for crackpots, a pain in the neck for judges and legislators, and a goldmine for lawyers" have turned out to be right'.[3] Fear that courts would be swamped by applications does not appear to have materialised. An emerging trend seems to be that human rights points are being added to existing claims, but relatively few new claims based solely on human rights issues have been lodged. One exception to this, where human rights arguments frequently feature, is in the area of immigration and asylum, e.g. *R (Ben Abdelaziz)* v. *Haringey LBC* [2001] 1 WLR 1485. In part the scarcity of cases may be due to comments urging restraint, e.g. Lord Woolf, who insisted it was essential that counsel took a responsible attitude as to when it was appropriate to raise arguments based on the HRA 1998 and judges should be robust in resisting inappropriate attempts to introduce such arguments. In *Re F (Care: Termination of Contact)* [2000] 2 FCR 481, Wall J commented that he would be disappointed if the Convention were to be routinely paraded as a makeweight ground of appeal or if there were to be extensive citation of Strasbourg authorities in every case. It may also reflect the fact that many of the individuals whose rights are violated are themselves vulnerable and not naturally litigious. On a more positive note, Liberty urge bold and imaginative use of the Convention by lawyers and judges.

What does the HRA 1998 do?

The HRA 1998 incorporates the Convention for the Protection of Human Rights and Fundamental Freedoms (usually referred to as the European Convention on Human Rights (**ECHR**)) into UK domestic law. The Convention was ratified in 1951, British lawyers having made a major contribution to its drafting. It contains rights, prohibitions and freedoms arranged in sections referred to as articles.

The focus of the Act is on promoting and upholding rights. The United Kingdom, in contrast to most other democracies, has no written constitution or positive guarantees of rights. This is largely a result of the way the political and constitutional tradition has developed in the United Kingdom. '"Freedom" as it has emerged in this tradition rests largely on the (negative) freedom from government interference rather than positive human rights guarantees, enshrined in a written constitution or human rights instrument.'[4]

The long title describes the Act as one 'to give *further* effect' to the rights and freedoms of the Convention. Since 1966 it has been possible for an individual to directly petition the European Court of Human Rights in Strasbourg, bringing a claim against the United Kingdom for violation of one of the Articles. The European Court of Human Rights was established in 1959 and the first case which found a breach of the Convention by the United Kingdom was decided in 1975.[5] There were, however, a number of disadvantages to the process of petitioning the European Court, including financial cost. In essence, the process was expensive, cases costing as much as £30,000. It was necessary to show that all domestic remedies had been exhausted before reaching the European Court. This added to the expense and also contributed to delays of around five years. These factors often proved prohibitive. The case for full incorporation of the Convention was thus, partly, practical. The emphasis in the Act is on 'bringing rights home' (incidentally the title of the consultation paper which preceded the Bill),[6] making the Convention more accessible, so that remedies which would be available in Strasbourg can be ordered by the domestic courts. It will still be possible for cases against the United Kingdom to reach Strasbourg; however, the requirement that domestic remedies are exhausted first remains. This is to ensure that the domestic courts have the first opportunity to resolve any breach. The application to Strasbourg has to be made within six months of the final decision in domestic proceedings.

Incorporation of the rights into English law

There are three principal sections that effect the incorporation of the rights (summarised in Exhibit 5.1).

Section 2	Section 3	Section 6
Courts must take into account any judgment, decision or opinion of the European Court of Human Rights	So far as possible, legislation must be read and given effect in a way that is compatible with the Convention rights	It is unlawful for a public authority to act in a way that is incompatible with a Convention right

Exhibit 5.1   Incorporation of the Human Rights Act 1998

■ Consideration of case law

Section 2 of the HRA 1998 provides that a court or tribunal which determines a question which has arisen in connection with a Convention right must take into account any judgment, decision or opinion of the European Court of Human Rights. This imposes mandatory consideration of relevant Strasbourg jurisprudence on domestic courts. This requirement will impact on the doctrine of precedent. The House of Lords, as the superior court, will no longer simply be bound by its own decisions but must also consider European decisions as binding and not simply of persuasive authority. A criticism often directed at the system of precedent has been the fact that once a poor decision has been made it may stand for many years. In contrast, the Convention has been described as a 'living instrument which . . . must be interpreted in the light of present day conditions' (*Tyrer* v. *United Kingdom* (1978) 2 EHRR 1, para. 31). The effect of this is that case law should develop with circumstances in an organic way and reflect changes in society. It will not be necessary for existing case law to be specifically overruled where changes in society dictate the need for a different approach. As an example, the Court found in *Marckx* v. *Belgium* (1979) 2 EHRR 330 that the distinction between legitimate and illegitimate children was no longer compatible with the Convention.

■ Compatibility of legislation

Secondly, s. 3 provides that, so far as possible, primary and subordinate legislation must be read and given effect in a way that is compatible with the Convention rights. This is referred to as the technique of 'reading down'.[7] Where a provision has a range of possible meanings, the court must give effect to the meaning that is compatible with the Convention. This principle applies to past and future legislation, and to primary and secondary legislation. It encourages the courts to develop a more purposive approach to statutory construction and is not limited to cases of ambiguity.

If it is not possible to construe legislation to give effect to the Convention, the High Court may issue a 'Declaration of incompatibility'. The courts cannot quash primary legislation which in their view is not compatible; that remains the responsibility of Parliament. Absolute parliamentary sovereignty is thus retained. If a declaration is made, the Government can use a fast track process to introduce amending legislation. If the Government does not take this opportunity – and it will be under immense public and political pressure to do so – the declaration will act as a trigger for the aggrieved individual to take the case to Strasbourg. For example, in *R (H)* v. *London North and East Region Mental Health Review Tribunal* [2001] EWCA Civ 415, the court made a declaration that ss. 72 and 73 of the Mental Health Act 1983 were incompatible with Art. 5. The sections placed the burden of proof on the patient to show continued detention was unlawful, whereas to be compatible the burden should be on the tribunal to show that continued detention was lawful. Within family law, a declaration of incompatibility has been made in relation to the failure of the law to recognise transsexuals' acquired sex for the purposes of marriage: *Bellinger* v. *Bellinger* [2003] UKHL 21. The Gender Recognition Act 2004 gives effect to the required change in the law.

The obligation to interpret legislation compatibly with the Convention applies to old and new legislation. In terms of legislation passed after the Human Rights Act 1998, in theory, the interpretation requirement should present less of a difficulty. This is as a result of the requirements of s. 19. During a Bill's passage through the Parliamentary process the relevant minister is required to make a 'statement of compatibility' to the effect that in his or her view the Bill is compatible with the Convention.

∎ Public authorities

Thirdly, and of great significance for social work, a new responsibility is imposed on public authorities. Public authorities are of central importance under the Act. Under s. 6 it is unlawful for a public authority to act in a way that is incompatible with a Convention right (unless as a result of primary legislation the authority could not have acted differently).

A 'public authority' includes any court or tribunal, and any person certain of whose functions are functions of a public nature (s. 6(3)). This is likely to include local government, social services, the police, health authorities, probation, public utilities, inspection bodies and certain private bodies where they are exercising functions of a public nature, e.g. a professional regulatory body. It is possible for a person or body to have both private and public functions. For example, a general practitioner when undertaking NHS work will be a public authority but not when treating a private patient. The impact of the HRA 1998 will depend considerably on how widely the courts interpret the concept of a public function and whether it is an area where further litigation is likely. So far it appears that the courts have interpreted the term rather more restrictively than Parliament may have intended. The Court of Appeal, in *R (Heather)* v. *Leonard Cheshire Foundation* [2002] EWCA Civ 366, decided that a private charitable organisation managing a care home was not a 'public authority'. This was a disappointing decision given that the home was receiving public funding and was providing care which would otherwise have been provided by the state. Some of the argument focused on the fact that some of the residents had made private arrangements to enter the home; however, that seems a weak justification for withholding the obligation to give effect to the human rights of the residents, many of whom were vulnerable. Of some reassurance, however, in such a case is that the regulatory body is clearly a public authority. A subsequent decision, though not overruling the *Leonard Cheshire* case, adopted a wider interpretation of the term emphasising a functional approach (*Aston Cantlow and Wilmcote with Billesley Parochial Church Council* v. *Wallbank* [2003] UKHL 37. If enacted, the Care of Older and Incapacitated People (Human Rights) Bill (2006) will amend the HRA to extend the definition of public authority to include care homes regulated under the Care Standards Act 2000.

It is of crucial importance that public authorities, including Social Services Departments, examine policies and procedures for compliance with the rights. The Department of Health suggested in a local authority circular:[8] 'As the UK has been signed up to the ECHR since 1951, the expectation is that best practice in the services already respects the Convention.' Such confidence may be misplaced and, while scrutiny of policy may seem an enormous task, it is not acceptable for a public authority, which has a positive duty to comply with the Convention, to simply sit back and await challenge. It is also clear that public authorities will carry liability for their agents if they outsource, for example, delivery of certain services. As a minimum, any contracting-out arrangements should include terms that require contractors to comply with the public authorities' obligations under the Articles.

It is significant that courts themselves are public authorities. Taken with the rules of interpretation it is clear that courts are obliged to decide *all* cases before them – whether they arise in connection with a statutory or common law principle, and whether they involve public authorities or private individuals' compatibly with Convention rights. Wall LJ confirmed in *Re V (A Child) (Care Proceedings: Human Rights Claims)* [2004] EWCA Civ 54: 'Every court hearing proceedings under Part IV of the 1989 Act (that is the family proceedings court (FPC) the county court and the High Court) has a duty under s. 3(1) of the 1998 Act to give effect to the provisions of the 1989 Act in a way which is compatible with convention rights.' (The 1989 Act referred to is the Children Act 1989.)

This duty on the court can lead to indirect application of the Act, in private cases sometimes referred to as the 'horizontal' effect. Actions between an individual and a public authority are referred to in terms of the direct or 'vertical' application of the Act. In a private case between two individuals, e.g. where one individual applies for a non-molestation order against the other, even though there is no suggestion that a public authority has breached an article, in reaching its decision the court (as a public authority) must act compatibly with the Convention. In this example it could be argued that the making of a non-molestation order is a violation of Art. 8, the right to respect for private and family life.

Section 7 makes clear the significance of s. 6. Failure to comply with Convention rights will be a new ground for judicial review of a public authority. A new cause of action against public authorities is created, and Convention rights are available as a defence to actions brought by public authorities against individuals.

Section 7 provides:

s. 7

7. – (1) A person who claims that a public authority has acted (or proposes to act) in a way which is made unlawful by section 6(1) may –
(a) bring proceedings against the authority under this Act in the appropriate court or tribunal, or
(b) rely on the Convention right or rights concerned in any legal proceedings, but only if he is (or would be) a victim of the unlawful act.

(HRA 1998)

It is clear from s.7(1)(b) that a separate action under s.7 is not necessary (and the practice has been strongly discouraged) where there are ongoing proceedings. For example, in care cases where parents might wish to challenge the action of the local authority, relying on the Convention, the human rights arguments should be dealt with by the court hearing the care proceedings. The arguments should be brought to the court's attention as early as possible to avoid delay and it would only be necessary in exceptional cases to transfer the case to the High Court to address the human rights arguments: *Re L (Care Proceedings: Human Rights Claims)* [2003] EWHC 665 (Fam).

It is also important to note that an individual does not have to wait until the public authority has actually acted unlawfully before bringing a claim under s. 7. There is provision for proceedings where the public authority 'proposes to act'. This could apply, for example, to claims in respect of the content of a care plan before it is implemented, or a proposed change to policy or procedures.

In the application of the Act two further principles – proportionality and the margin of appreciation – are of enormous importance.

■ Proportionality

Any interference with a Convention right must be proportionate to the intended outcome. Even if an action which interferes with a Convention right pursues a legitimate aim, the means of achieving the aim must not be excessive. To coin a phrase, 'You must not use a sledgehammer to crack a nut'. Interference with a qualified Convention right may be justified if it is:

- in accordance with law
- for a legitimate purpose
- proportionate.

This principle was clearly applied in *Re O (A Child) (Supervision Order: Future Harm)* (2001) EWCA Civ 16, where the Court of Appeal decided that a supervision order rather than a care order provided a proportionate response. In the case Hale LJ found that a care order would be severe in three respects: power to the local authority to remove the child from her parents; power to the local authority to have parental control and responsibility; and a long period of time for its discharge. Any intervention of the court needed to be proportionate to the aim for protection of family life in the European Convention.

■ Margin of appreciation

The application of Convention rights will frequently involve a balancing exercise of competing claims. In recognition of this and of the various countries signed up to the Convention, the Court of Human Rights allows a 'margin of appreciation' to each country, rather than simply substituting its own view for that of the national authority. It allows for different countries to take different approaches to the rights, reflecting their different cultures and traditions, including religion, where it is acceptable for there to be differences in interpretation, e.g. the question of abortion. The principle was described in *Handyside* v. *United Kingdom* (1976) EHRR 737: 'By reason of their direct and continuous contact with the vital forces in their country, state authorities are in a better position than the international judge to give an opinion on the exact content of requirements.'

The Convention rights (s. 1)

The Articles contain rights, prohibitions and freedoms and fall into three categories. Some are absolute; others are limited or qualified (see Exhibit 5.2).

Absolute rights (Arts. 3, 4, 7) cannot be restricted in any circumstances and violation claims are not balanced against any general public interest.

Limited rights (Arts. 2, 4(2), 5, 6(1)) are those Articles where derogation is possible, in other words the right is established but there are some limitations. The existence of those limitations or specific exceptions, however, is not balanced against the public interest.

HUMAN RIGHTS ACT 1998		
European Convention on Human Rights and Fundamental Freedoms		
ARTICLES		
Absolute	Qualified	Limited
Art. 3: Prohibition against torture, inhuman or degrading treatment or punishment	Art. 8: Right to respect for private and family life, home and correspondence	Art. 2: Right to life
Art. 4(1): Prohibition of slavery or servitude	Art. 9: Freedom of thought, conscience and religion	Art. 4(2): Prohibition of forced or compulsory labour
Art. 7: Prohibition of punishment without law	Art. 10: Freedom of expression	Art. 5: Right to liberty
	Art. 11: Freedom of assembly and association	Art. 6(1): Right to a fair trial
High threshold but any breach is a violation of the Article	Right may be breached if: ▪ in accordance with law ▪ breach pursues a legitimate aim ▪ measures are proportional	Article contains a clear statement of circumstances which permit breach of the right

Exhibit 5.2 Human Rights Act 1998

Qualified rights (Arts. 8, 9, 10, 11) are Articles set in positive form but subject to limitation or restriction clauses, which enable the balance between individual rights and the general public interest to be weighed. A *prima facie* violation of a qualified right will be justified only if the limitation is prescribed by law, it pursues a legitimate aim, it is necessary in a democratic society, fulfils a pressing social need and is proportionate.

■ The Articles

It is appropriate to consider the Articles of most relevance to social work in turn, together with case law illustrations of their application. Clearly, some Articles are already proving to be subject to more litigation than others. It is also important to remember that in some cases a number of Articles may be argued and the decisions shed some light on the interrelationship of the Articles. The Articles are written in quite general terms and apply universally to all. There are no Articles that apply specifically to particular groups, e.g. children. The Articles provide for basic rights, and some areas that might seem significant and where individuals would wish to assert a 'right' are excluded, for example there is no 'right to employment'.

Article 2

ECHR

Everyone's right to life shall be protected by law.

(HRA 1998)

This Article is relevant to the debate about euthanasia, resource allocation, withdrawing treatment, and age-related treatment decisions. It relates to quality of life not simply life or death decisions. While the outcome of such cases may not change the reasons for taking a particular course of action, reasons will need to be clearly justified with reference to the Convention. In some circumstances there may be a positive obligation on a public authority to protect life. For example, in *Association X* v. *United Kingdom* (1978) 14 DR 31, a case which concerned a vaccination programme, the court stated that the Article 'enjoins the state not only to refrain from taking life intentionally but, further, to take appropriate steps to safeguard life'. Steps to protect life were taken by the court in *Venables and Thompson* v. *News Group Newspapers Ltd* [2001] 1 All ER 908, where injunctions were granted against publishing details (apart from their names) of the individuals who killed James Bulger, in response to the risk to their lives if they were found.

The right to life does not include the right to die at a time and manner of your own choosing and therefore a prosecution under the Suicide Act 1961, in respect of an individual who assists another to commit suicide, would not be in breach of the Article according to *Pretty* v. *United Kingdom (2346/02)(2002)* 35 EHRR 1. Unlike the House of Lords, the European Court did concede that Art. 8 was engaged.

Article 3

ECHR

No one shall be subjected to torture or to inhuman or degrading treatment or punishment.

(HRA 1998)

Article 3 is an absolute prohibition. It follows that it will be unlawful for any public authority to treat an individual in a way that violates the Article. Challenges may be brought based on various circumstances, e.g. use of ECT, experimental medical treatment, restraint, seclusion or force-feeding. It is necessary to consider existing case law to evaluate the likelihood of a finding of violation and much will hinge on the meaning of key terms used in the Article.

With regard to torture, the case of *Ireland* v. *United Kingdom* (1978) 2 EHRR 25 considered five 'techniques': wall standing, hooding, subjection to noise, sleep deprivation, food and drink deprivation. This behaviour was found not to constitute torture but did amount to degrading treatment. The term 'degrading' applied to the techniques used as they were such as to cause feelings of fear, anguish and inferiority, and were capable of humiliating and debasing the prisoners. The decision also ruled that the other factor, 'ill treatment', must attain a minimum level of severity to fall within Art. 3. That minimum level is relative and will depend on all the circumstances of the case, including duration of the treatment, its physical and mental effects, the age, sex and state of health of the victim.

In *A* v. *United Kingdom (Human Rights: Punishment of Child)* (1998) 27 EHRR 611, A was beaten by his stepfather with a stick. The stepfather was charged with assault occasioning actual bodily harm but was acquitted, having argued that the assault was permitted as 'reasonable chastisement'. It was found that the lack of clear guidelines as to what amounted to reasonable chastisement and the failure to protect A and provide a deterrent amounted to a breach of Art. 3. Further, in *Z* v. *United Kingdom* (2001) 34 EHRR 97, the European Court found the United Kingdom in breach of Art. 3 where a local authority had failed to act to protect children who had suffered 'horrific ill treatment and neglect' by their parents. The court awarded substantial damages and stressed the positive obligation on local authorities to protect individuals from the actions of others.

A further decision of the European Court which found a local authority in breach of Art. 3 for its failure to protect children is *E* v. *United Kingdom* [2003] 1 FLR 348. The court found that the local authority had failed in its duty to protect E and her brothers and sisters and to monitor the behaviour of a known offender who lived with the children and their mother. Damage caused to the children by the offender could have been minimised or avoided had they acted properly. As a result of the breach the children were entitled to an award in damages.

To send an individual to another country knowing that they will be likely to suffer torture or inhuman or degrading treatment, can amount to a breach of Art. 3. This is highly relevant to decisions about immigration and asylum.

Article 5

ECHR

> 1. Everyone has the right to liberty and security of person. No-one shall be deprived of his liberty save in the following cases and in accordance with a procedure prescribed by law:
>   (a) lawful detention of a person after conviction
>   (b) lawful arrest or detention of a person . . .
>   (c) detention of a minor . . . for the purpose of educational supervision . . .
>   (d) lawful detention of persons for the prevention of the spreading of infectious diseases, of persons of unsound mind, alcoholics or drug addicts or vagrants.
> 4. Everyone who is deprived of his liberty by arrest or detention shall be entitled to take proceedings by which the lawfulness of his detention shall be decided speedily by a court and his release ordered if the detention is not lawful.
>
> (HRA 1998)

This is not an absolute right, as deprivation of liberty is permissible in certain cases (those most relevant to social work are also set out in the box) prescribed by the Article, provided a procedure prescribed by law is followed. It is concerned with *deprivation* of liberty, rather than *restriction* of liberty, the distinction between deprivation of and restriction upon liberty being one of intensity or degree (*Ashingdane* v. *United Kingdom* (1985) 7 EHRR 528). This distinction is reflected in the Mental Capacity Act 2005. Under the Act it may be permissible for a person who is caring for another who lacks capacity, to restrain that person in their best interests, e.g. preventing an individual with dementia from stepping out into the traffic. Deprivation of liberty, however, can never be sanctioned by the Act.

Article 5 is a prohibition on arbitrary detention. Arbitrary detention could apply to restraint practices, lock-door policies, sedation, etc., in residential establishments, to the use of detention under the scheme of the Mental Health Act 1983 and has been argued (unsuccessfully) in relation to the use of secure accommodation under s. 25 of the Children Act 1989: see the case of *Re K* (A Child) *(Secure Accommodation Order: Right to Liberty)* [2001] Fam 377, discussed in Chapter 10. The Article was found to have been breached in the case of *HL* v. *United Kingdom* (2004) EHRR 761, the European Court judgment of the appeal of *R* v. *Bournewood Community and Mental Health Trust, ex parte L* [1998] 3 All ER 289. The case concerned informal detention of mental health patients who are mentally incapable of consenting to detention but are compliant. Under the Mental Health Act 1983 such patients are not entitled to the safeguards provided for formally detained patients such as the right of appeal to the Mental Health Review Tribunal (see further discussion in Chapter 15).

Article 6

ECHR

In the determination of his civil rights and obligations . . ., everyone is entitled to a fair and public hearing within a reasonable time by an independent and impartial tribunal established by law.

(HRA 1998)

This represents an extension to the principle of 'natural justice' or 'fairness', which permeates the legal system. It encompasses the concept of 'equality of arms', which requires a degree of balance between the parties in terms of legal representation and may have an impact in terms of requiring greater access to legal assistance and representation. In *Re O (Children); Re W-R (A Child); Re W (Children)* [2005] EWCA Civ 759, the Court of Appeal noted that Art. 6 ECHR was engaged in any application by a litigant in person for assistance of a McKenzie friend and that there was a presumption in favour of allowing this and ensuring a fair hearing.

A high proportion of cases before the European Court have been based on this Article, and it will often be employed in connection with another Article, e.g. where someone is a victim of restraint practices and has no means of challenge. The continued growth in numbers of administrative tribunals may be partly due to the influence of this Article. The Article would apply to conduct of case conferences and adoption panels.

The requirement of independence and impartiality has been called into question in the context of the adequacy of social services complaints procedures. This point was tested in *R (on the appllication of Beeson)* v. *Dorset CC* [2002] EWCA Civ 1812. This case began as a judicial review of a local authority decision that an individual had deprived himself of his property before entering residential care. It was decided initially that the local authority complaints procedure panel which comprised two councillors and one independent member, was not sufficiently independent and impartial for the purposes of Art. 6. On appeal, the Court of Appeal stated that the real question was whether the addition of judicial review to the process satisfied the standard. It found that if there was no substantive reason to question the integrity of the panel decision, whatever its appearance might suggest, the added safeguard of judicial review would usually satisfy the Art. 6 standard.

This principle is likely to apply across the range of complaints procedure panels, whether in relation to those established under the Children Act 1989 or the National Health Service and Community Care Act 1990. The argument advanced by the Court of Appeal is that, in any case where there is a concern that the panel was not sufficiently independent or impartial, the fact that the decision can be reviewed by judicial review in the High Court is sufficient to provide that element of the Art. 6 requirement. Looked at overall this may be so; however, it pays insufficient regard to the 'bringing rights home' philosophy which underpins the Human Rights Act 1998. It is expensive and time consuming for a claimant to take a case to judicial review and this may prove to be a deterrent for some. The preferable course would have been to ensure absolute and transparent independence and impartiality at the panel stage by extending the requirement for independence to at least two members.

In *T* v. *United Kingdom, V* v. *United Kingdom* (2000) 30 EHRR 121, trial of children for murder in an adult court was found to be a violation of Art. 6 with regard to effective participation. In *B* v. *United Kingdom, P* v. *United Kingdom* (2002) 34 EHRR 19 it was found that to hear a custody case and pronounce judgment in public would frustrate the aim of protecting the privacy of children and the practice of hearing children's cases 'in camera' did not breach Art. 6. This position has been confirmed in *Pelling* v. *Bruce-Williams* [2004] EWCA Civ 845.

Recognition of the detrimental effect of delay on proceedings has lead to a number of initiatives to ensure speediness in resolving disputes. It is important, however, that the pressure to promote cost efficient and speedy disposal of cases does not override the need for proper examination of the facts. In *Kaur* v. *Dhalisal* [2005] EWCA Civ 743, the Court of Appeal found that there had been a breach of the right to a fair trial in a contested contact and residence order case. Limited court time meant that issues were not fully explored and key individuals including the child's paternal grandmother, whom it was proposed would offer daily care, did not give evidence. There was as a result, an 'impression of overall unfairness within Art 6 terms' (Wall LJ)

Article 8

ECHR

(1) Everyone has the right to respect for his private and family life, his home and his correspondence.
(2) There shall be no interference by a public authority with the exercise of this right except such as is in accordance with the law and is necessary in a democratic society in the interests of national security, public safety or the economic well being of the country, for the prevention of disorder or crime, for the protection of health or morals, or for the protection of the rights and freedoms of others.

(HRA 1998)

Broad interpretation is likely regarding this Article, which has frequently been invoked, and may supplement the lack of any real privacy laws in the United Kingdom. There is potential for it to be relied on, e.g. in the context of vulnerable adults, moving from independent living in the community to residential accommodation, sharing rooms, being offered only communal meals, no provision for couples to be together, lack of after-care services, covert surveillance, physical integrity, e.g. tagging, and violations which relate to a person's dignity as an aspect of private life. Case law discussed below relates to provision of community care services.

It may be used as a defence against unwanted interference, including over-zealous investigations, because any interference by the state with a person's private and family life, home or correspondence must be justified by one of the exceptions. It is pertinent to note that the Act applies to all; it may also be argued by an alleged abuser that his or her removal from home may constitute a violation of his or her rights. It will be increasingly important to recognise the existence of rights conflicts within a family, whether as between a child and his parents or between adults.

Family life is interpreted broadly under the Convention, beyond the boundaries of married couples and immediate relatives. In *B* v. *United Kingdom* (1988) 10 EHRR 87, a contested contact case, the court stated that 'the mutual enjoyment by parent and child of each other's company constitutes a fundamental element of family life'. The prison policy of separating babies from their mothers at 18 months of age was challenged under this Article, but found not to be a breach of the mother's right to family life, in *R (P)* v. *Secretary of State for the Home Department* [2001] EWCA Civ 1151. Article 8 includes protection of physical integrity and protection from sexual abuse: *X and Y* v. *Netherlands* (1985) 8 EHRR 235. The right to privacy has applied to enjoyment of homosexual sexual relations (*Dudgeon* v. *United Kingdom* (1981) 4 EHRR 149) and in *Pretty* v. *United Kingdom* (2002) 35 EHRR 1, it was described as,

> . . . a broad term not susceptible to exhaustive definition. It covers the integrity of the person. Elements such as, gender identification, name and sexual orientation and sexual life fall within the personal sphere protected by Article 8. Article 8 also protects a right to personal development and to establish and develop relationships with other human beings and the outside world.

The second part of Art. 8 expressly qualifies the right. In doing so, the Act seeks to balance rights of individuals with other public interests. This is known as *proportionality*, as any limitations must be proportionate to the end achieved. The question to be posed will be whether the interference is prescribed by law, serves a legitimate objective and is necessary in a democratic society. Such questions could be applied to justify the inclusion of an individual's name on the list of people unsuitable to work with vulnerable adults, established under the Care Standards Act 2000, or with children, under the Protection of Children Act 1999. Inclusion could arguably be an interference with the right to privacy; however, it is prescribed by law, is intended to protect the rights and freedoms of others, and has been deemed necessary in UK society. It is significant that inclusion on the list is intended to be for ten years and there is a right to challenge initial inclusion. Indefinite inclusion without these safeguards might be considered not proportionate, as the term is explained in the following quote: 'Inherent in the whole of the Convention is the search for the fair balance between the demands of the general interest of the community and the requirements of the protection of the individual's human rights' (*Soering* v. *United Kingdom* (1989) 11 EHRR 439).

Medical treatment can be an aspect of family life, as illustrated in *Glass* v. *United Kingdom* [2004] 1 FLR 1019. Here, a 12-year-old boy who was severely disabled became seriously ill following surgery. At the hospital his mother opposed the medical view that he should not be resuscitated if his heart stopped and also did not wish him to be given morphine. Despite expression of these views, a DNR (do not resuscitate) note was placed on the boy's notes and he was given diamorphine. His condition deteriorated further and at one point during an argument about treatment a fight took place on the ward between the doctors and the boy's family. The European Court found that Art. 8 had been breached. To impose treatment against the parent's wishes clearly interfered with the boy's right to respect for private and family life. The Court stated that the Trust should have sought court intervention through a declaration as it was not a situation of necessity. This case clearly places the onus on hospital authorities to seek court intervention before administering treatment where there is a dispute.

Finally, a significant case for social services illustrates the broad interpretation of Art. 8. In *R (Bernard)* v. *Enfield London Borough Council.* [2002] EWHC 2282 (Admin) the Court found that human rights were violated by failure to provide adequate community care services. Damages were awarded.

The facts of the case are quite complex and revolve around housing needs of a family comprising husband and wife and six children aged between 3 and 20. The wife, aged 48, suffered right-side paralysis following a stroke, was largely immobile, reliant on an electric wheelchair, doubly incontinent and diabetic. Her husband cared for her and the children.

The family had lived in house adapted by Enfield Borough Council but were forced to sell due to mortgage arrears. They held a tenancy of a second house for 15 months (not adapted). At the end of that tenancy they moved to a third house, provided by Enfield's Housing Department. They then moved to a fourth house, which had no adaptations and was provided as temporary accommodation, the family having been considered intentionally homeless in June 2000.

In September 2000 social services assessed the needs of claimants and their family and concluded that the fourth house was totally unsuitable for the following reasons:

- The wife was unable to use wheelchair in house.
- The only accessible toilet was in a lean-to in the back garden, down stairs so she was unable to get there without her husband's help.
- The bath was also in the lean-to.
- The wife was forced to live in the lounge, where her husband and youngest two children also slept.
- The front door opened directly into the lounge.
- There were steps to the front door so the wife was unable to leave house by herself.

Enfield accepted that it needed to provide residential accommodation to meet the family's needs under s. 21 of the National Assistance Act 1948 and the current house could not be suitably adapted, but no action was taken. The family actually moved into suitably adapted accommodation the day before the hearing of their claim, some two years after the initial assessment.

The judgment makes clear that application of the HRA 1998 means that community care functions must be exercised compatibly with Convention rights. The court noted that the family had lived in deplorable conditions, but the circumstances of the case did not meet the threshold of mistreatment required for Art. 3, i.e. minimum level of severity (though the arguments were 'finely balanced'). It was relevant that mistreatment had arisen by 'corporate neglect' rather than deliberate mistreatment. The claim that Enfield had acted incompatibly with Art. 8 was successful.

The court noted that private life includes a person's physical and psychological integrity (*Botta* v. *Italy* (1998) 26 EHRR 241) and[9] that 'the fundamental element of family life is the right to live together so that family relations can develop naturally and that members of a family can enjoy one another's company'. The obligation is to do more than protect individuals from arbitrary interference with Art. 8 rights – it can require a positive act by state authorities, noting 'those entitled to care under s. 21 are a particularly vulnerable group. Positive measures have to be taken (by way of community care facilities) to enable them to enjoy, so far as possible, a normal private and family life.'

When applying Art. 8 the court will ask the following question: Is there an interference? The answer will be 'Yes': if provision would secure a person's physical and psychological integrity and development of personality in relations with others; if provision would allow family relations to develop naturally and allow family members to enjoy one another's company; if there is a direct link between the services that could be provided and the users private/family life.

Bernard was clearly an extreme case highlighting apparent bad practice. Not every service user who is dissatisfied with the outcome of a community care assessment will be able to mount a human rights claim. Whether there has been a breach of human rights will always depend on the circumstances of the case and not all failures will equal breach. *Bernard* is, however, a significant application of the human rights philosophy and demonstrates the court's willingness to enforce the duty of public authorities to act in compliance with the articles of the European Convention.

The following extract from the judgment in *Bernard* summarises the human rights issues in the case:

Following the assessments in September 2000, Enfield was under an obligation not merely to refrain from unwarranted interference in the claimants' family life, but also to take positive steps, including the provision of suitably adapted accommodation to enable the claimants and their children to lead as normal a life as possible, bearing in mind the second claimant's severe disabilities. Suitably adapted accommodation would not merely have facilitated the normal incidents of family life, for example she would have been able to move around her home to some extent and would have been able to play some part . . . in looking after their children. It would also have secured her 'physical and psychological integrity'. She would no longer have been housebound, confined to a shower chair for most of the day, lacking privacy in the most undignified of circumstances, but would have been able to operate again as part of her family and as a person in her own right, rather than being a burden, wholly dependent upon the rest of her family. In short it would have restored her dignity as a human being.

A further decision, *Anufrijeva* v. *Southwark London Borough Council* [2003] EWCA Civ 1406, is more restrictive and suggests that a public authority in a similar position should only be liable where there is negligent culpability.

A series of questions must be considered in a systematic way in determining whether there has been a breach of Art. 8. For ease of reference these questions are set out below.

Art. 8 ▷

- Does the issue concern an aspect of the right to respect for private and family life, home and correspondence?
- Has there been an interference with the right?
- Has the interference been by a public authority, or a body exercising a public function, or the State?

If the answer to any of the above questions is NO then there is NO BREACH. Where an interference is established proceed with the following questions:

- Is the interference lawful?
- Is the interference necessary in a democratic society?
- Is the interference proportionate?

If the answer to the above is YES there is NO BREACH.

Article 9

ECHR ▷

Everyone has the right to freedom of thought, conscience and religion; this right includes freedom . . . to manifest his religion or belief, in worship, teaching, practice and observance.

(HRA 1998)

The terms of Art. 9 should encourage residential homes to respect different religious ceremonies depending on their residents' beliefs. It may also apply in respect of dress codes. In *R(SB)* v. *Headteacher and Governors of Denbigh High School* [2005] EWCA Civ 199, a muslim schoolgirl asserted her right to wear religious dress (a *jilbab*) in school. As she had missed time off school the Court of Appeal also found an infringement of her right to education under Art. 2, protocol 1 but the decision was later overturned by the House of Lords ([2006] UKHL 15). Reference to religious belief will not justify inappropriate behaviour that might violate other rights, e.g. chastisement of children based on religious belief, the subject of *R (Williamson)* v. *Secretary of State for Education and Employment* [2005] UKHL 15.

It was argued in *Williamson* that s. 548 of the Education Act 1996, which bans corporal punishment in all schools, interfered with the claimants' freedom to manifest their religion in accordance with Art. 9 of the European Convention on Human Rights. The claimants were a group of teachers and parents of pupils at independent schools. They sought a declaration by judicial review that s. 548 did not prevent a parent delegating to a teacher the right to administer corporal punishment. The schools provided a Christian education based on biblical observance. Various sections from the Bible were cited to support the use of corporal punishment. For example: 'Do not withhold correction from a child for if you beat him with a rod, he will not die. You shall beat him with a rod and deliver his soul from hell.' The claim was dismissed. The court held that under Art. 9 there was a difference between freedom to hold a belief and freedom to manifest a belief. Freedom to manifest a belief was qualified. Section 548 interfered with the parents' rights but it was justified as the legislature had taken the view that corporal punishment at school was unnecessary and undesirable and other non-violent methods of punishment were available.

Article 10

ECHR

Everyone has the right to freedom of expression. This right shall include freedom to hold opinions and to receive and impart information and ideas without interference by public authority . . .

(HRA 1998)

Most cases under Art. 10 have related to the freedom of the press to publish information in matters of local, national and international interest. Article 10 issues often conflict with a corresponding individual right to privacy, e.g. *Douglas* v. *Hello! Ltd* [2001] 2 All ER 289, which concerned publication of a celebrity couple's wedding photographs. In employment law, this Article should override any gagging clauses designed to prevent whistleblowing and supports the provisions of the Public Interest (Disclosure) Act 1998. This right also extends to the right to receive information (*Open Door Counselling and Dublin Well Woman* v. *Ireland* (1992) 15 EHRR 244), and may have implications for local authorities' publications relating to available services.

It is important that information the local authority may publish, about its services and also about human rights, is in an accessible format, for example, to reflect languages spoken in the locality. Information should also be accessible to people with disabilities. The British Institute of Learning Disabilities (BILD) has produced a useful guide to the HRA which considers implications for people with learning disabilities illustrated by shared experiences.[10] An accompanying poster translates the rights into more accessible language, for example:

- I should be able to say what I like as long as I respect other people, and expect people to listen to me (Art. 10).
- I should have my rights respected (Art. 6).

- I should be safe at home and have time to myself (Art. 8).
- I can speak out and complain if something is wrong (Art. 10).
- I can get married and have children (Art. 12).
- It is wrong for anyone to shout at me, call me names, hit or hurt me (Art. 3).
- It is wrong for anyone to lock me in or stop me going out (Art. 5).

Article 12

ECHR

> Men and women of marriageable age have the right to marry and to found a family, according to the national laws governing the exercise of this right.
>
> (HRA 1998)

It is apparent from the wording of Art. 12 that it is limited to heterosexual relationships and there have been cases where transsexuals have been denied the right to marry (*Rees* v. *United Kingdom* (1986) 9 EHRR 56; *Cossey* v. *United Kingdom* (1991) 13 EHRR 622). In *Goodwin* v. *United Kingdom* [2002] 2 FLR 487, the ECHR found that the United Kingdom's refusal to allow people who had undergone gender reassignment the ability to alter their gender on their birth certificate was in breach of Convention rights. Legislation to remedy this position has been introduced in the form of the Gender Recognition Act 2004. It is possible that decisions to sterilise young women with learning disabilities may be subject to closer scrutiny in future, given the application of the right to found a family under Art. 12 (*Re F* [1990] 2 AC 1). Article 12 is also relevant to adoption as a means of founding a family. However, it is unlikely to support an argument that an individual has a right to fertility treatment.

Article 14

ECHR

> The enjoyment of the rights and freedoms set forth in this Convention shall be secured without discrimination on any ground such as sex, race, colour, language, religion, political or other opinion, national or social origin, association with a national minority, property, birth or other status.
>
> (HRA 1998)

Article 14 prohibits discrimination (based on a wide range of grounds) in individuals' enjoyment of the rights contained in Articles of the European Convention on Human Rights. It is not a freestanding Article but is directly linked to the other Articles.

Sexuality is not specifically listed in Art. 14 as a ground of discrimination but case law has shown that discrimination on the grounds of a person's sexuality does fall within the Article. This position was confirmed in the case of *Ghaidan* v. *Mendoza* [2004] UKHL 30. The issue in this case was whether Mr Mendoza was entitled to succeed to a tenancy under the Rent Act 1977, i.e. was he entitled to carry on the tenancy of the property in which he lived with his same-sex partner, when his partner died, the tenancy having been in his partner's name. The relevant paragraph in the regulations refers to a surviving spouse or 'a person who was living with the tenant as his or her wife or husband'. Applying the duty to read legislation compatibly with the Convention, the court interpreted 'as his or her wife or husband' to mean, 'as if they were his or her wife or husband', thus including homosexual couples. The court commented that issues of discrimination have 'high constitutional importance'.

First Protocol

The First Protocol contains Articles that were added to the Convention following ratification:

Article 1: Protection of property may be relevant to cases of financial and material abuse suffered by vulnerable adults and to the operation of systems whereby management of property and finances are delegated to another person or body.

Article 2: Right to education could be relevant in general terms to people with a learning disability and to provision for special educational needs, and specifically to the provision of sex education.

▪ Using the HRA 1998

To bring a claim under the HRA 1998, the individual must be a 'victim'. This means that they are directly affected by the measure or at least at risk of being affected, or a person closely or personally related to one affected. It is not possible to complain in abstract about behaviour. This formulation is more restrictive than the existing criterion for judicial review applications of having a 'sufficient interest' in an issue. It will be possible for interest groups, e.g. MIND and BAAF, to bring an action only if their members are themselves victims. It is possible for a company or group of individuals to make a claim as a victim. In fact, case law suggests that the term 'victim' is not unduly restrictive. For example, in *Campbell and Cosans* v. *United Kingdom* (1982) 4 EHRR 293, a case which challenged the use of corporal punishment in schools, the applicants were classed as victims because their children went to state schools where corporal punishment was permitted; the applicants' children had not actually been punished.

▪ Remedies

If a court finds that there has been a violation of one of the Articles, there are a range of possible remedies available to the person whose rights have been breached. These remedies are: injunctions, declarations, declaration of incompatibility, and an award of 'just satisfaction' in financial compensation. Damages awarded under the HRA 1998 will be assessed in a slightly different manner from the normal calculation of damages in civil cases but may nevertheless be substantial. In *Smith and Grady* v. *United Kingdom* (1999) 29 EHRR 493, the discharge of the applicants from the armed forces following an investigation into their sexual orientation was found to be a violation of their right to respect for private life (Art. 8). In the circumstances they were awarded £19,000 each. The total cost to the Government, including costs and expenses, far exceeded the amount paid in damages. This serves as a further useful reminder of the value of local authorities' reviewing procedures in search of any areas of non-compliance. Litigation is expensive and if a local authority is found to be in breach it may be faced with a substantial bill.

Weakness of the HRA 1998

There is no body equivalent to the Equal Opportunities Commission or the Commission for Racial Equality to assist people who wish to bring a case under the provisions of the HRA 1998. Such a body does exist in Northern Ireland, where a Human Rights Commission has been created. The Parliamentary Joint Committee on Human Rights has reported a compelling case for establishing a human rights commission in England and Wales. It suggests that respect for human rights is not at the heart of public authorities' policies and practices, and that bodies such as local councils and hospitals act defensively, in aiming to avoid litigation but no more.[11]

More recently, the Government has proposed a Commission for Equality and Human Rights, which would draw together the functions of existing equality commissions, e.g. the Commission for Racial Equality, but with an extended remit to include human rights issues. One of the duties of the Commission will be to promote human rights and to raise public bodies' awareness of their obligations under the HRA 1998. The role of the Commission is considered in more detail in Chapter 6.

Influence of European and international law and Conventions

The discussion above explains how the European Convention on Human Rights has been fully incorporated into our domestic law. There are other European and international Conventions which it is useful to be aware of, even though they do not carry the same force of law and are best described as morally persuasive statements of intent.

Universal Declaration of Human Rights

The Universal Declaration of Human Rights 1948 contains a number of Articles which are similarly worded to the ECHR, e.g. Art. 33: 'Everyone has the right to life, liberty and the security of person.' It is, however, a broader statement of rights, starting with Art. 1, which states that 'All human beings are born free and equal in dignity and rights.'

Other significant Articles include:

Article 6: Everyone has the right to recognition everywhere as a person before the law.

Article 14: Everyone has the right to seek and to enjoy in other countries asylum from persecution.

Article 16: Men and women of full age, without any limitation due to race, nationality or religion, have the right to marry and to found a family. Marriage shall be entered into only with the free and full consent of the intending spouses. The family is the natural and fundamental group unit of society and is entitled to protection by society and the state.

Article 21: Everyone has the right to take part in the government of his country, directly or through the freely chosen representatives. Everyone has the right of equal access to public service in his country.

■ United Nations Convention on the Rights of the Child

The United Nations Convention on the Rights of the Child 1989 provides a useful guide for good practice for promoting children's rights. Whilst the rights are not enforceable in a court of law in the same way as the right within the HRA 1998, the rights are nevertheless persuasive and have been referred to in domestic judgments. The United Kingdom has experienced a high level of criticism by the UNCRC Committee on the Rights of the Child, which conducts reviews of states' compliance with the Convention. Recently, this criticism may arguably have been partly responsible for the introduction of the Children's Commissioner in England.

The articles include a range of rights which position the child's best interest as priority, provide for children to participate in decisions affecting them, and ensure the protection from harm and provision of basic needs. The following Articles are particularly significant, starting with a commitment to anti-discrimination.

Article 1

States parties shall respect and ensure the rights set forth in the present Convention to each child within their jurisdiction without discrimination of any kind, irrespective of the child's or his or her parent's or legal guardian's race, colour, sex, language, religion, political or other opinion, national, ethnic or social origin, property, disability, birth or other status.

Article 3

1. In all actions concerning children, whether undertaken by public or private social welfare institutions, courts of law, administrative authorities or legislative bodies, the best interests of the child shall be the primary consideration.

2. States parties undertake to ensure the child such protection and care as is necessary for his or her well-being, taking into account the rights and duties of his or her parents, legal guardians, or other individuals legally responsible for him or her, and shall take all appropriate legislative and administrative measures.

3. States parties shall ensure that the institutions, services and facilities responsible for the care or protection of children shall conform with the standards established by competent authorities, particularly in the areas of safety, health, in the number and suitability of their staff, as well as competent supervision.

Article 9

States parties shall ensure that a child shall not be separated from his or her parents against their will, except when competent authorities subject to judicial review determine, in accordance with applicable law and procedures, that such separation is necessary for the best interests of the child. Such determination may be necessary in a particular case, such as one involving abuse or neglect of the child by the parents, or one where the parents are living separately and a decision must be made as to the child's place of residence.

Article 12

States parties shall assure to the child who is capable of forming his or her own views the right to express those views freely in all matters affecting the child, the views of the child being given due weight in accordance with the age and maturity of the child.

It is clear that the rights outlined in the above Conventions extend further than the rights that have been incorporated into domestic law via the Human Rights Act 1998. For example, the HRA 1998 does not include reference to the right of access to public services, nor does it specifically recognise the special status of a child.

Chapter summary

- The Human Rights Act 1998 will have a significant influence on the future development of vast areas of English law, but particularly on the role and responsibilities of public authorities, which includes Social Services Departments.
- The Human Rights Act 1998 incorporates the European Convention on Human Rights into domestic law, making its rights, freedoms and prohibitions more directly enforceable in the domestic courts.
- The Articles of the ECHR are incorporated in three main ways. First, courts are bound to take into account judgments of the European Court when determining

any question in connection with a Convention right; second, legislation must be read and given effect in a way that is compatible with the Convention rights; third, it is unlawful for a public authority to act in a way that is incompatible with the Convention rights.

■ Public authorities including central and local government, police, courts, social services, CAFCASS, regulatory bodies and others exercising functions of a public nature may be faced with compensation claims if they violate or propose to violate individual rights.

■ The ECHR Articles contain rights prohibitions and freedoms which may be absolute, limited or qualified. Some interference with the rights may be permissible but must be proportionate.

■ Rights which are particularly relevant to social work practice are: the prohibition against torture or inhuman or degrading treatment or punishment (Art. 3); the right to liberty and security of the person (Art. 5), the right to a fair and public hearing (Art. 6); the right to respect for private and family life (Art. 8).

■ To make a claim under the HRA 1998, a person must be a 'victim', i.e. directly affected by the measure, or at risk of being affected, or closely related to such a person.

■ A new Commission for Equality and Human Rights is to be established. One of its objectives will be to promote human rights.

■ Other international and European Conventions exist which, although not carrying full force of law in this country, are nevertheless morally persuasive.

Exercise

In the following scenarios, consider which and whose human rights have been breached and how any competing rights might be balanced:

1. Julie and Adam, parents of Josie, aged 2, are regular drug users. Their neighbour, Mrs Thomas, sees Josie crying at the window one evening and assumes Julie and Adam are out when they do not answer the door to her. In fact they are in the back garden. She reports this to the police and social services. Julie and Adam are known to social services and have a history of being uncooperative. Their elder child, Jack, was born addicted to heroin and taken into care at birth. A case conference is held the next day and the health visitor expresses concern over Josie's development. Julie and Adam are not invited to attend. The local authority apply for an *ex parte* emergency protection order and Josie is removed to foster carers who live 40 miles away. Julie and Adam have no means of transport.

2. Mrs Jones has multiple sclerosis and is aged 72. She is a resident in Ferndale Nursing Home. She has lived there for four years. Her husband lives alone in the matrimonial

home and is becoming increasingly frail. Mr and Mrs Jones would like to share a room in the home and have been on a waiting list for a double room for 15 months. Mrs Jones' daughter is concerned that at times when she has visited the home, Mrs Jones' door has been locked from the outside. The staff say it is because she has a tendency to wander and might fall. Mrs Jones says she is happy at the home, although she does not like getting up at 7 a.m. for breakfast in the dining room and, as a Jehovah's Witness, she does not like having to join the other residents to watch 'Songs of Praise' on Sundays. The home owner has announced that his profits are down and he intends to close the home at the end of the month. Mrs Jones had assumed she would end her days at the home and does not want to move.

3. Linda and Tony both have learning disabilities and live in a small community home with two other adults and a care worker. They enjoy each other's company and have recently become engaged. Linda is upset because her mother has told her she will not be able to get married because of her learning disability. When she asked John, the care worker, about this he agreed, saying that marriage is not really for people like Linda and Tony. Linda's mother is concerned that Linda and Tony might be having sexual relations and has been to see a consultant about a sterilisation for Linda. Neither Linda nor Tony have ever had any sex education. Before she moved into her current home Linda lived in a residential home for young people with learning disabilities. While there she was raped by another resident. Linda told Amy, her favourite care assistant, about this, around a week after it happened and they went to the police. At the station the policeman who interviewed Linda said it would not be possible to prosecute the other resident because Linda would not be able to give evidence. He said it was better to keep things like this informal. He went to the home and had a word with the resident. The home owner was furious at having the police visit the home and sacked Amy.

Websites

Information on the Human Rights Act 1998 is available from Liberty. The site gives an overview of the HRA and also considers the rights of particular groups, e.g. immigrants, travellers, children and young persons and prisoners:
www.yourrights.org.uk

Decisions of the European Court of Human Rights are available from:
www.echr.coe.int/echr

The Human Rights Unit at the Department for Constitutional Affairs includes a useful 'What's New' section:
www.humanrights.gov.uk

Further reading

There is a wealth of information available on the Human Rights Act 1998, some of it geared specifically to particular areas of interest, such as social work. General texts include:

Wadham, J. and Mountfield, H. (2006) *Blackstone's Guide to the Human Rights Act 1998* (4th edn). London: Blackstone Press. (A comprehensive guide to the law, including a copy of the Act.)

Hoffman, D. and Rowe, J. (2006) *Human Rights in the UK: An introduction to the Human Rights Act 1998* (2nd edn). Harlow: Pearson. (Very accessible and easy to understand, also including a copy of the Act.)

Articles with a particular focus on the impact on social work include:

Williams, J. (2001) '1998 Human Rights Act: Social Work's New Benchmark' 31 *British Journal of Social Work* p. 831. (This article outlines the effect of the Act illustrated by reference to examples from social work practice.)

McDonald, A. (2001) 'The Human Rights Act and social work practice' 13(3) *Practice* p. 5. (Discussion of the implications of the Act for social work practice and the relationship between human rights and anti-oppressive practice.)

Specific areas of social work practice are covered by:

Clements, L. and Read, J. (2003) *Disabled People and European Human Rights: A Review of the Implications of the 1998 Human Rights Act for Disabled Children and Adults in the UK*. Bristol: Policy Press.

Harris-Short, S. (2005) 'Family Law and the Human Rights Act 1998: judicial restraint or revolution?' 17(3) *Child and Family Law Quarterly* p. 329.

Johns, R. (2004) 'Of Unsound Mind? Mental Health Social Work and the European Convention on Human Rights' 16(4) *Practice* p. 247.

British Institute of Human Rights (2003) *Something for everyone; The Impact of the Human Rights Act and the Need for a Human Rights Commission*. London: British Institute of Human Rights, Kings College. Available from www.bihr.org. (Argues that the Act has failed to make a real impact on the lives of disadvantaged groups such as children, refugees, older people and people with disabilities, and makes the case for an independent body to promote and protect human rights.)

Clements, L., Clements, L.J. and Thomas, P. (eds.) (2006) *Human Rights Act: A Success Story.* Oxford: Blackwell. (A collection of critical essays.)

Watson, J. and Woolf, M. (2003) *Human Rights Act Toolkit*. London: Legal Action Group Books. (A useful practical guide to the Act designed for non-lawyers working in relevant organisations such as health and social services. Includes checklists which can be applied in order to test and demonstrate compliance with the Act.)

Notes

1   J. Wadham and H. Mountfield (2006) *Blackstone's Guide to the Human Rights Act 1998* (4th edn). London: Blackstone Press.

2   D. Lammy MP, Parliamentary Under Secretary at the Department of Constitutional Affairs. Third Anniversary of Human Rights Act Audit Commission Conference speech, 2003, www.dca.gov.uk/speeches/2003/dl061103.htm.

3   Sedley LJ (2003) 'The rocks or the open sea: where is the Human Rights Act heading?'. LAG Annual Lecture.

4   Ibid.

5   *Golder* v. *UK* (1975) 1 EHRR 524.

6   Home Office (1987) 'Bringing Rights Home'.

7   R. Edwards (2000) 'Reading down legislation under the Human Rights Act' 20(3) *Legal Studies* pp. 353–71.

8   LAC (2000) 17.

9   Citing from R. Clayton and H. Tomlinson *Law and Human Rights*. Oxford: Oxford University Press.

10 A. Hughes and P. Coombs (2001) *Easy guide to the Human Rights Act 1998: implications for people with learning disabilities*. Kidderminster: BILD Publications.

11 See 'The case for a Human Rights Commission' published by the Joint Committee on Human Rights on 19 March 2003, available at www.publications.parliament.uk.

6 Discrimination

Learning objectives

To develop an understanding of the following:

- A range of references in legislation and guidance which support anti-discriminatory practice.
- The legal basis of the requirement for anti-discriminatory practice in social work.
- The implications of the Human Rights Act 1998 for discrimination.
- An outline of existing legislation, which outlaws discrimination on grounds of race, sex, disability, religion and age.
- The meaning of discrimination.
- Ways in which the right not to be discriminated against may be enforced, including the role of the new Equality Commission.
- Law reform.

Introduction

If we are committed to anti-oppressive practice then we have a duty to ensure that the rights of users are not violated. Legislation can be used to deny rights but we need to be aware of our role in minimizing the oppressive aspects of practice and the law and we must endeavour to maximize the rights to which all people are entitled. It is for this reason that we see the law as an instrument to protect people's rights. It is a powerful instrument but it one that we can control and we should not therefore become subservient to it.

(Dalrymple and Burke, 1995)[1]

Discrimination issues are identified throughout this book, with an emphasis on promoting anti-discriminatory and anti-oppressive practice. The objectives of this chapter are twofold: first, to draw together the various references to discrimination in legislation and guidance, beyond specific anti-discrimination legislation, some of which direct social services to act in a non-discriminatory fashion. Challenging discrimination is not confined to the use of specific anti-discrimination legislation and it is necessary to take a broad perspective and consider all options. The second objective is to outline the legislation that outlaws discrimination on the grounds of race, sex, disability, religion and age. This legislation is considered from two perspectives: its impact on social work practice; and as an aspect of the law which a service user may be affected by in, for example, the field of employment. An aspect of good social work practice is ensuring that service users are aware of their rights not to be discriminated against. There may also be circumstances where social workers experience discrimination directly, whether it is in the form of racial or sexual harassment from service users or colleagues, or discrimination in relation to training, working conditions and career opportunities. As a minimum, support from managers and colleagues should be forthcoming where discrimination is experienced. In some circumstances, just as for any employee, it may be necessary to have recourse to an employment tribunal.

Reliance on law to combat discrimination has a number of limitations. This is an area where good practice has developed far beyond the minimum legal requirements. Anti-discriminatory practice extends to recognition of other forms of discrimination which are not addressed by existing anti-discrimination legislation. The aim of the anti-discrimination legislation of the 1970s was to alter entrenched attitudes and to promote change. It is clear that, despite that anti-discrimination legislation, much systematic discrimination exists. The role of law as an instrument of social change must be questioned; however, it is important that the legislation does provide a framework for certain discriminatory practices to be challenged.

It has also been noted that the law itself can operate in a way that is discriminatory. Such discrimination may be explicitly defined by statute: for example, until recently part-time staff enjoyed lesser employment protection rights than full-time staff. Discrimination may also manifest itself as a facet of the composition of the legal workforce. Despite growing numbers of women and people from ethnic minorities, the profession is still dominated by white, middle-class males, and this is nowhere more evident than in the courts, where, amongst the senior judiciary (High Court, Court of Appeal and House of Lords), there is just one ethnic minority judge. It has also been noted that some legal terms are themselves discriminatory and direct use of the terms should be avoided unless necessary for accuracy: e.g. reference to 'blind, deaf or dumb' in s. 29 of the National Assistance Act 1948.

A useful starting point for a social worker employed in the statutory sector is to become familiar with the local authority equal opportunities policy for guidance on good practice. In addition, the British Association of Social Workers (BASW) Code of

Ethics, which contains principles that prescribe professional responsibility of the social worker, includes the following statement: 'Basic to the profession of social work is the recognition of the value and dignity of every human being, irrespective of origin, race, status, sex, sexual orientation, age, disability, belief or contribution to society. The profession accepts a responsibility to encourage and facilitate the self-realisation of each individual person with due regard to the interest of others' (para. 6, 1996). Recognising diversity is central to the social work role and the GSCC Code of Practice requires social care employers to put into place and implement written policies and procedures to deal with dangerous, discriminatory or exploitative behaviour and practice. The Code also requires social care workers to protect the rights and promote the interests of service users and carers by, promoting equal opportunities, and respecting diversity and different cultures and values.[2]

An obvious limitation of the anti-discrimination laws in this country is their scope of application. The existing law, which has developed in a piecemeal fashion, is contained in the following legislation and addresses discrimination on the grounds of race, sex, disability, and most recently, religion and age:

- Sex Discrimination Act 1975
- Equal Pay Act 1970
- Race Relations Act 1976
- Disability Discrimination Act 1995
- Disability Rights Commission Act 1999
- Race Relations (Amendment) Act 2000
- Special Educational Needs and Disability Act 2001
- Employment Equality (Religion or Belief) Regulations 2003
- Employment Equality (Sexual Orientation) Regulations 2003
- Disability Discrimination Act 2005
- Employment Equality (Age) Regulations 2006

Within the areas of race, sex and disability there are further limitations, which are explored under each piece of legislation, such as the limited recognition of discrimination relating to sexual preference. It has been argued that consolidation of all UK anti-discrimination statutes into a single coherent piece of legislation would be beneficial, in part because of the changing face of disadvantage and discrimination, social and employment practices.[3] The law in England and Wales does not contain a general prohibition of discrimination in broad terms. This contrasts with other countries which have a modern constitution often expressed in a Bill of Rights. For example, the Canadian Charter of Rights and Freedoms 1982 provides: 'every individual is equal before and under the law and has the right to equal protection and equal benefit of the law without discrimination based on race, national or ethnic origins, colour, religion, sex, age or mental and physical disability'. The pro-active stance of this particular charter is further evidenced by its explicit legitimisation of affirmative action programmes.

However, it is also relevant that the United Kingdom is a signatory to various international and European treaties which include commitment to anti-discrimination. Article 1 of the Universal Declaration of Human Rights 1948 (UDHR) provides:

Art. 1

All human beings are born free and equal in dignity and rights.

(UDHR)

Article 2 expands on this principle:

Art. 2

Everyone is entitled to all the rights and freedoms set forth in this Declaration, without distinction of any kind, such as race, colour, sex, language, religion, political or other opinion, national or social origin, property, birth or other status.

(UDHR)

The United Kingdom is also a signatory to the Convention on the Elimination of All Forms of Discrimination against Women 1981 and to the UN Declaration on the Elimination of All Forms of Racial Discrimination 1963. As signatory to these declarations, the United Kingdom agrees to abide by their terms; however, as aspects of international law, the rights contained within them are not directly enforceable in the United Kingdom.

The introduction of the Human Rights Act 1998 has meant that the anti-discrimination article of the European Convention on Human Rights is directly enforceable in domestic courts. Article 14 provides:

Art. 14

The enjoyment of the rights and freedoms set forth in this Convention shall be secured without discrimination on any ground such as sex, race, colour, language, religion, political or other opinion, national or social origin, association with a national minority, property, birth or other status.

(ECHR 1998)

The forms of discrimination envisaged by this Article are significantly broader than those covered by existing discrimination legislation. The term 'other status' would suggest that the Article would apply to forms of discrimination which have not, as yet, been widely recognised. However, the application of this Article is qualified; it is not a freestanding article, but is limited to discrimination in relation to the 'enjoyment of the rights and freedoms set forth in this Convention'. Chapter 5 set out the

153

Articles of the Convention. As an example, it could be argued in relation to Art. 12, the right to marry and found a family, that a restriction on availability of fertility treatment to women above a certain age, or of a particular religion, is discriminatory. The Article could not be relied on for matters not covered by the ECHR, such as the right to employment or to welfare benefits.

In other cases, where Art. 14 is argued alongside another Convention right, if the court finds a violation of the other Convention right, it may consider it is unnecessary to make a finding under Art. 14. For example, in *Smith and Grady* v. *United Kingdom* (1999) 29 EHRR 493, the applicants had been discharged from the armed services following an inquiry into their sexual orientation. It was found unanimously by the European Court of Human Rights that their right to respect for private and family life under ECHR, Art. 8 had been violated. In addition to Art. 8, the applicants also complained under Arts. 3, 10 and 14, the latter relating to discriminatory treatment by the Ministry of Defence policy against homosexuals in the armed forces. The court decided that the Art. 14 complaint did not give rise to any issue separate to those already considered and did not therefore make a specific finding under Art. 14.

As yet, the British government has not signed Protocol 12 of the European Convention on Human Rights (November 2000), which provides: 'the enjoyment of any right set forth by law shall be secured without discrimination on any ground such as sex, race, colour, language, religion, political or other opinion, national or social origin, association with a national minority, property, birth or status.' As this Protocol applies to any rights set forth by law and is not limited to enjoyment of Convention rights, it would significantly enhance the existing discrimination legislation.

Evidence of discrimination

It is beyond the scope of this text to present detailed evidence of the many and various forms of discrimination that exist within society. A brief summary, however, serves as a reminder that, for many of the service users social workers will encounter, discrimination is an aspect of their everyday experience.

- Black children are over-represented in the care system.[4]
- Children with dual black and white parentage are over-represented among looked after children.[5]
- There is also an over-representation of black children in referrals for physical abuse.[6]
- Black children are more likely to be permanently excluded from school than white children.[7]
- The stereotypical view of the African Caribbean grandmother as ever resourceful and able to cope was in part considered to be a cause of the failure to provide adequate support by social services in the Tyra Henry Inquiry.[8]

- A disproportionate number of care orders are made in respect of children whose parents have a learning disability.[9]

- There was a fourfold increase in the number of racist incidents reported to and recorded by the police between 1995 and 1999.[10]

- A black male is more likely to be detained under the criminal provisions of the Mental Health Act 1983, to be in a secure ward and to receive higher doses of medication.[11]

- Disabled people are over six times as likely as non-disabled people to be out of work and claiming benefits.[12]

It is also important to recognise that perceptions of discrimination vary. A Home Office Citizenship Survey in 2003 found that respondents from ethnic minorities were more likely than white respondents to think organisations would treat them badly. For example, black respondents felt that police, immigration, prison, courts, CPS and armed forces were more likely to treat black respondents worse than people of other races.

■ Institutional racism

Racism and other forms of discrimination may be manifest at an individual level based on prejudice. It is also becoming recognised that racism may operate at an institutional level. Some of the evidence cited above would suggest that institutional racism is present in social care agencies including social work.[13] The Macpherson report defined institutional racism as '[t]he collective failure of an organisation to provide an appropriate and professional service to people because of their colour, culture or ethnic origin. It can be seen or detected in processes, attitudes and behaviour which amount to discrimination through unwitting prejudice, ignorance, thoughtlessness and racist stereotyping which disadvantages minority people.'[14] The report stated further that 'it is incumbent on every institution to examine their policies and practices to guard against disadvantaging any section of our communities'. A clear outcome of this report is the extension of the Race Relations Act 1976 in respect of duties of public authorities, discussed below.

Discrimination – general

In combating discrimination, and acting in a non-discriminatory fashion, it is important to look beyond the major pieces of anti-discrimination legislation. A selection of references in legislation other than specific anti-discrimination legislation, and guidance and codes of practice, which are intended to prevent discrimination and promote anti-discriminatory practice, are set out below.

■ Legislation

- The Children Act 1989, s. 22(5) requires due consideration to be given to a child's racial origin, religious persuasion and cultural and linguistic background when making any decision about a looked after child (including placement decisions).

- The Children Act 1989, Sch. 2, Part 1, para. 6 states that local authorities are required to 'provide services designed . . . to minimise the effect on disabled children . . . of their disabilities, and to give such children the opportunity to lead lives as normal as possible'.

- The Criminal Justice Act 1991, s. 95 requires those involved in the administration of criminal justice to avoid discrimination. The Home Secretary must publish information to assist with this duty on an annual basis. Ethnic monitoring in police forces has been introduced as a result of this provision.

- The Crime and Disorder Act 1998, ss. 29–32 contains specific offences of racist violence and harassment.[15] There is a mandatory requirement to enhance the sentence if an offence was racially aggravated.

- The Public Order Act 1986 contains a number of offences of racial hatred, including broadcasts, written materials, use of words and behaviour with the intent to stir up racial hatred, or, having regard to all the circumstances, with the likelihood of racial hatred being stirred up (ss. 18–22). Consent of the Attorney-General is a prerequisite for the prosecution of these offences and cases have been rare.

- The Employment Rights Act 1996 makes a dismissal automatically unfair if it is for a reason related to pregnancy, childbirth, maternity leave, parental leave or time off for dependants.

- The Protection from Harassment Act 1997 introduced a criminal offence of harassment. Racial or sexual harassment could constitute a course of conduct required under the Act.

- The Adoption and Children Act 2002 provides at s. 1(5): 'In placing the child for adoption, the adoption agency must give due consideration to the child's religious persuasion, racial origins and cultural and linguistic background.' A late amendment to the Act allows adoption by 'couples' removing the previous limitation that adoption was only available to couples who were married.

- The Mental Capacity Act 2005 guards against stereotyping in the principles set out at the start of the Act. Section 2(3) provides that lack of capacity cannot be established merely by reference to age or appearance or a condition or aspect of an individual's behaviour which might lead others to make unjustified assumptions about his capacity.

■ Guidance

- ■ The Mental Health Act 1983 Code of Practice[16] contains a number of guiding principles which underpin the code, including: people to whom the Act applies should be given respect for their qualities, abilities and diverse backgrounds as individuals and be assured that account will be taken of their age, gender, sexual orientation, social, ethnic, cultural and religious background, but that general assumptions will not be made on the basis of any one of these characteristics.

- ■ 'No Secrets'[17], guidance on the development of adult protection policies and procedures, includes recognition of discriminatory abuse as a form of adult abuse, comprising racist, sexist, that based on a person's disability, and other forms of harassment, slurs or similar treatment.[18]

- ■ 'Working Together'[19] includes the following statement: 'Children from all cultures are subject to abuse and neglect. All children have a right to grow up safe from harm. In order to make sensitive and informed professional judgements about a child's needs, and parents' capacity to respond to their child's needs, it is important that professionals are sensitive to differing family patterns and lifestyles and to child-rearing patterns that vary across different racial, ethnic and cultural groups. At the same time they must be clear that child abuse cannot be condoned for religious or cultural reasons. Professionals should also be aware of the broader social factors that serve to discriminate against black and ethnic minority people. Working in a multi-racial and multi-cultural society requires professionals and organisations to be committed to equality in meeting the needs of all children and families, and to understand the effects of racial harassment, racial discrimination and institutional racism, as well as cultural misunderstanding or misinterpretation.'[20]

- ■ Further, at para. 10.12, 'Working Together' states: 'Professionals should guard against myths and stereotypes – both positive and negative – of black and minority ethnic families. Anxiety about being accused of racist practice should not prevent the necessary action being taken to safeguard a child. Careful assessment – based on evidence – of a child's needs, and a family's strengths and weaknesses, understood in the context of the wider social environment, will help to avoid any distorting effect of these influences on professional judgements.'

- ■ From the above statements the value of proper assessment is clear. Further guidance is provided in the 'Framework for the Assessment of Children in Need and their Families',[21] which recognises that 'since discrimination of all kinds is an everyday reality in many children's lives, every effort must be made to ensure that agencies' responses do not reflect or reinforce that experience and indeed, should counteract it'.[22]

- ■ A full chapter in the accompanying practice guidance expands on this principle of ensuring equality of opportunity.[23]

- ■ The Care Homes Regulations 2001 (SI 2001/3965) require homes where children are to be accommodated to include in their statement of purpose a description of the home's policy on anti-discriminatory practice in relation to children and children's rights.[24]

■ The Code for Crown Prosecutors includes a two-part test for decisions whether to prosecute: first, examination of the evidence, and second, whether prosecution is in the public interest. A factor in favour of prosecution is where the offence is motivated by any form of discrimination such as racial or sexual or hostility towards a victim based on his membership of a particular section of society. The Code itself is a public document produced in 14 different languages.

■ The Quality Protects Objectives apply to all children in need and children looked after but there is specific reference to ethnicity as follows. In objectives 3 and 4, ensuring that children in need and children looked after gain maximum life chance benefits from educational opportunities, health care and social care, this is to be achieved by making sure that black and ethnic minority children in care are as successful as possible, and black and ethnic minority children in need do as well as possible.[25]

■ Guidance to the Sexual Offences Act 2003 notes that whilst the act sets out new sexual offences where the victim has a mental disorder, 'It is important to appreciate that where a person with a mental disorder is able to consent freely to sexual activity, they have the same rights to engage in sexual activity as anyone else.'[26]

■ The National Service Framework for Older People (LAC (2001) 12) requires that NHS services are provided regardless of age, on the basis of clinical need alone. Also, social care services must not use age in eligibility criteria or policies to restrict access to services.

■ Other responses to discrimination

Existing anti-discrimination legislation provides some avenues for challenge of discrimination. In addition, it is important to be aware that issues of discrimination may feature in other types of cases and may be challenged on a number of different levels: e.g. use of the local authority complaints procedure or through specific criminal offences.

The case of *Thomas* v. *News Group Newspapers Ltd* [2001] EWCA Civ 1233, is illustrative. Miss Thomas had received race hate mail at her place of work following articles in the *Sun* newspaper. In this case the Protection from Harassment Act 1997 was applied to provide protection to the individual from harassment by the press. It was found that publication of three newspaper articles could constitute a course of conduct and therefore amounted to harassment.

Ethnic monitoring has been introduced into statistical collections on children's services. This should enable clearer analysis of how black and ethnic minority children fare in relation to the Quality Protects Objectives. It should produce information on the services children from ethnic minorities receive and how ethnicity relates to the reasons behind the need for services.[27]

Anti-discrimination legislation

The Race Relations Act 1976 and the Race Relations (Amendment) Act 2000 are discussed in relation to racial discrimination. The primary legislation which encourages equal treatment regardless of sex is the Sex Discrimination Act 1975. Disability discrimination gained statutory recognition more recently and is addressed by the Disability Discrimination Act 1995, the Special Educational Needs and Disability Act 2001 and the Disability Discrimination Act 2005. Following the European Equal Treatment in Employment Directive 2000, regulations have been introduced in respect of discrimination in employment and training on grounds of religion and belief, age or sexual orientation.

■ Race Relations Act 1976

The Race Relations Act 1976 (RRA 1976) makes discrimination on racial grounds illegal.

s. 1

> (1) A person discriminates against another in any circumstances relevant for the purposes of any provision of this Act if –
>   (a) on racial grounds he treats that other less favourably than he treats or would treat other persons.
>
> (RRA 1976)

'Racial grounds' includes race, colour, nationality, and national or ethnic origin.[28] Whilst most racial discrimination in the United Kingdom is against members of ethnic minorities, the Act applies to people of every background, race, colour and nationality and could equally be relied upon by a white person who suffers discrimination.

Case law has provided interpretation of certain aspects of the Act.

'Ethnic origins'

Interpretation of this phrase was the central issue in the leading case of *Mandla* v. *Dowell Lee* [1983] 2 AC 548, concerning a Sikh schoolboy. The House of Lords found that Sikhs are a distinct ethnic group though not of distinctive national origins. In fact, though religion is not specifically covered by the RRA 1976, racial identity could be centred on observance of a particular religion. Lord Fraser said that an ethnic group had to regard itself and be regarded by others as a distinct community with two essential characteristics: first, a long shared history of which the group is conscious and keeps the memory alive; and second, a cultural tradition of its own including family and social customs and manners often associated with religious observance. An earlier case,

Seide v. *Gillette* [1980] IRLR 427 ruled that Jews are a racial group. In contrast, in *Dawkins* v. *Department of the Environment, sub nom Dawkins* v. *Crown Suppliers (PSA)* [1993] IRLR 284, the Court of Appeal held, following the guidance given in *Mandla,* that Rastafarians did not comprise a racial group under the RRA 1976, partly because they did not fulfil the requirement of 'a long shared history'.

'National origins'

It has recently been decided that, although members of the United Kingdom, it could be possible for national origins to apply to discrimination between English, Welsh, Scottish and Northern Irish people. In *BBC Scotland* v. *Souster* [2001] IRLR 150[29] the court found that the race relations legislation could cover the situation of an Englishman discriminated against by a Scottish employer on account of his being English.

The RRA 1976 will also apply to a person who is affected by discrimination targeted at someone else: e.g. if services are withheld from a white person due to their marriage to a black person. A person who refuses to act in a discriminatory way will also be protected. In *Showboat Entertainment Centre Ltd* v. *Owens* [1984] 1 All ER 836, a white person was unlawfully discriminated against when he was dismissed after refusing to carry out an instruction from his employer to exclude black people from his place of work.

Discrimination may be direct, as envisaged by s. 1(1), by treating less favourably. There may also be *indirect discrimination* under s. 1(1)(b), meaning discrimination which by means of requirements or conditions discriminates in a way that is unjustifiable and detrimental against a racial group because a considerably smaller proportion of that racial group will be able to comply with the condition. It is for the employer or other potential discriminator to show that a condition can be justified. Indirect discrimination is sometimes referred to as disproportionate impact.

Examples of indirect discrimination include the following:

- Requiring high standards of English language competence, which indirectly discriminates against 'non-native' English speakers or requirements for specific UK-based examinations.
- Height requirements may discriminate against certain racial groups.
- Refusing to insure properties with certain postcodes or charging excessive rates may discriminate against certain racial groups living in a community. In the case of *Hussein* v. *Saints Complete House Furnitures* [1979] IRLR 337, indirect discrimination was found where a furniture store refused to employ people from Liverpool 8. Fifty per cent of the population of that area was black.

Permitted discrimination

In limited circumstances, behaviour which could be regarded as discriminatory will be permitted as a specific exception under the RRA 1976.

- A person who employs another individual to work in their own home may discriminate as to the person chosen.

- A genuine occupational requirement for a job may make it lawful to discriminate: e.g. employment of a Chinese person as a waiter in a Chinese restaurant, choice of a black male actor to play Othello for authenticity.

- A genuine occupational requirement defence may also apply where an employee provides persons of that racial group with personal services promoting their welfare and those services are most effectively provided by a person of that racial group: e.g. Asian care staff in a residential setting catering mainly for an Asian population whose first language is not English.

- Positive discrimination may be permitted where the objective is to rectify under-representation of a particular group in an area of employment: e.g. if black social workers are under-represented in senior posts or in a specialist field, additional training opportunities could be provided.

The Race Relations Act 1976 also established the Commission for Racial Equality (**CRE**). This is a publicly funded non-governmental organisation. Its functions include providing advice and assistance to individuals who feel they have suffered racial discrimination or harassment. The CRE works with public bodies and other organisations in improving policies and practices and it can investigate discrimination. Its role is discussed further below (under enforcement).

■ Race Relations (Amendment) Act 2000

The Race Relations Act 1976 has been amended by the Race Relations (Amendment) Act 2000. The Act specifically prohibits discrimination by a public authority:

s. 19B

> (1) It is unlawful for a public authority in carrying out any functions of the authority to do any act which constitutes discrimination.[30]
>
> (RRA 1976)

The Act also places a duty on public authorities to promote equality of opportunity and good relations between different racial groups, in all of the authorities' functions (s. 2). It will not be sufficient for an authority to respond to race discrimination; it must take positive steps to prevent race discrimination. The Act introduces a new s. 71 into the Race Relations Act 1976, effectively a new race equality duty:

s. 71

> (1) Everybody . . . shall, in carrying out its functions, have due regard to the need –
> (a) to eliminate unlawful racial discrimination; and
> (b) to promote equality of opportunity and good relations between persons of different racial groups.[31]
>
> (RRA 1976)

Under the new Act any functions of a public authority are covered by the legislation. Previously, public authorities had to abide by the terms of the Act in relation to employment, provision of goods, facilities and services, education and housing.

A public authority is given a wide definition under the Act. It will include public authorities such as central and local government, the National Health Service, the police and Social Services Departments. It also includes (in terms similar to those in the Human Rights Act 1998) anyone whose work includes functions of a public nature. Private or voluntary agencies would therefore be included if they carry out a public function, such as providing residential care or education.

Inclusion of the police stems directly from the recommendations of the Macpherson report. Chief officers of police become liable for acts of discrimination by any police officer within their command and individual officers who discriminate will also be liable for discrimination on racial grounds in relation to their functions, including arrest and detention of suspects, stops and searches, controlling demonstrations and assisting victims. Previously, although the 1976 Act made employers vicariously liable for acts of race discrimination committed by their employees in the course of their employment, as police officers are office-holders rather than employees, chief officers of police were not liable for their actions.

All public authorities are obliged to publish a race equality scheme, which identifies how they intend to meet their obligations to promote race equality. For many local authorities this has effectively been in place for some time in the form of an Equal Opportunities Policy. The race equality scheme has to include details of 'how the authority will ensure ethnic minorities have access to information and services, and arrangements for staff training on the duty to promote race equality'. Authorities must undertake ethnic monitoring and report on this annually alongside an evaluation of the effectiveness of their scheme.

A limited number of functions still remain outside the terms of the Act. Excluded functions are: decisions not to prosecute and judicial proceedings; security services functions; parliamentary functions; some immigration and nationality functions where discrimination is based on grounds of nationality or ethnic or national origin (not race or colour).

The Act gives powers to the Commission for Racial Equality to enforce the duties imposed on public authorities by the use of compliance notices. This is an improvement on the old RRA 1976, s. 71, which was considered largely unenforceable. The Commission may also issue codes of practice containing practical guidance on the performance of duties by public authorities.[32]

■ Sex Discrimination Act 1975

The Sex Discrimination Act 1975 (SDA 1975) is framed in terms broadly similar to the RRA 1976. It applies to direct and indirect discrimination and is supported by the Equal Opportunities Commission, which fulfils a role similar to the Commission for Racial Equality. The Sex Discrimination Act 1975 makes direct and indirect discrimination against women illegal in education, employment, recruitment and training, the provision of goods, services and facilities and the disposal and management of premises. Section 1 provides:

s. 1

> (1) In any circumstances relevant for the purposes of any provision of this Act, a person discriminates against a woman if –
>
> (a) on the ground of her sex he treats her less favourably than he treats or would treat a man, or
>
> (b) he applies to her a requirement or condition which he applies or would apply equally to a man but –
>
> > (i) which is such that the proportion of women who can comply with it is considerably smaller than the proportion of men who can comply with it, and
> >
> > (ii) which he cannot show to be justifiable irrespective of the sex of the person to whom it is applied, and
> >
> > (iii) which is to her detriment because she cannot comply with it.
>
> (SDA 1975)

Direct discrimination may include sexual harassment,[33] denying training opportunities to a woman because she is pregnant, appointing a man to a job when a female applicant is better qualified. In *Gill* v. *El Vino Company Ltd* [1983] 1 All ER 398 it was found that where a wine bar would only serve women at tables and not at the bar this directly discriminated against women, who were denied facilities and services on an equal basis. As with race discrimination, indirect discrimination will occur where practices appear fair in a formal sense but are discriminatory in operation and effect: e.g. a requirement that all employees must be a particular height where minimum height requirements bear no relation to the actual job.

Examples of requirements which may have a discriminatory effect on women include:

■ Redundancy criteria to select part-time workers first, where the majority of part-time staff are women.

■ An upper age limit for appointment to a particular job. This was found in the case of *Price* v. *Civil Service Commission* [1977] IRLR 291,[34] to indirectly discriminate against women, who were more likely to have taken time out from a career for child care responsibilities.

■ A requirement to work full-time, when part-time or job share would be suitable, may discriminate against women.

■ The requirement to comply with new rostering arrangements was indirect discrimination in a case where a female train driver could not comply because of her child care commitments (*London Underground* v. *Edwards (No. 2)* [1998] IRLR 364.

The SDA 1975 also applies in respect of less favourable treatment of men and of married people in employment. Since 1999 the Act has also applied to discrimination on the ground of gender reassignment.[35]

The SDA 1975 established the Equal Opportunities Commission (**EOC**). This is a publicly funded non-governmental organisation, which has a similar role to the

Commission for Racial Equality. In addition to its enforcement role, the EOC provides advice and information to individuals and employers, campaigns on equal opportunities issues and produces statistics and publications. The EOC can take action against discriminatory advertisers.

In addition to the SDA 1975, the Equal Pay Act 1970 (which came into force in 1975) placed on a statutory footing the principle that men and women should receive equal pay for equal work. A job evaluation, which can refer to 'like' work, will normally be required for a claim to be successful. There must be some material difference in the work carried out to justify unequal pay.

New regulations which came into force in October 2005, the Employment Equality (Sex Discrimination) Regulations 2005 (SI 2005/2467) include sexual harassment as a freestanding separate claim. Harassment includes unwanted conduct, and unwanted verbal, non-verbal or physical conduct of a sexual nature, where it has the effect of violating dignity, or creating an intimidating, hostile, degrading, humiliating or offensive environment. The specific right not to be discriminated against because of pregnancy or maternity leave is also included in these regulations, reflecting decided case law. (Dismissal on the grounds of pregnancy is illegal under the Employment Protection Act 1978. If dismissed, the woman will be entitled to compensation unless the employer is able to show that pregnancy genuinely made the work impossible and there was no suitable alternative work available.)

■ Disability Discrimination Act 1995

It is unlawful to discriminate against a disabled person in relation to employment and the provision of goods and services and selling, letting or managing of land or premises. In contrast to the race and sex legislation, the Disability Discrimination Act 1995 (DDA 1995) applies only to direct discrimination; there is no recognition of indirect discrimination. Disability is defined as:

s. 1(1)

> . . . a physical or mental impairment which has a substantial and long-term adverse effect on ability to carry out normal day-to-day activities.

(DDA 1995)

Guidance on the definition of disability was given to employment tribunals in the case of *Goodwin* v. *Patent Office* [1999] ICR 302, in which it was recognised that merely because a person was able to cope at home did not mean that he was outside the definition of a disabled person for the purposes of the DDA 1995. The case concerned a man who suffered from paranoid schizophrenia and had been dismissed following complaints from employees about his, at times, bizarre behaviour. The Employment Appeal Tribunal were surprised to find that, simply because the applicant was able to cope at home, the industrial tribunal found that he fell outside the definition of disability. The proper approach for tribunals is to adopt a purposive approach to construction of the definition, assisted by guidance and the Code of

Practice: Disability Discrimination Act (1996). The tribunal should look at all the evidence by reference to four different conditions – impairment, adverse effect, substantiality and long-term effect – and it might be helpful to address each separately, noting that substantial is used in the sense of more than minor or trivial.

'Long-term effect'

The effect of impairment is long term if it has lasted at least 12 months or it is likely to last for at least 12 months or for the rest of the life of the person.[36]

'Normal day-to-day activities'

This phrase is broad and can include, for example, putting hair rollers in and applying makeup.[37] The employment tribunal initially stated that, as this was an activity carried out almost exclusively by women, it could not be considered a normal day-to-day activity. The Employment Appeal Tribunal found to the contrary and added that anything done by most women or most men could be considered a normal day-to-day activity.

Severe disfigurement is specifically cited as an impairment which is to be treated as having a substantial adverse effect on the ability of the person to carry out normal day-to-day activities.[38]

Under Sch. 1, an impairment will be taken to affect ability to carry out normal day-to-day activities if it affects an area from the following list: mobility; manual dexterity; physical coordination; continence; ability to lift, carry or otherwise move everyday objects; speech, hearing or eyesight; memory or ability to concentrate, learn or understand; or perception of the risk of physical danger.[39] Certain impairments are excluded, including allergic conditions: e.g. hayfever, impairments caused by alcohol, tobacco and drug addictions, and personality disorders such as paedophilia.

Employment

A person is discriminated against in employment if their employer, for a reason which relates to the disability, treats the person less favourably than they would treat a non-disabled person and they cannot show that the treatment was justified. If an employer is unaware of an employee's disability then there can be no discrimination. In *O'Neill* v. *Symm & Co Ltd* [1998] IRLR 232, an employee was dismissed because of absence from work. Her employer was not aware that she suffered from ME, a disability under the Act. It was found, therefore, that she was dismissed because of absence from work, not because she had a disability. This case should have limited application, as, under para. 4.57 of the Guidance to the Act, employers are required to do all they could be reasonably expected to do to find out whether a person has a disability.

Furthermore, there is an expectation that an employer will provide reasonable adjustments to the working environment and if they fail to do so and cannot justify the failure that is also discrimination (ss. 5 and 6). Reasonable adjustments include modifying equipment and arranging training. Section 6 provides:

s. 6

> (1) Where –
>   (a) any arrangements made by or on behalf of an employer, or
>   (b) any physical feature of premises occupied by the employer,
> place the disabled person concerned at a substantial disadvantage in comparison with persons who are not disabled, it is the duty of the employer to take such steps as it is reasonable, in all the circumstances of the case, for him to have to take in order to prevent the arrangements or feature having that effect.
>
> (DDA 1995)

There is an exemption in relation to small businesses, with fewer than 15 employees.

In *Kenny* v. *Hampshire Constabulary* [1999] IRLR 76, the Employment Appeal Tribunal heard an appeal by a man who suffered from cerebral palsy whose offer of employment had been withdrawn because the necessary care assistance he required for going to the toilet could not be provided. It was recognised that he was a disabled person within s. 1 of the Disability Discrimination Act 1995 and that withdrawing the offer of employment was potentially discriminatory. It was found, however, that s. 6 did not extend to a requirement for employers to provide carers to attend to their employees' personal needs and the appeal was dismissed accordingly.

Discrimination against disabled people in the provision of services, goods or facilities is prohibited. Services include: access to and use of any public places; accommodation in hotels, etc.; facilities by way of banking or insurance or credit; facilities for entertainment, recreation or refreshment; and the services of any profession or trade or any local or other public authority.[40] It is arguable that social and legal services would be included in this provision. If a provider of services treats someone less favourably for a reason relating to their disability, which cannot be justified under the Act, this is discrimination. If a service provider has a practice, policy or procedure which makes it impossible or unreasonably difficult for disabled people to make use of the service, there is a duty to take reasonable steps to change that practice, policy or procedure so that it no longer has that effect. This would include, for example, ensuring that information about services is produced in a way that makes it accessible to people with disabilities, e.g. Braille translations and large print copies. In addition, if there is a failure (which cannot be justified) to make reasonable adjustments, e.g. adding a ramp or widening a doorway, this amounts to discrimination (DDA 1995, s. 20).

Education and transport services were specifically excluded from this part of the DDA 1995. The law on education has been altered by the Special Educational Needs and Disability Act 2001 (discussed below).

When the DDA 1995 was introduced, it simply established an Advisory Council, which had substantially fewer powers than the corresponding bodies under the Sex Discrimination Act 1975 or the Race Relations Act 1976. The Council was mandated to advise the Secretary of State on the operation of the Act and on the elimination of discrimination and to prepare a Code of Practice. Enforcement of the provisions of the Act thus relied entirely on individuals taking cases forward.

The Disability Rights Commission Act 1999 rectified this position with the introduction of the Disability Rights Commission (DRC). This body has a similar remit to the CRE and EOC and can issue non-discrimination notices.

The DDA 1995 abolished the 3 per cent quota system which was established by the Disabled Persons (Employment) Act 1944 as a means of ensuring that at least 3 per cent of the workforce were disabled. This requirement was difficult to enforce and largely ignored.

■ Special Educational Needs and Disability Act 2001

The Special Educational Needs and Disability Act 2001 (SENDA 2001) extends the provisions of the DDA 1995 to education by inserting a new Part IV into the DDA 1995. The new law is largely the result of recommendations of the Disability Rights Task Force to the Government.[41] The emphasis of the Act is on education of disabled children in mainstream schools if parents want this and it does not interfere with the efficient education of other children.[42] The discrimination provisions apply to schools and to education post-16 years of age. A school or higher education setting discriminates against a disabled child/person if, for a reason related to the child's disability, it treats the child less favourably than others to whom that reason does not apply and it cannot show that the treatment is justified. The duty not to discriminate is imposed on the responsible body of all schools; usually this will be the governing body or LEA. It applies to admissions, education and associated services, which would include, e.g. school trips, dinner arrangements and bullying policies, as well as access issues. Schools and colleges should anticipate the reasonable adjustments that are necessary so that a disabled pupil will not be substantially disadvantaged. Physical adaptations to buildings are not included in the reasonable adjustments duty for schools; LEAs, however, are under a duty to plan to increase access for disabled children.[43] Reasonable adjustments relating to physical adaptations of buildings are not exempted in the further and higher education settings. In post-16 settings 'student services' are also included. Providers of Social Work qualification courses will clearly be covered by these provisions and should take steps to ensure that disabled students are not disadvantaged.[44]

Parents make claims on behalf of school-age children to the SEN and Disability Tribunal. The Disability Rights Commission (DRC) can arrange conciliation services with the aim of resolving disputes and avoiding legal action. Compensation is not available but other remedies could include an apology, additional tuition or staff training. Where discrimination occurs in post-16 education, complaint is made to the county court and compensation may be payable.

■ Disability Discrimination Act 2005

The Disability discrimination Act 2005 amends the Disability Discrimination Act 2005 in similar terms to the race relations amendments. It imposes a 'disability equality duty' on public authorities. Specifically, s. 3 introduces a new duty on public authorities requiring them, when exercising their functions, to have due regard to the need to eliminate harassment of and unlawful discrimination against disabled persons, to promote positive attitudes towards disabled persons, to encourage participation by disabled persons in public life, and to promote equality of opportunity between disabled persons and other persons.

This represents a change of emphasis from law which was reliant on individual disabled people making complaints to a position where the public sector are required to be more pro-active in promoting equal opportunities for disabled people. Authorities are required to produce a Disability Equality Scheme and must involve disabled people in its production. A Code of Practice will accompany the Act, which is expected to be implemented by December 2006.

The Act also extends the definition of disability so that it includes people who have cancer, multiple sclerosis, or are HIV Positive, who will be deemed disabled from diagnosis.

▪ Influence of European Law

To give effect to Art. 13 of the Treaty of Amsterdam, the Council of Europe issued an Equal Treatment in Employment Directive in 2000, which requires member states to make discrimination unlawful on grounds of religion or belief, age or sexual orientation in the areas of employment and training. The United Kingdom has taken steps to comply with this directive by introducing the following regulations and should have given full effect to it by 2006.

▪ Employment Equality (Religion or Belief) Regulations 2003[45]

There have been some cases where religion or belief has been addressed as an aspect of ethnicity, e.g. Sikhism in *Mandla*. These regulations make it unlawful to discriminate against a person specifically because of his religion or belief in employment and training. The definition of religion or belief refers to 'any religion, religious belief, or similar philosophical belief'. It is likely to include all major religions and also strongly held views such as humanism or atheism. Perception by the discriminator about religious belief, even if untrue, will also be covered if the less favourable treatment was based on that perception.

▪ Employment Equality (Age) Regulations 2006[46]

Ageist attitudes may operate so that older people are treated less favourably in relation to employment and other areas, and legally there has been nothing to prevent an employer rejecting a job applicant because he is 'too old'. People may also be selected for redundancy on age grounds. An exception to this absence of protection is provided by *Marshall* v. Southampton and *South West Hampshire AHA* [1986] 2 All ER 584, where the different retirement ages for men and women was declared unlawful by the European Court of Justice. A voluntary code published by the Government contains guidelines for employers and continues to be relevant (a 'Code of Practice on Ageing in Employment' (2001)[47])

The draft regulations were published in July 2005 and it is expected that they will come into force by October 2006. The regulations prohibit direct or indirect age discrimination, prohibit ageist harassment and include a duty for employers to consider requests to work beyond retirement age.

As with race and sex discrimination, a 'genuine occupational requirement' defence can be relied on. Unfortunately, the new legislation does not extend to age discrimination in areas beyond employment, nor address provision of goods, services and facilities.

■ Employment Equality (Sexual Orientation) Regulations 2003[48]

From 1 December 2003, these regulations have prohibited discrimination on the grounds of sexual orientation in the employment field.

It was previously unclear whether discrimination on the basis of sexual orientation could be considered sex discrimination within the ambit of the SDA 1975. This issue was tested in the case of *Grant* v. *South West Trains Ltd* [1998] All ER (EC) 193. South West Trains refused to provide travel concessions to Grant's female partner. The travel concessions were available only to a spouse or cohabiting partner of the opposite sex of two years' duration. Grant argued discrimination based on sex, as her male predecessor had received benefits in an unmarried relationship with a female partner. She also argued that discrimination on grounds of sexual orientation was prejudice against people of a particular sex. The European Court of Justice rejected this argument. It was found that the condition applied regardless of the sex of the employee. The court stated that sex discrimination legislation was not to be read so as to include discrimination on the grounds of sexual orientation. It was up to Parliament to change the law. This position was confirmed in *Pearce v Mayfield Secondary School Governing Body* [2003] UKHL 34. Here a lesbian teacher suffered homophobic taunts at school. It was suggested that the acts complained of constituted sexual harassment and were a form of sex discrimination. The House of Lords ruled that she was not treated less favourably on grounds of sex. Sex related to gender and not sexual orientation, which fell outside the Act. Sexual harassment was not of itself less favourable treatment.

In other circumstances same-sex relationships have been recognised. For example, in *Fitzpatrick* v. *Sterling Housing Association* [1999] 4 All ER 705, gay partners were recognised by the Honse of Lords as 'family' for the purpose of inheriting the tenancy of their rented flat on death.

■ Enforcement

For disability, race and sex discrimination, an individual can complain about discrimination relating to provision of goods and services through civil proceedings in the county court. A claim should normally be brought within six months of the last act complained of. Damages and injunctions may be ordered. Questions of discrimination in employment may be dealt with by application to an employment tribunal. The duty not to discriminate in the employment field relates to employees and job applicants and includes duties not to dismiss or refuse employment on the basis of discrimination, discriminatory advertisements, training and other benefits. Strict time limits for applications to the tribunal apply. The tribunal can award compensation and can make declarations as to the complainant's rights, order the employers to take steps to prevent further discrimination and order that an equal opportunities policy be followed.[49] The power to award compensation used to be 'capped' at the same limit as for unfair dismissal claims: the maximum amount of compensation payable was around £12,000. This upper limit has since been removed and substantially higher awards may be made: e.g. in *HM Prison Service* v. *Johnson* [1997] IRLR 162 compensation of £21,000 for injury to feelings and £7,500 aggravated damages was awarded.

The Disability Rights Commission, the Commission for Racial Equality and the Equal Opportunities Commission have powers to carry out formal investigations into complaints of discrimination and can require production of relevant documents for that purpose. The Commissions can offer assistance to individuals; negotiate with employers to ensure compliance with the Act; and issue non-discrimination notices if they find evidence of discrimination. A non-discrimination notice requires the person or organisation not to commit discriminatory acts for a five-year period. If a non-discrimination notice is not complied with, it may be enforced by an injunction from the county court. Victimisation of someone because they have tried to exercise their rights under the SDA 1975, Equal Pay Act 1970 or RRA 1976 is prohibited.[50]

■ Reform – a unified Commission

The Government plans to introduce a Commission for Equality and Human Rights, which will replace the existing Commissions on Racial Equality, Equal Opportunities and Disability Rights. The reforms are set out in the Equality Act 2006 and follow proposals contained in the white paper, 'Fairness for All: A New Commission for Equality and Human Rights' (2004, DCA).

The Bill provides for the establishment of the Commission for Equality and Human Rights, a new body which will replace the Equal Opportunities Commission, the Commission for Racial Equality and the Disability Rights Commission, each of will be dissolved. There are persuasive arguments in favour of an SEB, equally there are concerns that without major legislative reform to ensure coherence across the different strands of discrimination, the SEB might institutionalise a hierarchy of equality rights.

The role of the Commission will include:

■ Promoting equality and diversity.

■ Working towards eliminating discrimination and harassment.

■ Promoting understanding of good relations between different communities.

■ Encouraging good practice in the treatment of disabled people and reducing isolation.

■ Promoting understanding, good practice and the protection of human rights.

■ Encouraging public authorities to comply with the ECHR.

■ Enforcement of the various equality laws.

To support this role the Commission has similar powers and functions to the existing Commissions, i.e. dissemination of information, issuing Codes of Practice, investigating cases, issuing notices, supporting a person taking legal action, and additionally the Commission has the power to cooperate with others interested in human rights, which might, for example, include the Children's Commissioners.

It is the Government's intention to appoint the Chair and Commissioners of the new body by 2006 so that the new body can be operational by 2007. The existing Commissions will be phased in to the new body until fully incorporated.

Chapter summary

■ Anti-discriminatory practice is an essential cornerstone of social work and is required by the BASW Code of Ethics and CCETSW.

■ The law relating to discrimination provides a minimum baseline on which to develop good practice. Legislation specifically makes discrimination based on sex, race or disability illegal.

■ Other legislation also contains references which support the principle of equality and the need to avoid discrimination: e.g. the Children Act 1989, s. 22(5). Policy guidance and codes of practice further support anti-discriminatory practice.

■ Since the introduction of the Human Rights Act 1998, Art. 14 of the European Convention on Human Rights outlaws discrimination on any ground in relation to the enjoyment of the Articles of the Convention: e.g. the right to respect for private and family life.

■ Discrimination under the Race Relations Act 1976 and the Sex Discrimination Act 1975 may be direct or indirect. Indirect discrimination occurs where a requirement or condition is stipulated, with which a disproportionate number of women or black and minority ethnic persons are unable to comply: e.g. a minimum height requirement. The Disability Discrimination Act 1995 relates only to direct discrimination.

■ The Race Relations (Amendment) Act 2000 extends the Race Relations Act 1976 by making race discrimination in any of the functions of a public authority illegal. It places a duty on public authorities to work towards elimination of unlawful discrimination and to promote equality of opportunity and good relations between persons of different racial groups. The Act also makes chief officers of police vicariously liable for acts of race discrimination by police officers.

- The Special Educational Needs and Disability Act 2001 extends the application of the Disability Discrimination Act 1995 to educational settings.

- The Disability Discrimination Act 2005 introduces a disability equality duty on public authorities.

- New regulations have been issued further to a European Directive, to extend anti-discrimination laws to cover discrimination on grounds of religion or belief, age and sexual orientation.

Exercises

In each of the following cases, consider whether there is discrimination, what action might be taken and whether existing law supports anti-discriminatory, anti-oppressive practice.

- Joan applies for a job as a fitness instructor at a newly opened sports complex. She is not offered an interview and when she queries this she is told that, because of her age, she did not meet the criteria for the position.

- An 'alternative' theatre, situated in the basement of an existing 1920s theatre, refuses access to Susan and her boyfriend Mike, who uses a wheelchair, because of 'health and safety'.

- Ranbir, aged 76, is offered a place at a day centre for elderly people. She is the only person there from an ethnic minority background and hears a member of staff and woman who attends the centre making racist comments about her.

- Jenny is a child from the travelling community. She has been attending primary school for three weeks when her teacher tells her that if she does not come to school in uniform the next day she will be given detention.

- Josh is removed from his mother's care under an emergency protection order and placed with white foster carers. He is black.

- Jane, a recently qualified social worker, has been off sick for five months with depression. Her manager invites her in for an informal chat and suggests to Jane that she probably isn't cut out for social work and might prefer to move to administrative duties. Jane is really upset and hands in her notice.

- Sam and Max are a gay couple in their mid-thirties. They have received a letter from the adoption panel rejecting them as suitable adopters. They are convinced this is because of their sexuality.

Websites

Web sites for the existing enforcement bodies include examples of cases they have supported. They are:

Commission for Racial Equality:
www.cre.gov.uk

Equal Opportunities Commission:
www.eoc.org.uk

Disability Rights Commission:
www.drc-gb.org

The Home Office has an Equality and Diversity section:
www.homeoffice.gov.uk/equality-diversity

Further reading

Dalrymple, J. and Burke, B. (2006) *Anti-oppressive practice: Social Care and the Law* (2nd edn.). Buckingham: Open University Press.

Commission for Racial Equality (1995) *Racial Equality Means Quality: the Commission's Standard for Local Government.* London: CRE.

Disability Rights Commission (1996) *Guidance on Matters to be Taken into Account in Determining Questions Relating to the Definition of Disability.* London: DRC.

Gooding, C. (1996) *Blackstone's Guide to the Disability Discrimination Act 1995.* London: Blackstone Press.

Dutt, R. (2001) 'Racism and social-work practice' in Cull, L.-A. and Roche, J. (eds) *The Law and Social Work: Contemporary Issues for Practice.* Basingstoke: Palgrave.

Hay, D. (2001) 'The Special Educational Needs and Disability Act 2001' *Education Law Journal* p. 72.

Help the Aged (2002) *Age Discrimination in Public Policy.* London: Help the Aged.

Hepple, B., Coussey, M. and Choudhury, T. (2000) *Equality: A New Framework, Report of the Independent Review of the Enforcement of the UK Anti-Discrimination Legislation.* Oxford: Hart Publishing.

Lester, A. (2001) 'Equality and United Kingdom law: past, present and future' *Public Law* SPR p. 77.

Macpherson, W. (1999) 'The Stephen Lawrence Inquiry: Report of an Inquiry by Sir William Macpherson of Cluny *et al.*' London: The Stationery Office.

McColgan, A. (2002) (ed.) *Discrimination Law handbook* London: Legal Action Group – a detailed guide to the law.

Nairn, J. (2006) *Discrimination Law. Text, Cases and Materials.* Oxford: OUP.

Notes

1   J. Dalrymple and B. Burke (1995) *Anti-oppressive Practice: Social Care and the Law.* Buckingham: Open University Press.

2   General Social Care Council (2002) Codes of Practice for Social Care Workers and Employers.

3   This is the principal recommendation contained in B. Hepple, M. Coussey, and T. Choudhury (2000) *Equality: A New Framework, Report of the Independent Review of the Enforcement of the UK Anti-Discrimination Legislation.* Oxford: Hart Publishing.

4   R. Barn, R. Sinclair and D. Ferdinand (1997) *Acting on Principle: An Examination of Race and Ethnicity in Social Services Provision for Children and Families.* London: BAAF/CRE.

5   Department of Health (2000) *The Children Act Report 1995–1999* (Cm. 4579). London: The Stationery Office.

6   J. Gibbons *et al.* (1995) in Department of Health *Child protection: Messages from Research.* London: The Stationery Office.

7   I. Brodie (1998) *Highlight: Exclusion from School.* London: National Children's Bureau.

8   London Borough of Lambeth (1987) *Whose Child? A Report of the Public Inquiry into the death of Tyra Henry.* London: London Borough of Lambeth.

9   T. Booth, W. Booth and D. McConnell (2004) 'Parents with learning difficulties, care proceedings and the family courts: threshold decisions and the moral matrix' 16 *Child and Family Law Quarterly* p. 409.

10 British Crime Survey, 2000.

11 D. Browne (1995) 'Sectioning – The Black Experience' in S. Fernando (ed.) *Mental Health in a Multi-Ethnic Society: A Multi-Disciplinary Handbook.* London: Routledge.

12 DfEE Disability Briefing (November 1999) cited in A. McColgan (2000) *Discrimination Law: Text, cases and materials.* Oxford: Hart Publishing.

13 See R. Dutt (2001) 'Racism and social-work practice' in L.-A. Cull and J. Roche (eds) *The Law and Social Work: Contemporary Issues for Practice.* Basingstoke: Palgrave.

14 W. Macpherson (1999) The Stephen Lawrence Inquiry: Report of an Inquiry by Sir William Macpherson of Cluny *et al.* London: The Stationery Office.

15 See discussion in Chapter 18.

16 (1999) London: HMSO.

17 Department of Health (2000) *No Secrets: Guidance on Developing and Implementing Multi-Agency Policies and Procedures to Protect Vulnerable Adults from Abuse.* London: Department of Health.

18 Paragraph 2.7.

19 HM Government (2006) *Working Together to Safeguard Children.* London: The Stationery Office.

20 Paragraphs 10.9–10.10.

21 Department of Health (2000) *Framework for the Assessment of Children in Need and their Families.* London: The Stationery Office.

22 Paragraph 1.42.

23 Department of Health (2000) *Assessing Children in Need and their Families: Practice Guidance.* London: The Stationery Office.

24 Schedule 5, para. 20. Note the same requirement has not been included in the regulations for homes providing accommodation for adults.

25 Department of Health (1999) *The Government's Objectives for Children's Social Services.* London: Department of Health.

26 HOC 021/2004.

27 Department of Health (2000) The Children Act Report 1995–1999 (Cm. 4579). London: The Stationery Office.

28 Race Relations Act 1976, s. 3.

29 See discussion in C. Munro (2001) 'When racism is not black and white' 6973 *New Law Journal* p. 314.

30 Section 1 of the Race Relations (Amendment) Act 2000 inserts a new s. 19B into the Race Relations Act 1976.

31 'Body' in this provision refers to public authorities.

32 RRA 1976, s. 71C, inserted by Race Relations (Amendment) Act 2000, s. 2.

33 Sexual harassment was recognised as a form of sex discrimination in *Strathclyde Regional Council* v. *Porcelli* [1986] IRLR 134.

34 In *Price* an upper age limit of 28 for entry as an executive officer in the civil service was found to indirectly discriminate against women.

35 SDA 1975, s. 2A(1).

36 DDA 1995, s. 2(1).

37 *Ekpe* v. *Commissioner of Police of the Metropolis* [2001] IRLR 605.

38 DDA 1995, s. 3(1).

39 DDA 1995, Sch. 1, para. 4(1).

40 DDA 1995, s. 19(3).

41 Disability Rights Task Force (1999) *From Exclusion to Inclusion: A report of the DRTF on civil rights for disabled people.* London: DfEE.

42 See discussion in Chapter 5.

43 DDA 1995, s. 28D.

44 This could include physical adaptations to buildings but also applies, for example, to teaching materials such as use of large print handouts, Braille translations, hearing loops, etc.

45 SI 2003/1660.

46 SI 2006/1031.

47 Eurolink Age, 2001.

48 SI 2003/1661.

49 RRA 1976, s. 56; SDA 1975, s. 65.

50 Victimisation would extend to ex-employees only where it includes refusing to provide a reference to a person who brought a discrimination claim.

Children and families

Part
2

Chapters:

7 Supporting children and families

Learning objectives

To develop an understanding of the following:

- The legal framework for social work practice with children and families provided by the Children Act 1989.
- Central principles of the Act, including the concepts of welfare and children's rights.
- The background to and effect of the Children Act 2004.
- The concept of a 'child in need' and range of services which may be available to support children in need and their families.
- Issues relating to children with a disability.

This chapter addresses four main areas. To begin with, the Children Act 1989 (**CA 1989**) is introduced, being the principal legislation providing the legal framework within which social work practice with children and families is situated. The key principles of Part I of the Act – that the welfare of the child is the court's paramount consideration, non-intervention and avoidance of delay – are outlined. This is accompanied by a broader discussion of some of the value positions of the Act, including welfare, children's rights and parental responsibility.

Second, the Children Act 2004 (**CA 2004**) is introduced. This legislation builds on the Children Act 1989 and places emphasis on safeguarding the wellbeing of all children. Discussion of the Climbié report provides some background to the Act, and 'Every Child Matters' documentation that set out the five aspects of children's 'well being' a term incorporated in the Act. The Act establishes a new role of Children's Commissioner in England to ensure that at national level issues affecting children and young people have a high profile. It also provides for some reorganisation in delivery of child care including new Director of Children's Services posts and Local Safeguarding Children Boards replacing area child protection committees. An overview of the

Act is included in this chapter and further reference to particular provisions is covered elsewhere as appropriate.

Support for families and preventive measures to combat child abuse are provided for within the framework of the Children Act 1989 in relation to children in the local authority area and specific responsibilities toward children in need. The concept of a child in need and the range of services which may be provided to support children in need and their family are discussed in the third section of the chapter.

Introduction to the Children Act 1989

The Children Act 1989 is a major piece of legislation comprising 108 sections, divided into 12 Parts, with a further 15 Schedules.

■ Summary of central themes and changes introduced by the Children Act 1989

Readers may not have any experience of the law relating to children that applied prior to introduction of the Children Act 1989. In order to appreciate the scale of reform which the Act introduced, a brief outline of some of the key changes is provided in this section.

The 1989 Act introduced a number of language changes. The familiar concepts of custody and access were replaced by s. 8 orders, principally residence and contact orders. Parental rights and duties became parental responsibility. In each case, although there is an obvious change in terminology, more significant conceptual changes were incorporated, as suggested by reference to responsibility rather than rights and duties.

The 1989 Act provides a single route into care. Section 31 provides a threshold for care and supervision orders. The only circumstances in which a care or supervision order will be made is on satisfaction of the s. 31 criteria, on the application of the local authority (or authorised person, e.g. the NSPCC). The system of voluntary care, which could be transformed into formal care by administrative action, was replaced by provision of accommodation, to be seen as a service for families and not a back door route into care.

Wardship (an aspect of the High Court's inherent jurisdiction) was one way in which a child could formally enter the care of the local authority prior to the Act. It is still possible for a child to be made a ward of court; however, the opportunities for a local authority to use wardship have been limited. Certain elements of the wardship jurisdiction have been retained and made more widely available via the new Specific Issue Order and Prohibited Steps Order contained in s. 8.

A range of new orders were introduced by the Children Act 1989, including the Child Assessment Order, Family Assistance Order, Specific Issue Order, Prohibited Steps Order and Education Supervision Order, as well as extending the circumstances in which interim orders could be made. Procedural changes were also made to support improvements in practice. A system of concurrent jurisdiction operates between the magistrates' family proceedings court, the county court and the High Court, and there is a provision for transfers between different levels of court. Hale J noted in 1999: 'The whole purpose of the Children Act 1989 was to give the court flexibility to meet the needs of the particular child in the particular circumstances and to do what was best for that child.'[1]

The 1989 Act was hailed as a charter for children's rights and certainly introduces greater opportunity for the voice of the child to be heard in some circumstances. In addition, provision is made for children's guardians to be appointed in a wider range of cases. The Act places great emphasis on the advantages of children being brought up in their own families. To further this aim there is a definition of a 'child in need' and a range of services which are to be provided to support children and families and ultimately to prevent children entering the care system, supported by the principle of working in partnership. The Act provided a comprehensive reform of law relating to children and significantly it brought together public and private law in one statute, areas which had previously been treated separately. However, it should also be noted that, despite the comprehensive nature of the reform, major areas of law relating to children remain outside the Act, notably adoption and youth justice, each of which is considered in separate chapters. A child is defined under the 1989 Act as 'a person under the age of 18' (s. 105).

Given its size, finding your way around the Children Act 1989 may seem daunting. Exhibit 7.1 maps out the parts of the Act and provides brief summaries of the key elements in each part as an initial guide.

The Children Act 1989 incorporates a number of value perspectives, which may at times appear to be in conflict. Fox-Harding (1997)[2] describes these as: laissez-faire and patriarchy; state paternalism; defence of the birth family; and children's rights. Each perspective is reflected in particular provisions throughout the Act. Opportunities for coercive state intervention should be minimal according to the laissez-faire perspective and the presumption of non-intervention in s. 1(5) and limitations on local authority use of wardship may be interpreted as reflecting this perspective. State paternalism places greater value on the role of the state to intervene to protect children's welfare as evident in the inclusion of 'future harm' in the threshold criteria and aspects of the Quality Protects initiative which place greater emphasis on using adoption as a child care resource. Defence of the birth family is reflected in the Children Act emphasis on providing support to families, including recognition of children in need and the provision of accommodation as an aspect of support to families. Finally, the increased role for children's guardians and opportunities for children to initiate proceedings and express their own views in certain circumstances would suggest that the children's rights perspective is also reflected in the Children Act 1989.

It is 16 years since the Act was implemented and certain parts of it have already been amended, expanded or revoked. Research has been conducted to evaluate how well different aspects are working (see 'Messages from Research' (1996) and 'The Children Act Now' (2001)) and has contributed to policy and legislative changes. Some commentators questioned whether a new Children Act was needed, including Freeman.[3]

Part I Introductory	Welfare principle and checklist, delay, non-intervention, parental responsibility, guardians, welfare reports
Part II Children in Family Proceedings	Residence, Contact, Specific Issue and Prohibited Steps Orders (s. 8), Change of Name and Removal from Jurisdiction, Family Assistance Orders (s. 16)
Part III Local Authority Support for Children and Families	Provision of services, definition of child in need, accommodation, duties to children looked after, secure accommodation, cooperation between authorities
Part IV Care and Supervision	Care and Supervision Orders, Interim Orders, discharge and variation, contact with children in care, exclusion requirements, appointment of children's guardian
Part V Protection of Children	Child Assessment Orders, Emergency Protection Orders, exclusion requirements, Police Protection, local authority duty to investigate
Part VI, VII and VIII Community Homes, Voluntary Homes and Organisations, and Registered Children's Homes	Now covered by Care Standards Act 2000
Part IX Private Arrangements for Fostering: Children	Privately fostered children, disqualification from fostering, as amended by the Children Act 2004
Part X Childminding and Day-Care	Now covered by Care Standards Act 2000
Part XI Secretary of State's Supervisory Functions and Responsibilities	Inspection of children's homes, inquiries, default powers
Part XII, ss 85–108 Miscellaneous – General	Includes litigation limit and LA restriction on use of wardship jurisdiction, interpretation
Schedules 1–15 Schedule 2	Schedule 2 includes requirements for the LA to maintain a register of disabled children; prepare children's services plans; prevent neglect and abuse; reduce the need for care proceedings or criminal proceedings against children; provide family centres

Exhibit 7.1   Contents of the Children Act 1989

This debate continued in the face of criticism that the tragedy surrounding the death of Victoria Climbié in 2000 suggested an inadequate child protection framework. Following the inquiry, new legislation, the Children Act 2004, was introduced and key features are discussed below. The essence of these changes can be described as providing for organisational changes and new duties to promote inter-agency working. The essential features of the Children Act 1989, relating to child protection (discussed further in Chapter 9) have not changed.

Central principles

∎ Welfare

Part I of the Children Act 1989 contains a number of principles which apply throughout the Act. The first and most influential is the welfare principle.[4]

> **s. 1**
>
> When a court determines any question with respect to
> (a) the upbringing of a child; or
> (b) the administration of a child's property or the application of income arising from it, the child's welfare shall be the court's paramount consideration.
>
> (CA 1989)

Section 1 of the Children Act 1989 provides that the welfare of a child is the court's paramount consideration. At first sight this might appear to be a straightforward proposition worthy of support. Closer examination prompts a number of questions as to the meaning of this phrase. Welfare is an indeterminate concept (Bainham, 1998),[5] which is open to wide-ranging interpretation, meaning different things to different people. Eekalaar (1986)[6] suggests that there are three aspects to welfare: 'basic' – general physical, emotional and intellectual care; 'developmental' – opportunity to maximise resources available through childhood; and 'autonomy' – freedom to choose one's own lifestyle and enter social relations according to one's own inclinations uncontrolled by the authority of the adult world, whether parents or institutions. It encompasses a spectrum of possible interpretation, from a paternalistic emphasis on protection to a more liberal stance which places greatest value on child autonomy. Herring (2005)[7] has provided an evaluation of the various criticisms of the welfare principle and ultimately concludes that the principle is defensible. A similarly worded welfare principle is included in the new Adoption and Children Act 2002, also supported by a checklist.

The welfare checklist

Given the difficulty inherent in interpreting welfare and reaching decisions, which are made in the best interest of the child, the welfare checklist contained in s. 1(3) is a valuable aid to interpretation for the court. The checklist gives some clarification and direction as to the matters that a court should consider when applying the welfare principle. It has a less direct influence on social work practice, though preparation of any case for court which did not show an awareness of its features could be criticised. The Law Commission[8] envisaged the checklist providing greater consistency and clarity and promoting a more systematic approach to decision-making. The checklist is not exhaustive, and should be considered as including a minimum range of issues to be considered. In many cases other matters absent from the checklist will be relevant, and equally other elements of the checklist will not apply in every case. The checklist is not written in order of importance, though it may be symbolic that the child's wishes and feelings are positioned first on the list (*Re J* [1992] Fam Law 229). The checklist also provides a useful framework for the preparation of evidence. If circumstances arose where an element of the checklist was not considered, this would provide good grounds for appeal.

The court must have regard in particular to:

s. 1(3)

> (a) the ascertainable wishes and feelings of the child concerned (considered in the light of his age and understanding);
> (b) his physical, emotional and educational needs;
> (c) the likely effect on him of any change in his circumstances;
> (d) his age, sex, background and any characteristics of his which the court considers relevant;
> (e) any harm which he has suffered or is at risk of suffering;
> (f) how capable each of his parents, and any other person in relation to whom the court considers the question to be relevant, is of meeting his needs;
> (g) the range of powers available to the court under this Act in the proceedings in question.
>
> (CA 1989)

The checklist does not apply in all proceedings. It applies to all public proceedings under Part IV of the Act, care and supervision orders, whether or not they are contested. However, the checklist applies only to private proceedings, s. 8 applications, where contested. Other exceptions include: applications for secure accommodation orders; leave applications under s. 10 (*Re A and W (Minors) Residence Order: Leave to Apply*) [1992] 3 All ER 872); and emergency and short-term order applications under Part V of the Act.

Each of the factors in the checklist will now be considered in more detail.

s. 1(3)

> (a) the ascertainable wishes and feelings of the child concerned (considered in the light of his age and understanding);
>
> (CA 1989)

This factor may be interpreted as a clear statement of the importance of taking a child-centred approach. It is further explained in the *Children Act Guidance* (Vol. 1): 'the Act aims to strike a balance between rights of children to express their views on decisions made about their lives and rights of parents to exercise their responsibilities'.[9] Examination of children's rights may provide some justification as to why it is appropriate for the court to be aware of the child's wishes and feelings. A key question remains as to how the child's wishes and feelings are to be ascertained.

Usually, the wishes and feelings of the child are presented to the court via a report produced by a ***children and family reporter*** or ***children's guardian*** whose role is to represent the best interests of the child. The report will usually be based on a number of meetings over a period of time prior to the hearing.

It is possible for a judge to see a child privately in chambers and directly discuss the child's wishes. In *Re W (A Minor) (Residence Order: Baby)* [1992] 2 FLR 332, the judge talked to children aged 10 and 12 who wished to see him, an approach that was in line with s. 1(3). The judge, however, was not bound to adopt their wishes. This approach may be problematic, however, in terms of confidentiality. If the child says anything which influences the judge's decision, it will be necessary to inform the other parties in order that they can comment. In addition, it may be argued that such an approach could increase the stress experienced by a child when involved in court proceedings. Research in Scotland, where children and young people are more likely to participate directly in hearings, often by meeting with the judge in chambers, would suggest otherwise (Raitt, 2004).[10]

It is clear that welfare is not synonymous with the child's wishes and feelings. In *Re P (Minor: Wardship)* [1992] Fam Law 229, Butler-Sloss LJ emphasised that the court was not bound by the wishes of children, in this case brothers aged 13 and 11, and should depart from them when their future welfare so required. Welfare has to be a decision of the court, not a preference of the child. Nevertheless, all other things being equal, in *Re P (A Minor) (Education: Child's Views)* [1992] FCR 145, the wishes of a 14-year-old boy to attend school daily rather than to reside at boarding school tipped the balance when his parents were in dispute. The age and maturity of the child is relevant to the weight to be attached to the child's views. In *Re S (A Minor) (Change of Surname)* [1999] 1 FLR 672, two children applied to change their name following allegations that their father had sexually abused the older daughter. Initially, the court granted the application for the eldest child (aged 16) but refused for the younger. The Court of Appeal overruled that decision stating that, at 15, the younger daughter was also '*Gillick* competent' and weight should also be given to her wishes.

s. 1(3)

(b)   his physical, emotional and educational needs;

(CA 1989)

The court should adopt a broad interpretation of the child's various needs and not attach great weight to material considerations. In *Re W (A Minor) (Residence Order: Baby)* [1992] 2 FLR 332, the court held that there was no presumption of law that a child of any age should be with one parent or another. The relevant legal principle to apply is paramountcy of the child's welfare. However, the court noted that the 'natural position' if other things were equal would be for a mother normally to have care of a baby of under four weeks of age.

s. 1(3) ▷

(c) the likely effect on him of any change in circumstances;

(CA 1989)

This is sometimes referred to as the 'status quo' principle. In *Re B (Residence Order: Status Quo)* [1998] 1 FLR 368, the Court of Appeal took the view that a decision to give a residence order to the child's mother when the child was 8 years old, having been cared for by his father since the age of 2, was plainly wrong.

Delay is clearly relevant to this factor. It is crucial that the court does not allow delaying tactics by one party to strengthen their case, on the basis of the status quo principle, weakening the case of an 'absent' party seeking to care for a child.

s. 1(3) ▷

(d) his age, sex, background and any characteristics of his which the court considers relevant;

(CA 1989)

Cases decided prior to the Children Act 1989 are relevant to this factor: e.g. *C v C (Minors: Custody)* [1988] 2 FLR 291 supports the principle that sibling groups should be kept together wherever possible. Under s. 22(5)(c), local authorities are bound to give due consideration to a child's religious persuasion, racial origin, and cultural and linguistic background, when making decisions, particularly relating to a child's placement. The phrase 'any characteristics of his', and reference to background would presumably incorporate such issues but it is suggested that explicit reference would reflect and support anti-discriminatory practice. Research suggests that provision of information to the courts regarding diversity is inconsistent and in some instances there is insufficient regard to families' heritage (Brophy, 2003).[11]

s. 1(3) ▷

(e) any harm which he has suffered or is at risk of suffering;

(CA 1989)

Harm is defined under the Children Act 1989 to include ill treatment or impairment of health or development. Significant harm is the basis of the criteria for care or supervision orders. In private law proceedings, there may be some concerns about harm that the child has suffered or is at risk of suffering, which falls short of the threshold for care proceedings but may influence a decision on residence and contact. The Adoption and Children Act 2004 has amended the definition of 'harm' to include 'impairment suffered from seeing or hearing the ill-treatment of another'. Where the court has concerns about harm, which has not been investigated by the local authority, it may direct the local authority to carry out an investigation with a view to commencing care proceedings, under s. 37.

s. 1(3)

> (f) how capable each of his parents, and any other person in relation to whom the court considers the question to be relevant, is of meeting his needs;
>
> (CA 1989)

This factor invites the court to consider the suitability of relatives, or new partners of a couple who have separated. The sexuality of new partners has been the subject of court scrutiny, as has religious conviction. In *S v. S (Custody of Children)* [1980] 1 FLR 143, the court stated that being brought up in a lesbian household would not promote the child's welfare and could cause social embarrassment for the child in the community. Subsequent cases have demonstrated a more open-minded approach. In *Re B and G (Minors) (Custody)* [1985] 15 Fam Law 127, the Court of Appeal found that the religious beliefs of a parent who belonged to the Church of Scientology could be damaging to the child.

s. 1(3)

> (g) the range of powers available to the court under this Act in the proceedings in question.
>
> (CA 1989)

This factor reminds the court that it is not limited to granting or denying orders applied for by the parties (in family proceedings) and is sometimes referred to as the 'menu' principle. The court may make an order of its own volition if it considers that would be the best way to promote the child's welfare. An example might be where a local authority applies for a care order for a child with a plan that the child should reside with grandparents. It may be preferable to make a residence order to the grandparents and maintain local authority involvement through a supervision order. The court may also exercise its powers to seek further information, possibly by requiring a report under s. 7 of the 1989 Act.

Conflicting welfare claims

How is the issue of welfare determined when both the parent and the child are minors? According to *Birmingham City Council v. H* [1993] 1 FLR 883, the welfare of neither should necessarily be given priority. In that case the court was faced with an application concerning the baby of a 16-year-old girl who was in care, and the welfare of the baby, as the subject of the application to court, was paramount.

■ Avoidance of delay

s. 1(2)

> In any proceedings in which any question with respect to the upbringing of a child arises, the court shall have regard to the general principle that any delay in determining the question is likely to prejudice the welfare of the child.
>
> (CA 1989)

The Act makes it clear that delay in court proceedings is generally harmful to children, because of uncertainty and harm to relationships. A statutory presumption that delay is prejudicial and to be avoided is introduced. This presumption is reinforced by a number of provisions, which move the onus of controlling progress of cases to the court and away from the parties. Section 11 requires the court in s. 8 proceedings to draw up a timetable and give directions to ensure the timetable is followed. Directions hearings have been introduced and court rules require guardians to assist and advise on progress. Witness statements are disclosed before the hearings, there are restrictions on the number of experts, and concurrent jurisdiction allows transfers of cases. In public law proceedings the 'Protocol for Judicial Case Management' (2003) provides a timetable to be adhered to.

The presumption against delay is rebuttable. The onus would be on the party seeking delay to argue that it is positively beneficial to the child. In *C v. Solihull Metropolitan Borough Council* [1993] 1 FLR 290, the court suggested that any delay must be planned and purposeful. An obvious example of delay being acceptable would be where detailed assessment was required in order to reach an informed decision.

Delay should also be distinguished from duration, as it would be expected that straightforward cases could be dealt with more speedily than complex cases. Use of experts invariably increases the duration of a case but (unless this causes excessive delay) should be viewed as purposeful in ensuring that the court has the best information on which to reach its decision. Unfortunately, procedural issues can be a significant source of delay, including the time taken to transfer a case to a higher court. A study found that, on average, transferring a case from the family proceedings court to a care centre (county court) added a further three months to the case and cases transferred to the High Court suffered greater delays with a further four and a half months added to cases.[12]

■ Non-intervention

s. 1(5)

Where a court is considering whether or not to make one or more orders under this Act with respect to a child, it shall not make the order unless it considers that doing so would be better for the child than making no order at all.

(CA 1989)

In other words, there should be a positive benefit to the child in making the order. This provision applies in public and private proceedings (and has been introduced in a similar form into adoption law by the Adoption and Children Act 2002). It aims to discourage unnecessary court orders being made as part of a standard package, and to encourage parties to reach agreement and avoid matters being litigated. Once a case reaches court the principle should ensure that careful thought is given to whether or not an order should be made. In private proceedings, this principle is backed up by the concept of parental responsibility, which may help to equalise the position of the parties and 'lower the stakes' in disputes relating to children. The principle does not equate with a practice of keeping cases out of the court system unless absolutely unavoidable, though research suggests that in the early period following implementation of the Act there was evidence of such a misinterpretation in practice.[13] Application of the *'no order' principle* has also been evident in practice in the greater use of accommodation compared with the previous use of 'voluntary care'.[14]

Application of the section was considered in *Re G (Children) (Residence Order: No Order Principle)* [2005] EWCA Civ 1283. Following difficult negotiations, the unmarried parents of two daughters reached agreement that the mother would have residence and the father would have contact and parental responsibility. The judge interpreted s. 1(5) as providing a presumption against making orders and decided that, since the parents were no longer in dispute, no order was necessary. At the Court of Appeal this view was rejected. The court ruled that s. 1(5) does not create a presumption. Rather it calls for courts to ask the question: 'Will it be better for the child to make the order than making no order at all?' In this case it was better for the children to have an order. It was clearly important to the mother's security of mind and would promote settled arrangements in the future, after a long period of difficult negotiation. Making an order respected the parents' views that an order would be beneficial.

■ Litigation limit

The power to restrict applications being made, the *litigation limit*, is not one of the Part I principles but is included here as it is a provision that applies throughout the Children Act 1989.

s. 91(14) ▶

> A court may order that no application for an order under the Act of any speci-
> fied kind may be made with respect to the child concerned by any person named
> in the order without leave of the court.
>
> (CA 1989)

This provision is designed to deter litigious people who might otherwise continually
reapply for orders whenever time limits permit. For example, it is possible to apply
for revocation of a care order every six months. The section is used infrequently and
is appropriate in circumstances where its use will avoid anxiety and uncertainty for
the child, and avoid wasting court time. In *Re F (Contact: Restraint Order)* [1995]
1 FLR 956, CA the provision was described as a draconian sanction of last resort
principally appropriate when there is a real fear that children might become distressed or have their security disturbed through vexatious or ill-judged or obsessive
pursuit by a party to the litigation process.

Re P (A Minor) (Residence Order: Child's Welfare) [1999] 3 All ER 734 provides
an example of use of the section and sets out guidelines. The case concerned an
application by the child's natural parents to vary a residence order, which placed the
child with foster parents. The child was born into an orthodox Jewish family. At 17
months of age, when her parents were unable through illness to care for her, she was
placed with foster parents of Christian faith. She was born with Down's syndrome,
had a strong attachment to her foster parents and had thrived in their care. The
child's natural religious and cultural heritage was found by the court to be relevant
to her welfare but not a paramount consideration.

In judgment, Butler-Sloss LJ commented that there was no guidance as to the circumstances in which a s. 91(14) restriction might be imposed. It was noted that this
omission was intended to give the court a wide discretion and authorities cited suggested that it would be most likely to apply where the applicant had already made
repeated and unreasonable applications with little hope of success. The section was
not limited, however, to oppressive or semi-vexatious applications and could operate in circumstances where there was no criticism of the applicant's conduct but in
the best interests of the child it was necessary to prevent future applications. Adding
that in each case a balancing exercise between the welfare of the child and the right
of unrestricted access of the litigants to court would have to be carried out, a number of guidelines were suggested:

1. Section 91(14) should be read in conjunction with s. 1(1), which makes the
   welfare of the child the paramount consideration.
2. The court had to balance all the relevant circumstances in exercising its discretion to restrict applications.
3. An important consideration was that the restriction was a statutory intrusion
   into the right of a party to bring proceedings.
4. The power was to be used with great care and sparingly: the exception and not
   the rule.

5. Generally it was useful as a weapon of last resort in cases of repeated and unreasonable applications.

6. On clear evidence the restriction might be imposed in cases where the welfare of the child required it even though there was no past history of making unreasonable applications.

7. In such cases the court should be satisfied that the facts went beyond the need for time to settle into a new regime and animosity between the adults; and there was a serious risk that without the restriction the child or primary carers would be subject to unacceptable strain.

8. The restriction can be imposed in the absence of a request.

9. The restriction can be imposed with or without time limitations.

10. The degree of restriction should be proportionate to the harm it was intended to avoid.

11. It would be undesirable to make the order *ex parte* in all but the most exceptional cases.

■ Concurrent jurisdiction

The Children Act 1989 creates a *concurrent system of jurisdiction* for matters classified as family proceedings in s. 8(3). This falls short of the creation of a 'family court', which was argued for before the Act was introduced, but does effectively unify the system. In essence, each of the three courts (family proceedings court, county court and High Court) can deal with any of the matters identified as family proceedings (in s. 8(3) and (4))[15] and must apply the same law.

Cases may be transferred between the magistrates' family proceedings court, the county court and the High Court on the grounds of:

(a) exceptional complexity, importance or gravity;

(b) the need to consolidate with other proceedings;

(c) urgency.[16]

Case law has provided further guidance on this area. In *Essex County Council* v. *L* [1993] Fam Law 458 it was stated that a protracted hearing over several weeks on non-consecutive days was inimical to the best interests of the child. Cases likely to run for more than three days and cases containing conflicting medical evidence should be transferred from the magistrates' to the county court. Further, in *W* v. *Wakefield Council* [1995] 1 FLR 170, the court advised that all proceedings regarding the same children, public and private matters, should be consolidated and heard together. In fact, as noted above, transfer to a different court has in practice proved to be a significant cause of delay.

■ Children's rights

The United Nations Convention on the Rights of the Child was ratified by the United Kingdom in 1989. It states in Art. 12(1) that children capable of forming their own views should be assured of the right to express those views freely in all matters affecting them. International obligations are influential but the Convention is not actually part of UK domestic law and it is not possible to directly challenge the United Kingdom if rights in the Convention are not being upheld. To find legal recognition of the concept of children's rights it is therefore necessary to consider UK case law and legislation.

A starting point when considering the development of children's rights and their expression in the Children Act 1989 is the decision in *Gillick* v. *West Norfolk and Wisbech Area Health Authority* [1986] AC 112. The case established what has become known as the mature minor principle or '*Gillick* competency'. The case concerned whether it was lawful for a doctor to give advice and contraceptives to a person under the age of 16 without parental consent. The Family Law Reform Act 1969, s. 8(1) states that a person may give informed consent to medical treatment at 16. In *Gillick* the court ruled that if a person under the age of 16 is of sufficient understanding that person may give consent to treatment in the absence of parental consent and it is not necessary to notify the parent. Lord Scarman stated: 'a minor's capacity to make his or her own decisions depends on the minor having sufficient understanding and intelligence to make the decision and is not to be determined by reference to any judicially fixed age limit'. The case was heralded as a landmark decision that provided authority for young people who were '*Gillick* competent' to make lawful decisions in a range of areas. The courts, however, were more cautious and subsequent decisions appeared to limit application of the principle. This is particularly evident in cases concerning refusal of medical treatment. In *Re W (A Minor) (Wardship: Medical Treatment)* [1992] 4 All ER 627 the court overruled the refusal to consent to treatment of a 16-year-old girl suffering from anorexia nervosa. The court (exercising its inherent jurisdiction) decided that the welfare of the girl required that her wishes be overruled. The courts have demonstrated that they are prepared to overrule the wishes of '*Gillick* competent' minors and their parents in order to reach the decision which is in the child's best interest.

There is no specific provision in the Children Act 1989 that promotes 'children's rights' but a number of areas have clearly been influenced by this notion. In the first section, in applying the welfare principle the court is required to have regard to 'the ascertainable wishes and feelings of the child concerned (considered in the light of his age and understanding)' s. 1(3)(a). The court is not, however, bound to follow those wishes. As discussed above, there may be difficulties in ensuring the child's voice is heard by the court. In most public law proceedings a children's guardian will be appointed to represent the child's interests. If the child disagrees with the guardian's view and is of sufficient maturity, he may directly instruct a solicitor to represent him. The checklist does not apply to all proceedings, however, and in private proceedings where an agreed application for s. 8 orders is being made, it is possible for the voice of the child to be hidden behind parental agreement.

Section 22 confers a duty on the local authority to consult a looked after child (or a child the local authority proposes to look after) so far as is practicable, before making a decision with respect to the child. The local authority must give due consideration to the child's wishes and feelings having regard to his age and understanding. This duty is reinforced by the child's role in the review process.

Other examples may be drawn from the 1989 Act. A child of sufficient understanding may refuse a medical or psychiatric examination or other assessment ordered under a Child Assessment Order, Emergency Protection Order or Interim Care or Supervision Order. In each case an assessment of the child's ability to make an informed decision will be conducted. Even the provisions which at first sight appear to support children's rights may be questioned. For example, the child's right to apply for an s. 8 order in respect of himself is subject to the court giving prior leave, whereas a parent has an automatic right to apply. In contrast, a child of sufficient understanding may apply to vary or revoke a special guardianship order directly whereas others require leave to do so. In adoption cases, in contrast to the position in Scotland the new Adoption and Children Act 2002 did not introduce a requirement that the child in question should formally agree to the adoption.

The children's rights debate embraces a spectrum of views from those who advocate the child's absolute right to self-determination to those who argue that children have the right to protection and for decisions to be taken by adults in their best interests. Whatever stance is taken, ensuring rights are upheld in practice can be problematic. Some authorities employ a children's rights officer to ensure children in care are aware of their rights and to assist them in making complaints.

Information about the existence of rights must be made available in an accessible form if children are to be enabled to exercise their rights. Greater access to advocacy schemes may prove to be the most effective strategy. In addition, at national level, in order to promote children's rights and monitor Government policy and practice, the argument has been successfully made for the creation of a post of Children's Rights Commissioner in England.[17]

■ Children's Commissioner

In response to a recommendation of the Waterhouse Report[18] a Children's Commissioner for Wales has been appointed under Part V of the Care Standards Act 2000,[19] taking up office in March 2001. The Welsh Commissioner has powers of independent investigation, exercised in Clwych into allegations of child sexual abuse in schools.[20] Subsequently, following widespread support of the notion, Children's Commissioners have also been appointed in England, Scotland[21] and Northern Ireland,[22] though the terms of reference of each varies, particularly in the extent to which they can take on individual cases.[23]

The post of Children's Commissioner in England is established by the Children Act 2004.[24] Aspects of the Commissioner's role include promoting the views and interests of children, with particular reference to five outcomes from 'Every Child Matters': children's physical and mental health; protection from harm and neglect; education and training; making a positive contribution to society; and children's social and economic well-being. The general function of the Commissioner, set out in CA 2004, s.2(1) is 'the function of promoting awareness of the views and interests of children in England'. In particular, the Commissioner may:

S.2

(2). . . (a) encourage persons exercising functions or engaged in activities affecting children to take account of their views and interests;
    (b) advise the Secretary of State on the views and interests of children;
    (c) consider or research the operation of complaints procedures so far as relating to children;
    (d) consider or research any other matter relating to the interests of children;
    (e) publish a report on any matter considered or researched by him . . .

(3) The Commissioner is to be concerned in particular with the views and interests of children so far as relating to the following aspects of their well-being –
    (a) physical and mental health and emotional well-being;
    (b) protection from harm and neglect;
    (c) education, training and recreation;
    (d) the contribution made by children to society;
    (e) social and economic well-being.

(CA 2004)

The Commissioner must take reasonable steps to involve children in discharging his functions, and make sure children are aware of his functions and how to contact him. He is expected to report annually to the Secretary of State for Education and Skills on progress and proposed work towards achieving the five outcomes. It is intended that the Commissioner will mainly be concerned with broad issues affecting children, rather than investigating individual cases; however, it is possible for the Secretary of State to direct that such an inquiry take place. The focus for the Children's Commissioner in England is on representing children's views and interests in relation to the five aspects of well-being, which could be described as a rather paternalistic role rather than actively promoting children's rights. Reports to the Secretary of State will provide more information about the Commissioner's remit in due course.

The Children Act 2004

The Children Act 2004 received Royal Assent on 15 November 2004. Its introduction can be directly traced back to events surrounding the death of Victoria Climbié in February 2000. It was published as the Children Bill in March 2004 following the green paper, 'Every Child Matters' (September 2003).[25]

Implementation of the Act underpins the policy set out in 'Every Child Matters'. As a major piece of legislation that will shape child care law, practice and policy, the Act is discussed in this chapter. Its full effects are not expected to be felt for some years, as the delivery of fully integrated services as envisaged by the Act calls for what Lord Laming described as a 'fundamental change in the mind-set of managers'. To secure improvement in outcomes for children and young people a radical change in child care systems is proposed. The reforms presented by the 'Every Child Matters' agenda and the new legislation aim to improve multi-disciplinary working and integrated service delivery and increase accountability. The need for this was clearly identified By L. Laming: 'I am in no doubt that effective support for children and families cannot be achieved by a single agency acting alone. It depends on a number of agencies working well together. It is a multi-disciplinary task' (para 130).[26]

New duties are created that focus on children and young people's 'well-being' and 'welfare'. 'Well-being' is based on five outcomes. Effective safeguarding and promoting of children's welfare supports well-being. Specific aspects of the Act are also addressed as relevant in other chapters. The Act does not introduce a range of new child protection powers, rather it sets the foundations for good practice in the use of existing powers through a holistic integrated approach to child care.

■ Background to the Act

Victoria Climbié died, aged 8 on 25 February 2000. Her great-aunt Marie Therese Kouau and her partner Carl Manning were convicted of her murder in 2001. Victoria came to live with her great aunt, to be educated in England, in November 1998. While she lived with her great aunt in London, Victoria had contact with a range of child care agencies, specifically, four social services departments, two child protection teams of the Metropolitan police, three housing departments, two hospitals and an NSPCC family centre. She did not attend school. Following her death the Government established three statutory inquiries, chaired by Lord Laming, known as the Victoria Climbié Inquiry. The report was published in January 2003: 'The Report of the Victoria Climbié Inquiry (Cm 5730). The Laming report found Victoria had suffered extreme abuse and neglect. It is a disturbing but important report to read.

The report identified a number of failings: 'The extent of the failure to protect Victoria was lamentable. Tragically, it required nothing more than basic good practice being put into operation. This never happened.' (para 1.17). It continues:

Not one of the agencies empowered by Parliament to protect children in positions similar to Victoria's – funded from the public purse – emerge from this Inquiry with much credit. The suffering and death of Victoria was a gross failure of the system and was inexcusable. It is clear to me that the agencies with responsibility for Victoria gave a low priority to the task of protecting children. They were underfunded, inadequately staffed and poorly led. Even so, there was plenty of evidence to show that scarce resources were not being put to good use. Bad practice can be expensive. (para 1.18)

In relation to management:

> The greatest failure rests with the senior managers and members of the organizations concerned whose responsibility it was to ensure that the services they provided to children such as Victoria were properly financed, staffed and able to deliver good quality services to children and families. They must be accountable.

The legal framework was described as fundamentally sound, the gap being in its implementation:

> I recognise the fact that over the years, successive governments have refined both legislation and policy, no doubt informed in part by earlier Inquiries of this kind, so that in general, the legislative framework for protecting children is basically sound. I conclude that the gap is not a matter of law but in its implementation. (para 130)

The report made 108 recommendations covering a wide range of issues, some of which have been taken up in the Children Act 2004 and through the 'Every Child Matters' agenda. Some recommendations are of general application; others specifically refer to particular agencies, e.g. recommendations 64–90 relate to health services and 91–108 relate to the police.

The Laming report was followed later in 2003 by 'Keeping Children Safe – Government's response to the Victoria Climbié Inquiry Report' and the Joint Chief Inspectors Report, 'Safeguarding Children', published at the same time as the green paper, 'Every Child Matters'.

'Every Child Matters'

The five outcomes for children's services were introduced in 'Every Child Matters' (ECM):

- be healthy;
- stay safe;
- enjoy and achieve;
- make a positive contribution;
- achieve economic well-being.

In slightly different wording, the outcomes are included as areas for improving the well-being of children in s.10(2) of the Act (see below).

The 'Every Child Matters' agenda has produced an enormous amount of literature covering all aspects of safeguarding and well-being and specific to the variety of professional groups and settings which will be affected. The green paper was followed by 'Every Child Matters: Next Steps' (2004) DfES, a response to consultation, published alongside the Bill. It described the Bill as, 'the first step in a long term programme of change. It creates the legislative spine for developing more effective and accessible services focused around the needs of children, young people and their families' (para 2.2). In 2004, following the Act, 'Every Child Matters: Change for

Children' was published, which includes a timeline of when statutory requirements come into effect.

Alongside the Act, several important volumes of guidance have been issued including:

Children Act 2004 Guidance

- ■ *Inter-agency co-operation to improve wellbeing of children: children's trusts* – sets out the features of co-operation and a strategic framework within which all children's services in an area will operate.
- ■ *Duty to make arrangements to safeguard and promote the welfare of children* – sets out the key arrangements agencies should make to safeguard and promote the welfare of children.
- ■ *Children and Young People's Plan* – local authorities are required to work with partners to produce a strategic plan describing how they will achieve the five outcomes.
- ■ *The Role and Responsibilities of the Director of Children's Services and the Lead Member for Children* – Guidance on the governance, leadership and structures required within the new strategic framework.
- ■ *Working Together to Safeguard Children: a guide to interagency working to safeguard and promote the welfare of children* (2006), a revised volume which includes an important chapter on *Local Safeguarding Children Boards.*

In addition to this guidance, a National Service Framework for Children, Young People and Maternity Services has been published (DH, DfES London: DH Publications 2004). It sets out a ten-year strategy for improvement in children and young people's health and well-being. Within the strategy there is a national standard for safeguarding and promoting the welfare of children and young people.[27]

■ Organisational changes

The Act introduces key structural changes within the organisation of children's services. Local authorities will have a Director of Children's Services covering children's social services and education (s. 18) (in place of the current Director of Social Services and Chief Education Officer). A Director of Adult Services will also be appointed. The functions of the Director of Children's Services are set out in s. 18(2) and include: education functions; children's social services functions; functions towards young people leaving care; functions delegated by the NHS relating to children. A Lead Council Member for Children will be appointed to provide political leadership on children's issues.[28]

Children's services authorities are defined in s. 65 as local authorities with social services and education responsibilities, i.e. county councils, metropolitan district councils, unitary authorities and London Boroughs. Integrated services are to be provided through a **children's trust.** According to the Department for Education and Skills, 'Children's trusts have been created to address the fragmentation of responsibilities for children's services.' Children's trusts draw together services for children and young people in an area, underpinned by the Children Act 2004 duty to cooperate. The intention of Government is that local areas should enjoy a degree of flexibility as to how they develop a children's trust. Children's trusts are not directly provided for in the legislation, as this might limit that flexibility. Children's trusts will normally be led by the local authority and provide a basis for partnership between organisations. A three-year independent national evaluation of different models of childrens trusts is due to be published in 2007.

Local Safeguarding Children Boards will be established to replace the previous non-statutory Area Child Protection Committees, providing direct local accountability, (discussed further in Chapter 9). The Laming report noted: 'Area Child Protection Committees (ACPCs), the organisations with responsibility for co-ordinating child protection services at a local level, have generally become unwieldy, bureaucratic and with limited impact on front-line services.' (para 1.33).

By 2008 all local authorities are expected to have children's trust arrangements in place, have appointed a Director of Children's Services and have a designated Lead Member for Children's Services.

At Central Government, responsibility for children's services and policies has moved to the Department for Education and Skills (DfES). In June 2003 the Prime Minister announced the creation of a new post in that department, a Minister for Children, Young People and Families. The minister's portfolio within the DfES includes many areas which were previously dealt with by the Department of Health, including: looked after children; adoption and fostering; the Quality Protects programme; and teenage pregnancies initiatives. Other areas included in the DfES include: the Children and Young Peoples Unit; Connexions; the Children's Fund; and Sure Start. Within the DfES the two Directorates, the Schools Directorate and the Children, Young People and Families Directorate, are expected to work in a 'joined-up' fashion.

Cooperation to improve well-being

Section 10 introduces a requirement to cooperate for best outcomes for children. Agencies can pool funds to facilitate this. The object of the section is to secure cooperation and facilitate joint working across a wide range of organisations described as 'relevant partners' of the children's services authority and 'other bodies or persons considered appropriate', the latter probably including voluntary organisations and schools. The children's services authority is broader than its social services and education functions and extends to other departments such as housing, planning and leisure. The following are relevant partners: district council; police authority; probation board; youth offending team; Strategic Health Authority and Primary Care Trust; person providing services under s. 114 of the Learning and Skills Act 2000 and the Learning and Skills Council for England. This provision has been in force since October 2005.

S.10

> (1) Each children's services authority in England must make arrangements to promote cooperation between –
>   (a) the authority;
>   (b) each of the authority's relevant partners; and
>   (c) such other persons or bodies as the authority consider appropriate, being persons or bodies of any nature who exercise functions or are engaged in activities in relation to children in the authority's area.
> (3) In making arrangements under this section a children's services authority in England must have regard to the importance of parents and other persons caring for children in improving the well-being of children.
> (5) The relevant partners of a children's services authority in England must cooperate with the authority in the making of arrangements under this section.
>
> (CA 2004)

Well-being

The five outcomes set out in 'Every Child Matters' (Be healthy; Stay safe; Enjoy and achieve; Make a positive contribution; Achieve economic well-being) are translated in the Act as aspects of well-being.

S.10(2)

> The arrangements are to be made with a view to improving the well-being of children in the authority's area so far as relating to –
>   (a) physical and mental health and emotional well-being;
>   (b) protection from harm and neglect;
>   (c) education, training and recreation;
>   (d) the contribution made by them to society;
>   (e) social and economic well-being.
>
> (CA 2004)

Duty to promote welfare

Section 11 explains the duty to make arrangements to safeguard and promote welfare. It is imposed on a wide range of bodies listed in s.11(1) to include the following: a children's service authority; district council; Strategic Health Authority; Primary Care Trust; NHS Trust; NHS Foundation Trust; police authority; British Transport Police Authority; probation board; youth offending team; governor of prison or secure training centre; and any person providing services under s. 114 of the Learning and Skills Act 2000 (Connexions). The duty also applies to any privatised or contracted services. Inter-agency working is the focus of this section and much of the Act. Inter-agency working is not a new idea, but the Children Act 2004 strengthens the legal basis of the concept. Guidance on this issue has been in existence since the Children Act 1989 as 'Working Together to Safeguard Children' (DH, 1999 revised version) and reinforced more recently with 'Safeguarding Children: A Joint Chief Inspector's Report on Arrangements to Safeguard Children' (DH, 2002) and the 2006 version of 'Working Together'.

S.11(2)

> Each person and body to whom this section applies must make arrangements for ensuring that –
> (a) their functions are discharged having regard to the need to safeguard and promote the welfare of children;
>
> (CA 2004)

Section 11 does not introduce any new functions for agencies; it applies to how they carry out existing functions. It introduces a statutory requirement to carry out their existing functions in a way that takes into account the need to safeguard and promote the welfare of children.

The duty to safeguard and promote the welfare of children is broader than preventing child abuse or responding to children in need. It is defined in Guidance as:

> protecting children from maltreatment; preventing impairment of children's health or development; and ensuring that children are growing up in circumstances consistent with the provision of safe and effective care; . . . and undertaking that role so as to enable those children to have optimum life chances and to enter adulthood successfully.[29]

Children and young people's plans

A children's services authority may be required to prepare and publish a children and young people's plan setting out their strategy for how services for children and young people will be provided (s. 17). Guidance has been issued on children and young people's plans. Planning requirements may vary as between authorities which have been judged as 'excellent' and weaker authorities. With the introduction of this planning requirement, others will no longer be required, such as Early Years Development and Childcare Plans, Education Development Plan and Adoption Services Plans. The details of the plans' content is set out in regulations and covers: the period of the plan; publication arrangements; review and consultation requirements.

Other provisions

Many of the other provisions of the Act are dealt with in more detail in other sections of this book.

- The role of Children's Commissioner is established in England under Part 1 of the Act (discussed above under children's rights).

- Information databases may be required to be established and operated by children's services authorities or the Secretary of State (s. 12) containing basic information about children and young people to help professionals in working together to provide early support to children, young people and their families. Case details are specifically ruled out.

- Section 52 Duty of local authorities to promote educational achievement: s 22 of the Children Act 1989, the general duty to safeguard and promote the welfare of looked after children, is amended to include in particular a duty to promote the child's educational achievement (see Chapter 12).

- An integrated inspection framework for children's services will be created (ss. 20–24) to inform future inspections of all services for children. Provision is made for regular Joint Area Reviews to be carried out to look at how children's services as a whole operate across each Local Authority area.

Exhibit 7.2 outlines the structure of the Act and provides a summary of the provisions.

Part 1	Children's Commissioner
s. 1	Establishes post
s. 2	Function
ss. 3–4	Inquiries initiated and held by Commissioner
ss. 5–7	Functions of Commissioner in Wales, Scotland and Northern Ireland
s. 8	Annual report of Commissioner
s. 9	Remit extended to care leavers aged 18–21
Part 2	Children's Services in England
s. 10	Cooperation to improve well-being
s. 11	Arrangements to safeguard and promote welfare
s. 12	Information databases
	Local Safeguarding Children Boards
s. 13	Establishment of Local Safeguarding Children Boards
s. 14	Function and procedure of LSCBs
ss. 15–16	Funding of LSCBs and supplementary
	Local authority administration
s. 17	Children and young people's plans
s. 18	Director of Children's services
s. 19	Lead member for Children's Services
	Inspection of children's services
s. 20	Joint area reviews
ss. 21–23	Review framework, co-operation, delegation and interpretation
s. 24	Performance rating for children's social services
Part 3	Children's services in Wales
ss. 25–34	Similar provisions as in Part 2 for Wales

Continued overleaf

Exhibit 7.2 Summary of provisions

Part 4	CAFCASS functions in Wales
	Responsibility for the Cafcass transfers from DCS to the Welsh Assembly
Part 5 ss. 44–47	**Miscellaneous** Strengthens private fostering notification scheme including power to register and inspect
s. 48	Adds a schedule on childminding and daycare registration
s. 49	Payments to foster parents
s. 50	Power of Secretary of State to intervene in CSA functions
ss. 51–52	Inspection of LEAs and duty to promote educational achievement
s. 53	Duty to ascertain children's wishes and feelings added to CA 1989, ss. 17, 20 and 47
s. 54	Information on individual children to Secretary of State
ss. 55–56	Update of Social Services Committees and functions
s. 57	Fees payable to adoption review panel members
s. 58	Limits defence of reasonable punishment
s. 60	Court can make a parenting order where child fails to comply with child safety order, but not a care order
Part 6	**General** Repeals, interpretation, regulations, commencement etc.
Schedules Schedule 1	Children's Commissioner
Schedule 2	Director of children's services
Schedule 3	Advisory and support services (Wales)
Schedule 4	Child minding and daycare
Schedule 5	Repeals

Exhibit 7.2 (continued)

Local authority support for children in need

Local authorities must provide a range of services and facilities to children in need and their families under Part III of the Children Act 1989. Actual provision will depend partly on whether it is provided for under a duty or power and also on levels of resources which impact on the whole area of service provision.

The duty of the local authority towards children in need is contained in s. 17(1).

The 1989 Act's philosophy is that the best place for a child to be brought up is usually in the child's own family and the child in need can be helped most effectively if the local authority, working in partnership with the parents, provides a range and level of services appropriate to the child's needs.[30] For this reason, services may be made available to members of the child's family as well as the child in need (s. 17(3)). 'Family' is defined to include any person who has parental responsibility for the child and any other person with whom he has been living (s. 17(10)). It would thus include not only the child's carers but also other family members such as siblings.

s. 17(1)

It shall be the general duty of every local authority (in addition to the other duties imposed on them by this Part) –

(a) to safeguard and promote the welfare of children within their area who are in need; and

(b) so far as is consistent with that duty, to promote the upbringing of such children by their families, by providing a range and level of services appropriate to those children's needs.

(CA 1989)

There is a limited range of duties owed to all children living in a local authority area, and powers to provide services to all children and families and duties towards children defined as 'in need'. Certain of the duties that apply to all children may be interpreted as operating to prevent children becoming children in need, e.g. the duty to provide family centres (Sch. 2, para. 9).[31]

Section 17(10) defines a child in need:

s. 17(10)

(a) he is unlikely to achieve or maintain, or have the opportunity of achieving or maintaining, a reasonable standard of health or development without appropriate provision for him of services by a local authority under this Part;

(b) his health or development is likely to be significantly impaired, without the provision for him or her of services by a local authority under this Part; or

(c) he is disabled.

(CA 1989)

Section 17(11) includes relevant definitions.

s. 17(11)

'development' means physical, intellectual, emotional, social or behavioural development; and 'health' means physical or mental health.

(CA 1989)

∎ Interpretation of need

Under Sch. 2 to the 1989 Act, the responsibilities of local authorities are presented in qualified terms, such as the local authority shall take *reasonable* steps or shall make such provision as they *consider appropriate*. There is no absolute duty to meet the needs of every individual child. The assessment of need is therefore a crucial stage as the reality of service provision is based on a system of prioritisation. Each local authority sets its own priorities, linked to the range of services available. For example, authorities may identify different levels of provision: e.g. indirect provision, including advice and counselling, referral on and information; low-level direct provision which may include support groups, small-scale adaptations and irregular contact; and high-level direct provision including intensive family support, and provision of accommodation.

R v. *Lambeth LBC, ex parte K (A Child)* (2000) 3 CCLR 141 ruled on the conduct of assessments. Assessments must accord with Guidance issued under s. 7(1), such as 'The Children Act Guidance'. The intended procedure is that local authorities first assess the needs of the child and, where appropriate, the carers and other family members; second, produce a care plan; and third, provide the identified services.

'The Children Act 1989 Guidance' recognises the breadth of the s. 17 definition.

> The definition of need . . . is deliberately wide to reinforce the emphasis on preventive support to families. It has three categories: a reasonable standard of health or development; significant impairment of health or development; and disablement. It would not therefore be acceptable for an authority to exclude any of these three – for example, by confining services to children at risk of significant harm which attracts the duty to investigate under s. 47.[32]

In fact, early implementation of s. 17 was problematic; studies found that eligibility criteria were often linked to the concept of risk but otherwise there was great inconsistency in the way authorities interpreted 'in need'.[33] Both eligibility for services and service provision were something of a regional lottery.

Guidance on assessment was produced with a principal aim being to promote a greater level of consistency across the country in terms of the factors to be taken into account in an assessment, 'The Framework for the Assessment of Children in Need and their Families' (2000) – commonly referred to as the 'Lilac book'. The Framework stresses the need to have a full picture of the child's circumstances and to take a child-centred approach. It is based around principles that assessment should be rooted in child development; involve children and families; build on strengths as well as identifying difficulties; be a process and involve inter-agency working (amongst others). The Framework will be used in cases where an assessment of need leads to service provision; equally, whilst it is important that need is not interpreted in the same way as 'at risk', the assessment will also be used in child-protection investigations under s. 47. Exhibit 7.3. illustrates the range of factors to be included in an assessment.

Three general areas are assessed: the child's development needs; parenting capacity and family and environmental factors. Each of these areas is broken down further into specific categories to be addressed in the report.

Not all services will be provided directly by the local authority. The authority has the central role of coordinating service provision. Inter-agency cooperation in provision of services is as important as inter-agency cooperation in child-protection investigations. Section 27 of the 1989 Act imposes a duty on the local authority to consider whether public authorities providing education, health and related services can assist

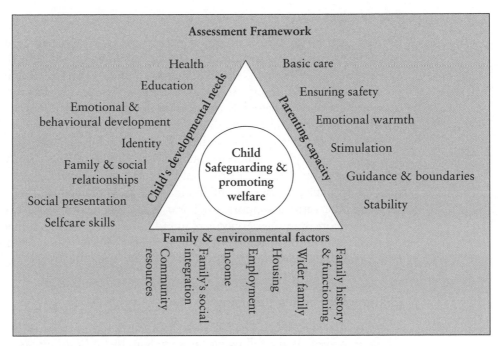

Exhibit 7.3 *The Framework for the Assessment of Children in Need and their Families*
Source: DH, DEE and Home Office (2000). HMSO, Crown Copyright.

in the exercise of its functions under Part III. If requested to help, an authority must provide assistance unless it is incompatible with its own duties. In addition there is significant scope for voluntary organisations and the private sector to provide services. The above discussion on 'well-being' extends the statutory basis of inter-agency cooperation.

A key element of the 'Every Child Matters' strategy is the introduction of the Common Assessment Framework (CAF), which supplements the Framework for Assessment. It provides a common approach to needs assessment that can be used by the whole children's workforce, it is common across services and may equally be completed by a health or social work or other professional. Effective use of CAF should lead to earlier holistic identification of children's needs and fewer assessments of individual children. The CAF consists of: a simple pre-assessment checklist to help practitioners identify children who would benefit from a common assessment; a process for undertaking a common assessment; and a standard form to help practitioners record, and, where appropriate, share with others, the findings from the assessment. Referral to specialist further assessment may be made following common assessment. In time electronic common assessment will be developed. CAF is being trialled in a number of authorities and should be in operation nationally by 2008.

An amendment by the Children Act 2004 requires local authorities to ascertain children's wishes and feelings regarding provision of services (including provision of accommodation) under s. 20), giving due consideration to them having regard to age and understanding, before determining what, if any, services to provide. This puts good practice on a statutory footing (s. 17(4A) CA 1989, inserted by s. 53 CA 2004).

The services

The services, which may be provided by the local authority, include giving assistance in kind or in cash. The specific services are contained in Sch. 2 to the Children Act 1989. Exhibit 7.4 contains duties towards children generally. Exhibit 7.5 contains those duties that are specific to children in need. Services in relation to disabled children are considered below. Services to children looked after by local authorities, which are provided for in Sch. 2, are discussed in Chapter 10.

As part of the 'Every Child Matters' strategy, each local authority has to prepare a 'service directory' for children, young persons and families. This should be a complete listing of services in the area, not just those provided by social services, including, for example, registered childminders, preschool facilities, teenage pregnancy services, bereavement support, toy libraries, mental health services, etc.

Where more than one service is required to meet a child's identified needs, a 'lead professional' will be allocated to act as a single point of contact and ensure coordinated service delivery.[34]

Challenging Service Provision

There is limited scope to challenge the local authority exercise of its duties towards children in need, as the following cases explain. In *Re J (Specific Issue Order: Leave to Apply)* [1995] 1 FLR 669, a 17-year-old boy was refused leave to seek a specific issue order that he was a child in need and required a local authority to provides services. The court held that the existence of Part III duties could not be the subject of judicial intervention other than through judicial review. However, in a subsequent case, *R v. Lambeth London Borough Council, ex parte A* [2001] EWCA Civ 1624,

---

Take reasonable steps, through provision of services, to prevent children suffering ill treatment or neglect (Sch. 2, para. 4)

The authority may assist a person to obtain alternative accommodation (assistance may be in cash) where a child who is living on premises is suffering or likely to suffer ill treatment at the hands of that person (Sch. 2, para. 5)

The local authority shall take reasonable steps:
- to reduce the need to bring proceedings for care or supervision orders
- to reduce the need to bring criminal proceedings against children
- to encourage children not to commit criminal offences
- to avoid the need for children to be placed in secure accommodation (Sch. 2, para. 7)

The local authority shall provide family centres, as it considers appropriate. A family centre is a centre at which the child, his parents or anyone with parental responsibility or caring for the child, may attend for occupational, social, cultural or recreational activities, advice, guidance or counselling (Sch. 2, para. 9)

Exhibit 7.4   Local authority duties to support children and families

Take reasonable steps to identify the extent of children in need (Sch. 2, para. 1(1)). Publish information about services provided by the local authority and others, including voluntary organisations, and take steps to ensure the information is received by those who might benefit from the services (Sch. 2, para. 1(2))

Where it appears a child is in need, the authority may assess his needs under the Children Act 1989 at the same time as an assessment under: the Chronically Sick and Disabled Persons Act 1970, the Education Act 1981, the Disabled Persons (Services, Consultation and Representation) Act 1986 (Sch. 2, para. 3)

Review provision of services and publish a plan (Sch. 2, para. 1A)

Where a child is living away from his family, take reasonable steps to enable him to live with them or promote contact (Sch. 2, para. 10)

The local authority shall provide, as it considers appropriate, for the following services to be available to children in need living with their families:

- advice, guidance and counselling
- occupational social control or recreational activities
- home help (including laundry facilities)
- travelling assistance to use a service
- assistance to the child and family to have a holiday (Sch. 2, para. 8)

In making arrangements for day care and to encourage people to act as local authority foster parents, the local authority shall have regard to the different racial groups to which children within the area, who are in need, belong (Sch. 2, para. 11)

The local authority shall provide day care for children in need in their area aged 5 or under and not at school, as is appropriate (s. 18)

Exhibit 7.5   Local authority services to children in need

the court ruled that the duty owed by a local authority under s. 17 of the Children Act 1989 was a target duty owed to children in general and was not justiciable by judicial review. The case concerned an application for judicial review of the local authority's failure to meet the housing need it had identified under the section. Two children were autistic with severe learning difficulties and the family were assessed as needing appropriate housing with a garden. The court described s. 17 as a duty to strive rather than to deliver and there was no requirement to perform particular tasks or to achieve particular results. Section 17 gives a local authority discretion rather than a duty to provide accommodation in any individual case. It was described as a hybrid provision, providing more than a power but less than a specific duty to, and enforceable by individuals. The case proceeded to the House of Lords as *R (G) v Barnet London Borough Council; R (W) v Lambeth London Borough Council; R (A) v Lambeth London Borough Council* [2003] UKHL 57. The Lords confirmed that s. 17 duties were correctly classified as duties of a general character not a specific duty owed to an individual child. Housing was the primary duty of the housing authority and not the primary purpose of s. 17. The authority providing accommodation to a child were not under a duty to provide accommodation for the family as a whole. Lord Nicholls and Lord Steyn gave dissenting judgments and noted with concern the potential impact on a child of separation from his family. In such circumstances it would be difficult for the authority to argue that its actions met the needs of the child.

An amendment to s. 17 introduced by the Adoption and Children Act 2002 clarifies that authorities have the *power* to provide accommodation to children in need and their families. Children provided with accommodation under s. 17 are not included in the definition of looked after children. Under s. 17 'Provision of services for children in need, their families and others', subsection (6) now reads:

s.17(6)

The services provided by a local authority in the exercise of its functions conferred on them by this section may include providing accommodation, giving assistance in kind, or in exceptional circumstances, in cash.

(CA 1989)

■ Children with disabilities

The term 'children with disabilities' will be used in this text rather than 'disabled children', in accordance with the philosophy of the Children Act 1989 that children with a disability are 'children first'[35] (and despite the fact that the Act refers to disabled children, e.g. Sch. 2, Part I, para. 6). It is also important to recognise that an argument exists in favour of using the term 'disabled children' as reflecting application of the social model of disability whereby children with disabilities experience social oppression and exclusion. A child may thus have a physical impairment but in fact is rendered disabled by a society that does not support the child to function to full potential because account is not taken of the impairment.

As seen above, a disabled child is clearly classified as a child in need for the purposes of the Children Act 1989, s. 17(10)(c). A disabled child is defined as a child who is:

S.17(11)

Blind, deaf or dumb or suffers from mental disorder of any kind, or is substantially and permanently handicapped by illness, injury or congenital or other disability as may be prescribed.

(CA 1989)

(Note that this is the same as the definition in the National Assistance Act 1948, s. 29 relating to adults, and that it utilises oppressive language.)

Services for disabled children are provided for by the Children Act 1989 by virtue of their status as a child in need. The 'Framework for Assessing Children in Need' (2000) provides the structure for assessment of need for services. In addition, however, there is a range of other legislation through which services can be accessed, such as the Chronically Sick and Disabled Persons Act 1970 (CSDPA 1970) and the Disability Discrimination Act 1995 (DDA 1995). Reference is made in Sch. 2, para. 3 to parallel assessments under the Children Act 1989 and other legislation.[36] It is important to be aware that there are differences between the various pieces of legislation as to whether there is a duty or a power to provide services. This was evident in the case of R v. *Bexley LBC, ex parte B* [2000] 3 CCLR 15. The court held that if a local authority is satisfied that a child needs a service which can be provided under the CSDPA 1970, s. 2, then the authority is under a duty to provide that service and cannot avoid a specific duty owed to a child with a disability by purporting to act under the more general provisions of the Children Act 1989. In addition to the legislation cited, assessment under the Carers (Recognition and Services) Act 1995, the Carers and Disabled Children Act 2000 and the Carers (Equal Opportunities) Act 2004 may be appropriate. Service provision is not the sole responsibility of Social Services and good levels of inter-agency cooperation with other agencies, specifically health and education, is central to effective provision of services. Some of the barriers to this objective include lack of agreement on definitions and priorities, and confusion about responsibilities for children with disabilities.

As a preliminary point, social services have a duty to provide advice, guidance and counselling services (CA 1989, Sch. 2, Part I, para. 8a). This may include advice on welfare benefits that disabled children and their families are entitled to, and referral to advocacy services so that an advocate may (amongst other things) assist the family in obtaining appropriate services.

A local authority can take resources of parents into account when deciding whether to provide services for disabled children. R *(Spink) v Wandsworth London Borough Council* [2005] EWCA Civ 302 concerned provisions under the Chronically Sick and Disabled Persons Act 1970, s. 2, which apply to disabled children as they do to disabled adults. The parents of two profoundly disabled boys were not eligible for a Disabled Facilities Grant to cover the adaptations required (these are means tested), which included a powered step lift and an adapted bathroom. The Court of Appeal found that the authority did not need to provide a service where it was reasonable to expect the parents, using their own resources, to meet those needs. It applied the three-stage approach to s. 2 set out in R v. *Gloucestershire County Council, ex parte Barry* [1997] 2 All ER 1, namely, there must be an assessment of need, the authority then considers whether it is necessary to meet those needs and, thirdly, if it decides it is necessary to meet those needs then services must be provided. At the second stage, the court ruled that when deciding whether it is necessary to provide a service, the authority can have regard to the parents' means.

Local authorities are required to 'provide services designed . . . to minimise the effect on disabled children . . . of their disabilities, and to give such children the opportunity to lead lives as normal as possible' (Sch. 2, Part I, para. 6). This provision is reinforced by the Quality Protects initiative, which includes an objective of increasing the use of services so that disabled children and their families can lead as ordinary lives as possible. The provision of services needs to be flexible in order to meet the variety of needs of disabled children and their families.

The local authority should maintain a register of disabled children (Sch. 2, Part I, para. 2). There is no duty to register; it is a voluntary process and service provision is not dependent on registration. Registration can help with service planning.

A significant proportion of looked after children are disabled. If a disabled child is looked after by the local authority, and provided with accommodation, s. 23(8) requires that the local authority must, as far as is reasonably practicable, ensure that the accommodation is not unsuitable for his particular needs. Care plans for disabled children should demonstrate that the proposed plan is the best way to meet the assessed needs of the particular child. In terms of education, the policy of the Department for Education and Skills is to promote the inclusion of disabled children in mainstream education and this should be reflected in the care plan.

Taken together, these responsibilities support work with children with disabilities in the context of the Children Act 1989, following the principle that children with disabilities are children first. In reality, because the law in this area is framed in terms of powers or qualified duties, children in need and their families, including children with disabilities, often experience limited support.

The impact of the Disability Discrimination Act 1995 is discussed in Chapter 6.

Chapter summary

- The Children Act 1989 introduced a number of themes including: parental responsibility; a new threshold for state intervention; concurrent jurisdiction; greater opportunities to hear the voice of the child; a preference for children to be brought up by their families with appropriate service input; and some new orders such as the specific issue and prohibited steps order.

- The central principles of the Act are mainly contained in Part I and include the principle that the child's welfare shall be the court's paramount consideration. This principle is supported by a welfare checklist, which guides the court as to a range of factors to be taken into account.

- There is a presumption that delay is prejudicial and to be avoided unless it can be shown to be planned and purposeful (CA 1989, s. 1(2)).

- Courts should not make orders unless there is a positive benefit in doing so, the principle of non-intervention (CA 1989, s. 1(5)).

- It is possible to impose a restriction that no application for an order in respect of a child can be made by a named person without leave of the court (CA 1989, s. 91(14)).

- The Children Act 1989 creates a system of concurrent jurisdiction operating for family proceedings in the magistrates' family proceedings court, the county court and the High Court.
- The Children Act 2004 was introduced following the Victoria Climbié Inquiry and provides statutory underpinning for the 'Every Child Matters: Change for Children' programme.
- There are new duties on local authorities and other relevant agencies to cooperate to improve children's well-being, and to make arrangements to safeguard and promote welfare.
- Children's Services Authorities are being established headed by a Director of Children's Services and including education as well as social services functions for children.
- Local authorities must provide a range of services and facilities to children and their families. In addition to general duties owed to all children, a number of services are designed for children in need, defined by CA 1989, s. 17 and including disabled children.

Exercises

Consider whether in any of the following cases there is a child in need. If so what, if any, support and services might be provided.

- Teachers at a primary school are concerned about Julie Anne, a 6-year-old child who has recently moved to the area. She often arrives at school dirty and dishevelled and hungry. She did not attend school at her previous address and cannot write, but she is a bright child who enjoys school.
- Lorna, aged 8, has asthma. She lives with her mum who has a mild learning disability. The local surgery have written to Lorna's mum three times asking her to bring Lorna in to their asthma clinic for a check-up but she has failed to do so.
- Althea's husband Jason died in an industrial accident. Following Jason's death, Althea moved with her daughter Janine, aged 3, to live with her elderly mother who has severe arthritis. Althea spends a lot of her time caring for her mother, who has consistently refused to consider getting any help from social services or any other body. Janine is very withdrawn and spends most of her time watching children's videos. Althea knows very few people in the area and is becoming increasingly depressed.
- Jonathan has Down's Syndrome. His parents both work full-time and they enjoy a good standard of living. Jonathan has a full-time nanny who cares for him during the day and takes him to a private preschool. The nursery teacher has expressed some concerns that Jonathon can be quite aggressive with other children.

■ Susan and Peter have three children, twin boys aged 9 and a daughter, Simone, who is 7 and has a learning disability. The boys have been selected to play for a football academy 40 miles away, on Thursday evenings when Peter is at work. After a couple of sessions, Susan decides she cannot manage the journey with all three children and the boys told her that some of the other footballers were laughing at Simone. Peter has been unable to change his work shift and, as a keen footballer himself, wants the boys to continue. They have no relatives close by and have never felt able to leave Simone with a babysitter. Susan overheard one of the twins saying that Simone spoils everything for them. The tension about this issue is causing arguments between Susan and Peter.

Websites

United Nations Convention on the Rights of the Child:
  www.unicef.org/crc/

The Children's Legal Centre produces a range of useful guides with an emphasis on children's rights:
  www2.essex.ac.uk

The Advisory Centre for Education (ACE) provides independent and confidential advice on all aspects of the education service:
  www.ace-ed.org.uk

Information about the Government agency, Connexions, can be found at:
  www.connexions.gov.uk

The organisation provides help and guidance for young people between 13 and 19 relating to health, housing, relationships, money, career and learning options.

Further reading

For this chapter and the following chapters relating to children and families it will be useful to refer to a number of specialist textbooks and key documents:

Bainham, A. (2005) *Children – The Modern Law* (3rd edn). Bristol: Family Law, Jordan Publishing.

Department of Health (2001) *The Children Act Now: Messages from Research*. London: The Stationery Office.

White, R., Carr, P. and Lowe, N. (2002) *The Children Act in Practice* (3rd edn). London: Butterworths.

Cretney, S., Masson, J. and Bailey-Harris, R. (2002) *Principles of Family Law* (7th edn). London: Sweet & Maxwell.

Allen, N. (2005) *Making Sense of the Children Act 1989: And Related Legislation for the Social and Welfare Services*. London: John Wiley and Sons Ltd.

In relation to children's rights see:

Fortin, J. (2003) *Children's Rights and the Developing Law* (2nd edn). Cambridge: Cambridge University Press.

Franklin, B. (ed.) (1995) *The Handbook of Children's Rights, Comparative Policy and Practice*. London: Routledge.

Freeman, M. (2000) 'The future of children's rights' 14(4) *Children and Society* pp. 277–93.

Sawyer, C. (1999) 'International developments: one step forward, two steps back, the European Convention on the Exercise of Children's Rights' 11(2) *Child and Family Law Quarterly* pp. 151–70.

Aspects of welfare are debated in:

Herring, J. (2005) 'Farewell Welfare?' 27(2) *Journal of Social Welfare and Family Law* p. 159.

James, A., James, A. and McNamee, S. (2003) 'Constructing children's welfare in family proceedings' *Family Law* p. 889. (Discusses the ways in which children's guardians and children and family reporters incorporate the principle of ascertaining the child's wishes and feelings, into their working practices.)

Read, J., Clements, L. and Ruebain, D. (2006) *Disabled Children and the Law: Research and Good Practice* (2nd edn). London: Jessica Kingsley Publishers. (A specialist text covering children with disabilities.)

Murphy, J. (2003) 'Children in need: the limits of local authority accountability' 23 *Legal Studies* p. 103.

Notes

1 *Re M (Leave to Remove Child from Jurisdiction)* [1999] 2 FLR 334 at 340.

2 L. Fox Harding (1997) *Perspectives in Child Care Policy* (3rd edn). London: Longman.

3 M. Freeman (1998) 'The next Children's Act?' 28 *Family Law* pp. 341–8. He suggests that any new legislation should be entitled the Children's Act rather than the Children Act, the latter title positioning the child as object rather than subject. The welfare principle should be extended to all decisions taken in court and beyond the courtroom to tribunals dealing with education issues and cases where one parent is trying to oust the other from the family home. 'The next Act should contain an interpretational presumption that, unless specifically excluded, all court and tribunal decisions relating to children should be governed by the paramountcy principle' (p. 343). He advocates following Scots legislation, which states that a child of 12 years of age or more shall be presumed to be of sufficient age and maturity to form a view and participate in decision-making. Again following the Scottish model, a list of parental responsibility should be specified in legislation. Corporal chastisement should be made unlawful and the defences providing for reasonable chastisement removed. Finally, new institutional structures are required, including a statutory duty to appoint children's rights officers, a network of Children's Legal Centres and a Children's Ombudsperson.

4   The welfare of the child is the paramount consideration in decisions taken by the court. In other circumstances a different position may apply: notably, under s. 17(4) the local authority must safeguard and promote the welfare of a child in need.

5   A. Bainham (1998) *Children – The Modern Law* (2nd edn). Bristol: Family Law, Jordan Publishing.

6   J. Eekelaar (1986) 'The emergence of children's rights' 6(2) *Oxford Journal of Legal Studies* p. 161.

7   J. Herring (2005) *Family Law* (2nd edn). Harlow: Longman Law Series.

8   Law Commission Report No. 172 'Review of Child Law: Guardianship and Custody' (1988).

9   Department of Health (1991) 'The Children Act 1989 Guidance and Regulations', vol. 1. London: HMSO.

10 Raitt, F.E. (2004) 'Judicial discretion and methods of ascertaining the views of a child' 16(2) *Child and Family Law Quarterly* p. 151.

11 J. Brophy (2003) 'Diversity and child protection', *Family Law*, pp. 674–8.

12 J. Brophy, P. Bates, L. Brown, S. Cohen, P. Radcliffe and C.J. Wale (2001) 'Expert evidence in child protection litigation: where do we go from here?' in Department of Health *The Children Act Now: Messages from Research*. London: The Stationery Office.

13 J. Hunt, A. Macleod and C. Thomas (2001) 'The last resort: child protection, the courts and the 1989 Children Act' in Department of Health *The Children Act Now: Messages from Research*. London: The Stationery Office.

14 J. Packman and C. Hall (2001) 'From care to accommodation: support, protection and control in child care services' in Department of Health *The Children Act Now: Messages from Research*. London: The Stationery Office.

15 Namely: under the inherent jurisdiction of the High Court; Children Act 1989, Pts I, II and IV; Matrimonial Causes Act 1973; Adoption Act 1976; Domestic Proceedings and Magistrates' Courts Act 1978; Matrimonial and Family Proceedings Act 1984, Pt III; Family Law Act 1996; Crime and Disorder Act 1998.

16 Children (Allocation of Proceedings) Order 1991 (SI 1991/1677).

17 See M. Rosenbaum and P. Newell (1991) *Taking Children Seriously: A Proposal for a Children's Rights Commissioner*. London: Calouste Gulbenkian Foundation.

18 R. Waterhouse (2000) 'Lost in care – Report of the Tribunal of Inquiry into the Abuse of Children in Care in the Former County Council Areas of Gwynedd and Clwyd since 1974, HC 201. London: The Stationery Office.

19 As amended by the Children's Commissioner for Wales Act 2001. See further discussion in K. Hollingsworth and G. Douglas (2002) 'Creating a children's champion for Wales? The Care Standards Act 2000 (Part V) and the Children's Commissioner for Wales Act 2001' 65(1) *Modern Law Review* pp. 58–78.

20 Children's Commissioner for Wales (2004) Clywch: Report of the Examination of the Children's Commissioner for Wales into allegations of child sexual/abuse in a school setting.

21 Commissioner for Children and Young People (Scotland) Act 2003.

22 Commissioner for Children and Young People (Northern Ireland) Order 2003 (SI 2003/439 (NI 11)).

23 See detailed discussion of the respective roles in J. Williams (2005) 'Effective government structures for children?: The UK's four Children's Commissioners' 17 *Child and Family Law Quarterly* p. 137

24 Previous attempts to introduce the role in Bills in 1999 and 2000 were unsuccessful.

25 (Cm. 5860) (Chief Secretary for the Treasury).

26 Secretary of State for Health, Home Secretary (2003) The Victoria Climbié Inquiry: Report of an Inquiry by Lord Laming. Cm 5730. Norwich: The Stationery Office. Also available at www.everychildmatters.gov.uk/publications.

27 See also: White Paper 'Choosing Health: making health choices easier (Cm 6374) – addresses how Primary Care Trusts can be involved in the new Children and Young peoples plans and integration of health services through Childrens Trust model.

28 See *The Role and Responsibilities of the Director of Children's Services and the Lead Member for Children.* London: DfES.

29 Statutory guidance on making arrangements to safeguard and promote the welfare of children under section 11 of the Children Act 2004, para. 2.8.

30 See further Department of Health (1991) 'The Children Act 1989 Guidance and Regulations', vol. 2 'Family support, day care and educational provision for young children'. London: HMSO.

31 See discussion in A. Bainham (1998) *Children: The Modern Law* (2nd edn). Bristol: Family Law, Jordan Publishing.

32 Department of Health (1991) 'The Children Act 1989 Guidance and Regulations', vol. 2 'Family support, day care and educational provision for young children' (para. 2.4). London: HMSO.

33 See Department of Health (2001) *The Children Act Now: Messages from Research.* London: The Stationery Office (in particular studies 1, 8 and 23).

34 See www.ecm.gov.uk/leadprofessional for more information.

35 Department of Health (1991) 'The Children Act 1989 Guidance and Regulations', vol. 6 'Children with disabilities'. London: HMSO.

36 Chronically Sick and Disabled Persons Act 1970; Education Act 1981; Disabled Persons (Services, Consultation and Representation) Act 1986; or any other enactment.

8 Children and family breakdown

Learning Objectives

To develop provide an understanding of the following:

- The meaning of parental responsibility.
- Private law provisions which regulate the exercise of parental responsibility.
- Residence and contact.
- Representation of children in private law disputes.
- Domestic violence.
- Divorce and relationship breakdown.
- Civil partnership.

Introduction

The focus of this chapter is children and family breakdown. Whilst social workers have major responsibilities in child protection, where the local authority may intervene in the private life of a family, it is also necessary to have an awareness of the law which operates to regulate aspects of private family life. Consideration of the orders that formalise arrangements made for children following divorce or separation of their parents, and the role of law in domestic violence, are included in this chapter. Failure to hear the child's voice in private disputes is a criticism often directed at the English legal system and the chapter therefore considers the circumstances when independent representation of children is permitted in private law cases.

The legal status of adult relationships, marriage, divorce, cohabitation, civil partnership and dissolution is examined, as is the relationship of adults to children with a focus on parental responsibility. The family is an ever changing concept[1] and whilst much family law is embedded in traditional concepts of the married, nuclear family, recently legal recognition has been given to broader notions of family life including same-sex partnerships in the Civil Partnership Act 2004 and adoption by unmarried couples (discussed in Chapter 11). It is an area where the balance between respecting privacy and protecting the interests of members of the family is a constant challenge and the rights enshrined in ECHR, Art. 8, the right to respect for private and family life, and Art. 12, the right to marry and found a family, are keenly debated.

Parental responsibility

Parental responsibility is a central tenet running through the Children Act 1989. It is defined as:

s. 3(1)

> All the rights, duties, powers, responsibilities and authority which by law a parent of a child has in relation to the child and his property.
>
> (CA 1989)

In terms of the philosophical position of the Children Act 1989, the Law Commission considered that the law failed to recognise parenthood in terms of responsibility and concentrated on parental rights. This position had become out-dated and misleading, particularly in view of the *Gillick* case, which builds on the previous case law[2] and makes it clear that any rights and powers of parents exist only for the benefit of the child and dwindle as the child reaches maturity. Whilst it may be argued that changing the wording away from rights to responsibility is largely symbolic, it was hoped that this would begin to reflect the everyday reality of being a parent.

The concept of parental responsibility is easier to understand in relation to a range of issues over which decisions about a child may be made, i.e. the exercise of parental responsibility. Parental responsibility covers: determination of the child's religion and education; choosing the child's name; appointing a guardian for the child; consenting to the child's medical treatment and adoption; representing the child in legal proceedings; lawfully correcting the child; protecting and maintaining the child; and having physical possession of the child.

In contrast to this position, the Children (Scotland) Act 1995 helpfully provides a list of parental responsibilities in s. 1(1): to safeguard and promote health, development and welfare; to provide direction and guidance in a manner appropriate to the stage of development of the child; to maintain personal relations and direct contact with the child on a regular basis, if the child is not living with the parent; and to act as the child's legal representative.

■ Who has parental responsibility?

If married, both parents of a child will have parental responsibility (s. 2(1), (3)). If the parents are not married, only the mother will have automatic parental responsibility and the father is classed as a parent without parental responsibility (and may also be referred to as the unmarried father). This position has changed somewhat under the Adoption and Children Act 2002. Under s. 111, which amends s. 4 of the Children Act 1989, where parents are not married but jointly register the birth of a child[3] and the father's name appears on the birth certificate, then the father will also have parental responsibility.[4] This provision came into force in December 2003 and applies to all registrations since that date. It is not retrospective. If an 'unmarried father' does not jointly register the birth, it would still be possible to use the existing Children Act options, i.e. parental responsibility order or agreement. This amendment was introduced because few unmarried fathers appear to have been aware of their status as a parent without parental responsibility or how to obtain it.

It is possible for a father without parental responsibility to take steps to acquire parental responsibility in two ways. The first is by way of a **recorded agreement** with the mother in the prescribed form (a parental responsibility agreement (s. 4(1)(b)). A degree of formality reflects the significance of the agreement. In *Re X (Parental Responsibility: Children in Care)* [2000] 2 All ER 66 the fact that children were subject to interim care orders did not prevent their mother from entering into a parental responsibility agreement with their unmarried father.

The second way to acquire parental responsibility is by *application to the court* (s. 4(1)(a)). An application is most likely to occur where there is a level of disagreement between the parents, often following separation. In *Re H (Minors) (Local Authority: Parental Rights) (No. 3)* [1991] Fam 151 the court established a three-point test to be applied in parental responsibility applications. The courts should consider: the degree of commitment shown by the father to the child; the degree of attachment between father and child; and the reasons for applying for the order.

In *Re S (A Minor) (Parental Responsibility)* [1995] 2 FLR 648, the Court of Appeal indicated that, where possible, an order should be made to a 'committed' father, but noting that any interference with the child's welfare could be addressed by use of s. 8 orders. *Re C and V (Contact: Parental Responsibility)* [1998] 1 FLR 392 stressed the importance for a child's self-esteem of having a positive image of the absent father, when determining applications for parental responsibility. In *Re P (Minors) (Parental Responsibility: Change of Name)* [1997] 2 FLR 722, however, a father who was serving a long prison sentence for robbery was unsuccessful in his application for a parental responsibility order. The court recognised that, realistically, he would be unable to exercise parental responsibility.

The Adoption and Children Act 2002 introduces new ways for step parents to acquire parental responsibility (s. 112, introducing a new s. 4A into the Children Act

1989). In a similar way to unmarried fathers the court may give parental responsibility by order or the step-parent may acquire parental responsibility by agreement with the other parent (who does not lose parental responsibility), e.g. a step-father would need the agreement of the birth father, unless he was not married to the child's mother and had not acquired parental responsibility. Agreement of both parents of the child is required where they were married and where the unmarried father had acquired parental responsibility, but not of the unmarried father without parental responsibility. In the absence of agreement the section also allows for the court to make a parental responsibility order. The other parent does not lose parental responsibility. This option is not available to an unmarried step-parent.

Parental responsibility may also be acquired by the holder of a residence order (s. 12), a person who is appointed as the child's guardian (s. 5), and a local authority with a care order in respect of a child (s. 33(3)). When a child is adopted, the adoptive parents acquire parental responsibility, and the birth parents lose their parental responsibility.

More than one person may share parental responsibility and it is not lost by virtue of another acquiring it (except in adoption). Where more than one person has parental responsibility, each may act alone and without the others in meeting that responsibility (s. 2(7)). This is consistent with the aim of encouraging both parents to feel responsible for their children. Practically, as there is no duty to consult the absent parent, the responsibility may prove to be symbolic only. If a care order or placement order is in force, the local authority has parental responsibility for the child and may determine the extent to which a parent may meet his parental responsibility for the child (s. 33(3)). There are some important limitations on the local authority's exercise of parental responsibility. It cannot change the child's name or religion, appoint a guardian or consent to an adoption order (s. 33(6)).

Margaret Thatcher once famously stated that 'parenthood is for life'. Parental responsibility for parents ends only on the death or adoption of the child or when the child reaches 18.[5] Parental responsibility gained by others, e.g. the local authority, may be brought to an end by a court order. Parental responsibility may not be surrendered or transferred but it can be delegated. There are numerous circumstances when a child will be in the care of someone aged 16 or over who does not have parental responsibility for that child. An obvious example is the child's teacher, who is often described as being *in loco parentis,* or a foster carer. Statutory authority for this position is provided by s. 3(5), which states that:

s. 3(5)

A person who –
(a) does not have parental responsibility for a particular child; but
(b) has care of the child,
may do what is reasonable in all the circumstances of the case for the purpose of safeguarding or promoting the child's welfare.

(CA 1989)

This would include obtaining urgent medical attention and arranging food for the child. If a child is placed with foster carers, an 'unmarried father' without parental responsibility would have no legal right to remove the child and the foster carers could rely on the *in loco parentis* provision to retain the child.

Other legislation may impact on the aspects of parental responsibility that may be delegated. A useful example is the issue of lawful chastisement. Corporal punishment was banned in state schools under the Education Act 1996. Foster carers may not resort to physical punishment[6] but in a controversial decision it was held that childminders may do so. In the case of *Sutton London Borough Council* v. *Davis* [1995] 1 All ER 53, the judge stated that a parent had a right to chastise his or her child to a reasonable extent and a parent could delegate this right to another person. This position has altered under Children Act 2004, which removes most defences that could formerly be relied on to justify reasonable chastisement or punishment. Section 58(2) states that: 'Battery of a child causing actual bodily harm to the child cannot be justified in any civil proceedings on the ground that it constituted reasonable punishment.'

The ability to exercise parental responsibility may be limited in reality. If a child is in care, the local authority can determine the extent to which parents exercise their parental responsibility. Even where a looked after child is provided with accommodation, though parental responsibility is not acquired by the local authority, the extent to which a non-resident parent can exercise parental responsibility is limited by practical circumstances. The same position applies to a parent with parental responsibility who is not living with the child. As more than one person, who may not be in a position to take all decisions jointly, may hold parental responsibility, it is exercisable severally so long as it is not inconsistent with any court orders.

Parental responsibility may be obtained by the grant of a residence order. This order, discussed below, settles with whom the child is to reside and confers parental responsibility on that person. Where the residence order is granted to a parent without parental responsibility, parental responsibility is acquired and is retained up to the child's sixteenth birthday even if the residence order is revoked. In all other cases, e.g. if a residence order was granted to a grandparent, parental responsibility is retained for the duration of the order.

Under an Emergency Protection Order, parental responsibility is conferred upon the local authority but limited to 'such action in meeting his responsibility for the child as is reasonably required to safeguard or promote the welfare of the child' during the order. The court must separately provide for important issues such as examination of the child and contact. See Chapter 9 for full discussion.

Where there is a dispute between persons holding parental responsibility, it may become necessary to resolve it by recourse to a Prohibited Steps Order or a Specific Issue Order.

Finally, parental responsibility may be acquired by a guardian, a person appointed by a parent to be the child's guardian in the event of the parent's death

Mother	■ CA 1989, s. 2(2)(a)
Mother and Father, if married	■ CA 1989, s. 2(1)
Father	■ Parental responsibility order (CA 1989, s. 4(2)(a))
	■ Parental responsibility agreement (CA 1989, s. 4(2)(b))
	■ Under a residence order
	■ Where the parents jointly register the birth: (ACA 2002, s. 111)
Step-parent	■ Adoption and Children Act 2002, s. 112
	■ Agreement or court order
Civil partner	■ Civil Partnership Act 2004, s. 75(2)
Relative/Other	■ For the duration of the residence order (CA 1989, s. 12(2))
Special Guardian	■ CA 1989, s. 14C(1)(a)
Guardian	■ CA 1989, s. 5(6)
Local Authority	■ Care order (CA 1989, s. 33(3)(a))[†]
	■ EPO§ (CA 1989, s. 44(4)(c))*
Prospective Adoptive Parents with whom child is placed	■ Placement order or placement with parental consent, ACA 2002, s. 25

Exhibit 8.1   Who has parental responsibility?

Notes: [†]Parental responsibility limited: LA cannot change the child's religion, consent/refuse adoption, appoint a guardian, change name, remove from the UK.

§ Emergency Protection Order.

*Shall only take such action in meeting his parental responsibility for the child as is reasonably required to safeguard or promote the welfare of the child (having regard in particular to the duration of the order).

(s. 5(3)). Exhibit 8.1 summarises the various ways in which parental responsibility can be acquired.

Private law orders – s. 8

Section 8 orders are new orders introduced by the Children Act 1989. Roughly speaking the orders of residence and contact replaced custody and access, and the new orders of specific issue and prohibited steps are drawn from wardship. The new orders are not simply changes in terminology; there are conceptual changes and a clear link to parental responsibility. Section 8 orders are used to control the exercise of parental responsibility and have provided a wider range of options to the courts in both public and private proceedings. The orders concentrate on practical questions relating to children's lives – where they live, who they have contact with, etc. – and, in the context of parental responsibility and the 'no order' principle, are less reliant on proprietorial connotations of ownership. The expression 'section 8 orders' includes any order varying or discharging an order (s. 8(2)). Conditions may be attached to the orders under s. 11(7).

The orders

s. 8(1)

'a contact order' means an order requiring the person with whom a child lives, or is to live, to allow the child to visit or stay with the person named in the order, or for that person and the child otherwise to have contact with each other;

'a prohibited steps order' means an order that no step which could be taken by a parent in meeting his parental responsibility for a child, and which is of a kind specified in the order, shall be taken by any person without the consent of the court;

'a residence order' means an order settling the arrangements to be made as to the person with whom a child is to live;

'a specific issue order' means an order giving directions for the purpose of determining a specific question which has arisen, or which may arise, in connection with any aspect of parental responsibility for a child.

(CA 1989)

■ Residence

Residence orders determine where a child is to live. Sir Stephen Brown stated in an early decision: 'it must be remembered that a residence order under the Children Act 1989 is not an order which connotes possession or which in any sense excludes the other parent. It is an order of the court which regulates where children live during a particular period.'[7]

Residence orders incorporate an element of flexibility that was absent under the previous framework for custody orders. This flexibility is most apparent in *shared residence arrangements,* which are legally provided for:

s. 11(4)

Where a residence order is made in favour of two or more persons who do not themselves all live together, the order may specify the periods during which the child is to live in the different households concerned.

(CA 1989)

The aim of this provision is to reflect the reality that children often do effectively live with both parents in a way that is not reflected by a residence order to one parent and a contact order to the other. This section overrules an earlier decision in *Riley* v. *Riley* [1986] 2 FLR 429, in which May LJ stated, in relation to an arrangement where a child spent alternate weeks with each parent: 'In my judgment to keep a child going backwards and forwards each week between Mother and Father with no single, settled home is prima facie wrong.' *Re A (A Minor) (Shared*

Residence Orders) [1994] 1 FLR 669 confirmed that the decision in *Riley* could not stand, given the new statutory framework, and that whilst joint residence orders need not be confined to exceptional cases there would need to be some positive benefit to the child in making the order. A shared residence order should not be made simply as a means of investing parental responsibility in the father (*Re WB (Minors: Residence)* [1993] Fam Law 395). A recent Court of Appeal decision provides guidance on the use of shared residence orders: in *Re D (Children) (Shared Residence Orders)* [2001] 1 FLR 495, the Court of Appeal held that, where a child was spending a substantial amount of time with both parents, a shared residence order could be appropriate despite the existence of a high degree of animosity between the parents. It was not necessary to demonstrate exceptional circumstances or a positive benefit to the child; it was sufficient to show that the order would be in the child's interests. In this case there would be positive benefits from the close relationship the children had with both parents being recognised by a shared residence order, which simply reflected the reality of the situation. A shared residence order could also be made when the parents lived some distance apart and the arrangements for the children involved them spending term times with one parent and most of the holidays with the other parent: *Re F (Children) (Shared Residence Order)* [2003] EWCA Civ 592.

In practice, shared care arrangements are most likely to work well where the parties are on good terms, in which case application of the 'no order' principle should negate the need for an order. It is difficult, therefore, to gauge how common such arrangements are.

In addition, a residence order can be made to more than one person, e.g. a parent and his or her new partner, and may be referred to as 'joint residence'.

If a residence order is made following parents' separation and they become reconciled for more than six months, the residence order will cease to have effect.

Exceptionally, a residence order may be made *ex parte*. This would be appropriate in a 'snatch' situation, where it was necessary to protect the child, as in *Re G (Minors)* [1993] 1 FLR 910. The holder of a residence order acquires parental responsibility. In the case of *B v. B (Grandparent: Residence Order)* [1992] 2 FLR 327, it was agreed that a child would reside with grandparents and, although application of the 'no order' principle might suggest that a residence order was not necessary, an order was made in order to vest parental responsibility in the grandparents and provide greater legal security.

Section 9 of the 1989 Act (restrictions on making s. 8 orders) is amended by the Adoption and Children Act 2002 so that for a local authority foster parent to apply for a residence order in respect of a child they are fostering, the child needs to have lived with them for one year out of five, rather than three years out of five. *R (W) v. Leicestershire County Council* [2003] EWHC 704 (Admin) (discussed in Chapter 10) illustrates the potential impact of this provision. A further amendment by the Adoption and Children Act 2002 to the scheme for residence order is made which enables the court, at the request of the person seeking residence, to direct that the order will continue in force until the child reaches the age of 18. So, whilst most residence orders will be made up to the age of 16, added legal security is provided for by the option of extending the order to the child's eighteenth birthday.

Enforcement

Section 14 provides a special enforcement provision for residence orders. Where a residence order is in force, if any other person is in breach of the arrangements, a person named in the residence order may enforce it under the Magistrates' Courts Act 1980, s. 63(3), ordering production of the child. Failure to produce the child would be contempt of court.

Change of child's name or removal from jurisdiction

Where a residence order is in force, no person may change the child's surname or remove the child from the United Kingdom without written consent of every person who has parental responsibility for the child or leave of the court (s. 13). An exception exists for the holder of the residence order, who may take the child out of the United Kingdom for up to one month without leave or consent, for holidays.

■ Contact

A contact order will be appropriate in situations where the child spends most of his time with one parent but retains links with the other. It may also be made for persons other than parents, e.g. grandparents. The emphasis in the contact order is different from the old access orders in that contact is seen primarily as the right of the child. Case law has recognised contact as an aspect of 'family life' under ECHR, Art. 8 and has positioned contact as a right of the adult also, though one which is qualified. For example in *Payne v Payne* [2001] EWCA Civ 166, the father argued that if the mother was allowed to take their 4-year-old child to live in New Zealand, this would infringe his right to contact as an aspect of his Art. 8 rights. The court nevertheless found that interference by allowing removal was necessary and proportionate in protecting the child's best interests.

The court can order any form of contact, including letters, phone calls, supervised contact and overnight stays. Conditions may be attached to a contact order via s. 11(7); however, a direction for a local authority to supervise contact between parent and child should be made by a Family Assistance Order, rather than s. 11(7), according to *Leeds County Council* v. *C* [1993] 1 FLR 269.

Decisions of the court have demonstrated a clear commitment to ongoing contact between parents and children. This proved problematic in a number of cases where mothers did not support contact between child and father, for reasons of fear of violence. The judiciary have coined the term 'implacable hostility' to describe such cases. It is unfortunate that this term implies a degree of unreasonableness or irrationality where the refusal may be grounded in genuine concerns for safety. The decision of *A* v. *N (Committal: Refusal of Contact)* [1997] 1 FLR 533 helpfully stated that where a mother had justification for refusing contact, due to fear of violence, this should not be regarded as implacable hostility.

Re O (Contact: Imposition of Conditions) [1996] 1 FCR 317 set out a number of principles relating to contact. (It was a case where the child's mother was described as displaying irrational repugnance to an indirect contact order.)

1. The welfare of the child is paramount and interests of the parents are relevant only if they affect the welfare of the child.

2. It is almost always in the interest of the child to have contact with the non-resident parent. There are long-term advantages to the child in keeping in touch.

3. Where direct contact is not possible there should be indirect contact.

4. The court should take a medium-term and long-term view of the child's development and not give excessive weight to short-term problems.

5. No parent should be allowed to think that the more intransigent, unreasonable, obdurate and uncooperative they are, the more likely they will be to get their own way.

6. Section 11(7) confers the power to require a parent to provide a progress report and to read communications from the other parent to the child.

In exceptional cases, parental refusal of contact has been found a contempt of court resulting in the mother's imprisonment, although this power should be used only as a last resort in urgent and exceptional cases (*Re M (Minors) (Breach of Contact Order: Committal)* [1999] 2 All SR 56. In the balancing exercise, the violent parties' willingness to change and understanding of the consequences of their violence are important factors according to *Re M (Minors) (Contact: Violent Parent)* [1999] 2 FLR 321.

The effect of domestic violence allegations on contact applications was the central issue in a Court of Appeal decision, which is now the leading authority on the matter. Four appeals, which raised similar issues, were heard jointly in the case of *Re L (A Child) (Contact: Domestic Violence); Re V (A Child) (Contact: Domestic Violence); Re M (A Child) (Contact: Domestic Violence); Re H (Children) (Contact: Domestic Violence)* [2000] 4 All ER 609. Dame Butler-Sloss, President of the Family Division, gave judgment. In each of the cases a father's application for direct contact had been refused against a background of domestic violence. Butler-Sloss commented on a report, 'Contact between Children and Violent Parents' (1999),[8] which was produced to the court. She stated that family judges and magistrates needed to have a heightened awareness of the existence and consequences on children of exposure to domestic violence. Decisions about contact should be child-centred and there should be no automatic assumption that contact with a violent parent was in the child's interests. The court always had to apply s. 1 of the Children Act 1989 (the welfare of the child is paramount) and should also take into account Art. 8 of the European Convention for the Protection of Human Rights. In each case the court had to balance the need to safeguard the child and promote his best interests with other issues, such as providing knowledge of religious and cultural background. Domestic violence is one material factor among many which might offset the assumption in favour of contact and this difficult balancing exercise is to be carried out.

Disputes about contact continue to produce much case law and debate and was the subject of a detailed report to the Lord Chancellor in 2002 which recommended increased funding for contact centres and a greater emphasis on resolving contact disputes by conciliation and mediation.[9] Pressure from a number of fathers' groups has brought the issue of contact and residence sharply into the public eye with the suggestion that the court structure is biased against fathers. In a green paper[10] the Government rejected the argument that there should be a statutory presumption in favour of contact whilst recognising that it is usually in the child's best interest to enjoy a continuing relationship with both parents following breakdown.

Many of these concerns were evident in the judgment of Munby, J in *Re D (Intractable Contact Dispute: Publicity)* [2004] EWHC 727 (Fam), in which, he observed, ' a wholly deserving father left my court in tears having been driven to abandon his battle for contact with his seven year old daughter'. The case was one that illustrated the 'appalling delays of the court system, . . . the court's failure to get to grips with the mother's (groundless) allegations; and the court's failure to get to grips with the mother's defiance of its orders, the court's failure to enforce its own orders'. Over a period of five years the case had 43 hearings conducted by 16 different judges, numerous adjournments and 905 pages of experts' evidence. The judge described delay as the scourge of the system and called for guidance in a comparable form to the Protocol for Judicial Case Management in Public Law Children Act Cases (2003) to be introduced. He expressed dissatisfaction with the frequent judicial response to contact problems, i.e. to list the matter for further directions with a reduction in contact in the meantime, obtain experts reports and further evidence that produced further delays and exacerbated difficulties.

In a move to ensure safety of children during contact, facilitate contact in the face of obstruction and provide enforcement measures, the Government has issued a Children and Adoption Bill, progressing through the House of Lords at the beginning of 2006. As set out above, the courts had also expressed some dissatisfaction with family law systems for dealing with contact and pressure group actions, particularly fathers groups, raised the profile of this issue.

The Bill inserts new provisions in to the Children Act 1989 after s. 11. These include, powers to impose 'contact activity directions' (s. 11A) and 'contact activity conditions' (s. 11B). Contact activities include attending an information session, or taking part in a programme, class, counselling or guidance session or other activity for 'assisting a person to establish, maintain or improve contact' and which may facilitate contact with a child by addressing a person's violent behaviour (s. 11E). A contact activity direction cannot require a person to undergo medical or psychiatric examination, assessment or treatment. A CAFCASS officer may be ordered to monitor compliance with activities with a power to report back to the court. If there is a breach of the terms of a contact order, without reasonable excuse, the court has additional enforcement mechanisms including unpaid work requirements. Again, CAFCASS will be expected to monitor compliance with the terms of the enforcement order. Clearly the reforms carry resource implications for CAFCASS. There is also a power to order one person to pay compensation to another for a financial loss caused by a breach.

Contact centres

There are 270 Child Contact Centres in England and Wales. They are predominantly staffed by volunteers. The centres aim to provide a neutral and safe place for contact to take place or for handovers. Referrals tend to be made by solicitors, court welfare officers and social services.

▪ Specific issue

Specific issue and prohibited steps orders are new orders introduced by the Children Act 1989, modelled on aspects of wardship, where the High Court enjoyed wider powers than the lower courts. These new orders should reduce the need to resort to wardship proceedings and are particularly suitable in cases concerned with a single issue or dispute as to exercise of parental responsibility. As the orders are available from the lower courts, they should be more accessible, cheaper and quicker to obtain. Approximately 3,000 orders are made annually.[11]

Specific issue orders are designed for situations where people with parental responsibility do not agree about an aspect of the child's upbringing, e.g. surname disputes, education issues such as choice of school, religion and medical treatment. The following case law examples are illustrative.

Dawson v. *Wearmouth* [1999] 2 WLR 960 concerned the issue of whether one parent can unilaterally change a child's surname and was dealt with by an application for a specific issue order. The choice of a child's name is an exercise of parental responsibility. A key issue, therefore, where there is a dispute between parents, will centre on whether the father has parental responsibility. In this case the father issued an application for a parental responsibility order and a specific issue order as to the child's surname. Applying the criteria in s. 1 (welfare principle and checklist), the House of Lords found that in this case it would not be in the interests of the child's welfare to change the surname.

In *Re C (A Child) (HIV Testing)* [1999] 2 FLR 1004 the local authority applied for a specific issue order to obtain a blood test to determine whether a child was infected with HIV. There was a concern that, as the child was being breastfed by her mother, who had HIV, she could become infected. The court was prepared to override the wishes of the parents and order the blood test; however, the law could not make an order that breastfeeding should cease.

In applications for specific issue orders, infringement of Art. 8 of the European Convention on Human Rights may be argued and under the Human Rights Act 1998 the court is of course obliged to reach a decision which is compatible with the Articles of the ECHR. For example, in *Re C (A Child) (Immunisation: Parental Rights)* [2003] EWCA Civ 1148, fathers applied for specific issue orders asking the court to order immunisation of their daughters. The Court of Appeal found that immunisation was in the girls' best interests but noted that courts invited to override parental wishes had to move extremely cautiously. The court could interfere with the rights of both the children and parents under Art. 8, in this instance on the exception permitting interference to protect the health of a child.

It may be possible for a specific issue order to be made to vest a particular area of decision-making (in the exercise of parental responsibility) in a named individual. For example, in *Re H (A Child: Parental Responsibility)* [2002] EWCA Civ 542, a specific issue order was made giving the mother sole responsibility for decisions relating to the child's medical treatment.

There are limits, however, to the use of specific issue orders. In *Re J (Specific Issue Order: Leave to Apply)* [1995] 1 FLR 669, a specific issue order could not be used to determine whether a child was a 'child in need'. Such determination was a matter for the local authority alone and not an exercise of parental responsibility. In another decision the court would not make a specific issue order to compel a local authority to supervise contact (*Re DH (A Minor) (Child Abuse)* [1994] 1 FLR 679). Section 9 of the Children Act 1989 prohibits the court from making a specific issue order in respect of a child who is in the care of a local authority and this has been extended by the Adoption and Children Act 2002, where a local authority is authorised by the court to place a child for adoption.[12]

■ Prohibited steps

A prohibited steps order presents a specific restriction on the exercise of parental responsibility towards a particular child. In *Re J (Child's Religions Upbringing and Circumcision)* [2000] 1 FCR 307, a prohibited steps order was made prohibiting the child's father from making arrangements for his son, aged 5, to be circumcised without the permission of the court. Circumcision was described as an irrevocable step in a child's life and, in the event of a dispute between people exercising parental responsibility, it was for the High Court to resolve the matter. A prohibited steps order was made to prevent a step-father visiting a child in *Re H (Minors) (Prohibited Steps Order)* [1995] 4 All ER 110.

Neither a specific issue nor a prohibited steps order should be made if this would achieve a result that could have been achieved by making a residence order, e.g. a specific issue order that a child attends a particular school which would involve a change of residence.

■ Who may apply for an order?

Section 10 sets out varying levels of eligibility to apply for s. 8 orders. As of right, any parent, guardian, civil partner in relation to whom the child is a child of the family, or person in whose favour a residence order is in force may apply for any s. 8 order. Note that this right is given to a parent rather than a parent with parental responsibility. It follows that a father who does not have parental responsibility is entitled to apply for a s. 8 order. Any other person, including the child, and other relatives, must obtain leave of the court to apply for an order.

The criteria for granting leave is contained in s. 10(9), which directs the court to have regard to:

s. 10(9)

> (a) the nature of the proposed application;
> (b) the applicant's connection with the child;
> (c) any risk of the application disrupting the child's life to such an extent that he would be harmed by it;
> (d) when the child is being looked after by the local authority, the authority's plans for the child's future and the wishes and feelings of the child's parents.
>
> (CA 1989)

Leave will be granted to a child if the court is satisfied that he has sufficient understanding to make the proposed application (s. 10(8)). If a child makes an application it will be heard in the High Court, as, for example, in *Re AD (A Minor) (Child's Wishes)* [1993] 1 FCR 573, where a child applied for a residence order to be made to her boyfriend's parents enabling her to leave home and reside there. In *Re J (Leave to Issue Application for Residence Order)* [2002] EWCA Civ 1346, Thorpe noted the need to 'recognise the greater appreciation that has developed of the value of what grandparents have to offer, particularly to children of disabled parents' and it has been argued (strongly by the Grandparents Association) that grandparents should not be required to seek prior leave of the court before making an application.

A s. 8 order can be made on application or the court may make an order of its own volition in any family proceedings. The court will hold an informal hearing before it lists a contested s. 8 application for trial, to ascertain whether conciliation is possible.[13] A number of restrictions on the court's power to make s. 8 orders are set out in s. 9.

(a) No s. 8 orders may be made in respect of a child in care, except for a residence order, which then discharges the care order. To provide otherwise could lead to private orders being used to control local authorities statutory responsibilities in conflict with the principle established by *A* v. *Liverpool City Council* [1981] 2 All ER 385.

(b) No residence order or contact order may be made in favour of the local authority. This issue was debated in *Nottinghamshire County Council* v. *P* [1993] 3 All ER 815. In this case the local authority sought a prohibited steps order which required that the father should not live in the same household or have any contact with his children. On analysis, it was held that the local authority was in effect seeking residence and contact orders, which it is debarred from doing, and the application for the prohibited steps order was refused.

(c) A s. 8 order will not be made for a child over the age of 16 unless there are exceptional circumstances.

(d) Local authority foster parents can apply for residence and contact orders only if they have the consent of the local authority, are a relative, or have cared for the child for one year out of the last five.

(e) If a care order is made, this discharges any s. 8 order.

Two other orders are closely linked to s. 8 orders:

▪ Section 37 – Investigation of the child's circumstances.
▪ Section 16 – Family Assistance Order.

▪ Investigation of the child's circumstances (s. 37)

It is not possible to apply for a s. 37 direction. A direction will be made by the court of its own motion in appropriate circumstances, i.e. where it appears that a public law order might be required (*Re L (A Minor) (Section 37 Direction)* [1999] 3 FCR

s. 37(1) ▶

> Where, in any family proceedings in which a question arises with respect to the welfare of any child, it appears to the court that it may be appropriate for a care or supervision order to be made with respect to him, the court may direct the appropriate authority to undertake an investigation of the child's circumstances.
>
> (CA 1989)

642), although it would be possible for parties in family proceedings to suggest this to the court. If a direction is given then the local authority must consider whether it should apply for a care or supervision order or provide services to the child or his or her family or take any other action (s. 37(2)). If the local authority decides not to apply for a care or supervision order it must inform the court of its reasons and whether any other service has been provided or any other action taken (s. 37(3)). The local authority has eight weeks in which to investigate and provide a report to the court. During this period the court can make an interim order. In addition the court may request a welfare report under s. 7 at any time. In *Re M (Intractable Contact Dispute: Interim Care Order)* [2003] EWHC 1024 (Fam), a 5.37 direction was made in circumstances where children whose contact with the non-resident parent was being denied, were suffering harm as a result.

■ Family assistance order

The family assistance order is a new order introduced by the Children Act 1989, s. 16. An order may be made in any family proceedings where the court has power to make a s. 8 order; the circumstances of the case should be exceptional; and consent must be obtained from every person named in the order, other than the child. The effect of the order is to require an officer of CAFCASS or a local authority officer to be available to, advise, assist and befriend any person named in the order. The persons who may be named in the order are set out in s. 16(2): any parent or guardian of the child, person the child is living with or who has a contact order in respect of the child, and the child himself. Guidance draws a contrast between the family assistance order and supervision order, the latter being designed for more serious cases where there is an element of child protection, whereas, 'a family assistance order aims simply to provide short-term help to a family, to overcome the problems and conflicts associated with their separation or divorce. Help may well be focused more on the adults than the child.'[14] The order is made by the court 'of its own motion' and cannot be directly applied for, though it is possible for a party to suggest to the court that an order would be appropriate. Orders for supervision of contact by the local authority should be made by way of a family assistance order rather than imposition of a condition under s. 11(7): *Leeds County Council* v. *C* [1993] 1 FLR 269. However, the local authority cannot be required to take on a family assistance order if it does not have the resources to do so: see *Re C (A Minor) (Family Assistance Order)* [1996] 1 FLR 424.

The order has been little used (1,009 in 1997, 864 in 1998). Research on the use of family assistance orders indicates that the majority of orders are made in response to issues arising over contact arrangements, and may be made alone or in combination with a s. 8 order. Family assistance orders tend to be made to the Court Welfare Service rather than the Social Services Department. In the area where the research was carried out, a high number of family assistance orders were made, the reason being that judges considered the order a useful and supportive means of promoting parental responsibility, and enabling more input to a case than is given in those cases where the court welfare officer's role is to produce a report. Equally, the Court Welfare Service supported the order as providing an opportunity for more sustained therapeutic work with families (Trinder and Stone, 1998).[15]

Plans to reform the family assistance order and make it more effective are included in the Children and Adoption Bill. The requirement that family assistance orders be made only in exceptional circumstances is removed, and the maximum duration of such orders is extended from six to twelve months.

Domestic violence

Domestic violence is:

> any form of physical, sexual or emotional abuse which takes place within the context of a close relationship. In most cases, the relationship will be between partners (married, cohabiting or otherwise) or ex-partners . . . Domestic violence also takes place . . . occasionally in heterosexual relationships where the man is the victim. However, research indicates that in the great majority of cases the abuser is male and the victim female . . . It is equally important to recognise that women from ethnic minority groups may face particular difficulties that result from a combination of sexism and racism.

The above definition of domestic violence is that used by the Association of Chief Officers of Probation, and is cited in a consultation paper on contact between children and violent parents.[16] The paper proceeds to note that:

> It is . . . important to remember that domestic violence not only takes many forms, but that it does not have to be physical or to result from a lack of impulse control. It can be psychological. It includes intimidation and harassment, in both their physical and psychological forms. It may be subtle emotional abuse of the other parent or children. It can be used as a means of one parent dominating and controlling the other. (para. 1.3)

Domestic violence is included in this chapter because the legal remedies available operate between individuals and are often associated with issues surrounding divorce and separation and applications for s. 8 orders. The effect of domestic violence in the context of contact applications has been discussed above. The law relating to domestic violence is essentially an aspect of private law. Nevertheless, the impact of domestic violence between adults upon children is increasingly being recognised in the context of child protection. This recognition is clear in the amended definition of 'harm' in the threshold criteria to include, 'impairment suffered from seeing or hearing the ill-treatment of another'.[17] In addition, under the Children Act 2004, authorities have a duty to ensure local cooperation to improve well-being and a duty to make arrangements to safeguard children in their area and this will include children who are living in households where there is domestic violence.

In court the dispute in domestic violence proceedings is essentially between adults and there may be cases where views of children are not made known to the court. There have been calls for s. 64 of the Family Law Act 1996 to be implemented. This section would allow for regulations to be made providing for separate representation of children in proceedings under Part IV of the 1996 Act, dealing with family homes and domestic violence.

Remedies for domestic violence are now provided principally by the Family Law Act 1996, Pt IV. Further, legislation the Domestic Violence Crime and Victims Act 2004 (**DVCVA 2004**) has been introduced to modernise the law on domestic violence and amends the Family Law Act. It aims to strengthen the rights of victims and witnesses, introduces new offences and includes tougher sanctions for perpetrators. Royal Assent for the Act coincided with publication of a joint report by the CPS and HM Inspectorate of Constabulary entitled 'Violence at Home' (2004). The report found that only 5 per cent of domestic violence cases result in a conviction and victims are often denied access to civil remedies because of limited access to legal aid.

Relief, in the form of non-molestation orders and occupation orders, can be sought against an 'associated person'. This term encompasses a wider range of people than previous domestic violence legislation, which was limited in its application to spouses and cohabitees. Section 62(3) defines the term as including parties: who are or have been married to each other; who are cohabitants or former cohabitants; who live or have lived in the same household (other than as employees or lodgers); who are relatives, including relatives of their spouse or cohabitee (or former); who have agreed to marry; who are parents of the child or have parental responsibility for the child. The definition is extended by the DVCVA to specifically include same-sex couples within the term 'cohabitants'. As cohabiting couples are already associated persons, the significance of this is that property owners, spouses and cohabitants are the only associated persons that can have apply for an occupation order. The list of associated persons is also amended to include people who have not married or cohabited but nevertheless 'have or had an intimate personal relationship with each other which is or was of significant duration'.

Case law suggests that the courts will give a wide, purposive interpretation to the definition. In *G v. F (Non-molestation Order: Jurisdiction)* [2000] 3 WLR 1202, justices initially refused to hear an application on the grounds that the parties were not associated persons. The parties had a joint bank account and a sexual relationship existed. The Family Division found that the justices should have found that the parties were former cohabitants, and noted that cohabitation can take many forms. The case of *JH* v. *RH* (*Child*) [2001] 1 FLR 641 illustrates the extension of the use of the occupation order beyond spouses and cohabitees. A 17-year-old, described as a truculent and violent teenager, was directed to vacate his parents' home and excluded from returning there.

The DVCVA includes a range of further relevant provisions. Breach of a non-molestation order is made a criminal offence punishable by five years' imprisonment on indictment (s. 1) and common assault becomes an arrestable offence (s. 10). The courts are given a power to impose a restraining order for the protection of a victim, even where a defendant has been acquitted of an offence relating to her, but the court believes an order is necessary to protect the victim (s. 12). Structural changes include the introduction of a new Code of Practice for the support and protection of victims which will apply across all criminal justice agencies (s. 32). A Commissioner for Victims and Witnesses is created (s. 48) with a role including monitoring and promoting good practice, ensuring the interests of victims and witnesses are heard in Government and keeping the Code of Practice under review. If the Code is not observed, it will be possible for a victim or witness to complain to the Parliamentary Commissioner (Ombudsman) (s. 42).

■ Social work and local authority involvement in domestic violence cases

The main statutory duty for social workers to become involved in domestic violence cases is triggered by the presence of children who may need protection or support. The role otherwise can be described as one of liaison and support and may include the following tasks: contacting the police; organising a refuge place; contacting a lawyer; arranging medical attention; arranging accommodation for the children; providing support at court hearings; giving evidence to the court; assisting with benefits claims; acting as an advocate to the housing authority; assisting with a criminal injuries compensation claim and generally acting as a coordinator ensuring that accurate advice and appropriate referrals are made.

There is a wider responsibility for local authorities in relation to domestic violence in their area. Local authorities must work with other agencies to reduce crime and disorder in their area. Domestic violence will be included in local crime reduction strategies and action plans, as required by the Crime and Disorder Act 1998.[18] Local authorities are responsible for the delivery of a wide range of services to people affected by domestic violence, including housing, and have duties to individuals accepted as homeless for domestic violence reasons. A Best Value Performance Indicator for domestic violence was issued in 2005 (BVPA 225) and is based on whether the authority has taken action to: produce a director of local services that can help victims; ensure a minimum of one refuge place per 10,000 population; employ or fund a voluntary sector based domestic violence coordinator; adopt a multi-agency strategy to tackle domestic violence; support and facilitate a multi-agency domestic violence forum; develop an information sharing protocol; promote a 'sanctuary' scheme that enables victims and children to remain safely in their own homes; reduce the number of homeless cases rehoused in the previous two years as a result of violence; include a specific clause in the council's tenancy agreement stating that perpetration of domestic violence can be a ground for eviction; develop a domestic violence education pack; and conduct multi-agency training of staff.

■ Family Court Welfare Service

The Family Court Welfare Service is now provided under the auspices of CAFCASS (established by the Criminal Justice and Court Services Act 2000). It was previously provided by the Probation Service, actually the responsibility of the Home Office. In private law proceedings, including s. 8 applications and domestic violence cases, a *children and family reporter* (formerly known as a court welfare officer) may be involved as court reporter. Section 7(1) provides that any court when considering any question with respect to a child under the 1989 Act may ask an officer of CAFCASS or local authority to report to the court 'on such matters relating to the welfare of that child as are required to be dealt with in the report'. In contrast to the role of the children's guardian in public proceedings, the children and family reporter is not specifically the child's representative as children are not normally parties to the application. (There is an exception relating to s. 8 applications commenced by the child with leave of the court – in these cases a guardian would be appointed.) In addition, the children and family reporter is not always appointed in private law proceedings.[21] A recent case may present a significant development in terms of representation of children in the private law: in *Re A (A Child) (Separate Representation in Contact Proceedings)* [2001] 1 FLR 715, a boy aged 14, who was concerned about his younger half-sister, aged 4, wanted to inform the judge that he believed it was dangerous for his sister to see her father. He had not been spoken to by the Court Welfare Service or social services. The Court of Appeal gave permission for the National Youth Advisory Service to intervene in the contact proceedings and act as guardian for the younger child. The court held that where there was a conflict of interest between the parents and child it could be necessary for a guardian to be appointed in private family law proceedings, bearing in mind the impact of the European Convention and that children were not always sufficiently seen and heard by the use of a court welfare officer's report.

A practice direction provides some clarity as to the circumstances where separate representation is likely to be appropriate, *Practice Direction (Family Proceedings: Representation of Children)* [2004] 1 FLR 1188. The Direction states that, before making a child party to proceedings, the court should give consideration to an alternative route such as asking an officer of CAFCASS to assist, referring the case to social services or obtaining an expert's report.

Circumstances that would merit making a child a party would include:

■ where a CAFCASS officer had notified the court of his opinion that the child should be made a party;

■ where the child had an interest which was inconsistent with or incapable of being represented by the adult parties;

■ where there was an intractable dispute over residence and where all contact had ceased, or where there was irrational but implacable hostility to contact or where the contact dispute might be causing the child to suffer harm;

■ where the child's views or wishes could not adequately be communicated to the court in a report;

■ where an older child opposed a proposed course of action;

■ where there were complex medical or mental health issues;

■ where there were international complications outside questions of child abduction which required discussion with overseas authorities;

■ where there were serious allegations of abuse or domestic violence, and

■ where there was a contested issue as to blood testing.

When directing whether to make the child a party the court would consider the risk that to do so would cause delay to the proceedings. The primary consideration would be the welfare of the child. If a child was made a party and a guardian was appointed, consideration should be given to appointing an officer of CAFCASS as guardian. A county court dealing with such a case would also consider whether the case was sufficiently complex or important to merit transfer to the High Court.

Mabon v Mabon [2005] EWCA Civ 634 concerned a residence order application where three boys aged 13, 15 and 17 sought separate representation. The court noted the need to recognise the right to freedom of expression and the risk of emotional harm that might be caused by denying participation in proceedings.

Section 122 of the Adoption and Children Act 2002 establishes the right to a children's guardian in complex residence and contact cases. New rules for this provision will be introduced when commissioned research has been analysed. Under the same legislation, separate representation for children placed for adoption has been implemented.

CAFCASS have published a new strategy with a clear emphasis on early intervention in appropriate cases ('Every Day Matters', 2005). The strategy proposes that in both public and private cases every referral should be allocated within two days and a case plan formulated before the first directions hearing. In private cases the emphasis of the guardian's work (in the absence of any allegations of significant harm) is to be on intensive dispute resolution and a shared parenting approach.

Divorce

It is necessary to have an awareness of divorce law, as it clearly affects a considerable number of families. In 2004, 153,999 divorces were granted, affecting 149,275 children under the age of 16.[20] Existing service users may ask questions of social workers about the law of divorce and the court's role in making orders consequent to divorce and wish to discuss their circumstances. In addition, at the time of divorce social workers may be directly involved in emergency work to protect children where separation follows violence, or in providing services for children and families, or supervising contact.

A brief consideration of marriage is necessary before turning to the law of divorce. It is important to note, however, that there has been a long-term downward trend in the number of marriages taking place each year, with more and more couples preferring to cohabit. From a peak of 490,285 marriages in 1972, there were 311,180 marriages in 2004.[21] There is also a tendency for couples to marry later in life.

▪ Marriage

The legal definition of marriage is drawn from *Hyde* v. *Hyde* (1866) LR 1 P&D 130. It is:

> The voluntary union for life of one man and one woman to the exclusion of all others.

Taking each element of this definition: first, the union must be voluntary; therefore, if there is no true consent it is possible to have the marriage annulled. Given the high divorce rate it is questionable whether reference to 'for life' remains a valid part of the definition.

A marriage will be void if the parties are not respectively male and female. This issue has been raised in a number of transsexual cases, where the national and European courts consistently stated that a person's sexual attribution is fixed conclusively at birth. In *Rees* v. *United Kingdom* (1986) 9 EHRR 56, the court found no violation of ECHR, Art. 8, the right to respect for private life, or Art. 12, the right to marry, when the United Kingdom refused to amend the birth certificate from female to male. That position was challenged recently in *Bellinger* v. *Bellinger* [2003] UKHL 21.[22] Legislation has subsequently been introduced to rectify the position. Now, under the Gender Recognition Act 2004 the acquired gender of transsexuals is recognised.

Reference to the exclusion of all others is reflected in adultery being included as one of the possible facts required to be proven before divorce.

▪ Ground for divorce

The sole ground for divorce is irretrievable breakdown of marriage, contained in the Matrimonial Causes Act 1973, s. 1(1). Irretrievable breakdown must be established or evidenced by one of five facts. The first three facts are referred to as 'fault' grounds and the latter two as 'no fault' grounds. A *petition* (application) for divorce cannot be brought during the first year of marriage, though subsequent petitions may rely on events which occurred during that first year. In divorce proceedings the parties are referred to as the **petitioner** (the person applying for divorce) and the **respondent.**

s. 1(2)

> (a) that the respondent has committed adultery and the petitioner finds it intolerable to live with the respondent;
>
> (MCA 1973)

Adultery means voluntary heterosexual intercourse (a relationship with a person of the same sex does not count as adultery). It is not possible to rely on this ground if the petitioner has lived with the respondent for six months or more following disclosure of the adultery. There are two elements to this fact: there must have been adultery, and the petitioner must find it intolerable to live with the respondent, but that does not have to be as a consequence of the adultery (*Cleary* v. *Cleary* [1974] 1 All ER 498).

s. 1(2)

> (b) that the respondent has behaved in such a way that the petitioner cannot reasonably be expected to live with the respondent;
>
> (MCA 1973)

This fact is commonly referred to as unreasonable behaviour. That phrase is misleading, as it is not the behaviour that has to be unreasonable; rather it is the expectation that the petitioner should live with the respondent. The principle to be applied was enunciated in *Livingstone Stallard* v. *Livingstone Stallard* [1974] 2 All ER 766, where Dunn J stated: 'Would any right-thinking person come to the conclusion that this husband has behaved in such a way that this wife cannot reasonably be expected to live with him taking into account the whole of the circumstances and the characters and personalities of the parties.' This is the most widely relied upon fact.

s. 1(2)

> (c) that the respondent has deserted the petitioner for a continuous period of at least two years immediately preceding the presentation of the petition;
>
> (MCA 1973)

This fact is rarely used and desertion has a technical legal definition.

s. 1(2)

(d) that the parties of the marriage have lived apart for a continuous period of at least two years immediately preceding the presentation of the petition . . . and the respondent consents to a decree being granted;

(MCA 1973)

Facts (d) and (e) are based on separation, which is perhaps the best evidence of the breakdown of marriage. The separation facts were introduced in 1969 in an attempt to move away from a fault-based divorce system. There are two elements to fact (d): the parties must have lived apart and the respondent must consent. The two years must be a continuous period; however, it will not be broken by periods of reconciliation totalling less than six months. In order to be living apart, the spouses must not be in the same household, sharing any aspect of domestic life (*Fuller* v. *Fuller* [1973] 2 All ER 650).

s. 1(2)

(e) that the parties to the marriage have lived apart for a continuous period of at least five years immediately preceding the presentation of the petition . . .

(MCA 1973)

For this fact, the fact of separation for five years must be proved but there is no requirement for the respondent's consent.

It is extremely rare to have a defended divorce. Most divorces are in fact straightforward, and it is the associated disputes relating to children and property that are complex. In an average case the decree nisi will be granted eight to twelve weeks after the petition is lodged, followed by the decree absolute, which may be applied for six weeks after decree nisi.

As an alternative to divorce, some couples prefer a judicial separation. This follows the same procedure as divorce up to decree nisi stage, but there is no actual termination of the marriage. There is no need to show irretrievable breakdown of the marriage for a separation; the five facts are themselves grounds for an order of judicial separation.

Reform?

Despite the introduction of no-fault grounds in 1969, the majority of divorce petitions continue to rely on adultery or behaviour. In both these cases the proceedings have a tendency to take on an adversarial nature. The Law Commission, through a process of consultation, recommended that new divorce law should be introduced which would enable marriages that had irretrievably broken down to be brought to an end with minimum distress to the parties and to children affected (Family Law Act 1996, s. 1).

A framework for new law was set up in the Family Law Act 1996. It continued to rely on irretrievable breakdown as the sole ground for divorce; however, the five facts were to be removed. Instead, a marriage would be taken to have irretrievably broken down if a statement to that effect had been made by one or both of the parties and a fixed period for reflection and consideration had ended. The proposals attracted considerable criticism from academics and practitioners, pilot studies of some aspects were unfavourable and the Lord Chancellor announced that the divorce reforms will not be implemented. It is unclear at this stage whether any alternative reforms will be pursued. In the meantime, the Matrimonial Causes Act 1973 continues to provide the law of divorce.

■ Civil partnership

The coming into force of the Civil Partnership Act 2004 enabled the first same-sex civil registrations to take place in December 2005.[23] It has been estimated that between 11,000 and 22,000 people will be in a civil partnership by 2010.[24]

The purpose of the Act is to enable same-sex couples to obtain legal recognition of their relationship by forming a civil partnership provided:

■ they are of the same sex;

■ they are not already in an existing civil partnership or lawfully married;

■ they are not within the prohibited degrees of relationships;

■ they are both over the age of 18 or are over 16 and have consent of the appropriate people or bodies (in England and Wales and Northern Ireland) or are 16 or over in Scotland.

The partnership is formed when the civil partnership document is signed by the partners in the presence of each other, the registrar and two witnesses in non-religious premises. The partners must give notice of their intention to enter into a partnership to the registration, then after a 15-day period the partnership may be registered. A civil partnership provides the same rights and responsibilities as a civil marriage: e.g. rights to occupy property of the partner; protection from domestic violence; the same rights as widows and widowers for a surviving civil partner, including succession rights to tenancies; equal treatment regarding social security and tax.

A civil partnership ends only on death, dissolution or annulment. A dissolution order (similar to divorce) will be made on the ground that the civil partnership has irretrievably broken down as evidenced by 'behaviour', two-year separation with consent or five-year separation without consent, or desertion (s. 44). These facts mirror those in divorce proceedings except that there is no adultery fact, though this might be included in the behaviour fact. The court may adjourn dissolution proceedings if it considers there is a reasonable prospect of reconciliation (s. 42). As with marriage, financial relief (lump sum, periodical payments, property adjustment, etc.) may be ordered following dissolution for the civil partner and any child of the family.

■ Children and civil partnership

Where there are children, a civil partner can acquire parental responsibility in a similar way to acquisition of parental responsibility by step-parents, and may apply for residence and contact orders. Parent is redefined in the Children Act 1989 to include any civil partner in a civil partnership (whether or not subsisting) in relation to whom the child concerned is a child of the family. It is possible for civil partners to adopt jointly, as a couple, recognised under the Adoption and Children Act 2002 as 'two people (whether of different sexes or the same sex) living together as partners in an enduring family relationship' (ACA 2002, s.144(4)(b)).

Chapter summary

- The concept of parental responsibility is introduced by the Children Act 1989. It may be held by a number of people in respect of a child and is defined as 'all the rights, duties, powers, responsibilities and authority which by law a parent of a child has in relation to the child'.

- Section 8 orders for contact, residence, prohibited steps and specific issues control the exercise of parental responsibility. Residence orders determine where a child is to live and may be made to more than one person. A contact order controls the type and level of contact which the child will enjoy with a range of adults. *Re L* [2000] 4 All ER 609 lays down guidelines on contact where there has been domestic violence. Specific issue and prohibited steps orders are modelled on aspects of wardship and can be used to determine disputes over the exercise of parental responsibility.

- In family proceedings the court may make an order for the local authority to investigate a child's circumstances and determine whether it is appropriate for a care or supervision order to be made (CA 1989, s. 37).

- The family assistance order can provide support to families following separation or divorce and can be used to facilitate supervision of contact.

- Social work involvement in domestic violence cases may be triggered by statutory child care responsibilities and extend to coordinating support and providing information. Non-molestation and ouster orders are provided by the Family Law Act 1996.

- The Civil Partnership Act 2004 provides for same-sex partnerships to be registered and to have the same legal effect as marriage.

Exercises

Consider what order, or combination of orders, if any, would be appropriate in the following circumstances. In each case consider the role of social services.

1. Sarah, aged 11, spends alternate weeks with each of her parents. They are in the process of an amicable divorce.

2. Tom and Louise are aged 6 and 4. They live with their mother during the week, spending weekends and part of the school holidays with their father. Their parents were not married. This arrangement has worked well until recently, when their father cancelled a couple of weekend visits at short notice and brought the children back early on another occasion. He recently announced his intention to marry his partner, who moved in with him two months ago.

3. Adam, aged 8, has been cared for by his grandparents since he was a baby. His mother is a drug user and has been unable to care for him. She sees him regularly but does not wish to care for him on a full-time basis. His grandparents want to plan for the future and would like some legal security.

4. Following his parents' acrimonious divorce, James, aged 5, has weekly contact with his father. He always returns distressed and has become enuretic. His parents regularly argue about contact in his presence.

5. Raymond and Eleanor have been married for six years. They have a 3-year-old son called Tom. Eleanor has been unhappy lately and finds Raymond irritating and insensitive to her needs. She would like another baby but he refuses to contemplate the idea. The couple lead increasingly separate lives. Raymond works away in London for much of the week and has a flat there. In an attempt to improve their relationship, Eleanor arranges for Tom to stay with his grandparents and drives to London to surprise Raymond. She lets herself in to the flat and finds Raymond in bed with another man. Eleanor wants to divorce Raymond and says if he is gay he can have no role as a father for Tom.

Websites

For further information about the work of contact centres, see the website of the National Association of Child Contact Centres:

www.nacc.org.uk

The Women's Aid website provides information to support women suffering violence including guides to the law:

www.womensaid.org

Further reading

Masson, J. (2003) The Impact of the Adoption and Children Act 2002: Part 1 – Parental Responsibility. Bristol: Family Law, Jordan Publishing, p. 580 (Provides an outline of the changes to the scheme for acquiring parental responsibility.)

Potter, G. and Williams, C. (2005) 'Parental responsibility and the duty to consult – the public's view' 17(2) *Child and Family Law Quarterly* p. 207. (An interesting analysis of views of the public on whether there should be a duty to consult others with parental responsibility before making decisions.)

Bainham, A., Lindley, B., Richards, M. and Trinder, L. (eds) (2003) *Children and their Families: Contact, Rights and Welfare.* Oxford: Hart Publishing. (A useful collection of essays.)

Private law orders have been considered in a range of articles:

Kaganas, F. and Piper, C. (2001) 'Shared Parenting – a 70% solution?' 14(4) *Child and Family Law Quarterly* p. 365.

Neale, B., Flowerdew, J. and Smart, C. (2003) 'Drifting towards shared residence?' 12 *Family Law* p. 904.

Butler-Sloss, E. (2001) 'Contact and domestic violence' 31 *Family Law* p. 355.

Seden, J. (2001) 'Family Assistance Orders and the Children Act 1989: Ambivalence about Intervention or a Means of Safeguarding and Promoting Children's Welfare?' *International Journal of Law, Policy and the Family* p. 226.

Smart, C. and May, V. (2004) 'Why can't They Agree? The Underlying Complexity of Contact and Residence Disputes' 26(4) *Journal of Social Welfare and Family Law* p. 347.

May, V. and Smart, C. (2004) 'Silence in court? – hearing children in residence and contact disputes' 16(3) *Child and Family Law Quarterly* 305. (Considers the extent to which children are consulted about their wishes and feelings, with examples of cases.)

Murray, C. (2004) 'Same sex Families: Outcomes for Children and Parents' 34 *Family Law* p. 136.

Notes

1   See A. Diduck (2003) *Law's Families*. London: LexisNexis UK.

2   *Hewer* v. *Bryant* [1969] 3 All ER 578: Lord Denning described the parental rights and duties of a parent with custody as a bundle of ever-dwindling rights and powers, which starts with a right of control and ends with little more than advice.

3   Births and Deaths Registration Act 1953.

4   This idea can be traced to a consultation paper issued by the Lord Chancellor's Department in 1998, 'Procedures for the Determination of Paternity and on the Law on Parental Responsibility for Unmarried Fathers'.

5   In limited circumstances the Human Fertilisation and Embryology Act 1990, s. 30 also provides for relinquishment of parental responsibility.

6   Foster Placement (Children) Regulations 1991 (SI 1991/910).

7   *Re W (Minors) (Residence)* (1992) CA *The Times* 3 March.

8   Children Act Sub-Committee of the Lord Chancellor's Advisory Board on Family Law (1999) 'Contact between Children and Violent Parents'.

9   LCD (2002) Making Contact Work: A report to the Lord Chancellor on the Facilitation of Arrangements for Contact Between Children and their Non-Residential Parents and the Enforcement of Court Orders for Contact.

10 Parental Separation: Children's Needs and Parents' Responsibilities (2004) (Cm. 6273).

11 S. Gilmore (2004) 'The nature, scope and use of the specific issue order' 19(4) *Child and Family law Quarterly* p. 367.

12 Adoption and Children Act 2002, s. 21.

13 Practice Direction (Family Division: Conciliation) [2004] 1 WLR 1287.

14 Department of Health (1991) 'The Children Act 1989 Guidance and Regulations', vol. 1 'Court Orders'. London: HMSO, p. 15.

15 L. Trinder and N. Stone (1998) 'Family assistance orders – professional aspirations and party frustration' 10(3) *Child and Family Law Quarterly* pp. 291–302.

16 Children Act Sub-Committee of the Lord Chancellor's Advisory Board on Family Law (1999) 'Contact between Children and Violent Parents: further consultation paper on the question of parental contact with children in cases where there is domestic violence'. See www.open.gov.uk/lcd/family/abfla/cvpcon.htm.

17 Amendment to the Children Act 1989 introduced by the Adoption and Children Act 2002, s. 120.

18 See: Home Office Violent Crimes Unit (2004) Developing domestic violence strategy – a guide for partnerships: www.crimereduction.gov.uk/dv08.htm.

19 J. Timms and J. Harris-Hendriks (1999) 'The separate representation of children in private law proceedings – which children need representation under section 64 of the Family Law Act 1996?' 12(1) *Representing Children*.

20 National Statistics: www.statistics.gov.uk.

21 National Statistics: www.statistics.gov.uk.

[22] See further discussion in A. Bradney (2003) 'Developing Human Rights? The Lords and Transsexual Marriages' *Family Law* p. 585.

[23] The Act can be traced back to June 2003, when the Government published, 'Civil Partnership – a framework for the legal recognition of same-sex couples' in England and Wales (a consultation document).

[24] Women and Equality Unit, cited in D. Gartland (2005) 'Dissolving civil partnerships' *New Law Journal,* p. 1661.

9 Child protection

Learning objectives

To develop an understanding of the following:

- Local authority responsibilities in child protection work.
- Current definitions of forms of child abuse.
- The duty to investigate referrals and concerns that a child might be suffering or at risk of suffering significant harm.
- The role of child protection conferences and reviews.
- The range and effect of short-term and emergency orders.
- The interpretation of the threshold criteria for intervention in family life, including leading case law.
- Care and supervision orders and interim orders.
- Procedural issues including the protocol for judicial case management in public law cases.
- The content and role of care plans.
- Independent representation for the child and the role of the children's guardian.
- The role of expert witnesses in care proceedings.
- The inherent jurisdiction and wardship.
- Types of inquiries, their purpose and influence.
- The criminal law and child abuse and special measures for child witnesses.

Introduction

Child protection is a high profile area of work where social work as a profession and, at times, individual social workers have become the subject of much criticism.

245

Inquiry reports published after child deaths or other situations of concern have identified individual and institutional culpability and repeatedly stated the importance of inter-agency work and good record keeping. There are examples of children who have been removed from their families where they suffered abuse only to be further abused in residential or foster placements, which were provided as a safe environment. Case law decisions are gradually removing the immunity from actions in negligence that local authorities enjoyed on public policy grounds.[1] In addition, the Human Rights Act 1998 has emphasised a clear duty on local authorities to protect children from abuse and enables compensation to be paid if a local authority fails in this duty.[2] As a result of the above it would be easy for a culture of defensive practice to develop in child protection and to forget the many success stories. It is essential that practice in this area continues to develop in line with research findings and that processes and procedures are rigorous and robust. The legal framework for intervention in child protection is largely contained in the Children Act 1989. The principles outlined in Chapter 7 are applicable and there is a body of guidance that should be adhered to.

The judgment in a recent decision specifically points out that social services can and should learn lessons from difficult cases and apply them to future similar cases. In *Re E (Care Proceedings: Social Work Practice)* [2000] 2 FCR 297, there was a history of social work intervention accompanied by a family's failure to cooperate with professionals, resulting in a pattern of abusive parenting over a long period. Lessons to be learnt included: the need to keep an up-to-date running chronology of significant events on the front of a social work file; recognition that lack of parental cooperation was never a reason to close the file or remove a child from a protection register; information given by health visitors and teachers in referrals is valuable and should be thoroughly investigated; a decision to take no action on a case should never be made without full knowledge of the file and consultation with the professionals who know the family; children who were part of a sibling group should always be considered in the context of the family history; and, in order to avoid drift, work with families had to be time-limited. In the particular case, Bracewell J commented that, had those matters been followed, effective intervention to protect the children would have occurred much earlier.

Child protection law and practice must be considered against the contect of the 'Every Child Matters: Change for Children' policy, and certain legal changes introduced by the Children Act 2004 (Chapter 7 provides an overview of these changes). There is a key role for child protection work as an aspect of the duties in respect of 'Safeguarding and promoting the welfare of children'. The new 'Working Together' clarifies that safeguarding and promoting the welfare of children means:

> The process of protecting children from abuse or neglect, preventing impairment of their health and development, and ensuring they are growing up in circumstances consistent with the provision of safe and effective care which is undertaken so as to enable children to have optimum life chances and enter adulthood successfully.[3]

This chapter begins with a brief outline of current definitions of child abuse. A discussion of the local authority duty to investigate where there are concerns follows, and includes consideration of the important role for child protection conferences and reviews in the investigative process. The next section outlines a range of short-term and emergency orders, which support the process of investigation and offer immediate protection to the child, followed by a section on care proceedings incorporating care and supervision orders, the significance of care plans, the role of the children's guardian and the expert witness in child protection proceedings. The inherent jurisdiction and wardship are explained next, followed by an evaluation of the role of inquiries. Finally, to consider child protection in a broad sense, the chapter continues with a section on the arrangements for screening child care workers; and guidance on interviewing the child; the position of the child as a witness and the role of criminal proceedings concludes this chapter.

Definitions of child abuse

It is difficult to offer a precise definition of child abuse, as knowledge and understanding and research findings mean that this is an evolving concept. 'Working Together to Safeguard Children' (2006) notes the variable circumstances of abuse stating that: 'Abuse and neglect are forms of maltreatment of a child. Somebody may abuse or neglect a child by inflicting harm, or by failing to act to prevent harm. Children may be abused in a family or in an institutional or community setting; by those known to them or, more rarely, by a stranger. They may be abused by an adult or adults or another child or children' (1.29).

It is commonly agreed that there are different types of abuse, namely emotional, physical and sexual abuse and neglect. These are the categories used in Child Protection Registers. Beyond these categories it has been argued that other forms of abuse should be recognised, such as institutional abuse, satanic or ritual abuse and medical abuse. Clearly, any professional working in the field of child protection needs to be alert to new research and open to the recognition of new or previously unidentified forms of abuse. In law the term 'significant harm' is central to any understanding of the state's powers to intervene in cases of child abuse. The term is explored fully in relation to s. 31, the threshold criteria, later in this chapter but it should be noted that it also features in other sections: e.g. applications for a child assessment order or emergency protection order.

The following extract from 'Working Together' (2006) provides a description of each of the four major types of abuse:

1.30 Physical abuse
Physical abuse may involve hitting, shaking, throwing, poisoning, burning or scalding, drowning, suffocating, or otherwise causing physical harm to a child. Physical harm may also be caused when a parent or carer fabricates the symptoms of, or deliberately induces illness in a child.[4]

1.31 Emotional abuse

Emotional abuse is the persistent emotional maltreatment of a child such as to cause severe and persistent adverse effects on the child's emotional development. It may involve conveying to children that they are worthless or unloved, inadequate, or valued only insofar as they meet the needs of another person. It may feature age or developmentally inappropriate expectations being imposed on children. These may include interactions that are beyond the child's developmental capability, as well as overprotection and limitation of exploration and learning, or preventing the child participating in normal social interaction. It may involve seeing or hearing the ill-treatment of another. It may involve serious bullying causing children frequently to feel frightened or in danger, or the exploitation or corruption of children. Some level of emotional abuse is involved in all types of maltreatment of a child, though it may occur alone.

1.32 Sexual abuse

Sexual abuse involves forcing or enticing a child or young person to take part in sexual activities, including prostitution, whether or not the child is aware of what is happening. The activities may involve physical contact, including penetrative (e.g. rape, buggery or oral sex) or non-penetrative acts. They may include non-contact activities, such as involving children in looking at, or in the production of, pornographic material or watching sexual activities, or encouraging children to behave in sexually inappropriate ways.

1.33 Neglect

Neglect is the persistent failure to meet a child's basic physical and/or psychological needs, likely to result in the serious impairment of the child's health or development. Neglect may occur during pregnancy as a result of maternal substance abuse. Once a child is born, neglect may involve a parent or carer failing to provide adequate food and clothing, shelter including exclusion from home or abandonment, failing to protect a child from physical and emotional harm or danger, failure to ensure adequate supervision including the use of inadequate care-takers, or the failure to ensure access to appropriate medical care or treatment. It may also include neglect of, or unresponsiveness to, a child's basic emotional needs.

■ Relevant publications

There are a number of important publications that inform the whole child protection process. The publications listed below include both relevant research findings and Government guidance. An awareness of their content is an essential prerequisite to good practice in this area.[5]

'Child Protection: Messages from Research' (1995)[6]

The Department of Health commissioned a number of pieces of research, published collectively, and effectively launching what became known as the *refocusing debate*.

The research found that the majority of families in the child-protection process experienced multiple disadvantages, and concluded that there needed to be greater emphasis on the need for assessment towards providing services as opposed to providing evidence for care proceedings. 'Messages' has had a clear influence on the approach taken in the following publications.

'The Government's objectives for children's social services' (1999)[7]

This publication and subsequent documents comprise the 'Quality Protects' initiative. Quality Protects is an aspect of the Government's strategy for tackling social exclusion in society, with a focus on disadvantaged and vulnerable children. It contains 11 objectives accompanied by measurable targets and performance indicators.[8]

Objectives 2 and 7 are most pertinent to the consideration of child protection.

2. Protecting children from abuse and neglect.

   By:

   ■ Reducing the number of deaths of children where abuse or neglect is a factor.

   ■ Reducing the incidence of child abuse.

   ■ Making sure as few children as possible suffer from repeated abuse.

7. Better assessment leading to better services.

   By:

   ■ Completing initial assessment within seven working days.

   ■ Completing a core assessment within 35 working days of the initial assessment.

'Working Together to Safeguard Children – A Guide to Inter-Agency Working to Safeguard and Promote the Welfare of Children' (1999, 2006)[9]

The original 'Working Together', was published in 1991, and an updated version has been in place since 1999. A new 'Working Together' has been published in 2006 following consultation and review. The new guidance is updated in line with the Children Act 2004 and other developments since 1999, and includes new chapters on Local Safeguarding Children Boards, the proposed child death review processes. The 1999 version of 'Working Together' was supplemented by two further documents, 'Safeguarding Children Involved in Prostitution' (2000), and 'Safeguarding Children in Whom Illness is Fabricated or Induced' (2002). They will continue to take effect alongside the latest version.

Part 1 of the new document is guidance issued under s. 7 of the Local Authority Social Services Act 1970 and, as such, 'it should be complied with by local authorities carrying out their social services functions unless local circumstances indicate exceptional reasons which justify a variation' (p. xxv). Part II is non-statutory practice guidance.

'Working Together to Safeguard Children' describes comprehensively how agencies should work together and gives guidance on investigations and conduct of case conferences.

'Framework for the Assessment of Children in Need and their Families' (2000)[10]

This publication replaces earlier Department of Health guidance on assessment, 'Protecting Children: A Guide for Social Workers Undertaking a Comprehensive Assessment' (1998) (often referred to as the 'Orange book'). The new framework is written in less prescriptive terms. It is relevant for all assessments, whether leading to provision of services to a child in need, or statutory intervention by court order.

'The Children Act Now: Messages from Research' (2001)[11]

'The Children Act Now' builds on the earlier messages from the research document of 1995. It is published in a similar format, incorporating research studies which evaluate the practical implementation of the Children Act 1989. Its potential impact is clear from the following quote from the Foreword:

> The findings point to the importance of the need to have an effectively integrated children's system for assessment and care planning, better management information, competent professional staff and a smooth interface between children's services and the court system. Heeding of the messages from these studies is essential for the improvement of our services for children in need and their families. (p. ix)

'Every Child Matters'

Child care law and practice, including child protection must now be understood in the context of the 'Every Child Matters: Change for Children' programme, arising from the death of Victoria Climbié. Numerous documents have been published as part of this policy and are accessible from the 'Every Child Matters' website, including the new Common Assessment Framework which builds on the Framework for Assessment and is to be utilised by all professions. The policy is discussed in more detail in Chapter 7.

■ Local Safeguarding Children Boards (LSCBs)

Under the Children Act 2004 reforms, Area Child Protection Committees (**ACPCs**) have been replaced by Local Safeguarding Children Boards as part of the drive to establish clearer accountability. The boards are established by s. 13 and their functions described in s. 14. In many respects the functions will be similar to those of ACPCs; however, a number of criticisms have been directed at ACPCs. The Joint Chief Inspectors Report on Safeguarding Children identified a number of concerns including lack of effective leadership of ACPCs, not all relevant agencies were members and levels of commitment varied and the ACPC lacked adequate authority to hold members to account. In a similar vein, the Climbié Report noted that 'Area Child Protection Committees (ACPCs), the organisations with responsibility for co-ordinating child protection services at a local level, have generally become unwieldy, bureaucratic and with limited impact on front-line services' (para 133). The introduction of LSCBs as statutory boards aims to address such concerns.

The board will be comprised of representatives of the children's services authority and each partner and including CAFCASS. Following consultation within the board it is also possible to add representatives of other bodies, 'of any nature exercising functions or engaged in activities relating to children in the area of the authority' (Children Act 2004 s. 13(6)). Senior representatives of agencies are likely to constitute an executive board with subcommittees to deal with specific areas, e.g. training. It is possible for two or more Children's Services Authorities to establish a LSCB for their combined area (Children Act 2004 s.13(8)). The function of the LSCB is to coordinate and ensure the effectiveness of each body represented on the board in safeguarding and promoting the welfare of children. Within that remit boards will produce their own policies and procedures, be consulted in the development of the Children's Services Plan, communicate best practice and hold serious case reviews) previously where a child died or was seriously harmed, the ACPC would conduct a review (Part 8).[12] According to 'Next Steps', it is likely that the Director of Children's Services will chair the board or, if more appropriate, there will be an independent chair. Guidance on LSCBs was published in advance of the new 'Working Together' and has become chapter 3 of that document.

Duty to investigate

Local authorities receive referrals from a wide variety of sources, including the professional and lay person (though there is no legal duty on a private individual to report concerns). Almost all referrals will require some level of investigation but a relatively small proportion will lead to statutory intervention. Referrals come from a variety of sources. Research by Gibbons[13] identified the following sources of referral: education – 23 per cent; health visitors, GPs and other health professionals – 17 per cent; household/lay – 17 per cent; social services professionals – 13 per cent; police and probation – 12 per cent; anonymous – 6 per cent; and others – 12 per cent. 'Working Together' provides some guidance on how social services should deal with initial referrals. The nature of any concerns, how they have arisen and the child's needs should be clarified with the person making the referral. If that person is a professional the referral should be confirmed in writing. There must be clarity about any action to be taken and by whom, and all decisions should be recorded in writing. A referral may lead to no further action, provision of support or further investigation and the possibility of an emergency short-term order. A strategy discussion will be held following a referral to decide whether further investigation should take place, and whether any short-term emergency action is required.

The local authority's duty to investigate is established under s. 47, which provides:

s. 47

(1) Where a local authority –
    (a) are informed that a child who lives, or is found, in their area –
        (i)   is the subject of an emergency protection order; or
        (ii) is in police protection; or
    (b) have reasonable cause to suspect that a child who lives, or is found, in their area is suffering, or is likely to suffer, significant harm, the authority shall make, or cause to be made, such inquiries as they consider necessary to enable them to decide whether they should take any action to safeguard or promote the child's welfare.

(CA 1989)

Further subsections elaborate on that central duty to make inquiries. When inquiries are being made, the local authority must take steps to obtain access to the child themselves or by a person authorised for that purpose, unless they are satisfied that they have sufficient information already (s. 47(4)). If issues arise in the course of inquiries relating to education, the local authority is directed to consult the relevant local education authority (s. 47(5)). Central to inquiries is the need for the local authority to see the child. If access to the child is denied or the local authority is denied information as to the child's whereabouts, the local authority shall apply for an emergency protection order, a child assessment order, a care order or a supervision order unless they are satisfied that the child's welfare can be satisfactorily safeguarded without doing so (s. 47(6)). If the local authority, on the conclusion of inquiries, decides not to apply for an order, it is directed to consider whether it would be appropriate to review the case at a later date and, if so, to set a date (s. 47(7)). The principle of working together is given statutory footing in s. 47(9), which provides for various persons to assist with the local authority's inquiries unless to do so would be unreasonable in all the circumstances of the case. The specified persons are: any local authority; any local education authority; any local housing authority; any health authority; and any other person authorised by the Secretary of State (s. 47(11)).

In addition to the above provision, s. 15 of the Crime and Disorder Act 1998 amends s. 47 by introducing a new subsection (1)(a)(iii), which reads: 'has contravened a ban imposed by a curfew notice'. In those circumstances the local authority is directed to commence inquiries as soon as practicable and, in any event, within 48 hours of the authority receiving the information. In relation to this subsection there is no reference to risk of harm. (The Crime and Disorder Act 1998 is discussed fully in Chapter 13.)

'Working Together' requires local authorities to refer parents to independent advice and advocacy agencies as soon as inquiries commence under s. 47.

The duty to investigate imposed on social services is distinct from any responsibility the police may have to conduct a criminal investigation, though a joint approach to some aspects such as interviewing the child may be appropriate. In *R (S)* v. *Swindon Borough Council* [2001] EWHC Admin 334, a man challenged a local authority's decision to continue its child protection investigation after he had been acquitted of indecent assault. The judge found that, as s. 47 required the local authority to have only 'reasonable cause to suspect' significant harm, not reasonable cause to believe, the duty to investigate was not removed by the acquittal. The judge also stated that the local authority duty to investigate remained the same before and after the coming into force of the Human Rights Act 1998. The threshold for investigation is thus quite low.

The investigation must be carried out 'properly'. In another recent case, a father and child claimed damages from the local authority after inquiries were pursued beyond the point required by s. 47 and damage resulted. Interviews had been held improperly with the child and information was wrongly withheld from the father (*L v. Reading Borough Council* [2001] EWCA Civ 346).

The checklist contained in the 'Framework for the Assessment of Children in Need and their Families', known as the referral chart (reproduced at Exhibit 9.1), is a useful starting point for information to be obtained and recorded at initial referral stage.

■ Case conferences and reviews

The first major recognition of the child protection case conference can be found in a 1974 DHSS letter following the Colwell inquiry.[14] Its recommendations were for area review committees to be formed in every local authority, child protection registers to be established and child abuse manuals to be drawn up. Case conferences were recognised as an invaluable tool for coordinating investigations into child abuse.

Case conferences are non-statutory bodies and, whilst occupying a central role in the child-protection process, neither their role nor their composition is set out in legislation. Due to the multi-disciplinary make-up of the case conference, it is not possible for conferences to make decisions about the conduct of cases; rather, recommendations are formulated which must be ratified by the Social Services Department with responsibility for child protection. The only decision which a case conference can make is on the issue of registration. Current guidance on case conferences is found in 'Working Together to Safeguard Children – A Guide to Inter-Agency Working to Safeguard and Promote the Welfare of Children' (2006) ('Working Together').

The initial child protection conference has three purposes:

- to bring together and analyse in an inter-agency setting the information which has been obtained about the child's developmental needs, and the parents' or carers' capacity to respond to these needs to ensure the child's safety and promote the child's health and development within the context of their wider family and environment;

- to consider the evidence presented to the conference, make judgements about the likelihood of a child suffering significant harm in future and decide whether the child is at continuing risk of significant harm; and

- to decide what future action is required to safeguard and promote the welfare of the child, how that action will be taken forward, and with what intended outcomes.

(5.80)

Referrals

Guide for use

This chart is designed to help you gather information at the initial referral stage. It is not exhaustive and should not be treated as a check list.

Please use the chart alongside the usual referral forms as a reminder of:

A. issues which may need to be checked

B. matters raised by the referrer that should be recorded.

What help is requested?

Material resources
Housing, beds, clothing, money, other

Practical help for parent/carer
Respite care, other

Support for parent/carer
Someone to talk to, advice/information, other

Support for referrer
Advice/information, discussion of current concern, other

Practical help for child
Accommodation, school place, specialist equipment, other

Support for child
Befriending, counselling, youth scheme, other

Protection for child
Home visit, immediate shelter, other

Is there a child in danger?

Source of information
- Problem observed by referrer
- Child talked to referrer
- Someone else told referrer of their concern – who?
- Referrer has general concerns – why refer now?

Why is the referrer worried?
- Is there a need for immediate medical treatment?
- Is there a physical injury – size, colour, shape and location?
- Is the child neglected – appearance, clothing, home conditions?
- Is there a lack of supervision – whereabouts and situation of child?
- Is child a victim of sexual assault – child's account or behaviour?
- Is the child emotionally abused – observed behaviour?
- Is there a person present who has been convicted of an offence against a child?
- Is there an explanation?

Details of:
- Child's current whereabouts
- Date child was last seen
- Any previous concerns
- Background to current concern
- Any specific injury or event causing concern
- When did it happen?
- Child's, parent's/carer's account
- Identity of alleged abuser – personal details assist police checks
- Alleged abuser's current whereabouts
- Any supporting medical or forensic evidence

Is there any other possible explanation the referrer can offer for their concern?

Additional information
- Willingness of referrer to be interviewed
- Discrepancies or inconsistencies in the report

Exhibit 9.1   Referrals involving a child (referral chart)
Source: Cleaver, H., Wattam, C. and Cawson, P. (1998), reproduced with permission of NSPCC.

Involving a Child

Family / household details

Child
Name, age, gender, ethnic origin, address and telephone number

Referrer
Name, address and telephone number

Referrer's relationship to the child

Parent / carer
Name, address, telephone number and age if under 18 years

Access to parent / carer
Is an appointment necessary?

Alternative carer(s)
Name, address and telephone number

Other significant relative(s)
Name, address and telephone number

Other children in the household
Age and gender

Primary language of family

Ethnic origin of family

Religion of family

Disability of parent or child

Other professionals involved with the family

School / nursery
Address, telephone number and name of head teacher

Health visitor
Name, address and telephone number

General practitioner
Name, address and telephone number

Probation service
Name, address and telephone number

Any other

Is any other help needed?

Remember this is not a check list. Record anything the referrer tells you about these or similar matters:

- Bereavement
- Child/parent conflict
- Drug/alcohol/ substance misuse
- Housing/homelessness
- Learning difficulties
- Non school attendance
- Physical disability
- Police involvement
- Racial harassment
- Violence
- Bullying
- Child behaviour
- Family/marital conflict
- Financial crisis
- Mental ill health
- Parenting
- Physical ill health
- Poverty
- Unemployment

Consider

- Is this the correct agency? – if not, refer elsewhere and tell referrer
- Have you sufficient information – if not where could you get more?
- Are they eligible for the service?
- Does the referrer want a visit immediately?
- Will an interpreter/sign language facilitator be needed?
- Are there mobility/access considerations?
- Are there any assurances you need to give? i.e. referrer's identity must be protected
- Feedback to the referrer about the action you will take
- How will you close the conversation – does anything else need saying, do they have any questions?
- Do you need to consult someone about the action to take?

Check

- Is the child/parent aware of the referral?
- Is the family/child known to the department?
- Is the family/child currently receiving services?
- If suspected child abuse – the Child Protection Register

Useful telephone numbers

Record your most used telephone numbers here:

_____
_____
_____
_____
_____
_____
_____
_____
_____
_____
_____
_____
_____
_____
_____
_____
_____

NSPCC

© NSPCC 1998

First published 1998 by NSPCC
42 Curtain Road, London, EC2A 3NH

NSPCC gives permission to photocopy this chart for use in connection with services to children and families.

Published as part of a pack in the NSPCC Policy Practice Research Series: Assessing Risk in Child Protection, by Hedy Cleaver, Corinne Wattam, Pat Cawson (ISBN 0 902498 81 9).

Registered charity number 216401

Exhibit 9.1 Continued

All initial child protection conferences should take place within 15 working days of the strategy discussion. Within that time band, there is a need to balance the urgency of the case and the need for adequate preparation and the initial assessment.

Levels of attendance will vary according to the circumstances of the case but 'Working Together' acknowledges that very large conferences can inhibit discussion and be intimidating for the family. It thus recommends that those attending 'should be there because they have a significant contribution to make, arising from professional expertise, knowledge of the child or family or both'. The LSCB should specify the required quorum. Written reports should be provided by agencies that are invited but unable to attend. In each case a written report should be provided to the conference by social services, summarising the information obtained through initial assessment and s. 47 inquiries, including a chronology of significant events and agency contact with the child. Exhibit 9.2 illustrates the range of potential members.

The conference will be chaired by a professional who is independent of operational or line management responsibilities for the case under discussion. The responsibilities of the chair include outlining the purpose of the conference, or setting an agenda, ensuring confidentiality, enabling full contributions to the discussion from all members and ensuring decisions are taken systematically. A chair should have appropriate skills including knowledge and understanding of anti-discriminatory practice.

Involvement of the child and family

'Working Together' states that parents should normally be invited to attend the conference and helped fully to participate with the option of bringing an advocate, friend or supporter. It is not clear what the term 'advocate' refers to in this context, but direct reference to a legal representative has been removed in the current version

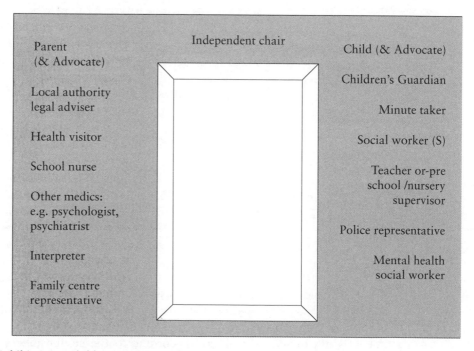

Exhibit 9.2   Child protection conference: possible membership

of 'Working Together'. An early decision of the European Court of Human Rights found breaches of Arts. 6 and 8 of the European Convention through failure to involve parents in decision-making regarding children in care (*R* v. *United Kingdom* [1988] 2 FLR 445). According to *R* v. *Cornwall County Council, ex parte LH* [2000] 1 FLR 236, the parents' solicitor cannot be refused attendance at the conference. In that case a blanket ban of solicitors attending child protection conferences and the withholding of minutes from a parent who had attended the conference was found to be unlawful. The decision relied on the status of guidance contained in 'Working Together', which envisaged a parent being accompanied by a friend or lawyer and stated that a copy of the minutes should be sent to all parties. The council had not articulated any good reason for departing from the guidance and the practice was thus found to be contrary to the statutory guidance and unlawful. (NB This case was decided when the relevant guidance, issued under LASSA 1970, s. 7 was 'Working Together under the Children Act 1989' (1991), the forerunner of 'Working Together' (1999) and (2006).) Although advocacy services are developing across the country, Lindley *et al.* (2001) found that, in relation to advocacy for parents in child protection cases:

> the absence of any national protocol and theoretical framework underpinning this service has led to much of the content and style of the work being developed 'on the hoof' resulting in wide variations in practice, both in terms of the service delivered, and how it is responded to by different local authorities.[15]

The child of sufficient age and understanding should also have the opportunity to attend and be supported by a children's advocate. Each conference will need to plan the level of involvement of family members, taking into account the need for professionals to be able to share information in a safe and non-threatening environment and for family members to speak to the conference in the absence of other family members. The chair may decide in exceptional circumstances to exclude a parent or carer from the child protection conference, perhaps where there is a risk of violence or intimidation or if the parent is subject to criminal prosecution in respect of the child. The chair should meet the child and family members before the conference and ensure they understand the procedure and purpose of the conference.

Professional practice has needed to develop to take on board greater involvement of family members in conferences and it is important for professionals to heed the advice in 'Working Together' that 'those providing information should take care to distinguish between fact, observation, allegation and opinion' (para. 5.101).

Registration

At an initial child protection conference it will be necessary to decide whether to register a child on the child protection register. The key question is: 'Is the child at continuing risk of significant harm?' If so, the child's name will be registered and a formal child protection plan will be drawn up. The chair will determine under which category the child's name should be registered. The categories used are physical, emotional, sexual abuse or neglect. The general category of grave concern is no longer applied. The reason for registration should always be made clear to the parents (and child of sufficient understanding), and also the implications of registration and procedure for removal of the child's name. Professionals who may have concerns about a child should be able to consult the register and ascertain the primary reason for registration. Approximately 32,000 children's names are on the register at any one time because they require a child protection plan (in England).[16] On average a child's name will remain on the register for about a year. Research suggests that, despite clarification of the criteria for registration, there is wide variation in child protection registration and re-registration figures between councils.[17]

When it is identified that the child is at risk of significant harm, the conference will appoint a key worker, identify a core group of professionals and family members to implement the child protection plan, identify what assessments are required and agree a date for the child protection review conference. The core group should meet within ten days of the initial conference and a core assessment should be completed within 42 days of the initial assessment, carried out in accordance with the 'Framework for the Assessment of Children in Need and their Families'. The review conference should be convened within three months, and thereafter every six months for as long as the child's name remains on the register. Exhibit 9.3 outlines the timescales for investigation.

Family group conferences

Family group conferences were described in the previous 'Working Together' as 'a positive option for planning services for children and their families' (para. 7.13). Family group conferences do not replace child protection conferences and they are more likely to be utilised to develop a plan for a child in need.[18]

Part V of the Children Act 1989 deals with orders for the protection of children. Where an application is made to court concerning a child, the proceedings will be conducted in private. This position has been upheld by the European Court in *B* v. *United Kingdom* [2001] 2 FLR 261.

Short-term and emergency orders

■ Child assessment orders

The child assessment order (**CAO**) was introduced by the Children Act 1989 broadly in line with a recommendation of the report 'A Child in Mind; Protection of Children in a Responsible Society' (1987) (the Kimberley Carlile Report).[19] It is designed to cover those situations where there are concerns about a child, and lack of cooperation from the child's carers is preventing full

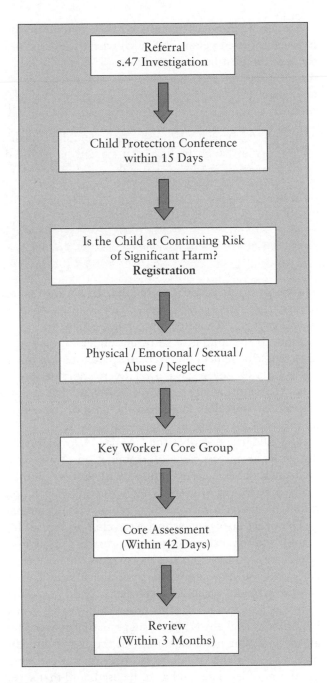

Exhibit 9.3 Child protection: timescales

assessment. The order is not intended to be used in obvious emergency situations. The court may treat an application for a CAO as an application for an emergency protection order if it feels the grounds for an emergency protection order exist.

Section 43 provides that a CAO will be made on the application of a local authority or authorised person (NSPCC) where the court is satisfied that all three limbs of the section must be satisfied:

s. 43

(a) the applicant has reasonable cause to suspect that the child is suffering, or is likely to suffer, significant harm;

(b) an assessment of the state of the child's health or development, or of the way in which he has been treated, is required to enable the applicant to determine whether or not the child is suffering, or is likely to suffer, significant harm; and

(c) it is unlikely that such an assessment will be made, or be satisfactory, in the absence of an order under this section.

(CA 1989)

The effect of the order is to require the child to be produced for assessment under the terms of the order. Directions can be included in the order relating to any aspect of assessment, such as the type of assessment and where and by whom it will be carried out. If the child is of sufficient understanding to make an informed decision, he may refuse a medical or psychiatric examination or other assessment (s. 43(8)). The order lasts for seven days, a relatively short period in which to carry out anything other than a primarily medical assessment. The seven-day period may commence at a specified start date later than the date of the court hearing, which would enable appropriate involvement of other professionals.

The guidance describes the CAO as 'A lesser, heavily court controlled order dealing with the narrow issue of examination or assessment of the child in specific circumstances of non co-operation by the parents and lack of evidence of the need for a different type of order or other action'.[20] An example is provided of a child who is failing to thrive, whose parents are unwilling or unable to face the child's condition.

The order does not authorise the child's removal from home unless directions are included in the order and it is necessary for the assessment (s. 43(9)). In exceptional circumstances, for example, this may include overnight stays if 24-hour monitoring is considered a necessary part of the assessment. The local authority does not acquire parental responsibility when a child assessment order is made.

It was anticipated that this order would rarely be used and research supports that hypothesis. Dickens (1993)[21] suggests that reasons for a lack of use in the immediate period after implementation of the Act included: lack of knowledge about the order; the fact that it is rare for parents not to be persuaded to cooperate, even if the threat of legal action has to be used; and that seven days is a very limited period for an assessment.

■ Emergency protection orders

Emergency protection orders (**EPOs**) were introduced by the Children Act 1989 to provide immediate protection for a child. An application may be made to a single justice but in most cases will be made to the family proceedings court. The grounds for an application for an EPO are contained in s. 44 of the Children Act 1989.

s. 44

(1) Where any person ('the applicant') applies to the court for an order to be made under this section with respect to a child, the court may make the order if, but only if, it is satisfied that –

(a) there is reasonable cause to believe that the child is likely to suffer significant harm if –

   (i) he is not removed to accommodation provided by or on behalf of the applicant; or

   (ii) he does not remain in the place in which he is then being accommodated;

(b) in the case of an application made by a local authority –

   (i) inquiries are being made with respect to the child under section 47(1)(b); and

   (ii) those inquiries are being frustrated by access to the child being unreasonably refused to a person authorised to seek access and that the applicant has reasonable cause to believe that access to the child is required as a matter of urgency; or

(c) in the case of an application made by an authorised person –

   (i) the applicant has reasonable cause to suspect that a child is suffering, or is likely to suffer, significant harm;

   (ii) the applicant is making inquiries with respect to the child's welfare; and

   (iii) those inquiries are being frustrated by access to the child being unreasonably refused to a person authorised to seek access and the applicant has reasonable cause to believe that access to the child is required as a matter of urgency.

(CA 1989)

The EPO operates as a direction to produce the child and gives authority to the applicant to retain or remove the child (s. 44(4)(a), (b)). Under an EPO the applicant acquires parental responsibility (s. 44(4)(c)) but this is limited to what is necessary to safeguard the welfare of the child having regard to the duration of the order. In other words, parental responsibility may be exercised in relation to day-to-day matters but long-lasting changes would not be authorised. In addition, specific directions will be included in an EPO in relation to contact with a child (s. 44(6)(a)), and to medical or psychiatric examination or other assessment of the child (s. 44(6)(b)). As with the CAO, a child of sufficient understanding to make an informed decision may refuse to submit to an examination or other assessment (s. 44(7)). Subject to any specific directions given by the court, the applicant (usually the local authority) must allow the child reasonable contact with his parents, any person with parental responsibility or with whom the child was living immediately before the order, and any person who has a contact order (s. 44(13)). The inclusion of this provision can be directly traced to events in Cleveland where parents whose children had been removed under place of safety orders (in some cases for 28 days) were denied any contact.

There is a power to return the child home if it appears safe to do so and to remove the child again if there is a change of circumstances. For example, if an EPO is made in respect of a child where sexual abuse is suspected, and the alleged perpetrator is charged and initially remanded in custody, it may be possible to return the child home provided that there is an individual who can care for the child. If the alleged perpetrator is granted bail and allowed to return home, it would be possible to move the child again, during the order (s. 44(12)).

Duration of the order

An emergency protection order lasts for eight days (s. 45(1)). It is possible for the order to be extended, once only, for a further seven days. An application for the EPO to be discharged may be made by the child, his parents, a person with parental responsibility or a person with whom the child was living immediately before the order, after 72 hours (s. 45(8)). This right of challenge does not apply if the person was given notice of the application and was present at the hearing. Applications for discharge will therefore normally be made in cases where the initial application was made *ex parte* (i.e. where notice was not given, because to do so would have placed the child in danger). Given the action that must be taken during an EPO the limited duration imposes significant pressure on the professionals involved in the case.

The applicant for an EPO may be any person, the local authority or the NSPCC as an authorised person. The grounds for the application are slightly different in each case. For any person the court must be satisfied that the applicant has reasonable cause to *believe* the child is likely to suffer significant harm. An example might be a doctor who wishes to prevent a child's removal from hospital or a youth worker who is concerned that a young person may be sexually abused on return home from a youth club. For the local authority there is an additional ground that where s. 47 inquiries are being made and are being frustrated by access to the child being unreasonably denied then an EPO application may be made. For the NSPCC the court must find that the applicant has reasonable cause to *suspect* that a child is suffering or likely to suffer significant harm.

It may be necessary to apply for an EPO very shortly after receiving an initial referral, or the need may arise due to a change in circumstances or exacerbation of events in ongoing involvement with a family.

An important decision has considered the impact of the Human Rights Act on emergency protection orders. Munby J gave the judgment in *X Council* v. *B (Emergency Protection Orders)* [2004] EWHC 2015 (Fam).[22] In this case the local authority were granted *ex parte* (without notice) EPOs in respect of three children (all of whom suffered severe illness) of a family with whom they had a long involvement. The authority's concerns centred on mother's failure to follow medical advice, engage with medical services and inappropriate management of medicines. An assessment of the children was required and the authority did not consider this was possible whilst the children were with their parents. The authority were criticised for seeking EPOs rather than child assessment orders, which would have been a more proportionate response. Munby J gave the following guidance on the use of EPOs. Without notice applications should only be made where there were 'compelling reasons to believe that the child's welfare would be compromised' and proof of imminent danger. Supporting evidence must be full and compelling. The order should not be made for longer than absolutely necessary. Arrangements for reasonable contact should not be limited by lack of resources.

Consider in the following scenarios whether an EPO, CAO or no order would be appropriate.

1. Julie is the mother of 3-year-old twins who live with her during the week and stay with their father, Ron, at weekends. Julie's older two children, Sam, aged 9, and Louise, aged 11, were removed from her care after their stepfather John was found guilty of sexual and physical assaults of them. He was imprisoned for six years. Julie began a short relationship with Ron, the twins' father, and agreed with social services that she would have no more contact with John. Since she separated from Ron, Julie has secretly resumed letter contact with John and social services have been informed that he will be moving in with Julie on release, expected next week.

2. Hopeshire Social Services have received several reports from neighbours of Jane and Peter, claiming to have heard persistent screaming from the house, which is believed to be their daughter Geraldine. They also say that Geraldine has not been seen going to nursery for several days but when they saw her in the back garden she had a black eye and bruises to her legs. A social worker goes to the house at 10.30 a.m. but is told by Jane that Geraldine is unwell, asleep and cannot be disturbed. When the social worker asks if she can come in for a chat, Peter comes to the door with their Rottweiler dog and tells the social worker in no uncertain terms to go away and stay away.

3. Joan, a health visitor, contacts Hopeshire Social Services to relay her concerns about Susie, a 3-year-old girl who lives with her mum, Amy, and her grandmother, Rosie. Her father, Jack, is currently in prison having breached an ouster and non-molestation order in respect of violence towards Amy. Amy appears very depressed and Joan suspects she is drinking heavily. Susie has a squint in one eye and appears under-nourished. She has very little speech and is clingy and withdrawn. Joan obtained a place for Susie at the local pre-school but Amy says it is too far to walk. Three appointments at the eye hospital have been missed and the hospital are reluctant to arrange any more. Joan arranged to collect and take Amy and Susie to the last appointment but they were out. Amy said at a later visit that she forgot. Rosie is schizophrenic and occasionally is verbally abusive to Joan and refuses to let her in.

■ Police protection

The police are able to remove and detain a child without reference to the court. Under s. 46:

s. 46

> (1) Where a constable has reasonable cause to believe a child would otherwise be likely to suffer significant harm, he may –
> (a) remove the child to suitable accommodation and keep him there; or
> (b) take reasonable steps to ensure the child's removal from any hospital, or other place, in which he is being accommodated is prevented.
>
> (CA 1989)

Police protection is a short-term remedy of no more than 72 hours' duration. The police must inform the local authority as soon as is reasonably practicable after taking a child into police protection. It may then be appropriate for the local authority to apply for an EPO in respect of the child. In that case the eight-day period runs from the start of police protection. The police must also take steps to inform the child's parents, any person with parental responsibility, or any person with whom the child was living immediately before being taken into police protection (s. 46(4)).

The Children Act 1989 does not give the police authority to enter property by virtue of s. 46; however, a warrant may be obtained under s. 48. There may be obvious emergency situations where obtaining a warrant will cause delay. For example, if a child can be seen at an upstairs window and appears to be at risk of falling, and the police cannot raise anybody to open the door, then reliance on s. 17 of the Police and Criminal Evidence Act 1984 enables the police to enter premises without a warrant, to save life or limb.

■ Recovery orders

It is a criminal offence to remove a child who is the subject of a care order, EPO or police protection, from the responsible person, or to keep the child away from the responsible person, e.g. by failing to return the child after a contact visit (s. 49). The responsible person is the person who had care of the child by virtue of the order. If a child has been taken away or is being kept away from the responsible person, has run away or is missing, the court may make a recovery order (s. 50). A person with parental responsibility (under an EPO or care order) or the designated officer, where the child is in police protection, may apply for a recovery order. Where an order is in force it is a direction to produce the child; it authorises removal of the child and it requires anybody with information as to the child's whereabouts to disclose that information to the police or an officer of the court. In addition, it authorises the police to enter specified premises and search for a child, using reasonable force where necessary, in addition to their general authority under the Police and Criminal Evidence Act, s. 17.

■ Children's refuges

Certain children's homes and also foster carers may be classed as providing a refuge for children who appear to be at risk of harm. A certificate will be issued by the Secretary of State to recognised refuges. A refuge can provide temporary accommodation to a child and, provided a certificate is held, the person providing the refuge will be exempt from prosecution for abduction or harbouring a child. A refuge can prove to be a vital resource, given some of the problems of institutional abuse that have been highlighted in recent years.[23]

■ Family Law Act 1996 – power of exclusion

New powers were introduced under the Family Law Act 1996 (amending the Children Act 1989 to include new s. 38A and 44A), which enable the court to exclude an alleged abuser from the home rather than having to remove the child. An exclusion order may be attached to an EPO or an interim care order.

Under s. 44A the court must be satisfied of three criteria:

(a) that there is reasonable cause to believe that if a person (the relevant person) is excluded from a dwelling-house in which the child lives, the child will cease to be likely to suffer significant harm, and enquiries will not be frustrated; and

(b) another person living in the same house, whether or not the parent, is able and willing to give to the child the care which it would be reasonable to expect a parent to give; and

(c) that person consents to the inclusion of the exclusion requirement.

A power of arrest may be attached to the order so that in the event of breach – for example, if the excluded person returns to the home – an arrest can take place without warrant. In *Re L (Children)* [2001] EWCA Civ 151, a case where an exclusion order had been breached repeatedly, a sentence of four months' imprisonment was given. The judge noted that the person in breach (the father) was unable to appreciate that orders had to be obeyed and needed to come to terms with the fact that the family situation had changed.

The exclusion order is available only if the person at home gives consent. In many cases this may be the mother, whose partner would be the subject of the exclusion order. There may be many reasons why she might not be able or willing to give consent, perhaps due to fear or unwillingness to recognise the possibility that her partner may have abused her child. It is most likely that the person being excluded will be a member of the household, e.g. step-father. It is also possible to exclude a person from without the household from entering the house or a defined area, e.g. a neighbour suspected of abuse whilst babysitting. The person remaining in the home must also be able to provide the standard of reasonable parenting. In many cases it will not be possible to clearly identify one person only as the abuser. If there were additional concerns relating to the standard of care the remaining parent would be able to provide, an exclusion order would not be appropriate.

Where an application for an Exclusion Order is made, a statement must be served on the relevant party (i.e. person to be excluded) in order that he is made aware of the evidence upon which the order is based so that he can make an informed decision as to whether to apply to vary or discharge the order. The statement must set out the facts on which the application for exclusion is based and evidence supporting an application for an interim care order or EPO. It must make clear what the person is required to do, e.g. leave the dwelling-house, not enter the dwelling or a defined area (*W v. A Local Authority (Exclusion Requirement)* [2000] 2 FCR 662). If the child is removed for more than 24 hours by the local authority the exclusion order will lapse.

Prior to introduction of the exclusion order, local authorities utilised a power contained in Sch. 2, para. 5. Where it appeared that a child was suffering or likely to suffer significant harm at the hands of a person living at the same premises, the local authority could assist that person to move from the premises. Assistance could be given in cash and often involved the local authority paying for bed and breakfast accommodation. The key difference between this power (which remains available to the local authority) and the exclusion order relates to the consent of the alleged abuser. In the former power the local authority could only assist an individual who was willing to move. The power to assist with alternative accommodation may be persuasive but the provision has no force if the individual wishes to stay in the premises. If that were the case the only alternative would be to remove the child. It appears that, despite its apparent advantages, the new power has been used infrequently.[24]

Care and supervision orders

The law relating to care and supervision orders is contained in Part IV of the Children Act 1989. It is possible for a care or supervision order to be made on the application of the local authority only in respect of a child under the age of 17.

'significant harm'

The grounds, which must be satisfied before an order can be made, are set out in s. 31 and are commonly referred to as the threshold criteria. Significant harm is the threshold justifying compulsory intervention. The Lord Chancellor described the criteria as the 'minimum circumstances which should always be found to exist before it can be justified for a court to even begin to contemplate whether the state should be enabled to intervene compulsorily in family life'. The phrase was intended to be broad and flexible in order to incorporate a wide range of circumstances; in fact it has caused major interpretational problems and a succession of case law decisions. 'Working Together' (2006) provides further explanation,

There are no absolute criteria on which to rely when judging what constitutes significant harm. Consideration of the severity of ill-treatment may include the degree and the extent of physical harm, the duration and frequency of abuse and neglect, and the extent of premeditation, degree of threat and coercion, sadism, and bizarre or unusual elements in child sexual abuse. Each of these elements has been associated with more severe effects on the child, and/or relatively greater difficulty in helping the child overcome the adverse impact of the maltreatment. Sometimes, a single traumatic event may constitute significant harm, e.g. a violent assault, suffocation or poisoning. More often, significant harm is a compilation of significant events, both acute and longstanding, which interrupt, change or damage the child's physical and psychological development. Some children live in family and social circumstances where their health and development are neglected. For them, it is the corrosiveness of long-term emotional, physical or sexual abuse that causes impairment to the extent of constituting significant harm. In each case, it is necessary to consider any maltreatment alongside the family's strengths and supports. (para 1.24)

It was anticipated when the Children Act 1989 was introduced, with its emphasis on partnership, prevention and provision of services and the 'no order' rule, that there would be fewer care proceedings. In fact judicial statistics show an increase in both the applications for and care orders made. There were 2,657 care applications in 1992 rising to 6,728 in 1998. This trend has been described as a 'care proceedings explosion'.[25] Nevertheless, research suggests that the Children Act 1989 has raised the threshold for intervention, and the children subject to care order applications have very serious problems. In addition, fewer appear to be instigated in a crisis, many children having been looked after or on the Child Protection Register before proceedings commenced.[26]

The relevant section is set out below:

s. 31

> (2) A court may only make a care order or supervision order if it is satisfied –
>   (a) that the child concerned is suffering, or is likely to suffer, significant harm; and
>   (b) that the harm, or likelihood of harm, is attributable to –
>   (i) the care given to the child, or likely to be given to him if the order were not made, not being what it would be reasonable to expect a parent to give to him; or
>   (ii) the child's being beyond parental control.
>
> (CA 1989)

In hearing cases it is necessary for all allegations to be determined, not just sufficient to meet the threshold criteria.

Certain of the terms used in the threshold criteria are further defined in subsection (9) and case law decisions have provided further clarification.

s. 31(9)

'Harm' means ill-treatment or the impairment of health or development; including, for example, impairment suffered from seeing or hearing the ill-treatment of another;

'Development' means physical, intellectual, emotional, social or behavioural development;

'Health' means physical or mental health; and

'Ill-treatment' includes sexual abuse and forms of ill-treatment which are not physical.

(CA 1989)

The definition of the meaning of 'harm' in the Children Act 1989 (s. 31) was extended to include 'impairment suffered from seeing or hearing the ill-treatment of another' by the Adoption and Children Act 2002, s. 120.

Subsection (10) introduces the concept of the similar child:

s. 31(10)

Where the question of whether harm suffered by a child is significant turns on the child's health or development, his health or development shall be compared with that which could reasonably be expected of a similar child.

(CA 1989)

There are three stages to the process of satisfying the threshold criteria and obtaining a care or supervision order. The first stage is to find 'significant harm'. Significant is not defined. A single act of abuse may constitute significant harm or there may have been a series of acts which taken together cause significant harm. Guidance suggests that 'the significance could exist in the seriousness of the harm or the implication of it'.[27] In *Humberside County Council* v. *B* [1993] 1 FLR 257, 'significant' was described as, 'considerable, or noteworthy or important'.

The following brief examples illustrate the difficulty in assessing significant harm.

- ■ A child aged 4 months has a broken rib.
- ■ A child aged 6 months has faint fingermark bruising around the mouth.
- ■ A child aged 2 years has 20 random bruises of differing ages around the knees and lower leg.

In the first case the injury is both substantial and significant. In the second case the harm caused may not be considered a substantial injury but it is significant in that the injury is unlikely to have been caused accidentally and may suggest that the child has been force-fed or a dummy has been forced into the child's mouth to stop crying. In the third case, 20 bruises is a substantial injury; however, given the age of the child and the position of the bruises it is likely that they are attributable to the usual tumbles and bumps that a 2-year-old child experiences. It is clearly not sufficient to look simply at the extent of an injury, but also to consider what the injury signifies.

'is suffering'

Re M (A Minor) (Care Order: Threshold Conditions) [1994] 3 WLR 558, a House of Lords decision (overruling the Court of Appeal), confirmed that the phrase 'is suffering' in s. 31(2) relates to the period immediately before the child protection process was implemented in respect of the child. In that case, at the time of the hearing, as the child was placed with a member of his wider family, it could not be said that he was suffering significant harm, nor that he was likely to suffer significant harm. The child had suffered significant harm when his father murdered his mother. The House of Lords ruled that it is incorrect to apply the words 'is suffering' literally as the present tense, to be applied at the date of the hearing. If that were the case, very few care orders would be made because the local authorities will have made arrangements to safeguard the child in the period before the final hearing. The correct interpretation is to apply 'is suffering' to the date of the initial statutory intervention. This may be the date of the initial care order application or the date of an EPO application. This interpretation clearly follows the spirit rather than the letter of the law.

In *Re G (Children) (Care Order: Evidence)* [2001] EWCA Civ 968, the Court of Appeal held that in determining whether the criteria were made out the court can take into account information later acquired, relating to the state of affairs at the relevant date (i.e. the point of initial intervention) and later events where they could help prove the state of affairs at the relevant date.

'likely'

Before the Children Act 1989 was introduced, it was possible to take action in respect of likely future harm only via the inherent jurisdiction. Inclusion of the word 'likely' in the threshold criteria has reduced the need to have recourse to wardship. Unfortunately, there is no indication of the degree of likelihood required, but it clearly invites risk assessment. In *Newham London Borough Council* v. *Attorney-general* [1993] 1 FLR 281, the court stated that it would be wrong to equate the phrase with 'on the balance of probabilities'. This part of the criteria may be relied upon in respect of newborn babies where there is a concern that parents will not be able to offer adequate care, and cases where harm arose during pregnancy, as in *Re D (A Minor)* [1987] AC 317, where the mother was a drug addict. It is not possible for a care order to be made simply on the basis that harm occurred in the past but, as in *Re D,* it may be possible to infer likelihood of future harm based on previous behaviour. It may also be used to retain a child being looked after when parents indicate that they want the child returned to them, if the local authority argues that the child is likely to suffer significant harm because of the state of affairs at home, perhaps due to the presence of an unsuitable adult. Likelihood of harm is linked to the ability of the parent to meet the emotional needs of the child for the years ahead: *Re H (A Minor) (Section 37 Direction)* [1993] 2 FLR 541, where Scott-Baker J stated: 'the likelihood of the harm is not confined to present or near future but applies to the ability of a parent or carer to meet the emotional needs of a child for years ahead.'

The application of 'likely' was further examined in the leading case of *Re H and R (Child Sexual Abuse: Standard of Proof)* [1996] 1 All ER 1. In this case a 15-year-old girl alleged that her step-father had sexually abused and had raped her on four occasions, over a period of seven years. He was prosecuted but acquitted of rape. The local authority applied for care orders in respect of three younger children on the basis that, as a result of the allegations of abuse made by their older sister, they were likely to suffer significant harm. In deciding whether the threshold criteria were satisfied, the House of Lords in a majority judgment (3:2) held that the question was whether there was a 'real possibility' that the child would suffer significant harm. The majority judgment included this statement from Lord Nicholls:

> When assessing the probabilities the court will have in mind as a factor, to whatever extent is appropriate in the particular case, that the more serious the allegation the less likely it is that the event occurred and, hence, the stronger should be the evidence before a court concludes that the allegation is established on the balance of probability . . . the more improbable the event, the stronger must be the evidence that it did occur before, on the balance of probability, its occurrence will be established.

In effect this decision means that the more serious or improbable the harm which is alleged to have taken place, the harder it will be for the local authority to prove. The standard of proof is not higher but more evidence will be required to prove something which is inherently less likely to have occurred. It may be harder, therefore, to obtain an order to protect the child who has suffered the worst abuse! This position has been followed in *Re U (Serious Injury: Standard of Proof); Re B* [2004] EWCA Civ 567, which also confirmed that responsibilities of local authority's and the applicable standard of proof in care order cases had not changed as a result of the Cannings case (R.V. *Cannings* [2004] ECWA Crim 1 [2004] 1 All ER 725).

'similar child'

Where concerns relate to the child's health and development, in determining whether the harm suffered is significant, the court must compare the child's health or development with that of a similar child (s. 31(10)). There is a danger that use of the similar child concept may provide a rather crude comparison. The court must compare the particular child before it with a hypothetical similar child. To illustrate, consider how in the following scenario a comparison with a white English 3-year-old child might lead to the wrong conclusions.

There are concerns about a 3-year-old child, who was born in England; her parents are from Pakistan. The health visitor is concerned that her development is slower than might be expected and mentions failure to thrive, describes the child as small and underweight for her age, listless and with limited language. In assessing the child as small and underweight, it is possible that development or centile charts have been used which may be Eurocentric and misleading when applied to different physiques. There are different expectations of development in different cultures, for example, as to potty-training or sleeping arrangements. English may not be the first language spoken at home and, if the child does not attend a pre-school, she may not encounter spoken English on a regular basis. In addition, experience of racism and possible unequal access to services may be a factor.

The similar child test may also be difficult to apply in respect of children with disabilities. A child who has Down's syndrome is not necessarily comparable with a notional child with Down's syndrome because the nature of the condition is so individualised.

In the case of *Re O (A Minor) (Care Proceedings: Education)* [1992] 4 All ER 905, a girl aged 15 had persistently truanted from school for three years. A care order was made on the basis that her intellectual and social development was suffering and was likely to suffer, and the harm was significant, as compared with a similar child. The judge stated that a similar child, in this context, meant 'a child of equivalent intellectual and social development, who has gone to school, and not merely an average child who may or may not be at school'.

The second stage of the process, once the court has found harm in s. 31(2)(a), is to find the cause for the harm.

'attributable to an absence of reasonable care'

Ground (b)(i) looks at standards of care and asks whether the harm or likelihood of harm is attributable to an absence of reasonable care which has been, or is likely to be, offered to the child. In other words, it questions whether the standard of care is below that which it would be reasonable to expect the parent of such a child to give to him. The phrase has both a subjective and an objective element. It is subjective in the sense that the care must meet the required standard for the particular child, a subjective test which will vary depending on the child's particular needs. The objective element requires the care to be reasonable in relation to the child's needs, not what is reasonable for the particular parent to provide (*a* parent not *the* parent). It is a child-focused test which addresses the particular needs of the child but makes little allowance for the characteristics of the particular parent.

For example, the care that a parent must give to meet the needs of a child with special needs, who is disabled or has suffered abuse, may be greater than that required for a child who does not have any special needs. The care given by the parent, however, may be that which the parent is able to give with the assistance of any support services to which the parent is entitled. The fact that the care which will be given in the future might be provided by another person and be adequate is not relevant at this stage. The court will look at the actions of the carer at the time the concerns became evident. So, in *Northamptonshire County Council v. S* [1993] Fam 136, it was not relevant that the grandmother would be likely to care for the child in the future, where significant harm had been caused by neglect by the mother.

Difficulties may arise where it is not possible to attribute the harm caused. This was precisely the issue in *Lancashire County Council* v. *B* [2000] 1 FLR 583,[28] where a 7-month-old baby suffered at least two episodes of shaking and it was not possible to determine whether this harm had been caused by the child's mother or father or the childminder. The House of Lords found that it was not necessary to exactly attribute the care or absence of care to a particular parent. If that were so, it would invite cases where parents collude to deny that either has caused harm. The court ruled that where care for a child was shared it was sufficient that the court was satisfied that the harm was attributable to any of the primary carers. Lord Nicholls stated that to decide otherwise could lead to 'the prospect that an unidentified and unidentifiable carer might otherwise be free to inflict further injury on a child he or she had already severely damaged'. This is an important and useful decision, as there may be many reasons why it is not possible to identify with certainty the perpetrator of abuse. Hayes (2000)[29] suggests the following reasons: child abuse is often met with denial; inaccurate information about the circumstances leading to abuse is often provided; it is common for there to be no witnesses to abuse; there may be a number of people who have had contact with the child who could be possible perpetrators; there may be evidential difficulties surrounding the child's account of abuse or a very young child may not be able to communicate at all.

The *Lancashire* interpretation was adopted in *Re O and N (Children) (Non-accidental Injury)*; *Re B (Children) (Non-accidental Injury)* [2003] UKHL 18, a conjoined appeal in the House of Lords. In 'uncertain perpetrator' cases, the phrase 'care given to the child' included the care given by any of the carers and it was not necessary to identify the perpetrator exactly in order to satisfy the threshold. The correct test is to ask whether there is a likelihood or real possibility that X, Y or Z was the perpetrator. At the welfare stage, the court has to proceed on the basis that each carer was a possible perpetrator.

Successful criminal prosecutions are unlikely in uncertain perpetrator cases, in part, due to the higher standard of proof required by the criminal law. In response to this predicament, a new offence of 'causing or allowing the death of a child' has been introduced by the Domestic Violence Crime and Victims Act 2004.

'beyond parental control'

This element of the criteria originates from the Children and Young Persons Act 1969, which provided the law on care proceedings before the Children Act 1989. It is a question of fact whether a child is beyond parental control and is not linked to parental culpability. In *M* v. *Birmingham City Council* [1994] 2 FLR 141, a 13-year-old girl was described as wayward and uncontrollable, sometimes violent and demonstrating a disturbed pattern of behaviour, including absconding and taking drug overdoses. Her mother was a caring parent who had attempted to obtain help for the child's problems. The girl in *Re O*, the truanting case mentioned above, was also found to be beyond parental control.

At the third stage, the court, having found that the child is suffering or likely to suffer significant harm which is attributable to care not being reasonable or the child being beyond parental control, must decide whether it is appropriate to make an order and, if so, which order. It has jurisdiction to make a care or supervision order if the threshold criteria are satisfied, but it is not *bound* to make an order.

In the Children Act 1989, Part I principles of welfare, non-intervention and the menu of orders come into play. In deciding whether the care order will provide a positive benefit to the child, the court will need to consider the local authority's plans for the child in the form of the care plan. The court also needs to consider the children's guardian's recommendations and give reasons if it decides not to follow those recommendations.

In *C v. Solihull Metropolitan Borough Council* [1993] 1 FLR 290, the local authority applied for a care order, but the court actually made a residence order to the parents, with a supervision order to the local authority.

In *Re D (A Minor) (Care or Supervision Order)* [1993] 2 FLR 423, the local authority was satisfied that a supervision order would allow proper monitoring of a situation but the court held that a care order was more appropriate. The case centred on risk assessment of a father towards his baby with a new partner, when he was thought to be responsible for serious injuries to a 2-month-old baby with his first wife and had served a prison sentence for cruelty to children.

In *Re O (A Child) (Supervision Order: Future Harm)* [2001] EWCA Civ 16, the Court of Appeal considered whether a supervision order or care order was most appropriate in the case in question in the context of the Human Rights Act 1998. The court stated that cases decided before the 1998 Act might not be appropriate to current and future care order applications. Hale LJ stated that a care order in this case would be severe in three aspects: power to the local authority to remove the child from its parents; power to the local authority to have parental control and responsibility; and a long period of time for its discharge. Any intervention by the state between parents and children should be proportionate to the aim of protection of family life in the European Convention.

To summarise, the court must work through three stages, as illustrated by Exhibit 9.4, before it can make a care or supervision order: it must find that significant harm occurred or is likely to occur; it must be satisfied as to the cause of that actual or likely harm; and it must apply the central principles of the Children Act 1989 before making an order.

▪ Effect of a care order

The local authority has parental responsibility for the child whilst a care order is in force, has authority to remove the child from home and to decide where he is to live (s. 33). The child's parents retain parental responsibility but the local authority has the power to determine the extent to which a parent may meet parental responsibility towards the child. A care order revokes any residence order previously in force.

▪ Interim care orders

During the investigation period, while appropriate assessments are carried out, the child can be protected via an interim care order. To obtain an interim care order the

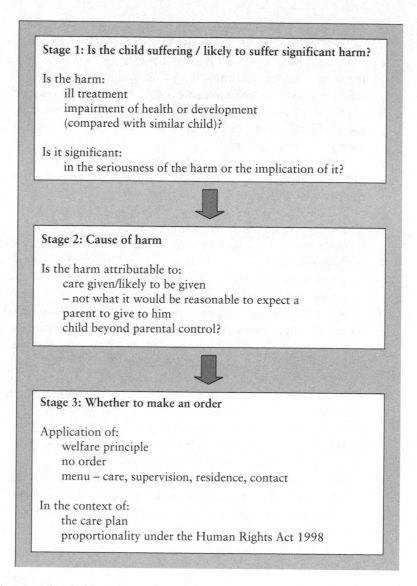

Exhibit 9.4   Threshold criteria

applicant must satisfy the court that there are reasonable grounds for believing the threshold criteria apply, for which evidence will be presented to the court at the final hearing. The first interim order is normally made for eight weeks (s. 38(4)), after which it may be renewed for further periods of four weeks (s. 38(5)). It is not usually necessary for all parties to attend court for renewals of interim care orders, provided there is agreement. Interim hearings should not be a rubber-stamping process, but at the same time it should not be necessary to go over all the evidence on each occasion. Evidence at interim care order applications may be limited to changes of circumstances and the impact of those changes on whether there should be an interim order: *Re B (Interim Care Orders: Renewal)* [2001] 2 FLR 1217. In practice, interim hearings will usually coincide with directions hearings so the court monitors the progress of the case. During an interim order the court has a wide jurisdiction to make directions for assessment to obtain necessary information for its decision (s. 38(6)). In *Re B (A Child: Interim Care Order)* [2002] EWCA Civ 25, this included a direction as to residence in a mother and baby unit. Directions for treatment alone would not be permissible under s. 38(6); however it is recognised that the line between assessment and treatment can be rather blurred (*Re G (Interim Care Order: Residential Assessment)* [2005] UKHL 68). The court can also make directions as to contact, for example in *Kirklees Metropolitan District Council v S* [2006] 1 FLR 333, an order was made by the Family Proceedings Court for daily supervised contact between a one-month-old baby and her mother. It was noted that this level of contact was unusual but appropriate in the circumstances as a short-term order.

It has been generally understood that an interim order should not be used to enable the court to keep the case under review whilst postponing the final hearing, nor where there is disagreement over the care plan (*Re L (Sexual Abuse: Standard of Proof)* [1996] 1 FLR 116). Such use would extend the court's involvement and control over the local authority. This position was questioned in *Re W and B (Children: Care Plan)* [2001] EWCA Civ 757, a Court of Appeal judgment which ruled that the trial judge should have a wider discretion to make an interim care order or defer final care order. The parts of the judgment in relation to care plans were overturned by the House of Lords (in *Re S (Children: Care Plan); Re W (Children: Care Plan)* [2002] UKHL 10) and are now addressed by amendments to the Children Act, discussed below. As to extended use of interim care orders, Lord Nicholls noted that it is not possible to provide a precise test as to when a court should continue interim relief and when it should proceed to make a care order, but it should always bear in mind the delay principle. If the uncertainty before the court needs to be resolved before the court can decide whether to make a care order, interim relief would be appropriate. In other cases if the uncertainty relates to an aspect of the care plan that is suitable for immediate resolution, a limited period of 'planned and purposeful' delay provided by interim relief can be justified. Beyond that, Lord Nicholls observed that 'when deciding to make a care order the court should normally have before it a care plan which is sufficiently firm and particularised for all concerned to have a reasonably clear picture of the likely way ahead for the child for the foreseeable future'. Such an analysis provided judges with a 'degree of flexibility' and appears to partially accept the stance of the Court of Appeal.

■ Care plans

The local authority duty to write a care plan for a child it is proposing to look after (by virtue of the Arrangements for Placement of Children Regulations 1991 (SI 1991/890)), has been further developed by amendments to the Children Act 1989 (by the Adoption and Children Act 2002), which provide that no care order can be made with respect to a child until the court has considered a s. 31A care plan. The new s. 31A states:

s. 31A

> (1) Where an application is made on which a care order might be made with respect to a child, the appropriate local authority must, within such time as the court may direct, prepare a plan ('a care plan') for the future care of the child.
>
> (2) While the application is pending, the authority must keep any care plan prepared by them under review and, if they are of the opinion some change is required, revise the plan, or make a new plan.
>
> (CA 1989)

It will normally be the responsibility of the social worker to prepare a plan; however, this must be done in consultation with the child, his or her parents, others likely to have a significant input into the child's life, and the children's guardian.

Guidance about planning for children was included in 'The Children Act 1989: Guidance and Regulations', vols 3 and 4, in the context of the Arrangements for Placement of Children Regulations 1991, and has been followed in care order applications, such as *Re J (Minors) (Care Proceedings Care Plan)* 1 [1994] FLR 253. Local authority circular LAC (99) 29 'Care Plans and Care Proceedings under the Children Act 1989', subsequently issued under LASSA 1970, s. 7, contains current guidance on preparation of care plans in care proceedings, supplementing the earlier guidance.[30]

The care plan should contain the following key elements:

1. Overall aim: A brief summary of the case and summary of timetables.

2. Child's needs including: contact; needs arising from race, culture and religion or language, special education, health or disability; the extent to which the wishes and views of the child had been obtained and acted upon; arrangements for and purpose of contact.

3. Views of others: the extent to which wishes and views of the child's parents and others with a sufficient interest in the child had been obtained and acted upon.

4. Placement details and timetable: the proposed placement; likely duration; arrangements for health care, education and reunification; other services to be provided; details of the parents' role in day-to-day arrangements. Where adoption is a possible option the authority should adopt a ***twin track*** approach.[31]

5. Management and support by local authority: who is responsible for implementing the overall plan and specific tasks; contingency plan; arrangements for input by parents, child and others into ongoing decision-making process; arrangements for making representations or complaints.

A separate care plan is required for each child who is the subject of proceedings, although large parts of the plan may be similar for sibling groups. The care plan should be specific to the particular child, not simply based on general policy considerations, as was challenged, for example, in *Berkshire County Council* v. *B* [1997] 1 FLR 171, where the local authority plan was adoption for all children under the age of 10. For a teenage child, the care plan will also need to consider the arrangements for leaving care.

Where an application for a care order has been made, the care plan is of great significance when the court, satisfied that the threshold criteria have been met, comes to decide whether or not an order should be made (applying the non-intervention principle of s. 1(5)). The court must determine whether the care plan is in the best interests of the child and will be better than making no order and returning the child to his former circumstances.

Under the Children Act 1989 as originally implemented, once a care order was made the court lost any power to control the arrangements for the child or ensure compliance with the terms of the care plan. Furthermore, the guardian's involvement would also end when a care order was made, there being no power to direct the guardian to continue to be involved (*Kent County Council* v. *C* [1993] 1 FLR 308). The court, however, had an important role, with which the guardian should assist in subjecting the care plan to 'rigorous scrutiny'.[32] The extent to which the courts could control aspects of the care plan was questioned in a Court of Appeal decision, *Re W and B (Children: Care Plan)* [2001] EWCA Civ 757, and its judgment (briefly) placed a clear duty on the local authority and/or guardian to return failing care plans to court, having 'starred' essential milestones in the care plan. The case was appealed to the House of Lords, as *Re S (Children: Care Plan); Re W (Children: Care Plan)* [2002] UKHL 10, whose judgment rejected the reasoning of the Court of Appeal, arguing the introduction of starred care plans went beyond the interpretation allowed under the Human Rights Act, stating: 'Under the proposed starring system courts would effectively exercise a newly created supervisory function.' The House of Lords did, however, give a clear indication in the following statement that this was an issue requiring further consideration:

> I cannot stress too strongly that the rejection of this innovation on legal grounds must not obscure the pressing need for the Government to attend to the serious practical and legal problems identified by the Court of Appeal . . . One of the questions needing urgent consideration is whether some degree of court supervision of local authorities' discharge of their parental responsibilities would bring about an overall improvement in the quality of child care provided by local authorities.

Parliament responded to these concerns with a further amendment to the Children Act 1989 (by the ACA 2002). Once a care order is made, there is now a provision for review of care orders and possible return to the court. Section 26 of the Children Act 1989 which deals with reviews for looked after children is amended to require, that the s. 31A plan is kept under review, and if some change is required, to revise the plan or make a new one. Local authorities are required to appoint a person (known as an Independent Reviewing Officer) in respect of each case to: participate in reviews; monitor the performance of the authority's functions in respect of the review; and refer the case to CAFCASS Legal if he considers it appropriate (s. 26(2A)). CAFCASS may then return the case to court for judicial directions in appropriate cases, most obviously where the local authority does not adhere to the care plan and this is not in the best interests of the child.

■ Procedure

Either the local authority or authorised person (NSPCC) can apply for a care order in respect of a child. If the NSPCC make the application the order will actually be made to the relevant local authority. Every person with parental responsibility for the child must receive at least three days' notice of the application. The father of the child must also be notified, or reasonable steps taken to trace him, even if he does not have parental responsibility. At the first hearing a children's guardian will be appointed (if one has not already been appointed at an EPO application). The principle of avoidance of delay will apply throughout care proceedings. Delay in children's cases has been acknowledged as a problem for some time and was considered in 'A Scoping Study on the Causes of Delay' (2002).[33] This study found that common reasons for delay included: unrealistic timetabling and poor enforcement of timetables, inadequate preparation time, more than one judge in a case and inadequate disclosure. In response to these and earlier concerns,[34] The Protocol For Judicial Case Management Of Public Law Children Act Cases [2003] 2 FLR 719[35] was published with a view to achieving a significant reduction in delay. The protocol aims to achieve more effective case management, address over-reliance on experts and ensure resources are used affectively. It provides a step-by-step account through a public law case, setting out what is required from the parties at each stage. Each care centre and magistrates' courts committee was required to produce an implementation plan and the impact of the protocol will be monitored. The protocol introduces a standardised procedure for dealing with care cases applicable to each level of court, whether proceedings are heard in the family proceedings court, the county court or High Court.

The objective is to enable the court to deal with each case justly, expeditiously, fairly and with a minimum of delay; in ways which ensure that parties are on an equal footing, the welfare of the children involved is safeguarded and distress to all parties is minimised; and in ways which are proportionate to the gravity and complexity of the issues and to the nature and extent of the intervention proposed in the private and family life of the children and adults involved (para 3.1 Practice Direction to the protocol).

Under the protocol it is intended that a considerable amount of preparation and work to take a case to trial will have been completed before proceedings are issued. By day 3 after issue of proceedings the local authority is expected to file and serve, the initial social work statement (including any proposals for twin tracking, the social work timetable, tasks and responsibilities), the social work chronology, the initial or core assessment, any s. 37 reports and existing expert reports. The protocol is divided into six steps, each with an objective and action required.

1. The application: day 1 to 3.
2. The first hearing in the Family Proceedings Court: on or before day 6.
3. Allocations hearing and directions: by day 11.
4. The case management conference: between day 15 and 60.
5. The pre-hearing review: by week 37.
6. The final hearing: by week 40.

Appointment of any expert witnesses will be considered at the case management conference and duties of the expert witness are codified in Appendix C of the protocol.

There is a target set by the Department for Constitutional Affairs to increase the proportion of cases completed in the courts within 40 weeks by 10 per cent by 2009.[36] Currently around 38 per cent of cases in care centres and 46 per cent in family proceedings courts are completed within that timescale. Against that target, however, it is important to note the comments in *Re G (Protocol for Judicial Case Management in Public Law Children Act Cases: Application to become Party in Family Proceedings)* [2004] EWHC 116 (Fam) that: 'The protocol is a tool to improving applying family justice and not, in the quest for speed and consistency to impair it.'

Guidance for social workers is set out in Appendix F, 'The Social Services Assessment and Care Planning Aide Memoire'.[37]

Split hearings

Some cases will be dealt with as split hearings. The case is effectively split into a fact-finding hearing to establish whether the threshold criteria are met, followed by a 'welfare' hearing at which the court exercises its discretion as to what will be in the best interests of the child. Active case management and timetabling is essential to avoid delay, which has sometimes been a feature of split hearing cases (*Re Y and K (Children) (Care Proceedings: Split Hearing)* [2003] EWCA Civ 669).

The case of *Re H (Children) (Summary Determination of Issues)* [2002] EWCA Civ 1692 recognises that, in the course of care proceedings, negotiations will take place between the local authority and the parents as to findings of fact the court needs to make in order to determine whether the threshold criteria are met. It is understandable that parents will wish to avoid adverse findings where there are allegations of serious risk. The case concerned a girl, aged 5 at the time of the hearing. The local authority case was that she had suffered significant harm as a result of the fictitious accounts of epilepsy made by her mother which led to unnecessary anti-convulsive medication being prescribed and administered, at a higher dosage than prescribed, by her mother. In addition, the local authority stated that the mother had failed to keep medical appointments for the child and the unruly behaviour of her brother had harmed her. The local authority were prepared to rely on the latter allegations which the mother conceded and, at first instance, findings were not made as to whether the mother had fabricated the epilepsy and overdosed the medication.

The child's guardian appealed and the Court of Appeal found that it was in the child's best interest for there to be findings as to the fabrication of epilepsy and overdose. Such findings were necessary in anticipation of future questions regarding access to the mother.

■ Human rights and child protection

The duty to protect children is reinforced by a number of European decisions. The United Kingdom has been found in breach of the European Convention on Human

Rights for failure to protect children in the case of *Z* v. *United Kingdom* (2001) 34 EHRR 97. This case was an appeal from the House of Lords decision in *X (Minors)* v. *Bedfordshire County Council* [1995] 3 All ER 353, where claims in negligence against the local authority were struck out. In this case four children suffered serious psychological disturbance and physical neglect by their parents. The European Court of Human Rights found the United Kingdom to be in breach of Art. 3, the right not to be subjected to inhuman or degrading treatment, by failing to protect the children from serious, long-term neglect and abuse. The local authority had a duty to protect the children from the time they first became aware of their treatment, in October 1987, but the children were not taken into care until April 1992. The court did not consider the application under Art. 8 (right to respect for family life), having found an Art. 3 breach. The court found, further, that as the children in these applications were unable to pursue a remedy in damages against the local authority, the United Kingdom was in breach of Art. 13, in not providing an effective remedy. The court therefore awarded damages and costs to the applicants. This decision limits further the extent to which claims against the local authority will be barred on grounds of public policy.

Procedural aspects of a case may also be challenged under the Human Rights Act 1998, as in the case of *TP* v. *United Kingdom* (2002) 34 EHRR 42. It was found that the local authority had failed to respect the family life of the mother (TP), contrary to Art. 8, as she was not properly involved in the decision-making process regarding her child who was taken into care. The local authority had failed to disclose all the information about the child's allegations of sexual abuse (in the form of a video).

In *P, C* and *S* v. *United Kingdom* (2002) 35 EHRR 1075, the court found that lack of legal representation in care proceedings violated the guarantee of effective access to courts under Art. 6 and the procedural guarantees of Art. 8.

The case concerned the child of a mother who had been charged in the United States of cruelty to her child (induced illness syndrome). The child was removed at birth. The mother represented herself in four-week care proceedings. Issues of contact were not dealt within those proceedings. The court commented that the 'procedures adopted not only gave the appearance of unfairness but prevented the applicants from putting their case in a proper and effective manner on the issues that were important to them'. It also warned that:

> . . . the taking of a new born baby into public care at the moment of its birth is an extremely harsh measure. There must be extraordinarily compelling reasons before a baby can be physically removed from its mother against her will . . . as a consequence of a procedure in which neither she nor her partner had been involved.

Human Rights complaints arising before the final care order should normally be dealt with in the context of the care proceedings by that court. There is no need for a separate application and any human rights claims should be brought to the court's attention at the earliest opportunity. If necessary the whole case may be transferred up to the High Court (*Re L (Care Proceedings: Human Rights Claims)* [2003] EWHC 665 (Fam), confirmed in *Re V (Care Proceedings: Human Rights Claims)* [2004] EWCA Civ 54).

■ Contact with children in care

There is a statutory presumption in favour of contact, contained in s. 34:

s. 34

(1) Where a child is in the care of a local authority, the authority shall . . . allow the child reasonable contact with –

(a) his parents;

(b) any guardian of his;

(c) where there was a residence order in force with respect to the child immediately before the care order was made, the person in whose favour the order was made; and

(d) where, immediately before the care order was made, a person had care of the child by virtue of an order made in the exercise of the High Court's inherent jurisdiction with respect to children, that person.

(CA 1989)

The local authority must apply to the court if it wishes to terminate contact, unless under s. 34(6) it is necessary to refuse contact in order to safeguard and promote the child's welfare. This power of refusal lasts for a maximum period of seven days, after which approval of the court is required. The arrangements for contact will receive court scrutiny as an integral part of the care plan and the purpose of contact must be clear. Section 34 may be used to achieve phased rehabilitation between parent and child or to enable a level of ongoing contact even if rehabilitation is unlikely. Subject to the restriction on terminating contact, after a care order is made, the contact arrangements are largely a matter for local authority discretion. The Court of Appeal held, in *Re W (A Minor) (Parental Contact: Prohibition)* [2002] 1 FCR 752, that the court could not prohibit a local authority into whose care a child had been placed from permitting parental contact with the child.

Re F (Minors) (Care Proceedings: Termination of Contact) [2000] 2 FCR 481 is a case which tested the human rights compliance of s. 34. The High Court found that nothing about s. 34(4) of the Children Act 1989, which gave the court power to authorise a local authority to terminate contact with children in its care, was not human rights compliant when used in appropriate cases as part of a care plan approved by the court. In this case, where there was no prospect of returning children to their mother, and the local authority care plan proposed adoption, leave to terminate contact had been granted. The mother claimed that this was an infringement of her rights under Arts. 6(1) and 8 of the ECHR. It was held that the court had correctly balanced the respective rights of the mother and the children to reach a conclusion which was in the children's best interests and had acted proportionately. A further decision on s. 34(4) gives guidance on its use and warns that 'a s. 34(4) order should not be made . . . merely against the possibility that circumstances may change in such a way as to make termination of contact desirable' (*Re S (Children) (Termination of Contact)* [2004] EWCA Civ 1397).

■ **Supervision orders**

The same threshold criteria must be satisfied for a supervision order as for a care order (s. 31). However, the effect of a supervision order is different from that of a care order. Under a supervision order the local authority does not acquire parental responsibility. The focus of a supervision order is ensuring that local authorities can provide certain services for the child and family and monitor the situation whilst the child remains with parents. The reasons for a supervision order being made rather than a care order were considered in the case of *Re O (A Child) (Supervision Order: Future Harm)* [2001] EWCA Civ 16, discussed above. It is crucial that the choice of order reflects a proportionate interference by the state with the right to family life.

A supervisor will be appointed to 'advise, assist and befriend' the child and to take steps to ensure the supervision order is complied with (s. 35). The supervision order may include a variety of requirements such as where the child is to live, for the child to take part in specified activities or present himself to a particular person at a specified place, for the parents' attendance at courses and for the local authority to supervise parental contact. However, the only real sanction for failure to comply with any of the requirements is for the supervisor to seek a variation or discharge of the supervision order. A supervision order initially lasts for up to one year; it can be extended by the courts for a maximum period of three years. It is possible for an interim supervision order to be made in the period prior to the full hearing of an application for a care or supervision order.

The role of the guardian during the operation of a supervision order was considered in, *Re MH (A Child) (Supervision Orders); Re SB (Children) (Supervision Orders)* [2002] 1 FCR 251. The court held that s. 12 of the Criminal Justice and Court Services Act 2000 (CJCSA 2000), which defines the function of CAFCASS, alters the position established in *Re G (A Minor) (Social Worker: Disclosure)* [1996] 2 All ER 65. In the latter case the court found that the guardian had no function once proceedings were completed. Section 12 states:

s. 12

> (b) . . . where a supervision order is made, the proceedings are not to be treated as concluded until the order has ceased to have effect.
>
> (CJCSA 2000)

The judge interpreted this provision so that the guardian's functions will continue after the order, effectively expanding the role of the guardian. This decision has major resource implications for CAFCASS, although it should be noted that the court retains the power to terminate the guardian's appointment.

■ **Discharge and variation**

Section 39 of the Children Act 1989 deals with discharge of a care or supervision order and variation, substitution or extension of a supervision order. It is possible for the child, local authority or any person with parental responsibility to apply for the discharge of a care order, or to substitute the order with a supervision order. An application to vary or discharge a supervision order can be made by the child, his supervisor or any person with parental responsibility, or the person with whom the child is living.

Discharge and variation of care orders

It was noted in Chapter 8 that, if a residence order is made, this will discharge a care order (CA 1989, s. 91(1)). The range of people who may apply for a residence order is wider than those entitled to apply for the discharge of a care order. In particular, only fathers with parental responsibility can apply for the discharge of a care order, whereas a parent, including fathers without parental responsibility, can apply for a residence order. There are no specific conditions to be met for discharge or substitution; the court will simply consider the welfare of the child. A children's guardian will be appointed, preferably the guardian who acted in the previous proceedings because prior knowledge of the case is likely to reduce delays.

Variation, extension or discharge of supervision orders

Supervision orders will initially be made for up to one year and may be extended to a maximum of three years on the application of the local authority (Children Act 1989, Sch. 3, para. 6). Supervision orders may be varied or revoked in relation to any specific obligation imposed on the supervisor, directions dealing with psychiatric and medical examination and treatment, where the requirements of the supervisor are not met. A supervision order cannot be varied to a care order. The child's welfare is the paramount consideration in any application to vary, extend or discharge a supervision order.

The role of the children's guardian

In 1984 the guardian *ad litem* service was established. Its origins can be traced to the Maria Colwell inquiry report, published in 1974, which stated: 'it would have been of assistance to the court to have had the views of an independent social worker'.[38] In addition, Art. 12 of the United Nations Convention on the Rights of the Child states:

Art. 12

(2) . . . the child shall in particular be provided the opportunity to be heard in any judicial or administrative proceedings affecting the child either directly or through a representative or an appropriate body in a manner consistent with the procedural rules of national law.

(UNCRC 1989)

The children's guardian (previously the guardian *ad litem*) is now one of three services, together with the Court Welfare Service and functions of the Official Solicitor in representing children, which have been amalgamated into the Children and Family Court Advisory and Support Service (CAFCASS).

The role of the guardian was extended by the Children Act 1989, as was the range of circumstances in which a guardian will be appointed. Section 41 of the Children Act 1989 (now amended to refer to an officer of the service (CAFCASS) rather than a guardian *ad litem*) provides that, in specified proceedings, the court shall appoint a children's guardian for the child concerned unless satisfied that it is not necessary to do so in order to safeguard his interests. Once appointed, the guardian is under a duty to safeguard the interests of the child (s. 41(2)(b)). Guidance and rules[39] expand on the duties of the guardian, which include: assisting the court with timetabling and avoidance of delay; ensuring that the child has an effective voice in court by representing the ascertainable wishes and feelings of the child; attending court and directions hearings; and preparing a report advising the court on matters including the child's level of understanding, the child's wishes, the order to be made, if any, and any other matter on which the court requests an opinion.

The guardian is a skilled professional, usually a professionally qualified social worker with at least five years' post-qualifying experience. Dale-Emberton (2001) describes the role as including: investigating the background to a case; accessing information and analysing and evaluating documents; gathering information through interviews with the child in a way that is sensitive and age appropriate, and also with the parents, other relatives and professionals; managing a case to avoid delay; and ensuring people with parental responsibility are aware of the proceedings.[40]

From the child's perspective, the guardian can provide the means to ensure that the child's own views are presented to the court and enable the child to feel part of the process, even if the child does not attend any court hearings. In research, where children were asked to name the most important characteristics of a guardian, 71 per cent said it was the ability to listen to children and 43 per cent said it was the guardian's role in explaining things to children.[41]

The guardian will also appoint a solicitor for the child. The solicitor will normally be appointed from the Law Society's Children Panel, being one with special expertise in child care cases. The solicitor's role is to give legal advice to the guardian and to present the case to court, instructed by the guardian. Even if the child is not likely to be present at any court hearings, it would be good practice for the solicitor to meet the child. There are some cases where the guardian's instructions to the solicitor are in conflict with the child's expressed wishes. In these circumstances, if the child is assessed as competent to give instructions, then the solicitor will take instructions direct from the child and advocate the views of the child, not a recommendation as to what is in the child's best interests. If the guardian requires legal representation, another solicitor will be appointed. The court ultimately decides whether the child is competent to give instructions, but will be advised by the guardian on this point (*Re M (Minors) (Care Proceedings: Child's Wishes)* [1994] 1 FLR 749).

The specified proceedings in which a guardian must be appointed are:

■ applications for a care order or supervision order;

■ family proceedings where the court has directed the local authority to investigate a child's circumstances under s. 37(1);

■ applications for discharge of a care order or variation or discharge of a supervision order;

■ an application to substitute a supervision order for a care order;

■ proceedings where the court is considering making a residence order for a child subject of a care order;

■ applications for contact with a child subject of a care order;

■ associated appeals;

■ applications for secure accommodation orders;

■ applications to change a child's surname or remove a child from the jurisdiction, in respect of a child subject to a care order;

■ applications to extend a supervision order;

■ applications for parental orders (Human Fertilisation and Embryology Act 1991, s. 30);

■ contested applications for adoption or placement.

In carrying out any of the above roles, the guardian has a right of access to local authority records. Section 42 of the Children Act 1989 provides that the guardian shall have the right at all reasonable times to examine and take copies of records held by the local authority relating to the child in question.

The guardian's report is an important document in care and other child-related proceedings. It will be read by the parties, including the child in some cases, their legal representatives, local authority social workers, the magistrates or judge, and any expert witnesses who may be called upon to comment on its contents. The exact format of the report will vary depending on the nature of the application but the Department of Health Guide[42] suggests the following sections:

■ front sheet (including a statement as to the confidential nature of the report);

■ information about the application (name of child, type of proceedings, date of hearing, name of guardian and solicitor);

■ contents list; experience and qualifications of guardian; summary of the case (initial causes of concern, orders sought and indication of parental responsibility);

■ summary of previous court hearings; enquiries undertaken (people interviewed, documents read, etc.);

■ family structure (a genogram may be useful);

■ family background history (e.g. detail of any abuse suffered by parents, family breakdown, involvement of social services);

■ parents (an assessment of the parents' ability and capacity to care for the child and the parents' own views);

- other relevant adults; the child (a comprehensive account of the child's needs);

- any significant harm suffered or likely to be suffered by the child; the child's wishes and feelings (and an assessment of the weight to be attached);

- expert assessments and professionals interviewed;

- local authority care plan (the guardian can present an independent scrutiny of the local authority care plan);

- summary, including the welfare checklist (this should ensure that the court considers all relevant matters);

- contact (the guardian may make a specific recommendation regarding contact);

- options available to the court and the suitability of each option, recommendation (a full explanation should be provided if the guardian's recommendation is significantly different from that of the local authority).

Research suggests that guardians make a significant contribution to the formulation of care plans (McCausland, 2000).[43]

In *R (Regester) v Children and Family Court Advisory and Support Service; R (Perkins) v Children and Family Court Advisory and Support Service* [2003] EWHC 235 (Admin), delay in provision of children's guardians for court hearings was challenged by judicial review. The court ruled that the duty on CAFCASS to provide children's guardians did not have to be discharged immediately but should be discharged as soon as practicable after a request was made.

CAFCASS has experienced some organisational difficulties and has issued a consultation paper which recognises some of these difficulties and identifies a new professional and organisational strategy, 'Every Day Matters: a New Direction for CAFCASS'. The final strategy is expected to be published in 2006, with a view to affecting cases from April 2007. Key elements of the new strategy relate to earlier intervention in cases in recognition of the problems of delay in allocating a case and commencing work. It is proposed that in both public and private cases every referral should be allocated within two days and a case plan formulated before the first directions hearing. Changes are proposed to report writing to include greater flexibility in format, so, for example, in some cases a letter to court rather than a report might be more suitable and ways of avoiding repetition, such as cross-referencing documents and endorsing aspects of the local authority report where there is agreement. Child-friendly care plans or statements of arrangements should be sent to the child at the end of proceedings.

Expert witnesses

The expert witness has a significant role in child care cases. In cases where sexual, physical or emotional abuse is suspected, medical evidence may be determinative.

Other types of experts may give evidence (e.g. addressing the effect of addictive behaviour or mental health problems, risk assessments and relationship assessments) and it is suggested that the courts are becoming increasingly reliant on expert evidence.[44]

Expert evidence in care proceedings, which should have a less adversarial tone than other proceedings, is adduced to assist the court in reaching its decision. An expert may be requested by one or other party or by joint request and the opinion given should not show bias towards any party. There is an expectation that the parties will use an 'agreed' expert where possible. In some circumstances a *witness summons* (formerly referred to as a subpoena) will be issued ordering a witness to attend court. This is often the case in practice for health visitors. As it would be contempt of court to disclose confidential documents to a person beyond the parties to the case, an expert can become involved only with the approval of the court, and will usually be appointed and terms of enquiry specified at a directions hearing. Specifically, an expert cannot examine or assess the child without leave of the court.[45] As expert evidence will include opinion it is essential that professional integrity is established and can withstand cross-examination. Opinion may be required as to whether a particular injury is consistent with the claim as to how it occurred. The decision will be reached on the 'balance of probability' already discussed in the context of *Re H (Minors) (Sexual Abuse: Standard of Proof)* [1996] 1 All ER 1. The judgment in *Re R (A Minor) (Expert Evidence)* [1991] 1 FLR 291 provides guidance on opinion evidence in family proceedings and suggests that expert opinion evidence should be objective, properly researched and based on consideration of all material facts.[46] In *Re A (Family Proceedings: Expert Witness)* [2001] 1 FLR 723, the court had the opportunity to comment on the role of the expert. In this case, a father who was having supervised contact with his two children at a contact centre surreptitiously videoed a session; the video was sent via his solicitors to a child psychologist, who was asked to provide a report on the father's interaction with the children. No permission had been sought from the court and no notice was given to the mother or her legal representatives. The judgment stated that in family proceedings it was wholly inappropriate for an expert witness to be instructed without the knowledge of the court; nor should experts accept instructions in the absence of court authority and awareness of the court order relating to their instructions.

The courts clearly have high expectations of experts. In *Re X (Non-Accidental Injury: Expert Evidence)* [2001] 2 FLR 90, an expert gave the opinion that a 20-month-old child's fractures were caused by temporary brittle bone disorder, a condition which other experts contested the existence of. Singer J was critical of the expert's evidence and his conduct and ruled that future applications to seek a report from him should not be granted without the sanction of a High Court judge.[47]

The protocol includes as Appendix C, a Code of Guidance on the use of experts. It suggests caution against overuse of experts and reminds: 'Expert evidence should be proportionate to the issues in question and should relate to questions that are outside the skill and experience of the Court.'[48]

Human rights arguments were raised in the case of *L (A Child)* v. *United Kingdom (Disclosure of Expert Evidence)* [2000] 2 FCR 145. The court in care proceedings ordered the mother to disclose an adverse expert's report. She argued that this was a breach of Arts. 6 and 8 of the ECHR. The court found that the obligation to disclose the report did not deprive the mother of her right to a fair trial as she had legal representation and was able to present her case. The court did find a breach of Art. 8 (right to respect for private and family life), but held that this was justified by Art. 8(2) because it was necessary for protection of the child's interest.

Wardship and the inherent jurisdiction

The High Court may deal with the same full range of family proceedings as the county court and the magistrates' family proceedings court. In addition, it may exercise the inherent jurisdiction and may make a child a ward of court. Wardship and the inherent jurisdiction are not one and the same. Wardship is in fact an exercise of the inherent jurisdiction under which the court obtains parental responsibility for the child and no major step in the child's life can be taken without the consent of the court. Prior to the Children Act 1989, local authorities were able to apply to make a child a ward of court and obtain a care order in respect of that child as part of the wardship jurisdiction.

Section 100 of the Children Act 1989 imposed restrictions on local authority use of wardship. This section provides that the High Court can no longer place a ward of court in the care or under supervision of a local authority, cannot require a child to be accommodated by a local authority, cannot make a child who is subject to a care order a ward of court or give the local authority the power to determine questions relating to the exercise of parental responsibility for a child. As a balance to this restriction other provisions in the Act were designed to reduce the need for local authorities to have recourse to wardship. Elements of the wardship jurisdiction were introduced in the form of specific issue orders and prohibited steps orders (s. 8: see discussion in Chapter 8) and the breadth of the threshold criteria covered situations where wardship would have been utilised to supplement the old grounds for intervention (e.g. in cases where concerns relate to future harm). It remains possible for local authorities to have recourse to the inherent jurisdiction in limited circumstances, having first obtained leave of the court (s. 100(3)). The court will grant leave only if the local authority could not achieve its objective through any other order available to the court, and there is reasonable cause to believe the child will suffer significant harm if the court does not act. So, in C v. *Salford City Council* [1994] 2 FLR 926, a wardship application by foster parents was dismissed because an application for a residence order gave the court all the powers it needed in the particular case.

The inherent jurisdiction lends itself to situations where a one-off major decision is required rather than cases where ongoing involvement of the court is required. Case law has produced examples of the types of circumstances that may justify leave being granted. Declarations may be made by the court in relation to the lawfulness of medical treatment and surgery. In *Re C (A Minor) (Detention for Medical Treatment)* [1997] 2 FLR 180, the inherent jurisdiction was exercised to authorise treatment of a 16-year-old child suffering from anorexia nervosa; and in *Re A (Children) (Conjoined Twins: Surgical Separation)* [2000] 4 All ER 961, a declaration was made by the court against the wishes of the parents. Wardship may be used in threatened child abduction cases where the court wishes to retain a child in this country because it automatically makes removal of the child from the jurisdiction illegal.

If there are concerns about a child having contact with an adult (not a parent), then wardship may be used to prevent the contact, as, for example, in *Re R (A Minor) (Contempt: Sentence)* [1994] 2 All ER 144, where a 14-year-old girl was having a relationship with a married man. An injunction prohibited contact and on breach the man was sentenced for contempt of court.

Screening child care workers

It has been possible for some time for criminal record checks to be made in respect of prospective workers who will work with children. Home Office guidance (1993)[49] provided that checks should be made where there will be substantial unsupervised access to children.

■ Protection of Children Act 1999

This Act established a protection of children register, which combines and places on a statutory footing the Department of Health's consultancy service index[50] and the Department for Education and Skills' 'List 99' on a statutory basis. Inclusion on the list prevents an individual from working with children. If a child care organisation intends to offer employment to an individual in a child care position it must check whether the individual is included in the list.[51] A person included in the list is considered unsuitable to work with children and should not be offered employment. A child care organisation is one that is concerned with the provision of accommodation, social services or health services to children, or the supervision of children. Appeals may be made to the Care Standards Tribunal, which will consider whether it is appropriate for a person to be included on the list. (NB the Care Standards Act 2000 establishes a similar list for adults unsuitable to work with a vulnerable adults – see Chapter 17.)

Criminal Records Bureau

The new Criminal Records Bureau, established under the Police Act 1997, holds information on criminal records, other relevant information held by the police (e.g.

applicant's association with drug users), the Protection of Children Act list and the Protection of Vulnerable Adults list. The Criminal Records Bureau is organised nationally and replaces the former system of police checks carried out by the local force. Local authorities (and other organisations) can obtain enhanced criminal records checks, full criminal record checks or criminal conviction certificates. The enhanced criminal records check will provide the most information. A charge will be levied for local authorities using the Bureau but voluntary agencies can obtain enhanced disclosures without cost.

Sex offenders

The names of sex offenders are held on the Sex Offender Register established under the Sex Offenders Act 1997. The Sexual Offences (Amendment) Act 2000 introduced an offence of 'abuse of trust' where a person has had a sexual relationship with a person they worked with and towards whom they were in a position of trust. A Criminal Records Bureau check will reveal convictions under this Act and also whether a person is named on the Sex Offender Register.

The Criminal Justice and Courts Services Act 2000 provides additional remedies to restrict unsuitable people from working with children. It is possible to add a disqualification order to the sentence of certain offenders who have abused children. The effect of this order is to ban the person from applying for paid or unpaid work, accepting or carrying out work with children for a period of at least ten years. Breach of the order is a criminal offence. The offences that can lead to a ban are contained in Sch. 4 and, in addition to sexual offences, include murder, assault or cruelty to a child. The disqualification order can be added only to a custodial sentence of 12 months or more.

Child abuse inquiries

The first major child abuse inquiry was held in 1945, following the death of Denis O'Neill, a child in foster care. It prompted the Children Act 1948 and the formation of children's departments. Since the 1970s the number of inquiries appears to have gradually increased[52] and in many cases the media have seized the opportunity to scapegoat individuals named in the reports and discredit Social Services Departments. Such an approach does little to instil public confidence in social services and can be very damaging to morale. In fact, inquiries can have a significant positive influence on both professional practice and the law. The positioning of law as a key element in social work training is partly attributable to the influence of inquiries. This section will consider the types of inquiries that may be held, their functions and the key findings of (a selection of) inquiries which have directly shaped the law.[53]

■ Types of inquiries

Inquiries will be held following the death or serious injury of a child (in care). The inquiry may be an internal case review, an external inquiry with an independent chair (which may be held in public or private), or an inquiry commissioned by the Secretary of State. It is possible for a public inquiry to be held following an internal case review of the same case. An inquiry may be conducted in either an inquisitorial or adversarial style. Chapter 7 of the new 'Working Together' deals with Child Death Review Processes, and Chapter 8 addresses LSCB's reviewing and investigative functions in serious case reviews.

The functions of an inquiry are to:

- ascertain the facts of the case;
- critically outline the role and functions of relevant agencies;
- make recommendations for legislation, guidance and practice;
- learn lessons for the future;
- meet public concern; and
- establish responsibility.[54]

■ Key findings from public inquiries

The most consistent findings of inquiry reports have been the failure of inter-agency work and cooperation, and the need for better training. Specific findings in particular reports have led directly to changes in professional practice and the law. A selection of examples are cited below.

Maria Colwell (1974)[55]

- Maria, aged 7, was killed by her step-father. She had been returned to her mother after a five-year period living with her aunt, following concerns over general neglect. Her care order was revoked and replaced with a supervision order. She was undernourished and severely beaten.
- DHSS instigated the system of Area Child Protection Committees, case conferences and at risk registers. The Children Act 1975 introduced the requirement for a guardian *ad litem* to act in cases where revocation of a care order was sought.

Jasmine Beckford (1985)[56]

- Jasmine died, aged 4, having been beaten over a period of time by her step-father and severely undernourished. He had previously been convicted of causing injuries to Jasmine and her sister in 1981. The children were home on trial when Jasmine died. She had been seen by her social worker only once in the ten-month period before her death. The report claims that her death was both predictable and preventable.
- DHSS placed greater emphasis on 'protection' and child abuse registers were renamed child protection registers.

Kimberley Carlile (1987)[57]

- Kimberley, aged 4, was killed by her step-father, who was subsequently convicted for her murder. She had multiple bruising and had scars and had previously been beaten and starved.

- The report recommended the introduction of a child assessment order, subsequently included in the Children Act 1989.

Tyra Henry (1987)[58]

- Tyra, aged 22 months, was killed by her father while a care order was in force. The report found that Tyra's mother was the main focus of social services work, rather than Tyra. The report addressed the issue of cultural stereotyping and noted that there was an assumption that Tyra's Afro-Carribean grandmother would find a way to cope.

- The introduction of 'care plans' can be traced back to this report.

The Cleveland Report (1988)[59]

- In 1987, 121 children were removed from their families in Cleveland under place of safety orders on suspicion of sexual abuse. Heavy reliance was placed on the use of the anal reflex dilatation test as a diagnosis of sexual abuse. Many of the parents were denied access to their children while under place of safety orders.

- The report made the notable statement that 'a child is a person not an object of concern'. It recommended greater rights for parents and children including statements that children should not be subjected to unnecessary medical examinations. Recommendations were incorporated into 'Working Together' guidelines including a policy change in favour of parents attending case conferences.

- A number of provisions of the Children Act 1989 may be traced to the Cleveland report, including: child's right of refusal of medical examination; local authority ability to make provision for an alleged abuser to be accommodated so that the child could remain at home; reduction in duration of emergency protection order (EPO) compared with longer place of safety order; presumption that parents will have access to their child during an EPO.

Pin-down (1991)[60]

- The Pin-down report found that physical and emotional abuse of children and young people in homes in Staffordshire masqueraded as accepted practice for the control and discipline of the young people.

- Following the Pin-down report, the Department of Health set up a general inquiry into the provision of residential care. The 'Utting Report'[61] ensued and contained recommendations designed to raise standards in residential care, many of which have been incorporated into the Care Standards Act 2000.

Victoria Climbié (2003)

- The report of the Victoria Climbié inquiry, chaired by Lord Laming was set up following Victoria Climbié's tragic death on 25 February 2000. The report details a catalogue of administrative, managerial and professional failure. It outlines a number of occasions upon which the most minor and basic intervention on the part of the staff concerned could have made a material difference to the eventual outcome.

Lord Laming made the following statement:

> . . . the legislative framework is fundamentally sound. The gap is in its implementation. Having considered all the evidence it is not to the often hapless front-line staff that I direct most criticism for the failure to protect Victoria. True their performance often fell well short of an acceptable standard of work. But the greatest failure rests with the senior managers and members of the organisations concerned whose responsibility it was to ensure that the services they provided to children such as Victoria were properly financed, staffed and able to deliver good quality services to children and families. They must be accountable.

- The report contains 108 recommendations. The full report will be essential reading for any practitioner working in child protection. Key recommendations have been implemented by the Children Act 2004 and the 'Every Child Matters: Change for Children' policy and include organisational changes for social services, establishment of Local Safeguarding Children Boards and a duty to cooperate to safeguard and promote welfare (see further discussion in Chapter 7).

Child protection and the criminal law

In addition to the civil structure for child protection provided by the Children Act 1989, in many cases of child abuse a criminal offence will be committed. These offences range from indecent assault through to rape and murder. The decision on whether to prosecute a perpetrator of abuse rests with the police and ultimately the Crown Prosecution Service. The possibility of a criminal trial does impact on the civil child protection process, however, particularly in relation to good practice in interviewing children (discussed further below), and inter-agency work with the police.

A list of offences against children is contained in Sch. 1 to the Children and Young Persons Act 1933, and the term, 'Schedule One Offender' has been used to refer to a person who has committed such an offence. Following a recent review of the Schedule, a Home Office Circular[62] to the police and social services (amongst others) states that the term 'is ill-defined and, to a certain extent, unhelpful'. It suggests that the term should be replaced by 'a person identified as presenting a risk, or potential risk, to children'.

Some of the criminal offences that may be committed against a child are outlined below:

■ Any person over the age of 16 who has responsibility for a child, who wilfully assaults, ill treats, neglects, abandons, or exposes him, or causes or procures him to be assaulted, ill treated, neglected, abandoned, or exposed, in a manner likely to cause him unnecessary suffering or injury to health, shall be guilty of an offence (Children and Young Persons Act 1933, s. 1).

■ To unlawfully abandon or expose any child, under the age of 2, whereby the child's life is endangered or health is likely to be permanently injured (Offences Against the Person Act 1861, s. 27).

■ A range of specific child sexual offences are contained in the Sexual Offences Act 2003,[63] including: sexual activity with a child (s. 9); causing or inciting a child to engage in sexual acitivity (s. 10); engaging in sexual activity in the presence of a child (s. 11); meeting a child following sexual grooming; abuse of position of trust offences (ss. 16–24); familial child sexual offences replace incest (ss. 25–29); abuse of children through prostitution and pornography; rape and assault of a child under 13 (ss. 5–8).

■ Sexual intercourse with a girl under 16 unless the man is under 24, believes her to be over 16 and it is a first offence (Sexual Offences Act 1956, s. 6).

■ Assault, grevious bodily harm or wounding (Offences Against the Person Act 1861, ss. 47 and 20).

■ Causing or allowing the death of a child (or vulnerable adult) also referred to as familial homicide (Domestic Violence Crime and Victims Act 2004, s. 5).[64] The offence carries a maximum sentence of 14 years. It will apply in circumstances where it is unclear who in the household actually caused a child's death. It will be possible to charge more than one person with causing or failing to protect the child.

■ Evidence of children[65]

In many cases of child abuse (particularly of a sexual nature) there will be no witnesses to the abuse. The child's account of what has happened can be the principal evidence relied upon. However the allegations of abuse initially came to light (e.g. the child made a comment to a teacher), it will need to be fully investigated and this process will entail interviewing the child. The chapter on interviewing children in the Cleveland report remains pertinent and valuable reading. Enduring messages from Chapter 12 of the report include:

■ undesirability of referring to 'disclosure' interviews which prejudge the situation;

■ interviews should be undertaken only by those with appropriate training and skills, and approached with an open mind;

- open-ended questions should be utilised;
- interviews should be at the child's pace and not be too long;
- the interview should take place in a suitable setting;
- the interview should be carefully recorded.

Where there is a possibility of legal proceedings (civil and/or criminal), it is essential that the purpose of any interview is clear. Due to rules of evidence, it is unlikely that a 'therapeutic' interview will be admissible as evidence in a criminal trial (*Re D (Minors) (Child Abuse: Interviews)* [1998] 2 FLR 11). In civil proceedings, as hearsay evidence is admissible, it is less likely that the child will be required to give evidence. This does not mean, however, that the above caution as to the purpose of the interview can be forgotten. Hearsay evidence of an interview which was carried out inappropriately, perhaps by excessive use of leading questions, will be of little value to the court.

Guidance as to the conduct of investigative interviews of children who are victims of abuse where a criminal prosecution is likely to be brought against the perpetrator, is contained in 'Achieving Best Evidence in Criminal Proceedings: Guidance for Vulnerable or Intimidated Witnesses including Children' (2001),[66] (replacing the 'Memorandum of Good Practice on Video Recorded Interviews with Child Witnesses for Criminal Proceedings' 1992[67]). The interview will be carried out jointly by officers from the police and social services who have received specialist training. The guidance extends beyond interviewing to pre-trial witness support and preparation at court stage. The guidance includes general principles for interviewing children which include: establishing rapport; truth and lies; establishing the purpose of the interview; raising issues of concern; obtaining a free narrative account; questions thereafter and closure.

The Youth Justice and Criminal Evidence Act 1999 makes further provision in the form of 'special measures' relating to the evidence of vulnerable and intimidated witnesses, including children. The court can exercise a degree of discretion as to the 'special measures' that may be made available to a witness but children under the age of 17 are automatically eligible for assistance (s. 16). Special measures include: use of screens so that the child cannot see the accused (s. 23); giving evidence by live link (s. 24); removal of wigs and gowns while the witness testifies (s. 26); giving evidence in private (in sexual offences cases), i.e. the press are removed (s. 25); video recording of evidence-in-chief (s. 27); video recording of cross-examination and re-examination (s. 28); examination of witness through an intermediary – this could be an interpreter or person with particular communication skills or a social worker (s. 29); and use of communication aids (s. 30). The case of *R (D) v Camberwell Youth Court* [2005] UKHL 4 confirms that the use of special measures for child witnesses is compatible with Art. 6 ECHR, the right to a fair trial.

The most important of the new measures is, arguably, the new facility of video recording cross-examination and examination-in-chief, which answers the deficiency identified in the old law.[68] It has been noted that an advantage of pre-recorded cross-examination is that it may be possible for therapy for the child to start earlier as the risk of contaminating the child's evidence and undermining credibility is diminished.[69] Guidance, 'Provision of Therapy for Child Witnesses Prior to a Criminal Trial' (2001), clarifies the position on provision of therapy prior to criminal trial, including evaluation of different therapeutic techniques.[70]

Chapter summary

- Child protection is a high profile area of work; it is crucial to be alert to new research, developments in recognition of abuse, changes in the law, and to learn from the findings of inquiry reports. The main types of child abuse are physical, emotional and sexual abuse, and neglect.

- The duty to investigate concerns relating to possible child abuse is clearly imposed on social services under s. 47 of the Children Act 1989. However, other bodies, such as the housing and health authorities, are required to assist with those inquiries.

- The child protection conference is a crucial part of the investigative stage. At the conference the decision whether to place the child's name on the child protection register will be taken, information about the child's circumstances analysed, and recommendations will be made as to the future action to be taken to safeguard the child and promote his welfare. The child's family, and the child if of a sufficient age, should normally be involved in the conference.

- Short-term orders introduced by the Children Act 1989 include the child assessment order (CAO) and emergency protection order (EPO). The CAO is designed to cover situations where there are concerns about a child and lack of cooperation is preventing full assessment. The EPO can provide immediate protection for a child, for a period of eight days (extendable in exceptional circumstances to 15 days). The applicant for an EPO may be any person, the local authority or the NSPCC. In addition, the police have a power to remove and detain a child for a maximum period of 72 hours.

- The Family Law Act 1996 introduces a new power of exclusion, which enables the court to exclude an alleged abuser from the home, rather than removing the child. The order may be attached to an emergency protection order or an interim care order.

- Care and supervision orders may be made on the application of the local authority, where the threshold criteria are satisfied. There are three stages that must be completed before an order will be made: first, significant harm must be established; secondly, the harm must be attributable to the care the child has received or his being beyond parental control; and thirdly, the court will apply the 'no order' principle and the menu of orders before deciding which, if any, order to make. Aspects of the criteria are defined in the legislation and a body of case law has developed, which defines further terms. Interim care or supervision orders may be made while the investigation continues. Expert witnesses will often provide evidence in child care cases.

- The local authority is obliged to prepare a care plan for a child it is proposing to look after, including children for whom an application for a care order is made. Its implementation will be kept under review by an Independent Reviewing Officer.

- There is a presumption in favour of contact between the child and significant others after a care order is made.

- In order that the child is independently represented in proceedings, a children's guardian, (CAFCASS), will be appointed. The guardian has a right of access to local authority records and must produce a report to court. If the child does not agree with the guardian's recommendation, and is of sufficient age and understanding, a separate solicitor may be appointed to represent the child.

- The High Court exercises the inherent jurisdiction and may make orders in respect of children according to their best interests, e.g. in relation to the lawfulness of proposed medical treatment. The wardship jurisdiction is also exercised by this court. Local authority access to wardship was restricted by the Children Act 1989. A local authority must obtain prior leave of the court before an application can be made.

- There have been developments in the law to prevent unsuitable people from being engaged in child care positions. The Protection of Children Act 1999 established the protection of children list and obliges child care organisations to check whether any prospective employee is included on the list. A central Criminal Records Bureau will deal with requests for information.

- There is a range of criminal offences against children that may be committed in child abuse cases. 'Achieving Best Evidence in Criminal Proceedings' provides guidance on how joint interviews of a child by the police and social services are to be conducted where there is the possibility of a prosecution. New special measures have been introduced to make the witness experience less stressful for children.

Exercises

1. David and Julie are married with one child, Lucy, aged 4. The health visitor has noted that Lucy appears uncomfortable with strangers, is clingy, underweight and has a slight hearing impairment. She passed on these concerns to social services three weeks ago and a social worker is planning to visit the family this week. When the social worker visits, Julie tells her that David has left after a violent incident, which she refuses to discuss in any detail. Julie tells the social worker that after he left Lucy said she was glad he had gone and she 'didn't like the way that he touches me at night'. Julie says she does not want him to see Lucy ever again. Later that day a senior social worker visits and Julie retracts her earlier comments, saying it was all a misunderstanding and that David is expected home shortly. The social worker is concerned that Lucy may be at risk. What action should be taken?

2. Richard and Helen are a married couple in their mid-thirties. They have two daughters – Anne, aged 14, and Clare, aged 6. They recently separated. Their relationship has deteriorated dramatically since Richard became unemployed and he now believes that Helen is having an affair with a woman. The children are currently living with Helen, but Richard wishes to care for them full time. Helen has petitioned for divorce and Richard has applied for a residence order. At the same time, Anne and Clare's teachers have become concerned about both the girls' behaviour. Anne's schoolwork is deteriorating and she has been involved in bullying. Clare's teacher is particularly concerned because she has noticed that Clare has become increasingly withdrawn whereas previously she was very lively. One day the teacher notices that Clare has bruises on her thighs, but she refuses to explain their cause. The teacher passes this information to social services. When the social worker contacts the parents, Helen claims that Richard must have caused the bruises when he took the girls out at the weekend. Richard denies the allegation. Anne has told the school nurse that her father smacks her and her sister but does not want the nurse to tell anybody about this. Consider how this case should progress.

Websites

The Department of Health and Department for Education and Skills sites includes many of the official publications referred to in this chapter, Circulars and Local Authority Social Services letters, and have useful 'What's New' sections:
www.doh.gov.uk
www.dfes.gov.uk

The CAFCASS website provides further information about the service and the role of the guardian:
www.cafcass.gov.uk

The National Society for the Prevention of Cruelty to Children (NSPCC):
www.nspcc.org.uk

Further reading

A detailed textbook with a particular focus on child protection is:

Lyon, C. (2003) *Child Abuse* (3rd edn.). Bristol: Family Law, Jordan Publishing.

A selection of articles provide critiques of various aspects of the child protection process:

In relation to short term intervention see:

Masson, J. (2002) 'Police Protection – Protecting Whom?' 24(3) *Journal of Social Work* p. 72.

Lavery, R. (1996) 'The child assessment order – a reassessment' 8(1) *Child and Family Law Quarterly* p. 41.

Masson, J. (2005) 'Emergency Intervention to Protect Children: Using and Avoiding Legal Controls' 17(1) *Child and Family Law Quarterly* p. 1.

Aspects of the child protection process and perspectives of professionals and parents are considered in:

Booth, T., Booth, W. and McConnell, D. (2004) 'Parents with learning difficulties, care proceedings and the family courts: threshold decisions and the moral matrix' 16(4) *Child and Family Law Quarterly* p. 409.

Larkin, E., McSherry, D. and Iwaniec, D. (2005) 'Room for improvement? Views of key professionals involved in care order proceedings' 17(2) *Child and Family Law Quarterly* p. 231.

Lindley, B., Richards, M. and Freeman, P. (2001) 'Advice and advocacy for parents in child protection cases – an exploration of conceptual and policy issues, ethical dilemmas and future directions' 13(3) *Child and Family Law Quarterly* p. 311.

Iwaniec, D., Donaldson, T. and Allweis, M. (2004) 'The plight of neglected children – social work and judicial decision making and management of neglect cases' 16(4) *Child and Family Law Quarterly* p. 423.

Cobley, C. (2004) '"Working Together?" – Admissions of Abuse in Child Protection Proceedings and Criminal Prosecutions' 16(2) *Child and Family Law Quarterly* p. 175.

Hann, J. and Owen, M. (2003) 'The Implementation of Care Plans and its Relationship to Children's Welfare' 15(1) *Child and Family Law Quarterly* p. 71.

Corby, B. (2004) 'Towards a new means of inquiry into child abuse cases' 25(3) *Journal of Social Work Law* p. 229.

The following address the role of the guardian:

Clark, A. and Sinclair, R. (1999) *The child in focus: the evolving role of the guardian* ad litem. London: National Children's Bureau.

McCausland, J. (2000) *Guarding Children's Interests*. London: The Children's Society.

Masson, J. and Winn Oakley, M. (1999) *Out of Hearing: Representing Children in Care Proceedings*. Chichester: NSPCC/Wiley.

Guidance on roles and responsibility in child protection are helpfully covered in:

Walsh, E. (2006) *Working in the Family Justice System. A Guide for Professionals* (2nd edn). Bristol: Family Law, Jordan Publishing.

Wilson, K. and James, A. (eds.) (2002) *The Child Protection Handbook* (2nd edn). Edinburgh, Bailliere Tindall.

Notes

1 See discussion in Chapter 4, and *Z* v. *United Kingdom* (2001) 34 EHRR 97.

2 *A* v. *United Kingdom (Human Rights: Punishment of Child)* (1998) 27 EHRR 611 *Z* v. *United Kingdom* (2001) 34 EHRR 97.

3 Glossary to 'Working Together' (2006) p. xxvii.

4 There is a supplement to 'Working Together' specifically addressing factitious illness (2002) 'Safeguarding Children in Whom Illness is Induced or Fabricated by Carers with

Parenting Responsibilities – Supplementary Guidance to Working Together to Safeguard Children'. London: Department of Health.

[5] Most of the publications listed are available on the internet via the Department of Health site www.doh.gov.uk.

[6] Department of Health. London: HMSO.

[7] Department of Health. London: The Stationery Office.

[8] There is a Quality Protects website at www.doh.gov.uk/qualityprotects/index/htm.

[9] Department of Health. London: The Stationery Office.

[10] Department of Health, Department for Education and Employment and Home Office. London: The Stationery Office.

[11] Department of Health. London: The Stationery Office.

[12] Often referred to as 'Part 8' Reviews, due to their introduction in Part 8 of the 1991 version of 'Working Together'.

[13] Department of Health (1995) 'Child Protection: Messages from Research'. London: HMSO, p. 29.

[14] Department of Health and Social Security (1974) 'Report of the Committee of Inquiry into the Care and Supervision Provided in Relation to Maria Colwell'.

[15] B. Lindley, M. Richards and P. Freeman (2001) 'Advice and advocacy for parents in child protection cases – an exploration of conceptual and policy issues, ethical dilemmas and future directions' 13(3) *Child and Family Law Quarterly* p. 311.

[16] Department of Health (2001) *The Children Act Now: Messages from Research*. London: The Stationery Office.

[17] Secretary of State for Health, Secretary of State for Education and Skills and Lord Chancellor (2001) 'The Children Act Report 2000'. London: HMSO.

[18] P. Nixon (2001) 'An Introduction to Family Group Conferences' in L.-A. Cull and J. Roche *The Law and Social Work: Contemporary Issues for Practice*. Basingstoke: Palgrave.

[19] Department of Health and Social Security. London: HMSO.

[20] 'The Children Act 1989 Guidance and Regulations', vol. 1 'Court Orders'. London: HMSO, para. 4.4.

[21] J. Dickens (1993) 'Assessment and control of social work: an analysis of the reasons for the non-use of the child assessment order' 15(2) *Journal of Social Welfare and Family Law* p. 188.

[22] For further analysis of this case see: Masson, J (2004) Emergency Protection, Good Practice and Human Rights. 34 *Family Law*: 882

[23] See, e.g. the Waterhouse Report: R. Waterhouse (2000) 'Report of the tribunal of inquiry into the abuse of children in care in the former county council areas of Gwynedd and Clwyd since 1974'. London: The Stationery Office.

[24] A. Pack (2001) 'Most efficacious, in every case? Exclusion requirements – an overview' *Family Law* p. 217.

[25] C. Beckett (2001) 'The Great Care Proceedings Explosion' 31(3) *British Journal of Social Work* p. 493.

[26] Department of Health (2001) 'The Children Act Now: Messages from Research', London: The Stationery Office (pp. 55–6).

[27] 'The Children Act 1989 Guidance and Regulations', vol. 1 'Court orders', London: HMSO (p. 24).

28 Discussed further in A. Perry (2000) '*Lancashire County Council* v *B*, Section 31 – threshold or barrier' 12(3) *Child and Family Law Quarterly* p. 301.

29 J. Hayes (2000) 'The threshold test and the unknown perpetrator' *Family Law* p. 260.

30 The circular was introduced to address concerns about consistency in care planning between authorities in terms of style, format, level of detail and contributors.

31 See *Re D and K (Care Plan: Twin Track Planning)* [1999] 2 FLR 872.

32 As discussed in *Re J (Minors) (Care Proceedings: Care Plan)* [1994] 1 FLR 253.

33 Department in Constitutional Affairs: available at www.dca.gov.uk/family/scopestud.htm.

34 See also M. Booth (1996) *Avoiding Delay in Children Act Cases*. London: Lord Chancellor's Department.

35 See E. Saunders (2003) 'The New Care Protocol' *Family Law* p. 774.

36 DCA SR 2004 Technical Notes for PSA Targets.

37 See D. Hershman (2004) *Working with the Child Care Protocol*. Bristol: Family Law, Jordan Publishing.

38 Department of Health and Social Security (1974) 'Report of the Committee of Inquiry into the Care and Supervision Provided in Relation to Maria Colwell'. London: HMSO.

39 Family Proceedings Rules 1991 (SI 1991/1247).

40 A. Dale-Emberton (2001) 'Working with children: a guardian ad litem's experience' in L.-A. Cull and J. Roche (eds.) *The Law and Social Work: Contemporary Issues for Practice*. Basingstoke: Palgrave.

41 J. McCausland (2000) *Guarding Children's Interests: The Contribution of Guardians ad Litem in Court Proceedings*. London: The Children's Society.

42 Department of Health (1995) 'A Guide for Guardians ad Litem in Public Law Proceedings under the Children Act 1989'. London: HMSO.

43 J. McCausland (2000) *Guarding Children's Interests: The Contribution of Guardians ad Litem in Court Proceedings*. London: The Children's Society.

44 For a full discussion of the role, see J. Wall (2000) *A Handbook for Expert Witnesses in Children Act Cases*. Bristol: Family Law, Jordan Publishing.

45 Family Proceedings Rules 1991 (SI 1991/1247), r. 4.18(1).

46 Further guidance on the appointment and role of expert witnesses is given in *Re G (Minors) (Expert Witnesses)* [1994] 2 FLR 291.

47 See also Expert Witness Group (1997) *The Expert Witness Pack for Use in Children Act Proceedings*. Bristol: Family Law, Jordan Publishing Ltd.

48 Annex to the Practice Direction: Principles of Application [2003] Fam Law 606.

49 Home Office (1993) 'Protection of children: disclosure of criminal background of those with access to children', Circular No. 47/93.

50 *R* v. *Secretary of State for Health, ex parte C* [2000] 1 FCR 471 ruled that the list maintained by the Department of Health of people who were thought to be unsuitable to work with children was not unlawful, nor was it operated unreasonably. At the time there was no statutory basis for the list, although that has now been supplied by the Protection of Children Act 1999. The judgment referred to guidance in circular LAC (93) 17, 'Protection of children', which stated that the object is to make sure that, as far as possible, unsuitable people are not appointed to positions involving contact with children or responsibility for them. Balancing the interests of an individual in safeguarding his reputation and livelihood against the interest

of children living away from home and the interest of the community which sought to safe-guard its more vulnerable members, the index was found not unlawful.

51   See further Department of Health (2000) 'The Protection of Children Act 1999: a practical guide to the Act for all organisations working with children'. London: HMSO.

52   According to Department of Health (1991) 'Child Abuse: A Study of Inquiry Reports 1980–1989'. London: HMSO, there were 37 inquiries between 1973 and 1989. Other commentators suggest the figure is higher: B. Corby, A. Doig and V. Roberts (1998) 'Inquiries into child abuse' 20(4) *Journal of Social Welfare and Family Law* p. 377.

53   Useful analysis of child abuse inquiries is presented in P. Reder, S. Duncan and M. Gray (1993) *Beyond Blame: Child Abuse Tragedies Revisited*. London: Routledge.

54   See C. Lyon and P. De Cruz (1993) *Child Abuse* (2nd edn). Bristol: Family Law, Jordan Publishing.

55   Department of Health and Social Security (1974) 'Report of the Committee of Inquiry into the Care and Supervision Provided in Relation to Maria Colwell'. London: HMSO.

56   Department of Health and Social Security (1985) 'A Child in Trust: Jasmine Beckford'. London: HMSO.

57   Department of Health and Social Security (1987) 'A Child in Mind: Protection of Children in a Responsible Society'. London: HMSO.

58   Department of Health and Social Security (1987) 'Whose Child?'. London: HMSO.

59   Butler-Sloss, LJ (1988) 'Report of the Inquiry into Child Abuse in Cleveland' (1987, Cmnd. 412). London: HMSO.

60   Staffordshire County Council (1991) 'The Pindown Experience and the Protection of Children: The Report of the Staffordshire Child Care Inquiry 1990'. Staffordshire County Council.

61   Sir W. Utting (1991) *Children in Public Care: A Review of Residential Care*. London: HMSO; followed by a further report, Sir W. Utting (1997) *People Like Us. The Report of the Review of Safeguards for Children Living Away from Home*. London: HMSO.

62   Home Office (2005) Guidance on Offences Against Children, 16/2005.

63   See J. Spencer (2004) 'The Sexual Offences Act 2003: Child and Family Offences' *Criminal Law Review* p. 347.

64   Follows Law Commission proposals in their September 2003 publication, 'Children – their non-accidental death or serious injury'.

65   See generally on child witnesses in criminal proceedings, J.R. Spencer and R. Flin (1993) *The Evidence of Children: the Law and the Psychology* (2nd edn.). London: Blackstone Press.

66   Home Office.

67   Following recommendations of the Pigot Report, 'Report of the Home Office Advisory Group on Video Evidence' (1989). London: HMSO.

68   For details of the Act and further information on special measures, see D. Birch and R. Leng (2000) *Blackstone's Guide to the Youth Justice and Criminal Evidence Act 1999*. London: Blackstone Press.

69   See discussion in P. Bates (1999) 'The Youth Justice and Criminal Evidence Act' 11(3) *Child and Family Law Quarterly* p. 289.

70   Home Office, Crown Prosecution Service, Department of Health. London: The Stationery Office.

10 Looked after children

Learning objectives

To develop an understanding of the following:

- The term 'looked after children'.
- The duties owed by local authorities towards looked after children.
- The duty to provide accommodation as an aspect of service provision.
- Outcomes for looked after children.
- The impact of the Quality Protects initiative.
- Local authority and private fostering.
- Residential accommodation and secure accommodation.
- The role of the independent visitor.
- Support for young people leaving care.

Introduction

Looked after children are those children who are accommodated by the local authority, away from their family, in a residential or foster placement, and all children who are the subject of a care order, even if they are living with their parents.[1] The accommodation (provided for a continuous period of more than 24 hours[2]) may be provided on a voluntary basis, or under the authority of a care order or other court order. Accommodation may be provided on a long-term basis or a series of planned short-term placements, including support foster care (formerly referred to as 'respite care').

There are a significant number of looked after children. On any one day 60,000 children are looked after. About 42 per cent of those children return home within eight weeks but many will need to be looked after in a planned way with a degree of permanence for a substantial part of their lives.[3] The majority live with foster carers (65 per cent), about 11 per cent live in residential accommodation and an equivalent number are actually placed at home but with social services input.[4]

This chapter will consider the duties towards looked after children, including the obligation to provide suitable accommodation. The material is structured to reflect the child's journey through placement leading to independence. For those looked after children for whom rehabilitation with their families is not possible, security and stability may be achieved through adoption. The law on adoption has undergone a major reform with implementation of the Adoption and Children Act 2002 and is considered fully in Chapter 11. There is a clear preference emerging from official publications for greater use of adoption for looked after children. The chapter moves on to consider a range of alternative options for looked after children offering some degree of permanence, namely fostering and residential accommodation, and includes discussion of secure accommodation. Finally, the responsibilities of local authorities towards looked after children who cease to be looked after under the Children (Leaving Care) Act 2000 (**C(LC)A 2000**) are considered.

Duties towards looked after children

A local authority has certain duties towards all looked after children. These duties are set out in the Children Act 1989, ss. 22 and 23.

s. 22(3)

> It shall be the duty of a local authority looking after any child –
>   (a) to safeguard and promote his welfare; and
>   (b) to make such use of services available for children cared for by their own parents as appears to the authority reasonable in his case.
>
> (CA 1989)

Local authorities have a duty of consultation before making decisions regarding looked after children. Specifically, they are directed to ascertain the wishes and feelings of the child, his parents, and any person with parental responsibility, and any other person whose wishes and feelings are considered relevant to the matter in hand (s. 22(4)). The authority is then directed to give due consideration to the views ascertained. In exceptional circumstances this duty of consultation may be limited as in *Re P (Children Act 1989, s 22 and 26: Local Authority Compliance)* [2000] 2 FLR 910, where restricted consultation was permitted because of the continuing risk the father posed to the children in placements outside the family. In addition, before making the decision, under s. 22(5) the local authority must also give due consideration to the child's racial origin, cultural and linguistic background. This factor is likely to be most relevant to placement decisions and would suggest that, where possible, a child's placement should be able to meet the child's cultural needs and be with a family of similar religious persuasion, racial origin, cultural and linguistic background. Where adoption is proposed for the child, the duty in ACA 2002, s. 1(5) applies, namely, 'In placing the child for adoption, the adoption agency must give due consideration to the child's religious persuasion, racial origin and cultural and linguistic background.'

Section 23(1)(b) states that the local authority must provide accommodation for the child and must 'maintain' the child. It is, however, possible to require a reasonable financial contribution from the child's parents where the local authority considers it is reasonable to do so.

There is a duty to promote contact between the child and his parents, any other person who has parental responsibility, and relatives and friends. This is not an absolute duty and is qualified in circumstances where it would not be reasonably practicable or is not consistent with the child's welfare (Sch. 2, para. 15(1)). The local authority must also ensure that parents (and others with parental responsibility) are kept informed of the child's whereabouts (Sch. 2, para. 15(2)), unless this would prejudice the child's welfare (Sch. 2, para. 15(4)(b)). To enable contact, the local authority *may* make payments to assist with travelling and subsistence costs incurred in visits to the child or by the child visiting his family, if undue financial hardship would be caused without the assistance.

■ Provision of accommodation

Perhaps the most important decision the local authority will take with respect to a looked after child is where the child is to be accommodated. Section 23 of the Children Act 1989 imposes a duty on the local authority to provide accommodation and maintain a looked after child and outlines a range of possible placements, namely a relative, a foster carer or a children's home. There is a preference for a child to be placed with her parents, a person with parental responsibility, a holder of a residence order, or a relative, friend or other person connected with the child unless it would not be reasonably practicable or consistent with the child's welfare (s. 23(6)). This preference will always be balanced against any risk presented by the household.

The accommodation should normally (if reasonably practicable and consistent with the child's welfare) be near to the child's home and be able to provide accommodation for siblings to stay together (s. 23(7)). Contact between looked after children and their families is important and the local authority is under a duty to promote contact between the child and his or her parents. In many cases this will be face-to-face contact and may include overnight stays. The importance of placing children near to their families in this context is obvious. In other cases contact may be by telephone, letters and cards, and other forms of indirect contact. If a looked after child is the subject of a care order an important element of the care plan will be the arrangements for contact.

Provision of accommodation on a voluntary basis is intended to be seen as a service to support parents and it is significant that s. 20, which deals with provision of accommodation for children in need, is contained in Part III of the Act: 'Local Authority Support for Children and Families'. The local authority must accommodate children in need who appear to require accommodation as a result of:

s. 20(1)

(a) there being no person who has parental responsibility for him;

(b) his being lost or having been abandoned; or

(c) the person who has been caring for him being prevented (whether or not permanently, and for whatever reason) from providing him with suitable accommodation or care.

(CA 1989)

The duty is to provide accommodation for a child, not for a parent and child. In *R (G)* v. *Barnet London Borough Council* [2003] UKHL 57 a mother and her 1-year-old child had come to the United Kingdom from Holland. The local authority were of the view that the child's best interests would be served by remaining in the care of his mother and they offered to pay their fare to return to Holland. This was rejected. The local authority therefore were found to have acted within the terms of the Children Act 1989 by offering to accommodate the child only, under s. 20.

A person may be prevented from providing suitable accommodation in a variety of circumstances including housing difficulties, hospital admission, illness, etc. The arrangement is voluntary and is an obvious area where the local authority must work in partnership with parents. A child cannot be accommodated under s. 20 if there is opposition from a person with parental responsibility who would himself be able to provide accommodation for the child. In such circumstances the only way the local authority could provide accommodation would be under the authority of a care order. Where a child is accommodated with the consent of the parents, the local authority does not have the power to move the child to live with foster carers against the parents' wishes. In *R* v. *Tameside Metropolitan Borough Council, ex parte J* [2000] 1 FCR 173, a 13-year-old girl with severe disabilities and autistic tendencies had lived in a residential home near to her parents' home for two years. Judicial review found that the local authority decision to move J against her parents' wishes was unlawful.

To reinforce the voluntary nature of s. 20 accommodation, there is no requirement for a person who wishes to remove the child to give notice to the local authority (s. 20(8)). A brief explanation of the law in operation before the Children Act 1989 illustrates the significance of this point. A child in 'voluntary care' could become subject to compulsion by an administrative process. Once a child had been accommodated for more than six months, it became necessary for a person wishing to resume care to give the local authority 28 days' notice of that intention. During that period local authorities could pass a parental rights resolution at committee level, which changed the position of the child to one in formal care. The parent could then challenge this status by application to the magistrates' court.

Nowadays, any question of notice and arrangements for the appropriate circumstances in which a child should be returned will be covered by negotiated agreement with parents. Such agreements are covered by the Arrangements for Placement of Children (General) Regulations 1991.[5] It is important to note that an agreement is not a binding contract and any notice provision it contains is unenforceable by the local authority. It may be argued that this renders such agreements pointless. Their value, however, rests on the fact that they should be negotiated with parents and relied upon in the spirit of partnership.

Further detail on local authority responsibilities towards looked after children is contained in Sch. 2 to the Children Act 1989. This Schedule provides for regulations to be made concerning placements with foster parents and the situation where a child in care is placed at home. Further detail is included about promotion of contact, arrangements for visits to or by children and the appointment of an independent visitor.

Reviews

The circumstances of looked after children should be reviewed regularly. Regulations made under s. 26 prescribe the detail. An Independent Review Officer (who will be a registered and experienced social worker) will chair the reviews and monitor the s. 31A care plan and may refer the case to CAFCASS if there are concerns; the CAFCASS officer may then return the case to court. A review should be held within four weeks of the initial placement, followed by a further review in three months' time and thereafter every six months. The review should consider the child's progress and whether his needs are being met in the placement, any changes that might need to be made to the plan and contact arrangements. The child (of sufficient age and understanding) will normally attend the review and parents are entitled to attend reviews unless given a specific reason as to why they should not, e.g. fear of violence. The relevant regulations which provide further detail on reviews are: the Review of Children's Cases Regulations 1991[6] the Review of Children's Cases (Amendment) (England) Regulations 2004[7] and the Review of Children's Cases (Amendment) (Wales) Regulations.[8]

The Children Act (Miscellaneous Amendments) (England) Regulations 2002.[9] (S I 2002/546) provide that health reviews of looked after children should be conducted every six months for children under 5 and at least once a year for children over 5. This follows an initial health assessment of the child's physical and mental health to be carried out as soon as practicable after the children becomes looked after.

■ Outcomes for looked after children

In comparison with other children in society, looked after children appear to fare less well on a number of levels. This includes levels of attainment, health,[10] levels of unemployment and numbers entering the prison population: 70 per cent leave care without any qualifications; 25 per cent of looked after children do not attend school regularly; up to 25 per cent of young women leaving care are pregnant or already have a child; those who have been looked after are 60 per cent more likely to be homeless than the general population; 39 per cent of male prisoners under 21 have been looked after.[11] Given the circumstances in which some children become looked after, having suffered neglect or abuse, and coming from disadvantaged backgrounds, these outcomes may not be a great surprise. Nevertheless, it is not appropriate simply to accept the inevitability of such outcomes, and the Government has adopted a position whereby it has set targets to significantly improve outcomes for looked after children. This should be seen in the context of the 'Every Child Matters: Change for Children' programme, which aims to improve outcomes for all children.

The primary vehicle for this initiative is the 'Quality Protects' programme ('Children First' in Wales). Associated initiatives have come out of the 'Modernising Social Services' agenda and include new systems of regulation under the Care Standards Act 2000, the 'Sure Start' programme and 'Connexions'.

■ Quality Protects

The whole area of care of looked after children must be seen in the context of the modernisation agenda for health and social services which the Labour Government has promoted.[12] Increasingly, services are being monitored with a view to improvement by the use of 'best value' initiatives, performance indicators and regulation. A key tenet of this agenda is the Quality Protects initiative, which was launched in 1998. Aspects of this strategy relate to all children likely to come into contact with social services but it is particularly targeted at children in need (discussed in Chapter 7) and looked after children. There are 11 main objectives, each accompanied by sub-objectives and performance indicators, published in 'The Government's Objectives for Children's Social Services' (1998).[13]

The Quality Protects objectives clearly call for greater use of adoption for looked after children. More recently, the Prime Minister's Review of Adoption lends further support to this, with the following quote drawn from the introduction: 'It is hard to overstate the importance of a stable and loving family life for children. That is why I want more children to benefit from adoption.'[14] This view is expressed with conviction, which is supported by new targets for increased numbers of adoption; yet it is difficult to evaluate how successful adoption is, as there have been no official statistics dealing with levels of disruption of adoptive placements.[15] The Government has recently announced its intention to amend the statistical collection for looked after children to provide national estimates of the number of children who are adopted from care whose adoption breaks down resulting in them re-entering care.[16]

Relevant Quality Protects objectives

1.0 to ensure that children are securely attached to carers capable of providing safe and effective care for the duration of childhood.

1.3 to maximise the contribution adoption can make to providing permanent families for children in appropriate cases.

Performance indicators

■ The number of looked after children adopted during a year as a percentage of children looked after at year ending 31 March.

■ The proportion of placements for adoption ceasing during the year which did result in adoption.

1.4 to minimise the period children remain looked after before they are adopted.

Performance indicator

■ The average duration of time looked after before adoption.

In addition to the Adoption and Children Act 2002, national standards on adoption have been introduced.[17] The standards aim to be child-centred and evidence-based and include sections for each of the key stakeholders. The number of children being adopted from care has risen and would seem to suggest that the Quality Protects objectives are being put into practice. There were 2,200 looked after children in England adopted in 1999 and 3,500 in the year ending March 2003.[18]

More recently, the Government has prioritised two areas for looked after children: improving the stability of placements for looked after children, and improving their educational achievement. These have been formalised into a Government public service agreement (PSA) target, to:

Narrow the gap in educational achievement between looked-after children and their peers, and improve their educational support and the stability of their lives, so that by 2008, 80% of children under 16 who have been looked after for 2.5 or more years will have been living in the same placement for at least 2 years, or are placed for adoption.

National performance indicators to measure this target include: the percentage of children aged 11, looked after for at least 12 months, who obtain level 4 in Key Stage 2 English and Maths; and the percentage of young people, looked after for at least 12 months and in Year 11, who achieve five or more GCSEs graded A*–C or equivalent. All looked after children should have a personal education plan covering achievement, development and educational needs, short-term targets, long-term plans and aspirations. Statutory guidance expects social workers to be 'effective advocates in dealing with school admissions, issues arising from behavioural problems and school discipline and school exclusions'.[19] The education of looked after children is considered further in Chapter 12.

In relation to stability, in 2005 a DfES study[20] found that 65 per cent of looked after children had been in the same placement for at least two years, but there was wide variation between different authorities. Factors which were most likely to lead to improvements in stability were improvements in placement choice and placement support.

Fostering

The term 'foster carer' is used in this text in preference to foster parent. It was acknowledged in The Children Act 1989 Guidance that although foster parent is the term used in legislation and regulations, and is understood by the general public, the term foster carer is more commonly used by professionals.[21] Fostering is a term that applies to a great variety of arrangements. It may be short- or long-term, provided in emergencies, as part of a planned provision of 'respite' care, by local authority, or private carers. There are some 'specialist' foster carers who cater, for example, for children who have been abused in a particular way or for gay teenagers.

Foster carers do not acquire parental responsibility by virtue of the fostering arrangement. They are *de facto* carers acting '*in loco parentis*', a situation which lacks legal security. If faced with a parent who wishes to resume care of their child, or a local authority who plans to move the child, there is little that the foster carers can do to prevent removal, other than to rely in the short term on s. 3(5) of the Children Act 1989 or to seek an emergency protection order (EPO). If foster carers wish to continue to care for a child on a long-term basis, they may seek a residence order, where the child has been living with them for one out of the last five years (CA 1989, s. 9(3)), or they have the consent of those with parental responsibility, or the consent of the local authority if they are relatives of the child. In other cases they must seek leave of the court. Section 113 of the Adoption and Children Act 2002 amended s. 9 of the Children Act 1989 so that local authority foster carers may apply to the court for a residence or adoption order in respect of a child who has been living with them for one year, instead of three years, as was previously the case.

The significance of this change is clearly illustrated in the case of *R (W) v Leicestershire County Council* [2003] EWHC 704 (Admin). The case concerned twins who were placed with a short-term foster carer with a care plan for them to be adopted. The foster mother became attached to the twins and wished to adopt them but the authority felt she would not be suitable. She gave notice to the authority that she intended to apply for an adoption order. The twins had lived with her for about a year. In response the authority removed the twins and terminated the foster placement.

The case illustrates the difficulties which may be experienced by foster carers who wish to strengthen their legal relationship with foster children. At the time, a foster carer could not apply for a residence order without the consent of the local authority unless a relative or the child had lived with her for three out of five years before the application CA 1989, s. 9(3), In this case the foster mother could not apply to make the children wards of court as they were placed under care orders (CA 1989, s.100(2)). Section 31 of the Adoption Act 1976 gave the local authority the power to give notice to a foster parent, who has given notice of intention to adopt, requiring the children to be returned within seven days. Failure to comply with the notice is a criminal offence.

In *R(W)*, an application for judicial review of the local authority notice was made by the foster mother. It was unsuccessful, as the court found that the foster mother's wishes and feelings were considered (as required by CA 1989, s. 22(4), making decisions in respect of looked after children). She was well aware of the local authority's reasons for assessing her as unsuitable to adopt. The court also rejected the argument that the authority had not given 'first consideration to the need to safeguard and promote the welfare of the children' (Adoption Act 1976 s. 6).

How would the position be different under the Adoption and Children Act 2002? Section 9 of the Children Act 1989 has been amended so that a foster parent may apply for a residence order where a child has lived with them for one year rather than three years in the preceding five. In this case, therefore, the foster mother could have applied for a residence order. Given the local authority's plan for adoption set out in the care plan, and the age of the children, such an application may not have succeeded. The foster mother was not considered suitable to adopt the 4-year-old twins in this case. Under s. 12 of the Adoption and Children Act 2002, the foster mother could seek a review of this decision. Under the new law, where a foster carer wishes to adopt a foster child, the foster parent must give notice of intention to adopt under s. 44 at least three months before the application to adopt. During the three-month period the local authority will prepare a report for the court. In the circumstances in this case, the local authority could remove the children only with leave of the court, or in exercise of its child protection functions.

Despite the legally insecure position of foster carers, their profile has been raised and there is a greater emphasis on the training and professionalism of foster carers. Foster carers frequently provide reports to case conferences and reviews, and may have to give evidence to court and keep records relating to a child. A Department of Health publication includes a useful checklist for foster carers to assist with the preparation of statements to be used in court.[22]

■ Local authority foster carers

A significant proportion of children looked after by the local authority are placed with local authority foster carers. Section 23 of the Children Act 1989 defines a local authority foster carer as someone with whom the local authority has boarded out a child. It may include a relative but not a parent. The foster carer's role is described in the Regulations as being: 'to care for any child placed with him as if the child were a member of the foster-parent's family and to promote his welfare having regard to the long and short term plans for the child'.

Fostering arrangements are governed by the Fostering Services Regulations 2002 (SI 2002/57), which provide for the approval process of foster carers and written placement agreements. 'The Children Act 1989 Guidance and Regulations', vol. 3 'Family placements', provides further guidance on practice issues. Some local authorities have difficulty recruiting sufficient foster carers to provide choice when placing looked after children. In particular, some local authorities have regular recruitment drives for ethnic minority foster carers. Paragraph 11 of Sch. 2 to the Children Act 1989 directs a local authority to have regard, in publicising and recruiting for the fostering service, to the different racial groups to which children in need in the area belong. This is important because a local authority must be satisfied that a particular placement is the most suitable way of performing its duty to safeguard and promote the child's welfare, and in particular it must consider the child's cultural background and racial origin.

Prospective foster parents must provide references and be assessed by the local authority or fostering agency before approval can be given. The assessment is comprehensive and includes consideration of health, age, marital status, religious persuasion, racial origin and cultural background, family members, employment record, accommodation, etc. Following approval a 'foster placement agreement'(reg. 34) will be drawn up concerning the foster carer's relationship with the authority and information about arrangements for the child including financial support. The agreement includes details of the training and support to be given to the foster carer, review and placement procedures, and the duties expected of the foster carer.[23] The foster carers should care for the child as if he were a member of the foster carers' family, not administer corporal punishment, and notify the authority of significant changes in the household or serious illness of the child. The agreement should contain all the information the authority considers necessary to enable the foster parents to care for the child. This information should include details of the child's personal history, religion, cultural and linguistic background and racial origin, health needs and education needs.

Information given to foster carers was found to be inadequate in the case of *W and Others* v. *Essex County Council* [1998] 3 All ER 111. Here, children of foster carers were given leave to sue the council and social worker for negligence on the grounds that they were not told that the foster child who was placed with them had previously sexually abused his sister.

The foster carer must comply with the terms of the agreement. Suitability of the foster carer should be reviewed annually and approval may be terminated.

A fostering allowance is paid to local authority foster carers. An enhanced rate may be payable to specialist foster carers. The National Foster Care Association recommends a minimum allowance based on the age of the child and the location. The Children Act 2004 introduces a power for the Secretary of State to set the level of payments made to foster carers caring for looked after children. *In R* (L) v. *Manchester City Council* (2001) *The Times,* 10 December, the council had a policy of financially assisting foster carers who were relatives or friends on a considerably smaller scale than other foster carers. This was found to be unlawful. The policy was '*Wednesbury*' irrational, fundamentally discriminatory and in breach of Art. 8 and 14 of the European Convention on Human Rights.

The local authority is not vicariously liable for the acts of foster carers. However, in *Barrett* v. *Enfield London Borough Council* [1999] 3 All ER 193, a claim was allowed for damages to be paid in respect of a child who suffered harm whilst placed with foster carers. Foster carers should take out their own insurance to cover their fostering role.

Local authority fostering services are subject to inspection under the Care Standards Act 2000.

■ **Private foster carers**

Private foster carers are those who foster a privately fostered child, defined in s. 66 of the Children Act 1989. A privately fostered child is under the age of 16 (18 if disabled); is accommodated by someone who is not a parent, does not have parental responsibility and is not a relative; and is accommodated for more than 28 days. A privately fostered child is not a looked after child under s. 22 of the Children Act 1989 and the local authority are not involved in making the arrangement. It is thought that as many as 10,000 children may be living in this type of arrangement.[24]

The local authority has responsibilities under Part IX of the Children Act 1989 and the Children (Private Arrangements for Fostering) Regulations 2005[25] to regulate and support private fostering. A person who is privately fostering a child or proposes to privately foster a child (and any person involved (whether directly or not) in arranging for the child to be fostered privately, and a parent of the child or other person with parental responsibility for the child) should notify the local authority and an officer will visit and report back to the local authority. Within the first year of the arrangement the child should be visited every six weeks, then every 12 weeks in subsequent years, and unless considered inappropriate the officer should speak to the child alone.

A person may be disqualified from private fostering under s. 68 of the Children Act 1989 and the Disqualification for Caring for Children Regulations 1991.[26] The grounds are: if a child of the individual has been the subject of a care order or otherwise removed from his care; the person has been convicted of a specified offence; or the person has been concerned with a registered home which has been deregistered or has had an application for registration refused; or the person has been prohibited from being a private foster parent. The local authority should be notified of private fostering arrangements.

The local authority must be satisfied that the welfare of privately fostered children is satisfactorily safeguarded and promoted. It may impose a fostering prohibition where: a prospective foster parent is not a suitable person; the premises intended to be used for fostering are not suitable; or it would be prejudicial to the welfare of the child to be accommodated by that foster parent in those premises (Children Act 1989, s. 69).[27]

The Children Act 2004 responds to the criticisms directed at the law on private fostering in the Climbié inquiry and strengthens the scheme for registration and monitoring of private fostering. Further regulations may require all private foster carers to register with the Childrens Services Authority, set requirements to be satisfied before registering, and grounds on which a person can be disqualified from being a private foster carer.

■ **Usual fostering limit**

A foster parent, whether private or local authority, may not foster more than three children, the 'usual fostering limit', unless the children are siblings or the foster parent has been exempted from the usual limit. Local authorities may impose a lower limit. If a foster parent exceeds the usual limit, he will be treated as a person carrying on a children's home and subject to the conditions governing the operation of children's homes.

Residential care

The Utting Report (1997) defined residential care as: 'Continuous residence in permanently staffed accommodation for more than three children, which provides or enables access to the care and services normally available to children and such additional measures of care, control and treatment as resident children require.' The report noted that residential care has a crucial role in the range of services available to children and should not be seen as a last resort. The number of children in residential care has steadily decreased, however. In providing residential care, the report emphasised the need for a planned approach, proper management, inspection and monitoring of the service, and the need for more professionally qualified staff.[28]

Practice and standards and the legal framework for residential care have been consistently challenged by successive inquiry reports, which have revealed the abuse of children and young people living in residential accommodation. A selection of those inquiry reports are listed below:

■ Report of the inquiry into the conduct of Leeways children's home (1985).

■ The Pin-down inquiry (1991).

■ The Leicestershire inquiry (1992).

■ Ty Mawr Community Home inquiry (1992).

■ The Aycliffe Centre for children (1993).

■ Report of the tribunal of inquiry into the abuse of children in care in the former county council areas of Gwynedd and Clwyd since 1974: 'Lost in care' (2000).

Guidance has been produced as a result of the findings of inquiry reports: e.g. following Pin-down, which was described as a 'regime intrinsically dependent on elements of isolation, humiliation and confrontation', the Department of Health published guidance on permissible forms of restraint in children's residential care. The key elements of that guidance provided that physical restraint, the positive application of force with the intention of overpowering the child, should only be used within the following framework:

■ necessary to prevent the child significantly injuring him or herself, others or causing damage to property;

■ dialogue and diversion to avoid need for a warning;

■ minimum force necessary;

■ the presence of other staff as assistance and witnesses;

■ gradually relax restraint once safe;

■ act of care and control, not punishment;

■ not used purely to enforce compliance with staff instructions if no other risks involved.

∎ Regulation of children's homes

Three types of children's home were provided for under the Children Act 1989. **Community homes** (Part VI of the Children Act 1989) provided by the local authority and known as maintained community homes, or partly financed by them and known as controlled or assisted community homes. **Voluntary homes** (Part VIII of the Children Act 1989) provided by voluntary organisations and charities. **Registered children's homes** (Part VIII of the Children Act 1989) provided on a profit-making basis by private individuals or companies and **small private children's homes,** which offer accommodation for fewer than four children. Different regulation and inspection frameworks applied to each type of home. This confusing situation changed with the introduction of the Care Standards Act 2000, which replaced the relevant provisions in the Children Act 1989, extended regulation to other areas, such as local authority fostering, and strengthened and streamlined the regulatory process (see discussion in relation to adult residential care in Chapter 14).

The 2000 Act established a National Care Standards Commission as the new registration authority for care homes (in Wales the National Assembly will be the equivalent registration authority). This body was subsumed into the Commission for Social Care Inspection which now has the responsibility for regulation and inspection.

The Act provides a new definition of a children's home, as an establishment which provides care and accommodation wholly or mainly for children (Care Standards Act 2000, s. 1(2)). This definition will incorporate community homes, voluntary homes and registered children's homes as they were defined under the Children Act 1989. Health service hospitals, independent hospitals and clinics, residential family centres and schools (other than boarding schools providing 295 days or more accommodation in a year) are exempt from the definition, as is accommodation provided by a foster carer, parent or relative, i.e. a domestic household.

National Minimum Standards for Children's Homes have been issued and are central to the registration and inspection function of the Commission for Social Care Inspection. The standards deal with planning for care, quality of care, complaints and protection, care and control, environment, staffing, management and administration, specialist provision including secure accommodation and refuges. Within each grouping there are a number of sub-groups, e.g. quality of care includes standards relating to consultation; privacy and confidentiality; provision and preparation of meals; personal appearance, clothing and pocket money; good health and well-being; treatment and administration of medicines; education; leisure and activities. They are intended to specify the minimum standard and many homes are likely to exceed the standards. The standards are available on the Department of Health and CSCI websites. Regulations also apply – The Children's Homes Regulations 2001.[29] (SI 2001/3967). Registration of homes is a compulsory requirement and is based on compliance with requirements in the regulations and legislation. The standards will also be taken into account. Registration may be cancelled if conditions of registration are not complied with. An appeal may be made to the Care Standards Tribunal against cancellation of registration or refusal of registration. The case of *William Mitchell* v. *Commission for Social Care Inspection* [2004] 0369. EA provides an example.[30] Mitchell unsuccessfully appealed against the CSCI decision to refuse his application to become the registered manager of a children's home. The criteria for managing a home are contained in the Children's Homes Regulations 2001, and stipulate that a person shall not manage a children's home unless he is fit to do so, and he will not be fit unless he is of integrity and good character, and he has the qualifications, skills, and experience necessary for managing the children's home (reg. 8). Standard 22.7 of the National Minimum Standards for Children's Homes was also relevant to the case, and states: 'Physical restraint is only used to prevent likely injury to the child concerned or to others, or likely serious damage to property.' The burden of proof is on the applicant to prove that he is 'fit'. Mitchell became employed in residential social work after he left the army. Concerns were raised and became subject of a disciplinary hearing, about physical intervention and restraint being used in a way that was not reasonable and appropriate. Evidence was produced concerning eight incidents including the following:

- A resident appeared to be encouraging another resident to cause damage by punching the walls. When she refused to leave the room she was physically restrained by the appellant and a co-worker and removed.
- A resident was found to have cigarettes in her room. She refused the appellant's request to hand them over and was physically restrained.
- A resident was being noisy and abusive. She appeared to be bleeding from her arm and had a history of self-harm. She was physically restrained for seven minutes on her bed.
- A resident was asked to leave the room of another resident as she was preventing her from getting ready for school. The appellant told her he would 'extract her from the room using non-violent intervention'. As he approached her, she began to throw punches, so the appellant placed his hand either on her lower throat or her breastbone, placed her on the bed, then grasped both her hands.

The regulation inspector gave evidence that, in her view, restraint had been used as a means of enforcing compliance and therefore inappropriately. A further expert witness was critical of the appellant's methods and expressed his opinion that the appellant failed to use effective de-escalation techniques and there was no indication that the use of physical intervention was a last resort. The tribunal found the appellant to be a sincere, honest man who had done well to gain the required paper qualifications in residential care following retirement from the army. He had, however, failed to discharge the burden to show he was a fit person, and the tribunal concluded: 'Whilst his use of physical restraint was well intended and at the time believed by him to be an appropriate intervention in difficult situations, critical analysis revealed lack of judgment and inadequate skills and training.'

The new structure for regulation is informed by 'Quality Protects' objective 9:

To ensure through regulatory powers and duties that children in regulated services are protected from harm and poor care standards.
By:

- Making sure that all staff and workers stick to the rules which protect children and which set standards of care.

Each child accommodated in a children's home should have a 'child placement plan,' which should address day-to-day care arrangements for the child, arrangements for health and accommodation and arrangements for contact (reg. 12).

A number of cases have ordered payment of compensation to adults who were abused in residential accommodation as children and are a further demonstration of the removal of the blanket immunity from actions in negligence formerly enjoyed by local authorities. In *C v. Flintshire County Council* [2001] EWCA Civ 302 the claimant was bullied by other residents in her first placement without staff intervention and in the second home she suffered physical, emotional and sexual abuse by staff and was illegally detained in a secure unit. She was awarded a total of £70,000 in damages for the local authority's negligence. In *KR v. Bryn Alyn Community (Holdings) Ltd* [2003] EWCA Civ 85, 14 adults were awarded damages for long-term psychiatric or psychological injury caused by sexual, physical and emotional abuse suffered whilst resident in children's homes in North Wales.

Secure accommodation

There are times when it is considered necessary for a child to be placed in secure accommodation, i.e. accommodation provided for the purpose of restricting liberty. There are a limited number of approved secure places in the country and a decision that a child needs to be in secure accommodation will often necessitate a move.

Section 25 of the Children Act 1989 provides:

s. 25

(1) . . . a child who is being looked after by a local authority may not be placed, and, if placed, may not be kept, in accommodation provided for the purpose of restricting liberty ('secure accommodation') unless it appears –

    (a) that –

        (i) he has a history of absconding and is likely to abscond from any other description of accommodation; and

        (ii) if he absconds, he is likely to suffer significant harm; or

    (b) that if he is kept in any other description of accommodation he is likely to injure himself or other persons.

. . .

(4) If a court determines that any such criteria are satisfied it shall make an order authorising the child to be kept in secure accommodation and specifying the maximum period for which he may be so kept.

(CA 1989)

Secure accommodation is defined in the Children (Secure Accommodation) Regulations 1991 (SI 1991/1505), reg. 2(1) as: 'Accommodation which is provided for the purpose of restricting the liberty of children to whom section 25 of the Act applies.'

A secure accommodation order may be made in respect of a child who is the subject of a care order or, providing there is parental consent, any other child to whom the criteria apply. If the child is not subject to a care order, the s. 20(8) provision applies to secure accommodation in the same manner as it does to any other accommodation for a looked after child. The effect of this is that a person with parental responsibility could remove a child (not subject to a court order) from a secure accommodation without notice.

It is possible for a child to be kept in secure accommodation for a total of 72 hours before an application is made to court. The 72 hours may be consecutive, or not consecutive within a period of 28 days. The court may make a secure accommodation order for a maximum initial period of three months, or it may make a 28-day interim secure order. A six-month order may be made if it is the second application for a child.

Secure accommodation is properly seen as a last resort, after all other alternatives have been considered (Children's Homes Regulations 1991 (SI 1991/1506)), and there is a duty imposed on the local authority to avoid the need for children to be placed in secure accommodation (CA 1989, Sch 2, para. 7(c)). The court must make an order if the criteria are satisfied but it will require detailed information about absconding patterns, what happens when the child absconds (e.g. any offences that are committed), where the child goes and with whom. In addition, the aims of a secure placement for the particular child, in the context of a care plan, should be presented to court. The local authority should not detain the child in secure accommodation if the criteria for detention cease to apply. As s. 25 applications are 'specified proceedings' under the Children Act 1989, a children's guardian should be appointed and the child must be legally represented.

The question whether human rights are breached by the imposition of secure accommodation orders under the Children Act 1989, s. 25 was considered in *Re K (A Child) (Secure Accommodation Order: Right to Liberty)* [2001] 1 Fam 377. Here the court refused an application for a declaration of incompatibility. It was accepted by the court that the purpose of s. 25 was to restrict liberty and it therefore fell within ECHR, Art. 5 as a deprivation of liberty. Article 5 is, however, a qualified article and the court held that detention under a secure accommodation order fell within the exception at Art. 5(1)(d):

Art. 5(1)(d)

> . . . the detention of a minor by lawful order for the purpose of educational supervision or his lawful detention for the purpose of bringing him before the competent legal authority.
>
> (ECHR)

A secure placement that did not involve educational or therapeutic provision might not subsequently be upheld, however.

Secure accommodation was the subject of a further Human Rights Act 1998 challenge in the case of *Re M (A Child: Secure Accommodation)* [2001] EWCA 458. In this case the Court of Appeal considered whether the procedure for obtaining a secure accommodation order was compatible with Art. 6(3) of the Convention. Article 6(3) concerns those charged with a criminal offence. It was decided that secure accommodation is protective in nature and therefore criteria applicable to criminal cases do not apply, even though there is a loss of liberty. The court found that the procedure for obtaining secure accommodation orders was compatible with Art. 6(3) but that any application should comply with the minimum requirements of Art. 6(3) relating to notice of the nature of the charge, adequate time to prepare a defence, the ability to defend oneself through legal assistance of one's own choosing, free assistance of an interpreter if required, and the opportunity to cross-examine witnesses.

Independent visitors

The Children Act 1989[31] introduced the role of the independent visitor. It is stated in para. 17 of Sch. 2 to the Act that:

Sch. 2, para. 17

Where it appears to a local authority in relation to any child they are looking after that –
(a) communication between the child and –
   (i) a parent of his,
   (ii) any other person who . . . has parental responsibility, has been infrequent, or
(b) he has not visited or been visited by (or lived with) any such person during the preceding 12 months and it would be in the best interests of the child for an independent person to be appointed, they shall appoint an independent visitor.

(CA 1989)

The duty of the independent visitor is to visit, advise and befriend the child. The independent visitor may also have a role in helping to prepare the young person for leaving care. An independent visitor will not be appointed (or an appointment can be terminated) if the child objects and the local authority is satisfied that his objection arises from the child's sufficient understanding to make an informed decision.[32]

Research carried out in the late 1990s found that only about a third of local authorities in England and Wales were using independent visitors but the young people in the study who had an independent visitor were very positive about the experience. Some charities such as NCH and NSPCC run independent visitor services, recruiting and training volunteers to work with local authorities.[33]

In addition to the independent visitor, advocates and children's rights officers are available in some areas and present a potential safeguard against institutional abuse.

Leaving care

Children leaving care tend to do so at an earlier age than children living with their own families and often experience multiple disadvantage. The Children Act 1989, s. 24 introduced a duty towards looked after children to advise, assist and befriend with a view to promoting their welfare when they cease to be looked after. The duty was owed to young people between the ages of 16 and 21. In support of this duty, guidance called for local authorities to act as 'corporate parent' for young people leaving care. Leaving care services and projects, however, proved to be provided in a patchy and under-resourced fashion, often failing to meet the needs of young people leaving care. Research continued to highlight the plight of children leaving care. The majority of young people leaving care have no educational qualifications, and up to 25 per cent of young women are pregnant.[34]

Recognition of the social exclusion of this group can be found in 'Quality Protects' objective number 5, which reads:

- To ensure that young people leaving care, as they enter adulthood, are not isolated and participate socially and economically as citizens.
- This objective is to be achieved by ensuring that young people who were in care at the age of 16 are studying, training or working when they are 19; making sure social services departments are still in touch with those young people when they reach 19; and making sure that young people leaving care are living in good accommodation at the age of 19.

The unsatisfactory picture emerging regarding children leaving care is partly attributable to the weakness of the Children Act 1989 provisions. A local authority circular related to leaving care 'strongly encouraged [local authorities] to prepare after care plans for individual children within the existing legal framework as a matter of priority and to base them on a multi-agency assessment of need'.[35] It also asked authorities to ensure that young people leave care only when ready and willing; to consider development of specialist leaving care schemes and to consider whether a care leaver would benefit from the assistance of a mentor or befriender. Many of the recommendations of the circular and findings of a consultation document[36] were included in law reform. This area is now covered by the Children (Leaving Care) Act 2000 (C(LC)A 2000). Central to the new Act is

Pathway Plans

1. The nature and level of contact and personal support to be provided, and by whom, to the child or young person.
2. Details of the accommodation the child or young person is to occupy.
3. A detailed plan for the education or training of the child or young person.
4. How the responsible authority will assist the child or young person in relation to employment or other purposeful activity or occupation.
5. The support to be provided to enable the child or young person to develop and sustain appropriate family and social relationships.
6. A programme to develop the practical and other skills necessary for the child or young person to live independently.
7. The financial support to be provided to the child or young person, in particular where it is to be provided to meet his accommodation and maintenance needs.
8. The health needs, including any mental health needs, of the child or young person, and how they are to be met.
9. Contingency plans for action to be taken by the responsible authority should the pathway plan for any reason cease to be effective.

The Pathway Plan must also record key details such as the name, age and contact details of the young person, the name and contact details of the personal adviser and those of any other people who will be actively involved in delivering aspects of the Plan. It will note the date due for review.

Children (Leaving Care) Act 2000 Regulations and Guidance.
(Para 21–22)

Exhibit 10.1 Pathway plans

the role of personal advisers for young people and pathways planning. The following is a summary of provisions:

- The C(LC)A 2000 amends the provisions of the Children Act 1989 requiring local authorities to provide support to those leaving care.

- Local authorities must comply with a new duty to meet the needs of eligible 16- and 17-year-olds in care (eligible children) or care leavers (relevant children) those who were eligible or relevant before reaching 18 (former relevant children).[37]

- There is a duty on local authorities to keep in touch with their care leavers until at least the age of 21.

- At the age of 16, each young person in care must have a comprehensive written pathway plan mapping out a clear route to their independence. The plan leads on from the care plan and should include information on education, health, accommodation and any contingency plans. The content specified by the guidance is set out in Exhibit 10.1 above. The plan is described by the guidance as 'pivotal to the process whereby children and young people map out their future' (para 7.2). It should be reviewed at least every six months.

- Personal and practical support must be provided by local authorities to 16- and 17-year-olds in care or care leavers to meet the objectives of their pathway plan.

- An adviser will be allocated to each young person to participate in implementation and review of the pathway plan, coordinate provision of support and assistance to meet the needs of the young person, and to be kept informed of his well-being. This may include helping the young person find training, employment or education opportunities and acting as the 'Connexions' adviser. The personal adviser should not prepare the plan.

- Assistance for care leavers aged 18–21 with education, training and employment shall be continuous.

- Accommodation should be suitable in relation to health and other needs and bed and breakfast accommodation should only be used in an emergency for 16- and 17-year-olds.

- In place of the current system of benefits, a new financial regime will be introduced and administered by the Social Services Department. Most care leavers will no longer be entitled to claim welfare benefits.

- All young people covered by the C(LC)A 2000 will have access to the Children Act 1989 complaints procedure.

- Unaccompanied asylum seeking children are covered by the C(LC)A 2000.

A High Court case has emphasised the importance of pathway plans. In *R (J) Caerphilly County Borough Council* [2005] EWHC 586 (Admin), Munby J gave guidance to local authorities as to what is expected in drawing up a pathway plan. The case concerned a 17-year-old, J, who had been in care for four years, having suffered abuse and disruption in his home life and with a number of criminal convictions. The local authority and other agencies had attempted to help J but he was uncooperative and unwilling to engage. Supported by the Howard League, J sought a declaration that the local authority has acted unlawfully in failing to assess his needs, prepare a pathway plan, appoint a personal adviser and provide accommodation. The court ordered the authority to produce a lawful assessment and a plan and gave the following guidance:

The child's personal adviser may be an employee of the local authority but it must be clear to the adviser and the local authority that the adviser was acting in the role of adviser to the child and not some other conflicting role. The personal adviser should not prepare the assessment and plan, the role being to liaise with the authority and focus on its implementation. The court described the personal adviser as a go-between between the child and the authority. In this case the local authority had failed to involve J in the process, which it had embarked on far too late. The plan had failed to specify key dates or identify specialist support. It was not a detailed operational plan. It failed clearly to identify the child's needs, what was to be done about them, by whom and by when. Where a child is unwilling to cooperate, this is not a reason for the authority not to carry out its obligations under the Act and Regulations. The child's lack of engagement should be clearly documented in the plan with the steps the authority has taken to engage the child, and proper thought should be given to contingency plans.

Chapter summary

- Looked after children are those children who are accommodated by the local authority, away from their family, in residential or foster placements, and all children who are the subject of a care order, even if they are living with their parents. There are approximately 60,000 looked after children on any one day.

- It is the duty of a local authority to safeguard and promote the welfare of all looked after children. Local authorities must consult the child, his parents, any person with parental responsibility and others whose wishes and feelings are relevant, before making decisions regarding a looked after child and give due consideration to the child's racial origin, cultural and linguistic background.

- The local authority must provide accommodation and maintain looked after children under CA 1989, s. 23. The accommodation should normally be near to the child's home and contact between the child and their family should be promoted. Accommodation provided on a voluntary basis is an aspect of service provision to families.

- The Quality Protects initiative includes a number of objectives that are particularly relevant to looked after children and includes maximising the contribution of adoption to providing permanent families for looked after children.

- Fostering covers a wide range of situations including short- and long-term arrangements and provision of respite care. There are private and local authority foster carers.

- Residential care continues to have a role to play in the provision of security and stability for some children. Standards in residential care have been challenged in a number of reports and a new regulatory framework is to be provided by the Care Standards Act 2000. An independent visitor will be provided to advise, assist and befriend certain looked after children. Sometimes a child will need to be placed in secure accommodation.

- The local authority has responsibilities towards young people leaving care, under the Children (Leaving Care) Act 2000, which develops earlier provisions of the Children Act 1989.

Exercises

The Beeches, a local authority children's home, provides accommodation for 15 young people. Consider whether any action should be taken in respect of the following incidents and what form it should take.

- A 17-year-old male resident and a 13-year-old female resident are discovered having sexual intercourse. They have not used any contraception and it is not an ongoing relationship.

The girl later tells a member of staff that she was being bullied by other girls in the home who called her frigid.

■ A 16-year-old male resident has been out shopping with a male member of staff in preparation for leaving the home. On the way back to the Beeches, they call at the member of staff's own home, drink a can of lager each and look at pornographic magazines.

■ A 14-year-old girl returns to the Beeches at 2 a.m., four hours after the agreed time. She is abusive to staff when they ask where she has been and tries to assault a female member of staff when she asks if the girl has been taking drugs. She is restrained by a male member of staff by twisting her arm behind her back, thereby sustaining a strained wrist. She is taken to her room and locked inside. The following morning she is prevented from telephoning her social worker and is told she has nothing to complain about.

Websites

Many of the relevant official publications relating to children looked after and adoption issues can be accessed via the Department of Health website, which has a section devoted to adoption issues:

www.doh.gov.uk/adoption

There is also a separate website dedicated to 'Quality Protects' issues:

www.dfes.gov.uk/qualityprotects

British Agencies for Adoption and Fostering (BAAF) provides a wide range of information and research publications:

www.baaf.org.uk

The Fostering Network (formerly known as the National Foster Care Association) is an organisation that aims to promote improvements in foster care through involvement with agencies and foster carers. It is also a useful resource for information on fostering, producing a range of publications and reports:

www.fostering.net/

The Every Child Matters website includes a section on fostering:

www.everychildmatters.gov.uk/socialcare/lookedafterchildren/fostercare

Voice for the Child in Care is a national organisation which provides independent advocacy and advice for children in care, care leavers, in custody and in need:

www.vcc-uk.org

Carelaw is an information site for children and young people in care in England and Wales, providing accessible information in a question and answer format:

www.carelaw.org.uk

Further reading

Relevant Government documents include:

Department of Health (1991) 'The Children Act 1989 Guidance and Regulations', vol. 3 'Family placements'; vol. 4 'Residential care'. London: DoH

Department of Health (1997) 'People Like Us: The Report of the Review of Standards for Children Living Away from Home' (the Utting Report). London: The Stationery Office.

Department of Health (1998) 'Caring for Children Away from Home: Messages from Research'. London: The Stationery Office.

Department of Health (1998) 'Quality Protects: Transforming Children's Services'. London: Department of Health.

Department of Health (1999) 'The Government's objectives for children's social services'. London: Department of Health.

Morgan R. and Lindsay, M. (2006) *Young Peoples Views on Leaving Care: What young people in and formerly in residential and foster care think about leaving care.* London: CSCI. (A comprehensive report written by the Childrens Rights Director for England.)

Sinclair, I. (2005) *Fostering Now: Messages from Research.* London: Jessica Kingsley Published (Sixteen research studies.)

Talbot, C. and Williams, M. (2003) 'Kinship Care' *Family Law* p. 502. (Considers outcomes for the increasing number of children living in kinship care arrangements.)

Residential care is specifically addressed in:

Waterhouse, R. (2000) 'Report of the Tribunal of Enquiry into the Abuse of Children in Care in the Former County Council Areas of Gwynedd and Clwyd since 1974'. London: House of Commons.

Butler, I. and Drakeford, M. (2005) *Scandal, Social Policy and Social Welfare.* Bristol: BASW/ Policy Press. (Analyses the concept of 'scandal' with chapters on residential care of children and 'Pin-down'.)

Stein, M. (2006) 'Missing Years of Abuse in Children's Homes' 11 *Child and Family Social Work* p. 11.

Notes

1 This includes children under an emergency protection order, police protection order, children placed or authorised to be placed for adoption, or where a placement application is pending, criminal supervision order with residence and children detained under the grave crimes provision of the Children and Young Persons Act 1933, s. 53.

2 Children Act 1989, s. 22(2).

3 www.everychildmatters.gov.uk/socialcare/lookedafterchildren/.

4 Department of Health (2000) 'Children Looked After by Local Authorities, Year Ending 31 March 2000, England'. Also at www.doh.gov.uk/public/cla2000.htm.

5 SI 1991/890, reg. 3.

6 SI 1991/895.

7 SI 2004/1419.

8 SI 2004/1449 (W149).

9 SI 2002/546.

10 See: I. Butler and H. Payne (1997) 'The health of children looked after by the local authority' 21 *Adoption and Fostering* p. 28.

11 Figures reproduced from the December 2000 white paper, 'Adoption: a new approach' (Cm. 5017).

12 See 'Modernising Social Services' (1998) (Cm. 4169). London: The Stationery Office.

13 Department of Health. London: HMSO. See also Department of Health (1998) 'Quality Protects: Transforming Children's Services'. London: Department of Health.

14 Tony Blair: Prime Minister's Review of Adoption (2000). Performance and Innovation Unit.

15 Levels of disruption measured in the studies contained in 'Adoption Now: Messages from Research' varied between 2 per cent and 24 per cent, though the studies are not really comparable as they occurred at different times, related to children of various ages, etc.

16 LAC (2001) 33.

17 Local Authority Social Services Letter LASSL (2000) 17.

18 DfES Statistics, Children adopted from care in England: 2002–03.

19 Statutory Guidance on the Duty on Local authorities to promote the Educational Achievement of Looked After Children under s 52 Children Act 2004, DfES. p. 23.

20 DfES (2005) *Qualitative Study: The Placement Stability of Looked After Children*. London: DfEs.

21 'The Children Act 1989 Guidance and Regulations', vol. 8 'Private fostering and miscellaneous', London: DfEs, p. 1.

22 J. Plotnikoff and R. Woolfson (2000) *Reporting to Court under the Children Act: a Handbook for Social Services*. London: Department of Health/The Stationery Office.

23 Foster Placement (Children) Regulations 1991 (SI 1991/910).

24 See: B. Holman (2003) *The Unknown Fostering*. Lyme Regis: Russell House.

25 SI 2005/1533.

26 SI 1991/2094.

27 See, further, 'The Children Act 1989 Guidance and Regulations', vol. 8 'Private fostering and miscellaneous' London: DfES.

28 Department of Health (1997) 'People Like Us: The Report of the Review of Standards for Children Living Away from Home' (The Utting Report). London: The Stationery Office.

29 SI 2001/3967.

30 Further decisions of the Care Standards Tribunal can be accessed on its website: www.carestandardstribunal.gov.uk.

31 See also Definition of Independent Visitors (Children) Regulations 1991 (SI 1991/892).

32 *Hereford and Worcester County Council* v. *S* [1993] 2 FLR 360. See also 'The Children Act Guidance and Regulations', vol. 4 'Residential care'. London: DfES.

33 A. Knight (1998) *Valued or forgotten? Disabled children and Independent Visitors.* National Children's Bureau in association with the Joseph Rowntree Foundation.

34 See B. Broad (1999) 'Young people leaving care: moving towards "joined up" solutions?' 13 *Children and Society* p. 81.

35 LAC (99) 16 'Leaving Care: The Government's Response to the Children's Safeguards Review', p. 2.

36 DoH (1999) 'Me, Survive, Out There? – New Arrangements for Young people Living in and Leaving care'. London: DoH.

37 The exact definitions are:

Eligible Children: Children aged 16 and 17 who have been looked after for at least 13 weeks since the age of 14 and who are still looked after.

Relevant Children: Children aged 16 and 17 who have been looked after for at least 13 weeks since the age of 14, and have been looked after at some time while 16 or 17, and who have left care.

Former relevant children: Young people aged 18–21 who have been either *eligible* or *relevant children,* or both.

Qualifying children and young people over 16: Any person under 21 (24 if in education or training) who ceases to be looked after or accommodated or privately fostered after the age of 16.

11 Adoption

Learning objectives

To develop an understanding of the following:

- The current law of adoption embodied in the Adoption and Children Act 2002.
- Background to the reforms introduced by the Adoption and Children Act 2002.
- National Standards for Adoption.
- Particular issues within adoption, including the question of who can adopt, placement, the role of parental consent and the development of 'open adoption'.
- Issues surrounding the adoption process, including the role of the adoption panel.
- Alternative routes to security and stability[1] including use of residence orders and special guardianship.

Introduction

Adoption may be described as the process whereby the legal relationship between the child and her birth parents is severed and a new relationship is created between the child and her adoptive parents. Adoption terminates parental responsibility and is permanent and irrevocable. The law on adoption is contained in the Adoption and Children Act 2002 (ACA 2002), which replaced and revoked the old law contained in the Adoption Act 1976. The main provisions of the Act are considered throughout this chapter following discussion of the context and background to the reforms. Towards the end of the chapter the amendments made to the Children Act 1989 are outlined with more detailed consideration of special guardianship, a new order introduced by the Act as one of a number of alternatives to adoption providing varying degrees of stability and legal certainty. The order is compared with both adoption and residence.

The opportunity was missed to reform adoption law and incorporate adoption into the Children Act 1989, despite the fact that a Department of Health review of adoption was ongoing at the time the Children Act was introduced; and a subsequent Adoption Bill in 1996 never became law. To a certain extent this defeated one of the objectives of the Children Act, which was to provide a comprehensive piece of legislation dealing with all aspects of child care, as a significant body of child law remained outside the Act. The Children Act did make some changes to adoption, which were described as minor and inconsequential by the guidance. In fact their impact has been significant.

Children Act 1989 changes to adoption

The following changes to adoption occurred as a result of the Act:

- The term 'parental responsibility' replaced parental rights and duties in the Adoption Act 1976.
- Adoption proceedings were designated family proceedings and hence the menu of orders principle applies. The effect of this is that, in proceedings where an adoption order is sought, it is possible for the courts to select an alternative order from the menu if it is considered appropriate. For example, if an adoption order is sought by a relative of the child, the court might consider that a residence order would be more appropriate. It is also possible, applying this principle, for the court to make formal contact orders alongside an adoption order.
- The Children Act 1989 established an Adoption Contact Register, whereby an adopted person, on reaching majority, could make contact with any birth relatives who had placed their names on the register.

Background to the Adoption and Children Act 2002 reforms

History suggests that some form of informal adoption has always been practiced; however, there was no formal legal adoption in England and Wales until the Adoption Act 1926 was introduced. This Act did little to regulate the process, simply giving legal recognition to *de facto* transfers. In 1927 there were 3,000 in adoptions. The next significant piece of adoption legislation was the Adoption Act 1958. In subsequent years a number of reports found levels of dissatisfaction with the absence of a clear legal framework to regulate the practice of adoption. The Houghton Committee reported in 1972, its recommendations leading to the Children Act 1975, the adoption provisions of which became the Adoption Act 1976. Over that period there were significant changes in society, which affected the numbers of children available for adoption. In 1968 adoptions were at a peak, with 27,000 adoptions registered. Since that time the numbers of children available for adoption have consistently fallen, contributory factors include the increased availability of contraception and abortion and less stigma surrounding single parenthood. At the same time, different children started to be considered available for adoption, with fewer and fewer newborn babies available. An influential report, 'Children Who Wait' (1973)[2] identified significant numbers of children languishing in care without appropriate plans for permanency. The emphasis of the Children Act 1975 was to position adoption as a local authority resource to provide permanency for children in care and to encourage greater long-term planning.

Many features of the new legislation can be traced back to a review of adoption law in the early 1990s which produced a number of background and consultation papers. An Adoption Bill was published in 1996 but, coinciding with a change in Government, it did not proceed. During the latter half of the 1990s a number of factors led to growing political interest in adoption and a commitment to introduce new legislation. The effects of Quality Protects, findings of the Waterhouse inquiry and research into children living away from home, were interpreted so as to locate a clear role for adoption. At the same time, a steady drop in the number of children leaving care through adoption had been identified through the 1990s[3] and concerns were expressed that the adoption system has been characterised by delays, with a quarter of children waiting more than three years for placement. These issues were taken up at the highest level in the Prime Minister's Review of Adoption, published in 2000. In the foreword, the Prime Minister states:

it is hard to overstate the importance of a stable and loving family life for children. That is why I want more children to benefit from adoption. We know that adoption works for children. Over the years many thousands of children in the care of local authorities have benefited from the generosity and commitment of adoptive families, prepared to offer them the security and wellbeing that comes from being accepted as members of new families. But we also know that many children wait in care for far too long. Some of the reasons are well known. Too often in the past adoption has been seen as a last resort. Too many local authorities have performed poorly in helping children out of care and into adoption.

This determination and commitment to adoption reform was reflected in a number of developments introduced prior to the new legislation. In October 2000 an 'Adoption and Permanence Task force' was established, its aim being to 'support local councils in improving their performance on maximising the use of adoption as an option for meeting the needs of looked after children'. A white paper, entitled 'Adoption: a new approach' followed in December 2000 and included a national target of increasing by 40 per cent the number of looked after children adopted from care. This target was subsequently incorporated into the Department of Health Public Service Agreement. In order to help agencies to identify matches of children and prospective adopters, a National Adoption Register was established in April 2001.

Finally, the Adoption and Children Bill was introduced in March 2001 (and reintroduced after the general election in autumn 2001).

The clear focus of the Bill reflected previous publications on the adoption of looked after children. It is essential to recognise that looked after children do not present as a homogenous group: there are different reasons for becoming looked after; there are differing legal statuses of being looked after; looked after children have different individual characteristics including age, disability and ethnic origin. This was acknowledged in the Prime Minister's Review which noted: 'adoption from care is not about providing couples with trouble free babies. It is about finding families for children of a range of ages, with challenging backgrounds and complex needs.'

New legislation on adoption has been largely welcomed in principle, having been consistently demanded by special interest groups. As the Bill progressed and the Act came into being, however, a number of critiques emerged (see Further reading) and the resulting legislation is complex and not very accessible. It is supplemented by a daunting amount of secondary legislation which contains much of the detail and procedure in the form of rules and regulations (at least 25 types identified in the Act).

Current law on adoption

■ Introduction

Adoption is a complex area of law and practice. A new statutory regime has been introduced by the Adoption and Children Act which was implemented in December 2005.[4] Its aim is to update the law, align adoption law with Children Act 1989, improve performance of adoption services and promote greater use of adoption for looked after children.

■ The adoption service

Adoption services are provided by approved *adoption agencies.* All local authorities are required by s. 2 of the Adoption and Children Act 2002 to provide a comprehensive adoption service in order to meet the needs of children who have been or may be, adopted, their parents, guardians and prospective adopters (the elements of what is sometimes referred to as 'the adoption triangle'). This comprehensive service includes provision of adoption support services (discussed below). Each local authority must prepare a plan for the provision of adoption services (s. 3). In addition to local authorities directly acting as adoption agencies, there are a number of registered adoption societies (previously known as voluntary adoption agencies, e.g. Barnardo's) in England and Wales providing services including recruitment of adopters, assessment and matching.[5] Under the Care Standards Act 2000 adoption agencies are regulated by the Commission for Social Care Inquiry. Local Authority

Adoption Service (England) Regulations 2003 require each local authority to provide a 'children's guide' to its adoption service, for children and prospective adopters.

Social workers involved with adoption cases will usually be experienced members of family placement teams specialising in adoption work. Regulation 10 requires there to be 'sufficient number of suitably qualified, competent and experienced persons working for the purposes of the adoption service'.

The new statutory guidance stipulates that adoption reports may only be prepared by social workers with 'necessary experience', which it defines as 'at least three years post-qualifying experience in childcare social work including direct experience of adoption work'.

If the child concerned has been the subject of care proceedings, adoption may have been identified in the care plan as the proposed plan for the child. In other cases the decision to place the child for adoption may follow unsuccessful attempts at rehabilitation with the child's family. Statutory child care reviews provide the focus for decisions following the care order. Once the decision is made to plan for adoption there may be a change of social worker, reflecting the different areas of expertise. The social worker in an adoption case is likely to have to work with the child, the birth family and the prospective adopters, each of which are likely to have a different perspective on the proposal and different needs (standards do provide for the birth family to have their own support worker). Adoption and placement orders can only be made by the court and the local authority legal adviser should work closely with the social worker in preparing the application and associated documentation.

■ National Standards

The new approach is underpinned by National Standards to promote consistency between authorities. The purpose of the introduction of National Standards is to ensure that all those involved in the adoption process have an understanding of what to expect and that there is consistency in adoption services across the country. A number of principles underpin the standards, which are expressed as values at the beginning of the document. For example:

The child's welfare, safety, needs and views will be at the centre of the adoption process.
The child's wishes and feelings will be actively sought and fully taken into account at all stages.
Delays in adoption can have a severe impact on the health and development of children and should be avoided wherever possible.
Children's ethnic origin, cultural background, religion and language will be fully recognized and positively valued and promoted when decisions are made.
Adoption has lifelong implications for all involved and requires lifelong commitment from many different organizations, professions and individuals who have to work together to meet the need for services of those affected by adoption.

Standards are likely to have a significant impact on good practice of the adoption service and the courts. The standards (and an addendum) are produced under

LASSA 1970, s. 7 as statutory guidance. The standards are arranged in sections of application to children; prospective adopters; adoptive parents; birth parents and birth families; councils (corporate and management responsibilities) and agency functions and voluntary adoption agencies. Each section begins with a key standard which is elaborated on further. For example in relation to adoptive parents: 'Children will be matched with approved adopters who can offer them a stable and permanent home and help and support will be provided to achieve a successful and lasting placement.'

A selection of other key standards are included below:

National Adoption Standards for England

- The child's need for a permanent home will be addressed at the four month review and a plan for permanence made.
- A match with suitable adoptive parents will be identified and approved by panel within 6 months of the agency agreeing that adoption is in the child's best interests.
- All children will have a named social worker who will be responsible for them throughout the adoption process.
- Children will be matched with families who can best meet their needs. They will not be left waiting indefinitely for a 'perfect family'.
- Foster carers who make a formal application to adopt children in their care will be entitled to the same information and preparation as other adopters and be assessed within four months.
- Before a match is agreed, adopters will be given full written information to help them understand the needs and background of the child and an opportunity to discuss this and the implications for them and their family.
- Birth parents will have access to a support worker independent of the child's social worker from the time adoption is identified as the plan for the child.
- Where it is in the child's best interest for there to be ongoing links, including contact, with birth parents and families (including siblings separated by adoption), birth families will be involved in discussions about how best to achieve this and helped to fulfil agreed plans, e.g. through practical or financial support.
- Councils will plan and deliver adoption services with local health and education bodies (including schools), voluntary adoption agencies, the local courts and other relevant agencies, including, where applicable, other councils.
- Agencies will plan, implement and evaluate effective strategies to recruit sufficient adopters to meet the needs of children waiting for adoption locally and nationally, especially those from diverse ethnic and cultural backgrounds and disabled children.

Guidance

Statutory Guidance to the Adoption and Children Act 2002 has been published (DfES, 2005). It is issued under s. 7 of the Local Authority Social Services Act 1970, and as such should be complied with unless there are exceptional local circumstances which justify a variation in practice. The guidance provides explanation of the regulations made under the Act and has a useful glossary at Annex G.

■ Principles

Part 1 of the Act introduces a set of principles in the section entitled 'Considerations applying to the exercise of powers'. The aim is to achieve consistency between the Children Act 1989 and the Adoption and Children Act 2002 through alignment of principles which put the child at the centre of the adoption process.[6]

Welfare

s. 1

> (1) This section applies whenever a court or adoption agency is coming to a decision relating to the adoption of a child.
> (2) The paramount consideration of the court or adoption agency must be the child's welfare, throughout his life.
>
> (ACA 2002)

Use of the word 'paramount' is a departure from the previous welfare provision in the 1976 legislation, where reference was made to 'first consideration being given to the need to safeguard and promote the welfare of the child throughout his childhood' (Adoption Act 1976, s. 6). Under the old law, welfare did not necessarily prevail over other considerations, including the birth parents' interests. It was the single most important factor but not overriding all other considerations, as paramountcy suggests. The section applies whenever a court or agency is coming to a decision. This is an area of difference between the Acts; in the Children Act 1989, the paramountcy principle applies to decisions of the court only, though of course agencies have this in mind in those cases which reach court. The test applies throughout the child's life, clearly recognising that the decision must reflect the long-lasting impact of an adoption order and extending beyond the previous test where consideration applied throughout childhood. The phrase 'coming to a decision' applies where orders that might be made include adoption or placement or granting leave.

Welfare checklist

The welfare principle is supported by a checklist, in similar but not identical terms to the checklist in the Children Act 1989. It is not intended to be exhaustive, nor in any order of priority. Every aspect of the checklist should be addressed in reports to court.

Children Act case law may be relevant to interpretation and application of aspects of the checklist.

s. 1(4)

(4) The court or adoption agency must have regard to the following matters (among others) –
(a) the child's ascertainable wishes and feelings regarding the decision (considered in the light of the child's age and understanding),
(b) the child's particular needs
(c) the likely effect on the child (throughout his life) of having ceased to be a member of the original family and become an adopted person,
(d) the child's age, sex, background and any of the child's characteristics which the court or agency considers relevant,
(e) any harm (within the meaning of the Children Act 1989 which the child has suffered or is at risk of suffering,
(f) the relationship which the child has with relatives, and with any other person in relation to whom the court or agency considers the relationship to be relevant, including –
  (i) the likelihood of any such relationship continuing and the value to the child of its doing so,
  (ii) the ability and willingness of any of the child's relatives, or of any such person, to provide the child with a secure environment in which the child can develop, and otherwise to meet the child's needs,
  (iii) the wishes and feelings of any of the child's relatives, or of any such person, regarding the child.

(ACA 2002)

Each factor in the checklist is worthy of fuller discussion.

s. 1(4)

(a) the child's ascertainable wishes and feelings regarding the decision (considered in the light of the child's age and understanding)

(ACA 2002)

The 1992 review of adoption suggested that a child of 12 plus should have to give consent to his or her own adoption, as is the case in Scotland. This position did at least recognise the need for a child's formal input during the process but was rejected and the familiar phrase 'considered in the light of the child's age and understanding' is included as preferable to a fixed age. Such an omission regarding a major life-changing decision is in flagrant disregard of children's rights. The judge in any particular case has discretion as to the weight to attach to the child's ascertainable wishes and feelings. Whilst actual consent of the child is not required, it is unlikely that adoption would proceed were the child to express a wish not to be adopted. Given the increase in older children being adopted, and the range of alternatives to adoption, this is a particularly important element of the checklist. The Guidance to the Act reinforces this aspect of the checklist stating: 'It is essential that an adoption agency, insofar as is reasonably practicable, involves and consults the child at all stages of the adoption process, ascertaining and taking into account his views in a way which is sensitive to, and consistent with, his age and understanding' (para 13).

s. 1(4)   (b)   the child's particular needs

This factor incorporates the child's physical, emotional and educational needs as expressed in the Children Act 1989 checklist and is likely to extend to other needs including social, psychological and health. The case of *Re M (Contact: Welfare Test)* [1995] 1 FLR 274 may be relevant here. It noted the fundamental emotional need of every child to have an enduring relationship with both of his parents. Emotional needs are also relevant when considering any continuing relationship with siblings as looked after children are often adopted apart from their siblings.

s. 1(4)   (c)   the likely effect on the child (throughout his life) of having ceased to be a member of the original family and become an adopted person

There are two important aspects of this factor: both ceasing to be and becoming a member of a family. The United Nations Convention on the Rights of the Child states that it is the fundamental right of every child to belong to a family, and Art. 8 of the ECHR, the right to respect for family life, is also relevant. In ceasing to become a member of the original family, there are risks to the child in terms of her sense of identity and possible feelings of abandonment. Becoming a member of the adoptive family may provide a sense of permanence and security for the child (and the adopters) and removes the uncertainty of possible further applications and moves. The comparable section in the Children Act 1989 considers the likely effect of any change in the child's circumstances. The provision here is clearly more focused on the effect of adoption. As with the welfare principle, the court must consider the effect on the child throughout his life, not just his childhood. By implication succession rights and interests and nationality could be a relevant consideration.

s. 1(4)   (d)   the child's age, sex, background and any of the child's characteristics which the court or agency considers relevant

The child's age is specified and this may be particularly relevant to issues of contact. Given the lifelong benefits, adoption of older children is clearly anticipated. The child's characteristics may include racial and cultural issues, though the court is specifically directed to their consideration under s. 1(5). Characteristics would also extend to consideration of any disability or special health needs.

s. 1(4)
> (e)   any harm (within the meaning of the Children Act 1989) which the child has suffered or is at risk of suffering

This factor refers to any harm, not just significant harm. Harm is as defined under the Children Act, which includes the amendment introduced by the ACA to 'impairment suffered from seeing or hearing the ill-treatment of another'.

s. 1(4)
> (f)   the relationship which the child has with relatives, and with any other person in relation to whom the court or agency considers the relationship to be relevant, including –
>   (i)   the likelihood of any such relationship continuing and the value to the child of its doing so,
>   (ii) the ability and willingness of any of the child's relatives, or of any such person, to provide the child with a secure environment in which the child can develop, and otherwise to meet the child's needs,
>   (iii) the wishes and feelings of any of the child's relatives, or of any such person, regarding the child

This factor is one of the provisions in the Act that calls on the court to consider contact. The term 'relationship' is not confined to legal relationships (s. 1(8)(a)), but allows the views of other important people in the child's life to be taken into account such as foster carers. It also includes the child's birth parents (without reference to parental responsibility). It is a factor that may be especially relevant to the older child with existing links to their birth family. It refers to 'ability and willingness' to meet the child's needs rather than 'capability', as in the Children Act 1989. Article 8 arguments are particularly important here in terms of continuation of some form of 'family life'.

Delay

s. 1(3)
> 1(3) The court or adoption agency must at all times bear in mind that, in general, any delay in coming to the decision is likely to prejudice the child's welfare
>
> (ACA 2002)

Again, the delay principle is drawn from the Children Act. The court will draw up a timetable for the avoidance of delay. The Protocol for judicial case management of Public Law Children Act cases ([2003] 2 FLR 719) will also have an impact on the overall timescales for a child between care proceedings and final placement.

There is also a close link to time limits set out in the National Standards, for example the commitment to make decisions about permanency at each looked after child's four-month review.

Culture

> (5) In placing the child for adoption, the adoption agency must give due consideration to the child's religious persuasion, racial origin and cultural and linguistic backgrouond
>
> (ACA 2002)

Discussion of adoption placements in recent years has been dominated by the role of ethnic origin and culture and it is perhaps not surprising that the new legislation includes a requirement to give due consideration to religious persuasion, racial origin and cultural and linguistic background as one of the principles. It is in the same terms as the duty on local authorities when considering making a decision about a looked after child (including placement) in CA 1989, s. 22(5). The debate has focused on whether it is good practice to place a black child with a white family and various terms have been employed, including trans-racial adoption and same-race placement. A limited amount of case law presents inconsistency in the way in which the law has approached the issue. For example, in *Re P (A Minor)* [1990] FCR 260, a mixed-race baby was placed with a white foster mother at five days old. It was intended to be a short-term placement but the child remained there for over a year. At the time of the hearing, the foster mother was not in a position to adopt the child, and the judge supported a move to a black adoptive family who could meet his cultural and identity needs; any trauma felt by the child in having to move could be limited by sensitive handling. In *Re O (Transracial Adoption: Contact)* [1995] 2 FLR 597, a black child of Nigerian parents had been in the care of white foster carers at the time of the hearing of the foster carers' application for adoption. The court made an adoption order to provide security for the family and an end to social work intervention. The parents' consent was dispensed with as being unreasonably withheld, despite the argument that adoption was anathema to Nigerian culture. A condition for contact with the mother was attached to the order.

Guidance in a circular entitled 'Adoption – Achieving the right balance' recognised the importance of a child's ethnic origin, culture and religion as significant factors to be taken into account, noting that 'placement with a family of similar ethnic origin is most likely to meet the child's needs as fully as possible'. It guards against agencies waiting indefinitely for a new family, and states: 'it is unacceptable for a child to be denied loving adoptive parents solely on the grounds that the child and adopters do not share the same racial or cultural background'.[7] The emphasis of formal guidance is therefore to find a family of similar ethnic background if possible. If that is not possible, the child should not be kept waiting and a family should be found which may not share the same characteristics as the child but is committed to assisting the child to understand his background and culture and be proud of his heritage. It is also important for the family to be able to deal with racism that the child might encounter, and this is a strong argument in favour of placing the child with a black family even though (particularly with children of mixed race) the family may not exactly match the child's ethnic background. This stance has clearly been influenced by concerns about the effect that delay has on a child waiting for an adoptive family, and a shortage of prospective adoptive parents (and foster carers) from ethnic backgrounds. The circular also encourages adoption agencies, in their planning strategy, to have programmes to develop and sustain recruitment of adopters from minority ethnic backgrounds.[8]

No order

s. 1(6)

> 1(6) The court or adoption agency must always consider the whole range of powers available to it in the child's case (whether under this Act or the Children Act 1989); and the court must not make any order under this Act unless it considers that making the order would be better for the child than not doing so
>
> (ACA 2002)

This principle incorporates the 'menu' principle of the Children Act and the 'no order' principle. The court is reminded of its obligation to consider whether other orders such as residence, care and supervision, contact and special guardianship might be appropriate instead of adoption, or in the case of contact, alongside an adoption order. This is particularly important given the courts' obligations under the Human Rights Act, the obvious interference with family life that an adoption order would effect and the need to act proportionately.

The court was faced with such an exercise in the case of *Re M (A Minor) (Adoption or Residence Order)* [1998] 1 FLR 570. Justice Ward identified two distinct and separate questions for the court. First, should the child live with the applicants or someone else, second, should the child live with that person under the aegis of adoption, care, residence alone, residence and s. 91(14) restriction, or no order at all. In reaching a decision it was necessary to have regard to the nature and effect of each order and the advantages and disadvantages each brings to the safeguarding and promotion of the welfare of the child.

The menu principle is supported by the requirement that the court must not make any order unless it considers that making the order would be better for the child than not doing so, the 'no order' principle. This again reflects the least interventionist approach and the need for proportionality. Whilst it may be argued that, in following that approach, adoption will be seen as a last resort, it does not mean that other 'least interventionist' orders have to be exhausted first. At planning stages the range of options should be considered for the individual child (not under a policy umbrella; e.g. all children under 8 are placed for adoption) and there should be evidence of such consideration.

■ Who can adopt?

Section 49 states that an application for adoption can be made by a couple, or one person (as long as certain conditions as to domicile and minimum age are satisfied, ss. 50–51).

Various factors beyond the basic legal requirement will actually determine whether an applicant(s) is considered suitable to adopt; this issue has been the subject of much controversy. A white paper issued in 1993[9] implored Social Services Departments to make 'common-sense and objective professional assessment and avoid reliance on ideology' (para. 4.28) in their judgments on suitability and not to be bound by dogmatic policies driven by ideas of political correctness.[10] The use of such a subjective term as 'common sense' is of little improvement. The reference is unhelpful and serves to undermine the skills required to assess suitability for adoption. It should be noted, however, that there has been considerable regional variation in the approach taken by different authorities, often driven by preferences of adoption panel members as well as authority policies. A number of specific cases are considered.

Step-parents

Adoptions by step-parents constitute about one-half of the total number of adoptions each year. Under the old law, in order to adopt it was necessary for the step-parent to apply jointly with his spouse. In most cases, therefore, where it is the step-father who wishes to adopt, his wife (the birth mother) had to adopt her own child. The adoption order extinguished the parental responsibility of the child's natural father (where he was previously married to the mother or where his responsibility was acquired by parental responsibility order or agreement), and may not always be appropriate for that reason. It has been suggested that in some cases there may be a 'quid pro quo' aspect to the adoption, in that motivation for the adoption may be that the child can take on the step-parent's surname and the birth parent is relieved of any continuing financial obligations.[11]

The new act changes the position on adoption by step-parents. Adoption is permitted by one person, under s. 51, where that person is the partner of a parent of the person to be adopted. The applicant, i.e. the step-parent must have lived with the child for six months minimum. This change in the law means that the parent of the child is no longer required to adopt her own child.

It should also be noted that as the term 'partner' is used, it is not necessary for the step-parent to be married to the child's parent. They may be in a cohabiting heterosexual or same-sex relationship. This is consistent with the late amendment to the Act which allowed unmarried couples to adopt jointly. It is inconsistent with the amendment to the Children Act (below) where a step-parent may acquire parental responsibility, only if married to the child's parent.

The step-parent must give three months' notice to the local authority of his intention to apply for an adoption order and the authority will prepare a report for the court dealing with suitability and following the s. 1 principles.

Single person

Policy documents have tended to refer to adoption by single persons as particularly suitable to the adoption of children with special needs against a preference in favour of married couples. Under the old law an adoption application was sometimes made by one person, who was part of a cohabiting or homosexual couple, with an application for joint residence to both of the couple. This was clearly the case in *Re W (Adoption: Homosexual Adopter)* [1997] 2 FLR 406.

Couples

A late amendment to the Act (following much debate) removed the previous restriction that only married couples could apply jointly to adopt a child. The preference for married couples rather than cohabitees was based on the argument that couples who have committed themselves legally to their relationship are more likely to be able to provide long-term stability for the adopted child. High divorce rates and the trend for more couples to cohabit both undermine this presumption and potentially limit the number of available prospective adoptive couples.

The new legislation allows adoption by single people or couples (s. 49) as defined by s. 144(4).

s. 144(4)

> . . . . a couple means –
> (a) a married couple, or
> (b) two people (whether of different sexes or the same sex) living as partners in an enduring family relationship.
>
> (ACA 2002)

In the assessment of suitability of adopters, regulations require that, 'in determining the suitability of a couple to adopt a child, proper regard is had to the need for stability and permanence in their relationship'. This change to the law will considerably widen the pool of prospective adopters.

Sexuality

The restriction against adoption by unmarried couples was also pertinent to the consideration of homosexual couples who wish to adopt. There was no specific reference to sexuality in the Adoption Act 1976 but early case law showed a judicial reluctance to approve adoption or other permanency options where the applicant was gay. For example, in *S* v. *S (Custody of Children)* [1980] 1 FLR 143, an application for custody by a lesbian mother was unsuccessful. In *Re P (A Minor) (Custody)* (1983) 4

FLR 410, the judge stated that there is disadvantage to a child of a homosexual parent, as 'a lesbian household would quite likely be the subject of embarrassing conduct or comment' (p. 405).[12] More recently, a less homophobic attitude can be detected from cases such as *Re W (A Minor) (Adoption: Homosexual Adopter)* [1997] 2 FLR 406, where the court stated the accurate position that there is nothing in law which prevents a single applicant for adoption being homosexual.

Age and health

The actual legal restrictions as to who may adopt are quite limited. In practice, other issues may effectively present a barrier to approval by the adoption panel. Most agencies have developed guidelines on the maximum age of prospective adopters, to ensure that the parents of adopted children will not be significantly older than non-adoptive parents of children of the same age, and so that there is a reasonable prospect of them being fit and healthy. Any age limit is most likely to apply to couples who wish to adopt a baby or young child. In practice, some couples who have exhausted fertility treatments before considering adoption may find that they are 'too old'. It may still be possible for an older individual or couple to adopt an older child or one with special needs. In practice, the medical member of the adoption panel can also influence agency policy on the extent to which health issues such as obesity or smoking should be taken into account in the assessment process.

▪ Who can be adopted?

A child under the age of 18 can be adopted. Consent of the child is not required, although her wishes and feelings will be ascertained by the children's guardian or reporting officer and will also be covered in the child's permanence report prepared by the agency social worker.[13]

A child must have been placed with the prospective adopters for a continuous period of at least ten weeks before the application is made (s. 42). In step-parent adoptions the child must have lived with the step-parent for a continuous period of six months preceding the application. A child must have lived with local authority foster parents for a year before they can apply to adopt. This 'probationary period' allows the relationship between the prospective adopters and the child to start to develop and allows the agency to see the child with the applicants. An order will not be made if the local authority have not had sufficient opportunities to see the child with the applicants in the home environment.

▪ Conditions for making an adoption order – placement and consent

An adoption order may not be made in England and Wales[14] unless one of two conditions is satisfied as set out in s. 47.

The first condition is that the court is satisfied that each parent or guardian consents to the adoption order, has consented under s. 20 (and has not withdrawn the consent) and does not oppose the making of the adoption order, or the parent's or guardian's consent should be dispensed with.

The second condition is that the child has been placed for adoption by an adoption agency with the prospective adopters in whose favour the order is proposed to be made, either with parental consent or under a placement order, and no parent or guardian opposes the making of the adoption order.

Placement and consent are considered in more detail below.

■ Placement

A new system of placement and placement orders prior to adoption is introduced by the Act. This system replaces freeing, a feature of some but not all adoption cases under the old law. Freeing is abolished by the ACA 2002, although transitional arrangements are in place for existing cases.

As a reminder, and to demonstrate contrast between the two systems, freeing could be described as an order which freed the child for adoption, vesting parental responsibilities in the adoption agency, extinguished pre-existing parental responsibility and extinguished any duty to make maintenance payments. The central issue in many freeing cases has been parental consent. Once a freeing order has been made, the birth parents will not be included as parties to subsequent adoption applications. One of the problems with freeing was that, whilst it was envisaged as a speedy mechanism, in practice freeing applications often took longer than full adoption orders (Murch *et al.*, 1991),[15] though this might be explained partly by the fact that freeing was more likely to be contested (75 per cent of freeing cases).

The introduction of placement orders and new rules on adoption agency placement of children for adoption is a major change to law and practice.

The new placement regime alters the timing of the courts' involvement in the process. The idea is that an earlier court decision on the child's placement avoids a fait accompli in circumstances where a child might have become settled with prospective adopters before the birth parents had an opportunity to challenge. The new regime formalises the placement stage. Placement is one of the most difficult aspects of the new legislation, rather technical and legalistic and dealt with in ss. 18–29.

The agency will be able to place a child for adoption, or allow a child who has been placed with another carer to stay with them as prospective adopter, only where the parents of the child have given consent or a placement order has been obtained. In the situation which is common under the current law, where a child is placed with prospective adopters following a care order, placement under the new provisions will inevitably be delayed if the birth parents did not consent, as obtaining a placement order from court will be a prerequisite. Experience of freeing cases and the delays associated with an additional court hearing support this view.

The exact procedure depends on whether parental consent to placement is forthcoming, so there are two possible routes: placement with consent and placement by court order. (The issue of consent is dealt with below.) Placement applies to all adoptions, including relinquishment cases, but it most obviously fits with adoption of looked after children.

343

Placement with consent (s. 19)

Where the adoption agency is satisfied that each parent or guardian of a child has consented to the child being placed for adoption, the agency is authorised to place the child for adoption. The consent may be to specific adopters or any who may be chosen by the agency. The parent may also state that he does not wish to be informed of any application for an adoption order. This is particularly relevant to cases where children are relinquished for adoption and the parent does not want any involvement in the process after giving consent.

Where a parent (with parental responsibility) agrees to a placement, they retain parental responsibility though exercise is subject to the control of the agency. The agency acquires parental responsibility and this is shared with the prospective adopters with whom a child is placed. The parent can ask for the child to be returned to her at any point up to the adoption application being made. Once an application is made, the court must sanction the child's removal. Having agreed to the placement, the parent cannot oppose the final adoption order without leave of the court, which will be given only if there has been a change of circumstances.

Placement orders (s. 21)

The placement order authorises the agency to place a child for adoption with any prospective adopters. The order will be made only if the child is subject to a care order or the court is satisfied that conditions for making a care order have been made out. Parents' consent is required unless the court is satisfied that their consent should be dispensed with. If parents do not agree to placement, a placement order must be sought. If the local authority plan is for adoption of a child under a care order or in (voluntary) accommodation (CA 1989, s. 20), it must apply for a placement order (s. 22). Where there are care proceedings and the care plan is for adoption, the local authority will also apply for placement order. The placement order authorises the local authority to place the child with any adopters it chooses.

The agency acquires parental responsibility when authorised to place by consent or placement order. Parental responsibility is given to prospective adopters while the child is placed with them. The birth parents retain parental responsibility but the agency may restrict the exercise of parental responsibility of any parent or of prospective adopters. When a placement order is made, any care or order is suspended and s. 8 orders and supervision orders are revoked. The placement order ends when the child is adopted, reaches 18 or marries. The order may be revoked by the court on application of the local authority or the child or others with leave of the court.

■ Parental consent

An adoption order cannot be made unless the court is satisfied that each parent or guardian of the child: consents to the making of the adoption order; has consented under CA 1989, s. 20 (and has not withdrawn the consent) and does not oppose the making of the adoption order; or that the parent's or guardian's consent should be dispensed with (s. 47).

A parent is the mother or married father or father with parental responsibility, i.e. not the unmarried father (without PR). Steps should be taken to contact the unmarried father of a child, counsel him and seek his views on adoption, even though he does not have to give his consent. The courts have found that there needs to be justification for excluding a natural parent from a child's life. These issues were examined in an appeal against the decision to make an adoption order to the natural father: *Re B (A Child) (Adoption by One Natural Parent)* [2001] UKHL 70.

The issue of involvement of natural fathers without parental responsibility was also considered in *Re H, Re G (Adoption: Consultation of Unmarried Fathers)* [2001] 1 FLR 646, in which the mother wished to conceal the existence of her baby from the father and her family. The court will consider whether the father has 'family life' with the child under ECHR, Art. 8, and in this case found that he did not. It will usually be appropriate to give notice of adoption proceedings to the natural father, however, and a mother's desire for confidentiality will normally not prevail over the requirement to give notice to the father. A further case, *Re J (Adoption: Contacting Father)* [2003] EWHC 199 (Fam) provides a further example of circumstances where it was considered lawful not to notify the father. In this case it was significant that the young mother had concealed her pregnancy from the community, she had split up with the father who had moved away from the area shortly after she became pregnant and she had only given the name of the father on an assurance from the social worker that he would not be informed.

Consent must be given unconditionally and with full understanding of what is involved. (s. 52). A mother cannot give a legally binding consent until after six weeks from the date of birth of the child concerned.

In cases where parental consent is an issue, the court should adopt a two-stage test. First, it will determine whether adoption is in the child's best interests; if so, secondly, it will consider the issue of agreement and, specifically, whether grounds for dispensing with parental consent exist at the time of the hearing: *Re D (A Minor)* [1991] 1 FLR 48.

There were six grounds for dispensing with parental consent, in the Adoption Act 1976, s. 16(2). The most widely used ground was that 'the parent is withholding his agreement unreasonably'. Under the new law there are only two grounds:

s. 52

> (1) The court cannot dispense with the consent of any parent or guardian of a child to the child being placed for adoption or to the making of an adoption order in respect of the child unless the court is satisfied that –
>   (a) the parent or guardian cannot be found or is incapable of giving consent, or
>   (b) the welfare of the child requires the consent to be dispensed with.
>
> (ACA 2002)

Whilst removal of connotations of 'unreasonable' parents is a positive change, this is nevertheless a significant erosion of the birth parents' position on such an important issue.

Ground (a), that the parent cannot be found or is incapable of giving consent, is reproduced from the 1976 Act. Every reasonable effort should be made to trace the parent, as it would be possible to set aside an adoption order if a parent came forward at a later date. Incapacity relates to mental or physical condition, e.g. parent in a coma.

■ Adoption application

After placement, when the child has lived with prospective adopters for ten weeks (in an agency placement) the prospective adopters may apply for an adoption order. As consent from birth parents will have been dealt with earlier, this should be relatively straightforward.

■ Effect of an adoption order

The effect of an adoption order under the new legislation is the same as the previous law. An adopted person is to be treated in law as if born as the child of the adopter(s) (s. 67). Parental responsibility is obtained by the adoptive parents; parental responsibility of the birth parents (and any other holder of parental responsibility) is extinguished. Any duties relating to maintenance payments and any liabilities under the Child Support Act 1991 cease to have effect.

■ Open adoption

Adoption has gradually moved on from the days when it was 'shrouded in secrecy' and there is now more openness about the process, operating on a number of levels. The concern and initial resistance to openness in adoption, particularly where the child has face-to-face contact with the birth family, was that it would impede the attachment process[16] and lead to placement breakdown. It is very difficult to assess the impact of contact, due to the variety in its nature, and the various research projects present an inconclusive picture.[17] However, the suggestion that contact weakens placements does not appear to be supported (Fratter, 1996).[18]

Adopted adults (adopted before commencement of the new Act) have the right to access their birth records from the Registrar General and to be provided with counselling support. The position is different for an adult adoptee who was adopted after commencement of the Act. That person cannot access information direct from the Registrar General, he must do so through an intermediary of the adoption agency. The Children Act 1989 introduced the Adoption Contact Register,[19] a register which is used to match up those adopted adults who wish to have contact with members of their birth family with any relatives who have registered their names.

Openness during adoption before the child reaches maturity has also increased in practice and gained legal recognition. Fratter (1996) describes openness in adoption as 'a range of options which depart from the exclusive, closed model of adoption'. Triseliotis[20] identifies three varieties of open adoption. Adoption with contact involves maintaining meaningful links, determined according to the child's needs, between the child and members of the birth family. Open adoption refers to the process in which the birth parent is actively involved in selecting prospective adopters. Semi-open adoption is the process where the agency provides full but non-identifying information about the birth and adoption families to each other, but they do not meet.

The advantages of contact have been summarised by Ryburn[21] in relation to the child, the birth parents and the adoptive parents. Contact enables the child to come to terms with difficult issues in their past, avoids speculation and fantasy, and provides reassurance that the birth family support the placement. Birth parents are helped to resolve the grief of their loss, and to move on; and adoptive parents gain a sense of security and permanence.

There has been an increase in case law where some form of open arrangement is recognised. The practice of open adoption has no doubt been influenced by the Children Act 1989 presumption of continued contact between the child and members of the birth family following care orders. In *Re E (A Minor) (Care Order: Contact)* [1994] 1 FLR 146 the Court of Appeal refused a local authority's application to terminate contact between two young children and their birth parents in order to move towards closed adoption, stating that 'the emphasis is heavily placed on the presumption of continuing parental contact'.[22] An order for contact may be achieved by adding a Children Act 1989, s. 8 contact order.

Re C (A Minor) (Adoption: Conditions) [1988] 2 FLR 159 was a landmark decision in which contact was ordered between siblings after adoption. Lord Ackner stated:

> In normal circumstances it is desirable that there should be a complete break, but . . . each case has to be considered on its own particular facts. No doubt the court will not, except in the most exceptional case, impose terms or conditions as to access to members of the child's natural family to which the adopting parents do not agree. To do so would be to create a potentially frictional situation which would be hardly likely to safeguard or promote the welfare of the child.

Clearly, formalised contact arrangements were envisaged by the judiciary as being appropriate only in exceptional circumstances and where the adoptive parents agreed.

Since the Children Act 1989, s. 8 contact orders may be made alongside an adoption order, as in *Re T (A Minor) (Adoption: Contact Order)* [1995] 2 FLR 251. If a birth parent applies for s. 8 contact, the application should be notified to the Official Solicitor and the local authority: *Re E (Adopted Child: Contact: Leave)* [1995] 1 FLR 57.

In many cases contact arrangements will be agreed informally and no order made. In *Re T (Minors) (Adopted Children: Contact)* [1995] 2 FLR 792, where there was no formal order relating to contact and the adopters had offered suitable indirect contact, the Court of Appeal stated that it would not allow adoptive parents to resile from agreed contact arrangements without good reason. Some form of contact will frequently be arranged and adoption agencies are beginning to use written contact agreements, which can help to clarify expectations and remove conflict.[23] In *Re G (adoption: contact)* [2002] EWCACiv 761, Ward LJ gave a significant statement on the benefit of contact:

> . . . in a case like this the benefit is the benefit that comes from the children simply knowing who the natural parental figures are. It is to remove the sense of the

ogre, as they reach adolescence and begin to search for their own identity . . . That is why the current research is in favour of some contact in adoption.

In most cases contact is an issue that must be agreed between the birth parents and the adoptive parents if it is to be workable, and increasingly prospective adopters are being prepared for adoption with some level of contact. In an exceptional case, *Re O (Transracial Adoption: Contact)* [1995] 2 FLR 597, a contact order was made on adoption without the consent of the adopters.

It is possible for a contact order to be made after the adoption order, but this will be limited to fairly exceptional circumstances. After an adoption order has been made, the birth parent is no longer a 'parent' under the Children Act 1989. He must therefore initially obtain leave of the court under s. 10(4) to make an application for contact. In considering whether leave should be granted, the court must consider the extent to which the proposed application would disrupt the child's life, and it is unlikely to be granted unless there has been a fundamental change in circumstances: *Re E (Adopted Child) (Contact: Leave)* [1995] 2 FCR 655. This may, however, be a possible avenue where an informal arrangement for contact has not been honoured after the adoption order and the birth parent seeks to formalise the original agreement.

■ Contact under the Adoption and Children Act 2002

The Adoption and Children Act 2002 does not introduce a presumption in favour of contact with adoption. It does, however, introduces provisions which oblige the court to consider arrangements for contact.

Where an agency is authorised to place a child with prospective adopters, existing contact orders under the Children Act 1989 are extinguished. Before making a placement order the court must consider arrangements which the adoption agency has made, or proposes to make for contact, and invite the parties to comment, and may make an order for contact under s. 26. Short-term refusal of contact is permitted by s. 27.

At the adoption application stage, s. 46(6) requires that, before making an adoption order, the court must consider whether there should be arrangements for allowing any person contact with the child; and for that purpose the court must consider any existing or proposed arrangements and obtain any views of the parties to the proceedings. If the court considers that an order for contact should be made, this is achieved by a s. 8 order. It is no longer possible to attach contact conditions to an adoption order.

Contact will also be considered as an aspect of subsection (f) in the welfare checklist as an element of the relationship which the child has with relatives, the likelihood of the relationship continuing and the value to the child of its doing so, and the wishes and feelings of any of the child's relatives, or of any such person, regarding the child.

■ Concurrent planning

The continually evolving practice around adoption and placement, which openness signifies, is also apparent in the development of concurrent planning[24] (also referred to as twin tracking and parallel planning). Its use is usually limited to particular children: those who are identified as at greatest risk of delay and repeated placements. The child will be placed with carers who are approved both as foster carers and prospective adopters. The birth family have a final opportunity to work towards rehabilitation of the child. It is made clear to all concerned that there are two plans:

1. The child will be returned home following the birth parents' satisfactorily working through the problems which led to the child entering care. The foster carers assist with this rehabilitation work.

2. If option 1 is not possible, the carers will adopt the child.

The whole process is time limited and involves intensive work, with suitable rehabilitation or education programmes. Early evaluation suggests that concurrent planning can be highly beneficial for the children concerned, who are protected from repeated moves and may be adopted sooner. Recruitment of sufficient carers may limit its availability in practice.[25]

■ The adoption panel

The Adoption Agencies Regulations 2005[26] require adoption agencies (usually the local authority) to establish an adoption panel. In a 2002 consultation, the Department of Health stated: 'In broad terms . . . the role of the adoption panel is: to provide an independent perspective, informed by a broad range of expertise to monitor and quality assure social work recommendations on adoption cases.'[27]

The adoption panel makes recommendations about three principle issues:

1. whether adoption is in the best interests of the child

2. the suitability of prospective adoptive parents; and

3. whether a prospective adopter is suitable for a particular child, i.e. matching child and adoptive parents.

Since October 2003, panels also make recommendations about adoption support. To make these recommendations the panel will need to ensure that it has received all relevant information and that the correct steps have been taken by the agency. There is clearly a 'quality assurance' aspect to the panel's role. The panel must keep a written record of the reasons for its recommendations, including any serious areas of dissent. The adoption panel will receive reports from the local authority social worker and its medical adviser will provide a medical report in relation to the child and the adoptive parents.

Membership of the adoption panel is specified by regulations. Since 1997, panel membership requirements have altered to shift the balance between professional and independent members, with a view to enabling panels to give more independent and informed advice and to be more representative of the local community.[28] Membership will include: an independent chairperson; an adviser; two social workers (each having at least three years' post-qualifying experience in child care social work including adoption work experience); an elected member of the local authority; a medical adviser; and at least three independent people with relevant experience (if possible including an adoptive parent and a person who has been adopted), up to a maximum of 11 people. As far as possible panels should be gender balanced and reflect the composition of the community.

All panel recommendations are reported to the Agency for a decision to be made (within seven days of the panel recommendation).

Representations to the panel

In *R* v. *Wokingham District Council, ex parte J* [1999] 2 FLR 1136, the court considered whether the mother of a child the local authority proposed to place for adoption should be able to make representations to the panel. The mother was not permitted to attend the panel, provide written representations or read the reports. Her claim that this amounted to a breach of natural justice was dismissed. The court suggested that it would be desirable to allow her to make written representations but held that a refusal was not unlawful. The panel was not making a final decision and she would be able to participate in any court hearing.

The position is different for prospective adopters, who are entitled to make representations to the panel after seeing their assessment report. Written observations will be considered by the panel or, because under the National Standards prospective adopters must be invited to attend panel, they may make oral representations. This position can be distinguished from the case above because, if prospective adopters are refused by the panel, there will not be any court proceedings in which they could make representations.[29]

The Adoption and Children Act 2002 establishes the *Independent Review Mechanism* under s. 12, as a form of external appeal. It provides an opportunity for the independent review of qualifying determinations, including decisions on prospective adopters' suitability to adopt. If prospective adopters are not approved for adoption, they have 40 days in which to decide whether to make representations to the agency or to apply to the independent review mechanism for fresh consideration of their application by an independent review panel (which will effectively 'mirror' adoption panels in their composition). So far, there have been few applications for reviews – only 10 cases in 12 months.[30]

■ Information to prospective adopters

A v. *Essex County Council* [2003] EWCA Civ 1848 is a further decision which addresses 'liability' of social services. A local authority was found to be vicariously liable for losses that arose from the failure of its social workers to ensure that prospective adopters were given full and relevant information concerning a child prior to placement.

In February 1996 two children were formally placed with A and B for adoption and on 1 May 1997 the court made adoption orders. The boy was subsequently diagnosed as suffering from Attention Deficit Hyperactivity Disorder (ADHD). A and B expected behavioural problems, their complaint was they were not prepared to accept the degree of disturbed behaviour that they were faced with. A and B alleged that the male child proved impossible to control to such an extent that he damaged A and B's home, health and family life. In press reports he was described as a 'wild child'. They claimed that the social workers had failed to give relevant information that they had to A and B or to ensure that it was given to them.

The court applied the precedent of *Phelps* v. *Hillingdon London Borough Council* [2001] 2 AC 619, and ruled that a local authority could be vicariously liable notwithstanding that the 'professional' was acting in furtherance of the authority's performance of a statutory duty, breach of which did not of itself result in damages. It was clearly in the public interest that professionals who are paid to offer their services to the public act to the appropriate standard. The court also noted that it was a cavalier attitude to the agency's own forms that permitted the lack of proper information for A and B to arise and continue undetected. The Form E did not give a full or fair picture of the male child. A and B were entitled to damages for such injury, loss and damage that they may prove they sustained during the placement but not thereafter. In effect, once the adoption order was made, the adoptive parents were taken to have accepted the child, whereas during the placement period they could have terminated the arrangement.

■ Adoption proceedings

Adoption proceedings may take place in the magistrates', county or High Court, but the majority are heard in the county court. Adoption proceedings are included in the definition of family proceedings under the Children Act 1989 and it is therefore possible for the court to exercise its powers under the Children Act 1989, s. 10 and make a range of orders. It will sometimes be necessary to consolidate the proceedings with other applications concerning the child, such as an application for a care order or applications for s. 8 orders. Certain county courts have been designated as adoption centres.[31] New court rules were introduced alongside the Act and include as r. 1 an overriding objective of enabling the court to 'deal with cases justly, having regard to the welfare issues involved'.[32] This includes a requirement to deal with each case fairly and expeditiously in a way that is proportionate to its nature and complexity, consistent with the delay principle. The rules provide the court with powers of case management including the power to extend or reduce time limits. The rules build on guidance for good practice issued in 2001[33] applicable to cases dealt with under the old law, which provided for all hearings and directions to be dealt with by an adoption judge and for each court to have a special adoption officer with a significant role in active case management, including tasks such as liaising with CAFCASS and the adoption agency.

To ensure confidentiality for the prospective adopters, a serial number may be applied for before commencing proceedings and the proceedings will then be conducted so as to ensure the prospective adopters are not seen by or made known to the birth parents. The structure of some court buildings can make this difficult and leads to split hearings in some cases.

The court will also receive an independent report from a reporting officer or a children's guardian. A reporting officer will be appointed where the application for adoption is not contested. It is the reporting officer's role to obtain the child's parents written consent. In addition, the reporting officer will briefly report on whether the adoption is considered to be in the best interests of the child. In contested cases a children's guardian will be appointed and will carry out a full investigation and make a report to the court as to whether adoption is in the best interests of the child. The guardian may also make other recommendations, e.g. that a residence order would be more appropriate than an adoption order, or as to orders for contact.

■ Adoption Support Services

The Adoption Support Services (Local Authorities) (England) Regulations 2003 (SI 2003/1348) came into effect ahead of the Adoption and Children Act, in 2003. These regulations were made in line with the duty imposed on social services authorities to make arrangements to provide adoption support services, including financial support.[34] Availability of support may increase willingness of prospective adopters to take on what may be a challenging task. The local authority must prepare and publish a plan for provision of adoption services (s. 5). Registered adoption societies may provide many support services and the need for a coordinated effort is noted by s. 3(5): 'The facilities of the service must be provided in conjunction with the local authority's other social services and with registered adoption societies in their area, so that help may be given in a co-ordinated manner without duplication, omission or avoidable delay.'

Adoption support services may be provided to:

- children who may be adopted, their parents and guardians:
- persons wishing to adopt a child;
- adopted persons, their parents, natural parents and former guardians (s. 3).

The local authority is under a duty to carry out an assessment of need for adoption support services at the request of any of the people named above (s. 3). If the authority decides that a person has needs for adoption support services, it must then decide whether to provide any. If the authority decides to provide services, it must plan the provision and keep the plan under review.

The new framework for adoption services includes: counselling, advice and information; a system for financial support; support groups for adoptive families; assistance with contact arrangements between adopted children and their birth relatives; therapeutic services for adopted children; an adoption support services advisor to help those affected by adoption to access support services; and development of adoption support plans for adoptive families.

■ Adoption or residence

The irrevocable nature of adoption and the degree of permanence it provides may be described as adoption's key features. Adoption does more than determine where a child is to live; it both creates and extinguishes parental responsibility. Whilst there are other ways of providing a degree of legal permanence, any order other than an adoption order may be perceived as less than ideal. It is clear, however, that the range of children requiring some form of security and stability has changed drastically since adoption in its current form was introduced, and there may be reasons in some cases why an adoption order is not the most appropriate way of providing that security and stability. This was precisely the issue the Court of Appeal had to consider in a complex case, *Re M (A Minor) (Adoption or Residence Order)* [1998] 1 FLR 570. In circumstances where the child had initially stated that she wanted to live with, but did not want to be adopted by, her long-term foster carers, a residence order (rather than an adoption order) was made, with a s. 91(14) restriction against further applications by the mother, for added security.[35]

■ Special guardianship

A new order, known as special guardianship, is introduced as an alternative order to adoption, providing a high level of legal security (ACA 2002, Part 2, s. 115).[36] It may be particularly suitable for older children who do not want the legal links to their birth family to be severed, but who need the security of a permanent alternative placement. The Prime Minster's Review of Adoption (PIU, 2000) envisaged special guardianship being appropriate for: 'Local authority foster parents, relatives, older children who do not wish to be legally separated from their birth family, children cared for on a permanent basis by their wider family, and certain minority ethnic communities with religious and cultural objections to adoption.'

A new s. 14A is inserted into the Children Act 1989 creating the new order. A 'special guardianship order' is an order appointing one or more individuals to be a child's *special guardian(s)*. A special guardian must be 18 or over and must not be a parent of the child (it is not therefore an order that could be made to parents who have separated in respect of their child). It is perhaps unfortunate that the term 'guardianship' has been chosen because this may cause some confusion with guardianship under the Children Act 1989, s. 5.

s. 14A

(1) A 'special guardianship order' is an order appointing one or more individuals to be a child's 'special guardian' (or special guardians).
(2) A special guardian –
  (a) must be aged eighteen or over: and
  (b) must not be a parent of the child in question.

(CA 1989, as amended)

Special guardianship is a private law order. Some individuals have an automatic entitlement to make an application for special guardianship, namely:

■ Any guardian of the child.

■ Any holder of a residence order in respect of the child.

■ A local authority foster parent with whom the child has lived for at least one year immediately preceding the application.

■ Any person the child has lived with for three years.

■ Any person with consent of holders of residence order; the local authority where child is in care; those with parental responsibility (alternatives).

Others falling outside that list require leave of the court. The court has the power to make the order in family proceedings of its own motion (i.e. it is not dependent on an application for special guardianship being made). It is not possible for a local authority to apply for special guardianship on another's behalf. When making a special guardianship order the court must also consider whether a contact order should be made, whether any s. 8 order be varied or discharged, and it may give leave for change of surname.

A person who intends to apply for special guardianship must give three months' notice to the local authority. This triggers a duty on the local authority to prepare a report which addresses the suitability of the applicant; the child's wishes and feelings and anything else it considers relevant. Regulation 21 of the Special Guardianship Regulations 2005[37] sets out the details that must be covered in the report. The court cannot make an order unless it has received a report from the local authority. These requirements inevitably draw the local authority into private law cases where it might otherwise not have had any involvement. It is a new area of responsibility with obvious resource implications.

Each local authority must also make arrangements for provision of special guardianship support services, to include counselling, advice and information. Support services may include financial assistance to the special guardian similar to a fostering allowance, and can include payment of legal fees associated with making the application. Authorities must also establish procedures to consider representations about special guardianship support services.

Effect of a special guardianship order

The order discharges any care order, contact order or other s. 8 order in respect of the child. The special guardian acquires parental responsibility and has the right to act exclusively in exercising parental responsibility. The birth parent retains parental responsibility but their ability to exercise it is constrained. Maintenance liability does continue alongside the order. The special guardian can appoint a person to be the child's guardian in the event of his death.

The order may be distinguished from adoption as it does not terminate birth parents' parental responsibility and it is revocable. It provides greater security than a residence order as there are restrictions in place on applications for variation.

Variation or discharge

To apply to vary a special guardianship order an applicant, including a birth parent, requires leave of the court, whereas to vary a residence order a parent can apply as of right.

Variation and discharge can be applied for by the special guardian, a parent or guardian of the child; an individual who has a residence order in respect of the child; an individual who has or had parental responsibility for the child immediately before the special guardianship order; the child (if he has sufficient understanding); a local authority with a care order in respect of the child. Other than in applications by the special guardian, leave of the court is required to make an application and with the exception of applications by the child, leave will normally only be granted if there has been significant changes in circumstances since the original order was made.

The court may vary the order itself in any family proceedings where the welfare of the child arises, for example, in child protection proceedings, or where the special guardians are divorcing and there is a dispute as to the arrangements for the child.

Exhibit 11.1 summarises the key differences between adoption, special guardianship and residence.

Order	Parental Responsibility (PR)	Duration	Permanence	Local authority (LA) support
Adoption	Acquired by adoptive parents (including step-parent adoption). Birth parents lose PR.	For life.	Irrevocable. Severs previous legal relationship.	Range of adoption support services available.
Special Guardianship	Acquired by special guardian (SG) and exercisable to the exclusion of others. Retained by birth parents but exercise is constrained.	Until 18.	May be varied or discharged by court. Leave required by all except SG and only granted if significant change in circumstances.	Range of special guardianship support services available.
Residence	PR to holder of residence order. PR retained by those with PR before order, discharges care order and PR of LA.	Until the child is 16, may be extended to 18.	May be varied or discharged by court. Parents and child may apply as of right. Leave required by others, s. 10(9).	LA *may* make contributions to child's maintenance.

Exhibit 11.1 Key differences between adoption, special guardianship and residence

Changes to the Children Act 1989

The Adoption and Children Act 2002 makes a number of amendments to the Children Act 1989, ranging from the relatively minor to introduction of special guardianship, a completely new order. A summary of the changes, which are contained in Part 2 of the Act ss 111–122, is set out below. Those which are directly relevance to adoption and permanence are considered in detail in this chapter. Other changes are considered within the relevant chapter, e.g. acquisition of parental responsibility by unmarried fathers on registration, is considered as part of the fuller consideration of parental responsibility in Chapter 8.

- Section 4 of the Children Act 1989 is amended so that an 'unmarried father' may acquire parental responsibility where he jointly registers the child's birth with the mother under the Births and Deaths Registration Act 1953 (s. 111). This provision came into force in December 2003 and applies to all registrations since that date.

- The new legislation gives greater recognition to the step-parent relationship and provides the means for a step-parent (who is married to a parent of the child) to acquire parental responsibility by agreement or by court order (s. 112) (discussed further in Chapter 8).

- A reduced time period for foster parents who wish to apply for a residence order for a child they are fostering, now the child needs to have lived with them for one year out of the previous five rather than three (s. 113).

- Courts are given the option of extending the duration of a residence order to the child's eighteenth birthday (s. 114).

- The introduction of a new permanence option, special guardianship (s. 115) and accompanying support services. It is designed to offer permanence through an alternative form to an adoption order.

- Section 17 of the Children Act 1989 is amended to confirm that services that may be provided to children in need include provision of accommodation (s. 116).

- There is provision for the local authority complaints and representations procedure to extend to representations about the discharge of functions under the ACA (s. 117).

- Following the important case of *Re W and B (Children: Care Plan)* [2001] EWCA Civ 757 which introduced (briefly) the concept of 'starred care plans', local authorities are required to appoint a person, known as an Independent Reviewing Officer, to keep the s. 31A care plan under review. Where they consider that some change is required, to revise the plan or make a new plan, if the reviewing officer may refer the case to CAFCASS, who may return the case to court (s. 118).

- Section 119 introduces a new s. 26A into the Children Act 1989 requiring local authorities to make arrangements to provide assistance, including advocacy services for children and young people making complaints.

- The definition of the meaning of 'harm' in the Children Act 1989 (s. 31) is extended to include 'impairment suffered from seeing or hearing the ill-treatment of another' (s. 120). This provision is welcome as an explicit recognition of (amongst other things) the damaging effect of witnessing domestic violence.

- A late amendment to the Act introduced statutory recognition of the care plan. The authority is required to prepare a care plan, giving prescribed information in a prescribed format, in any applications where a care order might be made and the court is required to consider the plan before it may make a care order (s. 121).

- In a section entitled 'Interests of children in proceedings', specified proceedings in which a children's guardian may be appointed under s. 41 of the Children Act 1989 are amended to include applications for making or revoking a placement order and for making, varying or discharging a s. 8 order (s. 122).

Chapter summary

- The Adoption and Children Act 2002 has reformed adoption law and replaced the previous law contained in the Adoption Act 1976. The Act is supported by National Standards and statutory guidance.

- The 2002 Act includes a set of principles applying to decisions about adoption: the paramount consideration of the court or adoption agency must be the child's welfare throughout his life; a welfare checklist supports the welfare principle, delay is likely to prejudice the child's welfare, the court must consider the whole range of powers available to it and apply the no order principle; the agency must give due consideration to the child's religious persuasion, racial origin and cultural and linguistic background.

- Adoption agencies (local authority) must provide a comprehensive adoption service in order to meet the needs of children who have been adopted or may be, their parents, guardians and prospective adopters (the elements of what is sometimes referred to as 'the adoption triangle'). The service includes provision of adoption support services Registered adoption societies also provide services.

- Adoption applications may be made in respect of a child under the age of 18, by a single person or a couple, married or unmarried. Step-parents may adopt or acquire parental responsibility.

- Adoption panels make recommendations about whether adoption is in the best interests of the child; suitability of prospective adoptive parents; and whether a prospective adopter is suitable for a particular child, i.e. matching child and adoptive parents.

- An adoption order may not be made unless each parent or guardian consents to the adoption order, or their consent should be dispensed with and the child has been placed for adoption by an adoption agency with the prospective adopters in whose favour the order is proposed to be made.

- There is increasing openness about the adoption process. Adopted adults are entitled to have access to their birth records and there is an Adoption Contact Register. Many adopted children will have some level of contact with their birth family throughout the adoption.

- A new order known as special guardianship is introduced as an alternative to adoption and provides a higher degree of legal security than the residence order as there are strict limitation on it variation.

- The Adoption and Children Act 2002 makes a number of amendments to the Children Act 1989, which are referred to elsewhere in the text, but are summarised in this chapter for ease of reference.

Exercise

John is 8 years old. He lives with his mother, Julie, and his step-father, David. Julie and David have been married 18 months. John's father, Ian, is serving a 14-year prison sentence. He writes to John occasionally and sends birthday and Christmas presents. John has not seen his father for four years. Since they married, David has said to Julie that he would like to adopt John, so that they can 'be a real family'. Ian will not agree to this as he believes it will mean he loses touch with John and John's surname will be changed. Julie is very anxious about any court proceedings because her divorce from Ian was very traumatic, and is nervous about a social work assessment of her relationship with David. He was also married previously and has no contact with his child from that marriage. John knows that David is not his real dad, but thinks if he is adopted he will not be teased as much about his father being in prison. Which (if any) orders would be appropriate in this scenario?

Websites

Information on adoption, including key publications can be found on the DfES (transferred over from DH) and 'Every Child Matters' sites:

www.dfes.gov.uk/adoption

www.everychildmatters.gov.uk/adoption

British Agencies for Adoption and Fostering (BAAF) provides a wide range of information and research publications:

www.baaf.org.uk

Barnardo's:

www.barnardos.org.uk

Further reading

Specialist texts include:

Allen, N. (2003) *Making Sense of the New Adoption Law: A guide for social and welfare services*. Lyme Regis: Russell House Publishing. (Provides an excellent contextual account of the Act placing its discussion in the wider social and political context and is written primarily for practitioners).

Bridge, C. and Swindells, H. (2003) *Adoption: The Modern Law*. Bristol: Family Law, Jordan Publishing (Offers a more detailed analysis of the provisions and includes a copy of the Act. Published in 2003 so does not refer to the most recent regulations or guidance).

Swindells, H. and Heaton, C. (2006) *Adoption: The Modern Practice*. Bristol: Family Law, Jordan Publishing. (Provides the additional detail not available in Allen or Bridge, above.)

For background to the Act and on development of its provisions see Department of Health publications:

Department of Health (1999) *Adoption Now: Messages from Research*. Chichester: Wiley.

Department of Health (2000) 'Adoption: a new approach' (Cm. 5017). London: The Stationery Office.

Further analysis of the Act and implications for practice is covered in a range of articles including:

Ball, C. (2005) 'The Adoption and Children Act 2002: A critical examination.' 29(2) *Adoption and Fostering* p. 6.

Cullen, D. (2005) 'Adoption – a (fairly) new approach' 17(4) *Child and Family Law Quarterly* p. 475.

Masson, J. (2003) 'The Impact of the Adoption and Children Act 2002: Part 2 – The provision of Services for Children and Families', *Family Law* p. 644. (Part 1 deals with parental responsibility and is at (2003) *Family Law* p. 580.)

Particular practice issues of contact, concurrent planning, partnership and adoption of looked after children are considered in:

Fratter, J. (1996) *Adoption with Contact – Implications for Policy and Practice*. London: BAAF.

Masson, J. (2000) Thinking about contact – a social or a legal problem? 12(1) *Child and Family Law Quarterly* p. 15.

Wigfall, V., Monck, E. and Reynolds, J. (2006) Putting Programme into Practice: the Introduction of Concurrent Planning into Mainstream Adoption and Fostering Services. 36 *British Journal of Social Work* p. 41.

Lindley, B. (1997) *Secrets or Links? Partnership with Birth Families in the Adoption Process; Report on a Trawl of Adoption Agency Practice*. London: Family Rights Group.

Thoburn J. (2003) 'The Risks and Rewards of Adoption for Children in Public care' 15(4) *Child and Family Law Quarterly* p. 391.

Notes

[1] The terms 'security' and 'stability' are preferred to 'permanence'.

[2] J. Rowe and L. Lambert (1973) *Children Who Wait: A Study of Children Needing Substitute Families:* London: ABAA.

[3] J. Triseliotis (1998) 'Is permanency through adoption in decline?' 22(4) *Adoption and Fostering* p. 41.

[4] A few provisions were implemented earlier than December 2005, for example the changes to parental responsibility for unmarried fathers.

[5] Department of Health (2001) Adoption and Children Bill 2001 Regulatory Impact Assessment: www. doh.gov.uk/regulatoryimpact/adoptionandchildren.htm.

[6] Similar principles contained in Part 1 of the Children Act 1989 are discussed in Chapter 7.

[7] LAC (98) 20 'Adoption – Achieving the right balance', Department of Health, paras. 13 and 14.

[8] LAC (98) 20, para. 39. See also H. Schroeder and D. Lightfoot 'Finding black families' 7(1) *Adoption and Fostering* p. 18 and R. Flynn (2000) 'Black carers for white children: shifting the "same-race" placement debate' 24(1) *Adoption and Fostering* p. 47.

[9] Department of Health, Welsh Office, Home Office, Lord Chancellor's Department (1993) 'Adoption: The Future' (Cm. 2288). London: HMSO.

[10] See also S. Jolly, and R. Sandland, (1994) 'Political correctness and the adoption white paper' *Family Law* p. 30.

[11] Justice Heald (1992) 'Whither Adoption' *Family Law* p. 29.

[12] Cited in R. Sandland (1993) 'Adoption, law and homosexuality: can gay people adopt a child?' 5 *Journal of Social Welfare and Family Law* p. 321.

[13] See J. Selwyn (1996) 'Ascertaining children's wishes and feelings in relation to adoption' 20(3) *Adoption and Fostering* p. 14.

[14] In Northern Ireland and Scotland a third condition applies, that the child must be freed for adoption. Freeing in England and Wales is abolished by the Act.

[15] M. Murch, N. Lowe, M. Borkowski, R. Copner and K. Griew (1991) 'Pathways to adoption research project'. London: HMSO; and N. Lowe, M. Borkowski, R. Copner, K. Griew and M. Murch (1993) 'Report of the research into the use and practice of the freeing for adoption provisions'. London: HMSO.

[16] J. Goldstein, A. Freud and A. Solnit (1980) *Before the Best Interests of the Child*. London: Burnett Books.

[17] See discussion in Department of Health (1999) *Adoption Now: Messages from Research*. Chichester: Wiley.

[18] J. Fratter (1996) *Adoption with Contact – Implications for Policy and Practice*. London: BAAF.

[19] Adoption Act 1976, s. 51A.

[20] J. Triseliotis (1991) 'Open adoption' in A. Mullender (ed.) *Open Adoption: The Philosophy and Practice*. London: BAAF.

21 M. Ryburn (1998) 'In whose interests? – post-adoption contact with the birth family' 10(1) *Child and Family Law Quarterly* p. 53.

22 [1994] 1 FLR 146 at 151e, per Sir Stephen Brown.

23 Social Services Inspectorate (1995) 'Moving Goalposts'. London.

24 And, more recently, the Coram project in London.

25 See L. Katz and B. Clatworthy (1999) 'Innovation in care planning for children' *Family Law* p. 108, and N. Wall (1999) 'Concurrent planning – a judicial perspective' 11(2) *Child and Family Law Quarterly* p. 97.

26 S1 2005/389.

27 DoH (2002) A Fundamental Review of the Operation of Adoption Panels London: DoH. p. 36.

28 LAC (97) 13.

29 See S. Pepys and J. Dix (2000) 'Inviting applicants, birth parents and young people to attend adoption panel. How it works in practice' 24(4) *Adoption and Fostering* p. 40.

30 'Independent Review Mechanism (England) End of Year One Statement, from www.dfes. gov.uk/adoption/update300605a.shtml.

31 New pilot specialist adoption courts were proposed in the white paper, 'Adoption: A New Approach, Cm. 5017, 2000.

32 Family Procedure (Adoption) Rules 2005 (SI 2005/2795).

33 Adoption Proceedings – A New Approach, by the President of the Family Division, from the Lord Chancellors Department (2001).

34 See LAC (2003) 12. Adoption Support Services Guidance has also been published alongside the new regulations.

35 See further discussion of this case: D. Savas and S. Treece (1998) 'Re M (Adoption or Residence Order) Adoption or Residence? Too many parents. . .?' 10(3) *Child and Family Law Quarterly* p. 311.

36 See also the Special Guardianship Regulations 2005 (SI 2005/1109).

37 SI 2005/1109.

12 Education

Learning objectives

To develop an understanding of the following:

- The legislative framework which underpins the provision of school education in England and Wales.
- The duty to ensure children receive efficient full-time education.
- Current areas of debate in educational provision, such as Special Educational Needs and exclusion of pupils.
- The role of the social worker with children and families as it touches on issues in education and schooling.
- The provision of sex education.
- The education of looked after children.
- The education supervision order.

Introduction

The law of education is complex. It is also an area of rapid change and new legislation appears frequently, providing a mass of statutory responsibilities. This chapter provides an overview of the framework and basic principles of education law, as issues which affect service users, in particular, matters of admission, exclusion and discipline. It continues with consideration of the role of social workers in education, education of looked after children, special educational needs, and the education supervision order. It is very likely that the role of the social worker in education related law will be enhanced by the current government initiative of 'Every Child Matters', as supported by the

Children Act 2004 (CA 2004). The emphasis in the Act is upon inter-agency working (particularly in Part 2, Children's Services) but, beyond that, there is a recognition of the interlinking of education and social welfare for children:

> Schools increasingly recognise their role in helping combat the barriers to learning and attainment that lie outside the school gates. Pupil performance and well-being go hand in hand. Pupils cannot learn if they do not feel safe or if health problems are allowed to create barriers to learning. Educational achievement is also central to lifting young people out of poverty and disaffection.[1]

Framework of education law

The law requires that all children[2] receive an education. Local education authorities (**LEAs**) are responsible for the provision of public education,[3] guided by the Department for Education and Skills (**DfES**).[4] The Education Act 1996 (**EA 1996**), which consolidated earlier education legislation, provides the basic framework of education law. However, that legislation has been supplemented by the Education Act 1997, the School Standards and Framework Act 1998 (**SSFA 1998**), the Special Educational Needs and Disability Act 2001 (SENDA 2001), the Learning and Skills Act 2000, the Education Act 2002 (EA 2002) and the Education Act 2005 (EA 2005).

Most of the duties and powers of the local education authority (LEA) are to be found in either the EA 1996 or the SSFA 1998. Note, however, that the EA 2002 (in keeping with apparent current Government policy) imposes rather wider and less specific responsibilities; for example, to safeguard the welfare of pupils (s. 175) and to consult with pupils on matters which may affect them (s. 176). This policy is emphasised in the 'New Relationship With Schools' initiative,[5] which has produced specific guidance on how schools can promote the welfare of pupils alongside the general aim to allow schools to improve their overall performance. There is a large quantity of specific advice and notes on these topics on the DfES website (listed, with others, at the end of this chapter).

The EA 2005 is largely concerned with arrangements for the inspection and organisation of schools. However, s. 75 establishes the Training and Development Agency for schools, which is charged with raising standards in teaching and ensuring that the workforce 'contributes to the well-being' of pupils following the definition in the Children Act 2004, s. 10. This is, perhaps, an example of the increased emphasis on seeing education within a larger picture of the overall welfare of the child. The CA 2004 itself, in turn, requires the Children's Commissioner to be concerned with 'education, training and recreation' (s. 2(3)(c)) as an aspect of children's well-being. It may reasonably be observed that education law inevitably reflects the political importance of education as a social policy issue. The consequence is frequent change and new legislation.

The corollary of the duty of LEAs to provide education is the legal obligation on parents to secure their child's education. Section 7 of the Education Act 1996 provides:

s. 7

The parent of every child of compulsory school age shall cause him to receive efficient full-time education suitable:
(a) to his age, ability and aptitude
(b) to any special educational needs he may have,
      either by regular attendance at school or otherwise.

(EA 1996)

'Parent' means anyone who has parental responsibility for or care of the child (EA 1996, s. 576(1)).

It is possible for parents to educate their child at home, and an increasing number do so. There is no requirement to seek permission from the LEA to educate at home (unless the child is at a special school) or to have regular contact with the LEA or to follow the National Curriculum (which applies only to registered pupils (EA 1996, ss. 351–353)).[6] If 'it appears' to an LEA that a child of compulsory school age is not receiving a suitable education, it may issue a notice to the parent requiring her to satisfy the LEA that the child is receiving a satisfactory education (EA 1996, ss. 437(1)) (*R* v. *Gwent County Council, ex parte Perry* (1985) 129 Sol Jo 737).

Parents should register their child at a school and ensure his attendance. If a child is not registered (and the parents cannot satisfy the LEA that the child is receiving suitable education), the LEA may serve a school attendance order, non-compliance being a criminal offence (EA 1996, s. 443). If not subject to a school attendance order, the parent still commits an offence (s. 444) if a registered pupil 'fails to attend regularly at school'. The offence is one of strict liability unless one of the statutory excuses applies, namely:

■ absence with leave;

■ sickness or other avoidable cause (both must relate to the child);[7]

■ religious observance;

■ the school is not within walking distance (two miles for a child under the age of 8 and three miles for a child over 8) and there are no suitable LEA arrangements for transport;

■ the child has no fixed abode (subject to certain conditions).

It may seem harsh and unproductive to prosecute parents for these offences but there has been at least one case of a pregnant mother being imprisoned for failing to secure the attendance of her child at school.[8]

It appears that there is a link to Government policy on crime because, inevitably, many of the children who do not attend school are in fact truanting. Whether that necessarily means the child is committing a criminal act is another matter but EA

1996, s. 444A (added by the Anti-Social Behaviour Act 2003, s. 23) allows an autho-rised officer (including a headteacher) to serve a penalty notice where he has reason to believe an offence has been committed under EA 1996, s. 444(1). The penalty is up to £100. There is little evidence at present as to the extent to which this power is used.

The ASBA 2003 has also introduced parenting contracts (s. 19), which, although voluntary, result in an agreement by parents to undergo a guidance programme. More punitive in nature is the parenting order, which is available when a parent breaches a school attendance order or fails to secure the regular attendance of a registered child at school. This power was introduced by the Crime and Disorder Act 1998 (CDA 1998), s. 8, and allows the court to impose an order for up to 12 months. Failure to comply may result in a fine or other community punishment.

From September 2005, the EA 2005 has extended provision for dealing with referrals for alternative provision for excluded pupils and the use of parenting con-tracts. A general drive to improve school attendance is a significant part of current Government education policy.[9]

Social work responsibilities

Significant statutory responsibilities towards children in education, set by the Education Acts and the Children Act 1989, are discharged by Education Welfare Officers (**EWOs**). This includes working with children (and their families) who do not attend school regularly (there are about 50,000 unauthorised absences on any one school day)[10] and bringing court proceedings in some circumstances. The EWO will carry out 'truancy sweeps' with the police under the Crime and Disorder Act 1998 and may also advise on home education and child protection issues, prepare reports in cases of SEN and will usually be the supervisor under an education super-vision order. In addition, social workers will frequently have direct contact with education professionals when working to support children in need and their fami-lies. A substantial amount of the child protection referrals to social services are from teachers and other education professions. Inter-agency cooperation between social services and education is therefore essential on a number of levels and is the basic principle of the 'Every Child Matters' initiative and the CA 2004.

A right to education?

The concept of children's rights is not central to the law of education,[11] despite ref-erences in international treaties, including the United Nations Convention on the Rights of the Child, Art. 28(1), to the 'right of the child to education' (though 'in considering for the purpose of his function under this section what constitutes the interests of children . . . the Children's Commissioner must have regard to the UNCRC', (CA 2004, s. 2(11))).[12]

The European Convention on Human Rights includes as Art. 2 of the First Protocol: 'No person shall be denied the right to education. In the exercise of any function which it assumes in relation to education and to teaching, the State shall respect the rights of parents to ensure such education and teaching in conformity with their own religious and philosophical convictions.' This right is phrased in negative rather than positive terms but arguably is upheld by the principle of compulsory education. However, there is no 'right' to education of a particular level or quality (*Belgian Linguistics Case (No. 2)* (1968) 1 EHRR 252) nor, necessarily, to one in compliance with parents' beliefs (*Valsamis* v. *Greece* (1996) 24 EHRR 294).

The right of parental preference is emphasised without direct reference to the wishes and feelings of the child. Practice would suggest, however, that it does not equate with an obligation to meet parents' wishes as, for example, in terms of admissions policy. The above Article was accepted by the United Kingdom subject to a reservation, initially contained in s. 9 of the Education Act 1996 but maintained in the Human Rights Act 1998 (HRA 1998), that pupils will be educated in accordance with their parents' wishes only so far as that is compatible with provision of efficient instruction and avoidance of unreasonable public expenditure.

It is probable that the HRA 1998 will make a significant impact upon education law given its central place in the public law jurisdiction. Articles of the Convention other than Art. 2 of the First Protocol which are most likely to arise for consideration in education law cases are: Arts. 3, 6, 8, 9, 10 and 14. (The detail of these Articles and the operation of the Act generally are dealt with in Chapter 5.) Two recent judgments of the HL (issued on the same day) are examples of the nuanced approach adopted by the judiciary in considering the interaction of the HRA with education law. In *R (on the application of Begum)* v. *Headteachers and Governors of Denbish High School* [2006] UKHL 15, a 14-year-old girl's request to wear a *jilbab* was rejected. Though Article 9 (Freedom of thought, conscience and religion) was invoked, the court held that a school's dress code, if proportionate in scope and effect, is a justifiable limitation on the manifestation of belief. In *Ali* v. *Headteachers and Governors of Lord Grey School* [2006] UKHL 14, their Lordships concluded that a partly unlawful exclusion did not give rise to finding of a breach of Article 2 of the First Protocol where suitable alternative educational provision had been made and the school had otherwise acted properly in difficult circumstances.

Resource implications will often be central to a local authority's decision-making in education matters, including any apparent reluctance or inability to meet parental preference. The courts are unlikely to support that view. In *R* v. *East Sussex County Council, ex parte Tandy* [1998] AC 714, a child suffering from ME was educated at home. The LEA reduced the teaching provided purely on financial grounds. The House of Lords held that the LEA had a duty (not merely a power) to provide home education in this case and consequently the question of the local authority's resources was not a matter to be taken into account. It is likely that cases such as this would also now fall to be considered within the ambit of legislation prohibiting discrimination on the ground of disability.

Local authority liability

It was claimed in *X (Minors)* v. *Bedfordshire County Council* [1995] 3 All ER 353 that the local authority had negligently failed to provide for the claimants' special needs. The House of Lords decided that it was not fair, just or reasonable to impose a duty of care on the LEA in respect of these statutory duties (i.e. public law functions), for example how to exercise its powers and discretions in relation to pupils with SEN. However, if an authority offers a service (e.g. an educational psychologist) it is under a duty to exercise reasonable care in the manner in which it runs that service and if it does so negligently, a claim may arise. This is what happened in *Phelps* v. *Hillingdon London Borough Council* [2001] 2 AC 619. The psychologist employed by the LEA failed to diagnose the claimant's dyslexia and was found to be in breach of her duty of care and the LEA vicariously liable as employer for that negligence. Damages of £45,000 were awarded and confirmed by the House of Lords. It seems unlikely that there will be a flood of claims based on this principle given the necessity to identify an individual who breached a duty of care to the claimant.

It may be noted that it was subsequently decided in the European Court in the case of *Osman* v. *UK* [1999] 1 FLR 193 that to confer a blanket immunity in respect of allegations of negligence was a violation of ECHR, Art. 6(1), a decision that may impact upon education cases even though this claim related primarily to Art. 2 and was directed against the police.

Role of governors

The SSFA 1998 classifies maintained schools into community, foundation, voluntary or special schools. Most are community schools and those which are voluntary are either voluntary controlled or aided and are familiar as the former 'church schools'. Governing bodies have overall responsibility for the governance and management of schools, (SSFA 1988, s. 38 and see also EA 2002, Part 3, Chapter 1 and Part 11, which introduces new arrangements from 2006). Note that s. 175(2) of the 2002 Act specifically charges governors to exercise their functions so as to safeguard and promote the welfare of children. Over recent years governing bodies have acquired many areas of responsibility previously the domain of LEAs. In particular, their role entails: determining and monitoring areas of the curriculum; ensuring the National Curriculum is delivered and daily worship takes place; appointing and dismissing staff; determining how the school budget is spent; developing policies (including policies on discipline, sex education and special needs); and reporting annually to parents on all of these issues. In the event that the proposals contained in the latest Government Bill,[13] based on the white paper 'Higher Standards, Better Schools for

All – More Choice for Parents and Pupils',[14] are put into effect, schools are likely to achieve greater independence of action, giving rise to 'an enhanced role for governors as schools become more autonomous'.[15]

Discipline

The purpose of discipline in school is to create an environment which is suitable for education and learning. SSFA 1998, s. 61 requires governing bodies to make a written statement of general principles to which the head 'must have regard' so as to ensure that the school follows policies designed to promote discipline and good behaviour. The governing body for each school must have a policy on discipline which is included in the school prospectus (the 'whole school behaviour policy') but on a day-to-day basis the head teacher is responsible for discipline (SSFA 1998, s. 61(4)).

Corporal punishment has been banned in the state sector since 1987 and is now illegal in all schools, including independent schools (SSFA 1998, s. 131). Any other action that teachers take to enforce discipline must be reasonable and proportionate and exceeding that limit could lead to action against the teacher for assault or battery. The Education Act 1997 provides some clarification in this difficult area through provision of a power for staff to use 'such force as is reasonable in the circumstances' to prevent a pupil committing an offence, causing personal injury or damage to property, or behaving in a way which prejudices the maintenance of good order and discipline at the school.[16]

Parents have their own role to play in supporting the school in matters of discipline. The use of home-school agreements is provided for in the SSFA 1998, ss. 110 and 111. Home-school agreements are not legally binding contracts but are designed to clarify the roles and expectations of schools for parents and pupils. They have been described as 'a method of soft control that sits alongside the more overtly disciplinary initiatives'.[17] The agreement is in fact a statement of the school's aims and values; the responsibilities of the school to educate pupils; the responsibilities of parents in connection with the education of their children; and expectations of pupils' conduct. Agreements typically cover the following areas.

The school agrees to: teach children and treat them fairly; provide a secure and happy environment in which to learn; respond to parents' concerns; keep them informed of children's progress and school activities.

Parents agree to: ensure that their child attends school regularly, is punctual and properly dressed; inform the school of any absence and concerns that might affect the child's behaviour; encourage their child; attend parents' evenings; and support the school.

Pupils agree to: treat others with respect; attend school; and observe the school's rules.

Recent policy, however, has been to adopt increasingly direct methods of encouragement to parents to impose discipline on their children in the form of parenting contracts and orders. There is a grading structure. Contracts are voluntary agreements between parent and school entered into after the child has truanted or been excluded. Orders are civil court orders compelling attendance at parenting classes and are available after a child has been permanently excluded and where parenting is considered a factor in the child's misbehaviour.[18]

Exclusions

Within a school's policy on discipline, exclusion should be the last resort. Nevertheless, figures for 2003/4[19] show that nearly 10,000 pupils were permanently excluded (0.13 per cent of pupils) and 344,500 fixed period exclusions were imposed, involving 2.6 per cent of all pupils. Of this latter group, 65 per cent were excluded on one occasion only and 19 per cent on two; 86 per cent of all fixed period exclusions were for less than one week. The exclusion rate for boys is about four times that of girls and the most likely age for exclusion is 13–14.

Certain children are disproportionately likely to be excluded. Children with special educational needs are four times more likely to be excluded than other children. Children of Afro-Caribbean origin (especially boys), traveller children and looked after children are significantly more likely to be excluded than children from other groups.

The power to exclude a pupil is exercisable by the head teacher (EA 2002, s. 52) who should follow DfES guidance.[20] An exclusion may be permanent or for a fixed period of up to 45 schooldays in any school year. The procedure of excluding pupils is tightly prescribed and it is essential that the correct procedures are followed. Exclusion by reference to race or disability would inevitably be discriminatory.

The headteacher must inform the 'relevant person' (the child's parents, and the pupil if over 18) of the reason for and period of the exclusion (or if it is permanent) of the right to make representations. Parents may make representations to the governing body (there are time limits) and will often request reinstatement. At least three governors should consider the representations and they must act independently (R(DR) v. *Head Teacher of St George's Catholic School* [2002] EWCA Civ 1822). There is no further right of appeal in respect of a fixed-term exclusion.

In relation to permanent exclusions, the parents may appeal to the independent exclusion appeal panel, which is arranged by the LEA and consists of three or five members constituted in accordance with the Education (Pupil Exclusion and Appeals) (Maintained Schools) (England) Regulations 2002 (SI 2002/3178). The panel may order reinstatement of the pupil and should give reasons if the exclusion is upheld. An LEA is under a duty to provide suitable education for excluded pupils by EA 1996, s. 19(1). This duty is increasingly fulfilled by placement in Pupil Referral Units, established by EA 1996, s. 19(2). These are effectively small schools which are relieved of many statutory obligations, e.g. there is no necessity to teach the National Curriculum.

Sex education

Sex education has a vital role to play in reducing the number of HIV and sexually transmitted infections contracted by young people and the number of conceptions among girls under 16. The law in this area attempts to strike a balance, involving the need to provide adequate education without undermining the role of parents. All secondary schools are required to provide sex education (EA 2002, s. 80), which must give due regard to moral considerations and the values of family life (EA 1996, s. 403). In primary schools, sex education is not compulsory but the governors must address the question and have a policy on the subject (EA 1996, s. 404). Under the Education Act 1996, s. 405 there is a statutory right for parents to withdraw their child from sex education classes without the need to give reasons. Governors and head teachers are required to have regard to guidance in terms of the content of sex education. The latest guidance places sex education within the framework for Personal, Social and Health Education and the study of citizenship, and there is a clear emphasis on reducing the numbers of teenage pregnancies and sexually transmitted diseases.[21]

Looked after children

Social services are under a duty to consult with LEAs where a child is looked after by the local authority (Children Act 1989, s. 28), with a view to ensuring suitable educational provision is made. Approximately 60,000 children are looked after at any one time.[22] Nevertheless, in recent years the educational underachievement of looked after children has been highlighted. The level of underachievement should not be underestimated and statistics paint a depressing picture. Figures for 2004[23] show that of some 45,000 children who had been looked after for a continuous period of at least 12 months: 27 per cent had statements of Special Educational Need; 12 per cent had missed at least 25 days from school; 1 per cent had been permanently excluded; 9 per cent of those aged over 10 had been cautioned for or convicted of an offence; and 9 per cent achieved five GCSEs at grade A*–C (compared with 54 per cent of all children entered for the exam).

The Quality Protects programme sought to address this need to improve outcomes for looked after children but this policy has effectively been overtaken by the 'Every Child Matters' initiative which (endorsing the findings of the Social Exclusion Unit's 2003 report, *A Better Education for Children in Care*) openly states its aspiration to deal with these 'unacceptably poor' educational outcomes. Crucially, CA 2004, s. 52 amends CA 1989, s. 22(3) to provide, with effect from July 2005, that the general duty to promote the welfare of looked-after children includes a duty to promote their educational achievement. There is statutory guidance on how to implement the duty

(Statutory Guidance on the Duty on Local Authorities to Promote the Educational Achievement of Looked After Children Under s. 52 Children Act 2004).[24] Further, CA 2004, s. 10 (the duty on agencies to cooperate) and ss. 18 and 19 (dealing with the roles and responsibilities of the Director of Children's Services) all seek to contribute to an increased awareness of the need to address the problems of looked after children. Other changes include: the introduction of Personal Education Plans for each child (to cover achievement, development and educational needs, short-term targets, long-term plans and aspirations); the use of Independent Reviewing Officers to monitor the local authority's effectiveness in its role of 'corporate parent'; and Joint Area Reviews to examine just how schools are meeting the needs of looked after children. EA 2005, s. 106 specifically requires maintained schools to give priority to looked after children in respect of admission policies.

It should perhaps be particularly noted that social workers are expected to be 'effective advocates in dealing with school admissions, issues arising from behavioural problems and school discipline and school exclusions'.[25]

Other relevant developments include the provisions of the Children (Leaving Care) Act 2000, which support continued education and training. A local authority has a duty to a 'relevant' child (one aged 16 or 17 who has been looked after for some period after age 16 (CA 1989, s. 23A). Local authorities must provide advice, assistance and support. See further discussion in Chapter 10.

Special Educational Needs (SEN)

The concept of Special Educational Needs arose largely out of the Warnock report published in 1978,[26] which concluded that, where possible, children with learning difficulties should be educated in mainstream schools. The overriding principle was one of inclusivity. Whilst that general principle continues to be endorsed in Government policy,[27] there has been criticism of the excessive legalism of the statementing system, not least by Dame Mary Warnock herself.[28] It remains to be seen, therefore, whether the current emphasis on providing for learning difficulties in mainstream schools will remain. However it is dealt with, the question of SEN is a significant one in school education. At January 2005[29] some 1.2 million pupils were recorded as having special needs but no statement and 242,600 pupils had statements of SEN. Twice as many boys as girls have SEN.

Legislation provides a detailed structure for assessment of special educational need. The law is to be found in the EA 1996, as amended by SENDA 2001. LEAs are required to have regard to the provisions of the Special Needs Code of Practice[30] issued under EA 1996. It is an extensive document and is accompanied by an even longer 'SEN Toolkit' in 12 sections.[31] For educational purposes, SEN is likely to mean in practice that the child has needs in the areas of communication and interaction, cognition and learning, emotional and social behaviour, and sensory and/or physical needs.

The legal definition of Special Educational Needs is to be found in the Education Act 1996, s. 312. SEN arises where a child has a learning difficulty which calls for special educational provision to be made. A learning difficulty arises where:

s. 312(2)

> (a) he has a significantly greater difficulty in learning than the majority of children of his age,
>
> (b) he has a disability which either prevents or hinders him from making use of education facilities of a kind generally provided for children of his age in schools within the area of the local education authority, or
>
> (c) he is under compulsory school age and is, or would be if special educational provision were not made for him, likely to fall within paragraphs (a) or (b) when of or over that age.
>
> (EA 1996)

Section 312(4) then defines special educational provision as provision which is 'additional to, or otherwise different from' the educational provision made generally for children of the same age in maintained schools.

EA 1996, s. 323 and Sch. 26 provide for the assessment procedure, after which:

> If, in the light of an assessment under section 323 of any child's educational needs and of any representations made by the child's parent . . . it is necessary for the LEA to determine the special education provision which any learning difficulty he may have calls for, the authority shall make and maintain a statement of his special educational needs. (EA 1996, s. 324(1))

If the LEA decides not to make a statement, the parent may challenge that decision by way of appeal to the Special Educational Needs and Disability Tribunal. The Code anticipates that only a small minority of pupils with learning difficulties will need to have an SEN. However, it is this aspect of special needs which has been most litigated because where a statement is made, the LEA has an absolute duty to arrange the provisions detailed in it. The consequence is that parents have sought statements to obtain additional specialist help for their children but LEAs are, because of limited resources, not always keen to incur the expenditure required to meet those perceived needs.

SENDA 2001, s. 1, substituted a new and stronger version of EA 1996, s. 316 which replaced a presumption with a *duty* to place children with SEN in mainstream schools. Section 316(3) provides:

> If a statement is maintained under s. 324 for the child, he must be educated in a mainstream school unless that is incompatible with:
>
> (a) the wishes of his parent; or
>
> (b) the provision of efficient education for other children.

A parental wish for their child to be educated in mainstream education will rarely be refused. Conversely, if a parent would prefer her child to attend a special school and this would be considerably more expensive for the LEA, it may prove more difficult to achieve this outcome. In any school there should be a SEN coordinator (the 'SENCO') and each child with SEN will have his own individual education plan (**IEP**).

As is apparent from the title, SENDA 2001 also seeks to address the question of discrimination against disabled people where this issue arises in an educational context. The Act extends the provisions of the Disability Discrimination Act 1995 to schools and colleges. Schools must not discriminate against disabled pupils, or disabled applicants for places at the school, by treating them less favourably than a non-disabled pupil without justification; nor by failing to make a reasonable adjustment in the provision of education so as to prevent a student being placed at a substantial disadvantage. There is a code of practice and much valuable information available from the Disability Rights Commission.[32]

Education supervision orders

Prior to the Children Act 1989 it was possible for care orders to be made in respect of 'truancy'. This route into care was abolished by the Act and in its place the *Education Supervision Order* was introduced in s. 36:

s. 36

(1) On the application of any local education authority, the court may make an order putting the child with respect to whom the application is made under the supervision of a designated local education authority.

(2) In this Act "an education supervision order" means an order under subsection (1).

(3) A court may only make an education supervision order if it is satisfied that the child concerned is of compulsory school age and is not being properly educated.

(4) For the purposes of this section, a child is being properly educated only if he is receiving efficient full-time education suitable to his age, ability and aptitude and any special educational needs he may have.

(CA 1989)

In practice, failure to comply with a *school attendance order* (SAO) will be good evidence to meet the criteria. In some cases the criminal court dealing with proceedings against parents for failure to comply with an SAO may direct the LEA to apply for a supervision order. The LEA must consult the Social Services Department before applying for an order. An order cannot be made in respect of a child in care. An Education Welfare Officer will usually act as supervisor and it is his responsibility to 'advise, assist and befriend' the child. Additionally, he may give directions to the child and parents to ensure the child's proper education and it is an offence for parents not to comply with these directions. The order is of one year's duration but may be extended to a maximum of three years. In any event, it will end when the child reaches school leaving age (16) or if a care order is made. The LEA, parents and the child can apply for discharge of the order. The Children Act 1989 Guidance suggests that a supervision order will be more effective in circumstances where parents experience difficulty in exercising proper influence over children, but if parents are 'hostile', a prosecution may be the more appropriate course.[33]

Other orders: care, section 8 and parenting orders

It is unusual now but possible for a care order to be made where the threshold criteria are satisfied largely because of concerns relating to education. In *Re O (A Minor) (Care Proceedings: Education)* [1992] 4 All ER 905, the court was satisfied that the 'social, intellectual and educational development' of a 15-year-old had suffered harm significant enough to warrant a care order. In that case she had truanted regularly over three years and had only attended school on 28 days in the last year.

Where there is a dispute between parents about the education of their child, which it is not possible to resolve informally, or where it is an issue to be determined following separation, the court may make an order under CA 1989, s.8. Determination of the child's residence with one parent or the other may effectively settle which school is attended. In other cases, where the dispute centres on different religious preferences, a specific issue order that stipulates the school may be made.

The criteria for making a parenting order under s. 8 of the Crime and Disorder Act 1998, include where a person has been convicted for failure to comply with a school attendance order or failure to secure regular attendance at school. In those circumstances the court may make a parenting order which requires the child's parent(s) to attend for counselling and guidance, and under which the parent(s) can be required to ensure that the child attends school. Failure to comply with a parenting order, which is a civil order, is a criminal offence.[34]

Chapter summary

- ■ Significant statutory responsibilities towards children in education law are discharged by Education Welfare Officers. Social workers will be directly involved with education professionals when working in child protection, with children in need and looked after children, whose educational attainment has been poor. There is a duty to promote educational attainment of all children.

■ There is a large amount of statute law which governs the management of schools and pupils; and various 'initiatives' from the Department for Education and Skills. The basic framework is contained in the Education Act 1996.

■ The law requires all children to receive an education. Local education authorities are obliged to provide education and parents are obliged to ensure their children receive efficient full-time education. This may be provided at home.

■ If a child is registered at a school the parents must ensure his attendance. Failure to do so may result in a school attendance order.

■ Schools may exclude pupils in limited circumstances. It is possible to appeal against permanent exclusions and reinstatement of the pupil may be ordered.

■ All secondary school are obliged to provide sex education; parents have a right to withdraw their child from sex education lessons.

■ Special educational needs are defined in legislation. Most children with SEN will be educated in mainstream education with some additional support.

■ Education supervision orders may be made where a child is not being properly educated.

Exercises

1. Tommy is aged 12 and lives with his mother, Jean, and his two siblings. Tommy is coming to the end of his first term of secondary school. His attendance record is poor with 18 days' unauthorised absence out of a possible attendance of 52 days. Jean says that she can no longer control Tommy and, though she does try to encourage him to attend school, if he does not want to go she accepts there is nothing she can do.

   When Tommy is at school, he is frequently involved in fights with other boys, who accuse him (often with justification) of being dirty and smelly.

   Tommy's form teacher has prepared a brief report, saying that Tommy is not a malicious child but he is large for his age, frequently clumsy, occasionally aggressive to his peers, and significantly behind his expected age-related attainment in reading and writing.

   What action do you consider taking to improve Tommy's current educational underachievement?

2. You are the supervising social worker for Ruth, an 11-year-old girl who has been in the care of your local authority for three years since there was a finding of sexual abuse by her father. Until the care order was made, Ruth lived in a 'traveller' community.

   Ruth has been placed in long-term foster care. She displays significant behavioural problems and has already suffered two brief, fixed-term exclusions from her junior school. She is due to start secondary school next term.

   The foster carer has reported to you that she has visited the headteacher of the new school to discuss Ruth's impending transfer. The head was frankly hostile. She commented that 'kids in care always drag down the exam results' and 'these traveller children are a particular nuisance'.

What support could you provide to Ruth in these circumstances, especially to deal with the transition to secondary school? Do any Human Rights Act considerations arise?

Websites

DfES:
www.dfes.gov.uk

DfES:
www.everychildmatters.gov.uk

DfES:
www.teachernet.gov.uk

Ofsted:
www.ofsted.gov.uk

Disability Rights Commission:
www.drc-gb.org

Special Needs and Disability Tribunal:
www.sendist.gov.uk

Advisory Centre for Education:
www.ace-ed.org.uk

British Dyslexia Association:
www.bdadyslexia.org.uk

Education Otherwise:
www.education-otherwise.org

Independent Panel for Special Educational Advice:
www.ipsea.org.uk

Further reading

Ford, J., Hughes, M. and Ruebain, D. (2005) *Education Law and Practice*. Bristol: Jordan Publishing. (A practical, up-to-date general guide.)

Horner, N. and Krawcczyk, S. (2006) *Social Work in Education and Children's Service*. Exeter: Learning Matters. (Has a social work focus.)

Ruff, A. (2002) *Education Law: Text, Cases and Materials*. London: LexisNexis (A good introduction to education law.)

Additional detailed texts useful for reference:

Hyams, O. (2004) *Law of Education*. Bristol: Jordan Publishing.

McManus, R. (2004) *Education and the Courts*. Bristol: Jordan Publishing.

Ruff, A. *et al.* (2000) *Butterworths Education Law Handbook*. London: LexisNexis. (Sets out all the statutory material.)

Critical articles on aspects of education include:

Harris, N. (2005) 'Empowerment and State Education: Rights of Choice and Participation' 68(6) *Modern Law Review* pp. 925–57.

Harris, N. (2005) 'Education: Hard or Soft Lessons in Human Rights?' in C. Harvey (ed.) *Human Rights in the Community*. Oxford: Hart, p. 81.

Monk, D. (2002) 'Children's rights in education: making sense of contradictions' 14(1) *Child and Family Law Quarterly* p. 45.

Monk, D. (2004) 'Undermining Authority? Challenging school exclusions and the problems of "reinstatement" ' 16(1) *Child and Family Law Quarterly* pp. 87–102.

For an interesting survey of the views of parents towards truancy and control methods; see:

Dalziel, D. and Henthorne K. (2005) Parents/Carers' Attitudes Towards School Attendance, DfES Research Report, RR618.

Notes

1 'Every Child Matters: Change For Children – Statutory guidance on inter-agency co-operation to improve the wellbeing of children': Children's Trusts, p. 9, para 1.20.

2 I.e. children of compulsory school age: 5–16 (Education Act 1944, s. 35).

3 The LEA must secure schools sufficient in number, character and equipment to provide for all pupils the opportunity of appropriate education: Education Act 1996, s. 14. This duty has been extended by the Schools Standards and Framework Act 1998 to include provision for all 4-year-olds.

4 Formerly the Department for Education and Employment (DfEE).

5 DFES-1290-2005; and *A New Relationship With Schools – next steps*, 1288–2005.

6 The National Curriculum includes core and foundation subjects for which there are attainment targets related to key stages at which Standard Assessment Tasks are set and applies to state schools. Parents who educate at home are not bound to follow its terms, however it is arguable that not doing so could lead to disadvantage when their children sit formal examinations.

7 *Bath and North-East Somerset District Council* v. *Warman* [1999] ELR 81.

8 *The Guardian*, 27 December 2002.

9 See the Replacement Guidance for LEAs and Schools in place of Circulars 10/99 and 11/99 at www.dfes.gov.uk/behaviourandattendance; and the Education (School Attendance Targets) (England) Regulations 2005 (SI 2005/58).

10 *Pupil Absences in England: 2004/2005 (Revised)*, DfES, SFR 56/2005.

11 See N. Harris (2000) 'Education law: excluding the child' 12(1) *Education and the Law* p. 31.

12 For a general consideration of the place of 'rights' in regard to children, see J. Fortin (2003) *Children's Rights and the Developing Law* (2nd edn). Cambridge: Cambridge University Press.

13 The Education and Inspections Bill, February 2006.

14 October 2005.

15 White paper, p. 101.

16 EA 1997, s. 4, adding s. 550A to EA 1996. (See DfEs Circular 10/98 S550A EA 1996; 'The use of force to control or restrain pupils'; and Circular 9/94, 'The Education of Children with Emotional and Behavioural Difficulties, and for current Government proposals on discipline generally, see the white paper 'Higher Standards, Better Schools for All' and A. Steer (2005) *Report of the Practitioner's Group on School Behaviour and Discipline*. London: DfES.

17 A. Blair (2001) 'Home-school agreements: a legislative framework for soft control of parents' *Education Law Journal* p. 79.

18 See D. Dalziel and K. Henthorne (2005) *Parents/Carers' Attitudes Towards School Attendance*. DfES Research Report, RR618.

19 *Permanent and Fixed Period Exclusions from Schools and Exclusion Appeals in England 2003/04*, DfES SFR 23/2005, 23.06.05.

20 *Improving Behaviour and Attendance: Guidance on exclusion from schools and pupil referral units*, DfES, 0354/2004, October 2004.

21 DfEE Circular 0116/2000 'Sex and Relationship Education Guidance'. See also D. Monk (2001) 'New guidance/old problems: recent developments in sex education' 23(3) *Journal of Social Welfare and Family Law* pp. 271–91. See also DfES Circular 116/2000, 'Sex and Relationship Education' and the DfES leaflet, 'SER – Schools' Responsibilities', 30.06.04.

22 *Children looked after in England 2004/2005*, DfES, SFR 5/2005.

23 *Outcome Indicators for Looked After Children: Twelve Months to 30.09.2004*, SFR 19/2005, DfES, 28.04.05.

24 DfES, 2083-2005 DOC-EN. This replaces Local Authority Circular (2000) 13.

25 Statutory Guidance, p. 23. And see *Who Does What: How Social Workers and Carers Can Support the Education of Looked After Children*, DfES, May 2005.

26 Cmnd. 7212 (1978).

27 *Removing Barriers to Achievement: the Government's Strategy for Special Educational Needs*, DfES, 0117/2004.

28 'Special Educational Needs: A New Look' (2005) Philosophy of Education Society Journal *Impact*, No. 11. See the critical report of the Education and Skills Select Committee HC478 of July 2006, commenting that the 'SEN framework is struggling to remain fit for purpose'.

29 *Special Educational Needs in England, January 2005*, National Statistics, Statistical First Release 24/2005, 30.06.05.

30 DfES, 581/2001

31 DfES, 0558/2001. See in particular section 11, *The Role of Social Services*.

32 Code of Practice for Schools, www.drc-gb.org.

33 Department of Health (1991) 'The Children Act 1989 Guidance and Regulations', vol. 7, paras 3.07–3.08.

34 Parenting Orders are discussed further in Chapter 13.

13 Youth justice

Learning objectives

To develop an understanding of the following:

- The context in which youth justice operates, with emphasis on significant changes introduced by a raft of new legislation.
- The role of the social worker in the youth justice system.
- The structural framework for dealing with youth justice issues, including Youth Offending Teams and provision of youth justice services.
- The duty to prevent youth crime imposed on the police and local authorities.
- Orders, which are designed to help prevent youth offending, including parenting orders, child safety orders and child curfew schemes.
- The age of criminal offending and abolition of *doli incapax*.
- The role of the appropriate adult.
- The range of disposal options available to the court, i.e. reprimands and warnings; reparation orders; action plan orders; anti-social behaviour orders; curfew orders; supervision; sex offender orders; community orders; detention and training orders; parenting orders; and referral orders.

Youth justice in context

Developments and trends in youth justice

Youth justice is an area that has been characterised by swings in policy and practice between a 'welfare' and a 'justice' approach, each reflected in a variety of legislation. Youth justice has always been and continues to be a live political issue.[1]

Two major pieces of recent legislation – the Crime and Disorder Act 1998 (**CDA 1998**) and the Youth Justice and Criminal Evidence Act 1999 (**YJCEA** 1999) – encapsulate current policy. In addition, the Powers of Criminal Courts (Sentencing) Act 2000 (**PCC(S)A** 2000) now consolidates a number of provisions relating to orders initially introduced in the Crime and Disorder Act 1998. The Introductory Guide to the Crime and Disorder Act 1998 states that 'action must be taken quickly to nip youth offending in the bud'. This appears to contradict the view that most children and young people simply grow out of offending behaviour and should not be introduced to the formal youth justice system if avoidable. Whilst it is true that a disproportionate amount of crime is committed by young people (e.g. in 1984, 25 per cent of known offenders were under the age of 18), the Act appears to have been driven by a profound error of judgement in terms of identifying groups. There is a significant difference between juvenile nuisance and juvenile crime, which the Act does not reflect. Whilst the focus is on orders that respond to the very young and the perceived threat to society from children, between 1986 and 1994 the peak age of offending in fact rose from 15 to 18. Prior to the new legislation, the Audit Commission published a report in 1996 entitled 'Misspent Youth'.[2] In its preparation, the remit was to establish how efficiently, effectively and economically the youth justice system was working. The report identified a number of criticisms, including: delay in processing young offenders through the courts; little being done to address offending behaviour; lack of preventive work with potential offenders; and uncoordinated work between the agencies involved in youth justice. These deficiencies were taken up in the white paper published by the newly elected Labour Government, 'No More Excuses: A New Approach to Tackling Youth Crime in England and Wales' (1997)[3] and was followed by the Crime and Disorder Act 1998.

Two further factors, in addition to the Audit Commission report, may be traced as providing the impetus for the Act: the murder of Jamie Bulger and the arrival of the 'persistent offender'. Media interest in both issues suggested a social crisis in which children frequently and increasingly committed the most serious crimes against other children and marauding gangs of young people made our streets unsafe to walk around in. Research does not support either position as accurate.

The new reforms are based on the principles underlying the concept of restorative justice, explained in the white paper as follows:

Restoration: young offenders apologising to their victims and making amends for the harm they have done;
Re-integration: young offenders paying their debt to society, putting their crime behind them and rejoining the law-abiding community; and
Responsibility: young offenders – and their parents – facing the consequences of their offending behaviour and taking responsibility for preventing further offending.

The Crime and Disorder Act 1998 enmeshes civil and criminal law (evident also in the Protection from Harassment Act 1997), a feature which is particularly important with regard to disposal and sentencing. For example, the anti-social behaviour order is a civil order made in civil court but, if breached, criminal sanctions may follow. This poses an inherent contradiction in that an order which is granted on satisfaction of the civil standard of proof, balance of probabilities, carries a criminal sanction if breached, whereas criminal sanctions would ordinarily follow only if the court had initially been satisfied beyond reasonable doubt. Criticism has also been levied at the Act to the effect that it criminalises certain behaviour in children before the age of criminal responsibility and that it reintroduces the possibility of making civil care orders for criminal acts, contrary to the spirit of the Children Act 1989.

■ Youth justice and 'Every Child Matters'

'Every Child Matters' (2003) set out five key outcomes for children's well-being, with an emphasis on early intervention and prevention and coordinated services. Criminal justice agencies are envisaged as having a role in securing the five outcomes for children and young people. The Children Act 2004 provided legal underpinning to the structural changes required for the delivery of child care services. The Act names police authorities, chief constables, probation boards and YOTs in the s. 10 duty to cooperate to improve well-being of children in the area. In addition, Local Safeguarding Children Boards will include chief constables, probation boards, YOTs and governors to secure training centres in their membership. The implications of the 'Every Child Matters' programme are addressed in a number of documents specific to particular services, including, 'Every Child Matters: Change for Children in the Criminal Justice System (2004). It notes that the key focus of the criminal justice system is on two of the outcomes:

- Making a positive contribution. A key element of this is encouraging young people to choose to engage in law-abiding and positive behaviour.
- Staying safe. Ensuring children and young people are safe from crime, exploitation, bullying, discrimination and violence is one of the major responsibilities of the criminal justice system.

In addition, 'Youth Justice – the Next Steps' (2003) was published as a companion document to 'Every Child Matters', and set out a range of possible reforms to develop the youth justice system. Responses to consultation on this document and the governments proposals on youth justice are set out in Annex B to 'Every Child matters – Next Steps'.

Many of the proposals will require legislation and a Youth Justice Bill is anticipated. Key proposals are:

- To retain the existing statutory framework on reprimands and final warnings because 'it provides speed, simplicity and effective sanctions for failure to comply'.
- Legislation will clarify that the main purpose of a sentence imposed by a court on conviction of a criminal offence by a juvenile should be to prevent their further offending.

- Preventing anti-social behaviour will be included in the duties of the Youth Justice Board and youth offending teams.

- Guidance will be issued to promote the fuller use of parenting measures, including Family Group Conferencing and family therapy, by youth justice agencies.

- A Young Defendant's Pack will be developed to help young people and their parents or carers understand and prepare for their court experience.

- Guidance on pre-sentence reports will be issued to ensure they are consistently well targeted and provide the information courts need.

- Proposals to encourage the use of remand fostering.

- Legislation will provide that 17-year-olds are to be treated as juveniles for the purposes of remand and bail.

- Legislation to introduce a new generic juvenile community sentence with a wide menu of interventions, known as a 'juvenile rehabilitation order'.

- Legislation to establish a new intensive supervision and surveillance order as a robust alternative to custody for the more serious or persistent offenders.

In 2005 the Government published a green paper, 'Youth Matters', outlining the future direction of policy on supporting young people. This has a much broader remit than youth justice. The focus is on engaging young people in positive activities; encouraging more volunteering and community involvement by young people; providing better information, advice and guidance for young people; and providing intensive personalised support for young people with serious problems or in trouble. A response to the green paper, 'Youth Matters: Next Steps' was published in March 2006.

■ Social worker's role in youth justice

In youth justice terms a 'child' is defined as under the age of 14 and a 'young person' as 14–17 years inclusive (CDA 1998, s. 117). The term 'juvenile' is used in this chapter to include children and young persons unless it is necessary to specify child or young person.

There are a variety of ways in which a social worker may be involved with youth justice issues. For example:

- Social workers are among the groups of professionals who will be represented on youth offending teams.

- Social workers may be the designated responsible officer under a child safety order and provide supervision of community sentences.

- Social workers frequently act as the appropriate adult under the Police and Criminal Evidence Act 1984 during police interviews of young people.

- Writing reports and attending court to present reports as an 'officer of the court'.[4]

- The local authority will be notified by the police if the decision is taken to prosecute a young person.

■ The local authority must provide support for a child or young person await-ing trial or disposal.

■ Social workers may be involved with the families of prisoners and have direct responsibility for children of prisoners, taking decisions about their long-term welfare and interim placement for the duration of the prison sentence.

■ Under the Children Act 1989 the local authority has a responsibility to reduce the need to bring criminal proceedings against children in its area.[5]

■ Research indicates that children living away from home are a particularly vul-nerable group and may come into contact with the criminal justice system. Social workers have responsibilities towards children who have left care under the Children (Leaving Care) Act 2000.

■ Social workers working in residential establishments, which provide secure and non-secure accommodation, may be responsible for young people who are placed on remand until their criminal trial takes place.

■ The case of *R (Howard League)* v. *Secretary of State for the Home Department* [2002] EWHC 2497 (Admin) confirms that provisions of the Children Act 1989 apply to those under 18 in prison establishments. In this judicial review application brought by the Howard League for Penal Reform the court made a declaration that the statement that the Children Act 1989 did not apply to people under the age of 18 in prison establishments (contained in Prison Service Order No. 4950) was wrong in law. As a result it will be necessary for social services departments to become more involved in meeting the needs of children in custody. Specifically, the judgment confirms that the duty to inves-tigate under CA, s. 47 and the duty to support children in need under CA, s. 17 apply to children detained in prisons. Munby J in the High Court stated that the case:

. . . on the face of it ought to shock the conscience of every citizen . . . if it really be the case that children are still being subjected to the degrading, offen-sive and totally unacceptable treatment described and excoriated by the chief inspector . . . then it can only be a matter of time . . . before an action is brought under the Human Rights Act 1998.

The changes introduced by the Crime and Disorder Act 1998 may be grouped into three areas:

■ institutional changes to the criminal justice system (Part III);

■ measures for the prevention of crime and disorder (Part I);

■ reform of the options for dealing with young offenders (Part IV).[6]

■ Institutional changes

The Crime and Disorder Act 1998 imposes responsibilities on local authorities as cor-porate bodies, not on the Social Services Department, as might have been expected. It follows that all local authorities, including district, county, metropolitan and unitary authorities will have responsibilities under the Act. The implications of the Act are central to each authority's community safety strategy,[7] on which audits take place. Responsibilities fall into three areas:

1. to create *youth offender teams* (YOTs);
2. to develop *youth justice plans;*
3. to provide and coordinate *youth justice services.*

Within the youth justice system, all individuals and organisations must have regard to the aim of preventing offending set out in s. 37:

s. 37

(1) It shall be the principal aim of the youth justice system to prevent offending by children and young persons.
(2) In addition to any other duty to which they are subject, it shall be the duty of all persons and bodies carrying out functions in relation to the youth justice system to have regard to that aim.

(CDA 1998)

Section 5 imposes a responsibility on the local authority and the police to create crime and disorder reduction strategies in their area; s. 6 calls on the local authority and the police to implement the strategy. Prior to formulation of the strategy a crime and disorder audit will take place, which reviews levels and patterns of crime and disorder.

Youth Offending Teams

Youth Offending Teams (YOTs), required by CDA 1998, s. 39 have a multi-agency membership and are intended to provide the opportunity for agencies to work in partnership. Certain agencies are specified and must participate but others may be invited at discretion, e.g. housing, justice's clerks. They will consist of police, social workers, probation officers and representatives from education and health, at the very least.

Section 115 is an important provision relating to sharing information. It provides that:

s. 115

(1) Any person who, apart from this subsection, would not have power to disclose information –
     (a) to a relevant authority; or
     (b) to a person acting on behalf of such an authority,
shall have power to do so in any case where the disclosure is necessary or expedient for the purposes of any provision of this Act.

(CDA 1998)

A relevant authority includes the police, local authorities, probation and health authorities. This is a wide-ranging provision and, in practice, agencies in each area are likely to produce information-sharing protocols. It is perhaps surprising that the Prison Service was not included in the list of those bodies that are required to share information with YOTs.

Section 38 stipulates that there must be at least one YOT for each county council or unitary area. The main function of the team is to provide youth justice services in the framework of the youth justice plan.[8]

Youth justice plan

Each Social Services Department must produce a youth justice plan every year (CDA 1998, s. 40) with its strategy and local targets designed to meet national objectives. This remains a separate requirement from the statutory children and young people's plans required by the Children Act 2004.

Youth justice services

Local authorities must ensure youth justice services are available. Youth justice services may include:

- provision of appropriate adults when children and young persons are detained or questioned by the police;
- assessment of children and young persons for rehabilitation programmes to prevent reoffending, where the young person receives a reprimand or final warning;
- provision of support for children and young persons remanded or committed on bail awaiting trial or sentence;
- placement in local authority accommodation when remanded or committed to the care of the local authority;
- provision of court reports for criminal proceedings;
- allocation of responsible officers for parenting orders, child safety orders, reparation orders and action plan orders;
- supervision for young persons sentenced to supervision, community rehabilitation, community punishment/community punishment and rehabilitation or orders;
- supervision of children and young persons sentenced to detention and training orders or supervision orders;
- post-release supervision;
- any other functions assigned in the youth justice plan.

Youth Justice Board

A National Youth Justice Board has been established under CDA 1998, s. 41 and Sch. 2. The Board is based in the Home Office, comprising 10 or 12 individuals representing a wide-ranging membership. The role of the Board is to oversee the delivery of youth justice services and includes advising the Home Secretary on National Standards, promoting and disseminating good practice. The Board publishes an annual report and other materials and its website is a useful source of information.[9]

Prevention of youth crime

Section 17 of the CDA 1998 imposes a duty on local authorities and police authorities in exercising their various functions to consider the crime and disorder implications and the need to do all they reasonably can to prevent crime and disorder in their area. It is questionable whether this actually adds anything to the existing provisions contained in the Children Act 1989, Sch. 2, para. 7, which requires the local authority (though in practice this has often been confined to social services) to take steps to reduce the need to bring criminal proceedings against children in its area.

Particular provisions, which are relevant to prevention of youth crime, are contained in Part I of the CDA 1998 and include:

- child curfew schemes – a curfew may be set for a particular area and the police have powers to return home any child who is in breach of the curfew;
- local authority duty of investigation;
- child safety orders – available for children under the age of 10 who are at risk of becoming involved in crime or already involved in anti-social or criminal behaviour;
- parenting orders – an order designed to reinforce parental responsibility;
- anti-social behaviour orders to protect people from harassment, alarm or distress.

▪ Child curfew schemes

s. 14

> A local authority may make a scheme . . . if . . . the authority considers it necessary to do so for the purpose of maintaining order.
>
> (CDA 1998)

The use of the word 'may' suggests that this is a permissive rather than a mandatory option for the local authority. A local authority can develop a child curfew scheme, following a requirement to consult with the police and other local bodies.

It must then be submitted to the Secretary of State and, if confirmed, the local authority is then free to implement the child curfew scheme. It is obliged to publicise the scheme by posting the notice in a conspicuous place and other ways the authority views as appropriate (CDA 1998, s. 14(7)).

A curfew scheme may be made for a specified period up to 90 days. It is a ban on children of specified ages (under 10) being in a public place within a specified area, during specified hours within the period from 9.00 p.m. until 6.00 a.m. Different time limits may be set for different ages of children: e.g. 10.00 p.m. may be considered appropriate for 9-year-olds (CDA 1998, s. 14(6)). The scheme applies to all children of the specified age unless they are under the effective control of a responsible person over the age of 18. The objective of the order is to prevent criminal tendencies from developing. It may be argued that this is an extreme type of order to be applied to children under the age of 10 when there is little evidence that that age group pose a significant threat to society and, until abolition of *doli incapax,* were not considered capable of committing a criminal offence. Application of a blanket scheme fails to recognise that there may be legitimate reasons for a young child to be in breach of the curfew. The most obvious example is where a child is effectively escaping from violent or abusive behaviour in their home.

The order formalises the surveillance role of the police and is unlikely to promote positive relations between children and the police. A police officer is required to take a child in breach of a curfew to his or her home, unless he has reasonable cause to believe that the child would, if removed to that place, be likely to suffer significant harm (CDA 1998, s. 15(3)). If there is no responsible adult at home, it is expected that the child will be taken to the police station temporarily.

Where a child has been found unsupervised during the operation of a curfew, the police will inform the local authority (s. 15(2)), who must then visit the child's family within 48 hours to determine whether there is any need for intervention or support (s. 15(4)). The Children Act 1989 is amended to incorporate this requirement. A new provision is inserted regarding local authority investigations. Section 15 of the Crime and Disorder Act 1998 amends s. 47 of the Children Act 1989, introducing the following provisions:

s. 47

(iii) has contravened a ban imposed by a curfew notice. . .
and
. . . the inquiries shall be commenced as soon as practicable and, in any event, within 48 hours of the authority receiving the information.

(CA 1989, as amended)

Contravention of a ban therefore becomes an additional trigger in the s. 47 criteria for investigation. In contrast to the other aspects of s. 47, there is a specific time period for the investigation written into the Act (48 hours); however, there is no enforcement provision should a local authority fail to meet this requirement.

Significantly, in this new limb of s. 47 there is also no reference to risk of harm as justification for state investigation. It is clear, therefore, that failure to comply with a curfew notice has the potential to lead to much greater state intervention.

Consider how a police officer might react on finding the following children in breach of a curfew order set in respect of children aged between 5 and 10 years old from 9 p.m.

- John, aged 9, is out with a group of four boys of similar ages. All but John run out of sight when the police officer approaches. John has a spray paint can in his pocket and fresh paint on his hands.

- Lucy, aged 7, is with her 13-year-old sister, on their way to fetch fish and chips. Their mother gave them the money to fetch a takeaway because she did not have time to cook any tea and has now gone out with her boyfriend for 'a quick drink'.

- Jane and Susan, sisters aged 8 and 9, are walking to their grandmother's house which is about half a mile away from their home. They have to walk past the local shopping centre, where youths have a tendency to congregate in the evening. It is 10.30 p.m. and they are concerned that they cannot wake their mother who is diabetic.

Research has evaluated the experience of other countries' use of curfews for children and young people. There is little evidence to suggest that curfews are effective in reducing the rate of juvenile crime and a further concern arises in that experience in the United States suggests that curfews have been used in a discriminatory way to target children from ethnic minorities. In addition, the Joint Committee on Human Rights, in its first report, has expressed a concern over the human rights implications of child curfew schemes. The Criminal Justice and Police Act 2001 extends the scheme to those under 16 and allows the police as well as the local authority to establish schemes (ss. 48–49) though there has been limited take up of curfew scemes.

■ Anti-social Behaviour Act 2003

The Anti Social Behaviour Act 2003 (ASBA 2003) introduced further powers which have a similar aim to curfew powers. Section 30 provides for designation of an area where the behaviour of young people has been problematic. The grounds are:

s. 30(1)

(a) that any members of the public have been intimidated, harassed, alarmed or distressed as a result of the presence or behaviour of groups of two or more persons in public places in any locality in his police area, and

(b) that anti-social behaviour is a significant and persistent problem in the relevant locality.

(ASBA 2003)

The police have the power to designate an area but are required to obtain the consent of the local authority. The designation must be publicised and can be of up to six months' duration. Designation triggers two further powers: dispersal and removal to place of residence. A police officer can order a group to 'disperse' in a designated area if he has reasonable grounds to believe their presence has resulted or is likely to result in any member of the public being 'intimidated, alarmed or distressed' (s. 30(3)). It then becomes an offence for a person to knowingly contravene that order. The police also have the power to remove a person, believed to be under 16, from a designated area, between the hours of 9 p.m. and 6 a.m. and take them to their place of residence. The power applies only where the child or young person is not under the effective control of a parent or adult and would not apply where the police officer has reasonable grounds to believe that if removed to the place of residence the child would 'be likely to suffer significant harm' (s. 30(6)).

■ Child safety order

Child safety orders (CDA 1998, ss. 11–13) tackle an issue in the family proceedings court, which would appear to be part of the criminal law. There is an overlap in the remit of the order with emergency protection orders and interim supervision orders. The child safety order is made in the family proceedings court on the application of a local authority (with social services responsibilities) in respect of a child under 10. As applications for child safety orders are family proceedings, the welfare of the child will be paramount in these proceedings (i.e. the welfare test of the Children Act 1989 applies). Other aspects of the Children Act 1989 do not, however, apply. A children's guardian will not be appointed as these are not specified proceedings under CA s. 41, nor will the child receive separate legal representation. An order can be made for a child less than 10 years of age where one of the following conditions applies:

s. 11(3)

(a) the child has committed an act which, if he had been aged 10 or over, would have constituted an offence;
(b) a child safety order is necessary for the purpose of preventing the commission of an Act as mentioned in paragraph (a) above;
(c) the child has contravened a ban imposed by a curfew notice;
(d) the child has acted in a way that caused or was likely to cause harassment, alarm or distress to one or more persons not of the same household as himself.

(CDA 1998)

There are procedural requirements that the court must take into account before making an order. These are explained in the Introductory Guide:

before a court makes a child safety order it will be required to obtain and consider information about the person's family circumstances; explain the effect of the order, the requirements imposed and the consequences which may follow if the child fails to comply with those requirements; and avoid, as far as practicable, any potential conflict with a parent's religious beliefs and any interference with the child's attendance at school.

The order lasts for a maximum of 12 months (it was originally only three months but s. 60 of the Children Act 2004 extends the maximum duration). The child is placed under the supervision of a responsible officer and is required to comply with specified requirements. The requirements are any: 'which the court considers desirable in the interests of – (a) securing that the child receives appropriate care, protection and support and is subject to proper control; or (b) preventing any repetition of the kind of behaviour which led to the child safety order being made'. Examples of requirements that may be set are: preventing the child being in certain places, e.g. a shopping centre; preventing the child associating with certain children; or requiring involvement in a particular activity, such as a homework club. The order can require the child to be home at a certain time and may in effect provide a curfew for a specific child.[10] A responsible officer may be a member of the YOT or may be a social worker in the Social Services Department. Before the court can make an order, s. 12 sets out a number of preliminary requirements. The court must obtain and consider information about the child's family circumstances and likely effect of an order on those circumstances. The court must explain to the parents, in ordinary language, the effect of the order and any requirements, the consequences of non-compliance and the court power to review the order. In considering any requirements to be imposed, the court must avoid any that would conflict with the parent's religious beliefs or interfere with school attendance.

Concern has been raised that the use of child safety orders could criminalise children before the age of criminal responsibility and introduce them at an early stage into the youth justice and care systems.[11]

The child safety order can be varied, or it may be discharged on application of the parent or responsible officer or if the child fails to comply with any requirements of the order. If the child fails to comply with the order the court can make a parenting order. The Children Act 2004 removed the power of the court to make a care order on breach of a child safety order. This provision had been widely criticised as introducing a further route into care which was not based on satisfaction of the threshold criteria.

■ Parenting order

The parenting order is introduced by s. 8 of the Crime and Disorder Act 1998. It is a free-standing order, which the court can make in conjunction with a range of other orders. It is an order designed to help and support parents or guardians in addressing their child's anti-social or offending behaviour. The order can be made in civil proceedings in the family proceedings court or other civil work of the magistrates' court, or in criminal courts including the youth court, adult magistrates' court and Crown Court. Section 8 provides that the order may be made in the following circumstances:

s. 8(1)

. . . where in any court proceedings –
(a) a child safety order is made in respect of a child;
(b) an anti-social behaviour order or sex offender order is made in respect of a child or young person;
(c) a child or young person is convicted of an offence; or
(d) a person is convicted of an offence under section 443 or section 444 of the Education Act 1996.

(CDA 1998)

Section 443 of the Education Act 1996 is the offence of failing to comply with a school attendance order and s. 444 is the offence of failing to secure regular attendance at school of a registered pupil.

There are two aspects to the order:

1. Compulsory attendance by the parents at counselling or guidance sessions.
2. The order may contain specific requirements, which the parent must comply with. This aspect of the order may last for up to a year.

The effect of the parenting order is to require parents to attend counselling or guidance sessions once a week for up to 12 weeks. The court is obviously limited to making orders where such facilities are available. It may include other requirements, e.g. specific to that child's behaviour, and these requirements may extend for up to 12 months. Examples include the parent ensuring that the child avoids visiting certain areas unsupervised, is at home during certain hours, or attends certain extra-curricular activities. Parents may be subject to a fine or probation order if they fail to comply with requirements in a parenting order. A responsible officer will be appointed by the court to ensure the order is carried out effectively. There is a tension between the objectives of an order that purports to provide support to parents but is formally enforceable. It also seems to imply that children offend because their parents have not acted responsibly, when often it is clearly not the case. The order may present a further burden on a dysfunctional family, which invites breach of the order.

The High Court had the opportunity to consider parenting orders in the case of *R (M)* v. *Inner London Crown Court* [2003] EWHC 310 (Admin) and confirmed that parenting orders comply with the Human Rights Act. The facts were that a mother appealed against the making of a parenting order and a compensation order, following conviction of her 13-year-old daughter for wounding. The court stated that the decision whether to make a parenting order was an exercise of judgment, not a finding of fact, and there was no applicable guidance for magistrates to follow. In response to the mothers claim that the order breached her Art. 8 rights, the court found that there was no breach. It applied the test of proportionality and noted that there is a pressing social need to address problems of juvenile crime, parenting orders were introduced to confront juvenile crime, and such orders are necessary in a democratic society. The decision to make the order in this particular case had, however, been irrational and it was quashed.

■ Parenting contracts

The Anti-social Behaviour Act 2003 has made it possible for parents to voluntarily enter into parenting contracts, in specified circumstances. Where a child has been excluded from school or failed to attend school regularly, or the child has been referred to a YOT and a member of the team has reason to believe the child has engaged or is likely to engage in criminal conduct or anti-social behaviour, schools, local authorities and YOTs may enter into a parenting contract with parents. The parenting contract contains an agreement from the parent to comply with the contract requirements for a specified period and a commitment from the school, LA or YOT to support the parent to help him comply with the requirements. If a parent refuses to enter into a parenting contract or breaches its terms then it is likely that a parenting order would be sought.

■ Removal of truants

Section 16 (CDA 1998) allows the police to remove truants from a public place to premises that have been designated to receive them (e.g. a school or local authority office), or the school from which they are absent. This provision relates to children and young persons of compulsory school age. The provision was suggested by the Schools Exclusion Unit. Its justification is the suggestion that truanting children in public places may be tempted to commit crimes or anti-social behaviour.

■ Anti-social behaviour orders

The anti-social behaviour order (**ASBO**) is established under s. 1 of the Crime and Disorder Act 1998. It is considered in this section because, although it is a court order responding to anti-social behaviour, it is an order made in the civil court rather than a disposal in the youth court, and is intended to prevent further anti-social behaviour. It may be made in respect of a child over the age of 10 or an adult. The responsible authority, i.e. the police or district council in consultation with each other; registered social landlords (housing associations); housing action trusts and British Transport Police, may apply for the ASBO. In either case the relevant Social Services Department and the YOT must also have been consulted. It is also possible for magistrates to make an ASBO following conviction of a criminal offence.

The order may be made in respect of an individual or a group, e.g. a family. The Introductory Guide to the Act states: 'it is intended that the order will be targeted at criminal or sub-criminal behaviour, not minor disputes between neighbours, or matters which can be dealt with effectively under existing legislation'. Between 2000 and 2003, 52 per cent of all ASBOs were imposed on 10–17 year olds.

This new order is something of a hybrid order, being made in civil proceedings on the balance of probabilities, yet breach of the order being a criminal offence (carrying a maximum penalty of five years' imprisonment) and the guidance referring to criminal or sub-criminal behaviour. A House of Lords ruling, *R (McCann)* v. *Crown Court at Manchester; Clingham* v. *Kensington and Chelsea Royal Borough* [2002] UKHL 39, has confirmed that anti-social behaviour order proceedings are civil. It follows that they cannot be challenged under the fair trial provisions of the Human Rights Act 1998 (ECHR, Art. 6(2) and 6(3)) and are not subject to the strict rules of evidence applied in criminal cases. In this case police officers gave evidence of allegations of anti-social behaviour made by members of the public who were too frightened to give evidence or could not be identified.

The House of Lords also considered the standard of proof to be applied in ASBO applications. Precedents exist for civil standard of proof, the balance of probabilities, to be heightened in cases where the matters alleged have a particularly serious bearing on the reputation of the person. This heightened standard of proof, which equates to the criminal standard of proof, is to apply in ASBO applications when deciding whether the defendant acted in an anti-social way.

Anti-social behaviour is not defined in the CDA 1998; however, guidance[12] refers to harassment, alarm and distress. These terms are very similar to those employed in the Protection from Harassment Act 1997. It is designed to be a lengthy order, for not less than two years' duration (CDA 1998, s. 1(7)). It is possible to attach specific prohibitions to the order, necessary for the purposes of protecting people in the local government area from anti-social acts by the defendant, for example not entering a particular shop.

The grounds for an application for an anti-social behaviour order are:

s. 1(1)

(a) that the person has acted, . . . in an anti-social manner, that is to say, in a manner that caused or was likely to cause harassment, alarm or distress to one or more persons not of the same household as himself; and

(b) that such an order is necessary to protect persons in the local government area in which the harassment, alarm or distress was caused or was likely to be caused from further anti-social acts by him;

(CDA 1998)

For example, an ASBO might be appropriate in the following cases.

■ Three men with learning disabilities live together in a terraced house and attend a nearby day centre. Regularly, when they walk home two youths aged 15 and 17 shout abuse at them, leave litter on their doorstep and try to trip them up.

■ A man in his early thirties drives around very slowly following groups of children walking to and from school, staring at them and occasionally pulling up in front of them. He is known to the police but has not committed any criminal offence. Many parents have started walking with older children to school as the children are becoming frightened of this man.

■ A 20-year-old man has committed acts of physical and financial abuse of his grandmother and shown threatening behaviour towards her and other elderly residents in a sheltered housing scheme.

The case of *R (M)* v. *Sheffield Magistrates' Court* [2004] EWHC 1830 (Admin) deals with the situation where the child who is subject of an application for an ASBO is in care and the Social Services Authority are the applicant. The facts of the case are set out in full, as the case illustrates a range of youth justice issues.

The claimant (M) sought judicial review of the imposition of an interim anti-social behaviour order (ASBO) against him. M was made subject to a care order at the age of 6 under the Children Act 1989, s. 31. Parental responsibility was shared by the local authority and M's mother. M lived in a series of residential care homes, but was ultimately placed temporarily with his maternal grandmother. An ASBO panel held a conference, which concluded that anti-social behaviour involving M had been proved. Following a report from social services, which suggested that M might be suffering from a disability and that an ASBO would not solve his problems, the panel nevertheless agreed that an ASBO was necessary. Following allegations that he had been involved in an attempt to steal a motor vehicle, the magistrates' court placed M on an intensive supervision and surveillance programme (**ISSP**) attached to a supervision order. The local authority issued a summons, which alleged that M had behaved in an anti-social manner, and the orders were revoked following M's conviction of two offences and breaching the conditions of the order. At the same time, M was made subject to a curfew order and sentenced to a further ISSP programme. The application for an ASBO was made by the local authority. M's social worker declined to a be a witness for M, as he wished to be a witness for his employer the local authority. M was unable to call anybody from the local authority as a witness discharging parental responsibility on his behalf. The local authority was granted a without notice interim ASBO and M was granted permission to apply for judicial review.

The issues for the court were: (1) how the interests of a child in care could be protected when the authority responsible for a child's care made an application for an ASBO against the child; (2) whether it had been appropriate to apply for an interim ASBO.

The court ruled that a conflict of interest would arise when a local authority, having parental responsibility for a child under the 1989 Act, exercised its power under the Crime and Disorder Act 1998 to apply for an ASBO. The conflict had prejudiced M, but had not precluded the authority from making an application under the 1998 Act against a child in its care. The 1989 Act contemplated the local authority remaining empowered to act to fulfil its duty to the public. The problem areas were as follows:

■ a decision to apply for an ASBO was a decision within s. 22(4) of the 1989 Act, which required the authority to ascertain the wishes and feelings of the child and any person having parental responsibility for that child. In this case the wishes and feelings of M, his grandmother and his social workers had not been obtained;

■ the relevant social worker should not participate in the decision to apply for an ASBO;

■ the social services/workers for the authority should be available to assist and be witnesses at court, if requested, for the child in question;

■ no court should, save in exceptional circumstances, make an order against a child in care, without someone from the social services who could speak to the issue;

■ once a decision had been taken to apply for an ASBO there should be no contact between the ASBO team and social services without the consent of the child's legal representative.

As to the interim ASBO, the court stated that the order should not have been granted without notice and where there was no-one present from social services. The ASBO should have had regard to the existing ISSP and prevailing curfew. There could be no further progress in the ASBO application until the steps above had been completed. In all the circumstances, and as the interim order had expired, no relief was necessary.

In addition to the use of ASBOs, 'acceptable behaviour contracts' have been introduced, as a preliminary stage. The young person meets with the police and local authority housing department and is asked to sign a contract agreeing not to engage in any further anti-social behaviour. A copy of the contract will be forwarded to the YOT, the young person and his parents. The contract would not stand as legally enforceable but if breached could be provided as evidence in a subsequent application for an ASBO.

Individual Support Orders are introduced under ss. 322–323 of the Criminal Justice Act 2003 to provide support to young people subject to ASBOs in the interests of preventing any repetition of the kind of behaviour which led to the making of the ASBO. The orders will run by YOTs and may require the young person to take part in activities and education.

Offending and orders

However commendable the aims of orders that seek to prevent young people engaging in criminal behaviour, there will inevitably be those who do commit offences, are discovered by the police and a decision taken to prosecute their behaviour. The remainder of this chapter will consider in chronological order the stages in the youth justice system, culminating in discussion of the range of disposal orders, some of which were introduced by the CDA 1998 (mostly consolidated into PCC(S)A 2000).

At this point it is useful to remember that Art. 37 of the United Nations Convention on the Rights of the Child states that the 'arrest, detention or imprisonment of the child . . . shall be used only as a measure of last resort and for the shortest appropriate time' and to evaluate the following provisions of the youth justice system in the light of that Article.

■ Offending behaviour

The age of criminal responsibility in England and Wales is 10.[13] Under that age there is an irrebuttable presumption that a child cannot be guilty of an offence.[14] From that age a child is presumed capable of committing and being held responsible for a criminal act. The Crime and Disorder Act 1998 abolishes the *doli incapax* (incapable of evil) rule for those aged 10–14 years. This rule covers the age at which criminal responsibility is acquired. For those aged under 10 the *doli incapax* rule applies and a child is considered incapable of evil and is immune from prosecution. For those aged 10–14 before the Crime and Disorder Act 1998, the *doli incapax* rule applied but was a rebuttable presumption. The prosecution therefore had to prove that the child appreciated the seriousness of his wrongdoing. This more flexible approach allowed for different levels of maturity within that age band. All children will now acquire criminal responsibility at the age of 10. This is arguably at odds with the approach elsewhere of the law relating to children that they develop autonomy and responsibility gradually and at different rates, as the familiar phrase 'considered in the light of his age and understanding' suggests. This is significantly lower than most other European countries. For example, it is 12 in Greece, 13 in France, 14 in Germany, 16 in Spain and 18 in Belgium.

There are no offences that are specific to juveniles. A person aged between 10 and 17 may be charged with any of the offences for which an adult may be charged. In addition, the process for dealing with juveniles charged with a criminal offence is broadly the same as for an adult, with a few notable differences, which are discussed below. Chapter 18 deals with adult offenders in detail.

One of the main aims of the youth justice reforms, which culminated in the Crime and Disorder Act 1998, was to speed up the process of dealing with young offenders within the criminal justice system. Reducing delays is particularly important where the young person is identified as a persistent offender. A target of halving the time from arrest to sentence for persistent young offenders by 2002 was included in the Government manifesto. The overall target for 2000 was for 65 per cent of cases to reach sentence within 71 days. The average time in 1996 was 142 days.[15] In support of this target, guidelines on the length of time each stage of the youth justice process should take have been set:

- arrest to charge – 2 days;
- charge to the first appearance – 7 days;
- first appearance to start of trial – 28 days;
- verdict to sentence – 14 days.[16]

These time periods are considerably shorter than those contained in the Prosecution of Offenders (Youth Courts Time Limits) Regulations 1999.[17]

Persistent young offender is defined as follows:

> . . . a persistent young offender is a young person aged 10–17 who has been sentenced by a criminal court in the UK on three or more separate occasions for one or more recordable Offences, and within three years of the last sentencing occasion is subsequently arrested or has an information laid against them for a further recordable offence.[18]

The Court of Appeal, however, in *R v. C (A Juvenile) (Persistent Offender)* (2000) *The Times*, 11 October, held that whether a person was a persistent offender for the purposes of making a detention and training order under CDA 1998, s. 73(2) was a matter of fact in each case and was not defined by the Government circular. In this case the appellant 'had burgled and had then done it again' and that behaviour demonstrated a sufficient degree of persistence.

■ Arrest and charge

If a juvenile is arrested, he should not be detained in a police cell unless there is no other secure accommodation available and the custody officer believes that it is not practical to supervise the child unless he is in a cell, or that the child will be more comfortable in a cell than any other secure accommodation at the station (PACE 1984, Code of Practice C, para. 8.8). The juvenile should not come ino contact with adult suspects.

If the juvenile is charged with an offence, the custody officer will have to consider the question of bail. If police bail is refused the child must be remanded to appear before the youth court at the earliest opportunity. Until then, the child should be accommodated by the local authority (PACE 1984, s. 38(6)). If the child is over the age of 12 this may be secure accommodation. The Children and Young Persons Act 1969 (CYPA 1969), s. 23 provides that the court shall remand a child committed for trial or sentence to the local authority. Under CDA 1998, s. 97 the court can make the remand for 12–16-year-olds direct to secure accommodation, provided the criteria in CYPA 1969, s. 23(5) are satisfied. Section 67(1) of the Criminal Justice Act 1967 provides for the period spent in custody while waiting for trial sentence to be taken into account when calculating a custodial sentence. To apply to a juvenile, the remand must have been in accommodation provided for the purpose of restricting liberty. In *R v. Secretary of State for the Home Department, ex parte A* [2000] 2 AC 276, the House of Lords found that this provision was not triggered in circumstances where a juvenile's liberty had been restricted by use of a curfew; it was limited to periods in secure accommodation.

Section 98 of the CDA 1998 amends the provision for remand of 15- and 16-year-old boys. At present they may be remanded to prison as an alternative to local authority secure accommodation; this happens increasingly as a result of the lack of local authority secure places. Now, if a boy of 15 or 16 is defined as vulnerable

(CDA 1998, s. 98(3)), he will be remanded to local authority secure accommodation. Other boys of that age will be remanded to a remand centre or prison. Girls will not be remanded to prison until aged 17.

Section 58 of PACE 1984 provides that, if a child is detained at the police station, he is entitled to have someone informed of his whereabouts and is entitled to free legal advice under the duty solicitor scheme or provided by a solicitor of the child's choice.

■ The appropriate adult

In addition to a solicitor, an appropriate adult should be present during any interview of a juvenile under the age of 17.[19] The appropriate adult can exercise the child's right to legal advice. It is important to distinguish the role of the appropriate adult from that of the solicitor. The Police and Criminal Evidence Act (PACE) 1984, Code C, para. 11.16 provides:

> Where the appropriate adult is present at an interview, he shall be informed that he is not expected to act simply as an observer; and also that the purposes of his presence are, first, to advise the person being questioned and to observe whether or not the interview is being conducted properly and fairly, and secondly, to facilitate communication with the person being interviewed.

The Crime and Disorder Act 1998, s. 38(4)(a) further describes the role of the appropriate adult as to 'safeguard the interests' of children and young persons detained by the police. At the interview, but not before, the police have a responsibility to inform the appropriate adult of what the role entails. This is unhelpful, as the appropriate adult should be proactive and take certain action before the interview. This would include looking at the custody record, making sure that the young person knows why they are detained and that they are aware of their rights, e.g. to make a phone call and to require legal advice.

The appropriate adult for a child or young person will be drawn from the following list (PACE 1984, Code C, para. 1.7):

1. the parent or guardian (or local authority or voluntary organisation if the juvenile is in care);
2. a social worker or a member of a local youth offending team;
3. failing either of the above, another responsible adult aged 18 who is not a police officer or employed by the police.

In most cases the juvenile's parents, or a person with parental responsibility for the juvenile, will act as appropriate adult. There may be circumstances, however, when that person is not available or is not considered suitable to act as the appropriate adult (for example, in *DPP* v. *Blake* [1989] 1 WLR 432 the confession of a juvenile was found to be inadmissible, as it was obtained in the presence of her estranged father with whom she had a poor relationship). In those cases a social worker will frequently be called upon to act as appropriate adult. A social worker should not act as appropriate adult if he called the police or is a witness, as he may not be perceived as independent (*DPP* v. *Morris,* 8 October 1990, unreported).[20] One of the youth justice services that a local authority (in cooperation with the police, probation committee and health authority) is required to provide is sufficient people to act as appropriate adults.

Recently there has been an increase in the number of volunteer schemes that provide appropriate adults. This is specifically endorsed in a Home Office circular, which suggests that volunteers may take the role of appropriate adult, possibly through partnership arrangements with local voluntary organisations.[21] Clearly, if volunteer appropriate adult schemes are to be successful, the volunteers will require a level of training and support. In a case where a volunteer appropriate adult claimed compensation for post traumatic stress disorder suffered as a result of sitting in interviews related to the Frederick West trial, the court held that the police had no duty of care to prevent psychological harm to the applicant.[22] Such a decision may deter future volunteers.[23] The desire for training is not confined to volunteers and it is imperative that if social workers are to fulfill this role they should also receive appropriate training.

If a parent does not act as appropriate adult, it is now open to question whether this might be in breach of their right to family life under the Human Rights Act 1998. On a wider level, the role of the appropriate adult may be questioned as part of the suspect's right to a fair trial under Art. 6 of the European Convention on Human Rights. The duty imposed on public authorities, which includes the police and the local authority, to comply with the terms of the Convention reinforces the responsibilities to provide appropriate adults and to ensure that the appropriate adult is always present and is informed of the terms of the role.

If a young person is not provided with an appropriate adult, this would probably be considered a significant and substantial breach of PACE rules and the court then has the power to exclude any evidence obtained (PACE 1984, s. 78). As well as being present during any interviews, the appropriate adult should be present when the young person is informed of his or her rights, is charged, takes part in an identification parade or is searched, and where the police issue a warning or reprimand.

Police powers are considered further in Chapter 18.

■ The youth court

The youth court deals with the majority of criminal cases taken against juveniles. It is part of the magistrates' court and was formerly known as the juvenile court. There are a number of features that distinguish the youth court from the adult criminal court. The magistrates who sit in the youth court are drawn from a special panel based on particular relevant experience and having received appropriate training. A stipendiary magistrate may hear a juvenile case alone but normally the bench will consist of three magistrates, including both sexes. The proceedings are not open to the public[24] and, although the press are entitled to be present, any reports must not contain information that would identify the accused. There is a power in s. 49(4A) of the Children and Young Persons Act 1933 to dispense with reporting restrictions in criminal proceedings concerning a juvenile, thereby identifying the juvenile. This power should be exercised with great care, caution and circumspection, according to the Divisional Court in *McKerry* v. *Teesside and Wear Valley Justices* [2000] Crim LR 594. The Lord Chief Justice stated that the reporting restrictions provisions should be read against the background of international law and practice, which the European Court had considered in the Thompson and Venables (Bulger) case. It was noted that there was a tension in this case, where a newspaper wished to publish the name of a 15-year-old found guilty of theft, between the competing principles of Art. 8 (the right to privacy) and Art. 10 (freedom of expression). The court found that the power to dispense with anonymity had to be exercised with great care and it would be wrong to dispense with this right as an additional punishment. The Lord Chief Justice continued that '[i]t was also extremely difficult to see any place for "naming and shaming"'.

In addition, s. 44 of the Youth Justice and Criminal Evidence Act 1999 prohibits the publication of information relating to any person under the age of 18 who is involved in any offence, in the period prior to proceedings being commenced. This section has a wide remit, relating not only to offenders but also to witnesses and victims, and it is hoped that it will encourage more young people to come forward as witnesses.

Access to court is limited to the people who are directly involved in the case. This will involve the magistrates and court staff, the parties and the young person's parents, legal representatives, social workers and probation officers. The proceedings are intended to be less formal than in adult court and the layout of the court should reflect this. Magistrates should sit at a table rather than a raised dais. The young person sits in front of the magistrates, not in a dock, and his parent(s) and social worker sit next to or behind him. The magistrates and the clerk address the juvenile by his first name and should explain the charge and other matters in ordinary language. Where the juvenile and other witnesses give evidence, they will promise rather than swear to tell the truth. At the outcome of the case the magistrates make a 'finding of guilt' rather than a 'conviction' and make a 'disposal on a finding of guilt' rather than a 'sentence'. The court must have regard to the welfare of the child under s. 44 of the Children and Young Persons Act 1933.

A juvenile may be tried in the adult magistrates' court where he is jointly charged with an adult. In the serious cases outlined below, a juvenile will be tried in the Crown Court.

■ Serious offences

Certain serious offences defined by s. 90 of the Powers of Criminal Courts (Sentencing) Act 2000 (formerly Children and Young Persons Act 1933, s. 53) will be tried and sentenced in the Crown Court. Commonly, reference has been made to 'section 53s'. Section 90 refers to murder. Section 91 refers to a range of offences including manslaughter and offences that carry a maximum penalty of 14 years or more where committed by an adult. Where the youth court considers that, if the case is proven, a term of detention is the likely disposal, then the case will be heard in the Crown Court.

■ Dangerousness

The concept of 'dangerousness' and the dangerous offender was introduced by the Criminal Justice Act 2003. It provides a further method by which the youth court can commit a youth to the Crown Court on satisfaction of certain criteria. An offender is 'dangerous' if the court considers there is a 'significant risk to members of the public of seious harm occasioned by the commission by him of further specified offences' (CJA 2003, ss. 225). There is a presumption (rebuttable if unreasonable) that an adult offender who has previously been convicted of a relevant offence, is dangerous. For youths the presumption does not apply, the court will take into account information about the nature and circumstances of the offence, and pattern of behaviour and information about the offender, in deciding on dangerousness. The court will assess serious risk in each case.

If an offence is a specified or a serious offence of sex or violence the court will consider a determinate extended sentence or an indeterminate sentence of imprisonment for public protection. Specified offences include a range of violent and sexual offences such as actual bodily harm, manslaughter and rape. Serious offences are those punishable by life imprisonment or imprisonment for ten years or more. Those serving an indeterminate sentence for public protection will be released only when the Parole Board considers it is safe, having served a minimum term set by the court. Release is not automatic. Extended sentences include a custodial term and an extended licence period.

As the youth court cannot impose an indeterminate sentence for public protection or an extended sentence, the court will send youth offenders charged with a specified offence, who appear dangerous, to the Crown Court.[25]

Disposal

Youth courts must follow the principle of proportionate sentencing established under the Criminal Justice Act 1991. These principles have been restated in the Powers of Criminal Courts (Sentencing) Act 2000 (PCC(S)A 2000). Effectively, this means that the court will consider how serious the offence is, taking into account any aggravating and mitigating factors, and reflect the level of seriousness in the choice of sentence. Furthermore, CDA 1998, s. 80 requires the Court of Appeal to consider producing sentencing guidelines in suitable cases, and CDA 1998, s. 81 establishes a new Sentencing Advisory Panel to provide advice on sentencing to the Court of Appeal. Section 153 of the Powers of Criminal Courts (Sentencing) Act 2000 specifically provides for sentences to be increased where an offence is racially aggravated. The judge is required to impose a higher sentence and state in open court that the offence is racially aggravated. This provision is relevant to all offenders whatever the sentence. There are also a number of specific racially aggravated offences created by the Crime and Disorder Act 1998, which provide for enhanced maximum penalties for existing offences (e.g. criminal damage) where racial aggravation is proved. This applies to juveniles and adults.

In addition to the orders that can be made in respect of the juvenile, the court can make a range of orders affecting parents. It is usual for the court to require the attendance of parents at the hearing. In addition, it can impose *parental bindovers,* compensation orders and fines.

In summary, the disposal options available since the Crime and Disorder Act 1998 reforms are:

- reprimands and final warnings – these replace cautions
- reparation order – reparation may be made to the victim of a crime, a person otherwise affected or the community at large
- action plan orders
- curfew orders
- supervision orders
- referral orders – a referral is made to a YOT for assessment and participation in a programme to prevent reoffending
- community orders (formerly probation, community service and combination orders) may be made for 16–17-year-olds only
- attendance centre orders
- drug treatment and testing orders
- detention and training orders – replace a variety of custodial options
- sex offender orders.

Each option is discussed more fully below.

■ Reprimands and final warnings (CDA 1998, ss. 65–66)

Cautioning as a formal alternative to prosecution is abolished by the CDA 1998 (in respect of juveniles) and replaced with a system of reprimands and warnings.[26] A first offence may be dealt with by a reprimand, warning or charge, depending on seriousness.

A reprimand or warning can be issued if:

- there is sufficient evidence
- the young person admits the offence
- he has no previous convictions
- a prosecution is not in the public interest.[27]

The warning or reprimand will be issued at the police station and an appropriate adult must be present.

Where a final warning is given, further intervention will follow, as the young person will be referred to the YOT for assessment and possible participation in a rehabilitation programme to prevent reoffending. Where a final warning is given, guidance and support will be provided but any further reoffending will lead to court action. The courts have been advised not to conditionally discharge someone who is convicted within two years of a warning. A reprimand is a stand-alone formal police warning. A warning or reprimand does not count as a criminal conviction; however, it can be brought to the court's attention in sentencing for a further offence.

■ Referral orders (PCC(S)A 2000, ss. 16–20)

A new sentencing disposal was introduced by the Youth Justice and Criminal Evidence Act 1999 in the form of the referral order, now consolidated in ss. 16–20 of the PCC(S)A 2000. It is a compulsory sentence for children and young persons aged 10–17 who plead guilty and are convicted for the first time by a court. The court can make a referral order for a minimum period of three months and no longer than one year, the actual period depending on the seriousness of the crime. The young offender is referred to a youth offender panel (**YOP**). Panels should be convened within 15 days of the court hearing and are intended to offer a less formal meeting than court, where the young offender and his/her family and the victim can consider the circumstances of the offence and draw up a 'contract'. It is an expectation that a parent(s) will attend panel meetings with the young offender (if under the age of 16) and, to reinforce this expectation, if parents fail to attend without reasonable excuse, contempt proceedings may result. When the order is made it will be usual practice for the court to order parents to attend. If the young offender does not attend the panel, and cannot give an acceptable reason for non-attendance, then the offender will return to court for re-sentencing. Also, if the young offender will not agree to a contract he or she will return to court for re-sentencing. The panel will reconvene for interim progress reports, after one month and then every three months. As the conviction is spent as soon as a referral order has been completed, this may in practice prove to be the incentive for offenders to agree and comply with contracts.

Youth offending panels should be made up of a representative group of the community, though early indications are of a majority of women, and few unemployed members. In their work, YOPs should be guided by the principles of 'restoration, reintegration and responsibility', which underlie restorative justice (Home Office (1997) pp. 31–2).

Success of the referral order must depend in large part on the range of programmes of activities that are available to be included in a contract. Contracts may include an element of reparation (e.g. a written apology to the victim), and the programme should be designed to prevent further offending. Contracts may include educational activities, intensive work with a YOT officer, sporting activities, involvement in a support group, family group conferences and curfews.

Pilot schemes for referral orders were set up in 11 areas in England and Wales and they were available nationally from April 2002. The pilot schemes were overseen by the Youth Justice Board. Of the orders made in the pilot schemes up to April 2001, 80 per cent were for six months or less and largely for acquisitive offences.[28] Full evaluation of the order will not be possible for some time; however, it is clearly another example of an order that stresses parental responsibility for a young offender's behaviour.[29]

■ **Reparation order (PCC(S)A 2000, ss. 73–75)**

As the name suggests, where a reparation order is made, the offender is involved in supervised direct reparation. The order may be made for a juvenile over the age of 10. Reparation orders provide for the offender to make reparation to the victim of the crime, any person otherwise affected, or the community at large (the victim's consent must be obtained). A maximum of 24 hours' reparation is permitted, to be completed within three months. Reparation conditions can also be attached to supervision orders. The Introductory Guide suggests that reparation might include writing a letter of apology or apologising to the victim in person, cleaning graffiti or repairing criminal damage. Again, before making an order, the court must consider a written report by a probation officer, social worker or member of the YOT, outlining the type of reparation proposed, availability of appropriate work, and the attitude of the victim to the proposed reparation. The order will be supervised by a social worker, probation officer or member of a YOT. Pilot studies conducted prior to full implementation of the CDA applied a range of methods of reparation, for example, distributing crime leaflets, designing a leaflet outlining help available to young drug users, voluntary work at a hospice.[30]

■ **Community orders**

Community orders which can be made in relation to juveniles are:

- community order
- supervision order
- action plan order
- drug treatment and testing order
- attendance centre order
- curfew order.

A community order may be made only if it satisfies the criteria in s. 35 of the Powers of Criminal Courts (Sentencing) Act 2000. In essence, the order shall in the opinion of the court be the most suitable on its own or with another sentence for the offender and the restrictions it places on the offender's liberty must in the opinion of the court be commensurate with the seriousness of the offence, or combination of associated offences.

Action plan orders (PCC(S)A 2000, ss. 69–72)

Where an action plan order is made, the offender will take part in an intensive three-month programme of supervised and directed activities. This new order, which is available for a juvenile over the age of 10, shares similarities with the old intermediate treatment condition. It is a community penalty, designed to address offending. In essence, it is a combination of elements of reparation, punishment and rehabilitation for the offender, together with parental involvement. Before an order is made, the court must consider a written report by a social worker, member of a YOT or probation officer, which outlines the proposed content of the action plan order, the benefits to the offender, and the attitude of the offender's parents to the order. The action plan order is intended to be fairly intensive and a hearing should take place within 21 days of the order to review its effectiveness. Requirements of the order must not conflict with religious beliefs or education or work commitments.

Curfew order (PCC(S)A 2000, ss. 37–40)

A curfew order may require an offender to remain in a specified place for a specified period of between 2 and 12 hours in any day. The curfew should avoid any conflict with the offender's religious beliefs or any requirement in another community order and should not interfere with normal attendance at work or school. The offender must consent to the order and there must be a responsible person to monitor the offender's whereabouts during the curfew period. An order may be made in respect of juveniles aged 12–17 years. Duration of the order is limited to three months if the offender is under the age of 16, and six months if the offender is aged 16 or 17. A curfew order may be enforced by electric monitoring or tagging (PCC(S)A 2000, s. 38). An electronic device is attached to the offender so that a monitoring station can check whereabouts during the curfew.

Attendance centre order (PCC(S)A 2000, ss. 60–62)

Attendance centre orders are available for juveniles over the age of 10. Attendance centres are run by the police in a variety of settings (e.g. schools) to provide a structured and disciplined atmosphere. The juvenile loses leisure time by attending as the orders often operate on Saturdays. The order can be made for between 12 and 36 hours and is usually spent in two-hour blocks. The order can be made only if the juvenile can access a centre within a reasonable distance.

Drug treatment and testing order (PCC(S)A 2000, s. 52)

A drug treatment and testing order may be made for an offender aged 16 or over with the agreement of the offender. The court must be satisfied that:

(a) the offender is dependent on drugs and has a propensity to misuse them, and

(b) his dependence is such as requires and may be susceptible to treatment.

Treatment may be ordered for between six months and three years and can include a residential requirement. The offender will regularly provide samples to see if he is clear of drugs, and the court will review the order on a monthly basis.

Community orders

The community rehabilitation order (probation), the community punishment order (community service orders), the community punishment and rehabilitation order (combination orders), used to be available for juveniles over the age of 16. The Criminal Justice Act 2003 has set out a new structure for community sentences (discussed in

Chapter 18). The previous orders, for those over 16, are replaced by a community order, which may be made for up to three years for offenders aged over 16. The order can include any one or more of the following requirements: an unpaid work requirement; an activity requirement; a programme requirement; a prohibited activity requirement; a curfew requirement; an exclusion requirement; a residence requirement; a mental health treatment requirement; a drug rehabilitation requirement; an alcohol treatment requirement; a supervision requirement; and an attendance centre requirement.

Supervision orders (PCC(S)A 2000, ss. 63–68)

Sections 63–68 of the PCC(S)A 2000 amend the Children and Young Persons Act 1969 and aim to strengthen the community penalty of a supervision order. The supervision order has a similar effect to the community rehabilitation order but is available for the full age range of 10–17 years. The supervisor will be a member of a YOT or could be a social worker or a probation officer if the juvenile is 13 or older. The duty of the supervisor is to 'advise, assist and befriend' the juvenile and the order can be made for up to three years.

Section 63 of the PCC(S)A enables reparation conditions to be attached to the supervision order. It also deals with the power to attach a residence condition to a supervision order. In effect, a supervision order with a residence requirement resembles the old criminal care order. A requirement to live in local authority accommodation can be imposed for up to six months where a juvenile previously failed to comply with a requirement attached to a supervision order, or was found guilty of an offence during a supervision order, and the court considers that this was due to a significant extent to the young person's living arrangements and that a residence requirement will help rehabilitation. Requirements can also be attached which stipulate that the juvenile should not live with a specified person, education requirements and night restriction orders.

Section 72 deals with breaches of supervision order requirements. In the event of a breach the court can vary the supervision order; impose a fine, a curfew order or an attendance centre order; or re-sentence for the original offence.

Intensive supervision and surveillance programmes

Existing statutory powers may be used to admit a young person onto an intensive supervision and surveillance programme (ISSP) scheme, as part of a community penalty, supervision or community rehabilitation or as a condition of community supervision in the second half of a detention and training order. It is inaccurate to refer to an 'ISSP order'. ISSP is intended to be the most rigorous non-custodial intervention available for young offenders. It may include a minimum of 25 hours' carefully programmed contact time each week, for three months, with support during evenings and weekends as the supervision element with a minimum requirement of two surveillance checks per day, which can be increased to 24-hour monitoring, including tagging and voice verification. ISSPs are available in all YOTs.

■ Custodial sentences

The UNCRC clearly states that custodial sentences should be considered as a last resort for juveniles. The principle of 'proportionality' discussed above applies to custodial sentences and under the PCC(S)A 2000, s. 79 the court must be satisfied that:

(a) the offence, or the combination of the offence and one or more offences associated with it, was so serious that only such a sentence can be justified for it; or

(b) that the offence is a violent or sexual offence, and that only such a sentence would be adequate to protect the public from serious harm from the offender.

Detention and training order (PCC(S)A 2000, ss. 100–107)

Section 73 of CDA established the detention and training order, followed by supervision. It is a generic new custodial sentence replacing the existing sentences of a secure training order and detention in a young offender institution. An order may be made in respect of juveniles aged between 12 and 17. A child under the age of 15 must be a persistent offender to become the subject of an order. The maximum period of detention is two years. Specific periods up to that maximum are designated, i.e. 4, 6, 8, 10, 12, 18 and 24 months. The period of detention will be spent in a secure training centre, a young offender institution, a youth treatment centre or local authority (or other) secure accommodation. Supervision will be provided after release, in the community, normally after 50 per cent of the detention element is complete.

Sex offender orders (CDA 1998, ss. 2–3)

New sex offender orders were created by CDA 1998, s. 2. The police are the applicants for an order, which is made by the magistrates' civil court after there has been a conviction for a sexual offence. The order will be made where a person is a sex offender (defined in the Sex Offenders Act 1997) and there is a risk of serious harm to the public. The order is intended to be preventative and requires sex offenders to register under the Sex Offenders Act 1997. An order will last for a minimum period of five years and will contain prohibitions designed to protect the public from harm by the defendant (e.g. staying away from particular premises), but it cannot require treatment of the individual. Breach of the order is a criminal offence. In the majority of cases it is anticipated that sex offender orders will be made in respect of adults; however, they can be made for anyone over the age of criminal responsibility.

■ Powers of Criminal Court (Sentencing) Act 2000, s. 90

Where a child is found to have committed a grave crime (e.g. murder), he or she must be detained during Her Majesty's pleasure, the exact place and period to be directed. Under s. 60 of the Criminal Justice and Court Services Act 2000, in the case of a murder committed by a person under the age of 18 the trial judge will now fix the *tariff* in open court. Tariff is the minimum period that must be served before first consideration for an early release. This change was occasioned by the European Court of Human Rights ruling in *T* v. *United Kingdom; V* v. *United Kingdom* (2000) 30 EHRR 121 (the 'Bulger case'). Previously, the judge would make a private recommendation to the Lord Chief Justice, who could adjust the tariff; the papers were then passed to the Home Secretary, who could make a further adjustment. In the Bulger case, the trial judge recommended that Venables and Thompson serve a minimum period of eight years; this was raised to 15 years by the Home Secretary at the time, Michael Howard. The case was taken to the European Court of Human Rights, which found breaches of the European Convention on Human Rights in terms of sentencing practice and also that the defendants did not receive a fair hearing in accordance with Art. 6(1).

A practice direction followed the case.[31] The practice direction is an important development in youth justice, which tackles many of the difficulties apparent in the Bulger case and suggests changes necessary to ensure compliance with the European Convention on Human Rights as required by the Human Rights Act 1998. The practice direction provides for special measures to be introduced to ensure a fair hearing at trial. The measures required will vary depending on the particular child's needs, assessed by the trial judge, 'the steps which should be taken to comply with the direction should be judged, in any given case, taking account of the age, maturity and development (intellectual and emotional) of the young defendant on trial'. (para 2). The added pressure of being tried with an adult is acknowledged by the practice note and it states that a court should order separate trials for juveniles and adults, unless it is in the interests of justice to do otherwise. It also recommends that young defendants should visit the court out of hours to become accustomed to the setting. The level of formality of the trial should be reduced, including removal of wigs and gowns, changes to the courtroom and limitations on access. Many of these features are already present in the youth court. Of course, a murder trial will always be conducted in the Crown Court, whatever the age of the defendant. The practice direction suggests that in the court everyone should sit at the same level, and the defendants should be able to sit next to their family and near the lawyers. (In the Bulger trial the defendants actually sat in a raised dock so that they could view the proceedings.) The practice direction suggests that only people with a direct interest in the outcome of the trial should be allowed into the court but if press access is restricted, a provision should be made for the trial to be viewed through a TV link into another area. The practice direction raises a number of issues that have been addressed in the Youth Justice and Criminal Evidence Act 1999 in respect of child witnesses. These provisions are discussed in Chapter 9.

Chapter summary

- The law relating to youth justice is substantially contained in the Crime and Disorder Act 1998, the Youth Justice and Criminal Evidence Act 1999 and the Powers of Criminal Courts (Sentencing) Act 2000. There is an increasing emphasis on the prevention of youth crime.

■ The role of a social worker in youth justice is varied and may include: membership of a youth offending team; acting as designated responsible officer on a child safety order; advising, assisting and befriending a young person under a supervision order; acting as an appropriate adult; and contact with young people in secure accommodation.

■ The Crime and Disorder Act 1998 introduced new structures for youth justice. Institutional changes are underpinned by s. 37, which introduces a statutory aim to prevent offending by children and young persons. Youth offending teams with multi-agency membership have been introduced and every Social Services Department must produce a youth justice plan.

■ Youth justice services may include: assessment of children and young persons for rehabilitation programmes; provision of support whilst children and young persons are remanded on bail; placements in local authority secure or non-secure accommodation; provision of court reports; supervision of young persons and post-release supervision. A National Youth Justice Board is established to oversee the delivery of youth justice services.

■ Section 17 of the CDA 1998 imposes a duty on local authorities and police authorities to do all they reasonably can to prevent crime and disorder. Parenting orders, child safety orders, child curfew schemes and an enhanced local authority duty of investigation are particularly relevant orders in respect of preventing youth crime.

■ The anti-social behaviour order is a new civil order to prevent harassment, alarm or distress, breach of which is a criminal offence.

■ Since the abolition of the *doli incapax* rule, all children will now acquire criminal responsibility at the age of 10.

■ Targets have been introduced for reducing delays in the youth justice system, with particular emphasis on persistent young offenders, defined as 'a young person aged 10–17 who has been sentenced by a criminal court in the United Kingdom on three or more separate occasions for one or more recordable offences, and within three years of the last sentencing occasion is subsequently arrested or has an information laid against them for a further recordable offence.'

■ If a child is interviewed at the police station, he should be accompanied by an appropriate adult, whose role is to safeguard the interests of children and young persons detained by the police, and 'not . . . to act simply as an observer; . . . the purposes of his presence are, first, to advise the person being questioned and to observe whether or not the interview is being conducted properly and fairly, and secondly, to facilitate communication with the person being interviewed.'

■ Most criminal cases taken against juveniles will be heard in the youth court in which magistrates drawn from a special panel hear cases. Proceedings are not open to the public and there are restrictions on press reporting. Certain serious offences (murder and offences carrying a maximum penalty of 14 years) will be tried in the Crown Court.

■ If the court makes a finding of guilt, a range of disposal options are available. Reprimands and final warnings have been introduced and replace cautioning.

Orders which may be made include, supervision, action plan orders, reparation orders, community orders with attached requirements and curfew orders.

■ Detention and training orders replace a number of custodial options previously available. The period of detention may be spent in a secure training centre, a youth offender institution, a youth treatment centre or local authority accommodation.

Exercises

1. Jeannie, aged 15, has recently started going out with James, who is 28. Her parents are very unhappy about the relationship and think she may also be taking drugs. She has failed to attend school today and is picked up by the police in an area of town known for prostitution, in possession of £100 cash and £50-worth of cosmetics. Just as the police are about to drive off, James rushes over, shouting at Jeannie not to talk, and damages the police car with an iron bar. At the police station the custody officer calls Jeannie's parents, who state that 'she is no longer our daughter' and refuse to come to the station. A social worker is called to be with Jeannie and notices injection marks on her arm. Jeannie admits to theft of the cosmetics but denies any knowledge of the money. She has no previous convictions. Initially she claims not to know James, but after a four-hour period of questioning she breaks down and states that he is her pimp, the money is for him, but she is frightened that he will beat her up if he finds out she has told the police.

   Consider the responsibilities of the social worker called to the station. If the social worker fulfils the role adequately, what changes to the above scenario might occur. What are the options for responding to Jeannie's situation?

2. Michael, a 15-year-old, has had a turbulent childhood; he has been living in a residential children's home for the last two years and frequently fails to attend school. He has received cautions from the police for criminal damage. Recently he has become friendly with Joe, who is aged 19 and lives in a bedsit near Michael. Joe has had three appearances before the youth court for shop theft, criminal damage and public order matters. One night Michael is stopped on the street by two police officers who have been notified of a break-in at a local off-licence store. The police had been informed that two youths were seen running away from the store and suspect that Michael is one of them. Michael denies any knowledge or involvement in the break-in. The police are still suspicious and take Michael to the police station to assist them with their inquiries. After two hours of questioning, Michael confesses and tells the police where Joe lives; the police then contact Michael's social worker. At Joe's flat the police find ten bottles of gin and, on further searching, discover a quantity of cannabis. Joe is charged with burglary and possession of drugs and Michael is charged with assisting burglary.

   Were the correct procedures followed at the police station? If the offences are prosecuted, which court will hear the case against Michael? If the case is proven, what is the likely disposal?

Websites

The Home Office site provides a mass of information on the Crime and Disorder Act 1998 and associated youth justice reforms. The introductory guide to the Act, and guidance on each of the new orders is available. Criminal statistics and research publications are also available:

www.homeoffice.gov.uk

For a copy of 'The Youth Court 2001, The changing culture of the Youth Court, Good Practice Guide':

www.homeoffice.gov.uk/documents/ythcrt01

The Youth Justice Board website provides a wealth of information on youth justice issues

www.youth-justice-board.gov.uk

Further reading

A number of specialist texts consider youth justice in more detail:

Goldson, B. (ed.) (2000) *The New Youth Justice*. Lyme Regis: Russell House Publishing.

Leng, R., Taylor, R. and Wasik, M. (1998) *Blackstone's Guide to the Crime and Disorder Act 1998*. London: Blackstone Press.

Moore, T. and Wilkinson, T. (2001) *Youth Court Guide*. London: Butterworths.

Muncie, J (2005) *Youth and Crime: A Critical Introduction* (3rd edn). London: Sage.

Dugmore, P., Angus, S. and Pickford, J. (2006) *Youth Justice and Social Work*. Exeter: Learning Matters.

Relevant Government publications provide background to the Crime and Disorder reforms, review the reforms in operation, outline further reforms and situate youth justice in the 'Every Child Matters: Change for Children' policy:

Home Office (1997) *No More Excuses – A New Approach to Tackling Youth Crime in England and Wales* (Cm. 3809). London: Home Office.

Home Office (1997) *Tackling Youth Crime: A Consultation Paper*. London: Home Office.

Audit Commission (2004) *Youth Justice 2004: a review of the reformed youth justice system*. London: Audit Commission.

Home Office (2003) *Youth Justice – The Next Steps* (Companion document to 'Every Child Matters').

Home Office (2005) *Every Child Matters: Change for Children in the Criminal Justice System*.

DFES (2005)Youth Green Paper, 'Youth Matters'.

Critical examination of the youth justice system features in the following articles:

Arthur, R. (2005) 'The Youth Justice System in England and Wales: complying with international human rights law' 3 *International Family Law* p. 3–13.

Ball, C. (2004) 'Youth Justice? Half a Century of Responses to Youth Offending' *Criminal Law Review* p. 167.

Fionda, J. (1999) 'New Labour, old hat: youth justice and the Crime and Disorder Act 1998' *Criminal Law Review* p. 36.

Gelsthorpe, L. and Morris, A. (1999) 'Much ado about nothing – a critical comment on key provisions relating to children in the Crime and Disorder Act 1998' 11(3) *Child and Family Law Quarterly* p. 209.

Smith, R. (2005) 'Welfare versus Justice – Again!' 5(1) *Youth Justice* p. 3.

For further information and discussion of ASBOs and the Anti-Social Behaviour Act 2003 see:

Waddington, M., Carr, H. and Blair, A. (2004) *Anti-Social Behaviour Act 2003: A special bulletin*. Bristol: Jordan Publishing.

Pema, A. and Heels, S. (2004) *Anti-Social Behaviour Orders: A Special Bulletin*. Bristol: Jordan Publishing.

Ashworth, A. (2004) 'Social Control and "Anti Social Behaviour" 120 *Law Quarterly Review* p. 263.

MacDonald, S. (2006) 'A Suicidal Woman, Roaming Pigs and a Noisy Trampolinist: Refining the ASBO's Definition of "Anti-Social Behaviour"' 69(2) *Modern Law Review* p. 183. (Suggests that ASBOs have been employed for social control at the expense of more constructive forms of intervention.)

Notes

1 For a full review of changes in policy see: C. Ball (2004) 'Youth Justice? Half a Century of Responses to Youth Offending' *Criminal Law Review* 167.

2 Audit Commission (1996) 'Misspent Youth: Young People and Crime. A Consultation Paper', London: Audit Commission.

3 Home Office (1997) (Cm. 3809). London: The Stationery Office.

4 See report writing section in Chapter 4.

5 Children Act 1989, Sch. 2, para. 7.

6 This classification is adopted by A. Bainham (1998) *Children: The Modern Law*, Bristol: Family Law, Jordan Publishing.

7 The term 'community safety' is increasingly used in preference to crime prevention.

8 Home Office (1998) 'Establishing Youth Offending Teams' provides some guidance on the role of YOTs.

9 See www.youth-justice-board.gov.uk.

10 See discussion by L. Gelsthorpe and A. Morris (1999) 'Much ado about nothing – a critical comment on key provisions relating to children in the Crime and Disorder Act 1998' 11(3) *Child and Family Law Quartely* pp. 209–21.

11 C. Piper (1999) 'The Crime and Disorder Act 1998: child and community "Safety"' 62(3) *Modern Law Review* pp. 397–408.

12 Home Office (1998) 'Introductory Guide to the Crime and Disorder Act 1998'. London: Home Office.

13 UNCRC, Art. 40(3) requires establishment of a minimum age below which children shall be presumed not to have the capacity to infringe the penal law.

14 Children and Young Persons Act 1933, s. 50.

15 HM Crown Prosecution Service Inspectorate (2001) 'A Report on the Joint Inspection of the Progress made in Reducing Delay in the Youth Justice System'. London: HMSO.

16 See discussion in J. Black (1999) 'Justice delayed . . . is justice denied?' 143(16) *Solicitors Journal* p. 394.

17 S1 1999/2763.

18 Inter-departmental circular (1997) 'Tackling delay in the youth justice system'.

19 For further discussion of this role see: B. Littlechild (1998) 'Appropriate Adult Services' 144 *Childright* pp. 8–9, and H. Pierpoint (1999) 'Appropriate practice? Young suspects' rights under UNCRC' 162 *Childright* pp. 8–10.

20 Cited in T. Moore and T. Wilkinson (2001) *Youth Court Guide*. London: Butterworths.

21 Home Office (1998) 'Inter-departmental circular on establishing youth offending teams'. See www.homeoffice.gov.uk/cdact/yotcirc.htm.

22 *Leach* v. *Chief Constable of Gloucestershire* [1999] 1 All ER 215.

23 For the evaluation of a volunteer scheme, see T. Nemitz and P. Bean (1998) 'The effectiveness of a volunteer appropriate adult scheme' 38(3) *Medicine, Science and the Law* pp. 251–6.

24 Children and Young Persons Act 1933, s. 47(2).

25 Crime and Disorder Act 1998, s. 51A (inserted by CJA 2003).

26 See Home Office (2000) 'The Final Warning Scheme: Guidance to Youth Offending Teams'. London: The Stationery Office.

27 Home Office (1998) 'Introductory Guide to the Crime and Disorder Act 1998'. London: Home Office.

28 Youth Justice Board (2001) 'The Preliminary Report on the Operation of the New Youth Justice System'. Youth Justice Board, London: HMSO.

29 The first interim evaluation report is available at www.homeoffice.gov.uk/rds/index.html.

30 P. Tain (1999) 'Youth Justice' *Solicitors Journal* 18 June, p. 581.

31 Practice direction (Crown Court: trial of children and young persons) (2000) 2 All ER 285.

Vulnerable adults

Part 3

14 Community care

Learning objectives

To develop an understanding of the following:

- The legal context to work with adult service users.
- The categories of adults defined in legislation in respect of whom a range of powers and duties exist.
- The legal framework for 'community care'.
- Care management – the duty to assess for community care services, provision of services via the care plan and implications of resources.
- The principles of charging for services.
- Avenues for complaints in respect of community care assessment and provision.
- The role of carers and provision of support for carers.
- The provision and regulation of domiciliary and residential services.

Introduction

This chapter is divided into three sections: introducing the legal framework for work with adult service users; community care and assessment for services; and two particular areas of service provision – domiciliary care and residential accommodation.

Social work with adult service users is the focus of the next four chapters. Adult service users will present a variety of needs and dilemmas for the social work practitioner. It is important that this diversity is fully recognised and that generalised assumptions are not made. The law, however, tends to operate here in relation to particular categories of people or particular needs or scenarios. That approach is necessarily followed in this text. As a preliminary issue, therefore, it is appropriate to start with a consideration of the categories of service users that the law recognises.

Working with adult service users

Increasingly in adult services work the term 'vulnerable adult' is being utilised, particularly in relation to community care services and adult abuse. A definition of a vulnerable adult was included in the Law Commission work on Mental Incapacity and it is significant that this term has been included recently in statutory form in the Care Standards Act 2000 (CSA 2000). It reads as follows:

s. 80

> (a) an adult to whom accommodation and nursing or personal care are provided in a care home;
> (b) an adult to whom personal care is provided in their own home under arrangements made by a domiciliary care agency; or
> (c) an adult to whom prescribed services are provided by an independent hospital, clinic, medical agency or National Health Service body.
>
> (CSA 2000)

This is a broad definition introduced in the context of regulation of services, which incorporates the groups of people specified separately in previous legislation, namely service users who are old, have a physical disability, a mental disorder or a learning disability. A further statutory definition of 'vulnerable adult' has been included in the Domestic Violence Crime and Victims Act 2004. Not surprisingly this has a different emphasis, in the context of a criminal offence the focus is on impairment of the ability of a person to protect himself. Different definitions do, however, invite confusion. In the context of adult protection, the Association of Directors of Social Services (ADSS) describes the use of the term 'vulnerable adults' as contentious and prefers to simply refer to adults and to 'safeguarding' rather than protecting. See further discussion in Chapter 17.[1]

Whilst the law can separate individual characteristics of adults, and organisational teams may also reflect these categories, the reality of the individuals encountered in everyday practice is less clear cut. For example, some elderly people will also have a physical disability, which may or may not be associated with old age; equally, people with mental illness grow older and other elderly people may suffer from a mental illness associated with increasing years. The following brief paragraphs outline the main characteristics of adult service users.

■ Adult service users

Older people

The term 'older people', rather than elderly people, will be adopted in this text following acceptance of this term in the field of gerontology as a value-free description of later life, i.e. persons over the age of 65.[2] In legal terms there is no clear definition of an old person (in contrast, a child is clearly defined as a person under the age of 18 (Children Act 1989, s. 105)). Entitlement to state pension in this country accrues at different ages for men and women, although discrimination in the use of different retirement ages in employment has been found to be unlawful (*Marshall* v. *Southampton and South West Hampshire Area Health Authority* [1986] 2 All ER 584). Even in respect of specific legal duties, different terms are used without definition, such as 'aged', or 'by reason of old age'. What is clear is that, given increasing longevity (and with more people reaching 100 years of age each year), it is inappropriate to speak collectively of the needs of older people. It is worth noting that there are more women than men in the older age bracket. In the context of community care, there will be people who are being cared for by carers who are themselves older people. Older people will increasingly come to the attention of mental health services, given that the incidence of depression and dementia in older people is high (approximately one in five of those aged over 85). A significant number of older people live in residential settings, though the majority retain independence living in the community. There is an increasing awareness of the law relating to older people, particularly concerning issues surrounding management of financial affairs and mental capacity. The Employment Equality (Age) Regulations 2006 will prohibit direct or indirect age discrimination in employment but do not extend to other areas such as provision of goods and services, areas where some discrimination may persist. Article 14 of the European Convention on Human Rights is relevant if an older person is discriminated against in terms of enjoyment of the other Articles in the Convention: e.g. if different practices exist in respect of older and younger residents relating to the privacy enjoyed in a residential setting.

People with a mental disorder

The legal framework for social work with people with a mental disorder is provided by the Mental Health Act 1983, discussed fully in Chapter 15. The Act contains definitions of the term 'mental disorder' and other specific forms of mental disorder, including 'mental illness'. Many people with mental disorders are able to live in the community. Others may spend time in hospitals or mental nursing homes as informal patients, or, in limited circumstances, may be compulsorily detained in a hospital for a fixed period of time. The criminal law may make specific orders with regard to mentally disordered offenders (discussed in Chapter 18). People with a mental disorder may be entitled to a range of services to enable them to live in the community under a care plan, they may be supported by a guardianship order, or in receipt of after-care services following a period of formal detention. The law relating to mental health is in the process of reform.

People with a learning disability

People with learning disabilities will occasionally fall under the compulsory detention provisions of the Mental Health Act 1983 where their learning disability is accompanied by 'abnormally aggressive or seriously irresponsible behaviour'. Guidance states that services for adults with learning disabilities should be arranged on an individual basis, taking account of 'age, or needs, degree of disability, the personal preferences of the individual and his or her parents or carers, culture, race and gender'.[3] A white paper, 'Valuing People – A New Strategy for Learning Disability' (2001), provides the framework for provision of services for people with learning disability. The strategy recognises the need to raise the skill levels and qualifications of people who work in learning disability services, and there is likely to be much greater emphasis on training in this field, given that 75 per cent of 83,000 people in England working in learning disability services have no relevant qualification.

Many people with learning disabilities live in the community with their families or in supported group homes and some may live in residential accommodation (51,000 residential care places available in 1999). Considerable research has shown that people with learning disabilities are particularly vulnerable to sexual exploitation.[4] A range of specific sexual offences against people with 'mental disorder' is outlined in Chapter 17.

People with a physical disability

People with a physical disability may receive services to reduce the impact of their disability. The Disability Discrimination Act 1995 (**DDA 1995**) makes it unlawful to discriminate against disabled people in the provision of goods and services. The definition of disability in the Act includes people with a physical or mental disability.

> **s. 1**
>
> A physical or mental impairment, which has a substantial and long-term adverse effect on their ability to carry out normal day to day activities.
>
> (DDA 1995)

People with a physical disability may register on the register of disabled persons compiled by social services but are not obliged to do so, and registration is not a prerequisite for service provision. Registration data is held under the following categories: very severe handicap; severe or appreciable handicap; and other persons.[5] Children with disabilities will normally be entitled to support as 'children in need' (Children Act 1989, s. 17), discussed in Chapter 7.

■ Powers and duties in respect of vulnerable adults

Given the difficulties inherent in the use of strict categories focusing on different characteristics of vulnerable adults, and the inevitable overlaps, the powers and duties contained in the law are set out in date order rather than by specific service user group. This is a complex area of law containing a mixture of rights, duties and powers.

National Assistance Act 1948

Local authorities are enabled by s. 29(1) of the National Assistance Act 1948 (**NAA** 1948) to promote the welfare of people:

s. 29(1)

> . . . aged 18 or over who are blind, deaf or dumb or who suffer from mental disorder of any description and other persons who are substantially and permanently handicapped by illness, injury or congenital deformity or other such disabilities as may be prescribed.
>
> (NAA 1948)

In effect, this power provides a statutory definition of disability. The terminology is that adopted in 1948. Obviously there have been significant developments since 1948 in practice, social circumstances and the balance between state and private provision; and the language employed in the definition now appears at best archaic and at worst offensive. Use of the terms in the definition should be limited to circumstances when it is necessary to make direct reference to the exact wording of the statute. In everyday practice, reference to 'special needs', and terms such as 'hearing impaired' and 'without speech' are preferable.

Section 21 of the NAA 1948 (together with Guidance at LAC 93/10) contains the duty of local authorities to provide residential accommodation for persons who, by reason of age, illness, disability or any other circumstances, are in need of care and attention which are not otherwise available to them. The role of this section in providing a safety net has recently been questioned in cases involving asylum seekers. In *R v. Hammersmith and Fulham London Borough Council, ex parte M* (1998) 30 HLR 10 the Court of Appeal described 'circumstances', which included 'lack of food and accommodation . . . their inability to speak the language, and their ignorance of Britain and the fact that they had been subject to the stress of coming to this country in circumstances which at least involved their contending to be refugees'. (See further discussion of asylum law in Chapter 20.)

Section 47 of the NAA 1948 contains a power to remove a person from their own home in specific circumstances. This section is discussed further Chapter 17.

Health Services and Public Health Act 1968

Section 45 of the Health Services and Public Health Act 1968 (**HSPHA** 1968) provides that a local authority may make arrangements for promotion of the welfare of old people. As this provision is expressed as a power, some regional variation in the level and types of services is inevitable. Services which may be provided include: provision of meals and recreation in the home and elsewhere; visiting and advisory services and social work support; information about available services; practical assistance in the home, including adaptations; warden services; assistance with boarding out; and assistance in travelling to services.[6]

Chronically Sick and Disabled Persons Act 1970

Section 1 of the Chronically Sick and Disabled Persons Act 1970 (**CSDPA** 1970) requires local authorities to inform themselves of the number of people who fall within the definition contained in s. 29 of the National Assistance Act 1948 (above) and the need to make arrangements for them.

Local authorities are required under s. 2 to assess individual needs and provide services to meet the needs of disabled persons. An occupational therapist will normally be involved in the assessment. The specific services authorised by the CSDPA 1970, s. 2(1)(a)–(h) are:

- provision of practical assistance in the home;
- provision of wireless, television, library or other recreational facilities (or assistance in obtaining);
- provision of lectures, games, outings or other recreational facilities or assisting the person to make use of educational facilities;
- provision or assistance with travelling to services;
- provision of adaptations in the home or disability aids and equipment for greater safety, comfort or convenience;
- facilitating holidays;
- provision of meals at home or elsewhere;
- provision of or assistance in getting a telephone or special equipment necessary to use a telephone.

The majority of home care is provided under this statute. Adaptations and aids could include, e.g. toilet raisers, hand rails and stair lifts.

National Health Service Act 1977

Schedule 8, para. 3(1) of the National Health Service Act 1977 (**NHSA** 1977) introduced a duty on local Social Services Authorities to provide home help:

Sched. 8, para. 3(1)

> . . . for households where help is required owing to the presence of a person who is suffering from illness, lying in, an expectant mother, aged, handicapped as a result of having suffered from illness or by congenital deformity.
>
> (NHSA 1977)

There is also a power in the same Schedule (para. 2(1)) to provide other services for people who are physically or mentally ill, including day centres, laundry facilities, and meals and social work support. Services for people with mental health problems and people suffering from HIV/AIDS can be provided under this Act.

Mental Health Act 1983

An approved social worker is under a duty to make applications for compulsory detention in hospital or for guardianship in respect of people with a mental disorder under s. 13 of the Mental Health Act 1983 (**MHA** 1983) where satisfied that such an application ought to be made. Section 117 contains a duty to provide after-care in the community following detention of certain classes of formally detained patients. This duty is imposed jointly on health and social services. It is not possible for local authorities to charge for services provided under section 117.

Disabled Persons (Services, Consultation and Representation) Act 1986

Major sections of the Disabled Persons (Services, Consultation and Representation) Act 1986 (**DP(SCR)A** 1986), which would have provided an entitlement to advocacy services, have never been implemented.[7] The provisions that are in force require the local authority to assess the needs of a disabled person for services under the CSDPA 1970 if asked by a disabled person or their authorised representative or carer and to inform a disabled person of their right to an assessment (DP(SCR)A 1986, s. 4). Under s. 8 the local authority must take into account the ability of a carer to continue to provide care when assessing the needs of a disabled person who is living at home. Section 9 provides that the local authority must ensure information is available about relevant services provided by the local authority and other relevant organisations.

National Health Service and Community Care Act 1990

The National Health Service and Community Care Act 1990 (**NHSCCA** 1990) introduced new provisions for the assessment of eligibility for 'community care' services provided under a range of other pieces of legislation. The main terms of the Act are discussed below.

Disability Discrimination Acts, 1995 and 2005

The Disability Discrimination Act 1995 (**DDA** 1995) makes it unlawful to discriminate against a person on the grounds of disability, which may be mental or physical, in the provision of goods and services. The Disability Discrimination Act 2005 imposes a 'disability equality duty' on public authorities, requiring them, when exercising their functions, to have due regard to the need to eliminate harassment of and unlawful discrimination against disabled persons, to promote positive attitudes towards disabled persons, to encourage participation by disabled persons in public life, and to promote equality of opportunity between disabled persons and other persons.

Under the Human Rights Act 1998, Art. 14 of the European Convention on Human Rights makes it unlawful to discriminate in the enjoyment of the rights and freedoms guaranteed under the Convention on broader criteria than those covered by domestic anti-discrimination laws.

Carers (Recognition and Services) Act 1995

The Carers (Recognition and Services) Act 1995 (**C(RS)A** 1995) provides for an assessment of a carer's ability to provide and continue to provide care for a person. The results of the carer assessment must be taken into account in the assessment of individual need under s. 47 of the National Health Service and Community Care Act 1990.

Carers and Disabled Children Act 2000

The Carers and Disabled Children Act 2000 (**CDCA** 2000) provides carers with entitlement to an assessment of their needs independently of an assessment of the person cared for. Services may be provided which will help the carer to care for the person they care for. It also authorises local authorities to make direct payments to carers, and short-term break vouchers. This Act recognises carers as anyone over the age of 16.

Carers (Equal Opportunities) Act 2004

This Act amends the earlier carers legislation (1995 and 2000 above). Local authorities are now required proactively to inform all carers of whom they are aware that they may be entitled to an assessment. The Act also addresses the scope of assessment, which must include consideration of whether the carer works or wishes to work, is undertaking, or wishes to undertake, education, training or any leisure activity.

Community care

■ Introduction to community care

The key statute applying to community care is the National Health Service and Community Care Act 1990, which was implemented in 1993. The idea of community care predated this statute and is evidenced, for example, by provisions in the Chronically Sick and Disabled Persons Act 1970, which provides for services to enable people to live independently in their own homes. The essential aim of community care law and policy is to enable people to continue to live in their own homes rather than move by necessity into residential settings. The background developments to the NHSCCA 1990 included an Audit Commission report on community care in 1986, which found increasing demand for community care services and under provision of actual services.[8] This was followed in 1988 by the Griffiths Report, 'Community Care, an agenda for action',[9] which found levels of confusion about responsibility for community care across local and central government, the National Health Service, the voluntary and private sectors. The principal recommendation of the report provided for the role of Social Services Departments to change. Local authorities were to become the lead agency for coordinating community care services through arranging and purchasing in a mixed economy of care, but would not have a monopoly on providing services. In 1989 the white paper,

'Caring for People – Community care in the Next Decade and Beyond',[10] a key document, was published and built on the themes of the Griffiths report. The white paper (para. 1.1) included a useful definition of community care:

> Community care means providing the services and support which people who are affected by problems of ageing, mental illness, mental handicap or physical or sensory disability need to be able to live as independently as possible in their own homes, or in 'homely' settings in the community. The Government is fully committed to a policy of community care which enables such people to achieve their full potential.

The NHSCCA 1990 was subsequently introduced. It is essential to appreciate that the NHSCCA 1990 does not provide a unified and coherent system for adult care services, along the same lines as the Children Act 1989. Rather, it exists in conjunction with pre-existing duties and responsibilities and introduces changes in structure and the ways in which social care is provided rather than in substance. It is an area of law that affects a wide range of individuals who have very different needs.

Since the 1990 Act, a variety of further legislation has impacted on community care, including three pieces of 'carers' legislation, the Disability Discrimination Acts of 1995 and 2005 and the Community Care (Direct Payments) Act 1996. In addition, guidance has been developed such as 'No Secrets',[11] which places significant emphasis on the prevention of abuse, in part by provision of support services.

It is clear that community care remains a problematic area of practice, which has become dominated by concerns over inadequate resources. 'Modernising Social Services' (1998)[12] describes (at para. 2.3) the challenges faced in 1998:

> Decisions about who gets services and who does not are often unclear, and vary from place to place. Eligibility criteria are getting ever tighter and are excluding more and more people who would benefit from help but who do not come into the most dependent categories. Decisions about care can still be service driven, and concentrate on doing things for people according to what is available, rather than tailoring services to the needs of individuals and encouraging those who are helped to do what they can for themselves. Overall, people feel ill-informed about how they should find out about services, what they may be asked to contribute themselves, who will be providing the care, and how they can influence it. This is particularly true for certain groups such as older people from ethnic minorities.

■ Future direction?

The Government has set out proposals for the future direction of adult social care in a green paper, 'Independence, Well-Being and Choice (2005)[13] and a white paper, 'Our health, our care, our say: a new direction for community services'(2006).[14]

The white paper advocates a new strategic direction for all the care and support services that people use in their communities and neighbourhoods by putting people more in control of their own health and care, enabling and supporting health, and greater partnership working between councils and PCTs. New outcomes for social care were set out in the green paper, which will be used to measure how well social care is moving towards the Government's ideas for more preventative services, greater choice and independence for individuals who will be at the centre of any assessments and in some cases will carry out self assessment. The outcomes are:

- improved health
- improved quality of life
- freedom from discrimination and harassment
- economic well-being
- personal dignity
- making a positive contribution
- exercise choice and control.

The Director of Adult Social Services will have a key strategic role and potential new roles for social workers have been proposed as 'care navigators' and 'care managers'. It seems likely that closer partnerships will be developed between the NHS and local and the voluntary sector in service delivery. Legislation to merge the Healthcare Commission and Commission for Social Care Inquiry will provide a unified inspectorate to support the changes. Both the green and white paper emphasis commitment to a long term strategy of gradual changes over the next 10–15 years.

■ What are community care services?

A definition of community care services is provided in NHSCCA 1990:

s. 46(3)

> Community care services means services which a local authority may provide or arrange to be provided under any of the following provisions –
> (a) Part III of the National Assistance Act 1948;
> (b) section 45 of the Health Services and Public Health Act 1968;
> (c) section 21 of and Schedule 8 to the National Health Service Act 1977; and
> (d) section 117 of the Mental Health Act 1983;
>
> (NHSCCA 1990)

The range of services provided for under the above legislation includes support for people with physical and mental handicaps, older people, and expectant and nursing mothers, services to prevent illness and for the after-care of people who have suffered from illness as a result of mental illness, drug or alcohol dependency. The range of services includes home helps and laundry assistants, and accommodation for people who need accommodation because of their age, illness, disability or other circumstances.

■ Care management

Care management is the term used in guidance (but does not feature in legislation) to define the whole process of assessment, provision of services and review or reassessment. The essentials of care management can be broken down into the following list:

1. Screening to determine whether the person appears to be in need of community care services at all.
2. Criteria to determine the urgency of the case and the depth of assessment required.
3. Determination of eligibility for services.
4. Determination of priorities of assessed needs.
5. Agreed objectives for each prioritised need.
6. Provision of a care plan.
7. Assessment of the service user's financial resources in order to reach a decision on whether to make charges.
8. Reconciliation of the user's preferences with available resources.
9. Any unmet need should be identified.
10. Review – reassessment of the person's needs, preferences and eligibility in the light of changing need, policies and eligibility criteria.[15]

■ Assessment

'The objective of assessment is to determine the best available way to help the individual.'[16] In assessment, procedural fairness and reasoned decision-making is essential and will be subject to closer scrutiny since the advent of the Human Rights Act 1998. The key provision is s. 47, which provides for assessment of needs for community care services.

s. 47(1)

... where it appears to a local authority that any person for whom they may provide or arrange for the provision of community care services may be in need of any such services, the authority –
(a) shall carry out an assessment of his needs for those services; and
(b) having regard to the results of that assessment, shall then decide whether his needs call for the provision by them of any such services.

(NHSCCA 1990)

There are three crucial elements in this section, indicated by the words, 'for whom they may provide', 'shall', and 'decide'.

'for whom they may provide'

The phrase 'for whom they may provide' sets the parameters for application of this assessment provision. If a person falls within a legal definition as belonging to a category to whom there is provision for services, then *prima facie* that person is, as a matter of law, eligible for a s. 47 assessment. Refusal to assess may be challenged by judicial review and the local authority should give reasons if it is not going to carry out an assessment. Given the breadth of the phrase 'where it appears', the scope to decline an assessment is extremely limited. This aspect of the provision was tested in *R* v. *Bristol City Council, ex parte Penfold* [1998] 1 CCLR 315. In this case the council refused to assess a woman for community care services because it had decided she had no real prospect of eventually being provided with services. The court described the first step in the key three-stage process of s. 47 as providing a very low threshold test. The duty to assess was triggered by the appearance of need for any service which could be provided, not which was actually likely to be provided. If a person is seeking a particular service and appears to be in need of community care services, the local authority must carry out an assessment even if it does not provide or arrange the service in question, provided it has the power to do so. The effect of the judgment is to prevent councils screening out individuals prior to assessment and, in all but the most extreme cases, if an individual requests a needs assessment, he or she should be provided with one. Screening might, however, be used for depth and urgency of assessment. Assessment levels are acknowledged in guidance as contact, overview, specialist and comprehensive.[17] Scott-Baker LJ, giving judgment in the *Bristol* case, also made the point that, even if it is unlikely that needs identified in the assessment will be met, the assessment is still useful in terms of identifying unmet needs, which will be useful for future strategic planning. Unmet need recorded as such is lawful if outside the eligibility criteria. The emphasis is firmly placed on the local authority to assess people who might be eligible for services, rather than on the individual to request an assessment. The community care plan, the local authority is obliged to produce under s. 46 (see below) should provide an indication of the number of people in the area that may require community care services and the range of needs

'shall'

Once the 'appearance' of need is established, the use of the word 'shall' in para. (a) indicates a mandatory obligation or duty on the local authority to carry out an assessment of need. A specific time limit in which assessments should be carried out is not included in the legislation or guidance, but by implication an assessment should be completed within a reasonable time. Timescales may be stipulated by a local authority in its community care plan to prioritise the most urgent cases, where an identifiable risk is apparent before assessment. Where there is unreasonable delay it would be appropriate to utilise the complaints procedure or complain to the local government ombudsman (see ombudsman decision below as an example).

'decide'

The use of the word 'decide' in para. (b) introduces an element of discretion into the provision. The link between this discretion and limited resources has been subject to challenge in a number of cases and will be considered further.

There is an explicit link to the provision of services for disabled people under other legislation in subsection (2).

s. 47(2)

> If at any time during the assessment of the needs of any person under subsection (1)(a) above it appears to a local authority that he is a disabled person, the authority –
> (a) shall proceed to make such a decision as to the services he requires as is mentioned in section 4 of the Disabled Persons (Services, Consultation and Representation) Act 1986 without his requesting them to do so under that section; and
> (b) shall inform him that they will be doing so and of his rights under that Act.
>
> (NHSCCA 1990)

The application of s. 47 by local authorities has produced a significant body of case law with particular focus on local authority resources and eligibility criteria. *R* v. *Gloucestershire County Council, ex parte Barry* [1997] 2 All ER 1 remains the leading decision in this area. This decision appeared to suggest that resources could be a relevant factor for councils to take into account when assessing need for all community care services. The case came to court as a judicial review application in the following circumstances. In 1995, Gloucestershire County Council, facing funding cuts of £2.5 million, withdrew or cut provision of home care services to 1,500 service users and changed its eligibility criteria. Mr Barry challenged the decision of the authority to withdraw services provided to him under section 2 of the Chronically Sick and Disabled Persons Act 1970 (for assistance with laundry and cleaning), on the basis that, although the authority's funding position might have changed, his needs had not. In the House of Lords' judgment there was recognition of the difficulties faced by local authorities in managing resources to fulfil duties in the complex area of community care. The court held, by a majority, that resources might be taken into account when assessing or reassessing whether an individual is in need of services. The concept of need has to be considered in the context of other relevant factors, including an authority's own resources. Since the *Gloucestershire* decision, it is clear that local authorities are justified in using eligibility criteria as a means of rationing resources. Eligibility criteria must be satisfied by an individual before his needs will be met. Local authorities would not be justified, however, in failing to provide services to an individual with an established need simply because the end of a financial year is looming and resources have run out. Eligibility criteria have to be set so as to anticipate such situations and operate to identify what levels of need will attract services. Eligibility criteria may be reset periodically and resources taken into account when setting new criteria. As a result, those in receipt of services under the old criteria would need to be reassessed before any reduction in services.

Guidance was issued following the *Gloucestershire* decision.[18] In response to concerns over the judgment, the guidance confirmed that the judgment did not provide authority for decisions to be taken on the basis of resources alone and that resource pressures were not an excuse for taking arbitrary or unreasonable decisions.

Possible challenges to the local authority would arise if an authority had no eligibility criteria. This would suggest poor administration and it would be difficult to demonstrate reasoned decision-making. If the authority had eligibility criteria that were so tight that people at risk did not qualify for services, this would conflict with the *Killigrew* decision (discussed below) and breach the overarching need for reasonableness in the way an authority carries out its responsibilities. Each case must be considered individually and therefore application of blanket criteria, such as 'we never provide this service to older people', would be unlawful (LAC (2002)13 para 23). It is essential that all service users are assessed under the current criteria. It would be inappropriate, therefore, where eligibility criteria are tightened and published, for them to be applied only to new assessments and not to existing users, to avoid provoking complaints. This would result in inequitable differences between service users with similar means living within a local authority boundary.

■ Fair access to care services?

The current guidance on assessment and eligibility criteria is found in 'Fair Access to Care Services?' LAC (2003) 12 published by the Department of Health. Implementation of the new framework, after consultation with local stakeholders is intended to lead to fairer and more consistent eligibility decisions across the country. The guidance is issued under s. 7(1) of the Local Authority Social Services Act 1970 and as such, councils risk breaching the law if (in the absence of a good reason) they do not follow the guidance. The guidance is clearly a response to the disparate arrangements that have existed around the country and challenges to community care decisions often based on judicial review and leading to a body of case law some of which has been discussed. It is also a step towards fulfilment of part of the National Service Framework for Older People relating to tackling age discrimination. The guidance identifies four eligibility bands – critical, substantial, moderate and low – which relate to individuals' needs and risks to independence. The bands should include consideration of immediate needs as presented and also longer-term risks including needs which are likely to worsen without help, as identified through risk assessments. The guidance emphasises that councils should operate only one set of criteria based on the eligibility bands outlined. Separate criteria relating, for example, to the depth and type of assessment and for specific services should be abolished. The guidance draws a distinction between presenting needs, as those issues that are identified when social care support is sought, and eligible needs as those needs that fall within the council's eligibility criteria. Presenting needs which do not fit into eligibility criteria have been known as 'unmet needs', a term which is implicitly discouraged by the new guidance. Many authorities have set a threshold for meeting need between the 'moderate' and 'substantial' band, i.e. those with presenting needs falling into the critical or substantial risk to independence bands will be eligible for services whereas those whose needs present a moderate or low risk to independence will not.

The categories are set out in Exhibit 14.1.

In most cases the bands are differentiated by the degree to which each factor is affected by the risk to independence, as indicated by the words in bold, for example, vital/the majority of/several/one or two family roles cannot be sustained. Additional factors are included in the more serious bands, e.g. life will be threatened.

Critical risk to independence	Substantial risk to independence	Moderate risk to independence	Low risk to independence
Life is/ will be threatened			
Significant health problems have developed/will develop			
There is/will be **little/no** choice and control over vital aspects of the immediate environment	There is/will be only **partial** choice and control over the immediate environment		
Serious abuse or neglect has occurred/ will occur	Abuse or neglect has occurred/will occur		
There is/will be an inability to carry out **vital** personal care or domestic routines	There is/will be an inability to carry out **the majority of** personal care or domestic routines	There is/will be an inability to carry out **several** personal care or domestic routines	There is/will be an inability to carry out **one or two** personal care or domestic routines
Vital involvement in work, education or learning cannot/will not be sustained	Involvement in **many aspects** of work, education or learning cannot/will not be sustained	Involvement in **several aspects** of work, education or learning cannot/ will not be sustained	Involvement in **one or two aspects** of work, education learning cannot/ will not be sustained

Continued overleaf

Exhibit 14.1   Eligibility bands for care services

Critical risk to independence	Substantial risk to independence	Moderate risk to independence	Low risk to independence
Vital social support systems and relationships cannot/will not be sustained	The **majority** of support systems and relationships cannot/will not be sustained	**Several** support systems and relationships cannot/will not be sustained	**One or two** support systems and relationships cannot/will not be sustained
Vital family and other social roles and responsibilities cannot/will not be undertaken	The **majority** of family and other social roles and responsibilities cannot/will not be undertaken	**Several** family and other social roles and responsibilities cannot/will not be undertaken	**One or two** family and other social roles and responsibilities cannot/will not be undertaken

Exhibit 14.1   (continued)

Whilst one of the objectives of the guidance is fairer and more consistent eligibility decisions, it will still be possible for councils to take account of their adult social care resources when setting eligibility criteria. Councils do need to be able to respond to the needs of their particular adult population and a measure of flexibility is welcomed, however, there will still inevitably be regional variation in the services provision for people with similar needs living in different parts of the country.[19]

■ Choice, preference or need?

The question of preference or need is more than simply a matter of semantics. In the case of *R* v. *Avon County Council, ex parte M* [1994] 2 FCR 259, the local authority was under a duty to make arrangements for residential accommodation for a 22-year-old man with Down's syndrome. The man's preference, which was described as 'entrenched', to go to a particular home was rejected by the council – it wished to place him in a home which it claimed would meet his needs but which was cheaper. In fact it was found that the entrenched position of this man was a psychological need, rather than a preference, and the authority were obliged to meet that need.

A move to another part of the country, perhaps to be closer to relatives, has also been recognised as a possible aspect of individual need. If the preferred area was typically more expensive than the accommodation costs the placing authority would normally pay, to meet the need of such an individual the authority would pay the normal rate in the more expensive area.[20]

Further case law has limited the reality of individual choice in community care provision. In *R* v. *Lancashire County Council, ex parte Ingham* (1995) 5 July QBD: CO/774, the court upheld the local authority's decision to provide for an assessed need for 24-hour care in a nursing home rather than in the elderly woman's own home. The local authority could take resources into account in deciding which service to provide to meet her needs. This position was confirmed when the case was consolidated with another appeal. In practice, local authorities often set a financial 'ceiling' as the maximum amount of care that they will provide to an individual at home. Provided that the alternative way of providing care (usually in a care home) will meet the individual's need, and the decision has been taken following an individual reassessment, this is lawful practice. In practice, if high levels of care at home will cost more than an appropriate type of residential care, the latter is likely to be offered as the means of meeting individual need. The Choice of Accommodation Directions 1992[21] provide that an individual has the right to choose a home, subject to it being suitable, there being a room available in the home, and it being available at a price which is no more than the authority will normally pay for that level of need. If no accommodation were available at that cost, the local authority would have to pay a higher rate.

■ Home closures

There have been a number of case where residents have sought to challenge local authority decisions to close care homes. In *R (on the application of Dudley, Whitbread and Others)* v. *East Sussex County Council* [2003] EWHC 1093 (Admin), the High Court found that closing a home is not necessarily incompatible with residents' rights under Art. 8, a persons right to respect for his home. Any interference with residents' rights must be proportionate and the court stressed the need for the process leading to closure to be managed properly including a consultation exercise. In times where authorities are having to deal with scarce resources and closing homes may result in cost savings the court showed a reluctance to interfere with the authority's decision.

The court rejected evidence that care home closures and associated transfer of residents lead to increased mortality, describing the statistical evidence as 'massively overstated'. It also rejected arguments under Art. 3, which provides that no-one shall be subject to inhuman or degrading treatment. The court stated that closure of the centre and subsequent transfer of residents did not come close to the threshold required for treatment to be inhuman or degrading.

■ Principles of assessment

Assessments should be carried out in a multi-disciplinary fashion with the individual and carers participating fully. The assessment should provide and support choices and self-determination and allow an element of measurable risk. The procedure should be flexible and supported by individual and central case management and monitoring of the assessment process and outcome. The assessment should take into account the wishes of individual carers and the carer's ability to provide care.[22]

It is essential that all agencies and professionals involved with the individual are brought into the assessment procedure as necessary in order for the multi-disciplinary object of assessment to be realised. Statutory support for this principle is provided in NHSCCA 1990, s. 47(3), which states that where it appears to the local authority that there may be a need for that person to be provided with services by the

433

health or housing authority, 'the local authority shall notify that [health authority] or local housing authority and invite them to assist, to such extent as is reasonable in the circumstances, in the making of the assessment; . . .[23] A multi-disciplinary assessment could include an extensive range of individuals and agencies, such as social workers from hospital or the community, community nurses, general practitioners, community psychiatric nurses, physiotherapists, occupational therapists, home care assistants, housing agencies, sheltered housing wardens, hospital consultants (e.g. geriatricians), members of the family and social network, interpreters and, of course, the service user.

The assessment should be comprehensive and is likely to include the following issues: biographical details, self-perception of needs, physical health, mental health, use of medicines, abilities, aptitudes, transport, social networks and support, care services and needs of carers, housing, finance, risk, race and culture. *R* v. *Haringey, ex parte Norton* (1997–98) 1CCLR 168 supports the principle of a comprehensive assessment and considered what needs to be assessed. The authority, which considered itself bound only to assess and meet personal care needs, was mistaken in law. An authority must assess for all the potential services in the Chronically Sick and Disabled Persons Act 1970, s. 2. In this case the authority had not assessed for social needs. All options must be assessed in line with the eligibility criteria.

In addition, the NHSCCA 1990 envisages service provision and responsibilities beyond the local authority Social Services Departments. If the local authority considers that there may be need for health services or services of the local housing authority, it should notify the authority and invite that authority to assist in the assessment (s. 47(3), above). The local authority can also take into account any services that are likely to be provided by the health authority or local housing authority when making its own decision on provision of services. Whilst these sections are intended to promote a seamless service provision and provide the foundation for cooperation between different agencies, in practice it can result in a degree of 'buck passing' and gaps in service provision.

The fact that the housing authority has responsibilities to provide housing does not remove from Social Services Departments the responsibility to arrange and provide accommodation in some circumstances. For example, in *R* v. *Islington London Borough Council, ex parte Batantu* (2001) 33 HLR 76, the community care assessment of need included the need for more spacious ground-floor accommodation. In this case the assessment found that the existing accommodation (a small twelfth-floor flat for B, his wife and four children) contributed to his mental health problems. There was a duty to provide appropriate accommodation and not to treat this as a pure housing issue, which would have left B waiting several years for more appropriate accommodation. Housing and accommodation needs may thus be included as part of the care package. Of further significance is the interpretation of the National Assistance Act 1948, s. 21 in relation to asylum seekers. In *R* v. *Hammersmith and Fulham, ex parte M* (1998) 30 HLR 10, asylum seekers (who were not eligible for benefits) were found to be entitled to residential accommodation to meet their need for care and attention 'not otherwise available to them'. This interpretation effectively supplemented Home Office responsibilities towards asylum seekers who were 'destitute or likely to become destitute' (see further discussion in Chapter 20).

It may not even be possible to carry out an assessment in some circumstances, particularly where the individual refuses access. The only possible forms of compulsion would be via use of the Mental Health Act 1983 and the National Assistance Act 1948, s. 47.

More recently, Community Care Assessment Directions 2004 have confirmed that there should be a 'single assessment' for older people, local authorities must consult the person to be assessed, take all reasonable steps to reach agreement with the person and where appropriate any carers of that person on the community care services which they are considering providing to meet his needs. The accompanying circular (Circular LAC (2004) 24) reinforces the Directions and reminds us that a carer should not be excluded from care planning where he does not want to be assessed for care services; carers should be as involved as possible where the person cared for lacks capacity; disagreements between the cared for person and the carer should be handled sensitively (it may be appropriate to involve independent or statutory advocacy) and if it is not appropriate to involve the carer a written account of the reasons should be kept.

■ Anti-discriminatory practice and assessment

Adherence to principles of anti-discriminatory practice is an essential aspect of any type of assessment process carried out by social services. The characteristics of many adult service users make them especially vulnerable to discrimination and an awareness of the relevance of anti-discrimination law can help to promote good practice in this area. Fuller discussion of discrimination law can be found in Chapter 6.

The focus of anti-discrimination law (and case law decisions) has settled around employment issues. Most of the early decisions under the Disability Discrimination Act 1995 (DDA 1995) dealing with interpretation of terms were arrived at by the Employment Appeal Tribunal and it is clear that many people who are disabled under the terms of the Act are or have been unemployed. As there is a level of consistency in the approach of each of the three pieces of anti-discrimination legislation, in relation to employment, this raft of legislation is discussed in more detail in relation to employment in Chapter 6. Here, the focus will continue to be on service provision and the specific anti-discrimination sections relating to service provision. A preliminary point should be made regarding procedure. If an individual claims he has suffered discrimination in an area not related to employment (i.e. goods and services), the action will be brought in the county court and damages may be awarded as compensation.

The DDA 1995 was initially implemented in respect of employment matters. Provisions now in force have extended its application to obtaining goods and services, education and transport. Disability is defined in the Act as follows:

s. 1(1)

> A person has a disability for the purposes of this Act if he has a physical or mental impairment which has a substantial and long-term adverse effect on his ability to carry out normal day-to-day activities.

(DDA 1995)

435

Section 19 provides that it is unlawful for a provider of services to discriminate against a disabled person:

s. 19(1)(a)

> In refusing to provide, or deliberately not providing, to the disabled person any service which he provides or is prepared to provide, to members of the public.
>
> (DDA 1995)

The definition of services specifically includes services of any local or other public authority (s.19(3)). It also includes access to and use of: any public places; accommodation in hotels; banking, insurance and credit facilities; entertainment, recreation or refreshment. As many of the services discussed in this chapter are specifically targeted at people with disabilities, the application of these provisions may seem limited. If, however, a local authority had a policy (for example) of not exercising their power to make direct payments to disabled people but did so for older people, this would be discriminatory. A challenge of such a policy would also be supported by Art. 14 of the European Convention on Human Rights, which prohibits discrimination on a wide range of grounds, including disability, in the enjoyment of the rights and freedoms of the Convention. Section 21 may also have a direct impact on practice. It states:

s. 21

> Where a provider of services has a practice, policy or procedure which makes it impossible or unreasonably difficult for disabled persons to make use of a service which he provides . . . to other members of the public, it is his duty to take such steps as it is reasonable, in all the circumstances of the case, . . . to change that practice, policy or procedure so that it no longer has that effect.
>
> (DDA 1995)

An obvious example, which would be covered by this provision, is if information provided in leaflet form was not also available for people with a visual impairment. The Act is supported by a Disability Rights Commission. The Commission's role is to oversee implementation of the Act, disseminate good practice, issue Codes of Practice and conduct investigations. The Commission will be amalgamated into the new Commission for Equality and Human Rights in the future. Under the Disability Discrimination Act 2005 local authorities are required to produce a Disability Equality Scheme.

Anti-discrimination laws do not anticipate 'multiplicity' of characteristics in the construction of separate legal categories for the purpose of recognising discrimination. A black woman with a learning disability may suffer discrimination on a number of levels and it may not be clear which legal route for challenge should apply.

Anti-discrimination legislation should be seen as additional to other possible avenues of challenge, such as the local authority complaints process.

The NHSCCA 1990 (in contrast to the Children Act 1989) does not make specific reference to race, religion, language and culture. It is perhaps not surprising that particular problems relating to community care for black and ethnic minority people have been identified, including under-use of services and restricted choice of services,[24] and assumptions being made about extended family networks of support, despite changing employment patterns and reduction in family size in the Asian community.[25] Service provision must, however, comply with the provisions of the Race Relations (Amendment) Act 2000 (RR(A)A 2000). This legislation places a duty on all public bodies,[26] including local authorities, to promote equality of opportunity and good relations between different racial groups, in all of its functions (s. 1). This strengthens provisions in the earlier legislation, the Race Relations Act 1976. It will not be sufficient for an authority to respond to race discrimination; it must take positive steps to prevent race discrimination. In community care this duty will extend to the assessment process, planning, publishing information and provision of services. The Commission for Racial Equality (**CRE**) will have powers to investigate public authorities that do not comply with the terms of the Act. The measures taken to ensure equality of opportunity in community care should be addressed in each authority's race equality scheme. Specific codes of practice for public authorities are to be published by the CRE.

■ Services pending assessment

The normal assessment process will take some time, particularly if it is to be comprehensive as outlined. In recognition of this, NHSCCA 1990, s. 47(5) authorises the local authority to arrange provision of community care services before an assessment. As that provision will not formally be as the result of an assessment, it is possible that the final level of service may be different and some of the services introduced pending assessment may be withdrawn.

■ The care plan

The care plan is an important document. All individuals in receipt of community care services, however limited or extensive, should have a care plan. The essential contents of the care plan will be the assessment of need of the individual and the services that will be provided. Further detail to be included should relate to risk management, role of carers, whether the service user agrees the plan, a named coordinator and contact, costs to the service user and any unmet need. Social and recreational needs as well as personal care needs should be addressed in the care plan. The plan may be implemented in a variety of ways, drawing on providers from the public, private and voluntary sectors and with scope for direct provision and direct payments to enable the service user to arrange their own services. The plan should be reviewed regularly and, particularly, where needs of the individual change, e.g. where a physical disability worsens or a person who has provided a substantial amount of care can no longer do so. If it is not possible to reach agreement about an aspect of the plan, any points of difference should be recorded.[27] Care providers, such as care homes and domiciliary agencies should also have care plans in respect of each service user.

A complaint about the content of a care plan would initially be dealt with through the Complaints and Representations Procedure. In *R (Lloyd)* v. *Barking and Dagenham London Borough Council* [2001] EWCA Civ 533, the Court of Appeal held that judicial review should be the last resort as a means of challenging the local authority's care plan, in this case made in respect of a disabled person.

■ Delay

Timescales for carrying out assessments are not stipulated in the legislation and in the absence of a clearly identified period, the law expects that assessments should be carried out within a reasonable time. This will vary dependent on the circumstances and most authorities include timescales and priority groups in their own policies. Excessive waiting times have featured in many local government ombudsman decisions, and local authority complaints and generally staff shortages have not been found to justify delays.[28] A case which reached the courts was *R (J)* v. *Newham London Borough Connai* [2001] EWHC Admin 992 in which the court decided that 35 days was too long a delay. Having carried out an assessment, delay in implementing the care plan should also be minimised. Again, the expectation is that the duty to meet needs by implementing the care plan will be carried out within a reasonable time, that varying depending on the circumstances of the case.

Legislation has been introduced specifically to tackle delay associated with 'bed blocking'. The Community Care (Delayed Discharges etc.) Act 2003 received Royal Assent despite widespread opposition. The Act provides for social services departments to be fined on a daily basis where they are considered responsible for any delay in discharging a qualifying patient from hospital (likely to be patients receiving acute or geriatric hospital care). This will usually be due to unavailability of an appropriate package of care. The NHS must give notice to the Social Services Authority (for the area where the patient normally lives) of the patient's likely need for community care services on discharge. Social services will have to complete an assessment which focuses on the patient's needs in order to be discharged safely. An assessment will need to be completed regardless of whether the individual has previously had an assessment for community care services. The NHS body must also notify Social Services of the intended day of discharge. Explanatory notes to the Bill stated:

> It provides for payment to be made to the healthcare provider per day of delay from the point at which responsibility for an NHS patient's care should have transferred from the acute sector to social services. This provides an incentive for social services to make prompt assessment of a patient's community care needs and make appropriate service provision for them in timely fashion.

▪ Community care and human rights

Challenges within the field of community care have been brought under the Human Rights Act 1998. The case of *R (Bernard)* v. *London Borough of Enfield* [2002] EWHC 2282 (Admin), where failure to provide community care services was found to be a violation of Art. 8, is discussed fully in Chapter 5. In *Anufrijeva* v. *Southwark London Borough Cannai* [2003] EWCA Civ 1406, similar arguments about the positive obligations arising from Art. 8 were rejected. The court's decision reflects a concern to discourage HRA claims based on failures to provide services. Where such claims are made they should be linked to an application for judicial review or preferably, dealt with by the Local Government Ombudsman. The court approved the *Bernard* decision but suggested that it would be unusual to find circumstances where failure to provide services would breach Art. 8 and not Art. 3 except that a breach under Art. 8 alone may arise where the family life aspect of Art. 8 was significant. In cases where it is alleged that Art. 8 has been breached through failure to provide services, *Anifrijeva* rules that claimant needs to demonstrate 'culpability' on the part of the authority and serious consequences for the individual arising from the failure.

The case of *A* v. *East Sussex County Council* [2003] EWHC 167 (Admin) centred on a dispute about manual handling for two severely disabled sisters. The judgment includes a number of statements about the application of Art. 8 (right to respect for private and family life) to disabled people.

> The other important concept embraced in the 'physical and psychological integrity' protected by Art. 8 is the right of the disabled to participate in the life of the community and to have what has been described as 'access to essential economic and social activities and to an appropriate range of recreational and cultural activities'. This is matched by the positive obligation of the state to take appropriate measures designed to ensure to the greatest extent feasible that a disabled person is not 'so circumscribed and so isolated as to be deprived of the possibility of developing his personality.

▪ Monitoring and reviewing and reassessment

The care plan should be monitored and kept under review. This aspect of care management enables changing needs to be identified and as a result services may be adapted to meet current needs of the individual. Guidance provides that care needs for which services are being provided should be reviewed as a matter of routine within the first three months of services being provided, then annually, or more often if necessary (LAC (2002) 13).

A reassessment of needs should be carried out in the same way as the initial assessment. Reassessment may be prompted by a change in the circumstances of the service user or their carer, or it may be required because the authority has changed its eligibility criteria. The most obvious reason for the authority to change its criteria is due to budget changes. If budgets are reduced, eligibility criteria may be drawn tighter and, ultimately, an individual whose needs have not actually changed may find on reassessment that he is only entitled to a reduced level of services. The important point here is that the authority cannot reduce services without first carrying out a reassessment. Furthermore, the case of *R* v. *Birmingham City Council, ex parte Killigrew* [1999] 3 CCLR 109 states that services can be reduced only if the person would not be left in 'serious physical risk'. In this case services were reduced from 12 hours to 6 hours daily. The decision was quashed because reassessment failed to address why services, which she had been assessed as needing, were no longer needed. In other words, there is a level below which service provision cannot be reduced, no matter what the financial circumstances of the authority, if the result would be unacceptable risk.

■ Community care plan

Each Social Services Department must publish a plan for community care in its area (NHSCCA 1990, s. 46), arrived at following consultation with relevant organisations (including the health authority, housing departments and organisations representing service users and carers). It must be updated regularly to ensure that services meet the particular needs of the community (e.g. a separate day care service for Muslim women). The plan should demonstrate how local arrangements for delivering community care services meet the Government's six key objectives:

- to promote development of domiciliary, day and respite services to enable people to live in their own homes;
- to ensure service providers make practical support for carers a high priority;
- to make proper assessment of need and good care management the cornerstone of high quality care;
- to promote the development of a flourishing independent sector alongside quality public services;
- to clarify the responsibilities of agencies and hold them to account for their performance;
- to secure better value for taxpayers' money by introducing a new funding structure for social care.[29]

It is disappointing that reference to race and culture did not feature in the six key objectives of the white paper, though it does include the following paragraph:

2.9 The Government recognises that people from different cultural backgrounds may have particular care needs and problems. Minority communities may have different concepts of community care and it is important that service providers are sensitive to these variations. Good community care will take account of the circumstances of minority communities and will be planned in consultation with them.

Policy guidance makes publishing information the first step in care management; and NHSCCA 1990, s. 46 requires local authorities to publish community care plans as public documents, which should list available services. Consumer surveys, however, suggest that service users are often ill-informed. Article 10 of the European Convention on Human Rights (the right to freedom of expression) may be relevant to this issue. The right extends to the right to receive information (*Open Door Counselling and Dublin Well Woman Centre* v. *Ireland* (1992) 15 EHRR 244, and may have implications for local authorities' publications relating to available services. Questions about, for example, whether there are sufficient leaflets, in accessible places, in different languages, become relevant.

■ Charging for services

The Health and Social Services and Social Security Adjudications Act 1983 (**HASSASSAA 1983**), s. 17 provides that local authorities have the power to make reasonable charges for non-residential community services (and they have been encouraged to use this power) where it is reasonably practicable for the service user to pay.[30] Community care services that can be charged for include: welfare services for disabled people, for older people and for prevention of illness, or provision of care, after care, home help and laundry facilities. Charges vary between different regions but guidance has been issued, providing a framework for charging which should reduce regional variation. Each authority should have a clear policy on charging and provide information about the system. Guidance suggests that charging policy should not reduce income to income support levels, the means of other members of the family should not be taken into account and service users should be made aware that they can ask for a review of a charge or make a complaint.[31] If an individual does not pay the required charges, the local authority should not withdraw services but may attempt to recover the debt, through the courts if necessary.

Regulations provide for some services to be provided free of charge. Under the Community Care (Delayed Discharges etc.) Act (Qualifying Services) (England) Regulations 2003,[32] Social services are required to provide the first six weeks of a period of 'intermediate care' free of charge, including residential accommodation. Intermediate care refers to the care provided on discharge from hospital to help an individual maintain or regain the ability to live in his own home. Social services are required to provide community equipment services free of charge. This includes provision of aids, minor adaptations to property, valued at less than £1,000, to assist with nursing at home or daily living.[33]

After-care services provided under s. 117 of the Mental Health Act 1983 are excluded services and cannot be charged for (confirmed in *R* v. *Richmond London Borough Council, ex parte W* [1999] 2 CCLR 402).

Local authorities are under a duty to apply charges in respect of the provision of residential accommodation (nursing care in all settings is free of charge). Regulations covering assessment of a person's ability to pay for residential accommodation are referred to as 'CRAG', the Charging for Residential Accommodation Guide[34] (issued under Local Authority Social Services Act 1970, s. 7(1)).

In summary, a person will be liable to pay the full cost of residential accommodation if they have in excess of £20,500 of capital. A sliding scale of contributions applies if there is between £12,500 and £20,500 of capital; below £12,500, the capital is disregarded. In many instances capital will be in the form of a property. The local authority must ignore the value of a person's property for the first three months of their stay, if their stay in residential accommodation is temporary, and also where the resident's spouse or dependant continues to live in the property. If the property is not eligible to be disregarded, then the local authority may create a charge on the property, until it is sold, when the money will be claimed.

There may be a scenario where an older person, having considered that a move to residential accommodation is imminent, decides to transfer their property to a relative, e.g. a son or daughter. If the local authority considers that they have in fact deprived themselves of capital assets in order to reduce or avoid any charges they would have to pay, they may be deemed still to have the capital. The local authority might be able to recover the property from the son or daughter if the resident deprived himself of the assets within six months of entering residential accommodation. To do so, the local authority must show that the transfer was done knowingly and with the intention of avoiding charges.[35]

A person who is entitled to residential accommodation has the right to choose which particular home to go to under the National Assistance Act 1948 (Choice of Accommodation) Directions 1992 through the concept of 'preferred accommodation'. That choice is subject to the important limitation of cost (and also suitability in relation to needs and availability). The local authority will set a level or cost ceiling which they are prepared to pay to meet that person's needs and the individual can choose a home which has a room available at that cost. This is supplemented by new choice directions guidance, issued in October 2004 relating to choice for those assessed as needing to move into a care home.[36] It confirms that, if requested (where an individual has chosen to move into a home that has higher fees than those agreed by the council with local independent care home providers), the council should arrange for care in a home more expensive than it would usually fund, provided a third party or, in certain circumstances, the resident, is willing and able to top up the fees. If, however, a person has to move into a care home whose fees are higher than standard because of the level of care they need, the council should meet the additional costs.

■ Direct payments

Local authorities are obliged to make direct payments to certain individuals, so they can purchase their own non-residential services including equipment, by virtue of the Community Care (Direct Payments) Act 1996,[37] the Health and Social Care Act 2001 and regulations[36] when certain conditions are met. Government policy is to make direct payments available to as many eligible people as possible in order to 'give recipients control over their own life by providing an alternative to social services provided by a local council'.[38] A possible disadvantage of direct payments may be greater susceptibility to abuse and lesser regulation of certain services. Payments are made to people who appear capable of managing a direct payment by themselves or with assistance. To be eligible for a direct payment,

- the individual must have been assessed as needing services and the payment is made in lieu of direct provision of services;
- the service to be purchased must meet the assessed need;
- the individual must consent to receipt of direct payment;
- the individual must be capable of managing a direct payment by himself or with assistance.

Direct payments can be made to any community care service users over 18 and informal carers over 16, who meet the criteria above. It is possible to have a combination of services and direct payments. Direct payments can provide greater control to the individual and guidance suggests that local authorities 'should seek to leave as much choice as possible in the hands of the individual, and allow people to address their own needs in innovative ways, whilst satisfying themselves that the person's assessed needs are being met, and that public funds are being spent appropriately and with best value.'[39] Direct payments cannot be used where the individual is subject to guardianship under the Mental Health Act 1983, or to pay for services that the National Health Service should provide, or for permanent (more than four weeks in a year) residential care. The local authority may make the payment subject to appropriate conditions, e.g. financial procedures. Rate of payment must be 'equivalent to the reasonable cost of securing the provision of the service concerned' (HSCA 2001, s. 57). A person using direct payments to arrange care services should be advised to go to a reputable agency and to draw up a contract of employment.[40]

The Carers and Disabled Children Act 2000 gives local authorities powers to make direct payments to carers instead of providing services. For example, this might enable a carer to pay somebody to carry out shopping and other chores, or free up more of the carer's time to provide care.

Grants are also available to disabled people from the Independent Living Fund, which can be used to employ personal assistants for personal and domestic care. (See further, Chapter 19).

■ Inspection of community care services

s. 48

> Any person authorised by the Secretary of State may at any reasonable time enter and inspect any premises . . . in which community-care services are or are proposed to be provided by a local authority, whether directly or under arrangements made with another person.
>
> (NHSCCA 1990)

The inspector is entitled to examine the management, records, premises, facilities, fire regulations and services of the establishment, e.g. a day centre. Registration of care homes is considered separately under the Care Standards Act 2000 later in this chapter.

It is arguable that the local authority could be in breach of its responsibilities under the Human Rights Act 1998, as a public authority, if it fails to monitor services adequately and prevent providers breaching users' rights.

▪ Complaints procedure

In assessment, procedural fairness and reasoned decision-making is essential. An avenue for challenge is equally important if a level of accountability is to be achieved. Article 6 of the European Convention on Human Rights may have some application here. The Article provides for fair determination of a person's civil rights and a person probably has a civil right to a service, having passed through eligibility criteria. Failure to provide a service, or to cut it without a lawful reassessment, might amount to a breach of human rights, if the decision has been taken unfairly. A fair decision-making process should involve a chance to make representations, proper reasons being given for a decision based on close consideration of individual needs rather than general application of policy. All relevant matters should be taken into account in an assessment and all irrelevant matters disregarded.

Section 50 of the NHSCCA 1990 amends s. 7 of the Local Authority Social Services Act 1970, giving the Secretary of State the power to order Social Services Authorities to establish a complaints procedure. The local authority must establish a procedure for considering representations (including complaints) made by qualifying individuals relating to the discharge or failure to discharge any of their social services functions in respect of that individual.[41] There are three stages to the process: an informal stage; the formal or registration stage; and the review stage. A complainant may go direct to the formal stage. At the review stage a panel is convened, which must include a person who is independent of the authority.[42] It may be helpful for an individual who wishes to make a complaint (and to participate fully in the community care process outlined in this chapter) to have the support of an advocate. There is no general legal right to an advocate although there are references to advocates in guidance, such as the importance of advocates 'taking a full part in decision-making',[43] and local authorities are encouraged to develop advocacy services.[44] Carers will often effectively take on the role of advocate, though there can be conflicts between the carer and the person cared for, in which case an independent advocate is preferable. There is also a significant growth of self-advocacy groups such as 'People First', who define self-advocacy as speaking for yourself, standing up for your rights, making choices, being independent and taking responsibility for yourself.[45] (Complaints are discussed further in Chapter 4.)

The requirement of independence and impartiality contained in ECHR, Art. 6 may call into question whether complaints procedures under s. 26 of the National Health Service and Community Care Act 1990, or those operating in, for example, residential homes, are adequate. *R (Beeson)* v. *Dorset County Council* [2002] EWCA Civ 1812 found that a local authority social services panel did not lack sufficient independence to comply with the fair trial provisions of ECHR, Art. 6(1). The review panel in this case had to decide whether the deceased person had deprived himself of assets before a move to residential accommodation. The panel was comprised of one independent person and two county councillors and the final decision was taken by the council's director of social services. The High Court found that failure to comply with Art. 6(1) could be remedied by appointment of a fully independent panel. On appeal, the Court of Appeal stated that the real question was whether the addition of judicial review to the process satisfied the standard. It found that if there was no substantive reason to question the integrity of the panel decision, whatever its appearance might suggest, the added safeguard of judicial review would usually satisfy the Art. 6 standard.

Financial compensation is not provided for under the complaints process.

Local government ombudsman

A reported decision illustrates the role of the local government ombudsman as providing a useful means of challenging the actions of local authorities in the field of community care. The role of the ombudsman is to consider whether there has been maladministration in a case. *Investigation into Complaint No. 97/A/2959 against Hackney LBC* [1998] 2 CCLR 66 concerned two brothers aged 41 and 39, both with learning difficulties. They had been attending a day centre for about ten years. In 1995, Hackney transferred management of the centre to a charity as part of reorganisation of services for people with learning difficulties and reorganisation of the community care division. The transfer took place on the understanding that Hackney and the charity would reassess the needs of all users of the centre within six months. Despite reminders from the charity and Edward and Robert's parents, Mr and Mrs Foster, the assessment did not commence until 1997. Mrs Foster lodged a complaint, which was upheld in January 1997 by the Social Services Complaints Review Panel, concluding that Hackney had been negligent and recommending that the reassessment be carried out within three months. The Director of Social Services wrote explaining that the cause of the delay was lack of resources. By November 1998 Hackney had still not completed risk assessments or a care plan for Edward or Robert.

The local government ombudsman reached the following conclusions:

1. The delay in carrying out reassessments (about 22 months) amounted to maladministration.
2. Hackney had still not completed a risk assessment at the time of the investigation; record keeping was poor, as were communications with Mr and Mrs Foster, to whom they had failed to explain the nature and purpose of the reassessment. These faults all amounted to maladministration.
3. Injustice had been caused by the maladministration. In particular, Mr and Mrs Foster had suffered anxiety and had been put to considerable time and trouble. Also, Edward and Robert had missed the opportunity of benefiting from earlier provision based on proper assessment.

It was recommended that Hackney should pay £1,500 compensation to Mr and Mrs Foster. Of general application, it was recommended that Hackney should review the needs of other people using the day centre; review provision of written information about the community care assessment process; review supervision arrangements for care managers and implement a system to ensure recommendations of review panels are implemented without unreasonable delay. This case provides a clear example of the damaging effect of delay relating to service provision for vulnerable adults. The full report is particularly interesting to read for the insight it gives into the extent and process of the detailed investigation carried out by the ombudsman.

Other avenues for complaint, the role of the monitoring officer, judicial review, default powers of the Secretary of State and action for damages, are all discussed in Chapter 4.

■ Carers

Carers play a vital role in community care, providing most support.[46] There are approximately 6 million carers throughout Britain, including some carers providing care for a few hours a week and others providing literally 24-hour care. Women are more likely to be carers than men and carers are most likely to be aged 45–64 (although there are a significant number of 'young' carers who may be caring for their parents). Carers may also have their own community care needs.

One of the NHSCCA 1990 objectives was to ensure service providers make practical support for carers a high priority. Building on this provision, the Carers (Recognition and Services) Act 1995 (C(RS)A 1995) was introduced.[47] Concerns were expressed at the time of implementation as to the impact of this provision because no additional funding was provided. Section 1 of the Act provides for the assessment of a carer's ability to provide or continue to provide care:

s. 1(1) ▶

. . . in any case where–

(a) a local authority carry out an assessment under section 47 (1)(a) of the National Health Service and Community Care Act 1990 of the needs of a person ('the relevant person') for community care services, and

(b) an individual ('the carer') provides or intends to provide a substantial amount of care on a regular basis for the relevant person,

the carer may request the local authority . . . to carry out an assessment of his ability to provide and continue to provide care for the relevant person.

(C(RS)A 1995)

In those circumstances, the local authority is obliged to carry out an assessment and must take the results of that assessment into account in making its decision. The assessment must be requested and the number of requests is likely to be linked to the authority's efforts in providing information to carers about their rights under the Act. The C(RS)A 1995 does not apply to all carers. Carers who are volunteers provided by a voluntary organisation or who are paid will not be included. As the wording of the Act refers to a substantial amount of care on a regular basis, occasional and minimal levels of care will also be excluded. Early guidance provides that consideration of the type of tasks the carer undertakes; the amount of time spent providing assistance; how much supervision the user requires; and whether this is a continuing commitment, will indicate whether the care provided is substantial and regular.[48] Subsequent guidance[49] stresses the importance of assessing the impact of the caring role on the carer, as to whether the care provided is regular and substantial:

> . . . it is not only the time spent caring that has an impact on carers. For some, such as those caring for disabled children or adults with learning disabilities, the caring role can have the additional impact of being a life long commitment. Others, for example people caring for those with mental health problems or some neurological conditions, may have responsibilities that are not necessarily based on physical tasks and the caring role may be sporadic or preventative in nature. The carer may not be physically or practically caring at all times but may still be anxious or stressed waiting for, or trying to prevent, the next crisis. In addition, caring responsibilities may conflict with other family responsibilities such as parenting or holding down a job. Any assessment of the carer's need for support has to look at the impact of the whole caring situation.' (para 49)

The Carers and Disabled Children Act 2000 (**CDCA 2000**) extends and supplements the C(RS)A 1995 (it does not repeal it). The Act gives carers (providing regular and substantial care) the right to an assessment (on request) whether or not the cared for person is being assessed (even where the cared for person has refused any assessment). There is an absolute duty to assess but not directly to provide services. The carer's ability to care is assessed and the local authority must consider the assessment, then decide:

1. whether the carer has needs in relation to the care provided;
2. whether the local authority could meet those needs; and
3. if so, whether services should be provided.

Care services are described loosely under the Act as 'any services which the local authority sees fit to provide and will in the local authority's view help the carer care for the person cared for' (s. 2(2)). This gives authorities a wide measure of discretion. However, services of an intimate nature are expressly excluded from the range of services which may be delivered to the person cared for (s. 2(3)(b)). Guidance notes the need for flexibility:

> Services to carers are not defined as such in the 2000 Act. The local authority may provide any services they see fit to provide and which in their view will help the person care. These services may take any form, for example, a gardening service or assistance around the house for a carer who devotes most of his or her time to providing intimate care for the person cared for. Practitioners carrying out carer assessments are encouraged to consider flexible and innovative use of services which would help minimize the impact of the caring role on the carer's own life. (para 52)

The cared for person must agree to any services to be delivered direct to him. Carer support groups and information for carers can be provided by the authority without any assessment. The detail of how any services provided to the carer will assist the person being cared for should be contained in the care plan. Carers may be required to pay for services they receive.[50] Carers may receive direct payments to purchase services.

Both the 1995 and 2000 carers legislation is amended and extended by the Carers (Equal Opportunities) Act 2004 (**C(EO)A**). Section 1 amends s. 1 of the Carers (Recognition and Services) Act 1995 where the right to assessment only crystallises once an assessment is requested. The 2004 Act amends the 1995 Act so that the local authority, when carrying out an assessment of a person's needs for community care, is now obliged to inform the carer of his right to an assessment. The CDCA 2000 is similarly amended so that local authorities are required to proactively inform all carers of whom they are aware that they may be entitled to an assessment under 2000 Act.

Further amendments address the scope of assessment (s. 2). Assessments must include consideration of whether the carer:

- works or wishes to work,
- is undertaking, or wishes to undertake, education, training or any leisure activity.

That should be built into care plans, so for example, if a carer has a part-time job or attends a regular evening class, other arrangements for care will need to be made during that time.

The final amendment deals with the issue of cooperation between local authorities and other statutory agencies. Under s. 3(1) of the CEOA 2004, a local authority may request other bodies to assist it in planning the provision of services to carers and persons cared for. Other bodies include other local authorities, Social Services Departments, local education authorities and housing and NHS bodies. Those bodies must give 'due consideration' to the request. Under s. 3(3), where the local authority is of the view that the carer's ability to provide care would be enhanced by provision of services by those bodies, it may request the other body to provide the service. That body must again give 'due consideration' to the request. It is perhaps unfortunate that the wording here – to give due consideration – is quite weak and unlikely to prompt a major change in practice.

Meeting need: particular services

This section will describe the provision and regulation of residential care and domiciliary services. At the outset, however, it is important to remember that services cannot be imposed on someone against their will. This may prove to be a crucial issue in adult protection cases.

A decided case confirms that, in limited circumstances, a person's refusal of care may allow a local authority to consider that it has discharged its statutory duty even where no services have been provided. In *R* v. *Kensington and Chelsea – Royal*

London Borough Council, ex parte Kujtim [1999] 4 All ER 161, an asylum seeker was twice evicted from hotel accommodation for threatening behaviour. The local authority accepted that the person was in need of care and attention not otherwise available and they were under a duty to provide him with accommodation. The Court of Appeal noted, however, that services could not be imposed on a person against their will. If someone refuses to comply with reasonable conditions (in this case good behaviour in multi-occupancy establishments) then the authority is entitled to regard such a stance as 'unequivocal and persistent rejection' of the service offered. The statutory duty is then regarded as discharged. (Note that if anti-social behaviour is an aspect of need, this case would not apply. There must be a rejection by a service user who is responsible for his own actions.)

If a person responsible for his own actions makes it impossible for the local authority to purchase appropriate care, then the person is rejecting appropriate offers of help. This is not, therefore, a case about the exercise of discretion; it is about not being able to coerce people into accepting services against their wishes.

▪ Residential accommodation

At first sight, consideration of residential accommodation does not sit easily in a chapter on community care and could be described as the very antithesis of care in the community. It is included here because residential accommodation may be provided for short periods of time as part of a care package, in circumstances where the individual will return to the community. Also, residential accommodation may be arranged for an individual through the assessment or reassessment process and may follow a period of community care support in the community.

Local authorities must make arrangements for the provision of residential accommodation for persons aged 18 or over who, by reason of age, illness, disability or any other circumstances, are in need of care and attention which is not otherwise available to them (NAA 1948, s. 21). In order to fulfill this obligation, local authorities can make arrangements with private and voluntary sector organisations.[51] In making the arrangements, the authority must have regard to the need for providing accommodation of different types suited to the different types of people who might need residential care through age, illness, disability or other circumstances. The term 'any other cricumstances' maintains flexibility in the interpretation and application of s. 21. It has, for example, been found to include the circumstances of some asylum seekers (*R (Westminster City Council)* v. *National Asylum Support Service* [2002] UKHL 38 – see further discussion in Chapter 20). The Community Care (Residential Accommodation) Act 1998 inserted a new subsection 21(2A) into the National Assistance Act 1948, confirming the case law decision of *R v. Sefton MBC, ex parte Help the Aged* [1997] 4 All ER 532. It is now clear that, in deciding whether care and attention is otherwise available to a person, the first £20,500 of a person's capital must be disregarded.

A range of types of accommodation will need to be available. *R v. Bristol County Council, ex parte Penfold* [1998] 1 CCLR 315 was a case which questioned the meaning of residential accommodation under s. 21(8) of the National

Assistance Act 1948. Under that provision accommodation is generally provided in the form of residential care homes for elderly people in shared accommodation. In *Penfold* it was decided that an ordinary flat or house could also be provided under this subsection if it answered the individual's needs, confirmed in *R (Bernard)* v. *Enfield London Borough Council* [2002] EWHC 2282. This is distinct from any obligation to provide accommodation under the Housing Act 1996, the key being that under s. 21 accommodation fulfils a community care need.

Accommodation provided must be suitable for the person's needs. There are human rights dimensions to the question of suitability. For example, ECHR, Art. 9 provides that 'everyone has the right to freedom of thought, conscience and religion; this right includes freedom . . . to manifest his religion or belief, in worship, teaching, practice and observance'. The terms of this Article should encourage residential homes to respect different religious ceremonies depending on their residents' beliefs.

■ Regulation of residential accommodation

A system of regulation of residential and nursing care with a view to upholding standards has been in place since 1986. The Care Standards Act 2000 (CSA 2000) presents a major reform of the regulatory system for care services in England and Wales with a wider remit than the former legislation, the Registered Homes Act 1984 (RHA 1984). 'Modernising Social Services',[52] which followed the Burgner report,[53] identified three main criticisms of the old law and practice. There was a lack of independence, lack of coherence and lack of consistency in the regulatory process. The Care Standards Act 2000, supported by National Standards, set out to address these areas and provide protection for vulnerable people from abuse and neglect and to promote high standards in quality of care.

The legislation is supported by national minimum standards and regulations. Central to the regulation of residential accommodation is the requirement that an individual is registered as the proprietor of a care home, possibly with a manager also registered; that individual must be a fit person (a central but undefined term in the RHA 1984), and has responsibility to fulfill the requirements of the regulations and national standards. Part I of the CSA 2000 established the regulatory body; Part II contains regulatory procedures; and Part V contains details of the list of individuals unsuitable to work with vulnerable adults (discussed in Chapter 17).

Commission for Social Care Inspection

The Care Standards Act 2000 established an independent body to fulfil the regulation task known as the National Care Standards Commission.[54] In April 2004 it was replaced by the Commission for Social Care Inspection (CSCI).[55] The CSCI is an amalgamation of the functions of the National Care Standards Commission, the Audit Commission and the Social Services Inspectorate. It has a broad remit, including responsibility for care homes, domiciliary care agencies, children's homes, family centres, fostering agencies, adoption agencies, nursing agencies and adult placement schemes. The Commission for Healthcare Audit and Inspection (CHAI) is responsible for independent hospitals, clinics and medical agencies.

What will be registered?

Regulatory requirements under the CSA 2000 will extend to local authority provision, which will be required to meet the same standards as independent and voluntary sector providers.

The proprietor (and manager if in place) of a care home must be registered. The following definition of a care home is introduced in s. 3:

s. 3

. . . the establishment is a care home if it provides accommodation, together with nursing or personal care, for any of the following persons:
(a) persons who are or have been ill;
(b) persons who have or have had a mental disorder;
(c) persons who are disabled or infirm;
(d) persons who are or have been dependent on alcohol or drugs.

(CSA 2000)

Hospitals, independent clinics and children's homes are excluded from the definition. The old distinction between residential homes, which offer accommodation and personal care, and nursing homes, offering nursing care, has been removed and replaced with one category of home: a care home. That does not mean that all homes will provide the full range of facilities and be able to accommodate people who need both nursing and personal care. The exact services that will be offered by a home and the people that the home can cater for will be prescribed in the conditions of registration.

The issue of grant or refusal of registration, dealt with in CSA 2000, s. 13, is central to registration. The registration authority may grant registration only if regulation requirements are complied with. Regulation 9 of the Care Homes Regulations 2001[56] provides that: 'A person shall not manage a care home unless he is of integrity and good character . . .' This was questioned in *Jones* v. *National Care Standards Commission* [2004] EWCA Civ 1713. The court confirmed that fitness is an essential requirement for registration and the burden of proving 'fitness' rests with the person seeking registration; it is not for the CSCI to show 'unfitness'. The application may be granted unconditionally or subject to such conditions as the registration authority thinks fit. At any time, the registration authority can vary or remove conditions or impose additional conditions. Conditions may be generic or specific, e.g. specifying the categories of patients or number of residents that can be accommodated or stipulating that a particular door is to be kept locked to prevent confused residents from wandering directly on to a busy road. Criteria for cancellation of registration are contained in CSA 2000, s. 14 and include failing to comply with requirements or conviction of a relevant offence. Offences under the CSA 2000 include failing to comply with conditions (s. 24), contravening regulations (s. 25), false description of an establishment (s. 26), false statements in applications (s. 27), failing to display certificate of registration (s. 28), obstructing an inspector (s. 31). Conditions are likely to be set so as to reflect the national standards; hence, failing to meet national standards could ultimately lead to cancellation of registration. In urgent cases there is a provision for the magistrates' court to order immediate cancellation (s. 20).

It will be possible for a care home owner to appeal to the Care Standards Tribunal against a decision of the Commission for Social Care Inspection to refuse or cancel registration. Reports of such cases may be accessed from the Care Standards Tribunal website.[57]

National minimum standards have been published by the Department of Health in the document 'Care Homes for Older People' (2003).[58] The standards are designed to help protect people living in care homes while promoting their health, welfare and quality of life. There are 38 standards, each with a number of sub-categories, grouped into seven areas:

■ choice of home
■ health and personal care, with emphasis on respecting dignity
■ daily life and social activities, with emphasis on greater choice over arrangements including bedtimes, mealtimes and social activities
■ complaints and protection, to ensure complaints are properly dealt with
■ environment – standards to ensure a safe, well-maintained environment with minimum-space requirements
■ staffing – standards relating to greater employment checks, the new list of adults unsuitable to work with vulnerable adults, and specific training requirements
■ management and administration – a requirement is introduced that managers hold a relevant qualification and are fit for the task.

Standards are accompanied by outcomes. As an example, standard 31 (relating to the qualities of the registered manager) is set out below:

Standard 31

31.1 the Registered manager is qualified, competent and experienced to run the home and meet its stated purpose, aims and objectives.

31.2 the manager has at least two years' experience in senior management of a relevant care setting within the past five years; and is qualified at level 4 NVQ and, where nursing care is provided, is a first level registered nurse.

31.3 the Registered manager is responsible for no more than one establishment.

31.4 the Registered manager can demonstrate he has undertaken periodic training to update knowledge, skills and competence.

31.5 the manager and senior staff are familiar with conditions and diseases associated with old age.

31.6 the job description of the manager enables him to take responsibility for fulfilling his duties.

31.7 there are clear lines of accountability within the Home and with any external management.

The overall outcome of compliance with standard 31 is:

Service users live in a home which is run and managed by a person who is fit to be in charge, of good character and able to discharge his or her responsibilities fully.

Lay assessors have been included in the inspection process since 1994. Their role is detailed in circular LAC (94) 16;[59] it is essentially to complement the work of the registration and inspection officers. It may be appropriate for the lay assessor to spend more time talking with residents than the inspector and form a view on quality of life issues.

■ Domiciliary services

Domiciliary services may be provided to an individual as part of their community care package or may be arranged independently of any social services assessment. Domiciliary services may include home helps or meals on wheels and help with bathing and dressing. Prior to implementation of the Care Standards Act 2000 there had been no formal regulation of domiciliary agencies. It was possible for any person regardless of qualifications and expertise to set up an agency without any external scrutiny. The exception was if a local authority chose to contract with an agency to provide community care services as part of an individual's care plan. In that situation a local authority would have to have been satisfied with regard to the standards of care provided and could stipulate standards through its contracting arrangements. Even in those circumstances, however, there was no formal role for the inspection unit. In fact, some authorities introduced registers for domiciliary agencies but these ran on an entirely voluntary basis. The CSA 2000 now requires all domiciliary care agencies to register and be inspected annually if they provide personal care services.

As already noted, there is no consolidating piece of legislation drawing together the extensive range of powers and duties towards adult service users in one framework. The law in this area has developed in a piecemeal way and can be confusing and difficult to understand. Exhibit 14.2 summarises the main provisions, in chronological order, in an attempt to present a quick point of reference.

Legislation	Section	Summary
National Assistance Act 1948	29	Local authority power to promote the welfare of people aged 18 and over who are blind, deaf or dumb or who suffer from mental disorder of any description and other persons who are substantially and permanently handicapped by illness, injury or congenital deformity
	21	Duty to provide residential accommodation for persons who by reason of age, illness, disability or other circumstances are in need of care or attention which is not other wise available to them
	47	Power of removal from home (see Chapter 17)
Health Service and Public Health Act 1968	45	Local authority may make arrangements for promotion of welfare of old people
Chronically Sick and Disabled Persons Act 1970	1	Local authorities to inform themselves of number of people within NAA 1948, s. 29
	2	Duty to assess needs and provide services to disabled people
National Health Service Act 1977	Schedule 8	Duty to provide home helps for households where help is required owing to the presence of a person who is suffering from illness, lying in, an expectant mother, aged, handicapped as a result of having suffered from illness or by congenital deformity
Mental Health Act 1983	117	After-care services (see further Chapter 15)
Health and Social Services and Social Security Adjudications Act 1983	17	Local authority power to make reasonable charges for non-residential community services

Exhibit 14.2 Summary of legal provision relating to adult service users

Legislation	Section	Summary
Disabled Persons (Services, Consultation and Representations) Act 1986	4	Right to an assessment
	9	Provide information about services
National Health Service and Community Care Act 1990	46	Community care plans
	46(3)	Definition of community care services
	47	Assessment of need for community care services
	47(5)	Services pending assessment
	48	Inspection of premises where community care services provided
	50	Complaints procedure
Disability Discrimination Act 1995	1 and 19	Unlawful to discriminate on the grounds of disability in the provision of goods and services
Carers (Recognition and Services) Act 1995	1	Assessment of a carer's ability to provide and continue to provide care for a person
Community Care (Direct Payments) Act 1996	1	Power to make direct payments
Carers and Disabled Children Act 2000	1	Carer entitlement to assessment independent of assessment of person cared for
	2	Definition of care services
Carers (Equal Opportunities) Act 2004	1	Obligation to inform carer of right to assessment
	2	Assessment to include carer's wishes as to work, education, training and leisure
	3	Cooperation between local authority and other bodies

Exhibit 14.2   (continued)

- The National Health Service and Community Care Act 1990 provides the statutory basis for the principle that people should be supported and enabled to live in their own homes for as long as possible. There are a range of powers and duties contained in pre-existing and subsequent legislation, which are accessed via a community care assessment, in respect of older people, people with physical or learning disabilities and people with mental heath problems.

- A local authority must produce and publicise a community care plan containing information about available services. An individual may be charged for services.

- An individual who is assessed as needing community care services, having met eligibility criteria, will be provided with a care plan, which should be reviewed regularly.

- Many people in receipt of community care services will also have a carer. Carers are entitled to assessment of their needs in order to provide care.

- There is a body of case law dealing with judicial review applications relating to the provision of community care services. It is also possible to raise concerns about community care services via the complaints procedure or to the local government ombudsman or monitoring officer.

- Short periods of residential accommodation may be included in a care plan or an individual may move to residential accommodation on a permanent basis when no longer able to live at home. The provision of residential accommodation is regulated by the Care Standards Act 2000.

Exercises

1. Surinder is an 18-year-old woman with Down's Syndrome. She lives at home with her parents; her two older brothers left home some years ago and have their own families. She attended a local comprehensive school until she reached the age of 16 and has stayed at home with her parents since then. The family have not received any support from social services. Her parents are very protective of Surinder and she is always accompanied by them if she goes out, even to the local shop. Surinder would like to go to college and meet up with her old school friends but her parents will not allow her to travel alone. Her parents are growing older and her father, who drove until recently, has lost his driving licence due to poor eyesight. Surinder's sister-in-law, Jasmin, has said that Surinder could move in with her family and help to look after her children but Surinder's parents will not allow this. They have a row with Jasmin and tell Surinder not to have any further contact with her. Surinder is becoming depressed and is eating very little. Jasmin contacts social services to see if they can help Surinder to gain more independence.

What steps might a social worker take, once contacted by Jasmin?

2.   Annie is 88 years old and cared for by her daughter, Dorothy, aged 66. They live in a third-floor flat, which Annie bought from the council. Annie is losing her sight and suffers from arthritis. She is on a waiting list for a hip replacement. She cannot use the stairs and the lift at the flats is often out of order. She does not want to go out much in any case as she is anxious about falling. She has recently become incontinent and needs attention at night. They have no washing machine and the laundry is a bus ride away.

Dorothy is finding caring for her mother very stressful and feels unable to leave her for more than a short time. She has not been able to do any of the things she had planned on retirement. She contacted social services and explained their situation. Three months later a social worker visited. She spent approximately half an hour at the flat. She offered Annie a place at a day centre for elderly people, four miles away, one day a week but said she could not help with transport to get her there. She said that at the moment she could not offer any help such as meals on wheels or home help but she would come back in six months' time, at the start of the next financial year. In response to Dorothy's concerns that she was finding it hard to care for her mother, the social worker said Annie could move to a residential home but that the flat would have to be sold to pay for it.

What are the legal and practice issues raised in this scenario?

Websites

Information about carers may be found at the Carers UK website:
   www.carersuk.org

and the section of the Department of Health site, 'Caring for Carers':
   www.carers.gov.uk

For Government publications and information relating to disability:
   www.disability.gov.uk

The website of the British Council of Disabled People:
   www.bcodp.org.uk/

The website of the Disability Alliance provides advice and useful publications:
   www.disabilityalliance.org

The British Institute of Learning Disabilities (BILD) website includes a wide range of information and research about learning disability:
   www.bild.org.uk/

Association for Residential Care:
   www.arcuk.org.uk

Age Concern is a national organisation with regional offices providing a wide range of information and advice relating to older people:
   www.ace.org.uk

A guide to the scheme for direct payments is available at:
www.doh.gov.uk/Policy and guidance/organisation Policy/Finance and Planning/
Direct Payments/fs/en

Further reading

There are a number of texts on community care law:

Clements, L. (2004) *Community Care and the Law* (3rd edn). London: Legal Action Group. (The most up-to-date and detailed text, including relevant guidance and case law.)

Dimond, B. (1997) *Legal Aspects of Care in the Community.* London: Macmillan.

Johns, R. and Sedgewick, A. (1999) *Law for Social Work Practice – Working with Vulnerable Adults.* London: Macmillan.

McDonald, A. (1999) *Understanding Community Care: A Guide for Social Workers.* London: Macmillan.

Means, R. and Smith, R. (1998) *Community Care: Policy and Practice.* London: Macmillan.

Mandelstam, M. (2005) *Community Care Practice and the Law* (3rd edn). London: Jessica Kingsley Publishers.

Goodenough, A. (200) *An introductory guide to community care.* London: Age Concern.

Easterbrook, L. (2000) *Moving on from Community Care.* London: Age Concern.

With a particular focus on older people:

Ashton, G. (2005) (2nd edn) *Elderly People and the Law.* London: LexisNexis Butterworths.

Fenge, L.-A. (2001) 'Empowerment and Community care – projecting the 'voice of older people' 23(4) *Journal of Social Welfare and Family Law* pp. 427–39.

On carers:

Clements, L. (2005) *Carers and their Rights: the Law Relating to carers.* London: Carers UK.

Carers UK (2003) *Missed Opportunities: The impact of new rights for carers.* London: carers UK. (This report publishes the findings of a survey of 2,000 carers as to the extent to which the Carers National Strategy, and carers legislation, have improved their lives.)

In relation to disability see also:

Cooper, J. (ed.) (2000) *Law, Rights and Disability.* London: Jessica Kingsley Publishers.

Gray, B. and Jackson, R. (2002) *Advocacy and Learning Disability.* London: Jessica Kingsley Publishers.

Notes

1 ADSS (2005) 'Safeguarding Adults: A National Framework of Standards for good practice and outcomes in adult protection work'. London: ADSS.

2 See discussion in A. Brammer and S. Biggs (1998) 'Defining elder abuse' 20(3) *Journal of Social Welfare and Family Law* p. 285.

3 Department of Health LAC (92) 15 'Registered Homes Act 1984: I. Small residential care homes. II. Inspection'. London: Department of Health.

4 See the Bulletin 'NAPSAC' produced by the National Association for the Protection from Sexual Abuse of Adults and Children with learning disabilities, and the work of H. Brown, including H. Brown, J. Stein and V. Turk (1995) 'The sexual abuse of adults with learning difficulties: report of a second two-year incidence survey' 8(1) *Mental Handicap Research* p. 3.

5 Department of Health LAC (93) 10 'Approvals and directions for arrangements from 1 April 1993 made under Schedule 8 to the National Health Service Act 1977 and sections 21 and 29 of the National Assistance Act 1948'. London: Department of Health.

6 Department of Health and Social Security (DHSS) (19/71) 'Welfare of the elderly: implementation of s. 45 of the Health Service and Public Health Act 1968'. London: DHSS.

7 Sections 1–3 provided for the appointment of 'representatives' to support individuals in the assessment process.

8 Audit Commission (1986) 'Making a Reality of Community Care'. London: HMSO.

9 R. Griffiths (1988) 'Community Care, an agenda for action: a report to the Secretary of State for Social Services by Sir Roy Griffiths'. London: HMSO.

10 Secretaries of State for Health, Social Security, Wales and Scotland (1989) 'Caring for People: community care in the next decade and beyond' (Cm. 849). London: HMSO.

11 Department of Health (2000) 'No Secrets: Guidance on developing and implementing multi-agency policies and procedures to protect vulnerable adults from abuse'. London: Department of Health.

12 Department of Health (1998) 'Modernising Social Services: Promoting independence, improving projection, raising standards' (Cm. 4169). London: The Stationery Office.

13 DH (2005) Cm. 6499.

14 DH (2006) Cm. 6737.

15 See Department of Health, Social Services Inspectorate (1991) 'Care Management and Assessment: Practitioners' Guide'. London: HMSO.

16 Secretaries of State for Health, Social Security, Wales and Scotland (1989) 'Caring for People: community care in the next decade and beyond' (Cm. 849). London: HMSO, para. 3.2.3.

17 HSC 2002/001.

18 LASSL (97) 13 'Responsibilities of local authority social services departments; implications of recent legal judgments'.

19 The guidance is issued as a local authority circular, LAC (2002) 13, and is accompanied by practice guidance in the form of frequently asked questions.

20 Department of Health LAC (92) 27 'National Assistance Act 1948 (Choice of Accommodation) Directions 1992'. London: Department of Health.

21 National Assistance Act 1948 (Choice of Accommodation) Directions 1992, annexed to Department of Health Circular LAC (92)27.

22 Department of Health, Social Services Inspectorate (1991) 'Care Management and Assessment: Practitioners' Guide'. London: HMSO.

23 See also: National Health Service Act 1997, s. 22; Housing Act 1999, s. 29; and Housing Act 1996, s. 213(1) – as examples of further statutory provisions which try to foster corporate responsibility.

24 M. Butt (1996) 'Social Care and Black Communities: A review of recent research studies'. London: HMSO. See also W. I. U. Ahmad and A. Atkin (eds.) (1996) *Race and Community Care*. Buckingham: Open University Press.

25 H. Cowen (1999) *Community Care, Ideology and Social Policy*. London: Prentice Hall Europe.

26 The definition of public authority is based on that contained in the Human Rights Act 1998, discussed in Chapter 2.

27 Department of Health (1990) 'Community Care in the next decade and beyond'. London: HMSO, para. 3.25.

28 See M. Mandelstam (2005) (3rd edn) *Community Care Practice and the Law*. London: Jessica Kingsley, pp. 152–9 for a full discussion of such cases.

29 Secretaries of State for Health, Social Security, Wales and Scotland (1989) 'Caring for People: community care in the next decade and beyond' (Cm. 849). London: HMSO, para. 1.11.

30 LAC (94) 1.

31 LAC (2001) 32 'Fairer charging policies for home and other non-residential social services: guidance for councils wth social services responsibilities'. London: Department of Health.

32 S1 2003/1196.

33 See also LAC 2003(14) the Department of Health Circular about the regulations.

34 Updated to take account of LAC (2005) 7.

35 Health and Social Services and Social Security Adjudication Act 1983, s. 21.

36 It is issued under LASSA 1970, s. 7 as LAC(2004)20.

37 See also LAC (97) 11; LASSL (97) 9; and Department of Health (1997) 'Community Care (Direct Payments) Act 1996: policy and practice guidance', London: Department of Health. Community Care, Services for Carers and Children's Services (Direct Payments) (England) Regulations 2003 (SI 2003/762).

38 Department of Health (2003) 'Direct payments guidance: community care, services for carers and children's services (direct payments)'. London: Department of Health.

39 Department of Health (1997) 'Community Care (Direct Payments) Act 1996: policy and practice guidance'. London: Department of Health.

40 Note the role of the National Care Standards Commission to regulate domiciliary care agencies.

41 Local Authority Social Services (Complaints Procedure) Order 1990 (SI 1990/2244).

42 See further guidance on this area: Department of Health (1991) 'The right to complain'. London: HMSO.

43 Department of Health, Social Services Inspectorate (1991) 'Care Management and Assessment Practitioners' Guide'. London: HMSO, para. 38.

44 Department of Health (1990) 'Care Management and Assessment: Managers' Guide'. London: HMSO.

45 People First (1993) 'Self-Advocacy Starter Pack'. London: People First.

46 See: www.carers.gov.uk, www.carersuk.org, www.carersinformation.org.uk,

47 See policy guidance: Department of Health (1996) 'Carers (Recognition and Services) Act 1995: policy guidance'. London: Department of Health.

48 Department of Health (1996) 'Carers (Recognition and Services) Act 1995: practice guidance'. London: Department of Health.

49 Carers and Disabled Children Act 2000 and Carers (Equal Opportunities) Act 2004 Combined Policy Guidance (issued under s. 7(1) of the Local Authority Social Services Act 1970).

50 Health and Social Services and Social Security Adjudication Act 1983, s. 17.

51 NHSCCA 1990, s. 42(2).

52 Department of Health (1998) 'Modernising Social Services: Promoting independence, improving projection, raising standards' (Cm. 4169). London: The Stationery Office.

53 T. Burgner (1996) 'The regulation and inspection of social services'. London: Department of Health/Welsh Office.

54 The NCSC was set up to operate from eight regions based on NHS boundaries, replacing 150 health authorities and 100 local authorities with regulatory functions under the RHA 1984.

55 In Wales the Care Standards Inspectorate for Wales is the regulatory body

56 SI 2001/3965.

57 www.doh.gov.uk/int/index.htm contains all the reported decisions of the tribunal. For an analysis of RHT decisions, see A. Brammer (1994) 'The Registered Homes Act 1984: safeguarding the elderly' 4 *Journal of Social Welfare and Family Law* p. 423.

58 See also: National Minimum Standards for Adult Placement (2003); National Minimum Standards for Care Homes for Adults 18–65 (2003); National Minimum Standards for Adult Placement Schemes (2004).

59 Department of Health LAC (94) 16 'Inspecting Social Services'. London: Department of Health.

15 Mental health

Learning objectives

To develop an understanding of the following:

- The legal framework for practice in the area of mental health provided by the Mental Health Act 1983.
- Major provisions of the Mental Health Act 1983, which define mental disorder.
- The role of the approved social worker.
- The role of the nearest relative.
- Powers of compulsory detention and guardianship.
- Patients' rights and treatment in hospital.
- Arrangements for discharge, including the role of the Mental Health Review Tribunal.
- Provision for after-care and for supervised discharge.
- Mental health and children and young people.
- The distinction between mental disorder and mental incapacity.
- Proposed reforms to mental health law.

Introduction

Mental health is a significant area of social work practice. A statutory framework is provided by the Mental Health Act 1983 (**MHA** 1983), but it remains something of an ethical minefield. Tension abounds in the form of conflicting claims and wishes of the patient, the safety of the patient and the protection of members of the wider community, and the position of the nearest relative. In resolving these various issues the social worker is often at the forefront of decision-making but must work alongside a range of other professional groups. It is perhaps not surprising that many aspects of social work practice in mental health are invested in a specially qualified social worker, the *'approved social worker'*. Nevertheless, all social workers are likely to encounter service users with mental health difficulties at some point and it is useful therefore to have an overview of the relevant law. For example, a child protection social worker may have concerns about the care being provided to a child by his parent who has enduring mental health problems.

The extent of mental health problems in society is surprisingly high. One in four people suffer from some form of mental health problem at some point in their lives and a substantial amount of sickness absence from work is attributable to some form of mental or emotional disturbance, including depression. The extent of mental illness is likely to increase further with demographic changes, given that approximately one in five people over the age of 85 suffer from some form of dementia. The range of mental health problems is extensive. There is an unfortunate perception in society that people with mental health problems are dangerous. This has no doubt been fuelled by media attention given to exceptional cases such as Christopher Clunis,[1] and the Government's current proposals to reform the Mental Health Act 1983[2] lend some support to that position. In fact, research suggests that there is no significant increase in the risk of homicide posed by people with a mental illness.[3]

The key legislation is the Mental Health Act 1983; however, this must be viewed in the context of community care law and policy. Many people with mental health problems will receive community care services under a care plan, as discussed in Chapter 14. The Act was produced following a period of review in the 1970s[4] and proposals for reform of aspects of the previous legislation, the Mental Health Act 1959. The current law is undergoing further review and reform of the Act is anticipated in the near future. The Mental Health Act 1983 is accompanied by a Code of Practice (1999),[5] which adds detailed guidance on the application of the Act. The Code commences by setting out principles:

People to whom the Act applies should:

■ Receive recognition of their basic human rights under the European Convention on Human Rights.

■ Be given respect for their qualities, abilities and diverse backgrounds as individuals and be assured that account will be taken of their age, gender, sexual orientation, social, ethnic, cultural and religious background, but that general assumptions will not be made on the basis of any of these characteristics.

■ Have their needs taken fully into account, though it is recognised that, within available resources, it may not always be practicable to meet them in full.

■ Be given any necessary treatment or care in the least controlled and segregated facilities compatible with ensuring their own health or safety or the safety of other people.

■ Be treated and cared for in such a way as to promote to the greatest practicable degree their self determination and personal responsibility, consistent with their own needs and wishes.

■ Be discharged from detention or other powers provided by the Act as soon as it is clear that their application is no longer justified.

This statement of principles should be read in conjunction with the discussion of values at the start of the book to provide a basis for good practice in mental health. According to *R (Munjaz)* v. *Mersey Care NHS Trust* [2005] UKHL 58, the Code provides 'guidance not instruction'. It is not binding in law but is nevertheless good practice to follow the code.

The term 'patient' is used throughout the Mental Health Act 1983 to refer to 'a person suffering or appearing to suffer from mental disorder' (s. 145) (within the definition provided by the Act) even where the person is not residing in hospital, e.g. a person who is the subject of a guardianship order and living in the community. For consistency the same approach will be taken in this chapter.

Mental incapacity is considered separately in Chapter 16 and has been subject of major law reform with the introduction of the Mental Capacity Act 2005. Mental capacity and mental illness are commonly confused though quite different in nature and in legal terms. A person with a mental illness as defined by the Mental Health Act 1983 may also lack mental capacity. For many people, however, the mental illness will not have a significant impact on the ability to make a range of decisions, including consent to medical treatment. For other individuals, capacity to make complex financial decisions may be limited but the majority of other more routine decisions may be still be within their capacity. There are other individuals who lack capacity to make a range of decisions but who would not fall within the definitions of mental illness under the Act. An obvious example would be an individual with a mental impairment or learning disability who does not display any 'abnormally aggressive or seriously irresponsible conduct'. The consequences in terms of any legal interventions will vary depending on whether the key issue is one of mental capacity or mental illness and further on the type of mental illness and associated behaviour. Proposals to reform the law on mental health and mental capacity were introduced at around the same time but as yet new legislation has only been produced in respect of capacity. The Government has indicated that codes of practice will be published when the new Mental Hill Bill is introduced into Parliament dealing with the interface between the Mental Health Bill and the Mental Capacity Act 2005.

National Service Framework

Over recent years the Government has introduced National Service Frameworks (**NSFs**) as long-term strategies for improving specific areas of care. The NSF for mental health was launched in 1999, and addresses planning, delivery and monitoring of mental health services for adults aged up to 65, until 2009. The Framework comprises seven standards with targets covering five areas: health promotion and stigma; primary care and access to specialist services; needs of those with severe and enduring mental illness; carers' needs; and suicide reduction. In addition to the standards, the Framework endorses a set of ten guiding values and principles:

- involve service users and their carers in planning and delivery of care
- deliver high quality treatment and care which is known to be effective and acceptable
- be well suited to those who use them and non-discriminatory
- be accessible so that help can be obtained when and where it is needed
- promote their safety and that of their carers, staff and the wider public
- offer choices which promote independence
- be well co-ordinated between all staff and agencies
- deliver continuity of care for as long as this is needed
- empower and support their staff
- be properly accountable to the public, service users and carers.

There is an obvious emphasis on prevention within the standards and they are of multi-agency application.

1. Health and social services should:
   - promote mental health for all, working with individuals and communities
   - combat discrimination against individuals and groups with mental health problems, and promote their social inclusion.
2. Any service user who contacts their primary health care team with a common mental health problem should:
   - have their mental health needs identified and assessed
   - be offered effective treatments, including referral to specialist services for further assessment, treatment and care if they require it.
3. Any individual with a common mental health problem should:
   - be able to make contact round the clock with the local services necessary to meet their needs and receive adequate care
   - be able to use *NHS Direct*, as it develops, for first-level advice and referral on to specialist helplines or to local services.
4. All mental health service users on the Care Programme Approach (CPA) should:
   - receive care which optimises engagement, prevents or anticipates crisis, and reduces risk
   - have a copy of a written care plan which:
     - includes the action to be taken in a crisis by service users, their carers and their care co-ordinators
     - advises the GP how they should respond if the service user needs additional help
     - is regularly reviewed by the care co-ordinator
   - be able to access services 24 hours a day, 365 days a year.

5. Each service user who is assessed as requiring a period of care away from their home should have:

   ■ timely access to an appropriate hospital bed or alternative bed or place, which is:

     – in the least restrictive environment consistent with the need to protect them and the public

     – as close to home as possible

   ■ a copy of a written after care plan agreed on discharge, which sets out the care and rehabilitation to be provided, identifies the care co-ordinator, and specifies the action to be taken in a crisis.

6. All individuals who provide regular and substantial care for a person on CPA should:

   ■ have an assessment of their caring, physical and mental health needs, repeated on at least an annual basis

   ■ have their own written care plan, which is given to them and implemented in discussion with them.

7. Local health and social care communities should prevent suicides by:

   ■ promoting mental health for all, working with individuals and communities (Standard one)

   ■ delivering high quality primary mental health care (Standard two)

   ■ ensuring that anyone with a mental health problem can contact local services via the primary care team, a helpline or an A&E department (Standard three)

   ■ ensuring that individuals with severe and enduring mental illness have a care plan which meets their specific needs, including access to services round the clock (Standard four)

   ■ providing safe hospital accommodation for individuals who need it (Standard five)

   ■ enabling individuals caring for someone with severe mental illness to receive the support which they need to continue to care (Standard six).

   and in addition:

   ■ supporting local prison staff in preventing suicides among prisoners

   ■ ensuring that staff are competent to assess the risk of suicide among individuals at greatest risk

   ■ developing local systems for suicide audit to learn lessons and take any necessary action.

A report looking at the impact of the NSF, five years on, concludes that 'the mental health NSF has had substantial benefits and has triggered a period of major change in the care that service users receive'.[6]

The record of achievement varies across the standards and the report notes that there is still much work to be done in respect of mental health promotion and social exclusion (Standard 1) and, on support for carers (Standard 6).

Anti-oppressive practice

It is important to be aware that many people with mental health problems will experience discrimination in various areas of life. This discrimination may be intensified if the person is also a member of an ethnic minority. There is evidence that in practice race is considered an index of dangerousness in the mental health field. In comparison to a white man, a black man is more likely to be detained under the criminal provisions of the Mental Health Act 1983, to be in a secure ward and to receive higher doses of medication.[7] The NSF notes that refugees are especially vulnerable to diagnosis of higher rates of mental health problems than the general population. A target for the next five years of the NSF is to develop 'services for ethnic minorities, abolishing inequalities in care and earning the confidence of people from minority communities'.[8]

A 2005 mental health and ethnicity census was conducted jointly by the Mental Health Act Commission, the Healthcare Commission and the National Institute for Mental Health in England. It provides confirmation of earlier research with findings that black African and Caribbean people are three times more likely to be admitted to hospital and up to 44 percent more likely to be detained under the Mental Health Act.[9]

Definitions

Definitions of types of mental health problems are of central importance to an understanding of the Mental Health Act and are contained in s. 1 of the Mental Health Act 1983. These are legal definitions and may appear to contrast with medical or social understanding of mental health:

s. 1

. . . (2) In this Act –
'mental disorder' means mental illness, an arrested or incomplete development of mind, psychopathic disorder and any other disorder or disability of mind;
'severe mental impairment' means a state of arrested or incomplete development of mind which includes severe impairment of intelligence and social functioning and is associated with abnormally aggressive or seriously irresponsible conduct on the part of the person concerned;
'mental impairment' means a state of arrested or incomplete development of mind (not amounting to severe mental impairment) which includes significant impairment of intelligence and social functioning and is associated with abnormally aggressive or seriously irresponsible conduct on the part of the person concerned;

> 'psychopathic disorder' means a persistent disorder or disability of mind (whether or not including significant impairment of intelligence) which results in abnormally aggressive or seriously irresponsible conduct on the part of the person concerned.
>
> (3) Nothing in subsection (2) above shall be construed as implying that a person may be dealt with under this Act as suffering from mental disorder, by reason only of promiscuity or other immoral conduct, sexual deviancy or dependence on alcohol or drugs.
>
> (MHA 1983)

Each of the definitions will now be considered.

■ Mental disorder

Mental disorder is a generic concept, which is further defined into four specific categories. As the widest term, it tends to apply to short-term powers under the MHA 1983. The phrase 'arrested or incomplete development of mind' is wider than severe mental impairment and the addition of 'any other disorder' takes in conditions that would not be included in any of the other grounds. This definition has remained the same since the 1959 Act; however, the list of circumstances where a person will not be treated as suffering from mental disorder was extended so that, on its own, promiscuity, sexual deviancy or dependence on alcohol or drugs will not be sufficient evidence of mental disorder.

At times it is clear that the Mental Health Act 1983 has been used inappropriately to provide statutory authority for action which is in fact unlawful. A clear example of this was provided in the case of *St George's NHS Trust* v. *S* [1998] 3 WLR 936. It was suggested in that case that a woman's irrational and bizarre behaviour in refusing to undergo a caesarian section and thereby placing herself and the baby at risk was evidence of mental disorder. The caesarian section went ahead but the court ruled that the Mental Health Act 1983 should not have been utilised in this way and that a caesarian section was not treatment for the purposes of the Act.

■ Mental illness

The term 'mental illness' is not defined in the MHA 1983 or in the code of practice. It remains a question for the professionals involved (including approved social workers) to identify its presence. Practice would suggests that the term includes illnesses such as depression, certain types of obsessive behaviour and psychoses including schizophrenia, and more recently recognised, anorexia nervosa.[10] The Court of Appeal declined the opportunity precisely to define mental illness in the case of *W* v. *L* [1974] 3 WLR 859. This case concerned a patient, aged 23, whose behaviour included putting a cat in a gas oven, making another cat inhale ammonia, hanging a puppy, threatening his wife with a knife and threatening to push her downstairs to cause a miscarriage. At the time, prior to the Mental Health Act 1983, his behaviour was considered sufficient for him to be classified as having a psychopathic disorder but in order to be detained for longer than 28 days it was necessary to determine whether his condition also fell within the definition of mental illness. The court found him both psychopathic and mentally ill; Lawton LJ provided the following statement on the meaning of mental illness:

> [The words 'mental illness' are] ordinary words of the English language. They have no particular medical significance. They have no particular legal significance. How should the court construe them? The answer in my judgment is . . . that ordinary words of the English language should be construed in the way that ordinary sensible people would construe them. That being in my judgment the right test, then I ask myself, what would the ordinary sensible person have said about the patient's condition in this case if he had been informed of his behaviour? In my judgment such a person would have said: 'well, the fellow is obviously mentally ill'.

Such an approach is less than helpful to those seeking a precise definition. The lack of precision may be advantageous in accommodating expanding knowledge of different types of mental health problems, e.g. anorexia nervosa has been recognised as a mental illness (*Re KB (Adult) (Mental Patient: Medical Treatment)* (1994) 19 BMLR 144). Conversely, it also permits inclusion of those with eccentric or unconventional behaviour. Other attempts to define mental illness proved too lengthy to include in legislation but can provide some insight. For example, in 1976 the Department of Health and Social Security suggested that mental illness could encompass the following symptoms: more than a temporary impairment of intellectual functions shown by a failure of memory, orientation, or comprehension, and learning capacity; more than a temporary alteration of mood of such a degree as to give rise to the patient having a delusional appraisal of his situation, his past or his future, or that of others, or to the lack of any appraisal; delusional beliefs, persecutory, jealous or grandiose; abnormal perceptions associated with that delusional misinterpretation of events; thinking so disordered as to prevent the patient making a reasonable appraisal of his situation or having reasonable communication with others.[11]

■ Severe mental impairment

The term 'severe mental impairment' replaced 'severe subnormalities' in previous legislation. The term refers to handicap rather than illness, conditions which are less likely to be cured and which would currently be referred to as 'learning disabilities'. The arrested or incomplete development of mind must be associated with abnormally aggressive or seriously irresponsible conduct to come within the terms of the MHA 1983. This provision was introduced in response to concern that compulsory detention would not normally be appropriate for people with learning disabilities and could be stigmatising. Incorporation of the requirement for abnormally aggressive or seriously irresponsible conduct was intended to include only those people with mental impairment who need hospital detention for their own safety or that of others. A legal loophole remains, however, which became evident in the Beverley Lewis case, where a 23-year-old, deaf, blind, black woman died wrapped in newspaper and weighing only 5 stone. The authorities were at a loss to act where a woman with learning disabilities exhibited passive behaviour. It is questionable whether or not her self-neglect in that case could have been interpreted as seriously irresponsible conduct.[12] There is no clear legal guidance as to what is meant by abnormally aggressive or seriously irresponsible conduct. The code of practice suggests:

> Abnormally aggressive behaviour. Any assessment of this category should be based on observations of behaviour which lead to a conclusion that the actions are outside the usual range of aggressive behaviour, and which cause actual damage and/or real distress occurring recently or persistently or with excessive severity.
>
> Irresponsible conduct. The assessment of this characteristic should be based on an observation of behaviour which shows a lack of responsibility, a disregard of the consequences of action taken, and where the results cause actual damage or real distress, either recently or persistently or with excessive severity. (para 30.5)

A recent case found that past history of irresponsible conduct could be sufficient in finding severe mental impairment as indicating a propensity to such conduct (*Lewis v. Gibson* [2005] EWCA Civ 587).

Mental impairments will be judged by comparison with people of average intelligence and social functioning and with learning disabled people generally. Various tests are utilised, including IQ assessments. The Code of Practice advocates a holistic approach:

> No patient should be classified under the Act as mentally impaired or severely mentally impaired without an assessment by a consultant psychiatrist in learning disabilities and a formal psychological assessment. This assessment should be part of a complete appraisal by medical, nursing, social work and psychology professionals with experience in learning disabilities, in consultation with a relative, friend or supporter of the patient. (para 30.4)

■ Mental impairment

The same definition is provided for mental impairment as for severe impairment except that it talks about significant rather than severe impairment. Again there is no legal guidance as to the factors that would distinguish 'severe' from 'significant'; it is a question of degree.

■ Psychopathic disorder

The phrase 'abnormally aggressive or seriously irresponsible conduct' features again in the definition of psychopathic disorder. In this case, however, the conduct must actually be caused by the psychopathic disorder rather than associated with it. In

R(P) v *Mental Health Review Tribunal (East Midlands and North East Region)* [2002] EWCA Civ 697 Pill LJ in the Court of Appeal stated that 'the absence of contemporaneous symptoms amounting to abnormally aggressive or seriously irresponsible conduct did not result in the conclusion that the patient no longer suffered from the underlying disorder' as, 'the absence of such symptoms might indicate either that the underlying disorder had resolved or that it continued to exist but without recent manifestations of aggressive or irresponsible behaviour'.

Treatment must be likely to alleviate or prevent the deterioration of the condition.

Reform

The reform option favoured by the Mental Health Act review (considered later in this chapter) was to reject the four specific categories and introduce a sole (and extremely broad) category of mental disorder, which is defined as 'any disability or disorder of mind or brain, whether permanent or temporary, which results in an impairment or disturbance of mental functioning'.

The role of the approved social worker

The majority of social work functions under the MHA 1983 are invested in the approved social worker. The *approved social worker* (ASW) must have appropriate competence in dealing with persons suffering from mental disorder (MHA 1983, s. 114(2)). Each Social Services Authority must provide approved training and ensure that it has sufficient approved social workers (for 24-hour cover) to deal with mental health work (LAC (93) 10).[13] This is currently the only aspect of social work that legally requires a further qualification. Nevertheless, it appears there is substantial variation in the arrangements for training and supervision of ASWs and ratios of ASWs to population, across the United Kingdom.[14] Huxley *et al.*[15] conducted a national survey of ASW numbers in England and Wales in 1992 and 2002 and suggest that there has been a decline in the ratio of ASWs per 100,000 population of over 50 per cent. They call for specific action to determine the numbers of mental health social workers needed in modernised community mental health services.[16] Perhaps the most significant aspect of the work of the approved social worker is their statutory role in arranging compulsory admission to hospital; however, it is important to note that the everyday work of a mental health social worker is much broader than this. The ASW is under a duty set out in s. 13(1) 'to make an application for admission to hospital or reception into guardianship in respect of any patient if he is satisfied that such an application should be made'. This is an individual duty invested in the approved social worker to be exercised on the basis of their own judgement rather than at the behest of others. Protection against liability is offered by the MHA 1983, s. 139. An ASW will not be liable to civil or criminal proceedings for any act done under the Act, rules or regulations, unless the act was done in bad faith or without reasonable care.

It will be important for ASWs to establish good working relationships with other professionals including psychiatrists and the police. Many ASWs are now employed in multi-disciplinary Community Mental Health Teams. It is vital for the approved social worker to keep a full record of their reasons for making (or not making) an application. Failure to keep such records might be found to be maladministration.

Where guardianship is arranged the ASW may be involved as the patient's guardian in some cases. Prior to an application for admission to hospital (where this is being considered), the approved social worker must interview the patient in a suitable manner and be satisfied that detention in hospital is the most appropriate way of providing care and treatment. In some cases it is difficult to satisfy this requirement and the code notes (at para. 2.11f): 'It is not desirable for a patient to be interviewed through a closed door or window except where there is serious risk to other people.' A genuine attempt to interview should be made, whatever the extent of communication difficulties or particular circumstances of the case. This may involve the use of trained interpreters or an ASW with appropriate communication skills.

The approved social worker will often work closely with the patient's nearest relative and must consult the nearest relative before making an application for treatment or guardianship. It is crucial that the ASW can ascertain the identity of the nearest relative, as any subsequent detention may be unlawful if the correct nearest relative was not consulted (*Re S-C (Mental Patient) (Habeas Corpus)* [1996] QB 599).

The emphasis of an ASW's assessment of an individual will be on the social effects of mental illness and consideration of community-based alternatives. In carrying out an assessment, the ASW will obtain appropriate information to enable a decision to be made as to the least restrictive way to offer appropriate help to the individual. The options will be dependent on the range of community-based resources available, which may, for example, support an individual who is willing to take prescribed medication at home. In addition, as an alternative to a section, the ASW should consider whether the individual would agree to admission as an informal patient. If an application for formal admission is made, the ASW should arrange the conveyance of the patient to hospital, accompany the patient and remain with him until medical examination can take place. The ASW should clearly explain his role to the patient and also explain the rights of the patient.

Other responsibilities of the approved social worker include providing social enquiry reports for the hospital or mental health tribunal; and making arrangements for after-care upon a patient's discharge. The ASW is not involved with decisions relating to treatment of the patient once in hospital. The ASW has no power to seek discharge of a patient.

A report of the Workforce Action Team on the mental health National Service Framework proposed the recruitment of non-qualified staff, to be known as support, time, recovery (STR) workers, to release ASWs from basic tasks. Their role is envisaged as promoting independent living, encouraging service users to take responsibility for practical needs and giving support with daily living activities. According to the Department of Health, 'an STR worker is someone who works as part of a team which provides mental health services and focusses directly on the needs of service users, working across boundaries of care, organisation and role. They will provide Support, give Time to the service user and thus promote their Recovery'.[17] They would not be involved with sectioning or coordinating the *care programme approach.*[18]

The nearest relative

The nearest relative (**NR**) has an important role in terms of admission, care and discharge of patients. A person's nearest relative is normally determined simply on the basis of priority on the list of adult relatives contained in s. 26, namely:

- spouse (disregarded if separated; cohabitee of six months or more is treated as a spouse)
- son/daughter
- parent
- sibling
- grandparent
- grandchild
- uncle/aunt
- nephew/niece.

Any other person with whom the patient resides and has done for five years shall be treated as a relative,[19] and priority is given to anyone on the list who cares for the patient (s. 26(4)). Same-sex partnerships are included within the term 'cohabitee' as the phrase 'living with the patient as the patient's husband or wife as the case may be' (s. 26(6)) will be read to include a same-sex partner.

Anyone who does not ordinarily reside in the United Kingdom, or anyone under the age of 18 will normally be ignored. Age takes precedence where there is more than one person in a category, e.g. elder sibling. If a child is in care the nearest relative will be the authority named in the care order. The nearest relative can delegate their powers to another person (MHA 1983, s. 26(5)).

The nearest relative is not the same as 'next of kin' and will not always be the person the patient would prefer to act in this capacity. The nearest relative is a 'public authority' under the Human Rights Act 1998 because he is able to exercise functions of a public nature. As such he is bound to comply with the Articles of the ECHR.

■ Role of the nearest relative

The NR must be consulted before an application for treatment or guardianship is made, and must not object to the application; he does not actually have to consent to the application. If the nearest relative objects to an application for treatment or guardianship, it will not be able to proceed.

The NR can apply directly for a s. 2 or 3 order and has a power to require the local Social Services Department to direct an ASW to consider a case with a view to making an application for admission to hospital. The NR has the right to appoint an independent doctor to visit the patient and view records; this is important in relation to the NR's power to discharge a patient.

▪ Choice of nearest relative?

The European Court considered the nearest relative in *JT* v. *United Kingdom* [2000] 1 FLR 909: a settlement was arrived at in an Art. 8 claim (right to respect for family and private life). The UK authorities agreed to amend the Mental Health Act 1983 so as to permit detainees to make an application to court to have their 'nearest relative' replaced where there was a reasonable objection to having a certain person acting in that capacity. In the instant case the patient wished to have her mother removed as NR due to their difficult relationship and the fear that her step-father, who allegedly had sexually abused her, would gain knowledge of her whereabouts. Further, in *R (M)* v *Secretary of State for Health* [2003] EWHC 1094 (Admin) it was held that where the patient reasonably objects to the nearest relative (in that case as there was no relationship of trust), another person should act. Similarly, in *R (E)* v *Bristol City Council* [2005] EWHC 74 (Admin) the High Court was able to interpret s. 11 MHA compatibly with the convention so that E's sister (the court had said that it would not be in E's interests for her sister to act as nearest relative) did not have to be consulted or informed in relation to applications for E's admission for assessment or treatment on the basis that it was not reasonably practicable. Practicability was not limited to availability and could also encompass whether it was appropriate to consult.

▪ Displacement of nearest relative

There is statutory provision for the nearest relative to be displaced under MHA 1983, s. 29 on the application of any relative of the patient, any other person with whom the patient is residing (immediately before, if admitted) or an ASW.

The county court may make an order that the functions of the nearest relative are exercisable by a proper person where the following grounds exist:

(a) the patient has no nearest relative, or it is not reasonably practicable to ascertain whether he has such a relative, or who that relative is;
(b) the NR is incapable of acting as such by reason of mental disorder or other illness;
(c) the NR unreasonably objects to the making of an application for admission for treatment or guardianship in respect of the patient;
(d) the NR has exercised, without due regard to the welfare of the patient or the interests of the public, his power to discharge the patient from hospital or guardianship, or is likely to do so.

Once an application has been made for displacement of the nearest relative, the nearest relative's power of discharge is immediately suspended. This provision provides in effect a 'veto' to the nearest relative's power of discharge, if it is likely to be exercised in a manner the authorities do not agree with. Interim displacement orders are possible (*R* v. *Central London County Court, ex parte London* [1999] 3 All ER 991).

In *Lewis* v. *Gibson* [2005] EWCA Civ 587, the Court of Appeal considered the relationship between displacement of nearest relative, guardianship and the inherent jurisdiction. The case merits some attention as it involves a number of related mental health issues.

The case concerned M, a 32-year-old woman with a severe learning disability (as a result of Down's syndrome), who lived with her mother. When her mother's health deteriorated, the council, concerned at the level of care she was receiving, removed M from home having obtained a warrant under s. 135 authorising entry to the house and removal of M to a place of safety. Once at the hospital an application was made under s. 2 for compulsory admission for assessment. M's mother, who was her nearest relative, sought to discharge her daughter, to which the responsible medical officer (**RMO**) responded with a s. 25 barring order preventing discharge on the basis that, if M was discharged, she would 'be likely to act in a manner dangerous to himself or others'. The approved social worker applied to displace M's mother as nearest relative; an interim order was made; M was received into the council's guardianship and placed in a care home in the community, where she apparently thrived. The county court, considering the application to displace the nearest relative, was asked to decide whether she unreasonably objected to the making of the guardianship order. The court approved the application and appointed the council as nearest relative.

M's mother argued, first, that her daughter did not fit within the category of mentally disordered person to which guardianship applied, as her mental impairment was not associated with 'abnormally aggressive or seriously irresponsible conduct', and therefore it could not be unreasonable for her to object to guardianship. This was rejected by the court on the basis that it was sufficient that M had a propensity to this conduct even though it was not exhibited at the time of the hearing. Secondly, M's mother argued that the criteria that guardianship is 'necessary in the interests of the welfare of the patient or for the protection of other persons' was not met. She argued that guardianship was not 'necessary' because the council could instead have applied to the High Court to declare whether it was lawful for them to remove M invoking the inherent jurisdiction and relying on the doctrine of necessity. This argument was also rejected. The Court of Appeal found that once the county court was satisfied that M met the criteria for guardianship, there was no gap for the High Court to fill with a declaration. The court did also note that guardianship confers 'extremely limited powers' and that it might be necessary at some point to seek a declaration for matters falling outside the guardian's powers. It seems, therefore, that a best interest declaration could be made alongside guardianship, or instead of guardianship to address matters not covered by guardianship. High Court declarations are discussed further in Chapter 16.

Compulsory powers

'Compulsory admission should only be exercised in the last resort' (para 2.7 Code of Practice, 1999).

In certain circumstances it will become necessary for an individual to be detained under a compulsory order in a hospital. The emphasis on the least restrictive intervention should mean that compulsory admission is considered as the last resort. Compulsory powers of detention in hospital are contained in ss. 2–5. Section 2 provides for admission for assessment and s. 3 provides for admission for treatment. Emergency admission for treatment is provided for by s. 4 and under s. 5 it is possible to detain a patient already in hospital.

Exhibit 15.1 summarises the elements of each section in terms of applicant, duration, medical involvement and criteria.

	Mental health category	Other criteria	Medical support	Duration	Applicant
s. 2	Mental disorder	Warrants detention for assessment In interests of own health or safety, or protection of other persons	2 doctors	28 days	NR or ASW
s. 3	One of four categories of mental disorder – nature or degree makes it appropriate to receive medical treatment in hospital	Treatability test for psychopathic disorder or mental impairment. Necessary for health or safety of the patient or protection of others Cannot be treated unless detained	2 doctors	6 months	NR or ASW
s. 4	Mental disorder	urgent necessity	1 doctor	72 hours	NR or ASW
s. 5	Mental disorder	urgent necessity	Doctor or nurse	72 hours (doctor) 6 hours (nurse)	Doctor or nurse

Exhibit 15.1   Compulsory powers under the Mental Health Act 1983

In each case there is no application to court, the operation of the sections outlined being essentially an administrative procedure. The application is made to the managers of the proposed hospital (MHA 1983, s. 11) and carries with it a power to convey the patient to hospital. Under the current proposals for reform, a new tribunal system would introduce an independent judicial aspect to the process.

∎ Mental health and risk

For each application the relevant mental health definition is stipulated, e.g. for s. 2 it is the broad category, mental disorder, whereas for s. 3 it is one of the further four categories. This diagnosis is not sufficient in itself. For each case there are further criteria as to the need for detention. For s. 2 the criteria are that he ought to be detained in the interests of his own health or safety, or with a view to the protection of other persons. Other persons could be members of the patients immediate family or the public. The protection could be required because of the risk of physical harm or the code suggests, 'serious persistent psychological harm' (para 2.9). For applications under s. 3 the criteria are more detailed. The mental disorder must be of a nature or dgree which makes it appropriate to receive treatment in hospital, i.e. not in the community or under guardianship. Failure to take medication in the community which leads to deterioration in the patient's mental health could prompt an application under s. 3. In respect of psychopathic disorder or mental impairment, the treatment must be likely to alleviate or prevent deterioration of the condition. If there is no potential benefit, then detention cannot be justified; however, the concept of treatability is broad. As with s. 2, there is a reference to detention for his own health or safety or with a view to the protection of other persons. Section 3 carries a stronger imperative however, it must be 'necessary' under s. 3 rather than 'in the interests of' under s. 2.

∎ Medical support

Applications under ss. 2 or 3 must have the support of two medical recommendations, the authors of which having examined the patient within five days of each other. One of the doctors must be a mental health specialist and the other, who should be familiar with the patient, will often be the patient's GP.

∎ Applicant

The applicant for an admission under ss. 2 or 3 may be the ASW or NR. The Code of Practice suggests that, as an application by the NR may damage the relationship he has with the patient, and given the training and knowledge of resources of the ASW, the ASW is usually the appropriate person to make the application. If the NR does make the application, the hospital managers should notify the local Social Services Department and a social worker will be required to provide a social circumstances report to the hospital (MHA 1983, s. 14).

■ Section 2

Detention under s. 2 is appropriate where there is no clear diagnosis of the patient's condition and in-patient assessment is necessary to produce a treatment plan. The broad category of mental disorder applies. If the applicant is an ASW he should take all reasonable steps to inform the person who appears to be the NR (MHA 1983, s. 11(3)) but the NR's consent is not required.

A person detained under s. 2 may be treated without consent if necessary. It is not possible to renew or extend a s. 2 admission. At the end of the 28-day period, the patient may leave the hospital, remain at the hospital as an informal patient or be detained at the hospital for treatment under s. 3.[20] The duty to provide after-care services under s. 117 does not apply following a s. 2 admission.

■ Section 3

The Code of Practice lists the range of circumstances where an admission under s. 3 might be appropriate, including where a patient has been admitted in the past and where a patient has been assessed recently and is known by the clinical team (para. 5.3). The patient need not always be detained for the full six-month period and can be discharged earlier by the responsible medical officer (the doctor responsible for the patient's treatment plan). Section 17 provides for leave of absence during the six-month period prior to discharge where a power of recall applies. If the nearest relative unreasonably objects to admission under s. 3, application can be made for the NR to be displaced (see above).

Admission for treatment under s. 3 is based on the existence of one of the four distinct categories of mental disorder (mental illness, mental impairment, psychopathic disorder or severe mental impairment), rather than the general term, mental disorder. For a compulsory admission it must also be shown that the mental disorder is of a nature or degree that makes it appropriate for him to receive medical treatment in a hospital. If a community-based alternative is available that should be the preferred option. The section may be renewed for a further period of six months, then 12 months (MHA 1983, s. 20). In *R (S)* v. *Mental Health Review Tribunal* [2004] EWHC 2958 (Admin), detention of a patient who was on leave was renewed to ensure that she continued to attend for weekly treatment.

■ Section 4

Section 4 provides for admission for assessment in an emergency. Its use should be limited to emergencies, where there is insufficient time to get a second medical recommendation; it should not be used for administrative convenience or because it is more convenient for the second doctor to examine the patient in hospital. A doctor who knows the patient, and who should confirm that admission is a matter of urgent necessity, should provide the medical recommendation in these circumstances. An emergency situation is evidenced by: immediate and significant risk of mental or physical harm to the patient or to others; danger of serious harm to property; or the need for physical restraint of the patient (para. 6.3). Once admitted, a the patient should be examined by a second doctor as soon as possible to determine whether the patient should be detained under s. 2.

■ Section 5

Section 5 provides holding powers under which an informal patient (including a patient receiving treatment for a physical condition) can be detained by a doctor or nurse. The section cannot be used for outpatients. Part IV of the MHA 1983 (treatment without consent) does not apply where the patient is detained under s. 5.

Where a doctor decides that admission under the MHA 1983 is appropriate, a patient may be detained for up to 72 hours starting from the hospital manager's receipt of the doctor's report (MHA 1983, s. 5(2)). It is good practice for a second doctor to examine the patient as soon as possible to determine whether the patient should be detained under a section. A nurse (registered under the Nurses, Midwives and Health Visitors Act 1979 for work with patients with a mental disorder) can exercise a similar power under s. 5(4) to prevent an informal patient leaving the hospital, but the duration is limited to six hours.

■ Human rights and detention

Aspects of the law relating to detention for reasons of mental illness have been considered in a number of cases before the European Court. Article 5 of the ECHR provides the right not to be deprived of liberty except in specified cases, including (Art. 5 (1)(e)) the lawful detention of persons of unsound mind. The leading case on this article is *Winterwerp* v. *The Netherlands* (1979) 2 EHRR 387, which set down the following minimum conditions for lawful detention of a person of unsound mind:

1. detention must be effected in accordance with a procedure prescribed by law;
2. the individual must clearly be of unsound mind on the basis of objective medical expertise;
3. the mental disorder must be of a kind or degree warranting compulsory confinement; and
4. continued confinement must be based on persistence of the mental disorder.

It has been found that *de facto* detention of informal, incapacitated patients may contravene the first requirement that detention must be in accordance with a procedure prescribed by law. This was precisely the issue argued in *R* v. *Bournewood Community and Mental Health NHS Trust, ex parte L* [1999] 1 AC 458, reported as *HL* v. *United Kingdom* before the European Court, discussed later in this chapter.

The fourth *Winterwerp* condition was relevant in the case of *Johnson* v. *United Kingdom* (1999) 27 EHRR 296: J was given a conditional discharge from hospital and a plan was drawn up for after care. Four years later he appealed to the Mental Health Review Tribunal, having continued to be detained, as it had not been possible to find a suitable hostel place for him. He was granted an absolute discharge. It was held that the four-year period of detention constituted an unreasonable delay and a breach of Art. 5(1)(e); and he was awarded £10,000 compensation for unlawful detention.

Informal patients in hospital

The discussion of compulsory powers of admission to hospital actually relates to only a relatively small number of patients in hospital at any one time (though numbers are increasing). The majority of patients have not been detained under a section; they are informal patients, sometimes referred to as 'voluntary patients'. Included in this group are patients with dementia who lack proper understanding of their situation, and others who may be compliant in the face of the 'threat' of formal detention.

A person over the age of 16 can become an informal patient and receive treatment in a hospital, and the informal nature of the admission is given explicit encouragement by the MHA 1983, s. 131:

s. 131

> Nothing in this Act shall be construed as preventing a patient who requires treatment for mental disorder from being admitted to any hospital or mental nursing home in pursuance of arrangements made in that behalf and without any application, order or direction rendering him to be liable to be detained under this Act, or from remaining in any hospital or mental nursing home in pursuance of such arrangements after he has ceased to be so liable to be detained.
>
> (MHA 1983)

If an informal patient attempts to leave the hospital, and this is not considered to be in their best interests, steps can be taken to convert the status of the patient to a formally detained patient through use of the holding power (MHA 1983, s. 5). The legal status of informal patients was called into question in the case of *R* v. *Bournewood Community and Mental Health NHS Trust, ex parte L* [1998] 3 All ER 289, which reached the House of Lords.

To recount the facts very briefly: L was an autistic man, aged 48, who was unable to agree or refuse treatment or give a valid consent to admission to mental hospital. He was admitted to hospital after becoming disruptive at the day centre he attended. His carers were anxious for him to return to their care; however, he remained in hospital as an informal patient. It was argued that he was not detained against his will, as he never made any attempt to leave.

The Court of Appeal found that L was detained and that the detention was unlawful. The implications of the Court of Appeal decision were that a significant number of patients who would not formerly have been compulsorily detained under the Mental Health Act 1983 would need to be. The court heard that there are approximately 13,000 detained patients on any one day in England and Wales. If the Court of Appeal judgment were followed there would be an additional 22,000 on any day and 48,000 additional admissions each year.[21] These figures do not include patients receiving treatment in mental nursing homes. Such an increase, it was noted, would have a significant effect on resources in terms of professionals and mental health services, as well as Mental Health Review Tribunals and the Commission.

Second, the Court of Appeal decision left areas of legal uncertainty. It was not clear whether mental nursing homes with patients such as Mr L in their care would have to become registered to receive patients under the 1983 Act, with the ensuing costs and staffing implications; and whether homes currently operating would be obliged to discharge patients. This could include a number of elderly patients who do not have capacity to consent.

Third, on a more positive note, if patients such as Mr L did have to be compulsorily detained, they would benefit from the safeguards contained in the MHA 1983, the current lack of protection being cited as a concern by the Commission. Again, the resource implications of such an extension were noted by Lord Goff, who continued by referring to the as yet unexercised power of the Secretary of State to direct the Commission to review care and treatment of patients not liable to be compulsorily detained.

The advantageous effects of the Court of Appeal judgment for patients such as L are clear from the following statement of Lord Steyn, which summarises the current differing status of formal and informal patients.

> Specifically, the beneficial consequences of the ruling of the Court of Appeal would be as follows. (1) Such patients could then only be admitted for assessment and detained . . . under s 2 or admitted for treatment and detained . . . under s 3 on the written recommendation of at least two doctors . . . (2) Such patients would gain the protection of s 58 which requires either the patient's consent or a second medical treatment before certain forms of medical treatment are given. (3) Such patients would have the advantage of applying to or being automatically referred to mental health review tribunals . . . (4) Such patients would become entitled to after-care services provided by health authorities and local authorities under ss 25A–25J and s 117. (5) Such patients would have the benefit of the Code of Practice to the Mental Health Act 1983 . . . (6) Such patients would be brought under the supervision of the Mental Health Act Commission (s 121).[22]

The House of Lords judgment in *Bournewood* focused on the question of whether L was detained and, if so, was the detention lawful; the interpretation of s. 131; and role of the common law doctrine of necessity. The House considered whether this section applied only to patients who have capacity and do consent to their admission ('voluntary patients') or whether a second group, patients who lack capacity to consent but do not object to their admission ('informal patients' such as L), are also covered. Where patients are admitted as informal patients under s. 131(1) but are unable to consent to treatment or care, the House found that the principle of necessity provides the basis for treatment and care. The case of *F* v. *West Berkshire Health Authority (Mental Health Act Commission intervening)* [1990] 2 AC 1, which sets out the circumstances when necessity would apply, was referred to in support. Under the principle, patients would receive treatment in their best interests.

The House then considered whether L had been unlawfully detained, as the Court of Appeal had decided. Lord Goff found that as detention has to be actual rather than potential, there was no false imprisonment in L's case. Lord Nolan and Lord Steyn found that L was detained and that the argument advanced that he was free to leave the hospital 'stretches credulity to breaking point',[23] but that the detention was justified by the principle of necessity.

Ultimately, the difference between the judgments of the House of Lords and the Court of Appeal can be summarised in terms of the extent to which we should rely on the exercise of professional judgement alone to safeguard the interests of informal patients. Lord Steyn explored the implications of this further:

> It is, of course true that health care professionals will almost always act in the best interests of patients. But Parliament devised the protective scheme of the 1983 Act as being necessary in order to guard amongst other things against misjudgement and lapses by the professionals involved in health care . . . Parliament was not content in this complex and sensitive area to proceed on the paternalistic basis that the doctor is always right.[24]

Lord Steyn felt that reversing the Court of Appeal decision left 'an indefensible gap in our mental health law'.[25] The case provides another argument in favour of major law reform. Department of Health guidance was issued following the *Bournewood* decision.[26] The guidance stated that lack of objection is not sufficient evidence of compliance with an informal admission. It also requires the wishes of the patient and his carers to be taken into account before an informal admission. As a matter of good practice, these requirements should have been followed irrespective of the *Bournewood* decision.

The case proceeded to the European Court of Human Rights and is reported as *HL* v. *United Kingdom* (2004) 40 EHRR 761). The Court found the law as described in the House of Lords judgment incompatible with the European Convention on Human Rights, specifically finding breaches of, Art. 5(1): 'Everyone has the right to liberty and security of the person. No one shall be deprived of his liberty save in the following cases and in accordance with procedure prescribed by law: . . . (e) the lawful detention of persons of unsound mind.' and Art. 5(4): 'Everyone who is deprived of his liberty by arrest or detention shall be entitled to take proceedings by which the lawfulness of his detention shall be decided speedily by a court and his release ordered if the detention is not lawful.' The first question the Court considered was whether L was detained. It found that the fact L had not attempted to leave the hospital was irrelevant to Art. 5. The key fact in L's case was that the healthcare professionals had complete and effective control over his care and movements and this amounted to a deprivation of liberty. Secondly, the Court considered whether the detention was 'in accordance with a procedure prescribed by law' and lawful under Art. 5(1). The court found that L was 'of unsound mind' and that the common law doctrine of necessity includes the minimum condition for lawful detention of persons of unsound mind. It went on to question whether there were sufficient safeguards to ensure the detention was not arbitrary and here the court was not satisfied: there was no formal admission process, nothing stating the exact purpose of admission, no timescales and no equivalent to the nearest relative. Thirdly, the court continued with consideration of Art. 5(4), and questioned whether L was able to challenge the lawfulness of his detention. In the absence of such an avenue, it found a further breach of human rights. In essence the lack of procedural safeguards of the doctrine of necessity was the incompatibility.

Following the European Court judgment, the Department of Health issued interim advice on the implications of the judgment.[27] In the advice the Government commits to introducing procedural safeguards which are effective, proportionate and deliverable in practice (para. 31). Until safeguards are established, the advice calls for NHS bodies to take steps to ensure that incapacitated patients continue to receive adequate care and that it falls short of a deprivation of liberty. Elements of such good practice which are likely to reduce the likelihood of legal challenge include: ensuring that decisions are taken (and reviewed) in a structured way, which includes safeguards against arbitrary deprivation of liberty; effective, documented care planning; ensuring that alternatives to admission to hospital or residential care are considered and that any restrictions placed on the patient while in hospital or residential care should be kept to the minimum necessary; ensuring appropriate information is given to patients themselves and to family, friends and carers (purpose and reasons for the patient's admission, proposals to review the care plan, etc.); and helping patients retain contact with family and carers. If it is considered that the only way of providing appropriate care will amount to deprivation of liberty, then it may be appropriate to use the formal powers of detention in the Mental Health Act 1983. The advice note warns against use of the MHA to be on 'the safe side' because of the stigma which may be attached to formal detention and the extra burden this would place on resources (ASWs, doctors, MHRT, etc.).

Subsequently, in a closely related area, the Court of Appeal has held that the European Convention requires there to be automatic reference to the Mental Health Review Tribunal for patients without the capacity to challenge their detention, in *R (H)* v. *Secretary of State for Health* [2004] EWCA Civ 1609. The case concerned a woman who was formally detained under the Mental Health Act. The court suggested that new legislation was required to place patients who lack capacity to bring proceedings to review their detention in the same position as patients with capacity. Automatic reviews should take place for incapacitated patients as frequently as the right to review if exercised by a capable patient i.e. once during a s. 2 28-day admission, once in the first six months of a s. 3 detention, once in the following 6 months and annually thereafter. It declared that the difference in this respect between capable and incapable patients was incompatible with Art. 5(4). However, the decision was subsequently overturned by the House of Lords ([2005] UKHL 60). This is a further matter to be addressed in reforming legislation.

Guardianship

Guardianship under the Mental Health Act 1983 provides a limited amount of control and support for patients who remain in the community. It is available only for patients over the age of 16. The criteria for an application are:

s. 7

> ... he is suffering from mental disorder, being mental illness, severe mental impairment, psychopathic disorder or mental impairment and it is of a nature or degree which warrants reception into guardianship, and it is necessary in the interests of the welfare of the patient or for the protection of others that the patient be received.
>
> (MHA 1983)

Application is made to the Social Services Department (MHA 1983, s. 11) rather than a hospital and must be accepted by the authority. The application may be made by the ASW (with agreement of the nearest relative) or the nearest relative and requires the written recommendations of two medical practitioners. The guardian may be either a local Social Services Authority or any other person (with agreement of social services and a statement from the guardian indicating his willingness to act).

The Code of Practice states that the purpose of guardianship is to enable patients to receive care in the community in those situations where it cannot be provided without compulsion. Paragraph 13.1 states: 'It provides an authoritative framework for working with a patient, with a minimum of constraint, to achieve as independent a life as possible within the community.' There is no treatability requirement.

Any application for guardianship should be accompanied by a comprehensive care plan (under the Care Programme Approach (CPA)) established on the basis of multi-disciplinary discussions, and guardianship should be used in a positive and flexible manner (para. 13.4). The plan should include details of local authority support for the guardian, the patient's accommodation, access to day care, education and training facilities, and the patient's willingness to work with the guardian. The Code of Practice also suggests that the guardian should be willing to advocate for the patient in relation to services (para. 13.6). There is a potential conflict here if the guardian is social services and is advocating on behalf of the patient for services to be provided by social services.

■ Powers of the guardian

The guardian acquires the following powers under the MHA 1983, s. 8:
  (a) to require the patient to live in a place specified by the guardian;
  (b) to require the patient to attend at specified places for medical treatment, occupation, education or training;

(c) to require access to the patient to be given at the place where he is living to any registered medical practitioner, ASW or other specified person.

Guardianship does not provide authority to detain the patient in the specified place, to remove him from it or convey him to it. If the patient is absent without leave from the specified place, he may be returned within 28 days. Guardianship does not authorise treatment to be given without consent. There are no legal sanctions against a patient who refuses to comply with the guardian's instructions. Despite the apparent statutory limitation on the powers of the guardian, a 1997 case suggests that the courts will adopt a more flexible approach. *R v. Kent County Council, ex parte Marston* (unreported, 9 July 1997) stated that guardians have a general implied power to act in the interests of the patient, exercisable in a variety of ways provided the behaviour falls short of totalitarian conduct.

Guardianship may be appropriate as a means of providing support to an individual who has suffered abuse or to some people with a learning disability (provided it falls within the definition of mental impairment or severe mental impairment), providing an element of supervision in the community and avoiding hospital detention. A person who has been detained in hospital may be discharged into guardianship by the hospital managers provided the proposed guardian and social services agree (s. 19).

The responsibilities of the guardian include visiting at least every three months, nominating a doctor for the patient and advising social services of any changes of address, of the death of the patient or his discharge from hospital.[28] The duration of guardianship is initially six months, with possible further renewals for six months then 12 months. It may be terminated at any point by the nearest relative, doctor or Social Services Authority (MHA 1983, s. 23).

Short-term powers

In addition to the compulsory powers of detention outlined above, there are a range of short-term powers, which may be utilised, in some cases prior to formal admission, to gain access to a patient or to remove a patient from a problematic situation.

s. 115

> An approved social worker . . . may at all reasonable times . . . enter and inspect any premises (not being a hospital) . . . in which a mentally disordered patient is living, if he has reasonable cause to believe that the patient is not under proper care.
>
> (MHA 1983)

There is no power of removal under s. 115; it would be necessary to apply for a warrant under s. 135 if removal is sought.

s. 135 ▷

> Where a person suffering from a mental disorder is being ill treated or kept otherwise than under proper control, or is living alone and unable to care for himself, a magistrate may issue a warrant authorising a police officer to enter, if need be by force, premises and remove him to a place of safety.
>
> (MHA 1983)

This power of removal is for a maximum duration of 72 hours. An ASW can apply to the court under the section following an attempted investigation under s. 115. A place of safety can be a hospital, Part III accommodation, a mental nursing home or a police station.

These powers may have some relevance to adult protection work where there are concerns for a vulnerable adult who is believed to suffer from a mental disorder.

s. 136 ▷

> Where a police constable finds a person in a public place who appears to be suffering from a mental disorder, he may remove him to a place of safety. The constable must be of the opinion that the person is in need of care and control and that removal is necessary in that person's interest or for the protection of others.
>
> (MHA 1983)

Detention is limited to 72 hours. Any area to which the public has access is included as a public place, e.g. a shopping centre. Police training clearly needs to encompass awareness and recognition of mental disorder.

Rights of patients in hospital

As a minimum, patients in psychiatric hospital have the right to a standard of basic care and accommodation. Successive inquiry reports and research suggest the converse is often true.[29] Conditions on wards are poor and patients' rights are given little credence. The rights provided by the European Convention apply to mental hospitals as to any other setting and the introduction of the HRA 1998 may engender greater awareness of rights and aid development of a rights-based culture in mental health.

The framework for dealing with adult abuse, set out in Chapter 17, applies to adults with mental heath problems and, in particular, the right to be protected from abuse is encapsulated in MHA 1983, s. 127. It is an offence for a manager or member of staff of a hospital or nursing home 'to ill-treat or willfully to neglect a patient . . . receiving treatment for mental disorder . . . or subject to guardianship'. The Director of Public Prosecutions or a Social Services Authority can institute proceedings. The new offence within the Mental Capacity Act 2005 is likely to be used in preference when in force as it is of broader application, carries a heavier penalty and does not require permission of the DPP to prosecute. Chapter 17 also sets out a range of sexual offences against people with mental disorder under the Sexual Offences Act 2003.

As a preliminary point, MHA 1983, s. 132 refers to a detained patient's right to be informed of their rights by the hospital managers. Information should be provided in writing relating to: treatment, applications to the Mental Health Review Tribunal, who has power of discharge, the role of the Mental Health Act Commission, and the basis of detention. The patient should also be informed that they will not be automatically discharged or detained at the end of the period of detention. A patient should also be given information about the Mental Health Review Tribunal and the role of the Mental Health Act Commission. The same information should be provided to the nearest relative. If the section under which the patient is detained changes, the patient should be provided with the information again.

There are a number of important restrictions on the rights of compulsorily detained patients. These restrictions relate to access to the courts, correspondence, voting rights and treatment.

■ Treatment

Informal patients are required to give consent to treatment just as any other hospital patient would for a physical injury or illness. Application of this principle can become difficult when the patient's mental disorder is such that he cannot give a legally valid consent. Treatment may be given using the authority of the common law doctrine of necessity. The criteria established by *F v. West Berkshire Health Authority* [1989] 2 All ER 545 are that the treatment must be given in the patient's best interests, it must be necessary to save life or prevent a deterioration or ensure improvement in the patient's physical or mental health, and accord with practice accepted by a reasonable body of medical opinion.

The situation is different for compulsorily detained patients in respect of treatment for mental disorder, which is generally permitted by the MHA 1983 without consent (s. 63). Treatment as been interpreted broadly with seclusion accepted as an aspect of treatment (*R (Munjaz) v Mersey Care NHS Trust* [2005] UKHL 58). The remit of s. 63 treatment was considered in *R (B) v Ashworth Hospital Authority* [2005] UKHL 20. Section 63 provides:

> The consent of a patient shall not be required for any medical treatment given to him for the mental disorder from which he is suffering, not being treatment falling within sections 57 and 58 above, if the treatment is given by or under the direction of the responsible medical officer.

The point considered was whether the section only permitted treatment for the mental disorder for which the patient was originally detained, or whether it extended to treatment for any mental disorder the patient was suffering from during the period of detention. The House of Lords adopted the broader construction, concluding that a detained patient could be treated for any mental disorder he was suffering from, whether or not he was classified as suffering from such on detention.

Part IV of the Act contains procedural safeguards for specific treatments, including psychosurgery: e.g. a lobotomy, surgical implant of hormones to reduce the male sex drive, electroconvulsive therapy (**ECT**) and courses of medication after three months. Some treatments require the patient's consent and a second medical opinion (MHA 1983, s. 57: psychosurgery and surgical implant of hormones). Before ECT can be administered or drugs continued beyond an initial three-month period, s. 58 requires the patient's consent or a second medical opinion supporting the need for treatment. This was tested in *R (PS) v Responsible Medical Officer* [2003] EWHC 2335 (Admin).

The patient had the capacity to make decisions on treatment, did not wish to have the proposed treatment (anti-psychotic medication), argued that his personal choice to refuse treatment should be respected and that to treat him under s. 58 on the basis of a second medical treatment amounted to an infringement of his Art. 3 and Art. 8 rights. The court refused the application for judicial review, and held that administration of the treatment was not an infringement of his rights under Art. 3 and Art. 8. Article 3 was contravened if the proposed treatment reached the minimum level of severity of ill treatment, applied, and the medical necessity for the treatment was not shown. Given the possible benefits to PS and the limited adverse consequences, the administration of the treatment to him did not reach the threshold. His rights under Art. 8 would not be infringed if the proposed treatment was justified under Art. 8(2) as being in the patient's best interests. This was satisfied by the evidence of the responsible medical officer and the doctor and was necessary for the protection of his health and the safety of others.

The safeguards provided by s. 57 and 58 are disregarded if treatment is needed urgently under s. 62. This will be the case if the treatment is immediately necessary to save life, stop the patient's condition seriously deteriorating, reduce serious suffering, or prevent the patient from behaving violently and being a danger to himself or to others. Complaints about treatment given without consent may be directed to the Mental Health Act Commission.

The above rules apply to treatment of mental disorder for compulsorily detained patients. Treatment for physical conditions cannot be given to a compulsorily detained patient without their consent, unless the patient lacks capacity to consent and the doctrine of necessity applies. Here it is important to remember that mental disorder and mental capacity are not one and the same. This was clearly illustrated in the case of *Re C (Adult: Refusal of Medical Treatment)* [1994] 1 All ER 819. C was 68 and suffered from paranoid schizophrenia. Against medical advice he refused to have his gangrenous leg amputated. The decision-making process was broken down into three stages: comprehending and retaining information; believing it; and weighing it in the balance to arrive at a choice. Regardless of his mental health problems, C was found to have the capacity to make a decision and refuse the amputation.

■ Voting rights

Patients who are compulsorily detained by a criminal court have no right to vote. Under the Representation of the People Act 2000 all other patients, informal and detained, are entitled to be registered to vote in local and parliamentary elections.[30]

■ Correspondence

Informal patients may send and receive correspondence without interference. Compulsorily detained patients may receive post, but hospital managers may confiscate any post sent to a person who has asked not to receive any post from the patient. Where a patient is detained in one of the special hospitals, e.g. Broadmoor, his post may be withheld if it is in the interests of safety of the patient or for the protection of others. The patient may be prevented from sending correspondence to a person who has notified the manager or if it is likely to cause distress or danger. Telephone calls of dangerous patients may be monitored: this was considered not a breach of Art. 8 in *R (N)* v *Ashworth Special Hospital Authority* [2001] EWHC Admin 339.

■ Visits

Detained patients enjoy the basic right to be visited by friends and relatives and the Code of Practice recognises that this is an important element of the patient's treatment and rehabilitation (para. 26.1). It is possible to exclude visitors on two grounds:

1. Clinical reasons, i.e. where the visit would be anti-therapeutic and could cause deterioration in the patient's mental health. In some cases the safety of the visitor may be the major concern.
2. Security restrictions, i.e. where the visitor has behaved in a way that is disruptive: e.g. bringing in alcohol or drugs or encouraging the patient to abscond.

Separate policies exist in most hospitals about visits by children and the emphasis will be whether the visit is in the child's best interests.[31] The case of *R (ML)* v. *Secretary of State for the Department of Health* (2000) 4 CCLR 59 unsuccessfully challenged guidance (HSC 1999/160) that restricts visits by children to offenders in special hospitals. Visits will be restricted unless the patient is the parent or relative of the child, had parental responsibility or the child was treated as a member of the patient's household.

■ Legal proceedings

A compulsorily detained patient cannot take legal action in respect of the exercise of Mental Health Act powers, e.g. by a doctor or approved social worker, without obtaining prior permission from the High Court (MHA 1983, s. 139).

Discharge

As a general principle, a patient should be discharged from hospital as soon as he is found not to be suffering from a mental disorder. Section 23 provides that the responsible medical officer (RMO), the hospital managers or the nearest relative hold the power of discharge. There are, however, some restrictions on the power held by the nearest relative. The nearest relative must give the hospital 72 hours' notice of intention to discharge the patient. The hospital may prevent this discharge if they do not agree with the nearest relative's proposal and are concerned that if discharged the patient would be a danger to himself or others (MHA 1983, s. 25). This action also prevents the nearest relative making any further attempts to discharge the patient within the next six months. The ASW can also prevent the nearest relative from acting by making an application to the county court to displace the nearest relative (MHA 1983, s. 29, outlined above).

The informal patient may discharge himself at any point, though detention (probably under MHA 1983, s. 5) can prevent this.

Following discharge it is possible for a fresh compulsory admission to be made as confirmed by the House of Lords in *R (von Brandenburg (aka Hanley))* v. *East London and the City Mental Health NHS Trust* [2003] UKHL 58. To avoid a breach of Art. 5 there must be some change in circumstances since the tribunal discharged the patient. This would include the emergence of new information not known to the tribunal.

■ Mental Health Review Tribunal

The patient or the nearest relative can also apply to the Mental Health Review Tribunal (**MHRT**) for discharge. Hospital staff should ensure the patient is aware of the right to apply for discharge. There are strict time limits within which applications can be submitted (MHA 1983, ss. 66 and 68). The patient can apply for discharge from a s. 2 admission within 14 days (i.e. half way through the period of detention), and for discharge from guardianship or admission for treatment the patient may make an application within the first six months. If, by the end of six months, no application is made, the hospital managers will automatically refer the case to the tribunal. There are also automatic reviews of detention by the tribunal if a long-term patient does not exercise the right to apply to the tribunal. This was introduced because many long-term patients never applied to the tribunal. If a patient detained under s. 3 does not apply to the tribunal within the first six months, the hospital manager must refer his case.

The MHRT proceedings are quite formal and a specialist mental health solicitor will normally represent the patient. The panel includes a legal, medical and lay member. A social work report will be submitted to the tribunal. The report should outline the circumstances leading to admission and the current situation. Tribunal rules also require the report writer to consider: the financial circumstances of the patient; the patient's home and family circumstances; the opportunities for employment or occupation and housing which would be available if the patient is discharged; the availability of community support; and medical facilities.[32] The tribunal has no jurisdiction to determine whether the original basis for detention was established. Its role is to consider whether continued detention is justified. The tribunal may also reclassify the type of mental disorder the patient is suffering from.

The provisions detailing criteria for discharge from hospital detention by the Mental Health Review Tribunal are contained in s. 72 and 73 of the MHA 1983. The wording of these sections presents a 'double negative' test and has been declared incompatible with the European Convention on Human Rights (Art. 5(4)) in the case of *R (H)* v. *London North and East Region Mental Health Review Tribunal (Secretary of State for Health intervening)* [2001] EWCA Civ 415.[33] Section 72 provides:

s. 72(1)

> . . . (b) the tribunal shall direct the discharge of a patient liable to be detained . . . if they are satisfied –
>> (i) that he is not then suffering from mental illness, psychopathic disorder, severe mental impairment or mental impairment or from any of those forms of disorder of a nature or degree which makes it appropriate for him to be liable to be detained in a hospital . . . or
>> (ii) that it is not necessary for the health or safety of the patient or for the protection of other persons that he should receive such treatment . . .
>
> (MHA 1983)

Section 73 relates to *restricted patients:*

s. 73

> ... the tribunal shall direct the absolute discharge of the patient if it is satisfied
>> (a) as to the matters in paragraph (b)(i) or (ii) of section 72(1) above; and
>> (b) that it is not appropriate for the patient to remain liable to be recalled to hospital...
>
> (MHA 1983)

The wording of s. 72 and 73 does not actually require the tribunal to discharge a patient if it cannot be shown that he continues to suffer from a mental disorder warranting detention. The central issue is that of the burden of proof. The court could not simply interpret a requirement that a tribunal had to act if satisfied that a state of affairs did not exist as meaning that it had to act if not satisfied that a state of affairs did exist. This was incompatible with the ECHR requirement that a person shall only be detained if it can be shown that he was suffering from mental disorder that warranted detention. Amending legislation has not yet been introduced.

R (AN) v. *Mental Health Review Tribunal (Northern Region)* [2005] EWCA Civ 1605 has confirmed that the standard of proof in Mental Health Tribunals is the civil standard, balance of probabilities. The patient's application for discharge under s. 73 was rejected by the tribunal. On appeal, Munby J rejected the patient's argument that the criminal standard should apply. He stated that the civil standard applies to the tribunals consideration of whether the patient is suffering from a mental disorder. The other elements of the detention criteria, nature or degree of the mental disorder and health and safety of the patient and others were matters of evaluation of judgment not fact and the standard of proof is therefore not relevant to them.

The above discussion relates to discharge of patients detained for treatment under s. 3. Where a patient is detained for a 28-day assessment under s. 2 it is also possible to apply to the MHRT for discharge. In that case a hearing date must be fixed within seven days (Mental Health Review Tribunal Rules 1983 (S1 1983/942) r. 31). It would be unlawful to fail to meet this timescale. The MHRT can set out conditions of discharge; however, a health authority is under no absolute obligation to comply with those conditions: *R (K)* v. *Camden and Islington Health Authority* [2001] EWCA Civ 240.

Article 5(4) of the ECHR provides: 'everyone who is deprived of his liberty . . . shall be entitled to take proceedings by which the lawfulness of his detention shall be decided speedily by a court and his release ordered if detention is not lawful'. The opportunity to challenge the lawfulness of detention currently applies only to detained patients (as discussed above in *Bournewood*). Guidance on the application of this Article was provided in the earlier decision, *Megyeri* v. *Federal Republic of Germany* (1993) 15 EHRR 584. According to this case, patients should enjoy the following rights:

- Detained patients are entitled to take court proceedings at 'reasonable intervals'.

- The procedure must have a judicial character and provide guarantees appropriate to the deprivation.

- Patients should have access to a court and the opportunity to be heard in person or when necessary by representation.

- Patients cannot be required to take the initiative in obtaining legal representation before having recourse to a court.

- Patients should receive legal representation.

As to speediness of the process, in *Barclay-Maguire* v. *United Kingdom* (1981) (Application No. 91/7/80, unreported) the Government undertook to ensure that tribunal proceedings were concluded within 13 weeks. This undertaking had not been honoured. Subsequent case law has found that delays of eight weeks meant that proceedings were not speedy and we may assume, therefore, that if a case arises where there is a delay of more than eight weeks it could form a legitimate challenge. In *R (C)* v. *Mental Health Review Tribunal* [2001] EWCA Civ 1110, the Court of Appeal found that the practice of routinely listing applications for the MHRT to be heard in eight weeks' time contravened Art. 5(4). The Master of the Rolls stated that such a policy was 'bred of administrative convenience not administrative necessity'. It is necessary to ensure that individual applications are heard as soon as reasonably practicable given the relevant circumstances of the case and within a maximum target of eight weeks.

After-care

s. 117

It is the duty of the [District Health Authority and Social Services Authority] to provide, in co-operation with relevant voluntary agencies, after-care services . . . until such time as . . . the person concerned is no longer in need of such services.

(MHA 1983)

This provision applies where a person has been the subject of a guardianship or treatment order. It does not apply where a person was detained under s. 2 for assessment or following a period in hospital, however lengthy, without compulsion (voluntary or informal admission). It is a free-standing, independent legal duty jointly imposed on the local and health authority. The duty continues until the health authority and local authority jointly agree that services are no longer needed by way of after-care. As the duty is joint, health authorities can be asked to pay for half of any after-care package. A person in receipt of after-care services will also be entitled to the highest rate of income support.

The patient is under no obligation to accept after-care and has the legal right to refuse. In reality, if there are concerns that the patient is unlikely to cooperate with plans for after care, including continuation of medication, the patient may be detained for a longer period in hospital. In a case where there are concerns that a patient's health is likely to deteriorate on discharge, an application for after-care under supervision, under a *supervised discharge order,* might be considered.

As part of the Care Programme Approach (CPA) (to which all patients should be subject, i.e. not limited to those included in s. 117) a multi-disciplinary care plan should be formulated for after-care. This process should include an assessment of the risks of discharge. A key worker should monitor implementation of the CPA.[34]

The status of the s. 117 provision was considered in the case of *R* v. *Manchester City Council, ex parte Stennett; R* v. *Redcar and Cleveland Borough Council, exparte Armstrong; R* v. *Harrow London Borough Council, ex parte Cobham* [2002] UKHL 34. There were four applications for judicial review based on similar facts. In each case the issue concerned whether each of the respondent Social Services Authorities could charge for residential accommodation provided as after-care services under the Mental Health Act 1983, s. 117. Each of the applicants had been detained in hospital under MHA 1983, s. 3. Upon discharge from hospital they had been provided with residential accommodation by the Social Services Authority. Evidence provided to the court showed that around half of all Social Services Authorities made a charge for residential accommodation provided pursuant to s. 117. It was also submitted that if authorities did not charge this would impose a cost of over £50 million. The arguments raised were based around differing interpretations of s. 117. It was agreed that residential accommodation was included in the term 'after-care services' and also that s. 117 did not directly confer a power to charge. The authorities did argue, however, that s. 117 should be seen as a 'gateway' section, imposing a duty on authorities to ensure after-care services were provided under other legislation. This would include s. 21 of the National Assistance Act 1948, which permits authorities to provide and recover the costs of residential accommodation.

The court concluded that the wording of s. 117 was clear. It did not impose a duty to secure provision of services under other legislation; it was a 'free-standing' duty to provide after-care services. It was therefore not possible to charge for the services by relying on s. 22 of the National Assistance Act 1948. A local government ombudsman decision applied this ruling in *Investigation into Complaint No. 98/B/0341 against Wiltshire CC (2000) 3 CCLR 60*. The local authority were ordered to repay several years' worth of charges made unlawfully for residential accommodation provided under MHA 1983, s. 117.

■ Supervised discharge

The Mental Health (Patients in the Community) Act 1995 introduced after-care under supervision, also known as *supervised discharge*. Application is made by the RMO, while the patient is still in hospital under a section, to the health authority with responsibility for after care. The application must be supported by a second medical recommendation, preferably by the Community Responsible Officer (**CRO**) (i.e. the doctor who will supervise the patient in the community) or the patient's GP. An ASW must also support the application but is not the applicant. The nearest relative should be consulted.

The criteria that must be satisfied before a supervised discharge order may be made are:

- the patient is detained under s. 3, s. 37, s. 47 or s. 48 of the MHA 1983 and is over 16 years of age;
- the patient is suffering from one of the four specific forms of mental disorder (i.e. mental illness, psychopathic disorder, mental impairment or severe mental impairment);
- there is a substantial risk of serious harm to the health or safety of the patient or the safety of others; *or*
- there is a risk that the patient will be seriously exploited if after-care services provided under s. 117 were not received; *and*
- placing the patient on a supervised discharge order is likely to help ensure the patient will receive after-care services (MHA 1983, s. 25A(4)).

The order can contain a number of conditions, including where the patient is to live and attendance at clinics, but it cannot impose a condition that the patient takes medication. These conditions are similar to those exercisable under guardianship. Failure to comply with the conditions might lead to re-sectioning.

■ Children and young people and mental health

The Mental Health Act 1983 also applies to children and young people, with the exceptions that a guardianship order can be made only from the age of 16 and the after-care provisions do not apply. The criteria for formal detention in hospital are the same for children and adults regardless of age.

If it is considered appropriate for a child to be admitted to hospital, this may be arranged informally provided there is parental consent. A young person of 16 or 17 years of age can give their own consent, as can younger children who are *Gillick* competent. Where a child is an informal patient, after three months the health authority must formally notify the local authority and the local authority must investigate to ensure that the welfare of the child does not require its intervention (CA 1989, s. 85). If neither the child nor the parents consent, as a last resort formal detention under the MHA 1983 may be appropriate. Use of the MHA 1983 provides the same safeguards for children as for adults, including recourse to the MHRT. Where there is a care order in force, the local authority can admit a child to hospital.[35] For children and young people who are not *Gillick* competent, parents can also consent to medical treatment, including treatment for mental disorder.

In addition to the MHA 1983, provisions of the Children Act 1989 may apply. It is arguable that the CA 1989 does not carry the same stigma as the MHA 1983. If proceedings are commenced in respect of the child, there is the advantage that a children's guardian will be appointed. There is no similar provision for independent representation of the child under the MHA 1983. A child may have mental health difficulties such that he would benefit from psychiatric intervention but does not fall within the MHA 1983 definition of mental disorder. Such a child may be within the definition of a 'child in need' (CA 1989, s. 17), and be eligible for support for the child and his family. Research suggests that there is a strong link between family income and the mental health of children, with children of families in Social Class 5 being three times more likely to have mental health problems than children of families in Social Class 1.[36] It is essential that consideration is given to mental health needs in any child assessment whether it leads to service input or formal intervention. Services and professionals that may be particularly relevant include the specialist Child and Adolescent Mental Health Service (**CAMHS**), primary child mental health workers, school health services, health visitors and advocacy services. As an alternative to formal detention it is possible for a child to be accommodated by the local authority with parental consent (CA 1989, s. 20). Particular treatment issues may be dealt with by specific issue orders (s. 8) or in the High Court through the exercise of the inherent jurisdiction where a declaration is sought.

The mental health of a child is clearly an aspect of emotional and behavioural development and it is possible that concerns relating to this aspect of development could lead to formal intervention to seek a care order. It is not unusual for psychologists and psychiatric services to work with children and families, carrying out assessments sometimes leading to the provision of reports to court. Recent research into the implementation of the CA 1989 found, however, that '[a] serious impediment to joint working for children with mental health problems was the absence of therapeutic or mental health services for children and young people'.[37] This is being addressed in part by the Department of Health strategy to improve provision of CAMHS (training and staffing levels), and liaison between CAMHS, primary care and social services.[38]

■ Criminal proceedings affecting those with mental illness

Chapter 18 includes discussion of the special position of those with mental health problems who are involved in criminal proceedings. It is appropriate here to note that in addition to the use of sections under the MHA 1983, an individual may be formally detained via the criminal justice system. A court can make a hospital order or guardianship order at the time of sentence. In addition, a prisoner may be transferred to a psychiatric hospital.

The Mental Health Act 1983 is a complex piece of legislation. Exhibit 15.2 provides an outline of the structure of the Act and summarises the main provisions discussed in this chapter.

Part I *Application of the MHA 1983*	s. 1 'mental disorder'
Part II *Compulsory admission to hospital and guardianship*	s. 2 Assessment s. 3 Admission for treatment s. 4 Emergency admission s. 5 Patient already in hospital ss. 7 and 8 Guardianship s. 13 Duty of ASW to make applications s. 23 Discharge of patients s. 26 Definition of nearest relative s. 29 Displacement of nearest relative
Part III *Patients involved in criminal proceedings or under sentence*	s. 37 Power of court to order hospital admission or guardianship s. 41 Restriction orders (see Chapter 18)
Part IV *Consent to treatment*	s. 57 Treatment requiring consent and a second opinion s. 58 Treatment requiring consent or a second opinion s. 62 Urgent treatment

Exhibit 15.2 Summary of key provisions of the Mental Health Act 1983

Part V Mental Health Review Tribunals	s. 66 Application to tribunals s. 68 Duty of hospital managers to refer cases to tribunal s. 72 Power to discharge patients
Part VI Removal and return of patients within United Kingdom	
Part VII Management of property and affairs of patients	
Part VIII Miscellaneous functions of local authorities and the Secretary of State	s. 114 Appointment of approved social workers s. 115 Power of entry and inspection s. 117 After care s. 121 Mental Health Act Commission
Part IX Offences Part X Miscellaneous and supplementary	s. 127 Ill treatment of patients s. 131 Informal admission of patients s. 132 Duty to give information to detained patients s. 135 Warrant to search for and remove patients s. 136 Mentally disordered persons found in public places

Exhibit 10.2   (continued)

Review of mental health services

Proposals for the reform of mental health law have grown out of the 'modernising agenda' for health and social services. An expert committee[39] was commissioned by the Government to make recommendations for reform (published almost simultaneously with a green paper) and was followed by a white paper which adopted some of those proposals in the Government's response.[40] A draft Bill followed but was subject to considerable criticism and did not proceed. A revised draft Bill was published in September 2004 (with explanatory notes). It was considered by Joint Committee which reported in March 2005 followed by the Government's response in July 2005. Questions and concerns remained about some of its provisions and the Bill was not introduced into Parliament as a formal Bill. A new amending Bill, to be substantially shorter than the

2004 Bill, will be introduced. The need for reform was linked directly to failures of the community care system and Government policy to tackle social exclusion and wide regional variation in the way provisions of existing legislation are applied. The strategy behind the reform proposals being to provide a new system which will be 'Safe, Sound and Supportive'[41] and which will apply the new provisions with greater consistency. A series of cases which have questioned compatibility of certain provisions in the existing legislation, with the European Convention require legislative changes to be made, e.g. *HL v United Kingdom* (2004) 40 EHRR 761.

∎ The shape of the new law

Whilst the new Bill, when introduced to Parliament, will be subject to further debate and is likely to undergo some amendment, the following elements are likely to feature in new legislation.

Principles underlying the provisions of the new law will be included in the Act as an aid to its interpretation, namely:

- Informal care and treatment should always be considered before recourse to compulsory powers.

- Patients should be involved as far as possible in the process of developing and reviewing their own care and treatment plans.

- Safety of both the individual patient and the public are of key importance in determining the question of whether compulsory powers should be imposed.

- Where compulsory powers are used, care and treatment should be located in the least restrictive setting consistent with the patient's best interests and the safety of the public.

A number of other principles recommended by the Expert Committee may feature in a Code of Practice, such as non-discrimination, patient autonomy, consensual care, reciprocity, respect for diversity, equality, respect for carers, effective communication and provision of information.

New legislation is likely to include a single definition of mental disorder in the following terms: 'any disability or disorder of mind or brain, whether permanent or temporary, which results in an impairment or disturbance of mental functioning'. Specifically excluded from this definition are disorders of sexual preference (e.g. paedophilia) and misuse of alcohol and drugs. The separate sub-categories of mental disorder will not be included in new legislation, nor will the 'treatability' test under s. 3.

The structure for compulsory orders is likely to change. A single pathway into care and treatment will replace the existing provisions in ss. 2–5. Recommendations suggest a formal assessment period of seven days prior to compulsory care. A further order for 21 days may be made and, beyond that, compulsory care and treatment would need to be authorised by an independent tribunal, chaired by a lawyer.

The nearest relative provisions will be amended to remedy incompatibility with the ECHR and encompass Civil Partnership Act 2004 changes.

The Bill will include Bournewood safeguards for people who lack capacity and are not under compulsion but are deprived of their liberty.

The approved social worker is likely to continue to be involved in applications for compulsory care; however, concerns have been expressed about the possibility of a reduced role for ASWs through a corresponding greater involvement of other professionals, and less emphasis on social circumstances and core issues of need, risk, vulnerability and disability.[42] The role may be renamed as Approved Mental Health Professional.

It remains to be seen whether the government's commitment to produce a shorter, streamlined Bill will satisfy critics of the 2004 Bill.

Chapter summary

- Mental health is a complex area of social work practice covered by the Mental Health Act 1983 and a Code of Practice. All social workers require a basic understanding of the Act but many specific functions are vested in a specialist worker, an approved social worker.

- The MHA 1983 defines mental disorder and other specific categories of mental disorder and provides a range of short-term and longer-term orders to detain a patient in hospital.

- The majority of people with mental health problems live in the community, possibly with the support of a guardianship order, but some will receive care and treatment in hospital either as an informal patient or detained under a section.

- Whilst in hospital there are a number of restrictions on the rights of detained patients and particular provisions relating to compulsory treatment.

- A patient may be discharged at an appropriate time by his nearest relative or at the behest of the hospital or by order of the Mental Health Review Tribunal.

- On discharge, after-care services should be provided to a patient who has been detained long term. A scheme for supervised discharge also operates.

- Mental incapacity is a distinct issue, but is often confused with mental disorder. A person may lack capacity to make a particular decision and in certain cases it will be possible to seek a declaration from the High Court dealing with the issue at stake. New legislation, the Mental Capacity Act 2005 has been introduced (see Chapter 16).

- Mental health law has been the subject of reform proposals and a new legislative frameworks is anticipated.

Exercises

1. George, aged 47, is susceptible to periods of depression and self-harming. He has been admitted to the local psychiatric hospital on a voluntary basis a number of times over the years. He recently lost his job, became depressed, stopped taking his medication and started to drink heavily. He refused to go back into hospital on a voluntary basis and has been detained for five months. His only relative, a sister whom he sees infrequently, has contacted the hospital and insists that George should be allowed home. His living accommodation is very poor and he has very few links in the community. He would also like to be discharged. The hospital are concerned that if discharged he will fail to take his medication and may start to self-harm again.

    Consider any options that would enable George to return safely to the community.

2. Jonathan, aged 33, has a history of manic depression and has received treatment in the past as a compulsorily detained patient. He lives with his mother who is diagnosed as suffering from schizophrenia and regularly fails to take her medication. Jonathan is found in the town shopping centre, dressed in pyjamas and acting in a bizarre fashion, shouting at passers by and threatening to throw himself off a balcony. The police are called and take him to the hospital. An approved social worker with no previous knowledge of Jonathan is called to the hospital and met by a consultant psychiatrist who instructs the ASW to do the necessary paperwork, saying that the only way forward for Jonathan is a course of ECT. At the same time, Jonathon's mother appears and insists that if he comes home she will take care of him.

    Consider the steps the ASW could take.

Websites

Mind – a national charity with over 200 regional offices:
  www.mind.org.uk

Mental Health Foundation:
  www.mentalhealth.org.uk

Mencap – the organisation which campaigns for equal rights for children and adults with a learning disability:
  www.mencap.org.uk

Department of Health website section on mental health:
  www.dh.gov.uk/policyandguidance/HealthandSocial CareTopics/MentalHealth/ fs/en

Young Minds – a charity focusing on children's mental health:
www.youngminds.org.uk

Further reading

Texts which provide more in depth coverage of mental health law include:

Brown R. *et al.* (2005) *Mental Health Law.* London: Hodder Arnold.

Bartlett, P. and Sandland, R. (2000) *Mental Health Law Policy and Practice.* London: Blackstone Press.

Jones, R. (2004) *Mental Health Act manual* (9th edn). London: Sweet & Maxwell. (A detailed reference source.)

Texts with an emphasis on social work practice in mental health:

Golightley, M. (2006) *Social Work and Mental Health* (2nd edn). Exeter: Learning Matters.

Brown, R. (2006) *The Approved Social Worker's Guide to Mental Health Law.* Exeter: Learning Matters.

Issues within the current law are discussed in:

Hatfield, B. and Antcliff, V. (2001) 'Detention under the Mental Health Act: balancing rights, risks and needs for services' 23(2) *Journal of Social Welfare and Family Law* pp. 135–53.

Richardson, G. (2002) 'Autonomy, Guardianship and Mental Disorder: one problem, two solutions' 65(5) *Modern Law Review* pp. 702–23.

A number of articles offer a critique of aspects of the reform proposals:

Cavadino, M. (2002) 'New mental health law for old – safety – plus equals human rights minus' 14(2) *Child and Family Law Quarterly* p. 75.

Eldergill, A. (2002) 'Is anyone safe? Civil compulsion under the Draft Mental Health Bill' 8 *Journal of Mental Health Law* p. 331.

Rapaport, J. (2004) 'A Matter of Principle: the Nearest Relative under the Mental Health Act 1983 and Proposals for Legislative Reform' 26(4) *Journal of Social Welfare and Family Law* p. 377.

Children and young people are considered in:

Darlington, Y., Feeney, J. A. and Rixon, K. (2005) 'Practice challenges at the intersection of child protection and mental health' 10(3) *Child and Family Social Work* p. 239.

Walker, S. (2003) *Social Work and Child and Adolescent Mental Health.* Dorset: Russell House.

Kay, H. (1999) *Bright Futures – Promoting Children and Young People's Mental Health.* London: The Mental Health Foundation.

Application of the Human Rights Act 1998 to mental health is the subject of two useful articles:

Hale, B. (2005) 'What can the Human Rights Act 1998 do for my mental health?' 17(3) *Child and Family Law Quarterly* p. 295.

Johns, R. (2004) 'Of Unsound Mind? Mental Health and the European Convention on Human Rights' 16(4) *Practice* p. 247.

Notes

1   Christopher Clunis killed Jonathon Zito shortly after release from detention in a mental hospital. Subsequently, in *Clunis* v. *Camden and Islington Health Authority* [1998] 2 WLR 902, it was held that Clunis had no cause of action against the health authority regarding provision of after care when he killed shortly after discharge. To provide otherwise would allow him to profit from his own wrong and the case was struck out by the Court of Appeal as against public policy.

2   Secretary of State for Health (1999) 'Reform of the Mental Health Act 1983: Proposals for Consultation' (Cm. 4480). London: The Stationery Office.

3   P. Taylor and J. Gunn (1999) 'Homicides by people with mental illness: myth and reality' 174 *British Journal of Psychiatry* pp. 9–14.

4   A number of influential documents were published at this time, including L. Gostin (1975) *A Human Condition,* vol. 1; (1977) Vol. 2. London: MIND; and the Butler Report on Mentally Abnormal Offenders.

5   Issued pursuant to s. 118 of the MHA 1983, succeeding earlier versions (first published in 1990 and revised in 1993). Department of Health and Welsh Office (1999) 'Mental Health Act 1983 Code of Practice'. London: The Stationery Office

6   L. Appleby (2004) *The national service framework for mental health – five years on.* London: Department of Health.

7   See D. Browne (1995) 'Sectioning: the black experience' in S. Fernando (ed.) *Mental Health in a Multi-Ethnic Society: A Multi-Disciplinary Handbook.* London: Routledge.

8   See NIMHE (2003): *Inside Outside: Improving Mental Health Services for Black Ethnic Communities in England.* London: Department of Health. See also Sir John Blofeld (2004) Independent Inquiry into the Death of David Bennett at (www.nscstha.nhs.uk/ 11516/David%20Bennett%20Inquiry.pdf).

9   'Count me in. Results of a national census of inpatients in mental health hospitals and facilities in England and Wales'. London: Commission for Healthcare Audit and Inspection.   The census day was 31 March 2005.

10 *Re KB (Adult) (Mental Patient: Medical Treatment)* (1994) 19 BMLR 144.

11 Department of Health and Social Security (1976) 'Review of the Mental Health Act 1959'. London: HMSO.

12 P. Fennell (1989) 'The Beverley Lewis case: was the law to blame?' 139 *New Law Journal* pp. 1557–8.

13 Department of Health LAC (93) 10 'Approvals and directions for arrangements from 1 April 1993 made under Schedule 8 to the National Health Service Act 1977 and sections 21 and 29 of the National Assistance Act 1948'. London: Department of Health.

14 J. Campbell, G. Wilson, F. Britton, B. Hamilton, P. Hughes and R. Manktelow (2001) 'The management and supervision of approved social workers: aspects of law, policy and practice' 23(2) *Journal of Social Welfare and Family Law* pp. 155–72.

15 P. Huxley, S. Evans, M. Webber and C. Gately, (2005) 'Staff shortages in the mental health workforce: the case of the disappearing approved social worker 13(6) *Health and Social Care in the Community* p. 504.

16 See also W. K. Fakhoury, and D. Wright (2004) 'A National Survey of Approved Social Workers in the UK: Information, Communication and Training Needs' 34(5) *British Journal of Social Work* p. 663.

17 Department of Health (2003) 'Mental Health Policy Implementaton Guide: Support, Time and Recovery (STR) Workers'. London: Department of Health.

18 The report of the Workforce Action Team may be obtained from: www.doh.gov.uk/mentalhealth/wat.htm#report.

19 The five-year residence rule would include carers who have fostered a mentally disordered person under an adult placement scheme.

20 For a discussion of the differences between admission under s. 2 or s. 3, see B. Hatfield and V. Antcliff (2001) 'Detention under the Mental Health Act: balancing rights, risks and needs for services' 23(2) *Journal of Social Welfare and Family Law* pp. 135–53.

21 Figures cited at p. 294d of the judgment.

22 [1998] 3 All ER 289 at p. 304.

23 Ibid, p. 306.

24 Ibid, pp. 304–305.

25 Ibid, p. 305.

26 HSC 1998/122.

27 DH (2004) 'Advice on the Decision of the European Court of Human Rights in the Case of HL v UK (The *Bournewood* Case)'.

28 Mental Health (Hospital, Guardianship and Consent to Treatment) Regulations 1983 (SI 1983/893).

29 N. Stanley and J. Manthorpe (2001) 'Reading mental health inquiries' 1(1) *Journal of Social Work* p. 77.

30 Section 5 of the Representation of the People Act 2000 amends the Representation of the People Act 1983, inserting new sections 3A, 7 and 7A.

31 See 'Guidance to Local Authority Social Services Departments on Visits by Children to Special Hospitals' (LAC (99) 23); 'Visits by Children to Ashworth, Broadmoor and Rampton Hospital Authorities Directions' (HSC 1999/160); and 'Mental Health Act 1983 Code of Practice: Guidance on the visiting of psychiatric patients by children' (HSC 1999/222, LAC (99) 32).

32 Mental Health Review Tribunal Rules 1983 (SI 1983/942), Sch. 1, Pt B.

33 The first remedial order to be laid before Parliament is to amend ss. 72(1) and 72(3) as declared incompatible with the European Convention: Mental Health Act 1983 (Remedial) Order, laid July 2001.

34 See Department of Health (1990) 'The Care Programme Approach for people with a mental illness referred to specialist psychiatric services' (HC (90) 23/LASSL (90) 11); and also Department of Health (1995) 'Building Bridges: a guide to arrangements for inter-agency working for the care and protection of severely mentally ill people'. London: Department of Health.

35 *R* v. *Kirklees MBC, ex parte C (A Minor)* [1993] 2 FLR 187.

36 Office of National Statistics (1999) 'Mental Health of Children and Adolescents' (Monograph series (99) 409) cited in Department of Health, Department for Education

and Employment, Home Office (2000) 'Framework for the Assessment of Children in Need and their Families'. London: The Stationery Office.

37 Department of Health (2001) *The Children Act Now: Messages from Research*. London: The Stationery Office, p. 106.

38 National Priorities Guidance for Health and Social Services 1999/2002, cited in Secretary of State for Health, Secretary of State for Education and Employment and the Lord Chancellor (2000) 'The Children Act Report 1995–1999' (Cm. 4579). London: The Stationery Office.

39 Chaired by Professor Genevra Richardson.

40 For a discussion of the expert committee and the green paper, see A. Parkin (2000) 'Contrasting agendas in the reform of mental health law; the expert committee and the green paper' 4 *Web Journal of Current Legal Issues*. The green paper was followed by a white paper, Department of Health (2000) 'Reforming the Mental Health Act'. London: The Stationery Office.

41 *Safe* – to protect the public and provide effective care for those with mental illness when they need it; *Sound* – to ensure that patients and service users have access to the full range of services that they need; and *Supportive* – working with patients and service users, their families and carers to build healthier communities.

42 P. Walton (2000) 'Reforming the Mental Health Act 1983: an approved social worker perspective' 22(4) *Journal of Social Welfare and Family Law* pp. 401–14.

16 Mental capacity

Learning objectives

To develop an understanding of the following:

- The current law on mental capacity.
- The meaning of 'capacity'.
- The role and status of relatives and next of kin.
- The use of High Court declarations and the doctrine of necessity.
- The status of advance healthcare decisions.
- The new statutory framework provided by the Mental Capacity Act 2005.
- Guiding principles of the Act including 'best interests'.
- Means of delegating decision making.
- The role of the new Court of Protection.

Introduction

Mental incapacity is often confused with mental disorder and, partly as a result of this confusion, a number of 'myths' abound. For example, it is commonly understood that:

- next of kin have decision-making rights
- capacity is a medical issue
- silence indicates consent
- irrational decisions are evidence of incapacity
- mental incapacity is very common amongst older people and people with learning disabilities.

In fact none of the above statements is entirely accurate, as will be explained below.

The question of mental capacity is especially important when considering whether a person can legally make a particular decision. This is an area of law which has developed largely through common law principles. There are gaps in the existing law and the chapter includes discussion of how the courts have attempted to fill some of these gaps with declaratory relief. Legally and ethically the uncertainty in the law has made this a complex area in which to practice. In recognition of this and movement towards greater recognition of the rights of adults whose capacity may be impaired new legislation has been introduced. The new law, the Mental Capacity Act 2005, establishes a much clearer framework for decision-making, provides a universal test of capacity and aims to promote empowerment of vulnerable adults by encouraging first-hand decision-making wherever possible. This chapter first considers the existing common law-based framework, then continues with an outline of the new law. The Mental Capacity Act is not expected to come into force until April 2007 and many of the rules and regulations which will supplement the legislation have yet to be produced.

Capacity and decision-making

In English law, for adults there is a presumption of capacity. This will be rebutted by evidence of incapacity. Whether X has capacity is a legal question, but medical evidence may be helpful to establish the level of capacity, whether it is permanent or transient and whether it is affected by external factors such as drugs or bereavement.

Capacity is not a fixed concept. The capacity required depends on the nature of the decision to be made, e.g. to vote, marry or execute a will. The level of capacity required to manage substantial property and financial affairs may thus be greater than the capacity required to exercise choice over a minor medical procedure. A person may thus have the capacity to make some decisions but not others. *Masterman-Lister* v. *Brutton & Co; Masterman-Lister* v *Jewell* [2002] EWCA Civ 1889 confirmed that the test of capacity is specific to the issue in question. It follows that no-one should be regarded as legally incapable in the total sense. The common law test of capacity is essentially in two parts: the individual must be capable of understanding what is proposed and its implications, and must be able to exercise choice. Capacity in an individual may fluctuate. Every effort should be made to ensure opportunities to take decisions during lucid periods. It is appropriate to consider different ways of promoting capacity. For example, an individual may find it difficult to understand an issue described in writing, but may follow an explanation using diagrams and flowcharts, or an oral explanation using appropriate vocabulary and concise sentences. Capacity may also be limited by communication difficulties. Again, communication aids such as Makaton (a sign and symbol language programme for people with communication difficulties) should be fully utilised in order to enable an individual to participate as fully as possible in decisions concerning himself.

Difficulties can arise where a person does not have capacity. If X cannot make the decision, who can? Currently, it is possible to delegate decision-making in a few areas only. The law recognises substitute decision-making only in relation to property and finance matters, not for welfare or medical issues. The various legal options (enduring power of attorney, involvement of the Court of Protection) for delegating decision-making regarding financial and property matters are discussed in Chapter 17 in the context of prevention of financial abuse.

■ Declarations

In other areas the High Court (Family Division) jurisdiction to make declarations has developed to fill the gap. A declaration states the legal position and will state that a proposed course of action is not unlawful. So, for example, if a surgeon carries out an operation, which has been 'approved' by a declaration, he will not be liable for assault. Someone closely connected, such as a carer or relative, or the local authority may seek a declaration. The Official Solicitor will normally represent the 'patient'. The case of *Re F (Adult: Court's Jurisdiction)* [2000] 3 WLR 1740, where a local authority sought a declaration to protect a young woman from possible abuse, is discussed in Chapter 17.

Declarations made by the court are guided by exercise of the best interests principle. The use of declarations is well established in medical cases. For example, in *Airedale NHS Trust* v. *Bland* [1993] 1 All ER 821, a declaration was made that it would be lawful to discontinue life-sustaining treatment for a person in a persistent vegetative state. The law as stated in *Bland* is compatible with ECHR, Art. 2, according to *NHS Trust A* v. *H* [2001] 2 FLR 501.

The leading decision of *Re F* v. *West Berkshire Health Authority* [1989] 2 All ER 545 establishes the principle that the doctrine of necessity may be relied upon and decisions taken based upon best interests. The best interests principle should strive for balance between autonomy and protection. In another area, where declarations have been utilised to authorise sterilisation of women with learning disabilities, it has been argued from a feminist perspective that the balance has tipped in favour of paternalism.[1] A survey of the case law is illustrative.

In *Re P (A Minor) (Wardship: Sterilisation)* [1989] 1 FLR 182, the court was willing to accept the unanimous decision of doctors regarding sterilisation as a form of contraceptive, without challenge. Further, a eugenic argument was accepted by the court: a 50 per cent chance that she would conceive a mentally handicapped child was seen as reason to justify sterilisation. The case also provides an example of an apparent lack of awareness amongst the judiciary about sexuality and learning disability, with the statement 'girls like T are readily seduced'. Further, in *Re B (A Minor) (Wardship: Sterilisation)* [1987] 2 All ER 206, which concerned a young woman showing signs of sexual awareness, the judge suggested she might 'become a danger to others'. The court considered the argument that sterilisation removed her right to reproduce, but stated that it was a right that existed only when reproduction would be the result of informed choice. The woman was unable to comprehend the link between intercourse and pregnancy; however, the court did not consider the quality of sex education she had received. Finally, in *Re W (An Adult: Mental Patient) (Sterilisation)* [1993] 1 FLR 381, the judge commented that a 20-year-old woman could not be taught to protect herself from unwanted advances and there was a risk that someone might take advantage of her. However, it was not noted that the elimination of the risk of pregnancy would do nothing to eliminate the risk of sexual abuse. Arguably, it might even increase the risk if it resulted in less vigilance by carers. The emphasis throughout these cases has been on eliminating the risk of pregnancy, yet there are no reported cases of male sterilisation. This was raised in the case of *Re A (Mental Patient: Sterilisation)* [2000] 1 FLR 549. A was a 28-year-old man with Down's syndrome, borderline severe/significant mental impairment. His mother sought a declaration that sterilisation was in his best interests, being concerned that, when she was no longer able to care for him, he might impregnate a woman and be unable to deal with the consequences. The judge adopted a broad definition of best interests, encompassing medical, emotional and other welfare issues. The judge took the view that, for any mentally incapacitated man, neither the birth of a child nor disapproval of his conduct was likely to cause him problems, and on that basis the application was refused. The court did state, however, that if evidence could be presented that after sterilisation A would enjoy greater freedom and the opportunity to develop sexual experience, it might reconsider the case.

Overall, the cases show deference to medical opinion, perpetuate sex discrimination and certain myths about sexuality, and appear to attempt to solve social problems by surgery.

Another line of cases has addressed the issue of contact with an adult who lacks capacity. *Re D-R (Adult: Contact)* [1999] 1 FLR 1161 considered a claim by a father for access to his adult daughter who had a learning disability. The Court of Appeal confirmed that, for an adult with a disability, the question the court must address was whether it was in her best interest to have contact, relying on *F* v. *West Berkshire Health Authority* [1989] 2 All ER 545. To determine best interests where there was family conflict, it was necessary to look at all the circumstances, which included the history and former relationship of the father and daughter, the current situation and the prospects for the future. There was no presumption of a right to contact. As the judge in the High Court had identified the relevant factors and had not erred on principle, the Court of Appeal saw no reason to intervene in the decision.

Capacity to marriage has been considered in two recent decisions. In *Sheffield City Council* v. *E* [2004] EWHC 2808 (Fam) an application was made by a local authority based on their concerns that a young woman of 21 with a learning disability (and described as having a mental age of 13) lacked the capacity to marry. The court agreed that she did not have the capacity to understand the nature of marriage and made a declaration to that effect. The second case, *M* v. *B* [2005] EWHC 1681 (Fam), concerned an arranged marriage proposed by the parents of a 23-year-old woman of Pakistani origin who had a severe learning disability. Her parents argued that they intended to take her to Pakistan for a family holiday. Again, the application was made by the local authority and the court made a declaration stating that she could not give a valid consent to marriage, and also declared that any marriage ceremony would be void and that it would not be in her best interests to leave the jurisdiction. The court noted that the injunction protected her right to private life, which would be jeopardised by her parents' attempts to arrange her marriage.

The cases have illustrated that declaratory relief has extended significantly beyond medical cases, into the area of social and welfare decision-making. Their use in an adult protection context on application by local authorities is discussed further in Chapter 17 and this expansion is evident in the comments of Mumby LJ in *Re S (Adult Patient) (Inherent Jurisdiction: Family Life)* [2002] EWHC 227 (Fam) at, para. 50: 'The court has jurisdiction to grant whatever relief in declaratory form is necessary to safeguard and promote the incapable adult's welfare and interest.'

■ Advance healthcare decisions

In limited circumstances a 'living will', also known as an 'advance directive', may be recognised as legally valid in relation to treatment decisions. A living will allows a person with capacity to make decisions about treatment should he lose capacity to do so at the time treatment is contemplated. The difficulty with a living will is that it must anticipate the exact treatment that may be needed or that to which the individual would not consent, so, for example, a refusal of treatment when contemplating a terminal illness may not be binding in circumstances following a road accident. There is no specific legal format for a living will but a variety of organisations, such as the Terrence Higgins Trust, have produced forms. The case of *Re T (Adult: Refusal of Treatment)* [1992] 4 All ER 649 ruled that an advance refusal of treatment will be legally binding if it is 'clearly established and applicable to the circumstances'. The case set out three criteria that must be fulfilled:

1. the maker must have had mental capacity at the time of expressing the refusal;

2. the maker must not have been subject to any undue influence;

3. the maker must have contemplated the circumstances that have arisen.

A living will cannot override statutory authority, such as detention under the MHA 1983 and its provisions for compulsory treatment.

The new provisions for 'advance directives', a statutory form of living will under the Mental Capacity Act 2005 are discussed below.

■ Litigation friend

A 'litigation friend' can assist a person who lacks mental capacity to instigate legal proceedings.[2] A person may act as a litigation friend as long as he can fairly and competently conduct the proceedings, has no adverse interest, undertakes to pay any costs which may be ordered, and can file a certificate of suitability covering these matters. (The term used before the civil procedure reforms was 'next friend'.)

The mental capacity of an individual will also be relevant where the court is considering making an order with which that person should comply. In *MJ Harris* v. *HW Harris (Acting by his Guardian ad Litem, the Official Solicitor)* (1999) LTL 22/4/99 (unreported), issues of domestic violence, enforceability of injunctions and mental health were aired. Mr and Mrs Harris, aged 82 and 62 respectively, were married in 1969. A decree nisi had been awarded in June 1998 and they both remained living in the former matrimonial home. Mrs Harris was granted a non-molestation order against her former husband in November 1998. Mr Harris appealed against the order. Mr Harris's GP advised his solicitors that Mr Harris was suffering from the early stages of dementia. The Official Solicitor agreed to act for Mr Harris and obtained a psychiatric report on Mr Harris. This indicated that Mr Harris appeared capable of understanding the order but, although it was possible he would comply with it, his recent memory was very poor and it was likely he would forget the details quite soon. The judge considered the case of *Wookey* v. *Wookey* [1991] 3 All ER 365, which involved a 72-year-old wife who sought an injunction against her 70-year-old husband. In *Wookey* it was decided that the fact of a disability was not in itself a bar to granting an injunction. In the case of mental incapacity, however, the question was whether the person understood the proceedings and the nature and requirements of the injunction. An injunction ought not to be granted where the person was incapable of understanding what he was doing or that it was wrong, because he would be incapable of complying with it, it would have no deterrent effect and would effectively be unenforceable as he would have a clear defence to an application for committal for contempt of court.

In the present case the judge felt that as Mr Harris was, according to the psychiatrist's report, capable of understanding the order, he did not come within the '*Wookey*' test. Mr Harris appealed. The case presented a borderline situation: Mr Harris knew that he must not molest Mrs Harris though he did not appreciate the consequences of so doing. In a case such as this, where some uncertainty regarding cognitive ability remained, it was for the legal advisers to keep an eye on the situation. The order here could not be continued given the changed circumstances.

It is consistent with presumptions concerning mental capacity that if an individual does not have the capacity to understand an order it should not be imposed upon him. It does, however, leave an individual such as Mrs Harris deprived of the protection that an injunction can provide. If a person in a position such as Mr Harris were then to molest, in the absence of a non-molestation order, the only recourse would be to seek protection from the police and criminal law.

Reform

The Law Commission examined this area in its report, 'Mental Incapacity' (1995), which was produced at the culmination of a five-year period of consultation. The opening statement sums up the need for reform: 'The law as it now stands is unsystematic and full of glaring gaps. It does not rest on clear or modern foundations of principle. It has failed to keep up with developments in our understanding of the needs of those with mental disability'.

Initially, it appeared that the report was unlikely to be adopted. A subsequent document in 1999, 'Making Decisions: the Government's proposals for making decisions on behalf of mentally incapacitated adults', contains a commitment to legislate when 'parliamentary time allows' but also made clear that the recommendations for public powers of protection would not be proceeded with. Government attention then focused on proposals to reform mental health law until publication of a Draft Mental Incapacity Bill in June 2003. In the interim, pressure for reform was maintained and a number of useful guides to the existing law on capacity and decision making were published by the Department of Health.[3] The draft Bill was reviewed and reported on by a Joint Scrutiny Committee and the Department of Constitutional Affairs published the Government's response in February 2004. A draft Code of Practice to accompany the Act was published in September 2004 and has been open for consultation. A number of amendments were to made to the Bill which ultimately became the Act, including a significant change to the name of the Act from 'Mental Incapacity' to 'Mental Capacity'. The Act applies to England and Wales. Similar legislation has been enacted in Scotland.[4]

The Mental Capacity Act 2005

The Mental Capacity Act 1995 received Royal Assent on 7 April 2005. Key elements of this long-awaited Act may be traced back to the recommendations of the Law Commission consultation exercise which began in 1989. It is important to note that the Act is not expected to be implemented before 2007. The existing law relating to mental capacity and decision-making pertains until the Act is brought into force. It is likely that we will continue to see applications for High Court declarations determining disputes as to the best interests of individuals who do not have capacity to make particular decisions.

The preamble to the Act describes it as,

> An Act to make new provision relating to persons who lack capacity; to establish a superior court of record called the Court of Protection in place of the office of the Supreme Court called by that name; to make provision in connection with the Convention on the International Protection of Adults signed at the Hague on 13th January 2000; and for connected purposes.

The legislation is divided into three main parts with accompanying schedules. Part I, entitled 'Persons who lack capacity', contains a set of principles to apply throughout the Act, provisions relating to the Lasting Power of Attorney (**LPA**), general powers of the court and the appointment of deputies; advance decisions to refuse treatment; research; and the independent mental capacity advocate scheme. Part II provides for the new Court of Protection and Public Guardian, with miscellaneous and general provisions contained in Part III. The Act applies to anyone over the age of 16. It will be relevant to people who have difficulty making decisions at any point in their lives, including adults with severe and profound learning disabilities, some people with autism, people with dementia, some people with mental health problems and some survivors of severe head injury. The Act applies to the full range of acts and decisions an individual might face, as described in the Code of Practice,

> The Act covers decisions made, or actions taken, on behalf of people lacking capacity, whether they relate to day-to-day matters or represent major life-changing events. Actions or decisions may range from choosing what to wear or doing the weekly shopping to carrying out a routine dental check-up, to deciding whether the person should move into residential care or deciding to undertake a major surgical operation. (para 2.3)

■ Principles

The principles set out in s. 1 of the Act are an important feature that restate some of the existing commonlaw principles with further elaboration. The principles are:

- A person must be assumed to have capacity unless it is established that he does not (s. 1(2)).

- A person is not to be treated as unable to make a decision unless all practicable steps to help him to do so have been taken without success (s. 1(3)).

- A person is not to be treated as unable to make a decision merely because he makes an unwise decision (s. 1(4)).

- An act done, or decision made for or on behalf of a person who lacks capacity must be in his best interests (s. 1(5)).

- Before the act is done, or the decision made, regard must be had to whether the purpose for which it is needed can be as effectively achieved in a way that is less restrictive of the person's rights and freedom of action (s. 1(6)).

As these principles are set out with the objective of assisting the range of people affected by the Act, restatement of the common law presumption in favour of capacity, as the first principle, is welcome. The code notes that 'this principle underpins a key message of the Act – that everyone has the right to make choices and decisions for themselves (the right to autonomy)' (para. 2.9). The burden to displace that presumption falls on the person who questions the individual's capacity. The Act also endorses good practice by requiring steps to be taken to encourage first-hand decision-making. The Explanatory Notes to the Bill suggested that such steps might include providing information relevant to the decision in a simple format, making sure the person is in an environment in which he is comfortable and there is minimal distraction, or involving an expert or person the individual trusts in helping the person express his views. The Act takes a functional approach to decision-making and does not exclude what might appear to be irrational or eccentric decisions provided the person making the decision has capacity. This 'reflects the fact that each one of us is an individual with our own values, beliefs, preferences and attitude to risk, which may not be the same as other people' (para 2.11). Decisions and actions must be in the person's best interests (discussed further below). Finally, the Act introduces a 'minimum intervention' principle, supporting practices which interfere least with the individual's freedom of action. This principle follows the spirit of Art. 8 of the European Convention of Human Rights (the right to respect for private and family life).

■ What is capacity?

The test of capacity is contained in s. 2:

s. 2

> (1) . . . A person lacks capacity if at the material time he is unable to make a decision for himself in relation to the matter because of an impairment of, or a disturbance in the functioning of, the mind or brain.
> (2) It does not matter whether the impairment or disturbance is permanent or temporary.
>
> (MCA 2005)

This is a diagnostic test which, the notes to the Bill explain, 'could cover a range of problems, such as psychiatric illness, learning disability, dementia, brain damage or even a toxic confusional state, as long as it has the necessary effect on the functioning of the mind or brain, which causes the person to be unable to make the decision'. There are two stages, establishing an impairment or disturbance, and a resulting inability to make the decision. Consideration of capacity is limited to the particular decision under consideration at the particular time. It is not a general assessment of capacity. A lack of capacity cannot be established merely by reference to a person's age or appearance, or a condition of his, or an aspect of his behaviour, which might lead others to make unjustified assumptions about his capacity. This rules out stereotyping. The question whether a person lacks capacity must be decided on the civil standard of balance of probabilities, i.e. more likely than not. Assessment of capacity will often be carried out on a day-to-day basis by people they are in close contact with such as carers and relatives. Professional involvement may be required for an assessment of capacity in some circumstances. The code advises that this is likely to depend on a number of factors, including;

■ The gravity of the decision or its consequences.

■ Where the person concerned disputes a finding of incapacity.

■ Where there is disagreement between family members, carers and/or professionals as to the person's capacity.

■ Where the person is expressing different views to different people.

■ Where the person's capacity to make a particular decision may be subject to challenge at the time or in the future (e.g. capacity to make a will).

■ The person is repeatedly making decisions that put him at risk or resulted in preventable suffering or damage. (para 3.37)

Being 'unable to make a decision', is addressed in s. 3.

s. 3

> (1) . . . a person is unable to make a decision for himself if he is unable.
>
> (a) to understand the information relevant to the decision,
>
> (b) to retain the information,
>
> (c) to use or weigh that information as part of the process of making the decision,
>
> or
>
> (c) to communicate the decision . . .
>
> (MCA 2005)

In most cases the first three criteria will apply. Appropriate assistance from speech and language therapists should mean that few people are unable to communicate a decision. Being unable to communicate a decision may be particularly relevant for people with the very rare condition of 'locked-in syndrome'. 'Relevant Information' includes the reasonably forseeable consequences of deciding or failing to make decision.

▪ Best interests

All circumstances must be considered in deciding whether something is in a person's 'best interests'. The Act gives further guidance on particular factors to be taken into account in s. 4, set out below. None of the factors carries any more weight or priority than another; the list is not exhaustive but should enable an objective assessment of what is in the person's best interest to be made. The person making the decision must first consider whether the person is likely to have capacity at some time and, if so, when. This suggests that non-urgent decisions might be postponed if there is a likelihood of the person regaining capacity. There is also a requirement to permit and encourage the person to participate as fully as possible in any act or decision.

The factors which must be considered include:

- the ascertainable past and present wishes and feelings of the person concerned (including any relevant written statements);
- the beliefs and values that would be likely to influence his decision if he had capacity (including religious beliefs and cultural values);
- other factors the individual would be likely to consider if able to do so (this might include a sense of family obligation);
- the views of others it is considered appropriate to consult including anyone so named, carers and others interested in the person's welfare and any donees of an LPA or deputies appointed under the Act.

In practice, whilst this list should help to structure decision-making, the concept of 'best interests' is likely to remain extremely difficult to apply in many cases.

■ Acts in connection with care or treatment

Section 5 provides some legal security for those people, including carers, making day-to-day decisions for a person who lacks capacity. In effect, it deems the person lacking capacity to have given consent to the person acting for him in providing care or treatment, in certain circumstances. It was previously referred to as a 'general authority to act reasonably' but the scrutiny process highlighted this as a negative and rather paternalistic term. Under the Act, where a person ('D') does an act in connection with the care or treatment of another person ('P'), he will not incur liability so long as he reasonably believes that P lacks capacity in relation to the matter, and that it will be in P's best interests for the act to be done. It is intended to be a positive permission-giving provision. The Code of Practice provides examples of acts in connection with personal care, including: assistance with washing and dressing; help with eating and drinking; shopping; help with mobility; acts performed in relation to domiciliary services required for the person's care (such as home care or meals on wheels) or in relation to other community care services.

There are limitations to the protection offered by s. 5. It will not authorise restraint unless it is necessary to prevent harm to P and is a proportionate response to the likelihood of P's suffering harm and the seriousness of that harm. The explanatory notes give examples of restraint including, pulling someone away from the road, putting on a seatbelt or administering sedatives before treatment. Further, s. 5 does not provide a defence to negligence, whether in carrying out a particular act or by failing to act where necessary. The general provision in s. 5 is overridden by decisions of a person acting as a deputy or donee of an LPA acting within their powers.

■ Lasting power of attorney

A new order, the *lasting power of attorney* (**LPA**) is created under ss. 9–14 (it had been referred to in the consultation process as a 'continuing power of attorney'). Where an individual has capacity but anticipates possible loss of capacity in the future he may execute a lasting power of attorney, conferring authority to the attorney to make decisions on his behalf. This replaces and extends beyond the currently used enduring power of attorney, and the Enduring Powers of Attorney Act (EPAA) 1985 will be repealed. Any validly registered power under the EPAA will continue to have effect, but will not extend beyond property issues

The most significant difference between the old EPA and new LPA is the extension to 'personal welfare' decisions. The attorney (or attorneys) may be authorised to make decisions about personal welfare, including healthcare, property and affairs where the donor no longer has capacity to make those decisions. As an example of a type of decision a welfare donee could be authorised to take, the code mentions arranging for the donor to access dental or optical treatment and applying for and having access to confidential documents relating to the donor such as personal files held by social services (para 6.7). The LPA can authorise the attorney to refuse life-sustaining treatment on behalf of the donor, one of the more controversial provisions of the Bill, discussed further below in relation to advance directions. An LPA may provide more flexibility in terms of refusal of treatment as the exact treatment and circumstances do not have to be anticipated and stipulated as they do in an advance decision.

This new power reflects the scope of decision-making seen in High Court declarations case law. An LPA can be constructed to deal only with health care or property matters or a combination and it can place restrictions on the exercise of powers within those areas. It thus allows a great deal of flexibility for individuals who wish to plan ahead.

Any person over the age of 18 may execute an LPA as long as they have capacity to do so. The LPA can also be revoked by the donor if he has capacity. To be effective the LPA must be registered with the Public Guardian and comply with certain procedural requirements in Sch. 1. It may be registered as soon as it is executed, contrasting with the current position on EPAs where registration takes place once the person loses capacity, and must be registered to take effect. As an additional safeguard, a 'prescribed person' (most likely to be a doctor) must certify that the donor has not been under any undue pressure which would persuade him to sign, and that he understands the effect of the LPA. If any disputes arise as to the exercise of an LPA the Court of Protection has jurisdiction to hear the matter and give directions. The donor does not lose his power to act as long as he has capacity even if the power has been registered.

■ Advance decisions

The common law has given some recognition to advance refusals of medical treatment, also known as living wills, advance statements and directives *(Re T (Adult: Refusal of Treatment)* [1992] 4 All ER 649). The MCA 2005 places this on a statutory footing with the introduction of advance decisions. It is also possible, as noted above, for health care decisions, including advance refusal of treatment, to be delegated under a lasting power of attorney. The greatest autonomy in advance decision-making will be secured by an individual utilising both procedures.

An advance decision to refuse treatment can be made by a person over the age of 18 with capacity. It must clearly specify the circumstances and the treatment which the person wishes to refuse. The treatment may be described in non-medical/lay terms, though this will be subject to interpretation by members of the medical profession. The more precise the terminology used as to both the treatment and the circumstances, the more likely the advance decision is to be followed. As treatments develop with advances in medicine, it is also important to keep the advance decision under review whilst the maker has capacity. The advance decision will also lose validity if the person acts inconsistently with its terms. As the advance decision should be an informed decision by the individual it must be demonstrated that the maker understood relevant information and the consequences of the decision. To this end, the Code of Practice recommends ongoing discussions with a healthcare professional. The code also sets out information which it considers useful to include: details of the person making the advance decision (date of birth, home address and any distinguishing features) details of general practitioner and whether they have a copy of the advance decision; a statement that the decision is intended to have effect if the maker lacks capacity to make treatment decisions; a clear statement of the decision, specifying the treatment to be refused and the circumstances in which the decision will apply or which will trigger a particular course of action; date of document; signature of maker and/or witness (para 8.16).

Unless the advance decision relates to life-sustaining treatment, it is not required to be in writing; however, evidentially this is likely to be the preferred option.

■ Court of Protection

A new Court of Protection is established under the Act will replace and take over the functions of the existing Court of Protection. Sections 15–23 deal with the powers of the court, and the appointment and role of deputies. Appeals from the court lie to the Court of Appeal. The court will have jurisdiction to determine disputes relating to capacity, by making declarations and single orders, including whether an individual has or lacks capacity to make a particular decision. The court may make declarations about particular issues, such as contact or residence and declarations as to the lawfulness of any act done or contemplated, including omissions. The court may make a will on behalf of the incapacitated person. The court also has power to revoke an LPA if the attorney has contravened his authority or acted other than in the best interests of the donor. The court can ask for a report from the Public Guardian, a Court of Protection Visitor and a local authority. The President of the Court of Protection is expected to issue a Practice Direction specifying cases which should be referred to the court. The Code of Practice describes the court's role as being available to 'settle serious and complex decisions'. It notes that 'it may often be more appropriate to explore alternative solutions to solving problems' and refers to advocacy, mediation and use of complaints processes. The scope of the court's jurisdiction and its accessibility as a regional forum would, however, suggest that more cases involving individuals with mental incapacity will be adjudicated on in a judicial setting. This has implications for staff who may be called upon to give evidence or to make applications and the need for training in court skills (see Chapter 4). The exercise of the court's powers is subject to the principles in s. 1 and best interests.

The new court will operate from a central office and registry, but significantly it 'may sit at any place in England and Wales on any day and at any time' (s. 45(3). In practical terms this means that there will be regional courts deciding matters under the MCA 2005 in a more accessible way. Procedure rules for the court will be developed and there is a power to make practice directions.

Applications to the court may be made as of right by:

■ the person who lacks capacity or is alleged to lack capacity
■ the attorney appointed under a lasting power of attorney
■ a deputy
■ a person named in an order of the court, if the application related to the order (e.g. a person who has been named in a contact arrangement with the incapacitated person).

Any other person requires leave of the court (s. 50(3)). In deciding whether to grant leave the court must consider: the applicant's connection to the person lacking capacity; reasons for the application; the benefit to the person lacking capacity of the proposed order and whether that benefit can be achieved in any other way (para. 7.7).

Deputies

The court may also appoint a 'deputy' to make welfare and financial decisions for a person who either has not made an LPA and subsequently loses capacity, or could not have made an LPA because of a long-term disability. This system will replace and extend the use of receivership currently operating from the Court of Protection. The Court will decide whether a proposed deputy (who must consent to the appointment), is suitable in terms of being reliable, trustworthy and competent. Deputies will be supervised by the Public Guardian. Appointment of deputies is subject to the principle that a decision by the court is to be preferred to the appointment of a deputy to make a decision, and the powers conferred on a deputy should be as limited in scope and duration as is reasonably practicable in the circumstances. A deputy does not have power to stop a named person from having contact with the incapacitated person. A deputy is treated as the agent of the adult lacking capacity and is entitled to reasonable expenses. A deputy cannot make a decision on behalf of the incapacitated person if 'he knows or has reasonable grounds for believing that he has capacity in relation to the matter' (s. 20(1)).

■ The independent mental capacity advocate service

The Act requires the Secretary of State for Health to make arrangements to make independent advocates available to represent and support people who lack mental capacity. Following scrutiny, the term *independent mental capacity advocate* (**IMCA**) was introduced in place of the term in the original Bill of independent consultee. An independent advocate will be involved: where serious medical treatment is proposed and there is no-one else who could be consulted about the patient's best interests; and where there is a proposal to accommodate a person in a hospital or care home. The advocate's role is to represent and support the individual, ascertain his wishes and feelings, obtain relevant information, which may include obtaining a further medical opinion, and consider available courses of action.

The independent advocate will be entitled to interview in private the person whom he has been instructed to represent, and may examine and take copies of records relevant to the independent mental capacity advocate's investigation (including records relating to health, social services and residential accommodation).

The consultation exercise on the role of the IMCA considered possible extension of the role beyond the criteria stipulated. One possible extension where an advocate should be appointed, regardless of the existence of family or friends, is where there is an adult protection investigation. Questions remain as to how the service will be provided in a way that ensures independence, what training and qualifications the advocates are required to possess and whether there are to be any links with the proposed Independent Mental Health Advocate set out in the Mental Health Bill.

Much of the detail of the independent advocate's role will be set out in regulations.

■ Criminal offence

Finally, the Bill introduces a new criminal offence in s. 44. A person is guilty of an offence if he has the care of a person who lacks capacity or is reasonably believed to lack capacity, or is the donee of a LPA or a deputy, and he 'ill-treats or wilfully neglects the person'. The offence is classified as an 'either way offence' (it may be prosecuted in the magistrates' court or Crown Court), and carries a maximum sentence of five years' imprisonment. The Code of Practice includes a separate chapter entitled 'Protection and Supervision', which addresses abuse and the responsibilities of professionals, agencies responsible for protecting adults, the role of the Office of Public Guardian and the new offence (see further discussion in Chapter 17).

■ Code of Practice

The Act is supported by a Code of Practice, the first draft of which was published in September 2004. A duty is imposed on various categories of people to have regard to the code when acting in relation to a person lacking capacity. This includes professionals, such as doctors and social workers; those receiving payment in connection with care of the person, such as a care assistant; the donee of a LPA and a deputy. It notes that, 'Failure to comply with the Code can be used in evidence in civil or criminal proceedings if relevant' (para. 1.10). The Code is not just intended as a resource for professionals:

> Other people, who are not placed under this legal duty will still be expected to follow the guidance in the Code. The Act applies to *everyone* who looks after, or cares for, someone who lacks capacity, including informal carers and family members, and the Code will help them to understand the Code and apply it. (para 1.11)

Chapter summary

- The current law on mental capacity is largely based on the common law, has developed piecemeal and contains a number of gaps or loopholes. A new statutory framework is provided by the Mental Capacity Act 2005. This legislation is expected to be brought into force in 2007 (at the earliest) and until then the common law applies.
- There is a legal presumption in favour of capacity. This means that adults are assumed to be autonomous and able to make their own decisions unless it can be

shown (on balance of probabilities) that they lack the capacity to make the decision in question.

■ Having capacity means that the individual is capable of understanding what is proposed and its implications, and is able to exercise choice. It varies depending on the nature of the decision to be made, e.g. to marry or to manage complex financial matters.

■ If an individual lacks capacity to make a particular decision, it is only possible formally to delegate that decision to another where it relates to financial and property matters or legal actions, via use of an enduring power of attorney, the Court of Protection or a litigation friend. In some circumstances advance health-care decisions have been given affect through a 'living will'.

■ In the absence of a framework for delegating health and welfare decisions, the High Court has developed and extended the use of 'declaratory relief'. Based on the common law doctrine of necessity, a declaration can state that a particular course of action is in the best interest of the individual and not unlawful. Such declarations have been made in respect of healthcare matters, e.g. sterilisations, contact and decisions about where an individual should live.

■ The new law, The Mental Capacity Act 2005 is the product of a lengthy consultation period and is based on recommendations of the Law Commission. It applies to anyone over the age of 16 in England and Wales. It is supported by a Code of Practice.

■ The Act starts with key principles: a presumption in favour of capacity; all practicable steps should be taken to help individuals to make their own decisions; an unwise decision does evidence lack of capacity; acts and decisions for a person who lacks capacity must be in his best interests; the least restrictive alternative is preferred.

■ A person lacks capacity if he is unable to make a decision for himself in relation to the matter because of an impairment of or a disturbance in the functioning of the mind or brain, whether permanent or temporary.

■ The Act provides for substitute decision making in various ways. Section 5 provides freedom from liability for acts in connection with care or treatment for a person lacking capacity and in his best interests, such as day-to-day care matters. A lasting power of attorney (LPA) is introduced to replace and extend the enduring power of attorney. An LPA may be prepared by a person with capacity, to take effect in the future should he lose capacity, and may relate to financial matters but also to health and welfare decisions. In addition, for medical matters, advance decisions to refuse treatment can be made by a person with capacity.

■ A new Court of Protection will have jurisdiction over all aspects of the Act. It can rule on whether a person has capacity for a particular decision, make one-off decisions and declarations, rule on the validity of LPAs and appoint deputies to make decisions for a person who does not have a LPA.

■ An independent mental capacity advocate will be appointed for an individual faced with a serious decision about medical treatment or where to live and there is no-one else to consult about the proposal, e.g. an attorney.

Exercise

Mrs June Jones is 54 years old. Her GP has recently diagnosed the onset of Alzheimer's disease. At times she is completely rational and lucid but there are spells when she does not recognise close relatives and believes she is in her 20s. At other times she appears unable to speak at all. Her husband, John, was planning to commence divorce proceedings prior to the onset of June's illness; he has been having a relationship with a colleague at work, Jemima, aged 35, for several years. He goes out most evenings to see Jemima. On two occasions he has returned to find that June has fallen and injured herself but cannot describe the circumstances. He feels that June should move into a residential home but he has been unable to gain a response to this suggestion from June. June has personal savings of £20,000, which John would like to manage on her behalf. He is concerned that she recently spent £2,000 on a motorbike (unused) and £1,000 fitting a jacuzzi to the bath. June's sight is deteriorating rapidly and she is waiting for a cataract operation. John cancelled her appointment for the operation, as June became agitated whenever it was mentioned. He considers it a waste of time anyway. Their only child, Julie, aged 32, lives 100 miles away and has a young family. She visited recently and was shocked at her mother's deterioration. She contacted the eye hospital and was furious to hear about the cancelled operation and requested a further appointment. She would like her mother to move in with her but is concerned that her husband will not agree and that it would mean moving her mother away from her friends. Julie has had little time for her father since she discovered his relationship with Jemima. Is any formal intervention appropriate in this scenario? How would your answer differ once the Mental Capacity Act 2005 is enacted?

Websites

To access the Mental Capacity Act 2005, the Explanatory Notes accompanying the original Bill and the draft Code of Practice, follow links from the Department of Constitutional Affairs website:

    www.dca.gov.uk

Further useful commentary is available from the Making Decisions Alliance website:

    www.makingdecisions.org.uk

The Official Solicitor has responsibility for representing minors or adults under legal disability, in county court or High Court proceedings in England and Wales, and in the Court of Protection:

    www.officialsolicitor.gov.uk

The Public Guardianship Office is the administrative arm of the Court of Protection:

    www.guardianship.gov.uk

Further reading

Specific texts covering the new legislation:

Ashton, G. (ed.) (2005) *Mental Capacity: The New Law.* Bristol: Jordan Publishing. (A detailed guide to the new law including a copy of the Act.)

Greany, N., Morris, F. and Taylor, B. (2006) *The Mental Capacity Act 2005: A Guide to the New Law.* London: The Law Society.

Bartlett, P. (2006) *Blackstone's Guide to the Mental Capacity Act 2005.* Oxford: Oxford University Press.

Kendrick, K. and Robinson, S. (2002) *Their Rights: Advance Directives and Living Wills Explored.* London: Age Concern. (A useful advice guide.)

Bartlett, P. and McHale, J. (2002) 'Mental Incapacity and Mental Health: The Development of Legal Reform and the Need for Joined-up Thinking' 25(4) *Journal of Social Welfare and Family Law* p. 313. (This introductory article is the first in an edition of JSWFL devoted to discussion of mental health and mental capacity. Written before introduction of the Mental Capacity Act 2005 and the latest Mental Health Bill, all the articles are nevertheless useful for their discussion of the principles involved.)

Bartlett, P. (2002) 'Adults, mental illness and incapacity: convergence and overlap in legal regulation' 25(4) *Journal of Social Welfare and family Law* p. 341. (A further article in the special edition mentioned above. This paper discusses procedural and substantive strengths and weaknesses of the proposed legislation, and the relationship between mental health, mental capacity and the inherent jurisdiction.)

Lord Chancellor's Department (1999) *Making Decisions.* London: Lord Chancellor's Department. (Outlines the Government position prior to publication of the draft Bill.)

Notes

[1] See K. Keywood (1995) 'Sterilising the women with learning difficulties' in S. Bridgeman and S. Mills (eds) *Law and Body Politics: Regulating the Female Body.* Aldershot: Dartmouth Publishing Co.

[2] Civil Procedure Rules 1998 (SI 1998/3132), r. 21.

[3] The series includes: 'A Guide for Social Care Professionals'; 'Planning ahead: a guide for people who wish to prepare for possible future incapacity' and 'A Guide for people with learning difficulties'.

[4] Adults with Incapacity (Scotland) Act 2000.

17 Adult protection

Learning objectives

To develop an understanding of the following:

- Adult abuse as a recently recognised social problem.
- Definitions, types and the extent of adult abuse.
- The policy framework provided by 'No Secrets'.
- Social services' responsibility to investigate and take action.
- The use of a range of existing laws to respond to cases.
- Opportunities to prevent abuse.
- Opportunities for the victim to take action.
- Opportunities for formal intervention.

Introduction

Recognition of the existence of adult abuse as a complex social problem, and the need to establish adult protection procedures in response, is of relatively recent origin. Many local authorities through their protection policies now focus on adult protection as a generic category, which encompasses abuse toward specific groups such as older people and people with learning disabilities. Greater consistency between policies around the country should be achieved under Department of Health guidance, 'No Secrets',[1] which requires local authorities to have policies in place to protect vulnerable adults from abuse. Initially, from the late 1980s and early 1990s responses to abuse were more likely to focus on distinct groups of vulnerable adults, with perhaps the most focus on elder abuse. An early reference had

523

described this phenomenon as 'granny bashing',[2] and was followed by Eastman's graphic account of cases of abuse in 1983.[3] A variety of terms have since been used, including elder mistreatment, old age abuse, inadequate care and miscare. At the same time, there was growing recognition of the vulnerability to abuse of adults with learning disabilities particularly (it seems) of a sexual nature.[4] A recent publication by the Association of Directors of Social Services expresses concern that the term 'vulnerable adults' is contentious, adding: 'One reason is that the label can be misunderstood, because it seems to locate the cause of abuse with the victim, rather than placing responsibility with the actions or omissions of others.'[5] In place of adult protection the ADSS prefers the term, 'safeguarding adults', and explains: 'This phrase means all work which enables an adult "who is or may be eligible for community care services" to retain independence, well-being and choice and to access their human right to live a life that is free from abuse and neglect.' The document sets out standards for good practice and outcomes in adult protection work.

There are issues of similarity to be drawn with the position of adults with learning disabilities and mental health problems and also with the experience of domestic violence and it is certainly helpful to place any discussion of specific victims of abuse against a context of vulnerable adults. It has also been argued that it is appropriate to address a continuum of 'family violence', ranging from child abuse to elder abuse, as the best way of understanding abuse.[6]

It is possible to detect a growing commitment from the Government to tackle adult abuse, and issues about vulnerable adults and ageing have become positioned in the policy against social exclusion. This commitment has not been translated into legislation prohibiting abuse and providing a structure for intervention but there is an emerging policy framework and the Mental Capacity Act 2005 is likely to have a significant effect. As with other areas of law concerning social work, the Human Rights Act 1998 is likely to have an impact.

Discussion of rights has been a central tenet of the debate over the relationship between autonomy and protection where adults are subject to abuse. Intervention, in reality, may be paternalistic (framed in terms of best interests and welfare) and may not always reflect the expressed preferences and rights of an individual. Under the Human Rights Act 1998 there will need to be very precise reasons, taken in a clear decision-making framework, to depart from the principle of autonomous decision-making by all adults.[7] It is clear that the focus under the Act will be on greater access to the courts for effective protection and enforcement of rights as 'the Convention is intended to guarantee not rights that are theoretical or illusory but rights that are practical and effective' (*Artico v. Italy* (1980) 3 EHRR 1, para. 33). Abuse is perhaps the most obvious violation of an individual's private and family life; and in *X and Y v. Netherlands* (1985) 8 EHRR 235, the court upheld that principle in finding that the sexual abuse of a young woman who was learning disabled violated ECHR, Art. 8.[8]

Adult abuse cases present complex practice and ethical issues for professionals. Central to these is the debate about 'protection versus autonomy'. This is perhaps the crucial defining difference between work with young children and work with adults. For the most part, adults are assumed to be autonomous, entitled to make their own decisions, however eccentric and risky they may appear. In an area where social care professionals are more focused on therapeutic interventions, use of the law may be considered a last resort.[9] Where it is appropriate to have recourse to legal intervention that action must be informed by values with appropriate emphasis on empowerment and self-determination and seek to achieve an outcome that improves the person's situation. It is also clear that, if legal action is contemplated, appropriate legal advice should be sought especially regarding the extent of evidence required. The need to distinguish this area of practice from child care has been noted. Nevertheless, there may be useful lessons to be learnt from child protection.[10] This is particularly so at operational level, where practice must develop to produce appropriate responses to abuse in the absence of a clear statutory framework for investigation.

This chapter includes a preliminary section considering the existence and definitions of abuse, and continues to focus on ways of responding to abuse under the headings of preventing abuse, action by the victim and formal responses, the latter incorporating consideration of the role of the criminal law.

Existence and definitions of abuse

There is no clear legal definition of adult abuse. Efforts to arrive at a suitable practice definition illustrate the difficulties inherent in attempting to define an emerging social problem in the absence of comprehensive research, professional consensus or significant grass roots pressure.[11]

■ Definitions

The first formal definition (which focused on older people) appeared in official practice guidelines in 1993.[12] 'Abuse may be described as physical, sexual, psychological or financial. It may be intentional or the result of neglect. It causes harm to the older person, either temporarily or over a period of time.' Though not obvious from the definition, it is apparent from the full title of the publication that the above definition focuses on abuse within domestic settings, i.e. the family or victim's home, to the exclusion of institutional care settings. The definition was adopted in a number of local authority policies, as was the following definition, which the Department of Health commissioned 'Action on Elder Abuse' to produce in 1994: 'Elder abuse is a single or repeated act or lack of appropriate action occurring within any relationship where there is an expectation of trust, which causes harm or distress to an older person.' The Action on Elder Abuse definition does not locate abuse within a physical setting but is problematic in other respects. What, for example, is meant by the term 'a relationship of trust'? It would appear to exclude abuse perpetrated by strangers.[13]

'No Secrets' (Department of Health, 2000) offers the following phrase as a basis on which to proceed: 'Abuse is a violation of an individual's human and civil rights by any other person or persons.' This is a much broader statement than earlier definitions of elder abuse, with a different conceptual emphasis which may be linked to the existence of the Human Rights Act 1998. Further elaboration is provided in para. 2.6:

> Abuse may consist of a single act or repeated acts. It may be physical, verbal, or psychological. It may be an act of neglect or an omission to act, or it may occur when a vulnerable person is persuaded into a financial or sexual transaction to which he or she has not consented or cannot consent. Abuse can occur in any relationship and may result in significant harm to, or exploitation of, the person subjected to it.

Categories of abuse

'No Secrets' goes on to note that beyond that definition there are certain categories of abuse over which some consensus has been reached. The categories are physical, sexual, psychological, financial and neglect, though abusive acts may embrace more than one category. In an area where our knowledge base is rapidly developing the importance of keeping an open mind to 'new' categories cannot be overstated. In some local authority policies, institutional and professional abuse have separate category status and chemical abuse is a sub-category of physical abuse. 'No Secrets' also refers to a separate category of discriminatory abuse including racist, sexist, that based on a person's disability, and other forms of harassment, slurs or similar treatment.[14] Discrimination may be a feature of each of the other categories. Physical abuse or name calling, for example, may be motivated by sexist, racist or ageist views.

Each category includes a variety of types of behaviour. Physical abuse includes hitting, slapping, pushing, unreasonable restraint, hair pulling and forced or over-medication, burning or biting. Sexual abuse has been described as a taboo subject, which is difficult to identify.[15] It may involve physical contact such as touching of genitals or breasts, masturbation or penetration. Equally, activities, which do not involve contact, such as photography, indecent exposure, sexual harassment or forced exposure to pornographic materials, may be considered abusive. Recent research by Stevenson and Jeary into sexual abuse of elderly people identified cases where abuse occurred in residential care, home care with domiciliary provision and independent living where no formal care was in place. The age of the abused women ranged from 60 to 98 and the abusers were between 16 and 70 years old. The types of cases ranged from sexual harassment through to rape, sexual assault and killing.[16] Psychological abuse includes verbal assaults, threats, humiliation, isolating the elder person, ignoring or being over-protective of the person, racial abuse or intimidation. The most common form of abuse is thought to be financial abuse, which includes theft, use of money or property without consent, forced transfer of assets, misuse of power of attorney or appointeeship and denial of access to funds or property. As one aspect of financial abuse, the Home Office has estimated that as many as 80,000 distraction burglaries and frauds by doorstep fraudsters take place each year targeting vulnerable elderly people. Neglect may be active, being the deliberate failure of a person to provide care; or passive, the unintentional failure to fulfil caring obligations due to inadequate knowledge or understanding. It includes failure to provide medical care, food, clothing, shelter or stimulation and failure to attend to personal hygiene needs of, for example, an adult who is incontinent.

For each category, possible indicators of abuse have been established. Whilst the existence of any of these indicators would not by itself be conclusive proof of abuse, it should arouse suspicion or concern. For example, injuries which are incompatible with history given or uncared for, untreated pressure sores, bruises in shapes of fingers or belts or other objects, poor skin condition, weight loss and absence of hair are all possible indicators of physical abuse. Certain injuries or medical conditions, e.g. bruising or bedsores, can occur very easily in older people. Where such a condition did not arise out of abusive behaviour it would nevertheless be a prompt for action to ensure appropriate attention or assessment by a relevant professional, e.g. involvement of district nurse.

'No Secrets' also recognises that abuse can take place in any context, whether the vulnerable adult lives alone, with a relative or other person, or in a residential setting. The perpetrator of abuse may be a relative, professional staff, paid care workers, volunteers, other service users, neighbours, friends and associates, people who deliberately exploit vulnerable people, and strangers.[17] The type of intervention (if any) will be dependent on the setting and the relationship of the perpetrator amongst other factors.

■ Prevalence

There has been one published UK study on the prevalence of elder abuse in the community, by Ogg and Bennett (1992).[18] This was carried out using an OPCS survey to interview adults over pensionable age in the general population about physical, verbal and financial abuse. The method used excluded adults in residential settings or adults who were disabled or ill. This is an important limitation, particularly when related to the risk factor, social isolation, and would suggest that the results are an underestimation. The resulting rates found that 1 in 20 older people had suffered verbal or financial abuse and 1 in 50 reported physical abuse. When the same definitions were used to ask adults under 60 if they had abused an older person, the survey produced rates of 1 in 10 for verbal abuse. The Ogg and Bennett study replicated prevalence figures from Pillemer and Finkelhor's 1988 Boston study.[19] It is likely that any measurement of abuse in the future will suggest that the phenomenon is increasing. An increase could be attributable to a number of factors, including demographic changes that have led to a larger population of elderly people, greater awareness and recognition of abuse and more sophisticated and reliable recording of referrals. Reports of the Action on Elder Abuse Helpline, provide further information on referral rates and types of abuse.[20]

Responding to abuse

■ A duty to investigate?

There is no specific statutory duty to investigate concerns of possible adult protection. Despite the recommendations of the Law Commission,[21] an equivalent to s. 47 of the Children Act 1989 does not exist. 'No Secrets' clearly envisages social services as the key agency with responsibility for coordinating procedures for adult protection. As guidance issued under s. 7 of the Local Authority (Social Services) Act 1970, 'No Secrets' does not carry the full force of law. It notes: 'This document gives guidance to local agencies who have a responsibility to investigate and take action when a vulnerable adult is believed to be suffering abuse' (para. 1.5) and, further: '. . . this document does not have the full force of statute, but should be complied with unless local circumstances indicate exceptional reasons which justify a variation' (para. 1.4). It is arguable that the Human Rights Act 1998, by imposing a duty on public authorities to comply with the ECHR, may effectively act to 'upgrade' this status, a position that would be welcomed by many who have been disappointed at the lack of primary legislation specifically addressing adult protection. The requirements of 'No Secrets' were in place by October 2001,[22] and procedures, developed from an inter-agency framework, are in place across the country. At least 90 local authorities have appointed a 'lead officer' for adult protection work since the publication of 'No Secrets'.[23]

'No Secrets' calls for better protection for individuals needing care and support. It requires that local authorities develop protection policies and a service development plan. The plan should identify relevant resources in the area, such as refuges and counselling services.

Any allegation of abuse will need to be investigated and local policies should reflect the following stages:

- reporting to a single referral point;
- recording, with sensitivity to the abused person, the precise factual details of the alleged abuse;
- initial coordination involving representatives of all agencies which might have a role in a subsequent investigation and could constitute the strategy meeting;
- investigation within a jointly agreed framework to determine the facts of the case; and
- decision-making, which may take place at a shared forum such as a case conference.[24]

Whilst social services are to take on the lead role, 'No Secrets' envisages working in partnership with other agencies, including: Commissioners and providers of health and social care services; providers of sheltered and supported housing; regulators of services; the police; the voluntary and private sector agencies; other local authority departments, e.g. housing and education; probation; DSS benefit agencies; carer support groups and user groups; advocacy services; community safety partnerships; and agencies offering legal advice.[25]

Some authorities hold 'at risk registers' as part of their response to adult abuse cases. For example, in Gloucestershire, case conferences are used in the assessment and decision-making process and the vulnerable adult would normally be invited to attend the conference. At the conference a care plan to manage risk is devised and the need for formal registration is considered. Whilst possible civil liberties implications of holding a register are acknowledged in Gloucestershire, registration (limited to substantiated cases) provides a useful reference tool to which agencies can speedily refer and generates accurate statistics on the incidence of abuse.[26]

■ Legal options

As each form of abuse may merit a range of legal responses (or none at all), the law covered in this chapter is arranged in order of levels of intervention rather than according to the specific category of abuse. 'No Secrets' recognises both the various nature of abuse and responses to it: 'Action should be primarily supportive or therapeutic or it might involve the application of sanctions, suspension, regulatory activity or criminal prosecution, disciplinary action or de-registration from a professional body. Remember vulnerable adults who are victims like any other victims have a right to see justice.' (para. 6.4).

Separate consideration is given to some of the particular issues, which may arise where the setting for abuse is the residential sector.

As a starting point guiding any intervention, it is useful to aim for the adoption of the following principle, as enunciated in the Law Commission report:

that people are enabled and encouraged to take for themselves those decisions which they are able to take; that where it is necessary in their own interests or for the protection of others that someone else should take decisions on their behalf, the intervention should be as limited as possible and concerned to achieve what the person himself would have wanted; and that proper safeguards be provided against exploitation, neglect and physical, sexual or psychological abuse.[27]

The legal framework for dealing with adult abuse lacks cohesion. A number of reasons have been given to explain underuse of the law in relation to adult abuse:

First, some legal procedures, particularly criminal prosecutions, are inappropriate in many cases of elder abuse because the perpetrators of abuse are themselves victims of the situation, for example, carers subject to an excessive degree of stress. Second, legal procedures are often under-utilised because of negative attitudes/lack of experience on the part of professionals such as lawyers and social workers. Third, the notion of abuse is seldom conceptualised in legal terms.[28]

These concerns are compounded by the lack of consensus over definitions and a limited UK research base. It is therefore necessary to be 'imaginative' in the use of existing law and guided by the above principle, which might be abbreviated to an objective of 'maximum autonomy, minimum intervention'.

Type of abuse	Legal remedies
Physical	Criminal prosecution – Offences Against the Person Act 1861 Civil action – assault, battery or false imprisonment (restraint) Family Law Act 1996 injunctions: non-molestation and occupation Criminal Injuries Compensation claim Mental Health Act 1983, ss. 115, 135, 127, 117 (after-care) Mental Capacity Act 2005 – ill teatment and neglect Police and Criminal Evidence Act 1984, s. 17 (power to enter to save life and limb) Care Standards Act 2000 – regulation of care homes and domiciliary provision, supported by National Standards National Health Service and Community Care Act 1990, s. 47 (support)
Sexual	Criminal prosecution – Sexual Offences Act 2003. NB specific offences against people with severe learning disabilities Civil action (as above) Family Law Act 1996 injunction for non-molestation Mental Health Act 1983 Care Standards Act 2000 Community Care support
Psychological	Protection from Harassment Act 1997 Care Standards Act 2000 Anti-discrimination legislation (race, sex, disability) Community care support Anti-social behaviour order – Crime and Disorder Act 1995, Anti Social Behaviour Act 2003
Neglect	National Assistance Act 1948, s. 47 (1951 Act, *ex parte*) Mental Health Act 1983, s. 127 Mental Capacity Act 2005 – ill treatment and neglect Criminal law – *R v. Stone* [1977] 2 All ER 341
Financial	Enduring power of attorney Court of Protection Criminal prosecution – Theft Act 1968 (*R v. Hinks* [2001] 2 AC 241)
NB	**Overarching effect of Human Rights Act 1998**

Exhibit 17.1 Possible legal remedies by abuse category
Source: Adapted from L.-A. Cull and J. Roche (eds) (2001).

Identification of a relevant legal provision will depend on the type of abuse and the desired outcome. Exhibit 17.1 summarises for ease of reference the relevant legal provisions by category of abuse to which they are most likely to be applicable.

Certain legal provisions will be more or less appropriate to particular types of abuse and some will be applicable only to specific categories: e.g. Sexual Offences Act 2003; Theft Act 1968. It is clear, however, that for most cases there will be a range of legal options. The selected option will depend on a number of factors including available evidence and seriousness of case. A major predisposing factor will be the desired outcome in tackling the abuse. Exhibit 17.2 offers a further classification of legal provision by desired outcome or objective. Discussion of the various legal options outlined in Exhibits 17.1 and 17.2 continues in the following sections, separated into law relating to the prevention of abuse, action which can be taken by the victim, and formal responses.

Objective	Legal provision
Support	NHSCCA 1990, s. 47 Domiciliary services Duty to promote welfare Mental Health Act 1983, s. 7 (guardianship) Carers (Recognition and Services) Act 1995 Carers and Disabled Children Act 2000 Carers (Equal Opportunities) Act 2005 Provision of accommodation – National Assistance Act 1948, regulated by Care Standards Act 2000
Prosecution	Criminal law – statute and common law Investigation by police and Crown Prosecution Service prosecution
Remove perpetrator	Family Law Act 1996 injunction Civil (law of tort) injunction Mental Health Act 1983
Remove subject	National Assistance Act 1948, s. 47 Mental Health Act 1983 (provision of accommodation) High Court Declaration
Compensation	Civil law Criminal Injuries Compensation Scheme Order of criminal court

Exhibit 17.2   Adult protection: legal objectives
Source: Adapted from L.-A. Cull and J. Roche (ed.) (2001).

Preventing abuse

'No Secrets' places great emphasis on the importance of prevention of abuse.

'The agencies' primary aim should be to prevent abuse where possible, but if the preventive strategy fails, agencies should ensure that robust procedures are in place for dealing with incidents of abuse' (para. 1.2). Social services are expected to be the lead agency dealing with a case of abuse and have a number of existing powers to provide services to older people, collectively known as 'community care services'. A vast amount of legislation focuses on support and provision of services in relation to specific 'categories' of vulnerable adults (e.g. National Assistance Act 1948, s. 29). In terms of interventions, except in the most serious cases, provision of an appropriate care package will often be the first step. Chapter 14 deals with assessment for and provision of community care services in some detail. In this context it is important to remember that an individual can legitimately refuse both assessment for and provision of services. In neglect cases such refusal may be one of the central concerns and an initial refusal of support should not be taken at face value.

In attempting to provide solutions to abusive situations, it is crucial that workers have confidence in the ability of any services offered to minimise the possibility of an already abused person being subject to further abuse. It was thus of concern that domiciliary or day-care services, often included in care packages, were not subject to any formal regulation prior to introduction of the Care Standards Act 2000, under which domiciliary services are required to register and will be regulated by the Commisssion for Social Care Inspection.

Support services to carers may help to lessen the risk of abuse to vulnerable adults. (There is no assumption here that carers form a significant body of 'abusers'. Early works on elder abuse suggested that 'carer stress' was a predisposing factor to elder abuse. In fact, research has not found this to be the case.) The Carers (Recognition and Services) Act 1995 (C(RS)A 1995) provides for a separate assessment of the needs of a person providing or proposing to provide care. Services can be provided to enable that person to better fulfil the caring role, e.g. support with shopping.

A National Strategy for Carers was produced in 1998 and, to further the aims of that strategy and supplement the C(RS)A 1995, the Carers and Disabled Children Act 2000 was introduced. The provisions of this Act allow for assessment of a carer's needs in relation to the care he provides, which can take place even if the cared for person refuses an assessment. The local authority has the power to provide direct services to carers such as assistance with household tasks through to training and counselling (but excluding intimate care). Greater flexibility is introduced through the local authority power to make direct payments to carers, which enable the carer to make his own arrangements for services. The Act also introduced the 'short-term voucher scheme'. The scheme is designed to offer more flexibility in timing and choice of carers' breaks. Vouchers are redeemable with providers approved by the local authority and typically arrange for another person to provide services in lieu of the care normally provided by the carer. The most recent carer legislation, the Carers (Equal Opportunities) Act 2005, amends and extends the earlier provisions in 3 key aspects. First, local authorities are now obliged to inform carers of their right to an assessment. Second, the scope of assessment is broadened to include consideration of whether the carer wishes to work or take part in education, training or leisure activities. Thirdly, local authorities may request other bodies (including the NHS) to assist in both planning provision of services to carers and cared for persons, and in actual provision of services.

■ Screening out unsuitable people

One of the most effective ways of reducing abuse must be to ensure that unsuitable adults do not come into contact with vulnerable adults in a caring role. The Care Standards Act 2000, s. 81 introduced a duty of the Secretary of State to keep a list of individuals who are considered unsuitable to work with vulnerable adults, the Protection of Vulnerable Adults (**POVA**) index.[29] This is in similar terms to the list established under the Protection of Children Act 1999. The scheme applies across the social care sector, i.e. registered care homes, registered domiciliary care agencies and registered adult placement schemes. It does not cover the NHS. Under section 82, a provider must refer a care worker to the Secretary of State if the worker has been dismissed on grounds of misconduct (whether or not in the course of his employment) that harmed or placed at risk of harm a vulnerable adult (or he would have been dismissed if he had not resigned, retired or been made redundant, or he has been transferred to a position which is not a care position, or he has been suspended). For these purposes a care worker is a person who has regular contact with a vulnerable adult in the course of his duties and is not limited to those people whose job title is care worker. In a residential home, for example, the cook might be classed as a care worker if the role regularly includes helping residents with eating. Equally, regular visitors to a home, such as hairdressers or chiropodists, would be included. In an adult placement scheme, it would include the adult placement carer. The worker shall be included on the list if the Secretary of State is of the opinion: (a) that the provider reasonably considered the worker to be guilty of misconduct which harmed or placed at risk of harm a vulnerable adult; and (b) that the worker is unsuitable to work with vulnerable adults (CSA 2000, s. 82(7)). Harm is defined broadly to include ill treatment or impairment of health or development.

The registration authority may also refer a care worker to the Secretary of State (CSA 2000, s. 84), for example the manager of a residential home that has been closed, and individuals named in the findings of inquiries may also be included on the list (s. 85). An individual who is included in the list may appeal to the tribunal against inclusion (s. 86), may apply to have his name removed from the list on the grounds that he is no longer unsuitable to work with vulnerable adults (s. 87) (leave of the tribunal is required for an application under s. 87); and an application may be made when a person has been included on the list for at least ten years and the individual's circumstances have changed since he was included. Under s. 89, it is the duty of care providers to check whether a person they propose to employ is included on the list. A check is made by application to the Criminal Records Bureau, and should accompany robust recruitment procedures e,g full references, verification of identity. Once the Mental Capacity Act 2005 is in place, the Public Guardian will be able to check whether a potential deputy is on the POVA list. The POVA scheme came into being in July 2004, having been deferred due to difficulties with the Criminal Records Bureau.

As at 31 August 2005, 2,520 people had been referred to the list. Of those 197 individuals are confirmed on the list and a further 970 are listed provisionally. An audit of the first 100 referrals has taken place. It found that just over a third of referrals concerned male workers involved in physical abuse, although they form a small proportion of the workforce (5 to 15 per cent). The majority of referrals were care assistants and support workers including some registered nurses; 81 per cent of referrals came from the residential sector and were most likely to concern neglect and physical abuse, whereas financial abuse was more common in domiciliary care.

Following the Bichard inquiry, a Safeguarding Vulnerable Groups Bill was published in March 2006. This provides for a joint list of those barred from working with children and vulnerable adults and should provide greater flexibility than exists under the current schemes. It is intended to enable wider access to information, for example, people receiving direct payments will be able to check the list and more information sharing across statutory bodies, such as the General Social Care Council and the Nursing and Midwifery Council. The new scheme is unlikely to be in place before 2007. In the meantime, good practice guidance on making referrals is being prepared.

In addition to POVA the Care Standards Act created the General Social Care Council (s. 4, a replacement for CCETSW) whose role is to ensure regulation of the social care workforce and promote high standards. Social care workers required to register are defined under s. 55:

- anyone who engages in relevant social work;
- a person employed in or managing a children's home, care home or residential family centre, or for the purposes of a domiciliary care agency, a fostering agency or a voluntary adoption agency;
- a person supplied by a domiciliary care agency to provide personal care in their own homes to persons who by reason of illness, infirmity or disability are unable to provide it for themselves without assistance.

Application of the registration requirement is being phased in and registration has initially been limited to qualified social workers and social work students. There is, however, a greater emphasis on training and qualifications for all social care staff (see National Standard 29)[30] and eventually the aim is that all social care workers will be registered. Any person can check the register via the GSCC website. The title 'social worker' may only be used by those people who are so registered. The Council will work to ensure high standards of practice and training and to disseminate good practice.

■ Preventing financial abuse

In cases of financial abuse[31] it is often difficult to recoup property and, in the longer term, greater emphasis on effective management of financial affairs as a means of preventing abuse may be more effective. If an individual is not able to manage part or all of their financial affairs, which may be due, for example, to a lack of mental capacity or physical difficulty in collecting a pension, there are a variety of ways to delegate that function. The options vary depending on whether the individual has mental capacity to manage their financial affairs. (For a fuller discussion of issues concerning mental capacity, see Chapter 16.)

Agency

Where a person has a mental capacity but needs another person simply to collect their benefits they may nominate an agent. In the short term, the declaration on the reverse of the benefit order is completed; for the longer term, an agency card from the Benefits Agency can be completed. There is no monitoring of agency agreements.

Third party mandate

A third party mandate can be used by a person with mental capacity to authorise another person to act on their behalf in bank or building society transactions.

Appointee

If the person is unable to act because of physical or mental incapacity, another person may be appointed to exercise the right to make claims, or receive and spend them for the sole benefit of the individual. This does not have to be a permanent arrangement. Normally, a close relative or friend or someone in regular contact with the adult is appropriate as an appointee. If there is no-one else suitable, social services or voluntary bodies may act. The Benefits Agency should be satisfied that the individual claimant is unable to manage his financial affairs and it should be satisfied as to the suitability of the person who intends to act. If the person is in residential or nursing home accommodation, the proprietor should be appointed only as a last resort as normally there should be no potential for conflict of interest. Although this provision applies where the individual entitled to benefits lacks capacity to manage the process of claiming etc., the Mental Capacity Act 2005 did not give separate consideration to it.

Power of attorney

A power of attorney is a legal document, which can be used by a person with mental capacity to authorise another person (or persons) to handle his financial affairs. The power may provide general authority or it may be limited to a specific action, e.g. sale of property. The power of attorney remains valid until revoked or the donor loses mental capacity.

Enduring power of attorney[32]

An enduring power of attorney (EPA) is a document, which provides for a person (the attorney) to deal with the financial affairs of an individual (the donor) in the future if that individual loses mental capacity. It is particularly suitable for people who are concerned that they may suffer from some form of dementia or Alzheimer's disease in the future. It must be prepared whilst the donor still has mental capacity and it must be registered with the Public Guardianship Office to take effect once the individual loses capacity. If there is any doubt as to whether the donor has capacity, it is normal practice for the solicitor drawing up the document to obtain medical opinion, having advised the doctor of the test of capacity (*Re K, Re F* [1988] 1 All ER 358). The doctor may also witness the donor's signature on the EPA. Prior to registration, the attorney must notify certain of the donor's relatives, who may object to registration on a number of grounds including that the donor is not mentally incapable or that the attorney is unsuitable to act. In *Re W (Enduring Power of Attorney)* [2001] 4 All ER 88, the capacity of the donor of an EPA was challenged, as was the question whether her daughter was suitable to act as attorney, given her acrimonious relationship with her siblings. It is for the person objecting to the validity of the EPA on grounds of incapacity to prove that the donor lacked the necessary understanding of the nature and effect of the power.

An EPA may be used to authorise an attorney to take control of affairs immediately and with authority to continue to act when mental capacity is lost. The public guardianship office[33] does not actually monitor enduring powers of attorney but it can consider complaints about its administration. The Court of Protection has power to revoke an enduring power of attorney if it is being abused. A common criticism of the EPA is that a significant number of attorneys do not register the power (it can be relied on once signed). Further, the Master of the Court of Protection has indicated that in 10–15 per cent of registered powers financial exploitation occurs and that percentage is higher with unregistered powers.[34] Currently, an EPA may be used only to deal with property and financial matters. When the Mental Capacity Act 2005 comes into force, a new order, to be known as a lasting power of attorney (LPA), will be created, under which it will be possible to delegate decision making relating to health and welfare matters as well as financial issues.

The Court of Protection is an office of the Supreme Court with jurisdiction to protect and manage the property and financial affairs of people who are incapable by reason of mental disorder of doing so. This body of people can include people with illnesses such as schizophrenia, people who have suffered brain damage, people with learning disabilities and people with forms of dementia (often associated with old age). An application to the court should be made if an individual is unable to manage their financial affairs and has not executed an enduring power of attorney. The court can appoint a receiver to act on the patient's behalf where there are assets of over £10,000. Prior to appointment the Public Guardianship Office will assess the needs of the patient. The receiver may be a relative or friend or a professional (such as a solicitor or accountant) or the local authority. Where a receiver is appointed, an annual administration fee is payable to the office and the receiver is entitled to reasonable expenses. Receivership has been criticised as outdated, bureaucratic, disempowering and expensive.

Where the case is straightforward and there are less substantial assets, the Public Trustee may make directions authorising certain use of funds, without the appointment of a receiver (previously known as the 'short order' procedure).

The Protection of Property Officer will normally be the individual within a local authority who acts as appointee, or in some cases will make an application to the Court of Protection in respect of an individual, where no-one else is able or willing to act.

Court of Protection and public guardianship office – Mental Capacity Act 2005 changes

When the Mental Capacity Act 2005 comes into force, the scheme outlined above will be replaced. Chapter 16 discussed the lasting power of attorney and the role of court appointed deputies as means of delegating decision-making in respect of financial, health and welfare matters. The new scheme is more extensive than the current law and will replace enduring powers of attorney, receivership and short orders of the Court of Protection. The Office of the Public Guardian (OPG) will have a role in supervision of attorneys under LPAs and deputies. This supervisory role will be conducted in conjunction with other protective measures and other relevant agencies, such as the police and social services, acting within the 'No Secrets' framework. The Public Guardian will maintain a register of LPAs and deputies and supervise deputies. The work of the Public Guardian is supported by Court of Protection Visitors, whose role includes visiting people who lack capacity and providing independent advice to the court and to the Public Guardian. If a concern is raised with the Public Guardian in relation to a LPA or deputy or in another respect, concerning an adult lacking capacity the Public Guardian may carry out investigations itself and/or cooperate with other relevant agencies, most obviously social services, following 'No Secrets', and the police. The draft guidance provides two examples where a referral might be made to another agency:

> Where a complaint has been raised that a welfare attorney is physically abusing a donor (his spouse). This would be referred to the relevant local authority adult protection committee and/or the police.
>
> Where a solicitor appointed as a financial deputy for an elderly person with dementia has been found to be defrauding that person's estate resulting in the loss of several thousand pounds. This would be referred to the police although the OPG, which would also conduct its own investigation, would prepare a report for the court recommending that the deputy's appointment be revoked. (paras. 9.17–9.18)

■ Residential settings

The framework for regulation (which implicitly includes prevention of abuse) of residential care homes and domiciliary care agencies is now provided by the Care Standards Act 2000,[35] supported by National Minimum Standards. This framework, which includes a registration requirement and provisions for attaching conditions and cancelling registration, is described in Chapter 14. The registration and inspection unit (initially the National Care Standards Commission as introduced by the Care Standards Act 2000, now the Commission for Social Care Inspection) operates independently of social services and clearly has a role to play where abuse takes place in a setting that is regulated. Social services will also have direct involvement with care homes in both their care management and commissioning roles.[36] Any concerns of possible abuse, which the home is aware of, should be notified to the registration authority. The Care Homes Regulations 2001[37] stipulate that the registered person for the care home should notify the Commission without delay of: any event in the care home which adversely affects the well-being or safety of the service user; any theft, burglary or accident in the care home; the death of any service user, including the circumstances of death; any serious injury to a service user; and any allegation of misconduct by the registered person or any person who works at the care home.[38]

If a complaint relating to abuse is received by the inspection unit, adult protection procedures should be clear about the role of the regulatory authority in investigations. Enforcement action (possibly cancellation of registration or prosecution) should be considered if abuse has occurred in a residential setting.[39] It should be recognised that abuse in a residential setting, as in the community, may take many forms. The abuse may relate to poor standards of care or the regime in a home[40] or it may be a single isolated incident, e.g. where a resident is sexually abused during a visit from a relative.

The practice of restraint in some care homes has been identified as an issue of concern.[41] Types of restraint include the use of furniture to prevent a resident moving around freely, bed sides, baffle locks and chemical coshes. Restraint without consent is clearly unlawful unless it can be justified as self-defence or to prevent a crime. The reality of the circumstances of many of the individuals who are subject to restraint means that individual legal challenge is unlikely. It is, however, an important aspect of the way a home is run and should be considered by the regulatory body. Regulation 13(7) of the Care Home Regulations 2001 states that: 'The registered person shall ensure that no service user is subject to physical restraint unless restraint of the kind employed is the only practicable means of securing the welfare of that or any other service user and there are exceptional circumstances.'

The following case provides an example of the need for close regulation of residential accommodation. It reached the Registered Homes Tribunal (whilst the Registered Homes Act 1984 was in force). In *Freeman and Goodwin* v. *Northamptonshire County Council* (2000) Decision 421, 20 December, the decision of the registration authority for cancellation was confirmed. The home in Northamptonshire was registered to accept 16 people with physical disability, or mental handicap and mental disorder. Mrs Goodwin, the Freemans' daughter, was registered manager. Reasons for cancellation included failure to care for a particular resident, Alan (AT), and recognise his care needs. Also there were concerns relating to inability to look after the financial needs of the residents: £19,000 of the residents' money was unaccounted for and some personal money had been used to pay for items for the home. In addition, employment practices, training, induction procedures and staff records were inadequate. Proper records had not been kept, including medication records, and records had been falsified on the instruction of the manager. Mrs Freeman had never played any part in running the home; she should not have been registered and was unfit to continue because of her complete inaction.

Mr Freeman felt it was not necessarily inappropriate for male staff to carry out intimate personal care for female residents. Previous experience of staff was not recorded. One resident, AT, had been kept in conditions of squalor and degradation, he had been deprived of his liberty, his dignity was ignored, his right to property compromised, and he was in pain with a dental abscess and no action had been taken to treat him. One of the inspection officers commented that she had never seen an animal kept in that way. He had effectively been abandoned by Essex County Council 12 years ago and kept in conditions reminiscent of those which led to the closure of many large mental institutions. He spent time sitting on a plastic chair dressed in only a ripped T-shirt, surrounded by urine, in a cold room with no bed linen and a high handle on the door to prevent escape. Of the 15 residents, only four had a care plan.

The human rights implications were noted in the judgment:

> We had in mind that Local Authorities now have a duty under the Human Rights Act 1998 to safeguard the rights of those, like AT, for whom they are responsible. We consider that both Essex and Northampton as public authorities by virtue of section 6 of the Act, behaved in a way which was incompatible with AT's Convention rights. Inspection units and Registered Persons should consider that it may be appropriate to look at how Convention (Human) rights are promoted and protected in Registered Homes when questions of Registration and 'fitness' arise.[42]

In *Freeman* it could be argued that aspects of the regime could amount to inhuman or degrading treatment under ECHR, Art. 3. Application of this article hinges on the definition of the terms used. In *Ireland* v. *United Kingdom* (1978) 2 EHRR 25 five techniques – wall standing, hooding, subjection to noise, and deprivation of sleep, food and drink – were held not to amount to torture but were degrading treatment. 'Torture' was defined as deliberate inhuman treatment causing very serious and cruel suffering; 'inhuman treatment' as intense physical and mental suffering and acute psychiatric disturbances; and 'degrading treatment' as behaviour which aroused in the victim fears of anguish and inferiority capable of humiliating and debasing them and possibly breaking their physical or moral resistance. The case also said that ill treatment must attain a minimum level of severity. That is a relative issue and will depend on all the circumstances of the case, including duration of treatment, its physical and mental effects, age, sex and state of health of the victim.

The right to enjoyment of private and family life contained in Art. 8 may also have an application in the residential sector. There is potential for it to be relied on in the following examples: moving from independent living in the community to residential accommodation; sharing rooms; communal meals only; no provision for couples to be together; lack of after-care services; covert surveillance; issues involving physical integrity, e.g. tagging; and violations which relate to a person's dignity as an aspect of private life.

The right to respect for a person's home formed part of the argument in *R* v. *North and East Devon Health Authority, ex parte Coughlan* [2000] 3 All ER 850. The health authority intended to close the home in which the applicant lived. Amongst other arguments, it was found that the health authority was in breach of Art. 8 on the basis that Mardon House was the applicant's home and their promise of a home for life for the resident had been broken. The savings the authority would make by closing the home did not outweigh the loss to the applicant of her home.

Action by the victim

It may be effective and empowering for an individual to take private law action to counter abuse. There are clear scenarios where this route would be available legally but may not be at the forefront of professionals' minds as an appropriate intervention. Behaviour, of a physical, psychological or sexual nature, which would ordinarily be classified as domestic violence, might be described as adult abuse where the victim is a vulnerable adult. The conceptual difference and complexities of definition are highlighted in the example of graduated domestic violence. If domestic violence has always been a feature of a couple's relationship, when they each turn 65 years of age does it suddenly become labelled elder/adult abuse? For these purposes the available law does not draw any distinctions based on age. Recourse may be taken to the Family Law Act 1996, the law of contract and the law of tort.

Where an individual lacks capacity to bring legal proceedings, a 'litigation friend' may be appointed to do so on their behalf (Civil Procedure Rules, r. 21) (as in e.g. *R* v. *Bournewood Community and Mental Health NHS Trust, ex parte L* [1998] 3 All ER 289). The implications of this may include the case being heard in a higher court than is routine for the particular application, and also possible involvement of the Official Solicitor.

■ The Family Law Act 1996

The Family Law Act 1996 provisions relating to domestic violence were discussed in Chapter 8. The potential availability of injunctions to prevent abuse in an adult protection context was significantly expanded by this Act. Previously, only where abuse took place between spouses or cohabitees, was recourse to injunctions available under a range of domestic violence legislation. The new legislation broadens the range of relationships that are covered.

Orders are available in respect of an 'associated person'. This term is defined in s. 62 and includes spouses, cohabitees (and previous spouses and cohabitees), people who have had an intimate relationship which is or was of a significant duration (who do not live together), people living in the same household (but not as lodgers or tenants) and relatives of the person or their spouse or cohabitee. Victims of abuse occurring within a homosexual relationship or at the hands of a grandchild (for example) can now apply speedily for injunctions under the Family Law Act 1996, whereas previously they were limited to an application in the law of tort.

All police forces now have specialist trained officers in domestic violence units (often also with responsibility for child protection) and a circular in 1990[43] directed the police to treat incidents of violence within a domestic setting as seriously as a violent assault by a stranger. A number of police forces now include adult abuse within the responsibility of domestic violence units. It is not currently possible for a third party to make an application for a domestic violence injunction. There is provision for this in FLA 1996 s. 60, but the provision has not been implemented. It is arguable that in some cases the victim of domestic violence would prefer a third party to make the application on their behalf and that investing the responsibility in, for example, social services would reinforce the state's responsibility to protect victims of violence. A possible disadvantage might be that if orders are sought by a third party then a police prosecution might be less likely.[44]

■ Contract

In addition to family law, an individual may also have recourse to the private law of contract and tort. Local authorities can require higher standards in homes they contract with than standards specified under legislation (*R* v. *Cleveland County Council, ex parte Cleveland Care Homes Association* (1993) 17 BMLR 122).

Particularly relevant to financial or property abuse, the law of contract offers protection whereby an individual who enters into a contract under duress or undue influence will not be bound by its terms. For example, if a vulnerable adult is falsely persuaded that it would be advantageous to transfer his house to a younger relative, the remedy in contract will be revocation of the contract or damages. In *Re Craig (deceased)* [1971] Ch 95, a will which was drawn up under undue influence was set aside. In certain circumstances a presumption of undue influence arises. In *Hammond v Osborn* [2002] EWCA Civ 885, an elderly bachelor transferred over 90 per cent of his assets, amounting to nearly £300,000, to a caregiver. The court was somewhat suspicious that major assets were transferred to a carer of recent acquaintance and found that it was for the carer to rebut the presumption of undue influence by reason of the relationship between them. If the elderly man had taken independent advice, the court would have been more likely to find that he had entered into the transaction of his own free will.

An alternative approach was evident in *R v Hinks* [2001] 2 AC 241. Acquiring property by accepting gifts from a vulnerable and trusting person amounted to 'appropriation' under the Theft Act 1968. The defendant, aged 38 was friendly with Mr Dolphin, a man described to be of limited intelligence, aged 53. In evidence before the House of Lords, a consultant psychiatrist described him as naïve and trusting and having no ideas of the values of his assets. Over a six-month period Mr Dolphin visited his building society daily and withdrew the maximum sum of £300, totaling around £60,000, the majority of his savings. The prosecution case was that the defendant had influenced and coerced Mr Dolphin to withdraw the money and she was found guilty of four counts of theft.

■ **Tort**

Under the law of tort, civil action may be instigated for assault (reasonable cause to fear direct harm), e.g. pointing a knife at someone; battery (actual direct and intentional application of force), e.g. a punch, unwanted kiss or removal of false teeth without consent; and false imprisonment (infliction of physical restraint not authorised by law), e.g. being tied to a chair or locked inside a room. The use of unauthorised restraint in the residential sector is well documented.[45] Criminal offences of assault, battery and false imprisonment also exist and a separate prosecution may be taken for the behaviour. Negligence may also be relevant (particularly regarding 'professional' care), where a duty of care is established, there is a breach of that duty, by act or omission, and harm is suffered as a consequence. As noted earlier, the previous public immunity enjoyed by local authorities is reduced and negligence claims are now more likely to succeed against local authorities where the elements of negligence are satisfied. Each claim will be decided on the facts, so, for example, a local authority was not found negligent for allowing a day centre bus to collect a service user (who was injured crossing the road) from the opposite side of the road to his house. The principal remedy is compensatory damages; however, there are examples of the use of injunctions to prevent further abusive acts (*Egan* v. *Egan* [1975] 1 Ch 218; *Patel* v. *Patel* [1988] 2 FLR 179). Vicarious liability may arise in respect of the negligent acts of another: e.g. a homeowner may be vicariously liable for the negligent actions of his staff.

Formal responses

Under the heading of formal responses, legal provisions, which are utilised or commenced by another party in a position of authority, are considered. The options include use of disciplinary proceedings, declaratory relief, the criminal law, the Mental Health Act 1983 and the National Assistance Act 1948, s. 47.

In any case where the abuser comes into contact with the vulnerable adult in the course of their employment (e.g. a nurse, care worker, teacher or social worker), disciplinary action may be taken in respect of that individual. Abuse of a patient or service user would almost certainly amount to a breach of contract of employment and could lead to dismissal. In addition, the relevant professional body may take action in relation to their code of conduct. For example, the UKCC, the professional body for nurses, found that breach of the client–practitioner relationship was the basis of 64 per cent of conduct hearings. More specifically, of those removed from the professional register each year, 10 per cent worked in the learning disability field, 15 per cent in mental health and 30 per cent were employed in the care of older people.[46] Closely linked to this, the Protection of Vulnerable Adults list has been discussed above.

When concerns arise in the workplace the role of whistleblowing becomes relevant (see discussion in Chapter 4). Whistleblowing in the context of adult protection is in the first instance likely to relate to a particular abuse scenario. It may also have a longer-term effect in preventing further abuse and helping to inform good practice. 'No Secrets' acknowledges whistleblowing, noting '. . . it is the responsibility of all staff to act on any suspicion or evidence of abuse or neglect (see the Public Interest Disclosure Act 1998) and to pass on their concerns to a responsible person/ agency' (para 6.2). For complaints and concerns about poor practice to be heard, well-publicised and accessible complaints procedures are vital. In the employment context, ECHR, Art. 10 states that everyone has the right to freedom of expression, which should override any gagging clauses designed to prevent whistleblowing and supports the provisions of the Public Interest Disclosure Act 1998.

■ Declaratory relief

There is a developing body of case law (in the High Court and above) based on declaratory relief to assist in the resolution of disputes about health and welfare issues for adults who lack capacity. Where proceedings are instituted, the Official Solicitor will be asked to represent the interests of the person whose capacity is at issue (as his litigation friend). There is no mechanism for the Official Solicitor to instigate proceedings. Cases have reached court on application by local authorities or family members. Declarations are used to determine the lawfulness of a particular position and can provide for injunctions. As interim injunctions are available, there is the potential to use declaratory relief in emergency cases, e.g. if a person is threatening to remove an adult who lacks capacity from their usual place of residence.

Declaratory relief cases originated in the area of medical intervention, and have been used in cases involving sterilisation and withdrawal of life-saving treatment. Their use has extended to the area of welfare decisions and it is this aspect that is most pertinent to adult protection. Decisions have been taken about residence, contact, religion and culture.

In *Re S (Hospital Patient: Court's Jurisdiction)* [1996] Fam 1, a cohabitant applied for a declaration that it was lawful for a man who lacked capacity to reside and be cared for in an English hospital, together with an injunction to prevent his family removing him from the jurisdiction. The court made the order and stated that declarations could be used to deal with 'serious justiciable' issues and with flexibility in order that the court could respond to social needs as manifested on a case-by-case basis. In a previous case, *Re C (Mental Patient: Contact)* [1993] 1 FLR 940, an injunction was granted to ensure that an adult could enjoy freedom of contact with an estranged parent.

In declaratory relief the decision of the court will be based on the best interests principle. This is discussed in more detail in Chapter 16 relating to mental capacity. In *Re MB* [1997] 2 FLR 426, Butler-Sloss LJ stated that this includes all relevant information about a person's circumstances and background. A significant case on declaratory relief and adult protection is now *Re F (Adult: Court's Jurisdiction)* [2000] 3 WLR 1740. The central issue in the case was whether the court had jurisdiction to grant declarations sought by a local authority as to the place of res-idence and contact arrangements for a mentally handicapped woman who was unable to care for herself. It was held that, where there was a risk of possible harm in respect of an adult who lacked the capacity to make decisions as to his or her own future, the court had power, under the inherent jurisdiction and in the best interests of that person, to hear the issue involved and to grant the necessary declarations. It was accepted that the woman concerned had the intellectual age of a 5–8-year-old child and she lacked capacity to make decisions as to her future. She did not come within the guardianship provisions of the Mental Health Act 1983, and, as she was aged over 18, the wardship jurisdiction could not be utilised.

The local authority based its application on concern that T was at risk of suffer-ing harm in the family home and sought to determine her residence in a local authority residential home and restrict contact with her mother, Mrs F. She had been placed in local authority accommodation prior to her seventeenth birthday with parental consent, which was since withdrawn. The family circumstances were com-plex and featured local authority involvement. T was the eldest of eight children; her seven brothers and sisters were in local authority care. The local authority case pro-vided evidence of chronic neglect, a lack of minimum standards of hygiene and cleanliness in the home, a serious lack of adequate parenting, worrying exposure to those engaged in sexual exploitation and possible sexual abuse of the children. Reference was made to the earlier case of *Re S (Hospital Patient: Court's Jurisdiction)* [1996] Fam 1 and the court found that there was a serious justiciable issue in this case, which could be dealt with under the common law doctrine of necessity. In response to argument that the court did not have jurisdiction to act, Butler-Sloss LJ noted:

> There is an obvious gap in the framework of care for mentally incapacitated adults. If the court cannot act and the local authority case is correct, this vulner-able young woman would be left at serious risk with no recourse to protection, other than the future possibility of the criminal law. That is a serious injustice to T, who has rights which she is unable, herself, to protect.[47]

The court was prepared to go beyond the local authority application for T to reside in local authority accommodation and was also prepared to sanction 'the use of such physical restriction as may be needed to keep T there and out of harm's way'.[48]

Newham London Borough Council v S (Adult: Court's Jurisdiction) [2003] EWHC 1909 (Fam) is a further example of a case instigated by the local authority. The facts concerned a 33-year-old woman with a moderate to severe learning disability. She was cared for by her parents in the family home, until 1995 when, following her mother's death, she was cared for by her father with support from care assistants. Newham sought a declaration that it would be lawful for them to remove S from the family home, place her in specialist residential accommodation and restrict access between her and her father, following an allegation that the father had punched her in the face and that he had a drink problem. As in other reported cases a declaration was the only legal avenue open to the council, as S did not fit the cri-teria for guardianship under the Mental Health Act 1983. It was agreed that S did not have the capacity to decide for herself where she should live and who should care for her.

In cases where a declaration is sought the court described the decision-making process in terms of 'four essential building blocks', i.e:

■ Is mental incapacity established?

■ Is there a serious justiciable issue relating to welfare?

■ What is it?

■ With welfare of the incapable adult as the court's paramount consideration, what are the balance sheet factors which must be drawn up to decide which course of action is in her best interests?

The court found that the factors against the authority's application were the father's love and sense of duty towards S and the fact that he had cared adequately for her since his wife's death. In favour of the application the court noted the relevance of the father's age and health, which meant his ability to care would diminish; contact with siblings which had ceased due to a rift between the father and his other children could resume if S were accommodated by Newham; the accommodation proposed was purpose-built for S and would enable her to socialise with people of her own age; independent evidence of a consultant psychiatrist supported Newham's plan as the best way of meeting her needs.

The allegations against the father were not substantiated. The court, however, rejected the father's argument that a 'significant harm' threshold needed to be satisfied (analogous to that in the Children Act 1989) before Newham could intervene. The court stated that, as long as the adult concerned lacked the capacity to make decisions about future care and there was a serious justiciable issue requiring resolution, the court's inherent jurisdiction was available to it. This case demonstrates a further extension of the court's willingness to invoke its jurisdiction, beyond cases where there is a significant risk of harm to the individual to scenarios where alternative arrangements are weighed to determine that which meets the best interests of the individual.

The use of High Court declarations as illustrated above is likely to be relatively short-lived, as the new framework provided by the Mental Capacity Act 2005 provides for the new Court of Protection to make declarations about single issues and appoint deputies to have a continuing decision making role. This is discussed in full in Chapter 16. Nevertheless, the reasoning adopted in these cases is likely to be followed by the Court of Protection if faced with similar issues.

■ Criminal law

In contrast to the United States, there is no specific offence of adult or elder abuse in the United Kingdom. An exception to this statement has been introduced by the Mental Capacity Act 2005 in relation to adults lacking capacity, and is discussed below. Abuse may nevertheless encompass behaviour that constitutes a criminal offence under common law and statute, such as assault, actual or grievous bodily harm, indecent assault, rape and theft. Reservations have been expressed questioning the appropriateness of applying the criminal law to elder abuse cases, particularly where family members are included. Williams argues that use of the word 'abuse' can undermine the impact of the act, which in other circumstances would clearly be seen as crimes.[49] However, Hugman suggests that, given the complexity and sensitivity of some abuse situations, where it may not be clear who the 'victim' is, criminalising all abusive acts is inappropriate.[50]

Increasingly, inter-agency guidelines will involve the police and provide for some level of joint investigation of elder abuse by the police and social services. Where there is a criminal investigation by the police, this will take priority over all other lines of enquiry. Early involvement of the police can have a number of benefits, including preservation of evidence and avoidance of multiple interviews of the victim.[51] Initially, to start the process it is normally necessary for the victim to make a complaint and be willing to press charges. Ultimately, the decision whether to bring a criminal prosecution rests with the Crown Prosecution Service, who must be satisfied that to prosecute is in the public interest and that there is a good prospect of conviction. Evidential difficulties, including the high standard of proof required, the fact that there will often be no witnesses to abuse and the perceived inability of adults with learning difficulties or older individuals, who may be mentally or physically frail, to give evidence, may influence the decision not to proceed. Encouragingly, the Youth Justice and Criminal Evidence Act 1999[52] introduces provision of *special measures* to assist 'vulnerable witnesses', including use of video-recorded evidence, intermediaries and the presence of a 'supporter' when a vulnerable witness is interviewed. Other practical steps, which can make giving evidence a less stressful experience, include court familiarisation, use of screens and the removal of wigs by judges and barristers.[53] In addition, extension of the role of the appropriate adult to situations where a vulnerable adult is being interviewed as a victim or possible witness, rather than as a suspect, has been suggested.[54] These provisions are discussed in more depth in Chapter 18. It is important not to deny the criminal route to vulnerable adults if they are willing to become involved in the criminal process, which serves to position acts of abuse as unacceptable criminal behaviour. 'No Secrets' clearly recognises this position:

> Some instances of abuse will constitute a criminal offence. In this respect vulnerable adults are entitled to the protection of law in the same way as any other member of the public. (2.8)

A Mencap study, in 1997, examined how the criminal justice system treats people with learning disabilities.[55] The findings present an overwhelming call for training for police, CPS, barristers, judges and magistrates. The study reports two major obstacles preventing people with learning disability from receiving justice. First, there is a reluctance to acknowledge crimes where people with learning disability are affected. This point echoes Williams' concerns that use of the term 'abuse' where a person with learning disabilities is concerned diminishes both the act in question and expectation of the consequences. This situation may be compounded by the fact that the victim may not realise a crime has been committed and is dependent on others to report it. This leads to the second point, that there is a significant lack of awareness about learning disability within the legal system. As a result, a learning disability may not be recognised or may be confused with mental illness.

Sexual abuse

The Sexual Offences Act 1956 provided specific designated sexual offences, which address sexual behaviour with an adult with learning disabilities, referred to in the act as a 'defective' where that adult is deemed incapable of giving consent.

The law on sexual offences has been the subject of major review and law reform. The terms of reference of the review of sex offences were to make recommendations, which would: provide clear and coherent sex offences to protect individuals, especially children and the more vulnerable, from abuse and exploitation; enable abusers to be appropriately punished; and be fair and non-discriminatory. The new legislation, the Sexual Offences Act 2003 (**SOA** 2003) replaces the Sexual Offences Act 1956. It is a complex piece of legislation, which covers sexual offences generally, including offences against children, adults whose capacity is impaired and familial sexual offences (incest). Under the new legislation all offences (rape excepted) are gender neutral, unless there is good reason to provide otherwise, so that a female carer who sexually abuses will also be culpable.

The Act includes a statutory definition of consent so that 'free agreement' to sexual relations becomes a prerequisite, and a broad definition of 'sexual activity'. There are particular offences against persons with a mental disorder which can be grouped into three categories – thankfully the old term 'defective' does not feature in the new law. Sections 30–33 cover offences against people who cannot legally consent to sexual activity because of a mental disorder impeding choice, i.e. because of the mental disorder he is likely to be unable to refuse. A person is unable to refuse if he lacks the capacity to choose whether to agree to engaging in the activity (whether because he lacks sufficient understanding of the nature or reasonably foreseeable consequences of the activity, or for any other reason), or he is unable to communicate such a choice.

Sections 34–37 cover offences against people who may or may not be able to consent to sexual activity but who are vulnerable to inducements, threats or deceptions because of a mental disorder. In such cases the person may appear to have agreed but consent cannot be deemed to have been given freely, because of inducements, threats or deceptions, e.g. telling the person that sex is an expected part of friendship or threatening to hurt family members. The new statutory scheme is not intended to interfere with the right to a sexual life of people who have capacity to consent, as the Guidance to the Act reminds: 'It is important to appreciate that where a person with a mental disorder is able to consent freely to sexual activity, they have the same rights to engage in sexual activity as anyone else.'

Care worker offences (breach of relationship to care) are the third category of offences against people with a mental disorder introduced by the Act. Where a care worker who has face-to-face contact through employment (which includes unpaid work) in a care home, NHS body or independent health setting engages in sexual activity with a person with a mental disorder, an offence is committed. The offences would prohibit relations between patients with a mental disorder and staff; residents and staff; persons receiving care in the community services and the care providers; doctors, therapists and their clients. Finally, a new offence of 'voyeurism' is proposed. Where a person in a building has a reasonable expectation of privacy and is observed without their consent or knowledge, this would amount to an offence and could be relevant in the residential sector. The existence of these special offences in relation to mental disorder of the victim do not preclude use of other general offences, such as rape, and it will be for the police and CPS to determine the most appropriate offence to charge.

In addition, under the Crime Sentences Act 1997, automatic life sentences will be imposed for anyone convicted of a second serious sexual offence.

Crime and disorder

Recent developments in the criminal law, which may impact on adult protection, have included certain provisions of the Crime and Disorder Act 1998, such as the introduction of sex offender orders. The anti-social behaviour order is outlined in the context of youth justice in Chapter 13. It is an order that may also be relevant to the abuse of vulnerable adults, particularly since stranger abuse has gained formal recognition in 'No Secrets'.[56] Anyone over the age of 10 may be the subject of an application by a council, Housing Action Trust or the police. An order may be made where a person has acted in an anti-social manner and it is necessary to protect persons living in the local government area from further anti-social acts. Anti-social behaviour is that which causes harassment, alarm or distress to people of another household. It is a civil order of not less than two years' duration, intended to deal with criminal or sub-criminal activity, to restrain anti-social behaviour which other individuals cannot be expected to tolerate. The scenario where a gang of youths are bullying and frightening older people or adults with learning disabilities would be an appropriate case for an order. Breach of the order is a criminal offence. Adult protection can be see as an aspect of community safety, a key focus of the Crime and Disorder Act, and addressed in partnership working between the police and local authorities via crime reduction and community safety strategies.

Harassment

The Protection from Harassment Act 1997 contains a number of harassment offences of possible application in certain adult abuse scenarios, particularly stranger abuse.[57] It is a piece of legislation that has a much broader remit than adult protection and which was not produced with a focus on adult protection. A general awareness of the Act will be useful as part of the law which may apply to a range of service users (and could also be relevant where a professional suffers harassment in the course of employment). The offences included in the Act are: knowingly harassing another person; pursuing a course of conduct amounting to harassment (summary offence); engaging in a course of conduct (at least two occasions) which causes the person to fear violence (either way offence). An offence will be committed if the person knew or ought to have known that his course of conduct would cause the person to fear violence. A course of conduct can include speech. In *R v. Director of Public Prosecutions* [2001] EWHC Admin 17 a 17-year-old youth was convicted for harassing the complainant and her family, all of whom are described in the law report as physically disadvantaged. Evidence was given relating to two incidents: first, where he had a knife and said 'I'm going to slash your . . . throat' and, secondly, where he said he would 'blow the . . . dog's brains out'. The defendant received a four-month detention and training order.

A restraining order (s. 5) prohibiting any specified action to prevent further harassment can be made by the court in addition to sentence. An example might be a restriction on contacting someone by telephone or letter or approaching within a specified area around a person's home or place of work. It is possible for a restraining order to be imposed without limit. The Court of Appeal provided some guidance on appropriate sentences in harassment cases in *R* v. *Liddle; R* v. *Hayes* [1999] 3 All ER 816. The court should consider the level of offence, seriousness of the conduct, the effect of the conduct on the victim and the victim's family, whether it was necessary to provide protection and whether the defendant expressed remorse and was prepared to undergo treatment or receive help.

■ Domestic Violence, Crime and Victims Act 2004

The Domestic Violence, Crime and Victims Act 2004 aims to tackle domestic violence and improve victim protection through reform of civil and criminal law. Strengthening of domestic violence is relevant to adult protection, but of particular importance for adult protection the act introduces a new offence of familial homicide and establishes domestic homicide reviews.

The new criminal offence, causing or allowing the death of a child or vulnerable adult (familial homicide), was introduced against a context of cases where a child had died as a result of abuse but it was not possible clearly to identify and therefore prosecute the perpetrator. At the same time, Action on Elder Abuse campaigned for vulnerable adults as well as children to be included in the ambit of the legislation.

The offence is punishable by up to 14 years' imprisonment, which places it at the higher end of the tariff, positioning both adult and child abuse as serious offences, and is likely to be used in the alternative to murder and manslaughter. Elements of the offence are that the vulnerable adult dies as a result of an unlawful act of a person who was a member of the same household, and who had frequent contact with him. The death must have either been caused by the defendant, or he was aware of the risk of harm and failed to take reasonable steps to protect the vulnerable adult. What constitutes 'reasonable steps' will depend on the person's circumstances and their relationship to the victim. Death must occur where there is an anticipated risk, for example where there is a history of violence or neglect and would not include accidents. The offence refers to death resulting from an 'unlawful act'. This term includes commission and omissions and therefore includes neglect. 'Vulnerable adult' in this Act means a person aged 16 or over whose ability to protect himself from violence, abuse or neglect is significantly impaired through physical or mental disability or illness, through old age or otherwise (s. 5(6)). This is a different definition from those contained in 'No Secrets' and in the Care Standards Act 2000.

Domestic homicide reviews (s. 9) are to take place where a person aged 16 or over dies as a result of violence, abuse or neglect from a person to whom he was related or with whom he was (or had been) in an intimate relationship, or someone of the same household. The multi-agency reviews are to be held with a view to identifying lessons to be learnt from the death. This will place on a statutory footing the 'serious case reviews' that some authorities already hold through their adult protection committees.

■ Mental Capacity Act 2005

The Act (expected to came into in force by 2007) introduces a new offence. A person is guilty of an offence if he has the care of a person who lacks capacity or is reasonably believed to lack capacity, or is the donee of a LPA or a deputy, and he ill-treats or wilfully neglects the person. The offence is classified as an 'either way offence' (it may be prosecuted in the magistrates' or Crown Court), and carries a maximum sentence of five years' imprisonment.

Compensation

Even if a criminal prosecution does not proceed, the criminal injuries compensation scheme may provide financial compensation. Payments may be made to those who have suffered personal injury directly attributable to a crime of violence (this term includes sexual abuse). (This scheme is discussed in more detail in Chapter 18.)

■ Mental Health Act 1983

In limited circumstances, the Mental Health Act 1983 may be utilised in respect of the victim or the perpetrator of abuse. An approved social worker has powers to enter premises in which a mentally disordered patient is living, if there is reasonable cause to believe the patient is not under proper care (s. 115). Further, under s. 135, where a person suffering from a mental disorder is being ill treated, neglected or kept otherwise than under proper control, or is living alone and unable to care for himself, a magistrate may issue a warrant authorising a police officer to enter premises, by force if necessary, and remove him to a place of safety for up to 72 hours. These short-term powers as part of an investigation may provide for an assessment of a situation causing concern, particularly if access is being denied.

Section 127 makes it an offence for a professional member of staff of a hospital or mental nursing home to ill treat or wilfully neglect a patient, subject to his guardianship or otherwise in his custody or care (whether by virtue of any legal or moral obligation or otherwise). The phrase in brackets would encompass almost any arrangement for care of a mentally disordered patient. The Director of Public Prosecutions must give consent before a prosecution can proceed and it appears that this section has been little used. The new offence introduced by the Mental Capacity Act 2005 is likely to supersede this offence.

It must be stressed that the definitions of mental disorder under the Act will restrict application of these powers to a limited proportion of vulnerable adults. The proposed reform of mental health law is considered in Chapter 15.

■ Removal from home: National Assistance Act 1948, s. 47

In exceptional circumstances an adult may be compulsorily removed from their home against their will. The National Assistance Act 1948, s. 47 provides this authority and is a provision which may be utilised in adult protection cases:

s. 47

> . . . for the purposes of securing the necessary care and attention for persons who –
> (a)   are suffering from grave chronic disease or, being aged, infirm or physically incapacitated, are living in insanitary conditions, and
> (b)   are unable to devote to themselves, and are not receiving from other persons, proper care and attention
> . . . in the interests of any such person . . . , or for preventing injury to the health of, or serious nuisance to, other persons, it is necessary to remove any such person . . .
>
> (NAA 1948)

If these criteria are satisfied, the provision authorises removal of the individual and detention in a suitable place for up to three months. This period may be extended further. Application is by the community physician to magistrates, who have been described by Hoggett as adopting a rubber-stamp approach to applications.[58] In more urgent cases it is possible for an application to be made to a single magistrate without notice to the subject for detention for a period of three weeks.[59]

A number of difficulties with the provision have been identified. Some may be attributable to the continued existence of a provision that was introduced in a different social climate when there was no concept of 'community care', as we know it, and considerably fewer very elderly people. Research indicates that there are between 100 and 200 cases a year. These figures have to be drawn from independent research, as central records are not held. Little or no administrative guidance has been given to interpretation of the section and applications are based on the individual judgement of the proper officer (the community physician). The wording of the section is ambiguous, over inclusive and open to broad interpretation, e.g. how old, how infirm? The section hints at neglect and in reality the majority of cases where it is used are based on situations of neglect of elderly people: Forster and Tiplady found that 43 per cent of cases of removal were because of self-neglect and 46 per cent of requests came from family doctors.[60] It is important to remember the principle that intervention should be a positive benefit and not place an individual in a different but worse situation. The significance of 'relocation effect' should not be underestimated. Forster and Tiplady found that, in Bradford, 91 per cent of people in their study died within one year of removal.[61]

From a civil liberties perspective, the section has obvious deficiencies. Legal Aid is not available to the subject. No appeals procedure or review tribunal exists. It is not even possible to make an application to revoke the order until six weeks of the detention period have elapsed. As is clear from the section, there is no requirement of any mental disorder/illness. Arguably, the ethical implications of s. 47 are thus even more disturbing than some MHA 1983 issues, as the individual concerned may have full control of their mental faculties. There is a suggestion that s. 47 applications are used for administrative convenience and, in some instances, that it is used defensively by professionals. In a climate of high criticism of social welfare professionals this is perhaps unsurprising; but of greater concern is the lack of a viable alternative. Ethical justifiability of the section has been widely questioned because of its paternalistic stance. As removal may be justified by reference to the benefit of other persons, it is clearly a provision that favours paternalism over personal autonomy without resolving the conflict between these positions.

It could be argued that s. 47 of the National Assistance Act 1948 breaches ECHR, Art. 6, the right to a fair trial: there is no provision for Legal Aid for representation; under the accelerated procedure removal may be ordered *ex parte;* and it is only possible to apply for the order to be revoked after a period of six weeks. In addition, it authorises a restriction of liberty contrary to ECHR, Art. 5, which is not covered by the lawful exceptions.

Chapter summary

- Adult protection is a relatively new area of social work practice. Concerns relating to possible abuse of vulnerable adults – which may include people with learning or physical disabilities, people with mental health problems and older people – are increasingly coming to the attention of social services and must be addressed.

- There is no clear legal framework that recognises adult protection or mandates practice. In the absence of a statutory duty to investigate, social services are nevertheless recognised as the lead agency with responsibility for adult abuse cases, under important guidance entitled 'No Secrets', which directs local authorities to draw up policies to respond to adult abuse.

- The main types of abuse are physical, sexual, psychological, financial neglect and discriminatory abuse.

- Existing law may be utilised to respond to concerns at three levels: prevention, action by the victim and formal intervention. In each case, respect for the autonomy of the adult is essential and any intervention should present a positive improvement of the situation.

- Prevention may include input of services to a vulnerable adult and support for carers. It can take the form of regulation of sectors of provision, notably residential settings; prohibition of unsuitable adults working with vulnerable adults; and mechanisms to delegate responsibility for an individual's financial and property affairs, particularly important where that person lacks mental capacity.

- The victim of abuse may take action themselves via domestic violence provisions in the Family Law Act 1996, the law of tort and the law of contract. An individual may require support for this and, if lacking mental capacity, a 'litigation friend' may be appointed.

- Formal intervention may be manifest through declaratory relief, criminal prosecution, use of the Mental Health Act 1983 or removal of the victim under the National Assistance Act 1948, s. 47.

- The Domestic Violence Crime and Victims Act 2004 introduces a new offence of causing or allowing the death of a vulnerable adult, and requires domestic homicide reviews to be held following the death of an adult as a result of violence, abuse or neglect from a relative or with whom he was (or had been) in an intimate relationship, or someone of the same household

Exercises

1. Albert is 82. He lives alone, but has a niece, Diana, who stays with him sporadically. She is an alcohol abuser. Diana collects Albert's pension for him but does not provide any other care. Albert has been physically fit until very recently, when arthritis in his hip has prevented him from walking far. His memory is poor and he is becoming increasingly disorientated. He sometimes gets lost and has mislaid keys and money. He was recently admitted to hospital with burns to his legs from sitting too close to the fire. Albert has unexplained bruising to his chest and upper arms; he spends time talking to a photograph of his daughter, assuming her to be his deceased wife, and has become aggressive towards his son-in-law. His relatives find it difficult to provide support for Albert, and do not approve of his relationship with Diana and their drinking sessions. He refuses to consider domiciliary or residential care.

    Albert often leaves the house unlocked, will let anyone in and has had some possessions stolen. He refuses to throw away rubbish or rotten food, which is piling up at the back of the house. He has a dog, which he can no longer exercise. His capacity for self-care (continence and diet) is decreasing. There is growing concern about his health and conditions in the home.

    What steps should social services take in this scenario?

2. Joe wants to complain about the way his cousin Lucy is being cared for at a residential care home for adults with learning disabilities. Lucy is 19 years old. On his last visit, Lucy told Joe that one of the care assistants is always rough with her and showed him bruising to her wrists. She also said she had been tied to her chair for several hours one day after she refused to eat any lunch. A member of staff told Joe that Lucy has been exhibiting extremely challenging behaviour lately and they have needed to become 'strict' with her, but denied any restraint. Joe explains that he would like to make a complaint and is told that the complaints procedures for the home are under review as they have an inspection looming.

Joe visits again the following week and finds that Lucy is sharing a room with an 82-year-old woman. There are cot sides on both beds in the room. He notices that the woman appears to be having difficulty focusing and is very sleepy; Lucy told him that earlier that day she fell asleep during her lunch. The manager of the home tells Joe that Lucy is only sharing the room temporarily whilst her room is being decorated. When questioned about the bruises on Lucy's wrists, the manager tells Joe that Lucy is very uncooperative at times and staff occasionally have to hold her by the wrist when walking to and from lunch. She tells Joe that he is welcome to check this with social services but will find that practice is the same in all local homes for adults with learning disabilities.

How would social services respond if contacted by Joe?

Websites

The Action on Elder Abuse site provides useful resources on elder abuse (the organisation also runs a telephone helpline):
www.elderabuse.org

Practitioner Alliance against Abuse of Vulnerable Adults:
www.pavauk.org.uk

Counsel and Care – provides advice and help for older people, with a particular focus on residential accommodation:
www.counselandcare.org.uk

VOICE UK is an organisation which supports people with learning disabilities who have experienced crime or abuse, their families and carers and campaigns for changes in law and practice:
www.voiceuk.org.uk

Services to people with learning disabilities who have experienced sexual abuse:
www.respond.org.uk

The Care Standards Tribunal website contains case reports detailing circumstances which have led to cancellation or refusal of registration of care homes:
www.carestandards.gov.uk

Further reading

The *Journal of Adult Protection* provides up-to-date coverage of adult protection issues incorporating policy, research, practice developments and law.

Department of Health (2000) 'No Secrets: Guidance on developing and implementing multi-agency policies and procedures to protect vulnerable adults from abuse'. London: Department of Health. (The key guidance in this area.)

ADSS (2005) 'Safeguarding Adults: A National framework of Standards for good practice and outcomes in adult protection work'. London: ADSS. (A guide for best practice drawing on experience since implementation of 'No Secrets'.)

Pritchard, J. (2001) (ed.) *Good Practice with Vulnerable Adults*. London: Jessica Kingsley Publishers. (A useful collection of essays.)

Particular types of abuse and appropriate responses are addressed in:

Action on Elder Abuse (1999) (Working Paper No. 4) 'Bags of money – the financial abuse of older people'. London: Action on Elder Abuse.

Jeary, K. (2004) 'Sexual abuse of elderly people: would we rather not know the details? 6 *Journal of Adult Protection* p. 21.

Perry, J. (2002) *Opening the gateways? People with Learning Difficulties and Partnership Action against Hate Crime*. London: Values into Action.

Williams, J. (2002) 'Public law protection of vulnerable adults: the debate continues, so does the abuse' 2(3) *Journal of Social Work* p. 293.

Comparisons with child protection are analysed in:

Stevenson, O. (1996) *Elder Protection in the Community: What can we Learn from Child Protection?* London: Age Concern Institute of Gerontology.

Stevenson, O. (1999) *Elder Protection in Residential Care: What can we Learn from Child Protection?* London: Age Concern Institute of Gerontology.

Notes

1 Department of Health (2000) 'No Secrets: Guidance on developing and implementing multi-agency policies and procedures to protect vulnerable adults from abuse'. London: Department of Health (hereafter 'No Secrets').

2 A. Baker (1975) 'Granny Bashing' 5(8) *Modern Geriatrics* p. 20.

3 M. Eastman (1984) *Old Age Abuse*. London: Age Concern.

4 H. Brown, J. Stein and V. Turk (1995) 'The sexual abuse of adults with learning disabilities: report of a second two-year incidence study' 8(1) *Mental Handicap Research* p. 3.

5 ADSS (2005) *Safeguarding Adults: A National framework of Standards for good practice and outcomes in adult protection work*. London: ADSS, p. 4.

6. P. Kingston and B. Penhale (1995) *Family Violence and the Caring Professions*. Basingstoke: Macmillan.

7 See further M. Preston-Shoot (2001) 'Evaluating self-determination: an adult protection case study' 3(1) *Journal of Adult Protection* p. 4.

8 See further A. Brammer (2000) 'Human Rights Act 1998: implications for adult protection' 3(1) *Journal of Adult Protection* p. 43.

9 O. Stevenson (1995) 'Abuse of older people: principles of intervention' in Department of Health and Social Services Inspectorate *Abuse of Older People in Domestic Settings: A report on two SSI seminars*. London: HMSO.

10 See O. Stevenson (1996) *Elder Protection in the Community: What can we Learn from Child Protection?* London: Age Concern Institute of Gerontology; and O. Stevenson (1999) *Elder Protection in Residential Care: What can we Learn from Child Protection?* London: Age Concern Institute of Gerontology.

11 See discussion in, A. Brammer and S. Biggs (1998) 'Defining elder abuse' 20(3) *Journal of Social Welfare and Family Law* p. 285.

12 Department of Health and Social Services Inspectorate (1996) 'No Longer Afraid: the safeguard of older people in domestic settings'. London: HMSO.

13 For a full discussion of a range of definitions, see A. Brammer and S. Biggs (1998) 'Defining elder abuse' 20(3) *Journal of Social Welfare and Family Law* p. 285.

14 'No Secrets', para. 2.7.

15 Action on Elder Abuse (2000) (Working Paper No. 5) 'The great taboo – sexual abuse of older people'. London: Action on Elder Abuse.

16 K. Jeary (2004) 'Sexual abuse of elderly people: would we rather not know the details?' 6 *Journal of Adult Protection* p. 21.

17 'No Secrets', para. 2.10.

18 J. Ogg and G. Bennett (1992) 'Elder abuse in Britain' 305 *British Medical Journal* pp. 998–9.

19 K. Pillemer and D. Finkelhor (1988) 'The prevalence of elder abuse: a random sample survey' 28(1) *The Gerontologist* pp. 51–7.

20 Action on Elder Abuse (2004) *Hidden Voices: Older People's Experience of Abuse.* London: Help the Aged.

21 Law Commission (1995) *Mental Incapacity* (Law Com. No. 231). London: HMSO.

22 D. Mathew, H. Brown, P. Kingston, C. McCreadie and J. Askham (2002) 'The response to No Secrets', 4(1) *Journal of Adult Protection* p. 4.

23 ADSS (2005) *Safeguarding Adults: A National framework of Standards for good practice and outcomes in adult protection work.* London: ADSS.

24 'No Secrets', para. 6.13.

25 'No Secrets', para. 3.3.

26 M. Linnett (2000) 'Chronicling care and registering concern: the use of an at-risk register for vulnerable adults' *Journal of Adult Protection* 2(4) p. 33.

27 Law Commission (1995) *Mental Incapacity* (Law Com. No. 231). London: HMSO, p. 26.

28 Griffiths *et al.* (1993) in P. Kingston and B. Penhale (1995) *Family Violence and the Caring Professions.* Basingstoke: Palgrave, pp. 198–9.

29 The scheme is administered by the DfES on behalf of the DoH.

30 Department of Health (2001) *Care Homes for Older People: National Minimum Standards.* London: The Stationery Office.

31 Financial abuse may also be described as financial or material exploitation, fiduciary, material or economic abuse.

32 Enduring Powers of Attorney Act 1985.

33 The Public Guardianship Office was known as the Public Trust Office until April 2001.

34 D. Lush (2001) 'The Court of Protection' in L.-A. Cull and J. Roche (eds) *The Law and Social Work: Contemporary Issues for Practice.* Basingstoke: Palgrave.

35 In force from 1 April 2002.

36 J. Stein and H. Brown (2001) 'Crossing the divide: the role of inspection units in protecting vulnerable adults' 3(1) *Journal of Adult Protection* pp. 25–34.

37 S1 2001/3965.

38 Care Homes Regulations 2001 (SI 2001/3965), reg. 37.

39 'No Secrets', para. 6.37.

40 Reports from the Care Standards Tribunal, previously Registered Homes Tribunal provide numerous examples of types of abuse occurring in residential homes, which have prompted the registration authority to take action. Reports can be accessed from the tribunal website (listed above) and see analysis in A. Brammer (1994) 'The Registered Homes Act 1984: safeguarding the elderly?' 4 *Journal of Social Welfare and Family Law* p. 423; and A. Brammer (1999) 'A fit person to run a home: registered homes tribunal interpretations of the 'fit person' concept in the United Kingdom' 10(1/2) *Journal of Elder Abuse and Neglect* p. 119.

41 See L. Bright (2001) 'Restraint: cause for continuing concern?' 3(2) *Journal of Adult Protection* p. 42; and A. Clarke and L. Bright (2002) *Showing restraint: challenging the use of restraint in care homes*. London: Counsel and Care.

42 Essex was the placing authority and Northamptonshire was the registration authority.

43 HO 60/1990.

44 For a full discussion of the arguments, see M. Burton (2003) 'Third party applications for protection orders in England and Wales: service provider's views on implementing Section 60 of the Family Law Act 1996. 25(2) *Journal of Social Welfare and Family Law* p. 137.

45 Counsel and Care (1992) *What if they hurt themselves*. London: Counsel and Care.

46 R. Bradshaw (2000) 'Preventing abuse of vulnerable adults' 2(1) *Journal of Adult Protection* p. 35. Concerns led to production of new guidance to practitioners: UKCC (1999) 'Practitioner–client relationships and the prevention of abuse'. London: UKCC.

47 [2000] 3 WLR 1740 at p. 1750H.

48 Ibid, p. 1756C.

49 C. Williams (1993) 'Vulnerable victims? Current awareness of the victimisation of people with learning disabilities' 8(2) *Disability, Handicap and Society* p. 161.

50 R. Hugman (1994) 'Social work and case management in the UK: models of professionalism and elderly people' 14 *Ageing and Society* p. 237 and R. Hugman (1995) 'The implications of the term "elder abuse" for problem definition and response in health and social welfare' 24(4) *Journal of Social Policy* p. 493.

51 'No Secrets', para. 6.7.

52 Based on recommendations of a Home Office Report, 'Speaking up for Justice'.

53 See Home Office (2002) 'Achieving Best Evidence in Criminal Proceedings: Guidance for Vulnerable and Intimidated Witnesses including Children'. London: The Stationery Office (a consultation paper).

54 J. Williams (2000) 'The inappropriate adult' 22(1) *Journal of Social Welfare and Family Law* p. 43.

55 Mencap (1997) 'Barriers to Justice'. London: Mencap.

56 'No Secrets', para. 2.10.

57 See: N. Addison and T. Lawson-Cruttendon (1998) *Harassment Law and Practice*. London: Blackstone Press.

58 B. Hoggett (1990) *Mental Health Law* (3rd edn). London: Sweet & Maxwell.

59 National Assistance Act 1951.

61 P. Nair and J. Mayberry (1995) 'The compulsory removal of elderly people in England and Wales under s. 47 of the National Assistance Act 1948' 24 *Age and Ageing* p. 180.

62 D.P. Forster and P. Tiplady (1980) 'Doctors and compulsory removal procedures: Section 47 of the National Assistance Act 1948' 1 *British Medical Journal* p. 739.

18 Criminal justice

Learning objectives

To develop an understanding of the following:

- The various constituents of the criminal justice system.
- The role of the social worker in the criminal justice system, including the 'appropriate adult'.
- The classification and elements of a criminal offence.
- An overview of the criminal process.
- Police powers as contained in PACE 1984.
- The range of sentences which may be ordered.
- Support for witnesses including 'special measures'.
- The scheme for state compensation for victims provided by the Criminal Injuries Compensation Authority.
- Recent reforms of the criminal justice system.

Introduction

Criminal justice is a highly politicised and complex area of law. Like youth justice, it has endured enormous policy changes driven by the agenda of whichever political party is in government. Recent years have seen an increasing commitment to get tough on crime, as evidenced by mandatory minimum sentences introduced in the Crime (Sentences) Act 1997. There is no specific Ministry of Criminal Justice; rather, responsibility for criminal justice cuts across the Home Office, the Department of Constitutional Affairs and the Crown Prosecution Service. The Office of Criminal Justice Reform, is a cross-department team to support criminal justice agencies reporting to the Home Office, the DCA and the Office of the Attorney-General.

The operation of the existing criminal justice system is certainly not without criticism. Some particular areas of reform may be prompted by the introduction of the Human Rights Act 1998 and its inevitable impact in increasing awareness of the rights of both victims and perpetrators of crime. It is also impossible to ignore the impact of miscarriages of justice and significant reports which have identified major failings in the system; notably, the Macpherson report,[1] which found institutionalised racism within the police.

Recent years have seen significant reforms and development across criminal justice. This has been achieved in large part through implementation of reforms proposed by the Halliday report[2] on sentencing matters and the Auld review of criminal courts.[3] Both the Halliday report and the Auld review were independent reports which must be viewed against the context of the earlier Government report, 'Criminal Justice: The Way Ahead'.[4] Certain of their proposals have been translated into legislation within provisions of the Criminal Justice Act 2003 and the Courts Act 2003.

The Criminal Justice Act 2003 provides for greater involvement of the Crown Prosecution Service in charging decisions, increases magistrates' sentencing powers and introduces a presumption against bail in some circumstances. It allows for judge alone trials in some cases and makes major changes to the sentencing framework. The various kinds of community orders (including community rehabilitation orders and community punishment orders) are replaced by a single community order with a range of attached requirements. A new Criminal Case Management Framework has also been introduced to facilitate active and efficient management of cases from pre-charge to conclusion. The impact of the measures introduced in the Crime and Disorder Act 1998 has also proved to be significant. As well as making new orders available, this Act blurs the line between civil and criminal responsibility: orders such as the anti-social behaviour order (ASBO), introduced as a civil order but with criminal sanctions for breach, will possibly draw more people into the criminal justice system. The Anti-social Behaviour Act 2003 extends this aspect of law.

Measuring the extent of crime accurately is always problematic. The British Crime Survey estimated that there were just over 10.8 million crimes against adults living in private households in 2004/5. This represents a 7 per cent fall in crimes compared with 2003/4. Fear of crime, however, may be as significant in influencing people's everyday behaviour as actual crime rates, e.g. choosing whether to walk alone after dark. The survey found that perceptions of the level of crime were still high, with 61 per cent of people believing crime in the country had increased in the previous two years – though this proportion is slightly lower than for 2003/4. Actual rates of crime have not increased as significantly as fear of crime.[5] Actual rates of crime recorded show a drop of 6 per cent in 2004/5 compared with 2003/4. The British Crime Survey, which is based on interviews and presents information on people's own experiences of crime, is now presented jointly with recorded crime figures, i.e. how many crimes are reported to the police to present a more accurate picture than could be obtained from either series alone.[6]

The focus in this chapter is on the criminal justice system as it affects adults, i.e. persons of 18 years and over. The criminal justice system relating to young offenders was considered in Chapter 13 and there are numerous areas of similarity and overlap. The chapter considers three broad areas: the machinery of the criminal justice system, the process of the criminal justice system and outcomes in the criminal justice system.

Machinery of the criminal justice system

■ Preventing crime and disorder

The Crime and Disorder Act 1998 (CDA 1998) introduced an important duty on local authorities.
   Section 17 provides:

s. 17

(1) Without prejudice to any other obligation imposed upon it, it shall be the duty of each authority . . . to exercise its functions with due regard to the likely effect of the exercise of those functions on, and the need to do all that it reasonably can to prevent, crime and disorder in its area.

(CDA 1998)

Local authorities, in cooperation with health authorities, probation committees, police and other agencies, are obliged to implement a strategy for tackling and preventing crime and disorder. This is no longer considered the sole responsibility of the police and it is recognised that a wide range of local authority responsibilities and functions may have an impact on local crime rates. Social workers and other professionals employed by local authorities in their various departments will need to be aware of community safety issues. Local authorities are expected to review all services, assessing crime and disorder implications of all aspects of work and develop a coherent plan for implementing the s. 17 duty. The duty is phrased in terms of the local authority doing all it reasonably can to prevent crime and disorder; however, it is unlikely that shortage of resources will be an acceptable reason for not acting. The impact of this section covers a diverse range of actions and responsibilities. For example, leisure departments may be expected to provide additional recreation to reduce boredom, which could lead to crime and disorder issues. Housing departments are expected to be particularly vigilant in relation to the anti-social behaviour of nuisance neighbours. Housing Action Trusts are now able to make applications for ASBOs directly. The risk of burglary and vandalism to a range of properties owned by a local authority, such as schools and libraries, may mean a greater emphasis on security measures, including CCTV cameras. Staff such as social workers who enter people's homes and may be at risk of violence could legitimately expect greater training to deal with conflict situations and perhaps the provision of mobile phones or pagers to call for assistance.

Social workers' responsibilities in the criminal justice system

Probation officers carry the vast area of social work within the adult criminal justice system, whilst local authority social workers are likely to have most responsibilities towards juveniles, as discussed in Chapter 13. Nevertheless, it is important that all social workers have an awareness of the elements and process of criminal justice. Service users to whom other responsibilities are owed may come into contact with the criminal justice system as victims, witnesses or offenders and the social worker may be asked about elements of the process. As the probation service is the main professional group working with adults in the criminal justice system, this chapter aims to give only a broad overview of the law. Reference to more in-depth texts is provided in further reading.

▪ Constituents of the criminal justice system

Police

It is the responsibility of the police to investigate crime and arrest and charge suspects. The decision whether to charge a suspect, and with what, was the sole responsibility of the police but under recent reforms has been invested in the Crown Prosecution Service. There are approximately 141,000 police officers in England and Wales, divided into 43 police forces, with a significant number of civilians, including traffic wardens, also employed by the service. In addition, the police are supported by 12,000 special constables (part-time volunteers) and 6,000 community support officers who have partial police powers and whose role focuses on community safety and deterring anti-social behaviour. In response to the recommendations of the Lawrence inquiry, police forces are taking steps to address diversity issues. The following examples are featured on the Home Office website:

- The Metropolitan Police encourage staff to register their knowledge and/or membership of a community, languages spoken, life-skills obtained as a result of ethnic origin, sexual orientation, race, religion and hobbies.
- The Greater Manchester Police have introduced a childcare voucher scheme to help staff balance work and childcare responsibilities.
- South Wales Police use gay officers to break down barriers between police and attendees at Cardiff's gay pride event.[7]

A Code of Practice on reporting and recording racist incidents was introduced in 2000 and the police are forbidden from membership of the British National Party, Combat 18 and the National Front, by the Police (Amendment) Regulations 2004.[8] Serious complaints against the police, including allegations of racism, are investigated independently by the Independent Police Complaints Commission (IPCC), established in 2004.

Crown Prosecution Service

The Crown Prosecution Service (**CPS**) was established under the Prosecution of Offences Act 1985 as an independent prosecution service. In essence, it is the Crown Prosecution Service's role to prosecute a person charged with a criminal offence. Within that role the Crown Prosecution Service will also assess whether sufficient evidence exists on which to charge a suspect, determine the appropriate charge, prepare cases for court and prosecute cases or instruct counsel to prosecute.

A Code for Crown Prosecutors[9] provides guidance on general principles to be applied to ensure fair and consistent decision-making. The fifth edition of the code was introduced in 2004[10] and recognises that the CPS is a public authority within the meaning of the Human Rights Act 1998. The key element of the code is the two-part test for prosecution: first, there must be sufficient evidence to provide a realistic prospect of conviction; and, secondly, that a prosecution is in the public interest. The code lists public interest factors in favour of prosecution. One important factor is where an offence involves racial, sexual or any other form of discrimination or hostility towards a victim based on his membership of a particular section of society. Other factors include the presence of a child at the scene of the crime and the impact of the crime on community confidence. The code is a public document and is currently produced in 14 languages.

In addition to the Crown Prosecution Service, a range of other public bodies may prosecute particular criminal offences. For example, environmental health departments regularly bring prosecutions in respect of food health offences in the restaurant trade, and there is a special body, the Serious Fraud Office, which prosecutes the most complex fraud cases.

Criminal Defence Service

A new Criminal Defence Service (**CDS**) was introduced in 2001 as part of the Legal Services Commission, to replace the Legal Aid scheme. Defence services are provided by salaried defenders and private practitioners for people involved in criminal investigations and proceedings.[11] A defendant will apply to the court for a right to representation when he wishes to be represented at public expense and must satisfy the interests of justice test before the request can be granted. The order is known as a representation order and any solicitor the defendant wishes to act for him must have in place a contract (a franchise) with the Legal Services Commission. The role of Citizens' Advice Bureaux, Law Centres and the provision of legal advice and assistance is covered in Chapter 3.

National Probation Service

The National Probation Service is defined as 'a law enforcement agency delivering community punishments, supervising and working with offenders within the terms set by the court or parole board in ways that help offenders to reduce their re-offending and better protect the public'.[12] The aims of the National Probation Service are set out as: protecting the public; reducing reoffending; proper punishment of offenders in the community; ensuring offenders' awareness of the effects of crime on victims of crime and the public; and rehabilitation of offenders.

The probation service carries out most social work functions within the criminal justice system, yet the above definition suggests something of a departure from the social work basis of probation, where the emphasis was traditionally framed in terms of advising, assisting and befriending. Their most important role is supervising offenders in the community (as supervising officers). The service is responsible for implementing community sentences and will provide supervision when the offender is on licence, having been released from prison. Each year the service takes on supervision of around 225,000 offenders. If a pre-sentence report is required, this is prepared by the probation service. Guidance on the contents of pre-sentence reports is contained in 'National Standards for Supervision of Offenders in the Community 2000'(revised in 2002). The service also provides bail information reports and risk and dangerousness assessments for parole and lifer review boards.

Probation officers may specialise in court-based work, prison-based work, or civil work, through care for prisoners and families and work in probation hostels. The probation service has undergone significant changes over recent years and is now part of a new body, the National Offender Management Service, which draws together the work of correctional services.[13] The prison service is also included. The new integrated service has a focus on 'end to end' management of offenders, and a target to reduce reoffending by 5 per cent by 2007/8.[14]

The probation service has also had a civil role in providing reports to the court in family proceedings as part of the Court Welfare Service. For these purposes work is allocated to officers of CAFCASS, the body which amalgamated the work of children's guardians, officers of the Official Solicitors Department and the Court Welfare Service (and may include some probation officers).

Prison service

There are approximately 77,000 people in custody: this is one of the highest prison population rates in Europe and some prisons are overcrowded, the prison population being 112 per cent of the certified normal accommodation. About 20 per cent of prisoners at any one time are on remand. In 2004–5 the number of remand prisoners increased by 13 per cent and young adults by 4 per cent. There are 139 prisons in England and Wales, divided into a variety of types, including remand centres, high security prisons, open prisons, dispersal prisons, female prisons and young offender institutions.

The prison service, as part of the National Offender Management Service, is responsible for the operation of the prison system, including prisons run by private companies such as Group 4. There is an Inspectorate of Prisons, which produces regular reports from scheduled and unannounced visits to prisons. Each prison has a Board of Visitors, which has a role in deciding offenders' disciplinary offences. Prisoners have different category status ranging from unsentenced prisoners held on remand through to Category A dangerous prisoners.

Courts

The courts which deal with criminal cases are the magistrates' court, Crown Court, Divisional Court, Court of Appeal (Criminal Division) and House of Lords. The characteristics of each court are described in Chapter 3. The Courts Act 2003 established a new executive agency, Her Majesty's Court Service, which brought together the Court Service (responsible for the Supreme Court) county courts and the Magistrates Courts Service into one organisation.

The witness service

The witness service, operated by the National Association of Victim Support Schemes, is a confidential and free service provided by a paid coordinator and teams of volunteers, operating from Crown Courts and magistrates' courts. The service can offer support to prosecution witnesses, victims and their family and friends, professionals accompanying victims and defence witnesses. This may include familiarisation visits to court, waiting areas, someone to accompany a witness to court, preparation for the outcomes of cases and practical help, e.g. with expense forms or referral onwards for further help.

Process of the criminal justice system

An offence may be defined by statute, e.g. theft, or it may have its origin in the common law, e.g. murder. Every offence is comprised of two elements, both of which must be proven. The actual commission of the offence, e.g. firing the gun which shoots another person, is known as the *actus reus*. It must be accompanied by the *mens rea*, which is the mental element, the criminal intent – sometimes referred to as the guilty mind. There are different levels of *mens rea*. Intent is required in most cases but there are also a range of offences which may be committed where the person is reckless as to the consequences of his actions. A group of offences exist which are classified as strict liability, where no *mens rea* is required. The commission of the act is sufficient, e.g. speeding, possessing a firearm without a certificate, and selling tobacco to a person apparently under the age of 16.

The standard of proof which must be satisfied in a criminal trial is 'beyond reasonable doubt'. The burden of proof is on the prosecution. Research by Zander (2000), which studied what the standard of proof means to different people, found that whilst there were differences between the understanding of members of the public (who might sit on a jury), magistrates and criminal justice professionals, the difference was not great. However, a higher proportion of the general public than of magistrates said they would need to be 100 per cent sure of guilt before convicting.[15] If the defendant is required to prove an issue, for example, that the knife he carried was for a legitimate purpose, then the lower, civil standard of proof will apply.

Offences are classified as summary, either way or indictable only. Offences which are triable summarily include most road traffic offences, breach of the peace, obstructing a constable, and criminal damage where the value of property is below £5,000. All summary offences are statutorily defined. They are dealt with by the magistrates' court and there is no entitlement to trial by jury. These offences are divided into five levels for the purposes of penalty, ranging from level 1 (a maximum £200 fine) to level 5 (a maximum £5,000 fine and/or six months' custody). For some summary offences it is possible to plead guilty by post and avoid attendance at court. There is generally no time limit within which a prosecution must be brought for an offence; however, as an exception to this principle, a summary prosecution must normally begin within six months of commission of the offence (i.e. the information must be laid). A person cannot be tried for the same offence twice.

Either way offences such as theft, indecent assault and misuse of drugs may be tried at the magistrates' court or the Crown Court. The choice of court will be decided in the magistrates' court following 'plea before venue'[16] and possibly mode of trial procedure. The defendant is asked to indicate his plea and will be dealt with by magistrates if the plea is 'guilty', unless the magistrates' sentencing powers are insufficient. If the plea is 'not guilty', the magistrates proceed to the mode of trial procedure. The magistrates will consider the nature of the case, its seriousness and whether their powers of sentence are adequate. If the magistrates decide that the case should be tried on indictment, the defendant is committed to Crown Court. In addition, the defendant currently has an absolute right to elect trial by jury.

Indictable only offences include the more serious crimes such as murder, rape and manslaughter. Since January 2001 the committal process has changed. Formerly, magistrates' courts decided whether there was a case to answer before committing to Crown Court for trial. Now the magistrates will send an indictable only offence straight to the Crown Court, having dealt with bail.

▪ Arrest

Criminal offences have also been classified as either an arrestable or non-arrestable offences. Arrestable offences included many serious offences such as murder, rape, manslaughter and robbery and a person suspected of committing or caught in the act could be arrested immediately, without a warrant. For non-arrestable offences, including the majority of driving offences, it was necessary to obtain a warrant from a magistrate for arrest or, more usually, issue a summons to appear at court. Since January 2006 when ss. 110 and 111 of the Serious Organised Crime and Police Act 2005 (amending PACE 1984) were brought into force, arrestable offences no longer exist. The police constables power of arrest will extend to all offences. Arrests will be subject to the test of necessity based upon the nature and circumstances of the offence and the interests of criminal justice. A new Code of Practice giving guidance concerning arrest will be issued.[17]

Each year the police make around 2 million arrests. When a suspect is identified and arrested he will be taken to a police station (as soon as practicable after arrest)[18] and usually placed in a cell. At that stage the suspect is entitled to free legal advice and to consult his solicitor privately. Even if a person has not been arrested, if being questioned by the police at the station he is entitled to free legal advice. A solicitor may be provided from the duty solicitor scheme or the individual may request another solicitor.

Section 28 of PACE 1984 sets out the elements of a valid arrest. The suspect must be informed of the arrest and of the ground of the arrest and must be cautioned in the following terms: 'You do not have to say anything, but it may harm your defence if you do not mention when questioned something which you later rely on in court. Anything you do say may be given in evidence.'

Since the Criminal Justice and Public Order Act 1994, if the accused remains silent during questioning, at his subsequent trial the court may draw adverse inferences from that silence. A police officer conducting an interview can also give a special warning where the suspect fails or refuses to account for any object or mark on an object or clothing at the time of arrest, or object found at the place of arrest or at the time of arrest, noting that the court can draw an inference if the suspect does not account for the relevant fact.

■ Time limits for detention

Having been arrested and interviewed by the police, the suspect may be charged with an offence, the police may issue a caution or he may be released with no further action. Once the suspect has been arrested and taken to the police station, specific time limits for his lawful detention apply. Section 37 of PACE 1984 provides that a suspect's detention (before charge) is lawful where it is necessary to secure or preserve evidence relating to an offence for which he is under arrest or to obtain that evidence by questioning. There is a requirement for an officer, independent of the investigation, to review the suspect's detention six hours after the suspect arrived at the police station and then every nine hours. In the majority of cases, a suspect should not be detained for longer than 24 hours, at which point, if there is insufficient evidence for a charge, the suspect should be released from police custody.[19] For serious arrestable offences the suspect may be detained for up to 36 hours without charge on the authority of an officer of superintendent rank.[20] Beyond that 36-hour period the police are required to obtain a warrant from the magistrates' court authorising further detention up to a maximum period of 96 hours.[21]

In some circumstances an individual will attend the police station on a voluntary basis (i.e. not under arrest) to help police with their inquiries. Such circumstances are covered by PACE 1984, s. 29, which states that the person must be informed immediately if placed under arrest. Until placed under arrest, the person is entitled to leave at any point.

■ Appropriate adult

The role of the appropriate adult in relation to young offenders was discussed in Chapter 13. An appropriate adult is also required where a vulnerable person, being mentally disordered or learning disabled, is being interviewed as a suspect. The police have a wide discretion in their interpretation of vulnerability and may also require an appropriate adult where, for example, the individual has speech or hearing difficulties. If the police have any suspicion or are told in good faith that the suspect is a vulnerable adult they should proceed on that basis and request an appropriate adult. Lack of police training on the recognition of mental disorder may lead to the police calling appropriate adults in only the most extreme cases.[22]

The role of the appropriate adult is described in Code C to the Police and Criminal Evidence Act 1984 at para. 11.16:

> he should be informed that he is not expected to act simply as an observer; and also that the purposes of his presence are, first, to advise the person being questioned and to observe whether or not the interview is being conducted properly and fairly, and, secondly, to facilitate communication with the person being interviewed.

An appropriate adult for a person who is mentally disordered or learning disabled may be one of the following:

■ a relative, guardian or other person responsible for care or custody;

■ someone who has experience of dealing with mentally disordered or mentally handicapped people but is not a police officer or employed by the police; or

■ some other responsible adult who is not a police officer or employed by the police.

The custody officer may therefore contact social services and ask the authority to provide an appropriate adult. An approved social worker or social worker on a learning disabilities team could act as an appropriate adult.

If the vulnerable adult is charged or cautioned, the appropriate adult must be present. The adult should not normally be interviewed or asked to provide a written statement unless the appropriate adult is present. The vulnerable adult is entitled to consult privately with the appropriate adult (and legal adviser) at any time. It may be appropriate for the vulnerable adult to consult separately with his legal adviser in the absence of the appropriate adult. One reason for this is that, unlike the solicitor, the appropriate adult is not covered by confidentiality or legal privilege. Appropriate adults may be asked to pass relevant information to the police and both the British Association of Social Workers and the Association of Directors of Social Services support the principle that social workers have a duty to assist in the prevention and detection of crime. In order to do that effectively, some awareness of police powers (as outlined below) is prerequisite.

The appropriate adult should take a proactive role and be prepared to challenge the progress of an interview. It would also be good practice to consult the custody record and to keep notes during the interview, noting who is present, what facilities are offered and any remarks which caused concern. If any aspects of detention are challenged (in particular as to the effect on evidence obtained), the appropriate adult may be called upon to provide evidence.

Exhibit 18.1 reproduces part of the custody record which must be maintained in respect of a detained person.

■ Police powers

To be an effective appropriate adult, some knowledge of police powers at the police station is essential. There are also some significant police powers, e.g. stop and search, which it is useful to have an understanding of in order to advocate for service users and recognise where individual civil liberties are threatened.

The majority of police powers are contained in the Police and Criminal Evidence Act 1984. This legislation was introduced at a time when serious miscarriages of justice had come to light and the old law, particularly reliance on the Judges' Rules to protect individuals at the police station, was recognised as inadequate. The Act provides a framework of police powers which are supplemented by codes of practice containing detailed guidance for the police and people likely to encounter the police. The codes were most recently revised with effect from Augsut 2004. The codes should be available at the police station to be consulted by the police, detained people, appropriate adults, legal advisers and the general public. There are five codes, covering the following areas:

Code A: Police powers to stop and search

Code B: Searching premises and seizing property

Code C: Detention treatment and questioning of suspects

Code D: Identification procedures

Code E: Tape-recording of police interviews.

Code C is most likely to be relevant to a social worker acting as an appropriate adult.

The designation of a police officer as custody officer was introduced by Part IV of PACE 1984. Features of the role of the custody officer can be outlined thus:

Characteristics

Sergeant rank or above

Independent of the investigation

Impartial

Role

Keeping a custody record

Determining whether there is sufficient evidence to charge the suspect or release on police bail or detain in police detention.

At the station the appropriate adult and the suspect's solicitor are entitled to access to the custody record. The suspect is entitled to a copy of the custody record on release, a right which also extends to the appropriate adult and solicitor for 12 months after the release. The custody record is an important source of information. It contains personal details about the detainee such as their name, address, occupation, age and also their ethnic appearance. The reason for arrest and details of arrest are recorded and the authority for continued detention, e.g. for preparation of charges, to secure evidence or obtain further evidence by questioning. The time that the appropriate adult was called and actually arrived should be recorded together with details of an

PART 3   D E T A I N E D   P E R S O N   D E T A I L S   A209(ii)
(Rev. 4/95)

Custody Record No. [＿＿＿＿＿＿＿＿＿]   Surname [＿＿＿＿＿＿＿＿＿]

┌ DETAINEE DETAILS ──────────────────────────

Mr/Mrs/Ms/Other . . . . Surname . . . .

Forename 1 . . . . Forename 2 . . . .

Maiden Name . . . . Nickname . . . .

Single	☐	Separated ☐
Married	☐	Divorced ☐
Co-habiting	☐	Widowed ☐

DOB [＿|＿|＿|＿|＿|＿]   Age [＿＿]   Marital Status:

Occupation . . . .

Place of Birth . . . .

Skin Colour: Ethnic Appearance:

White ☐   Non White ☐   Unknown ☐   1 White ☐   3 Indian/ ☐
SubContinent

                                     2 Black ☐   4 Other ☐

┌ ADDRESS DETAILS ──────────────────────────

Address Type (Home, Business etc) . . . .

Address . . . .

. . . .

. . . .

Post Code [＿＿＿＿＿＿＿]

Telephone 1 . . . . Telephone 2 . . . .

┌ APPROPRIATE ADULT ──────────────────────────

Mr/Mrs/Ms/Other . . . . Name . . . .

Address . . . .

. . . .

. . . .

Telephone 1 . . . . Telephone 2 . . . .

Relationship to Detainee . . . .

Exhibit 18.1   Detained person details
Source: West Mercia Police Authority, reproduced with permission.

PART 4   L E G A L   R I G H T S   A209(ii)
                                                               (Rev. 4/95)

RIGHTS

Rights Given on Arrival   Yes ☐   No ☐

A NOTICE SETTING OUT MY RIGHTS HAS BEEN READ TO ME AND I HAVE ALSO BEEN PROVIDED WITH A WRITTEN NOTICE SETTING OUT MY ENTITLEMENTS WHILE IN CUSTODY.

Signature . . . . TIM/DATE ☐☐☐ ☐☐☐☐☐
                     (Detainee)

Signature . . . . TIME/DATE ☐☐☐ ☐☐☐☐☐
                     (Appropriate Adult/Interpreter

LEGAL ADVICE REQUESTED

I want to speak to a solicitor as soon as practicable:

Solicitor's Name: . . . . Company: . . . .

Address: . . . .

. . . . Tel. No. . . . .

Signature . . . . TIME/DATE ☐☐☐ ☐☐☐☐☐
                     (Detainee)

Signature . . . . TIME/DATE ☐☐☐ ☐☐☐☐☐
                     (Appropriate Adult/Interpreter

LEGAL ADVICE DECLINED

I have been informed that I may speak to a solicitor IN PERSON or ON THE TELEPHONE:

Signature . . . . TIME/DATE ☐☐☐ ☐☐☐☐☐
                     (Detainee)

Signature . . . . TIME/DATE ☐☐☐ ☐☐☐☐☐
                     (Appropriate Adult/Interpreter

I DO NOT WANT TO SPEAK TO A SOLICITOR at this time:

Signature . . . . TIME/DATE ☐☐☐ ☐☐☐☐☐
                     (Detainee)

Signature . . . . TIME/DATE ☐☐☐ ☐☐☐☐☐
                     (Appropriate Adult/Interpreter

Reasons, if given, for not wanting legal advice: . . . .

. . . .

NAMED PERSON

YOU HAVE THE RIGHT TO HAVE SOMEONE INFORMED THAT YOU HAVE BEEN ARRESTED. DO YOU WISH TO HAVE SOMEONE TOLD?

| I DO |
| I DO NOT |

want someone informed. I understand that I can change this decision later if I wish. *(Delete)*

Named Person . . . .

Address: . . . .

. . . . Tel. No. . . . .

Signature . . . . TIM/DATE ☐☐☐☐ ☐☐☐☐☐☐
                     (Detainee)

Signature . . . . TIME/DATE ☐☐☐☐ ☐☐☐☐☐☐
                     (Appropriate Adult/Interpreter

DELAY OF RIGHTS

                                           TIME / DATE ☐☐☐ ☐☐☐☐☐

Legal Advice Delayed (S.58)   Yes ☐   No ☐

Intimation(s) Delayed (S.56)   Yes ☐   No ☐

interpreter (if used) and solicitor. The suspect will be asked whether they are suffering from any illness or receiving medication and the record should note whether a doctor is called. The detained person will also be asked to sign the form indicating receipt of the notice to detained persons and notice of entitlements and indicating whether legal advice was requested.

Rights at the station

Section 56 of PACE 1984 includes the right to inform someone of an arrest. The suspect should be informed of this right by the custody officer and is entitled on arrival at the station to have one person who is likely to have an interest in his welfare told of his whereabouts. If that person cannot be contacted, at least two further people should be tried.

Section 58 provides the right to legal advice. A suspect is entitled to receive advice in person or by telephone, in private, before questioning by the police. He is also entitled to consult a solicitor privately at any time during questioning and his legal adviser may be present during interviews.

The conditions of detention should be reasonable. Cells should have adequate heat and light and be clean and ventilated. The suspect should be provided with regular meals (taking into account any special dietary requirements) and have access to toilet facilities and outdoor exercise.

A breach of PACE or any elements of the code make a police officer liable to disciplinary action. Breaches may also have an effect on evidence. Any evidence which is improperly obtained may be excluded by the court. Section 76 relates to confessions where, in order to be admissible, it must be shown beyond reasonable doubt that the confession was not obtained by oppression or in circumstances likely to render it unreliable. Section 78 further includes an overall discretion to exclude evidence if its inclusion would make the trial unfair.

■ Remands

Once a case has been commenced, the court must decide on the issue of remand of the defendant. The court may remand either in custody or on bail. If in custody, the defendant will not normally be remanded for more than eight clear days at a time. Extended periods of up to 28 days are permissible on second and subsequent remands subject to a number of conditions having been met. In some areas prisons now have video links to the court so that it is not necessary for the defendant to attend court for each remand. Any time spent in custody on remand is generally deducted from the eventual sentence to be served. Nevertheless, a significant number of defendants who have been remanded in custody do not actually receive a custodial sentence and there is no compensation available to those who are acquitted of any offence.

The statutory framework for bail is provided by the Bail Act 1976 (as amended by the Criminal Justice Act 2003). Section 4 provides a statutory right to unconditional bail in certain circumstances, subject to defined exceptions. These exceptions should be compatible with Art. 5 ECHR. For an imprisonable offence, bail need not be granted if:

1. there are substantial grounds for believing that if released on bail he would:
    (a) fail to surrender to custody, or
    (b) commit an offence, or
    (c) interfere with witnesses or otherwise obstruct the course of justice;
2. he ought to be kept in custody for his own protection;
3. he is already in custody in pursuance of the sentence of the court;
4. there has not yet been time to obtain necessary information so as to take a decision about bail;
5. he has been arrested for having failed to surrender to custody after being released on bail in the current proceedings;
6. the proceedings have been adjourned for inquiries or a report and it would be impracticable to complete them without having the defendant in custody.

The prosecution will make representations to the court if they object to grant of bail for one or more of the above reasons. In addition, the probation service may be asked to supply a bail information report providing verified information for the CPS, e.g. as to the defendant's accommodation and employment, and an assessment of risk of harm to the public.

Bail may be granted conditionally or unconditionally. Conditions can be imposed if they are necessary to secure that the accused surrenders to custody, is available for reports, does not offend, does not interfere with witnesses or obstruct the course of justice. Examples of such conditions include daily reports to police, imposition of a curfew, stipulated residence, perhaps with a relative or in a bail hostel, avoiding certain areas or people and surrender of passport. The court may also request a surety or a security.

If bail is withheld, the court must state the statutory exception(s) which apply and must explain why it feels the exception(s) apply in the particular case. The defendant can apply for the decision to be reviewed by a judge. In *Caballero* v. *United Kingdom* (2000) *The Times*, 29 February, the European Court of Human Rights upheld the concession of the UK Government that automatic denial of bail pending trial was a breach of Art. 5(3) and 5(5) of the European Convention on Human Rights. Section 25 of the Criminal Justice and Public Order Act 1994 stipulated that bail could not be granted to defendants charged with or convicted of homicide or rape after previous convictions of such offences.

First appearance at court

Following charge, the defendant will appear before the magistrates' court. The court will take a plea from the defendant of either guilty or not guilty. If charged with a summary offence, the case may proceed straight to sentencing if the defendant pleads guilty. If there is to be a trial, i.e. where the defendant has pleaded not guilty, the case is likely to be adjourned for preparation of evidence. In either case there may be a further adjournment if reports are required to aid the sentencing decision.

Either way offences may be dealt with by the magistrates unless they decide, after a guilty plea, that their powers of sentence are insufficient, or, after a plea of not guilty, that the case is more suitable for a Crown Court trial or the defendant elects Crown Court trial.

Indictable only offences are committed to the Crown Court. In the Crown Court a plea and directions hearing will take place in which the *indictment* is prepared and the defendant is asked to plead.

■ Trial

A trial in the Crown Court is heard by a judge and jury. Before the trial commences, the jury must be selected and sworn in.

Trials in the magistrates' court and the Crown Court follow standard adversarial procedure as outlined in Exhibit 18.2.

Each witness must swear an oath or make an affirmation before giving oral evidence to the court. The terms of the oath and affirmation are set out in Chapter 13. Notes made contemporaneously (within reason) with the event may be referred to by the witness. The most obvious example of this is the police notebook.

Outcomes in the criminal justice system

■ Sentences

The sentencing process incorporates a wide range of both expectations and objectives. A number of sentencing theories have been identified including retribution, rehabilitation, deterrence, incapacitation, restitution and denunciation. A combination of aspects from each theory may inform a particular sentencing decision and can also be identified in particular policies.[23] The current sentencing framework has been revised significantly by the Criminal Justice Act 2003. It specifies the purpose or purposes of sentencing as: punishment; reduction of crime (including reduction by deterrence); reform and rehabilitation; protection of the public and reparation by offenders.

Sentencing decisions should be informed by the facts and seriousness of the offence, including culpability and dangerousness, the circumstances of the offender and be proportionate. There are four levels of culpability: intention to cause harm; recklessness as to whether harm is caused; knowledge of specific risks and negligence. Within the maximum penalty stipulated for an offence, the court has a wide discretion to fix an appropriate sentence. Appeals against sentence are not uncommon, although having fallen steadily from 14,355 in 2000 to 11,746 in 2003 they then rose to 12,578 in 2004. This represented 0.8 per cent of all defendants convicted in the

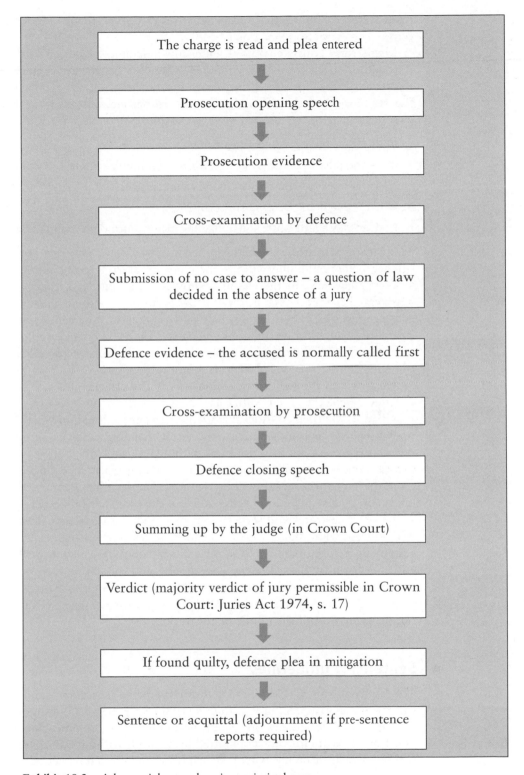

The charge is read and plea entered

Prosecution opening speech

Prosecution evidence

Cross-examination by defence

Submission of no case to answer – a question of law decided in the absence of a jury

Defence evidence – the accused is normally called first

Cross-examination by prosecution

Defence closing speech

Summing up by the judge (in Crown Court)

Verdict (majority verdict of jury permissible in Crown Court: Juries Act 1974, s. 17)

If found guilty, defence plea in mitigation

Sentence or acquittal (adjournment if pre-sentence reports required)

Exhibit 18.2   Adversarial procedure in a criminal case

magistrates' courts. Of these 19 per cent resulted in a change of sentence and 24 per cent in the conviction being quashed.[24]

Magistrates' courts now have sentencing guidelines produced by the Magistrates' Association to ensure greater consistency between benches. The guidelines' sentencing structure reaffirms the principle of 'just deserts' so that any penalty must reflect the seriousness of the offence and the personal circumstances of the offender. In every case magistrates are required to consider:

- Is discharge or a fine appropriate?
- Is the offence serious enough for a community penalty?
- Is it so serious that only custody will suffice?
- Are sentencing powers sufficient?
- Consider aggravating and mitigating factors, including victim personal statements.

Magistrates start the sentencing procedure by considering the seriousness of the offence before them and will use the guideline starting point contained in the sentencing guidelines. In the example shown in Exhibit 18.3, racially or religiously aggravated common assault, the starting point of 'is it so serious that only custody is appropriate' is a level higher than for common assault, where the guideline is 'is it serious enough for a community penalty'. They will consider culpability and risk of harm, then all the offence aggravating and mitigating factors, including relevant previous convictions or failure to respond to previous sentences, and determine the extent to which they affect the seriousness of the offence under consideration.

After completing their initial assessment of the seriousness of the offence, the magistrates will then consider the offender and any mitigation which has been given on his behalf, such as genuine remorse. If that mitigation is accepted they must reduce the assessment of seriousness, although this may be a minor revision only. If the assessment of seriousness remains at community penalty or higher, then a report from the probation service will be required. On deciding sentence, discount will be given for a guilty plea, note being taken of the timelines of the plea. In announcing sentence, magistrates will state their reasons. This is done in a structured way and will address: what makes the offence more or less serious than average, including a statement as to culpability (was the offence committed intentionally or recklessly etc), the harm or risk of harm, aggravating and mitigating factors relating to the offence and the offender. The magistrates will also state the main point of sentence as one or more of: punishment, reduction in crime/deterrence, reform and rehabilitation, protection of the public or reparation.

■ Sentencing guidelines

The Court of Appeal (Criminal Division) has issued sentencing guidelines from time to time. As an example, in R v. *Billam* (1986) 8 Cr App R (S) 48, Lord Lane set out principles to guide judges on sentencing in rape cases, commencing with a starting point of five years for rape committed by an adult without any aggravating factors, through to a life sentence where the behaviour manifested perverted or psychopathic

Criminal Justice Act 1988 s.39 Crime and Disorder Act 1998 s.29 Anti-Terrorism, Crime and Security Act 2001 Triable either way – see Mode of Trial Guidelines Penalty: Level 5 and/or 6 months	Racially or religiously aggravated common assault

CONSIDER THE SERIOUSNESS OF THE OFFENCE
(INCLUDING THE IMPACT ON THE VICTIM)

IS DISCHARGE OR FINE APPROPRIATE?

IS IT SERIOUS ENOUGH FOR A COMMUNITY PENALTY?

GUIDELINE: → IS IT SO SERIOUS THAT ONLY CUSTODY IS APPROPRIATE?

ARE YOUR SENTENCING POWERS SUFFICIENT?

THIS IS A GUIDELINE FOR A FIRST-TIME OFFENDER PLEADING NOT GUILTY

 ## CONSIDER AGGRAVATING AND MITIGATING FACTORS AND THE WEIGHT TO ATTACH TO EACH

for example	for example
Group action	Impulsive
Injury	Minor injury
Motivation for the offence was racial or religious	Provocation
Offender in position of authority	Single blow
On hospital/medical or school premises	*This list is not exhaustive*
Premeditated	
Setting out to humiliate the victim	
Victim particularly vulnerable	
Victim serving the public	
Weapon	
This list is not exhaustive	

If offender is on bail, this offence is more serious
If offender has previous convictions, their relevance and any failure to respond to previous sentences should be considered – they may increase the seriousness. The court should make it clear, when passing sentence, that this was the approach adopted.

TAKE A PRELIMINARY VIEW OF SERIOUSNESS, THEN CONSIDER OFFENDER MITIGATION

for example
   Age, health (physical or mental)
   Co-operation with police
   Evidence of genuine remorse
   Voluntary compensation

CONSIDER YOUR SENTENCE

Compare it with the suggested guideline level of sentence and reconsider your reasons carefully if you have chosen a sentence at a different level. Consider a reduction for a timely guilty plea.

DECIDE YOUR SENTENCE
NB. COMPENSATION – Give reasons if not awarding compensation

© The Magistrates' Association   *Issued October 2003 for implementation 1 January 2004*

Exhibit 18.3   Magistrates' Association sentencing guidelines for racially aggravated assault
Source: The Magistrates' Association, reproduced with permission.

tendencies. The Sentencing Guideline Council, an independent body, took over responsibility for developing comprehensive sentencing and allocation guidelines from the Court of Appeal and the Magistrates' Association in 2005. The Council receives advice from the Sentencing Advisory Panel on a particular sentencing topic and uses this to formulate sentencing guidelines on the subject. The court must state reasons if it intends to depart from sentencing guidelines. The Sentencing Advisory Panel, was established under CDA 1998, s. 81. It has issued consultation papers on offences involving child pornography, rape, domestic violence, and advice on offensive weapons, racially aggravated offences and minimum terms in murder cases.

Since 1988 it has also been possible for the prosecution to appeal against sentence (for indictable offences) on the ground that the sentence imposed is unduly lenient.[25] In 1997, of 70 referrals (by the prosecution) to the Attorney-General about lenient sentences, 43 resulted in an increased sentence.[26]

The levels of sentence currently available are discharges, fines, community sentences and custody.

■ Discharges

The court may order an absolute discharge or a conditional discharge. In both cases the conviction is recorded but no further action to sentence will be taken unless the offender commits a further offence during the period of a conditional discharge. If so, the offender can be re-sentenced for the original offence.

■ Fines

The most commonly used sentence is the fine, particularly for summary offences in the magistrates' court. In 2004, fines accounted for 73 per cent of all magistrates' sentences. The maximum fine is stipulated as a level (1–5) for each offence, and the overall maximum that the magistrates' court can impose is £5,000. There are no financial limits to the fines which can be ordered in the Crown Court. Fines may be recovered directly from income support or attachment of earnings. Prison is the ultimate sanction for non-payment of fines.

■ Fixed penalties

The Criminal Justice and Police Act 2001 introduced a variety of measures designed to combat crime and disorder including on-the-spot fines. The relevant offences where on-the-spot penalties can be issued are set out in s. 1 and include: wasting police time; being drunk in a highway, other public place or licensed premises; and disorderly behaviour while drunk in a public place. Any uniformed police constable can give a person over the age of 18 a penalty notice. The individual has 21 days to pay the penalty.

■ Compensation

When an offence which has resulted in a personal injury or damage to property is dealt with, the court must consider whether a compensation order should be made instead of or in addition to another order (Powers of Criminal Courts (Sentencing) Act 2000, s. 130). If a compensation order is made, that takes priority over a fine. The average amount of compensation ordered in 2004 was £226 in the magistrates' court and £1,494 in the Crown Court.[27] The amount of compensation will be determined in the light of medical evidence, the victim's age and sex and other relevant factors. Reasons must be stated if compensation requested is not given.

■ Community sentences

The Criminal Justice Act 2003 sets out the new structure for community sentences. The previous orders: community rehabilitation order (probation), the community punishment order (community service orders), the community punishment and rehabilitation order (combination orders), curfew orders, drug treatment and testing orders, no longer exist although elements of these orders are retained under the new structure. A community order may be made for up to three years for offenders aged over 16.

A 'community order' may include any one or more of the following requirements:

(a) an unpaid work requirement (s. 199);
(b) an activity requirement (s. 201);
(c) a programme requirement (s. 202);
(d) a prohibited activity requirement (s. 203);
(e) a curfew requirement (s. 204);
(f) an exclusion requirement (s. 205);
(g) a residence requirement (s. 206);
(h) a mental health treatment requirement (s. 207);
(i) a drug rehabilitation requirement (s. 209);
(j) an alcohol treatment requirement (s. 212);
(k) a supervision requirement (s. 213); and
(l) in a case where the offender is aged under 25, an attendance centre requirement (s. 214).

In determining which requirement or combination of requirements are imposed, the guiding principles are proportionality and suitability. Within the community sentence band, three sentencing ranges (low, medium and high) are set out in sentencing guidelines, based upon seriousness.

The low band covers offences only just crossing the community sentence threshold such as persistent petty offending and some thefts from shops. Suitable requirements might include 40 to 80 hours of unpaid work or a curfew requirement within the lowest range (e.g. up to 12 hours per day for a few weeks). In the high band, for offences that only just fall below the custody threshold, such as domestic burglary committed by a first-time offender, more intensive sentences may be appropriate. A combination of two or more requirements may be ordered, such as unpaid work order of between 150 and 300 hours and an activity requirement up to the maximum 60 days (Sentencing Guidelines Council).

Requirements

Unpaid work – this is similar to the previous Community Punishment Order and the number of hours will be between 40 and 300, to be completed normally within 12 months.

Activity – the offender is required to present at a specified place to participate in specified activities, for a total number of no more than 60 days.

Programme – the offender will participate in an accredited programme recommended to the court by a probation officer or YOT officer as suitable.

Prohibited Activity – this requirement prohibits the offender from participating in specified activities and specified days, e.g. avoiding a football ground on match day.

Curfew – the offender must stay at a specified place for between 2 and 12 hours in any 24-hour period, in a similar way to the old curfew. It can last for up to six months and will usually be monitored electronically.

Residence – after consideration of the home circumstances of the offender, a residence requirement directs the offender to live at a specified place.

Mental Health Treatment requirement – requires the offender (who must be willing) to undergo treatment by a named medical practitioner or chartered psychologist provided the condition is not so serious as to warrant a hospital or guardianship order.

Drug rehabilitation – the offender will have treatment with a view to reducing or elimination dependency and will provide samples. The treatment and testing period will be for between six months and three years.

Alcohol treatment – the period of treatment cannot be for less than six months and the offender must be willing to comply with treatment as resident or non-resident of an institution.

Supervision – similar to the previous community rehabilitation order, the offender must attend for appointments with the responsible officer with a view to promoting rehabilitation.

Attendance centre – where the offender is under 25 he may be required to attend a centre for between 12 and 36 hours, split into sessions of not more than three hours in a day.

For all community sentences the offender must keep in contact with their supervising officer (probation officer) and advise any change of address. Where an offender does not comply with a community order, the case may be returned to court and the court can revoke the order and impose a sentence which may include a custodial sentence.

Deferred sentences

Deferred sentences were introduced by Powers of Criminal Courts (Sentencing) Act 2000, ss. 1 and 2. These provisions have been modified by the CJA 2003. As well as requiring the consent of the offender, the court is able to impose a wide variety of conditions (including a residence requirement) for the period of deferment. The court can then review the conduct of the defendant before passing sentence.

Custody Plus

Sections 181 and 182 of the CJA 2003 make provision for a new sentence (described in the Halliday report as 'custody plus'), that will replace all short prison sentences of under 12 months (with the exception of intermittent custody). It will be made up of a short period in custody of up to three months (to fulfil the punishment purpose of the sentence), followed by a longer period under supervision in the community (to fulfil the reparation and crime reduction purposes of the sentence) of a minimum of six months. At the point of sentence the court will specify the lengths of the two parts and attach specific requirements, based upon those available under the generic community sentence, to the supervision part of the sentence so as to address the rehabilitative needs of the offender. This provision is not yet in force.

Suspended sentences

The suspended prison sentence was reformed so that offenders have to complete a range of requirements imposed by the court during the period of suspension. The prison sentence can be suspended for between six months and two years. The court can impose one or more requirements (as set out above for community sentences), and the requirements must be completed within a specified supervision period. The order can provide for periodical review hearings at which the offender must attend.

Pre-sentence reports are required before a community sentence can be imposed by the court. The report will be prepared by the probation service in accordance with 'National Standards for the Supervision of Offenders in the Community 2000'. Pre-sentence reports as defined by s. 3 of the Criminal Justice Act 1991 are designed to focus specifically on the offence, provide an analysis of why the crime was committed, the impact on the victim, the offender's attitude to the offence, an assessment of the risk of reoffending, a sentence proposal, and significantly less detail about the offender. The report should be objective, impartial, free from discriminatory language and stereotype, balanced, verified and factually accurate. It should be written following at least one face-to-face interview with the offender and will be based on the use of the **Offender Assessment System** (often referred to as **OASYS**). The court, offender, defence and prosecution will have a copy. The National Standards require that the report should be prepared within a maximum period of 15 working days. The format of the report is stipulated as follows:

Front sheet

Basic factual information on the offender and sources of information.

Offence analysis

The nature and circumstances of the offence, offender's culpability, impact on any victim, offender's attitude and any action to make reparation.

Offender assessment

Assessment of the offender, including his literacy and numeracy, accommodation and employment. Any special circumstances such as family crisis or substance abuse, patterns of offending, impact of racism on the offender's behaviour (if relevant) and personal background which may have contributed to motive.

Assessment of risk of harm to the public and likelihood of reoffending

The section should include any identifiable risks of self harm.

Conclusion

Evaluation of motivation and willingness to improve, suitability for a community sentence and a clear proposal for a sentence which will protect the public and reduce reoffending. An outline supervision plan should be included if the proposal is for a community sentence. The conclusion should include anticipated effects on the offender's family, employment or education if custody is likely.[28]

In addition, if a court envisages a specific sentence, e.g. community service order up to 100 hours or probation without additional requirements, a specific sentence report may be requested. This is a briefer report than a full pre-sentence report and is focused on suitability for a particular sentence. It should normally be available to the court on the day it is requested. There is a danger that the desire to speed up the process and avoid delay and the difficulty of trying to assess someone on the basis of one interview can lead to situations where the court is not made fully aware of important information regarding the suitability of a person for a community sentence.

■ Custody

An offender may be ordered to serve a prison sentence in a case where the offence is so serious that only custody is justified; it may be an offence of sex or violence where only a custodial sentence is considered sufficient to protect the public, or it may be imposed where an offender will not consent to a community sentence. The length of sentence for each type of offence is specified in legislation. The time actually served in prison will usually be less than that imposed by the court due to reductions for time spent on remand and the operation of remission. Under the CJA 2003, where a prison sentence of 12 months or more is imposed on an offender who is not classified as 'dangerous', that offender will be entitled to be released from custody after completing half of the sentence. The whole of the second half of the sentence will be subject to licence requirements

A life sentence is mandatory in cases of murder and may be imposed for other serious indictable offences. The Crime (Sentences) Act 1997 makes a life sentence mandatory for a person who commits a serious offence (attempted murder, manslaughter, attempted rape or rape, intercourse with a girl aged under 13 and armed robbery) having previously been convicted of a serious offence. This is sometimes referred to as the 'two strikes' rule. In addition, the 'three strikes' rule requires that a minimum sentence of three years is imposed for a third residential burglary. A prisoner on a life sentence may apply for release on licence and if released may be recalled to prison at any time. Time spent before release varies but there are few life prisoners who will literally spend the whole of their lives in prison. It is possible to suspend a custodial sentence (of up to two years) if justified by exceptional circumstances.

In 2004, 1,547,000 offenders were sentenced for indictable and summary offences in. In the magistrates' court: 73 per cent were fined (average level of fine was £140), 6 per cent given a conditional discharge, 12 per cent given a community sentence, 4 per cent sentenced to immediate custody and the remainder dealt with otherwise (including discharges). In the Crown Court: 61 per cent were sentenced to immediate custody, 30 per cent to a community sentence, 3 per cent were fined (average level of fine £650), 4 per cent received and the remainder were otherwise dealt with.[29]

■ Vulnerable witnesses

The Youth Justice and Criminal Evidence Act 1999 (YJCEA 1999) introduced measures to tackle problems relating to vulnerable witnesses. Special measures are available to witnesses on the grounds of youth, incapacity, or feelings of distress a witness is likely to suffer in giving evidence. It was recognised in 'Speaking up for Justice'[30] that giving evidence can be particularly stressful for some witnesses and the formality of the process may be intimidating and inhibit their giving best evidence. A vulnerable adult witness is defined as a person suffering from mental disorder or otherwise having a significant impairment of intelligence and social functioning (YJCEA 1999, s. 16(2)(a)), or a physical disability or disorder (YJCEA 1999, s. 16(2)(b)). In addition, a witness may also be eligible for special measures if the court is satisfied that the quality of evidence given by the witness is likely to be diminished by reason of fear or distress in connection with testifying (YJCEA 1999, s. 17). To determine eligibility there is a range of circumstances listed for the court to take into account, including: nature and circumstances of the offence; age of the witness; social and cultural background; ethnic origins; domestic and employment circumstances; religious and political beliefs; and any behaviour towards the witness by the accused or those associated with him, including anyone else likely to be an accused or a witness in the case. The court will make a special measures direction if measures are to be made available to a witness.

The following special measures are provided by the YJCEA 1999:

- ■ Screening the witness from the accused (s. 23);
- ■ Giving evidence via a live link (s. 24);
- ■ Removal of wigs and gowns during testimony (s. 25);
- ■ Giving evidence in private (intimidation and sexual cases) (s. 26);
- ■ Video recording of evidence in chief (s. 27);
- ■ Video recording of cross-examination and re-examination (s. 28);
- ■ Examination through an intermediary (s. 29);
- ■ Provision of aids to communication (s. 30).

Home Office guidance, 'Achieving Best Evidence in Criminal Proceedings: Guidance for Vulnerable and Intimidated Witnesses including Children' (2001) is in place. The various special measures have been implemented incrementally. All Crown Courts now have video link facilities. The use of intermediaries was piloted during 2004 with a view to national implementation. The intermediary will be a communication expert, such as a speech or language therapist and will act as intermediary between the witness and lawyers, judges and juries, will explain to the witness the questions posed and will explain the witness's response to the court.

▪ Mentally disordered offenders

There are a number of special provisions and orders affecting those with mental illness or disorder in the criminal justice system. In the Crown Court an accused person may be declared unfit to plead by the jury. The trial may proceed and, if the crime is proven, the court may order detention in a mental hospital, guardianship, or supervision and treatment (Criminal Procedure (Insanity and Unfitness to Plead) Act 1991).

After conviction, the court may remand a defendant to hospital for a report on his mental condition to be prepared, for up to 28 days (consecutive periods not to exceed 12 weeks) where there is reason to suspect that the accused person is suffering from mental illness, psychopathic disorder, severe mental impairment or mental impairment, and it would be impracticable for a report on his mental condition to be made if he were remanded on bail. The evidence of a registered medical practitioner is required (Mental Health Act 1983, s. 35). The Mental Health Act 1983, s. 36 provides that on the evidence of two medical practitioners the Crown Court can remand the accused person for treatment for a period of 28 days (consecutive periods not to exceed 12 weeks).

Specific orders may be made where mental disorder is apparent at the time of sentence. Under s. 37, a hospital order for six months, which period is renewable, may be made by the Crown Court, where it could have imposed a custodial sentence, on the evidence of two medical practitioners. The criteria are that the defendant is suffering from mental illness, psychopathic disorder, severe mental impairment or mental impairment which makes it appropriate for them to receive treatment (and it is likely to alleviate in the case of psychopathic disorder or mental impairment). The court must be of the opinion, having regard to all the circumstances, including the nature of the offence, character, antecedents, and other available methods of dealing with the offender, that the most suitable method of disposing of the case is by a hospital order.

An interim hospital order may be made under the Mental Health Act 1983, s. 38. A restriction order under s. 41 may be attached to a hospital order. It can be imposed when it appears to the court, having regard to the nature of the offence, character and antecedents of the offender and the risk of their committing further offences if set at large, that it is necessary to impose a restriction order for the protection of the public from serious harm.

A person who is serving a prison sentence may be transferred to a hospital on the direction of the Home Secretary and reports of two registered medical practitioners.

In hospital, the offender becomes a patient and is treated in the same way as any other patient compulsorily detained in hospital.

■ Racism and the criminal justice system

Recent years have seen an increasing awareness of and recognition of racist crimes. Section 95(1)(b) of the Criminal Justice Act 1991 introduced a requirement for the Home Secretary to publish information each year to assist those involved in the administration of criminal justice in fulfilling 'their duty to avoid discriminating against any persons on the ground of race, sex or any other improper ground'. As a result of this provision, ethnic monitoring in police forces was introduced with respect to stop and search, arrest, cautions, homicides and death in police custody. On average, this has shown that ethnic minorities are more than four times as likely to be stopped and searched as white people, and the proportion of black people arrested has been consistently higher than the proportion of white people.

A racial incident is defined by the Association of Chief Police Officers as 'any incident in which it appears to the reporting or investigating officer that the complaint involves an element of racial motivation; or any incident which includes an allegation of racial motivation made by any person' (ACPO, 1985).

A factor in favour of prosecution in the Code for Crown Prosecutors is whether the offence was motivated by any form of discrimination or racial motive. It is also relevant to sentencing decisions. The Crime and Disorder Act 1998 (CDA 1998) introduced racially aggravated offences (Part II of the Act) to deal with racist violence and harassment. Sections 29–32 provide that, where the prosecution is able to prove that the offence was racially aggravated, there is a mandatory requirement to enhance the sentence through additional fines or periods of custody. The prosecution must be able to show either the existence of racial hostility at the time of committing the offence, immediately before or after, or that the offence was motivated wholly or partly by racial hostility (s. 28). Use of racist language during an attack is an obvious example and in such a case the offence becomes a racially aggravated offence. The relevant offences are assaults, criminal damage, public order and harassment. Section 29 also creates three new offences: racially aggravated malicious wounding or racially aggravated grievous bodily harm; racially aggravated actual bodily harm; and racially aggravated common assault. When hearing such a case, the court must state in open court that it is dealing with a racially aggravated offence.

Prior to the introduction of the CDA 1998, it was possible for judges to take account of racial motivation and to increase the final sentence as an aspect of their sentencing discretion (*R* v. *Ribbans* (1995) 16 Cr App Rep (s) 698). Given the high profile of the Stephen Lawrence murder and subsequent inquiry, recognition of racial violence is currently high on the agenda. Earlier research suggested that there was significant under-reporting of racial incidents, many of which did not come to the attention of the police. The British Crime Survey 2000 found that, although racially motivated incidents had fallen between 1995 and 1999 (390,000 incidents to 280,000), the number of incidents reported to the police had increased by four times the previous rate, suggesting more reporting and better recording by the police.[31]

In determining racial aggravation, motivation and racial hostility are key issues. Prior to the CDA 1998 the offence of incitement to racial hatred existed, in s. 18 of the Public Order Act 1986, as well as the offences of possession of racially inflammatory material and causing harassment, harm and distress. The case of *R* v. *White* [2001] EWCA Crim 216 concerned an offence contrary to s. 4 of the Public Order Act 1986, racially aggravated for the purposes of s. 31 of the Crime and Disorder Act 1998. The court found that it was not tied to dictionary definitions in assessing a racial group and race in the case of racially aggravated offences. The defendant admitted calling a London bus conductress from Sierra Leone a 'stupid African bitch'. He asserted that this could not refer to a racial group within s. 28 of the 1998 Act; and there was no offence where the offender and victim were of the same racial group. The court found that African did describe a racial group and it was possible for a person to show hostility to another person of the same racial group. Further, in *R* v. *Saunders* [2000] 1 Cr App Rep 458, the Court of Appeal held that a person indulging in racial violence must expect a further term of up to two years to be added to their sentence for racial aggravation. This will be the case even if that resulted in a non-custodial sentence becoming custodial.

Sections 28(1) and 29(1)(b) and (2) of the Crime and Disorder Act 1998 provide guidance on the matters to be considered when passing sentence:

1. Nature of hostility demonstrated by language and/or use of a weapon.
2. Whether the location was public or private.
3. Number of demonstrators for and against.
4. Presence or absence of other features such as offensive remarks in a crowded area, such as a synagogue or mosque, or in an otherwise empty room.
5. Discount applied for genuine remorse, guilty plea, previous good conduct.

▪ Miscarriages of justice

The Criminal Appeal Act 1995 created the Criminal Cases Review Commission (**CCRC**) to investigate[32] cases of alleged miscarriage of justice. If the CCRC considers that a miscarriage of justice has occurred it will refer the case to the Court of Appeal. It is then possible for the Court of Appeal to quash a conviction on the basis that it is 'unsafe' (previous wording referred to 'unsafe and unsatisfactory'). Since the introduction of the Act, about 40 convictions have been quashed.

▪ Victims

A new code, issued by the Home Secretary under s. 32 of the Domestic Violence, Crime and Victims Act 2004 to give victims statutory rights for the first time came into force in April 2006. The Code of Practice for Victims of Crime sets out the services victims can expect to receive from the criminal justice system including:

- a right to information about their crime, including arrests and court cases, within a specified timeframe;
- a dedicated family liaison police officer to help bereaved relatives;
- clear information from the Criminal Injuries Compensation Authority (CICA) on eligibility for compensation;
- information about Victim Support, and a referral if sought;
- an enhanced service in cases of vulnerable or intimidated victims;
- the flexibility to opt out of unwanted services.

Victims will have the right to appeal if any of the service providers have not met their obligations.

Apart from the code, the Government's current programme of work for victims also includes:

- the establishment of Witness Care Units;
- a consultation on victims' advocates;
- the introduction of a Prosecutor's Pledge;
- the appointment of a Victims Commissioner by April 2006.

The Attorney-General is introducing a ten-point pledge that describes the level of service that victims can expect to receive from prosecutors. Prosecutors play a key role in protecting victims' interests, in particular when accepting pleas and during sentencing. The pledge is a further step towards the objective of placing victims at the heart of the criminal justice system and is applicable to all prosecuting authorities, including advocates instructed by the prosecuting authorities in the Crown Court.

Where there is an identifiable victim the prosecutor will:

- Take into account the impact on the victim or their family when making a charging decision.
- Inform the victim where the charge is withdrawn, discontinued or substantially altered.
- Where practical, seek a victim's view or that of the family when considering the acceptability of a plea.
- Address the specific needs of a victim and, where justified, seek to protect their identity by making an appropriate application to the court.
- Assist victims at court to refresh their memory from their written or video statement and answer their questions on court procedure and processes.
- Promote and encourage two-way communications between victim and prosecutor at court.
- Protect victims from unwarranted or irrelevant attacks on their character and may seek the court's intervention where cross-examination is considered to be inappropriate or oppressive.

■ On conviction, robustly challenge defence mitigation which is derogatory to a victim's character.

■ On conviction apply for appropriate order for compensation, restitution or future protection of the victim.

■ Keep victims informed of the progress of any appeal, and explain the effect of the court's judgment.

■ Criminal injuries compensation

The scheme for state provision of compensation to victims of criminal injuries is now governed by the Criminal Injuries Compensation Act 1995. Claims are made to the Criminal Injuries Compensation Authority (previously referred to as the Criminal Injuries Compensation Board). Applications are determined by claims officers and there is an appeal to the Criminal Injuries Compensation Appeals Panel.

A criminal injury is a personal injury (physical or mental) directly attributable to:

(a) a crime of violence;

(b) an offence of trespass on a railway; or

(c) the apprehension of an offender (or suspect), the prevention of an offence (or attempts to do so) or helping a constable.

Ground (b) was included to cover the circumstances where train drivers witness railway suicides or accidents on railway lines.

Claims must be made within two years of the incident that caused the injury. This time limit may be waived where it is reasonable and in the interests of justice to do so, given the particular circumstances of the case. For child victims, applications should be made by an adult with parental responsibility for the child (or, if in care, the local authority). The authority has been sympathetic to delayed applications made while the victim is still a child or on reaching majority in respect of an injury caused whilst a child. A payment will not be made if it is likely that the assailant will benefit or if it would not be in the child's interest. Child abuse cases comprise approximately 10 per cent of all applications and this is an issue which it is appropriate to raise during child protection conferences and reviews. Levels of compensation are fixed under the scheme and there is a minimum threshold of £1,000. If the injuries are likely to receive compensation of less than £1,000, this scheme does not apply. The maximum total amount payable is £500,000. Payments in respect of sexual abuse of children have ranged from £1,000 for minor isolated and non-penetrative indecent acts to £17,500 for repeated non-consensual vaginal and/or anal intercourse over a period exceeding three years.

Application of the scheme to injuries caused by domestic violence is limited. Under the original scheme, applications from incidents of domestic violence were excluded. Under the current scheme, compensation may be paid but only if the perpetrator has been prosecuted (or there are practical, technical or other good reasons for non-prosecution) and, where violence occurred between adults in the family, the perpetrator and the applicant ceased living in the same household before the application was made and are unlikely to live together again. Part of the justification for this rule is to prevent a perpetrator benefiting from an award of compensation.

The incident which caused the injury must normally have been reported to the police. Awards may be refused or reduced if the police were not informed, the applicant did not cooperate with the police or has not cooperated with the authority. It is also possible to refuse or reduce awards based on the authority's interpretation of the applicant's character as shown by his criminal convictions.

Case law has addressed issues of interpretation and procedure under the scheme. *R* v. *Criminal Injuries Compensation Appeals Panel, ex parte August; R* v. *Criminal Injuries Compensation Appeals Panel, ex parte Brown* [2001] 2 All ER 874, cases which were heard jointly in the Court of Appeal, considered the relevance of consent in determining whether a crime was a 'crime of violence' for the purpose of a claim. In each case sexual offences were committed against the claimants whilst children but with their consent. The court found that the applicant's consent or willing participation was highly relevant to deciding whether he had been a victim of violence. However reprehensible the conduct of the older man involved, a boy aged 13 who was a willing and active participant in an act of buggery with a man aged 53 was not a victim of a crime of violence so as to qualify for compensation.

The Criminal Injuries Compensation Authority is a creature of statute and a public body and, in order to conform to the basic public law requirement of sufficiency, it is obliged to provide proper reasons together with the gist of the supporting evidence for its decision to reduce or refuse claims for compensation. A failure to provide reasons is a form of procedural unfairness (*R* v. *Criminal Injuries Compensation Authority, ex parte Leatherland; R* v. *Criminal Injuries Compensation Board, ex parte Bramall; R* v. *Criminal Injuries Compensation Appeals Panel, ex parte Kay* (2000) *The Times*, 12 October).

A Government consultation document, 'Rebuilding lives – supporting victims of crime' (December 2005) includes proposals to simplify the Criminal Injuries Compensation Scheme.

■ Human Rights Act 1998 implications for criminal justice

When the Human Rights Act 1998 was introduced it was anticipated that a number of challenges to prisoners' rights would be voiced. As an example, in *R (P)* v. *Secretary of State for the Home Department; R(Q)* v. *Secretary of State for the Home Department* [2001] EWCA Civ 1151 the human rights implications of prison policy about babies in prison was considered. It was contended that the separation of mother and child once the child reached the age of 18 months was a violation of the right to respect for private and family life contained in Art. 8. The court held, however, that the Prison Service was entitled to adopt a policy allowing children to remain in prison with their mothers until the age of 18 months but not thereafter. The policy should, however, be applied flexibly, bearing in mind the effect of separation on the mother and child in each case and the alternative placement available for the child.

Chapter summary

- The National Probation Service is responsible for the majority of social work functions towards adults in the criminal justice system. It is important to recognise, however, that other service users will come into contact with the criminal justice system and for that reason it is essential that all social workers have an understanding of this area. In addition, recent legislation has introduced a duty on local authorities to do all they reasonably can to prevent crime and disorder in their area. This will impact on all aspects of social services work and other functions of local authorities.

- Key players in the criminal justice system are the police, the Crown Prosecution Service, the Criminal Defence Service, the National Probation Service, the Prison Service, and the witness service. Each organisation has defined areas of responsibility.

- Offences will comprise both a physical and mental element – the *actus reus* and the *mens rea*. The classification of an offence will dictate which court conducts the trial. Criminal offences may be defined by statute or the common law. An offence can be classified as summary, either way or indictable.

- The Police and Criminal Evidence Act 1984 (PACE) is an important piece of legislation which sets out the elements of a valid arrest, time limits for detention in custody, rights in the police station and other police powers. There are five codes of practice which accompany the Act, including Code C which addresses detention, treatment and questioning of suspects and outlines the role of the appropriate adult in respect to juveniles and vulnerable adults.

- Prior to the trial of a criminal offence the issue of remand must be determined. A suspect may be remanded in custody or on bail. The Bail Act 1976 includes a presumption in favour of bail unless specified circumstances apply.

- The court will proceed to sentence a defendant who has been found guilty. Sentences may be classified into the following groups: discharges, fines, community sentences and custody. A series of requirements can be added to community sentences and imposed during suspended custodial sentences.

- Regardless of the success of a criminal prosecution, a victim may apply for compensation for injuries caused by a crime of violence to the Criminal Injuries Compensation Authority.

- There are a range of special measures available for vulnerable witnesses to enable them to produce their best evidence to the court in a less intimidating environment.

- Specific disposals are available for people suffering from mental disorder who have committed a crime, including hospital orders. It is also possible for a person detained in prison to be transferred to a hospital because of mental disorder.

■ Various provisions have been introduced over recent years to address racism in the criminal justice system and to appropriately punish offences that are motivated by racism. The Crime and Disorder Act 1998 introduced a range of racially aggravated offences.

Exercise

The National Front attend a demonstration held in protest against 'loony left racist council policies' which have funded an Asian women's support group in Oldtown. The demonstration soon escalates into violence with others present who object to the National Front demonstration. The police make several arrests including James, aged 31 and white, who was seen attacking a black youth with a wooden post. He was found to be in possession of a large quantity of racially inflammatory material. During the course of his arrest he was racially abusive and spat in the face of the Asian officer arresting him. He is subsequently charged with several offences to which he intends to plead not guilty. The prosecution intend to oppose bail.

John, a friend of the youth who was attacked, is enraged by the demonstration and makes his way to the squat where James lives, intending to cause minor damage. Seeing racist posters through the window he loses his temper, forces his way in and sets fire to a pile of papers in the house. He was unaware that James' girlfriend and baby were upstairs at the time. They escape with minor injuries. John has a mild learning disability. He is seen running away from the property, is picked up by the police and taken to the station later that evening. The police refuse to call anybody to let them know of John's whereabouts until he tells them 'what he was up to'. They interview him alone, until he confesses to arson. John has never been in trouble with the police before.

Consider what offences James will have been charged with; whether the prosecution may successfully oppose bail; what issues might be dealt with in pre-sentence reports if he is found guilty; any breaches which there may have been to John's rights at the station and the consequences of breach. What is John's potential criminality?

Websites

Liberty:
www.liberty-human-rights.org.uk

The National Association for the Care and Resettlement of Offenders – an independent voluntary organisation working to prevent crime:
www.nacro.org.uk

The Home Office – including information about the police and the national offender management service:

www.homeoffice.gov.uk

The Criminal Justice System: includes a 'victims virtual walkthrough', an interactive guide to each step in the justice process:

www.cjsonline.org.uk

The Prison Service:

www.hmprisonservice.gov.uk

The Crown Prosecution Service, for information and a copy of the Code for Crown Prosecutors:

www.cps.gov.uk

The Independent Police Complaints Commission website has details of how to make a complaint:

www.ipcc.gov.uk

Further reading

Textbooks on criminal justice and guides to legislation include:

Zedner, L. (2004) *Criminal Justice.* Oxford: Oxford University Press.

Birch, D. and Leng, R. (2000) *Blackstone's Guide to the Youth Justice and Criminal Evidence Act 1999.* London: Blackstone Press.

Wasik, M. (2001) *Emmins on Sentencing* (4th edn). London: Blackstone Press.

Ward, R. and Wragg, A. (2005) *Walker and Walker's English Legal System* (9th edn). Oxford: Oxford University Press, chapters 12, 13, 18.

Specific aspects of criminal justice are addressed in the following publications:

White, C. (2002) 'Re-assessing the social worker's role as an appropriate adult' 24(1) *Journal of Social Welfare and Family Law* pp. 55–65. (This article suggests that more guidance and training is required if the role of appropriate adult is to be fulfilled in the spirit in which it was created.)

Bowling, B. and Phillips, C. (2002) *Racism, Crime and Justice.* Harlow: Longman.

Miers, D. (1997) *State Compensation for Criminal Injuries.* London: Blackstone Press.

Zander, M. (1995) *PACE Act* (3rd edn). London: Sweet & Maxwell.

Ellison, L. (2001) *The adversarial process and the vulnerable witness.* Oxford: Oxford University Press.

Winstone, J. and Pakes, F. (eds) (2005) *Community justice: issues for probation and criminal justice.* Cullompton: Willan Publishing.

Gray, N., Laing, J. and Noaks, L. (2002) (eds) *Criminal Justice, mental health and the politics of risk.* London: Cavendish.

Notes

1 M. Macpherson (1999) 'The Stephen Lawrence Inquiry' (Cm. 4262–1). London: The Stationery Office.

2 Home Office (2001) 'Making Punishments Work: Review of the Sentencing Framework for England and Wales' (The Halliday report). London: Home Office Communication Directorate.

3 Sir Robin Auld (2001) 'The Criminal Courts Review Report'. London: The Stationery Office.

4 Home Office (2001) 'Criminal Justice: The Way Ahead' (Cm. 5074). London: Stationery Office.

5 British Crime Survey 2000.

6 Home Office (2005) Crime In England and Wales 2004/5 (combined report of police recorded crime and the British Crime Survey). London: Home Office.

7 http://www.homeoffice.gov.uk/police/about/police-equality/?view=Standard

8 SI 2004/3216

9 The Code is issued under s. 10 of the Prosecution of Offences Act 1985.

10 The introduction to the code includes a useful section describing the role and structure of the CPS.

11 In matters concerning representation in criminal proceedings, the Access to Justice Act 1999 replaced the Legal Aid Act 1988.

12 National Probation Service for England and Wales and the Home Office Communication Directorate (2001) 'A New Choreography: An Integrated Strategy for the National Probation Service for England and Wales'. London: Home Office.

13 For the background to the creation of NOMS see: P. Carter (2003) 'Managing Offenders, Reducing Crime: A review of correctional services in England and Wales'. London: Home Office.

14 www.noms.homeoffice.gov.uk/background-to-noms/.

15 M. Zander (2000) 'The criminal standard of proof – how sure is sure?' 6956 *New Law Journal* p. 1517.

16 Plea before venue was introduced by the Criminal Procedure and Investigations Act 1996, s. 49.

17 For background to this and other changes to police powers see the Home Office Consultation paper, 'Policing: Modernising Police Powers to meet Community Needs' (2004).

18 PACE 1984, s. 30.

19 PACE 1984, s. 41.

20 PACE 1984, s. 42.

21 PACE 1984, s. 43.

22 See full discussion in J. Williams (2000) 'The inappropriate adult' 22(1) *Journal of Social Welfare and Family Law* pp. 43–57.

23 See M. Davies, H. Croall and J. Tyrer (2005) *Criminal Justice: an Introduction to the Criminal Justice System in England and Wales* (3rd edn) Harlow: Longman, for a detailed explanation of each theory and the types of sentences which most closely reflect each theory.

24 Home Office Research Development Statistics, Digest 4.

25 Criminal Justice Act 1988, s. 36.

26 Home Office Research Development Statistics, Digest 4.

27 Home Office Statistical Bulletin 15/05.

28 National Standards for the Supervision of Offenders in the Community 2000, s. B4–10.

29 Home Office Statistical Bulletin 15/05 for 2004.

30 The report which made recommendations on which the Act is based, Home Office (1998).

31 A. Clancy, M. Hough, R. Aust and C. Kershaw (2001) 'Ethnic minorities' experience of crime and policing: findings from the 2000 British Crime Survey' (Home Office Research Findings 146). London: Home Office.

32 Criminal Appeal Act 1995, s. 13.

19 Welfare and homelessness

Learning objectives

To develop an understanding of the following:

- The obligations of local authorities to provide advice and accommodation.
- The definition of homeless, priority need and intentionally homeless.
- Anti-social behaviour and housing.
- The range of welfare benefits.
- Application of the Human Rights Act 1998.

Introduction

This chapter focuses on three closely related areas: homelessness, housing and welfare benefits. Each area is characterised by complex regulation and frequent changes in law and policy. This chapter aims to provide an overview of the framework of law and regulation currently applicable. Social services' direct duties in these areas are limited; however, the impact of homelessness, housing and welfare provision on service users is often significant and may interrelate with other duties and powers of social services. These areas mainly fall within the aspect of social work law covering law that service users are likely to experience, though there may not be direct social work responsibilities. Councils have specific responsibilities towards homeless people exercised by the housing department. The principle duties are: to provide advice and assistance and suitable accommodation for people who are homeless and in priority need and did not become homeless intentionally. The role of the social worker is identified throughout and these are areas where it is important to be aware of avenues for further information and advice.

Homelessness

The Housing Act 1996 (HA 1996) is the key legislation on homelessness, as amended by the Homelessness Act 2002. Responding appropriately to homelessness is a key feature of the Social Exclusion Agenda and the 2002 Act includes an emphasis on strategies for preventing homelessness.

Causes of homelessness are many and varied. Changes to the housing market, including right to buy, demographic changes, unemployment and domestic violence all have their influence. Responses to homelessness have been highly politicised and it is unfortunate that negative perceptions, such as the idea that young women will get pregnant to jump the housing queue, still feature in the popular press. Against this context, and with a limited housing stock, councils have to assess each case on its merits.

This section considers relevant definitions, including homeless, priority need and intentionally homeless, duties imposed, review of decisions, homelessness strategies and the Code of Guidance.[1]

The Government is committed to reducing levels of homelessness and has set a target of a 50 per cent reduction in the number of homeless households in temporary accommodation by 2010. The Office of the Deputy Prime Minister (ODPM) holds statistics on the number of homeless people and has recently published research on homelessness and the ethnic minority population.[2]

It has also recognised that ethnic minority households are at a disproportionate risk of homelessness and has published two guides: 'Tackling homelessness amongst ethnic minority households – a development guide' and 'The causes of homelessness amongst ethnic minority populations' (ODPM 2005).

■ Specific duties

Councils have two principal duties:

- ■ **Advice and assistance** – Councils have to provide advice and assistance to any person who is homeless or threatened with homelessness who seeks their help.
- ■ **Emergency accommodation** – Beyond advice and assistance councils are also obliged to provide emergency accommodation in some circumstances.

The criteria are that the person is eligible for assistance, homeless and in priority need. Each of these criteria is discussed below.

Eligible

The rules on eligibility provide that most UK citizens are eligible for assistance. Individuals who have lived abroad, moved to the United Kingdom or come to the United Kingdom seeking asylum are ineligible for assistance (HA 1996, s. 185). The detailed rules on eligibility are quite complex. The Secretary of State is obliged to provide information to a housing authority requesting that information, to determine individual eligibility.

Homeless

A person is homeless if he has no accommodation in the United Kingdom or elsewhere in the world which is available for his occupation.

Potential homelessness is also covered by the Act, as a person is threatened with homelessness if it is likely that he will become homeless within 28 days (s. 175(4)). A person can be homeless even though they have some form of accommodation. For example, a person who is staying with friends or relatives but has been asked to leave, is at risk of violence at home or is about to be evicted, may be classed as homeless. Accommodation will be considered available for the applicant if it is available for him and any person who normally resides with him as a member of his family. If it is not 'reasonable to continue to occupy' (HA 1996, s. 175) accommodation it will be disregarded and the person can be considered homeless. For example, if the accommodation is in really bad condition, having taken into account general housing circumstances in the area (HA 1996, s. 177).

It is not reasonable to continue to occupy accommodation if doing so would result in violence to the applicant or a member of his family. 'Violence' includes threats of violence from another person which are likely to be carried out (s. 177(1A)). Violence is domestic violence where it is from a person who is 'associated' with the victim. The list of associated persons is set out in s. 178 and broadly replicates the list in the Family Law Act 1996 (i.e. married, cohabitants, live in the same household, relatives, parent relation to a child). Clearly there will be cases where social services have involvement with a family as a result of domestic violence concerns and one aspect to be addressed in ensuring protection of children is their housing situation.

It is also not reasonable to continue to occupy if the accommodation is unsuitable because the applicant cannot gain entry to it or it is a moveable structure and there is nowhere to place and reside in it, e.g. a caravan or boat. The cost of a property is also relevant to an assessment of whether it is reasonable to occupy. The housing authority must take into account the resources available to the individual, costs of the accommodation, any maintenance payments and reasonable living expenses.[3]

Priority need

A person has a priority need if the authority is satisfied that he or she falls into one or more of the following categories:

- A pregnant woman (or person the woman resides with).
- A person with whom dependent children would reside.
- A person who is vulnerable because of a disability, physical or mental health problems, or other special reasons (or a person he would reside with).
- A person who is homeless as a result of an emergency such as fire or flood.
- 16–17-year-olds, provided they are not the responsibility of social services (provided with accommodation under s. 20 of the Children Act 1989).
- 18–20-year-old care leavers.
- A person who is vulnerable having been in custody.

- A person who is vulnerable as a result of service in the armed forces.
- A person who is vulnerable having ceased to occupy accommodation because of violence or threats of violence which are likely to be carried out.

It is usual for the housing authority to require evidence from a midwife or doctor as to pregnancy, but it does not matter what stage of the pregnancy has been reached. From the above it is clear that the status of homelessness and priority need will attach not only to the applicant but also to people it would be reasonable to expect to live with him, i.e. a spouse or cohabitee, dependent children or relatives. In relation to dependent children it is not necessary to have a formal court order (residence, previously custody) before it would be reasonable to expect children to be living with the applicant (*R v Ealing London Borough, ex parte Sidhu* (1983) 2 HLR 45). The phrase 'dependent children' includes children up to the age of 16 and 16–18-year-olds living at home and in education or training. The crucial question will be the degree of permanence and regularity in the arrangement, so occasional ad hoc overnight contact would not be included, but 'joint residence' should be, even though the code notes that 'it will only be in exceptional circumstances that the child will be considered to reside with both parents' (para. 8.10).

Where the applicant may be considered 'vulnerable', the housing authority may liaise with social services and obtain medical opinion to assist with the assessment of vulnerability and suitable housing. A person may also be vulnerable due to old age but there is no automatic age limit. The phrase 'other special reasons' allows others who are not necessarily physically or mentally disabled to be considered as having a priority need.

In *Griffin v Westminster City Council* [2004] EWCA Civ 108, the Court of Appeal confirmed that the assessment of vulnerability is a matter for the council's discretion. A 33-year-old man applied as homeless to the council after leaving his mother's address. He had fallen out with his mother's partner and he had alcohol problems and reactive depression. The council provided temporary accommodation but decided he did not have a priority need. G sought a review of the decision. The review officer confirmed that the test to be applied was drawn from the case *R v Camden London Borough, ex parte Pereira* (1998) 31 HLR 317: 'whether G when homeless would be less likely to fend for [himself] than an ordinary homeless person so that injury or detriment to [G] would have resulted when a less vulnerable person would be able to cope without harmful effect.' G appealed, arguing that the correct test was contained in the Code of Practice, which required the authority to evaluate the risk of harm and likelihood of injury or detriment. The Court of Appeal confirmed that the *Pereira* test had been applied correctly and that likelihood of injury did not appear in the statute. The test is whether injury or detriment would occur, not likelihood of it occurring. The statute must prevail over the Code of Practice.

Where a person is vulnerable having ceased to occupy accommodation because of violence or threats of violence which are likely to be carried out, she has a priority need. This is not limited to domestic violence. The code notes: 'In cases involving violence, the safety of the applicant, and ensuring confidentiality must be of paramount concern. It is not only domestic violence that is relevant but all forms of violence, including racially motivated violence or threats of violence likely to be carried out' (para. 8.26).

Intentional homelessness

Section 191 of the Housing Act 1996 covers intentional homelessness:

s. 191

> A person becomes intentionally homeless if he deliberately does or fails to do anything in consequence of which he ceases to occupy accommodation which is available for his occupation and which it would have been reasonable for him to continue to occupy.
>
> (HA 1996)

A similarly worded provision applies to those threatened with homelessness (s. 196(1)). The definition can be broken down into four separate elements:

- A deliberate act or failure to act.
- As a consequence accommodation ceases to be occupied.
- The accommodation was available for occupation by the person.
- It was reasonable for him to continue to occupy the accommodation.

An act in good faith by a person who was unaware of a relevant fact will not be treated as deliberate, e.g. leaving accommodation before expiry of the notice period.

A person who leaves accommodation because of actual or threatened domestic violence should not be considered intentionally homeless. In *Bond v Leicester City Council* [2001] EWCA Civ 1544, the court confirmed that under HA 1996, ss. 177 and 191, when deciding whether it was reasonable for the victim to continue to occupy the former home, the authority should only consider whether it was probable that continued occupation would lead to domestic violence, and not whether preventative measures could have been taken by the victim. The variety of circumstances that can lead to homelessness, and about which there is argument as to intentionality, are endless. As examples, failure to pay rent or mortgage payments due to poor financial management is likely to be considered intentional, though if spouse A genuinely believed that spouse B was making payments, spouse A might be considered unintentionally homeless. Becoming homeless as a result of imprisonment is likely to be considered intentional.

Connection with the area

A person has a local connection with an area if he is or was normally resident in it as a matter of choice; is employed in the area; has family associations with the area; or there are other special circumstances which result in a local connection with the area. Establishing local connection is the key to which housing authority has the duty to provide accommodation for the applicant.

■ Duties of the authority

The responsibilities of the housing authority flow from inclusion in the categories outlined above and range from providing advice and information about homelessness to provision of accommodation.

Initially, where the authority is approached by an individual seeking accommodation or assistance, and it has reason to believe the person may be homeless or threatened with homelessness, it must make enquiries under HA 1996, s. 184 as to whether the person is eligible for assistance and, if so, what duties are owed to him. The individual does not have to apply in writing, and it should be possible for an application to be made at any time (24-hour access). Enquiries will include whether the person has a priority need and whether he is intentionally homeless. They should be carried out sensitively by the housing authority. Following enquiries, the applicant must be notified by the authority of its decision. It is possible to provide accommodation pending enquiries (s. 188). The Act does not stipulate a timescale for the conduct of enquiries, though the code suggests a target of completion within 33 days of the application (para. 3.18).

Possible decisions and corresponding duties:

Homeless but no priority need

If the applicant is eligible, homeless or threatened with homelessness, intentionally or unintentionally, but not in priority need, the authority has an obligation to assess his housing needs and provide advice and assistance (free of charge). This includes advice as to the likely availability of appropriate accommodation in the area. If the applicant is unintentionally homeless the authority may (but is not obliged to) secure accommodation for him. Much will depend on the resources in the area.

Priority need but intentionally homeless

In this situation the authority must assess the applicant's housing needs and provide advice and assistance. It must also ensure that temporary accommodation is made available for a period it considers will give him a reasonable opportunity to find his own accommodation.

Priority need but threatened with homelessness intentionally

The same advice and assistance duty applies, and once the homelessness occurs the applicant is entitled to a period of temporary accommodation.

Priority need and unintentionally threatened with homelessness

The duty here is to try to secure the accommodation does not cease to be available for the applicant to enable him to remain in the accommodation. If this is not possible, then accommodation must be provided once the homelessness occurs.

Priority need and unintentionally homeless

The full duty applies here – to ensure that accommodation is available for occupation by the applicant (and any family member who normally resides with him).

The authority has power to make reasonable charges for accommodation it provides. If the applicant refuses an offer of suitable accommodation, the council has discharged its duty and is not bound to provide an alternative. In terms of 'suitability' of accommodation the code advises housing authorities to:

> . . . have regard to all the relevant circumstances of the applicant and his or her household. Account will need to be taken of any medical and/or physical needs, and any social considerations relating to the applicant and his or her household that might affect the suitability of accommodation. Any risk of violence or racial harassment must also be taken into account. (para. 12.4).

Bed and breakfast accommodation for more than six weeks will not be classed as suitable accommodation for an applicant with family.

■ Review of homelessness decisions

Part VII of the Housing Act 1996 provides a scheme for reviewing homelessness decisions.[4] The authority may provide accommodation pending the outcome of a review. A request for review should normally be made within 21 days of notification of the authority's decision. The review should be conducted by a person of 'appropriate seniority . . . not involved in the original decision' (HA 1996, s. 203). There is a right of appeal to the county court on a point of law.

In *Runa Begum* v. *Tower Hamlets London Borough Council* [2003] UKHL 5, this was found to be compatible with Art. 6 ECHR. Article 6 was engaged as provision of urgent accommodation to disadvantaged people constituted a determination of civil rights. In terms of independence, the court found that the reviewing officer was not sufficiently impartial or independent, but looked at with the possibility of appeal to the county court, the scheme was compatible. This decision is in a similar vein to *R (on the application of Beeson)* v. *Dorset CC* [2002] EWCA Civ 1812, where the availability of judicial review was sufficient to make the social services complaints procedure compatible.

■ Cooperation with social services

Where an applicant with children is considered intentionally homeless (or threatened with homelessness intentionally), the housing authority must request the applicant's consent to refer the case to social services. Local government organisation means that in unitary and metropolitan areas this will be another department in the council, but in county areas the district council will be the housing authority with social services situated within the county council. There is scope under s. 17 of the

Children Act 1989 to provide accommodation to children in need and their families; however, as s. 17 provides a general duty, it would also be possible to provide accommodation just for the children.

Section 27 of the Children Act 1989 enables social services to request advice and assistance from the housing department where, for example, social services are concerned with an intentionally homeless family with children. The housing department might respond with advice as to availability of provide rented accommodation but is not bound to provide accommodation itself.

Where a housing authority receives an application for housing from a young person aged 16 or 17, cooperation with social services should enable a joint assessment of housing and other needs to be conducted.

■ Homelessness strategies

The Homelessness Act 2002 places a duty on housing authorities to publish a homelessness strategy. The strategy should be based on a homelessness review in the area, to include: the level (and likely future level) of homelessness in the area; actions taken to prevent homelessness; ensuring that accommodation is available for homeless people; and providing support for homeless people in the area, together with resources available to the authority and other bodies for such activities. The strategy should be prepared in consultation with social services (who will need to give detail of any activities they provide that are likely to meet the needs of the homeless), and other relevant organisations. The first strategy was to be published soon after the Act came into force and a revised strategy must be published every five years.

■ Code of Guidance

A Code of Guidance has been issued in support of functions under the Housing Act 1996. The code (2002) is published by the Office of the Deputy Prime Minister, the section of the Government with responsibility for housing and homelessness issues. Authorities are expressly required to have regard to the code.

What is a home?

The European Court of Human Rights has adopted a broad interpretation of 'home' for the purposes of Art. 8 (right to respect for private and family life).

Buckley v United Kingdom (1996) 23 EHRR 101 decided that: 'the concept of "home" within the meaning of Article 8 is not limited to those which are lawfully occupied or which have been lawfully occupied . . . Whether or not a particular habitation constitutes a "home" which attracts the protection of Article 8 will depend on the factual circumstances, namely, the existence of sufficient and continuous links.' This position was confirmed in *Harrow London Borough Council* v. *Qazi* [2003] UKHL 43, where it was held that there was no requirement for the occupier to have a legal interest in his home.

The right to respect for private and family life, his home and correspondence, in Art. 8, does not equate to a right to housing however (*Chapman* v. *United Kingdom* (2001) 10 BHRC 48). As with other areas of practice, it is essential that the housing authority (which is a public authority under the Human Rights Act 1998 and obliged to act compatibly with the Convention) makes decisions based on relevant information, follows procedures prescribed by law and makes proportionate decisions.

Anti-social behaviour and housing

Housing law is a complex area and it will almost always be necessary to seek further specialist advice on housing matters. Key legislation includes the Housing Acts of 1985, 1988 and 1996, the latter of which includes the duty of local housing authorities to provide advice and assistance; consider applications for housing under its housing allocation policy; and defines housing associations as registered social landlords. The Landlord and Tenant Act 1985 sets out the scheme for obligation to keep properties in good repair. The Protection from Eviction Act 1977 provides the scheme for legal eviction and provides protection against illegal eviction. With a focus on those areas most likely to come to the attention of social workers, the chapter continues with consideration of anti-social behaviour and housing.

Where a tenant is affected by anti-social behaviour, there are a number of ways in which this might be tackled:

- All social housing tenancy agreements should include clear clauses which prohibit anti-social behaviour by tenants and their guests, and outline the action that will be taken in response. Breach of the tenancy agreement may provide grounds for eviction. For some time tenancy agreements have included provisions prohibiting racial abuse.
- Under the Anti-social Behaviour Act 2003, all social landlords are obliged to publish their policies and procedures, including their approach to anti-social behaviour.
- Possession orders may be made by the county court under the ground of nuisance.
- When the court is considering possession, it must look at the impact of anti-social behaviour and the likelihood of it continuing.
- The Anti-social Behaviour Act 2003 gives the same powers to registered social landlords as local authorities to apply for injunctions to prevent anti-social behaviour, which causes nuisance or annoyance, including a power to exclude a person from a designated area or from their own home.

- Demotion orders were introduced by the Anti-social Behaviour Act 2003. These orders reduce the status and security of an existing tenancy, where the tenant has behaved anti-socially, and removes their right to buy.
- In addition to registered social landlords, the police and local authorities retain powers to apply for anti-social behaviour orders in their area.

Welfare

The Department for Work and Pensions (**DWP**) has overall responsibility for social security benefits, the policy surrounding benefits and their administration. This department is charged with implementing the Government's 'Welfare to Work' strategy and has assumed the responsibilities previously held by the Department of Social Security (DSS) and some aspects of the previous Department for Education and Employment. The Inland Revenue is a further key player in the welfare arena, with responsibility for various tax credits and child benefit. Responsibility for housing benefit and council tax benefit remains with local authorities. Jobcentre Plus is part of the DWP, and administers most pre-retirement benefits. It may do so through old local social security offices and jobcentres or combined centres offering a fully integrated service. Other parts of the DWP include the Pension Service, the Disability and Carers Service, the Child Support Agency and the Appeals Service. In certain circumstances, social services may make payments to support individuals and families, e.g. covering transport costs to enable parents to have contact with their looked after children.

An outline of the main benefits follows in alphabetical order. It is necessary to have on outline understanding of the main benefits and eligibility for those benefits (and the complexity which can be a feature of claiming), but this is an area where social workers will often need to refer service users for more detailed information and guidance. It is important to remember that, whilst the press often reminds us that some people will fraudulently claim benefits to which they are not entitled, there are in fact thousands of pounds of unclaimed benefits each year. Some people may choose not to claim benefits to which they are entitled, but for many others lack of awareness features and the complexity of the process may be daunting. Jobcentre Plus has benefit advisers and there are other statutory and voluntary organisations that provide information and guidance, such as Citizens' Advice Bureaux and the Disability Alliance, and some local authorities employ welfare rights officers. Even if an individual does not make a claim initially, it should be remembered that some benefits can be backdated. As noted in Chapter 14, individuals often have multiple characteristics and needs and may need to claim a package of different benefits to support their circumstances; for example, a disabled adult may have caring responsibilities for a child and an older adult relative, and be unable to work. For reference, the Child Poverty Action Group publishes an excellent 'Welfare Benefits Handbook' annually, with details of all benefits and their current rate.

Existing benefits can be grouped into various categories. Most benefits are financial payments, made by direct payments into an individual's bank account, in place of the old 'Giro' and order book system. There are also some other benefits that provide subsidised access to goods and services, such as free school meals. Some benefits, such as income support, are income-related or means-tested and others are paid at a flat rate regardless of income, e.g. child benefit. There are contributory and non-contributory benefits. Retirement pensions and jobseekers allowance are contributory benefits and income support and attendance allowance are examples of non contributory benefits. A further classification is into taxable and non-taxable benefits, the former including widows benefits, while maternity allowance is an example of the latter. 'Passport benefits' are payable alongside certain means tested benefits or tax credits, e.g. Income support is a passport to free school meals, health benefits such as free prescriptions and some social fund payments.

Attendance allowance

Attendance allowance (AA) is a tax-free benefit for people aged 65 or over who are physically or mentally disabled and need help with personal care. People under 65 may be able to get disability living allowance.

Carer's allowance

A taxable benefit, payable to carers, 'regularly and substantially engaged in caring', i.e. providing 35 hours per week or more (to a person receiving disability living allowance or attendance allowance). It applies to carers over the age of 16. The entitlement continues for eight weeks after the death of the person cared for.

Child benefit

Child benefit is paid for all children up to 16 (19 if in education). A higher rate is paid for the first child, then a lower amount for younger children. If the child is 'looked after' for more than eight weeks, the benefit may stop.

Council tax benefit

Council tax benefit is available to people on low incomes on a similar basis to housing benefit. In addition, where a person who is substantially and permanently disabled lives in a bigger property because additional space is required due to the disability, e.g. if extra space is needed for wheelchair use, it may be possible for council tax on the property to be charged at a band lower than the property is worth. To qualify, the property must have a room that has been modified for the disabled person's sole use or an additional bathroom, lavatory or kitchen or extra space to allow a wheelchair to be used inside.

Disability living allowance

People with care and mobility needs or who are terminally ill and under 65 may claim disability living allowance. A complex self-assessment form has to be completed. The benefit will cease in respect of the care element after periods in hospital or residential care. It is a tax-free benefit available to children and adults.

Guardians allowance

A benefit paid to a guardian of an orphan, or where one parent has died and the other is not available (whereabouts unknown, in prison, detained under the Mental Health Act, etc.).

Housing benefit

Housing benefit is paid by the local authority to people who have to pay rent to ensure that, after paying reasonable housing costs, tenants are left with at least equivalent to basic income support levels for day-to-day living expenses. The amount is calculated making allowances for each individual and dependent, including child care costs, and added premiums, such as lone parent or carer premiums.

In 2004/5 32 per cent of complaints to the local government ombudsman (England) concerned housing (including council house repairs) or housing benefit.

Incapacity benefit

Incapacity benefit is payable to people under pension age who cannot work because of illness or disability. There are short-term and long-term rates. Some part-time permitted work is allowed whilst claiming.

Income support

Income support is an income-related benefit for people between the age of 16 and 60 who are on a low income, not working, or working on average less than 16 hours a week. Savings of over £16,000 will affect eligibility. If the claimant's partner works, this will also affect the amount of income support awarded. To qualify for income support, most claimants will have to attend Jobcentres regularly (exceptions apply to lone parents, people who are sick or disabled or unable to work because they are caring for someone, or registered blind). Income support is made up of a basic personal allowance, allowances for dependent children and may include a family premium, pensioner premium, disability premium, severe disability premium and carer premium. Children under school age and expectant mothers are entitled to free milk and vitamins and children at school will have free school meals.

Jobseekers allowance

Jobseekers allowance is a taxable benefit paid to people who are registered unemployed and looking for work, up to pensionable age.

Social Fund

The Social Fund includes discretionary payments in the form of community care grants and crisis loans. Community care grants are made to people on income support or jobseekers allowance for various reasons, including: helping an individual remain in the community or move into the community after a period in residential care; helping an individual who has had an unsettled life settle into the community; and easing exceptional pressures on families.

Crisis loans are paid to people who, following an emergency or disaster, e.g. a fire, are without resources and the means to prevent serious risk or damage to their health or safety. The social fund also covers cold weather payments.

Chapter summary

- The Housing Act 1996 is the key legislation on homelessness, as amended by the Homelessness Act 2002. The legislation gives councils two principle duties: to provide advice and assistance to any person who is homeless or threatened with homelessness who seeks their help; and to provide emergency accommodation in some circumstances.

- The criteria for provision of emergency accommodation are that the person is eligible for assistance, homeless and in priority need.

- Priority need is defined as including: a pregnant woman; a person with dependent children; a person who is vulnerable because of a disability, physical or mental health problems, or other special reasons; a person who is homeless as a result of an emergency, such as fire or flood, 16–17 year olds, provided they are not the responsibility of social services (provided with accommodation under s. 20 of the Children Act 1989); 18–20-year-old care leavers; a person who is vulnerable having been in custody, as a result of service in the armed forces, or having ceased to occupy accommodation because of violence or threats of violence which are likely to be carried out.

- The council are not obliged to provide accommodation to a person who is considered intentionally homeless. A person becomes intentionally homeless if he deliberately does or fails to do anything in consequence of which he ceases to occupy accommodation which is available for his occupation and which it would have been reasonable for him to continue to occupy.

- Where children are part of a family which is considered intentionally homeless, social services may provide accommodation under s.17 of the Children Act 1989 as part of their general duty to children in need.

- Where a tenant is affected by anti-social behaviour, it is possible for registered social landlords to obtain an injunction to stop the behaviour and in some circumstances to obtain a possession order evicting the person causing anti-social behaviour. This is in addition to existing responsibilities of the police and councils to tackle anti-social behaviour.

■ Many of the people that social workers will be working with will be entitled to some form of welfare benefits. Benefits may be means-tested, contributory or non-contributory; some are taxable and some are passport benefits and are provided alongside an entitlement to another benefit. A summary of some of the key benefits is set out.

■ This chapter provides a brief overview of welfare and homelessness, as matters which will affect many service users but where social services do not generally hold key responsibilities. It will often be necessary to obtain detailed advice and further information when faced with cases that touch on these areas.

Websites

The Office of the Deputy Prime Minister, the Government department with responsibility for housing and homelessness, and to access a copy of the Code of Guidance:
www.odpm.gov.uk

The Department for Work and Pensions resource centre includes leaflets and guides to benefits and services, including downloadable forms:
www.dwp.gov.uk

Further advice and resources can be obtained from:
Citizens Advice Bureau:
www.citizensadvice.org.uk

Disability Alliance:
www.disabilityalliance.org

Child Poverty Action Group:
www.cpag.org.uk

HM Revenue & Customs:
www.hmrc.gov.uk

Shelter provides useful information and guides on all aspects of housing and homelessness and runs a helpline service:
www.shelter.org.uk

Further reading

Gervais, M. and Rehman, H. (2005) *Causes of Homelessness amongst the Ethnic Minority Population.* London: ODPM. (A research publication which identifies that ethnic minority households are three times more likely to become homeless than the majority white population, and attributes this to a complex cycle of deprivation.)

Arden, A. and Hunter, C. (2002) *Homelessness and Allocations.* London: Legal Action Group. (A detailed text including a copy of the Housing Act 1996, as amended by the Homelessness Act 2002 and the Code of Guidance.)

Arden, A. and Hunter, C. (2003) *Manual of Housing Law* (7th edn). London: Sweet & Maxwell. (A detailed resource on housing law by the same authors of *Homelessness and Allocations.*)

Rai, S. (2004) 'Accommodating Families with Children – The Final Chapter' *Journal of Housing Law* p. 21. (Considers social services responsibilities.)

Carlton, N., Fear, T. and Means, R. (2004) 'Responding to the Harassment and Abuse of Older People in the Private Rented Sector: Legal and Social Perspectives' 26(2) *Journal of Social Welfare and Family Law* p. 131.

Child Poverty Action Group. (2005) *Welfare Benefits and Tax Credits Handbook* (7th edn). London: CPAG. (A really useful and accessible text written with welfare advisers in mind.)

Wikeley, N. (2002) *The Law of Social Security* (5th edn). London: Butterworths. (A detailed and informative sourcebook.)

Notes

[1] See also 'Homelessness strategies – a good practice handbook', published for local authority use.

[2] M. Gervais and H. Rehman (2005) *Causes of Homelessness amongst the Ethnic Minority Population.* London: ODPM.

[3] Homelessness (Suitability of Accommodation) Order 1996 (SI 1996/3204).

[4] Allocation of Housing and Homelessness (Review Procedures) Regulations 1999 (SI 1999/71).

20 Asylum

Learning objectives

To develop an understanding of the following:

- The legislative framework for asylum seekers.
- Key provisions of the Immigration and Asylum Act 1999 and the background to its development.
- The application and appeals process for asylum seekers.
- The definition of refugee.
- Provision of support for asylum seekers.
- The position of unaccompanied children.
- Remaining responsibilities of social services for asylum seekers.
- Proposals for further reform.

Introduction

The plight of asylum seekers is rarely out of the public eye and for many it is an emotive issue. Notable events have drawn further attention to this issue, including asylum seekers' attempts to enter the United Kingdom via the channel tunnel and reports of deaths of asylum seekers during transit to the United Kingdom. Asylum seekers may flee their country and come to the United Kingdom, whereas others already in the United Kingdom on a temporary basis may apply for asylum if it would be dangerous to return to their country of origin. The number of asylum seekers coming to Britain rose consistently throughout the 1990s. Clearly many asylum seekers are fleeing from conflict, as for example in 2001, asylum seekers came to Britain in highest numbers from Afghanistan, Iraq, Somalia, Sri Lanka and the

Federal Republic of Yugoslavia. Home Office statistics reveal that asylum applications in 2005 had fallen to their lowest level since 1994, and there was an increase in the number of removals. In 2005 the greatest number of applications were from Iran, Eritrea and Afghanistan.

There have been five separate pieces of legislation relating to asylum seekers since 1993.[1] Current law is contained in the Immigration and Asylum Act 1999 (**IAA 1999**), a complex and detailed piece of legislation, based on a Government white paper, entitled 'Fairer, Faster and Firmer – A Modern Approach to Immigration and Asylum'.[2] It has been supplemented by the Nationality, Immigration and Asylum Act 2002 (**NIAA 2002**), which followed publication of a white paper entitled 'Secure Borders, Safe Haven: Integration with Diversity in Modern Britain'.[3] Finally, the Asylum and Immigration (Treatment of Claimants, etc.) Act 2004 (**AIA 2004**) was introduced and a further Immigration, Asylum and Nationality Bill 2005 has been published. No doubt the legislative activity has in part been an attempt to improve a system which has been characterised by delay and negative media reports concentrating on 'bogus' asylum seekers. A brief summary of each of the pieces of legislation is set out below.

Alongside the IAA 1999, a new body was created to administer the asylum support arrangements: the National Asylum Support Service (**NASS**), part of the Immigration and Nationality Directorate of the Home Office. New arrangements for support of asylum seekers by the NASS have been in force since April 2000. Section 115 of the Immigration and Asylum Act 1999 removed any previous entitlements to social security and housing benefits for new entrants. The law has restricted provision of support to asylum seekers, and allowed more de facto detention of asylum seekers whilst waiting for the outcome of tightened procedures for dealing with claims swiftly. It has been argued that over recent years, 'through the progressive hardening of asylum law, the asylum seeker has been subjected to a policy of deterrence, and on occasion of exclusion, either by the introduction of specific restrictive measures targeted at the asylum seeker, or by the categorization of the asylum seeker as *de facto* refugee, economic migrant, bogus refugee, or even quasi-criminal' (Stevens, 2004).[4]

For the purposes of this chapter, a person waiting for a decision on their application for asylum is referred to as an ***asylum seeker***. The term ***refugee*** applies to a person whose application for asylum has been accepted.

Outline of legislation

Asylum cases were originally dealt with under general immigration law, principally the Immigration Act 1971. The increase in numbers of asylum seekers in the late 1980s highlighted the particular needs of asylum seekers and led to the introduction of specific legislation, namely the Asylum and Immigration Appeals Act 1993 and the Asylum and Immigration Act 1996.

■ Asylum and Immigration Appeals Act 1993

Obligations under the Geneva Convention Relating to the Status of Refugees 1951 were incorporated into law by the Asylum and Immigration Appeals Act 1993. The Act also provided a right of appeal against refusals of asylum, within strict limits. The Act establishes the requirement for all asylum seekers to be fingerprinted and permits detention of asylum seekers whilst awaiting the outcome of an asylum claim.

■ Asylum and Immigration Act 1996

One of the features of this legislation was the establishment of a 'white list' of countries, which were considered by the Home Office not to pose a serious risk of persecution. Strict time limits were imposed for applications from asylum seekers from a white list country. The Act also prevented asylum seekers who had travelled through a safe third country from applying for asylum whilst in the United Kingdom. Entitlement to welfare benefits was restricted to asylum seekers who made an immediate application on arrival in the United Kingdom. This legislation heralded a much more restrictive regime, as indicated by the Home Secretary at the time when describing its objectives: 'first, to strengthen our asylum procedures so that bogus claims and appeals can be dealt with more quickly; secondly, to combat immigration racketeering through stronger powers; and thirdly, to reduce economic incentives, which attract people to come to this country in breach of our immigration laws.'[5]

■ Immigration and Asylum Act 1999

Much of the current structure for asylum is drawn from the Immigration and Asylum Act 1999, which followed the heavily criticised earlier legislation. It has not escaped criticism either and was been described as a missed opportunity.[6] The IAA 1999 repeals large parts of former immigration Acts including the 1993 and 1996 Acts referred to above. A complex and fragmented picture of legislation remains and there is a clear need for consolidating legislation.

The white paper leading to the Immigration and Asylum Act 1999 contained three objectives for a new support system:

1. support for those who would otherwise be destitute, whilst minimising costs;

2. separate provision for asylum seekers away from the main benefits scheme; and

3. minimise cash payments to deter abuse of the system by economic migrants.[7]

■ Nationality, Immigration and Asylum Act 2002

The Nationality, Immigration and Asylum Act 2002 is another lengthy and complex piece of legislation.

Key provisions include:

- ■ Section 70, which provides the statutory basis for the use of induction centres. An immigration officer may require and asylum seeker to reside at a 'specified place' for up to 14 days when an induction programmer is available there.

- Introduction of an application registration card to provide evidence of identity and nationality.

- The Home Secretary is given the power to establish accommodation centres (s. 16).

- Under s. 55, local authorities will be prevented from providing support to an asylum seeker who has not applied for asylum 'as soon as reasonably practicable' after arriving in the United Kingdom. Exceptions apply in cases where the asylum seeker has a dependent child living in the same household or if support is required to avoid a breach of the European Convention.

- Section 54 permits withdrawal or refusal of support for non-asylum seekers, being refugees granted status abroad, European Nationals, failed asylum seekers who have not cooperated with removal directions and the dependants of these groups.

■ Asylum and Immigration (Treatment of Claimants, etc.) Act 2004

This Act contains a controversial measure in s. 9. Families who have been refused asylum and have exhausted appeal rights can have any financial support and accommodation removed from them if they 'fail to take reasonable steps' to leave the United Kingdom. If the family becomes destitute, the children may be removed and taken into care.

This chapter concentrates on the impact of the three most recent Acts. It continues with an outline of the existing structure for dealing with asylum seekers' claims. The final section has a specific focus on the responsibilities of social services, with particular reference to unaccompanied children and the application of community care law.

Seeking asylum – the current law

It is important to recognise at the outset that discrimination will be a feature of the lives of many asylum seekers and a commitment to anti-discriminatory practice is essential – although it appears to have little support from the law.

■ Anti-discriminatory practice

Asylum seekers may experience discrimination on a number of levels and it may operate between different groups. At an institutional level, Shah argues, 'the legal system has consistently been favourable to European refugees, whilst it has consistently rejected or been hostile to, the presence of Asian or African groups'.[8] It has been argued that the specific experiences of women refugees are frequently neglected,[9] despite the fact that women and children constitute around 80 per cent of all asylum seekers. Gender persecution is also evident in some asylum seekers' cases, including instances where asylum is sought following extreme domestic violence from which the woman is unprotected in the country of origin, and cases where asylum is sought to escape the risk of female genital multilation.

Racism towards asylum seekers appears to have increased alongside the dispersal programme. The National Asylum Support Service has a racial harassment investigations team and asylum seekers dispersed away from London may be further disadvantaged because the majority of refugee community organisations, such as the Refugee Council, are based in London and there are fewer legal advisers with appropriate expertise away from the capital. In addition, communities with little experience of refugees may have been influenced by the negative reporting of the media and asylum seekers may suffer both discrimination and social exclusion.

■ National Asylum Support Service

The *National Asylum Support Service* (NASS) was established by the Home Office[10] and began to function on 3 April 2000. Based in Croydon, it was set up so that a single body would have the responsibility for providing support to asylum seekers whilst waiting for a decision on their asylum status. Before this time, support was provided by the Department of Social Security (DSS) and local authorities, principally through entitlement to welfare and housing benefits. Support provided by the NASS may be accommodation only, financial support only (if the person has somewhere else to stay, e.g. with relatives), or accommodation and financial support. Accommodation will usually be provided outside London at a number of dispersal centres. Support from the NASS is provided to asylum seekers who are destitute or likely to become destitute in 14 days, whilst the outcome of a decision on the asylum claim is awaited.

■ Refugee status

Asylum will be granted to a person who satisfies the definition of '*refugee*'.[11] This is set out in the Geneva Convention Relating to the Status of Refugees 1951[12] as a person who:

> . . . owing to a well-founded fear of being persecuted for reasons of race, religion, nationality, membership of a particular social group or political opinion, is outside the country of his nationality and unable or, owing to such fear, is unwilling to avail himself of the protection of that country; or who, not having a nationality and being outside the country of his former habitual residence . . . is unable or, owing to such fear, is unwilling to return to it.[13]

If a person is not found to meet this definition of refugee, he will normally be refused asylum. In some circumstances a person who does not fall within the 1951 definition may be granted leave to remain. In April 2003, exceptional leave to remain in the United Kingdom was replaced by 'humanitarian protection and discretionary leave'. This recognises that other individuals whose circumstances are not covered by the Convention may still require protection.

Interpretation of 'particular social group' has been an issue for the courts to consider. In *Islam* v. *Secretary of State for the Home Department; R* v. *Immigration Appeals Tribunal, ex parte Shah* [1999] 2 AC 629, the House of Lords reversed the decision of the Court of Appeal and found that Pakistani women sufferers of domestic violence were included. Whilst that might not be a sufficient consideration in other countries, it was noted that: 'in Pakistan women are unprotected by the State: discrimination against women in Pakistan is partly tolerated by the state and partly sanctioned by the State'.[14]

Fear of persecution must relate to current circumstances, as illustrated by *R* v. *Secretary of State for the Home Department, ex parte Adan* [1999] 1 AC 293. The applicant was granted exceptional leave to remain, having fled Somalia in 1988, at which time he had a fear of persecution from the Government. When he applied for his status to be converted to refugee, the House of Lords refused and found that, the Government of Somalia having changed, the applicant had no current fear of persecution. A claim of persecution based on the likelihood of punishment following failure to perform military service due to conscientious objection was not successful for individuals seeking asylum in the case of *Sepet* v. *Secretary of State for the Home Department* [2001] EWCA Civ 681. Interpretation of this key term is likely to continue to be subject to litigation.

An asylum seeker may be recognised as a refugee and granted asylum, not recognised as a refugee but granted humanitarian protection and discretionary leave, or not recognised as a refugee and required to leave the United Kingdom. If recognised as a refugee, the individual is entitled to settle permanently in the United Kingdom (settlement). If the person is granted leave to remain in the United Kingdom, settlement can be applied for after he has lived in the United Kingdom for five years. Once a person is recognised as a refugee or given leave to remain, they become entitled to apply for social security support and their NASS support will end.

■ Provision of support

Support may be provided for asylum seekers and their dependants who satisfy the criteria in s. 95 of the Immigration and Asylum Act 1999:

s. 95(1) ▷

> The Secretary of State may provide, or arrange for the provision of, support for –
> (a) asylum seekers, or
> (b) dependants of asylum seekers,
> who appear to the Secretary of State to be destitute or to be likely to become destitute within such period as may be prescribed.
>
> (IAA 1999)

Support is provided by the NASS; the prescribed period is 14 days. Destitute is further defined. A person is destitute if:

s. 95(3)

> (a) he does not have adequate accommodation or any means of obtaining it (whether or not his other essential living needs are met); or
> (b) he has adequate accommodation or the means of obtaining it, but cannot meet his other essential living needs.
>
> (IAA 1999)

Destitution is a subjective matter and the Secretary of State has a power rather than a duty to support asylum seekers who appear destitute. In providing accommodation, s. 97 directs that the Secretary of State (operating through the NASS) may not have regard to any preference of the asylum seeker or his dependants as to locality. Support can be refused if the person is intentionally destitute. The section below on social services responsibilities outlines the position where a person is not only destitute but has other needs.

■ The application process

Decisions on asylum claims are taken by the Home Office Immigration and Nationality Directorate. Relevant factors which will be considered include the political situation in the asylum seeker's country of origin, the human rights record of that country, and in some cases evidence of torture and abuse. Medical reports may be required for cases involving allegations of torture. The applicant must satisfy the definition of refugee set out in the 1951 Convention. Application is made on a 'Statement of Evidence Form', which runs to 19 pages and must be completed in English. Without support this will be very difficult for many asylum seekers and there are a limited number of legal and other advisers with expertise in this field. Section 70 of the NIAA 2002 provides for asylum seekers to spend the first 14 days living at a place where they will receive an induction programme, and after that they can be required to live at an accommodation centre.

During the induction process all claimants receive an Application Registration Card (ARC), containing their personal details. The card will act as an identity card, incorporating a photograph and the asylum seeker's fingerprints, name, date of birth, nationality, language and dependents.

Once an individual has made a claim for asylum, it will usually not be possible to remove him and his dependent spouse and children until the claim is determined (IAA 1999, s. 15).

Timing of application

Economic support may be withdrawn from asylum seekers who do not make their claim for asylum at the first opportunity. It is vital that applications are made swiftly because, under AIA 2004, s. 55, local authorities will only provide support to an asylum seeker who has applied for asylum 'as soon as reasonably practicable' after arriving in the United Kingdom. In reality, this almost always means immediately on arrival, or at least within the first 72 hours. Exceptions apply in cases where the asylum seeker has a dependent child living in the same household or if support is required to avoid a breach of the ECHR.

This provision was challenged, and the House of Lords gave its judgment in a combined appeal, in *R (Limbuela)* v. *Secretary of State for the Home Department* [2005] UKHL 66. Exclusion from NASS support under s. 55 left an asylum seeker sleeping rough in winter with no food or accommodation and no access to washing or toilet facilities. The House of Lords confirmed the decision of the Court of Appeal and stated that in the circumstances it was a breach of Art. 3 ECHR (inhumane and degrading treatment) to deny support to such a person who made a late application for asylum. NASS would have to consider all relevant facts and circumstances, including whether the person was male or female, their age and the length of time they had spent or might spend without support.

Exhibit 20.1 outlines the stages in the application process.

Accommodation

Whilst waiting for a decision on their asylum application, an asylum seeker and his dependents may be provided with accommodation by the NASS. The asylum seeker is offered no choice over the accommodation but it should reach a basic minimum standard. In order to ease the burden on London, Kent and the South East, as the areas that accommodated most asylum seekers before the 1999 Act, asylum seekers are now dispersed to cluster areas around the rest of the United Kingdom. The cluster area to which they are dispersed should be appropriate to their language and culture, but the asylum seeker cannot actually choose the area. However, in *R (Blackwood)* v. *Secretary of State for the Home Department* [2003] EWHC 97 (Admin), it was a breach of article 8 to send a woman (and her child) who had been brought up in London and had family there to a cluster area out of London. This was an unusual case, as the woman was seeking asylum having lived and become settled in London for some years. Regulations provide that an asylum seeker must not be absent from his accommodation for more than seven consecutive days and nights without permission or 14 days and nights within any six-month period. The accommodation offered is coordinated by the NASS but may actually be provided by private landlords, housing associations or local authorities. NASS housing inspectors check the standard of accommodation, but it need only be adequate and of a similar standard to temporary accommodation.

The NIAA 2002 introduced 'accommodation centres' which provide services (including food and essentials, healthcare and education) and accommodation to asylum seekers in one place. The maximum period an asylum seeker can be in an accommodation centre is six months (extendable by a further three months) (s. 25). An Accommodation Advisory Group will be appointed (s. 33) and has the power to visit the centre at any time.

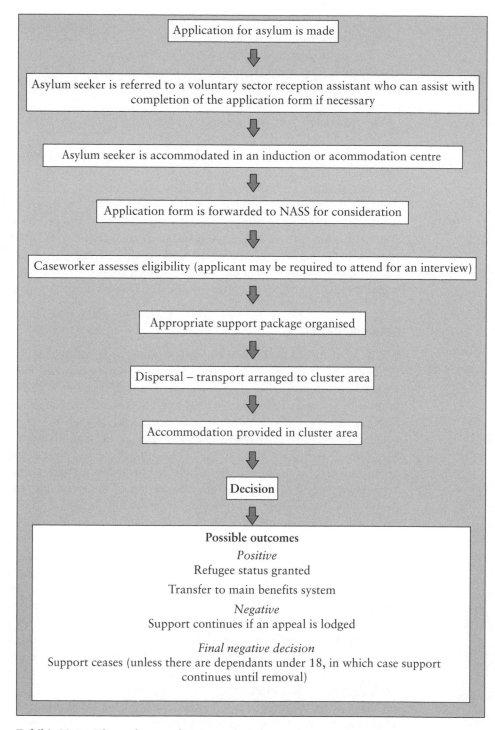

Exhibit 20.1   The asylum application process

Financial support

Support for asylum seekers' essential living needs was originally provided in the form of vouchers, which could be exchanged for necessities at specified shops and outlets. One of the objectives behind introduction of the voucher system and denial of welfare benefits was to act as a deterrent to asylum seekers with unfounded claims. The steady rise in the numbers of asylum seekers coming to this country would suggest that such an objective was not met and indeed challenges the assumption that asylum seekers were motivated to come to the United Kingdom for the cash benefits system. The voucher system was heavily criticised as discriminatory and stigmatising, and various organisations including the Refugee Council successfully campaigned for its abolition. Subsistence payments are now made, at a rate which is equivalent to about 70 per cent of income support rates. Where support is granted, it continues until the exhaustion of the application and appeal process, and for 21 days afterwards.

Appeals

The appeals system established by the 1999 Act was repealed by the 2002 Act. There is now one right of appeal against any of a list of immigration decisions (NIAA 2002, s. 82)

The key ground for appeal is contained in s. 84(1)(g) in the following terms: 'removal of the appellant from the United Kingdom in consequence of the immigration decision would breach the United Kingdoms obligations under the Refugee Convention or would be unlawful under section 6 of the Human Rights Act 1998 as being incompatible with the appellant's Convention rights'. The time limits for appeals are fairly tight and may not sufficiently accommodate the need to obtain specialist legal advice. Appeals are made to Asylum Support Adjudicators.

The 2002 Act allows for the Home Secretary to require the asylum seeker to return to a safe country he travelled through to arrive in the United Kingdom, and appeal from that country.

Removal of support

Schedule 3 to the NIAA 2002 removed the right to a range of defined services for failed asylum seekers. Services include accommodation, social services and promoting welfare under the Local Government Act 2000. Services to families with dependent children could still be provided until their removal from the United Kingdom. The AIA 2004, s. 9 takes that a stage further, with the insertion of a new paragraph into the Schedule. It allows financial support and accommodation to be removed from failed asylum seekers, who have exhausted their appeal rights, if it is considered that they are failing to take reasonable steps to leave the United Kingdom voluntarily or to place themselves in a position in which they are able to leave the United Kingdom voluntarily. This includes support to adults provided as part of a package of support for a child, e.g. accommodation provided to a 'child in need' and her family. Support will be withdrawn within 14 days of the Secretary of State certifying that the family has failed to cooperate. The only way in which a local authority will be able to continue to provide support to a family, and provision of accommodation is the crucial factor, is if the authority consider that to fail to do so would be in breach of the families' rights under Art. 3HRA 1998. Following the case of *Limbuela* (removal of support where an application is not made as soon as practicable), it may well be that such a human rights argument would succeed. The provision has been piloted in Leeds, London and Manchester and the Home Office is due to decide, in the face of strong opposition, whether to implement the provision nationally. It is difficult to see how this can be compatible with the Human Rights Act 1998.

There is a limited grant, the hard cases support grant, available to asylum seekers whose application for asylum has been refused, for whom there are no further appeal opportunities and who are unable to leave the country due to physical impediment or exceptional circumstances.

The grant will also be available to an individual who has been granted permission for judicial review of an aspect of his asylum application.

■ Voluntary sector

The voluntary sector plays an important role in the area of asylum. Voluntary organisations (with funding from the NASS) provide 'One Stop Services' for asylum seekers throughout the United Kingdom. The organisations are: Migrant Helpline; Refugee Action; Refugee Arrivals Project; Refugee Council; Scottish Refugee Council; and Welsh Refugee Council. Other voluntary agencies also provide support for asylum seekers but are not funded by the NASS. Asylum Support Advice Workers, from One Stop Services, can assist with applications for NASS support, explain rights and entitlements to asylum seekers and coordinate emergency accommodation.

■ Human Rights Act 1998 implications

There are a number of possible violations of the Articles contained in the European Convention on Human Rights in the area of asylum.[15] The Human Rights Act 1998 provides an opportunity to challenge the actions of the NASS, if thought to violate the Convention (by their actions or failure to act), because as a public body the NASS is bound to act in compliance with the Convention.[16] Appeals may be made where an individual alleges a breach of their human rights in connection with their asylum application.

The removal of an asylum seeker to a country where he is likely to face the death sentence could be a violation of Art. 2, the right to life. Article 3 contains an absolute prohibition against inhuman or degrading treatment, punishment or torture. Racial harassment may amount to inhuman and degrading treatment.[17] Again, removal of an asylum seeker to a country where he is likely, for example, to be tortured could be a violation. Article 5 provides the right to liberty and security, other than in specified circumstances in accordance with a legal procedure. The Article also provides for regular reviews of detention and speedy challenges to detention. This Article was relied on in a challenge by four Iraqi Kurdish asylum seekers who were detained for up to ten days in the Oakington Reception Centre whilst they were interviewed and decisions were taken on their claims. The High Court found that detention was lawful under domestic law but did breach Art. 5. The Court of Appeal, however, reversed the decision, allowing the Home Secretary's appeal. The exception in Art. 5(1)(f), 'the lawful arrest or detention of a person to prevent his effecting an unauthorised entry into the country or of a person against whom action is being taken with a view to deportation or extradition', applied and permitted detention whilst the state considered whether to authorise entry. The Court of Appeal decision is reported as *R (Saadi)* v. *Secretary of State for the Home Department* [2002] UKHL 41.

Article 6 provides for fair hearings by an independent tribunal. The independence of Asylum Support Adjudicators may be questioned, as they are appointed and financed by the Home Office. Also, support under IAA 1999, s. 95 has been found to be a civil right under ECHR, Art. 6 in the case of *R (Husain)* v. *Asylum Support Adjudicator* [2001] EWHC Admin 852. It was also noted in this decision that withdrawal of support could amount to inhuman and degrading treatment under Art. 3. Article 8 is a limited article, which provides the right to respect for private and family life. Any interference with this right must be proportionate. It may be argued that the dispersal policy could interfere with Art. 8 if, for example, its effect would be to move an asylum seeker away from a supportive base of friends and family (*Abdi* v. *Secretary of State for the Home Department* [1996] Imm AR 148). Article 14 relates to prevention of discrimination in enjoyment of the rights contained in the Articles. It is arguable that the provision of vouchers rather than cash could breach this Article when an asylum seeker's position is compared with others in receipt of welfare benefits.

Social services responsibilities

The majority of support for asylum seekers is now provided by the NASS. Beyond transitional support for asylum seekers whose application was lodged before the new Act came into force, three important areas, however, remain within the responsibility of local authorities: support for unaccompanied children; support for accompanied children who have needs for support not arising from destitution; and support for adults which is required not as a result of destitution. Some local authorities have specialist social services teams working in this area, e.g. Kensington and Chelsea has an Asylum Team and an Unaccompanied Minors Team.[18]

▪ Unaccompanied children

Social Services, rather than the NASS, are responsible for asylum seeking unaccompanied children. In addition to social services support, on entry to the United Kingdom an adviser from the Panel of Advisers for Unaccompanied Children will provide initial short-term support. As at 31 March 2004, there were 2,800 unaccompanied asylum seeking children being looked after, 70 per cent were boys and 30 per cent girls.

Unaccompanied (also sometimes referred to as separated) children are perhaps the most vulnerable of all asylum seekers, 'placed as they are at the intersection of two particularly vulnerable populations – refugees and children'.[19] Both groups, it should be added, are particularly vulnerable to discrimination. This disadvantaged position is acknowledged in Art. 22 of the UN Convention on the Rights of the Child 1989, which provides for the right of children seeking asylum or as refugees to 'appropriate protection and humanitarian assistance'. A Refugee Council Panel of Advisers for Unaccompanied Refugee Children (Children's Panel) was established in the United Kingdom in 1994 to provide independent support for children and counselling. Unaccompanied children are the responsibility of social services once they enter the United Kingdom (see below). Children will not be considered 'unaccompanied' by the Home Office if they have travelled with an adult member of their extended family, i.e. they are not 'unaccompanied' simply because they have travelled without their parents or legal guardians. A preferable interpretation is provided by the Separated Children in Europe Programme, which defines separated children as 'children under 18 years of age who are outside their country of origin and separated from both parents or their legal/customary primary caregiver'.[20] The children's panel adopts a broader definition of an unaccompanied child than that of the Home Office. The panel looks beyond the presence of an adult to consider the suitability of the adult to look after the child.

As a child in need, an unaccompanied asylum seeking child may be entitled to a range of services provided for in Sch. 2 to the Children Act 1989. Services include advice, guidance and counselling, home helps, assistance with travel to access services and occupational, social, cultural or recreational activities. Many unaccompanied children will be 'looked after' by the local authority and provided with accommodation under s. 20.[21] A local authority circular provides that where a child has no parent or guardian in the country there is a presumption that the child will be accommodated under s. 20.[22] The 'Quality Protects' initiative should have a positive impact on outcomes for unaccompanied children in the care of local authorities.[23] The Children (Leaving Care) Act 2000 will also apply, so that support continues after the young person reaches the age of 18 and should ensure that the young person will obtain accommodation in the local authority area rather than being dispersed to another part of the country.

Despite the application of the established framework of the Children Act 1989, the Audit Commission found that unaccompanied children were often receiving lower standards of care than other children in need and only one-third of local authorities produced individual care plans for asylum children in their area. Over one-half of unaccompanied children over the age of 16 were provided with accommodation in hostels and bed and breakfast. A further report produced by the Refugee Council and Save the Children (2001)[24] calls for closer coordination between the Department of Health, Home Office and Department for Education and Skills to improve service delivery. This report also identified as a trend the relatively few unaccompanied children who are successful in obtaining refugee status, noting that instead they are more likely to be awarded exceptional leave to remain, usually up to the age of 18, and may be required to leave the United Kingdom at that age. The results of a mapping exercise on numbers of unaccompanied asylum seeking children in the United Kingdom contained in a report produced by the BAAF and the Refugee Council (2001) are also worthy of note.[25] As with the Save the Children report, particular concerns were expressed about 16- and 17-year-olds, who tend to be treated as having the same needs as adults.

It is established that, for the purposes of support, an unaccompanied child is not classed as an asylum seeker and local authorities are responsible for providing support under s. 17 of the Children Act 1989 to them as 'children in need'. In most cases the local authority will also be bound to provide accommodation under CA 1989, s. 20, it being required due to there being no person with parental responsibility or the child being lost or abandoned. The practical difficulty for local authorities is that in many cases there will be no objective evidence as to the persons age. In *R (B) v Merton London Borough Council* [2003] EWHC 1689 (Admin), the High Court gave guidance to local authorities on how to assess the age of an asylum seeker who may be a child. The factors to be considered include:

- physical appearance and behaviour;
- medical evidence;
- personal history including educational background, ethnic and cultural information;
- documentary evidence, or the lack of.

The court also commented on the need for a fair process. It noted sensible advice contained in 'Practice Guidelines for Age Assessment of Young Unaccompanied Asylum Seekers', being piloted in Hillingdon and Croydon London Boroughs, namely: preference for two age assessment workers; taking account of 'the level of tiredness, trauma, bewilderment and anxiety' of the young person; key focus on ethnicity and culture; adoption of open ended, non-leading questioning; use of interpreters where appropriate; and the young person's understanding of the role of the assessors. If a provisional view is taken that the young person is lying, they must be given the opportunity to address that. The local authority should not simply adopt an earlier assessment, e.g. one undertaken by the Home Office. The local authority must give reasons for its decision, although these need not be long or elaborate. It would be possible for the High Court to interfere with an age assessment if it was one that no reasonable authority could make on the evidence before it.

■ Accompanied children

Accompanied children are excluded by their status from the support provision of the Children Act 1989, s. 17, except that asylum seeking children who have a disability will be covered by the Children Act 1989 definition of a 'child in need' (s. 17).[26] Section 122 of the IAA 1999 states that Social Services Departments may not provide assistance for children in need solely because the child or his family is destitute, so long as the asylum seeker's household (including the child) is entitled to NASS support under IAA 1999, s. 95. Needs not arising from destitution could be supported, e.g. if the child is disabled.

In *R (Ouji) v Secretary of State for the Home Department* [2002] EWHC 1839 (Admin), social services rather than NASS provided support to a 13-year-old asylum seeker in the care of her mother. The girl required additional bedding due to incontinence and suffered from other disabilities.

■ Education

Local education authorities are under a duty to ensure that children who are asylum seekers or refugees receive appropriate education from the age of 5 up to 16, just as any other child in the country is entitled to. They also have equal entitlement to pre-school facilities including playgroups and nurseries. Asylum seeking children qualify for free school meals. In practice, some children may not attend school as the cost of school uniform and transport to the school may be prohibitive. An Audit Commission report found that few local authorities collect information about the number of asylum seeking and refugee children in schools in their area.[27] The Commission recommend that the NASS should advise LEAs of the number of children likely to be placed in the area so that planning enables appropriate support to be provided.

■ Adult asylum seekers

It should be clear from the above discussion that, since 2000, support for asylum seekers has been the domain of the NASS. The position prior to 2000 was different, with asylum seekers entitled to welfare benefits support and housing benefit. Transitional arrangements have allowed local authorities to continue to provide support for individuals who applied for asylum before the creation of the NASS. There should be few people receiving such support now; however, the backlog in claims means that in London there are (at the time of writing) about 57,000 asylum seekers who continue to receive support from local authorities rather than the NASS.[28]

The Immigration and Asylum Act 1999 provides that local authorities are able to provide support in accordance with the arrangements made by the Secretary of State under s. 95 (the section which bases entitlement to support on the destitute test). This enables local authorities to provide support as part of the NASS arrangements, e.g. use of local authority housing stock. In fact, local authorities can be required by s. 100 to cooperate with the Secretary of State in the provision of accommodation under the s. 95 scheme, including providing information about their housing stock. Other local authority functions in relation to asylum seekers (which would have been available before the IAA 1999) have been removed by ss. 116–122. The effect of these provisions is that local authorities will continue to be involved with actual provision of support, but will do so as a NASS resource. In other words, local authorities, in assisting the Secretary of State to carry out his functions, will be secondary not primary providers of support.

▪ Community care

It may be useful to refer back to Chapter 14 for background discussion of the legal framework of community care. Under the terms of the 1996 Act, an asylum seeker who failed to make an immediate claim for asylum at the port of entry was ineligible to claim housing assistance, unlike those who made an immediate claim. This position undoubtedly led to some hardship, and the judiciary intervened to bridge this gap in the case of *R v. Hammersmith and Fulham LBC, ex parte M* (1998) 30 HLR 10. In this case s. 21 of the National Assistance Act 1948 was applied to the case of asylum seekers who failed to claim at the port of entry. The court found that a destitute asylum seeker (not entitled to welfare benefits) could be in need of care and attention not otherwise available under the reference to 'any other circumstances' in s. 21. The court suggested those words could include a lack of food and shelter, and also extended to factors such as inability to speak English, ignorance of the country and the stressful background resulting in the person seeking asylum. A further decision, *R v. Secretary of State for Health, ex parte Hammersmith and Fulham London Borough Council* (1998) 31 HLR 475, limited the application of this principle to payments in kind (such as food parcels) and provision of accommodation, rather than cash payments.

The combined effect of these cases was of clear benefit to asylum seekers and overcame the harsh ruling on immediate claims, but led to concern over the burden placed on local authorities. In response, the Immigration and Asylum Act 1999 amended s. 21 of the National Assistance Act 1948. Section 21 provides that a local authority must make arrangements to provide residential accommodation for people over the age of 18 who, by reason of age, illness, disability or any other circumstances, are in need of care and attention, which is not otherwise available to them. The amendment provides:

s. 21

> (1A) A person to whom section 115 of the Immigration and Asylum Act 1999 (exclusion from benefits) applies may not be provided with residential accommodation under subsection (1)(a) if his need for care and attention has arisen solely –
> (a) because he is destitute; or
> (b) because of the physical effects, or anticipated physical effects, of his being destitute.
>
> (NAA 1948, as amended)

Asylum seekers are people to whom s. 115 of the IAA 1999 applies. Asylum seekers applying under the new scheme provided by the IAA 1999 are excluded from benefits provision.

R (Westminster City Council) v. *National Asylum Support Service* [2001] EWCA Civ 512, is now the leading decision on interpretation of this section. Mrs Y-Ahmed, an Iraqi Kurd asylum seeker, was destitute and suffered from a spinal myeloma. The Social Services Department assessed her as needing assistance with mobility and personal care and accommodation with disabled access. The authority argued that as

Mrs Ahmed and her 13-year-old daughter were entitled to NASS support, it followed that care and attention was otherwise available to her; meaning she was not entitled to assistance under the National Assistance Act 1948. The NASS argued that she was not destitute because she had the means of obtaining accommodation through her entitlement under the National Assistance Act 1948, and she was therefore not entitled to asylum support. The Court of Appeal decided that the local authority were in fact responsible for meeting Mrs Ahmed's needs. Her need for care and attention did not arise solely because of her destitution or the effects of it. From this interpretation, it followed that s. 21(1A) of the National Assistance Act 1948 (inserted by the IAA 1999) did not exclude her from assistance under the National Assistance Act 1948. Destitute asylum seekers would have their needs met under the NASS, but would also be entitled to community care services if their needs for care and attention exist, even if in funds. This is a significant judgment, which Simon Brown LJ recognises 'raises an interesting and important question concerning the support of a particular category of asylum seeker. The category in question are those who are not merely destitute (that is, without adequate accommodation and/or the means of meeting their other essential living needs) but who in addition have community care needs.'[29]

The House of Lords judgment in this case, reported as *Westminster City Council v. National Asylum Support Service* [2002] UKHL 38, confirmed that the council was liable to provide accommodation to the asylum seeker under the responsibilities to provide accommodation imposed by the National Assistance Act 1948, s. 21. Lord Hoffmann stated that the 'infirm destitute' remain the responsibility of social services where they are in need of 'care and attention' under s. 21, as opposed to the 'able bodied destitute for whom NASS has a residual responsibility' under the IAA 1999, s. 95. He suggested further that if the local authority has a duty to provide accommodation under s. 21, NASS has no power to provide support.

In a further case, *R (Mani)* v. *Lambeth London Borough Council* [2003] EWCA Civ 836, the Court of Appeal confirmed that a disabled asylum seeker was entitled to care and attention under s. 21 of the National Assistance Act 1948, to meet needs arising from his disability.

It can be concluded that, whilst the majority of support is now provided by the NASS, asylum seekers may still be entitled to some support from the local authority and other organisations based on characteristics other than destitution. Community care legislation (as outlined in Chapter 14) therefore does apply to some asylum seekers.

■ Mental health

The Mental Health Act 1983 applies to asylum seekers as it does to other residents in the United Kingdom. If an asylum seeker is suffering from one of the categories of mental disorder contained in the Mental Health Act 1983,[30] in certain circumstances he may be admitted compulsorily (sectioned) to mental hospital, or made the subject of a guardianship order.[31] Where a person is detained in hospital under the Mental Health Act 1983, he cannot be removed (for deportation, for example) without the approval of a Mental Health Review Tribunal (*X* v. *Secretary of State for the Home Department* [2001] 1 WLR 740). The after-care provisions of the 1983 Act will apply when the person ceases to be detained or subject to guardianship.[32]

■ National Health Service

Medical treatment provided by the National Health Service is available to asylum seekers (and any dependants) whether they are awaiting a decision, appealing, awaiting deportation, granted refugee status or exceptional leave to remain. This includes the right to register with a GP. Most asylum seekers will also be exempt from prescription charges and related benefits. An interpreter should be provided by the health service where required.[33]

Chapter summary

- The law relating to asylum seekers is now contained principally in the Immigration and Asylum Act 1999, as amended by the Nationality, Immigration and Asylum Act 2002 and Asylum and Immigration (Treatment of claimants, etc.) Act 2004.

- A person who applies for asylum is known as an asylum seeker. A person whose application for asylum is successful is then classed as a refugee, having satisfied the 1951 Geneva Convention definition of refugee. A person who is not granted refugee status may nevertheless be granted 'exceptional leave to remain' in the country.

- The IAA 1999 introduced a new system for the support of asylum seekers. The system is administered by a new organisation, the National Asylum Support Service (NASS). Previous arrangements for the support of asylum seekers, in the form of welfare benefits and direct local authority support, have ceased to be available to any asylum seekers entering the country since the NASS was established.

- Where an asylum seeker (and his dependants) is found to be 'destitute' the NASS will provide support whilst a decision on the asylum seeker's application is reached. Support may be in the form of accommodation, subsistence for essential living needs or a combination of subsistence and accommodation. Initially, asylum seekers may be accommodated in 'induction centres'. Asylum seekers will be dispersed to accommodation in cluster areas throughout the country, away from London and the South East.

- Unaccompanied children seeking asylum remain the responsibility of Social Services Departments, as children in need. The sections of the Children Act 1989 relating to provision of support will apply, as will the Children (Leaving Care) Act 2000.

- Adult asylum seekers may also be entitled to local authority support under the community care provisions if they have needs which have not arisen solely as a result of their destitution.

- Support may be denied if an application for asylum is not made 'as soon as practicable' upon entering the country.

Exercise

Julianna is 15 and has lived all her life in a village in Kosovo. She witnessed the rape of her mother, her village was burnt down and she does not know what happened to her sister or her parents. She stayed with a family friend, Hugo, in the next village for one month but travelled to England with him and his daughter, Liza, in fear of their safety. Liza is 8 years old and was born physically disabled as a result of spina bifida. On entry to the United Kingdom they have only the clothes they are wearing and the equivalent of about £30. Hugo thinks that his uncle is living in London but cannot get a response from the telephone number he has. They are told initially that Julianna will stay in London and is likely to be accommodated in a hostel, whereas Hugo and Liza will be dispersed to Yorkshire. Julianna is terrified that she will be alone and separated from Hugo and Liza, the only people she knows from home. Hugo wishes to remain in London so that Liza will be able to access the medical support she needs.

Consider the type of support that should be provided to Julianna, Hugo and Liza and which agencies will be involved.

Websites

The Refugee Council provides advice and support to asylum seekers and refugees, campaigns on asylum issues and produces a range of reports and other publications:
www.refugeecouncil.org.uk

The Home Office site has an asylum and immigration section. It publishes statistical bulletins and NASS bulletins:
www.ind.homeoffice.gov.uk

The Home Office has launched a separate website for the 'National Refugee Integration Forum' established in 2000 and comprising representatives of public and voluntary sector. The Forum advises the Government on the development of the National Refugee Integration Strategy for England, 'Integration Matters':
www.nrif.org.uk

Separated Children in Europe website:
www.separated-children-europe-programme.org

Joint Council for the Welfare of Immigrants:
www.jcwi.org.uk

The UK Immigration Advisory Service,
www.iasuk.org.

Further reading

Hayes, D. and Humphries, B. (2004) *Social Work, Immigration and Asylum: Debates, Dilemmas and Ethical Issues for Social Work and Social Care Practice.* London: Jessica Kingsley Publishers.

A number of publications focus on the special position of asylum seeking children:

Rutter, J. (2003) *Supporting refugee children in 21st century Britain* (2nd edn). Stoke-on-Trent: Trentham Books.

Ayotte, W. and Williamson, L. (2001) *Separated Children in the UK: An overview of the current situation.* London: Save the Children and Refugee Council.

Kohli, R. (2006) 'The comfort of strangers: social work practice with unaccompanied asylum-seeking children and young people in the UK' 11 *Child and Family Social Work,* p. 1. (Considers social work practice (as criticised in a number of reports) in the complex area of resettlement of unaccompanied minors.)

Russell, S. (1999) *Most Vulnerable of All: The Treatment of Unaccompanied Children in the UK.* London: Amnesty International.

Coker, J., Finch, N. and Stanley, A. (2002) *Putting Children First: a guide for immigration practitioners.* London: Legal Action Group.

Williams, L. (2004) 'Refugees and asylum seekers as a group at risk of adult abuse' 6(4) *Journal of Adult Protection* p. 4. (This paper highlights the vulnerability of refugees to abuse and relates the forms of abuse contained in 'No Secrets' (see Chapter 17) to their situation, with strategies to reduce vulnerability.)

More general guides to asylum are listed below. Note, however, that the most recent changes in legislation and practice may not be included:

Cohen, S. (2001) *Immigration Controls, the Family and the Welfare State.* London: Jessica Kingsley Publishers.

Harvey, C. (2000) *Seeking Asylum in the UK: Problems and Prospects.* London: Butterworths.

Willman, S., Knafler, S. and Pierce, S. (2001) *Support for Asylum Seekers: a guide to legal and welfare rights.* London: Legal Action Group.

Symes, M. and Jorro, P. (2002) *The Law Relating to Asylum in the UK.* London: Butterworths.

Notes

[1] Asylum and Immigration Appeals Act 1993; Asylum and Immigration Act 1996; Immigration and Asylum Act 1999; Nationality, Immigration and Asylum Act 2002; Asylum and Immigration (Treatment of Claimants, etc.) Act 2004.

[2] Home Office (1998) 'Fairer, Faster and Firmer – A Modern Approach to Immigration and Asylum' (Cm. 4018). London: The Stationery Office.

3 Home Office (2002) 'Secure Borders, Safe Haven: Integration with Diversity in Modern Britain' (Cm. 5387). London: The Stationery Office.

4 D. Stevens (2004) *UK Asylum Law and Policy: Historical and Contemporary Perspectives*. London: Sweet Maxwell, p. 164.

5 Michael Howard, HC Official Report, vol. 268, series 6, col. 699 (11 December 1995) cited in E. Shorts and C. de Than (2002) *Human Rights Law in the UK*. London: Sweet & Maxwell.

6 D. Stevens (2001) 'The Immigration and Asylum Act 1999: A missed opportunity?' 64(3) *Modern Law Review* p. 413.

7 L.M. Clements (2001) 'Changing the support system for asylum seekers' 23(2) *Journal of Social Welfare and Family Law* p. 173.

8 P. Shah (2000) *Refugees, Race and the Legal Concept of Asylum in Britain*. London: Cavendish Publishing, p. 1.

9 C. Harvey (2000) *Seeking Asylum in the UK: Problems and Prospects*. London: Butterworths.

10 Under the Immigration and Asylum Act 1999.

11 Interpretation of the definition varies between different countries.

12 The Convention was initially restricted to European nationals. It was amended by the 1967 Protocol to have worldwide application.

13 Geneva Convention Relating to the Status of Refugees, Art. 1A(2).

14 Per Lord Steyn at p. 635.

15 See Separated Children in Europe website: www.sce.gla.ac.uk.

16 Human Rights Act 1998, s. 6.

17 See decision of the Asylum Support Adjudicators 00/12/0135.

18 See www.rckc.gov.uk/SocialServices/RefugeesAsylum/.

19 J. Bhabha (2001) 'Minors or aliens? Inconsistent state intervention and separated child asylum-seekers' 3(3) *European Journal of Migration and Law* p. 283.

20 For a fuller discussion of the Human Rights Act 1998, see Chapter 2.

21 See Chapter 7 for discussion of responsibilities towards looked after children.

22 LAC (2003) 13

23 Department of Health (1999) *The Government's Objectives for Children's Social Services*. London: Department of Health.

24 W. Ayotte and L. Williamson (2001) *Separated Children in the UK: An overview of the current situation*. London: Save the Children and Refugee Council.

25 BAAF and Refugee Council (2001) *Where are the children?*. London: Refugee Council.

26 See further discussion in Chapter 5.

27 Audit Commission (2000) 'A New City. Supporting Asylum Seekers and Refugees in London'. London: Audit Commission Publications.

28 S. Willman (2001) 'No change for asylum-seekers?' *Legal Action*, December, p. 8.

29 (2001) 4 CCLR 142 at p. 145B.

30 Section 1 defines the categories of mental disorder, mental illness, mental impairment, severe mental impairment and psychopathic disorder.

31 MHA 1983, s. 2 (admission for assessment), s. 3 (admission for treatment) and s. 7 (guardianship).

32 MHA 1983, s. 117.

33 See further HC (82) 15 and HSC 1999/018.

Glossary

Throughout the text the reader will notice occasional use of latin and technical legal terminology. I have attempted to limit this use being a supporter of the movement for plain speaking. There remain some situations, however, where certain terms which might not be part of everyday usage are still used regularly by lawyers or appear in legal documents. In order to be competent in legal settings and in dialogue with lawyers, an understanding of these terms is essential. Other terms and phrases which feature in *Social Work Law* are also included for ease of reference. This glossary attempts to provide clear explanations of terms in the context of social work practice. Terms used are defined consistently with their use in this book, therefore the definitions listed below may not appear as it would in a pure law dictionary

Ab initio from the beginning

Adoption Agency the body authorised to provide adoption services, either a function of the local authority or a voluntary agency

Affidavit a written sworn statement – now referred to as a 'Statement of Truth'

Affirmation evidence given in court by a person who objects to swearing an oath

Amicus curiae friend of the court

Antecedents previous convictions and other information provided to the criminal court

Appeal complaint to a superior court on the basis of 'injustice' by a lower court, e.g. against conviction

Appellant person making an appeal

Approved social worker a social worker with a recognised qualification in mental health, invested with a range of powers and duties under the Mental Health Act 1983

Asylum Seeker a person waiting for a decision on their application for asylum

Attorney person appointed to carry out wishes of another

Attorney General principal law officer, brings prosecutions on behalf of the Crown

Balance of probabilities the civil standard of proof

Barrister a lawyer who typically specialises in court advocacy – also referred to as counsel

Beneficiary person entitled under a will or trust

Beyond reasonable doubt the criminal standard of proof

Breach violation (usually of a right)

Burden of proof the responsibility to prove a point to the satisfaction of the court, often expressed as, he who alleges must prove

Care management in community care the term encompasses the process of assessment, provision of services and review or reassessment

Care programme approach a term which embraces the provision of services to people with mental health difficulties living in the community

Cause of action the basis of a civil case, the reason for suing

Children and family reporter a social work professional who provides reports to the court in private family proceedings – previously referred to as the court welfare officer

Children's guardian an independent officer who represents a child in court, part of the CAFCASS organisation (formerly known as a guardian ad litem)

Children's services authorities those authorities with social services functions, i.e. county, metropolitan and unitary councils

Children's trust an arrangement where services for children and young people in an area are collectively organised into a children's trust with the objective of working together to improve outcomes for children and young people

Codification drawing legislation in an area of law, e.g. criminal or family, into a code

Common law Case law, principles of law which can be extracted from decisions of courts of law

Community order a single generic sentencing option including a range of possible requirements, e.g. compulsory work. Replaces the community punishment order and community rehabilitation order

Compellable refers to a witness who may be forced to attend court

Competent being legally able to give evidence

Concurrent system of jurisdiction where the same types of cases can be delat within different levels of the court system

Consolidation bringing together fragmented pieces of legislation on the same topic into one statute

Contract a legal agreement

Counsel another term for a barrister

Cross examination evidence given in response to questions from the opponents advocate, which will challenge evidence already given 'in chief' and may attempt to discredit the witness

De facto in fact, actual

De minimus minimal or minor

Disclosure providing evidence to the other parties to a case, e.g. exchanging witness statements

Doli incapax the principle that a child of a certain age is incapable of committing an offence

Duty a mandatory obligation to carry out a particular function, something which the authority shall do

Education supervision order an order under s. 36 of the Children Act 1989 which may be made where there are concerns that a young person is not being properly educated

Examination-in-chief presenting oral evidence in court in response to questions from the advocate that calls the witness

Exceptional leave to remain an asylum seeker may be granted exceptional leave to remain and allowed to settle in the UK in circumstances where he is not recognised as a refugee

Ex gratia without charge or return

Ex officio by virtue of an official position

Ex parte an application made to court without giving notice to the other party, usually referred to as without notice

Fact in issue a point which parties to a case cannot agree upon and requires evidential proof

Family proceedings court the branch of the magistrates court which deals with family and child care issues

Green paper a command paper presented to government containing proposals for consultation

Guardian ad litem term replaced by 'children's guardian' with the introduction of CAFCASS. An independent person who reports to the court as to the best interests of the child

Habeus corpus literally you have the body, a remedy which can challenge legality of detention and order release

Hansard the official record of parliamentary proceedings

In camera a legal hearing which is held in private (press and public excluded)

Independent medical capacity advocate

Independent review mechanism a new review process under which prospective adopters may apply for a review of a decision not to recommend them as suitable to adopt

Indictment the official document in the Crown Court which contains the allegation (against the accused)

Injunction a court order which requires a person to do or refrain from doing a particular thing, e.g. non molestation injunction

In loco parentis in the position of a parent, see s. 5(3) Children Act 1989

Inter alia among other things

Inter parties between the parties

Intra vires within the powers that are legally given to the body in question, i.e. acting lawfully

Lasting power of attorney introduced by the Mental Capacity Act 2005 to replace the Enduring Power of Attorney, the LPA permits a person with capacity to appoint an attorney(s) to take decisions on their behalf, relating to health, welfare and financial matters, if they subsequently lose capacity

Liability legal responsibility for actions. Liability may be personal or vicarious, for example a residential home owner may be vicariously liable for the actions of staff employed there

Litigant in person a person who conducts a legal case without legal representation

Locus standi standing, the right to appear and be heard by a court on a particular matter

Mandamus a High Court order made in judicial review cases which orders action to be taken

National Asylum Support Service the body set up in 2000 to provide support and accommodation to asylum seekers whilst their claim for asylum is being considered

Natural justice more commonly referred to as fairness. The entitlement to the law applying fairly in accordance with its basic principles such as the right to make representations and to know of any allegations made against you, in order to have a fair hearing

Negligence a tort based on three principles: the existence of a duty of care, breach of that duty and damage resulting from the breach

No case to answer a submission made by the defence in a criminal case that the prosecution have failed to establish the existence of a case against the accused

No order principle the principle contained in the Children Act 1989 s. 1(2) that there should be a positive benefit to the child in making a formal court order

Obiter dicta things said by the way in a legal judgement, not binding comments

Ombudsman (Local Government) the local government ombudsman investigates complaints of injustice arising from maladministration by local authorities

Parens patriae 'parent of the country' the jurisdiction which used to be exercisable by the crown to safeguard adults who lacked mental capacity

Parental bindovers parent enters into a recognisance to ensure juvenile is of good behaviour and keeps the peace

Parental responsibility the term which replaces 'parental rights and duties' and is intended to encapsulate the areas in which a parent can exercise responsibility towards their child. Defined in the Children Act 1989 s. 3

Per in the opinion of, in the judgement of

Per curiam in the opinion of the court

Per se by itself

Petition an application for divorce

Power a discretion to act, often expressed as something which may be done

Precedent the principle by which decisions of the higher courts bind the lower courts so that case law develops consistently

Prima facie at first sight, on the face of it

Pro bono work carried out by solicitors and barristers free of charge

Proportionality the principle applicable to human rights that any intervention or violation of rights should be necessary and proportionate in relation to the matter in question

Public law law in which society has an interest, such as care proceedings, or law concerning constitutional matters

Private law the law which operates between individuals, e.g. contract

Ratio decidendi the principle of law on which a case is decided

Re-examination the final opportunity for a witness to present evidence to their own advocates questions. Limited to matters arising out of cross examination

Refocusing debate a debate which grew out of research findings was prevalent in the 1990s and signalled greater emphasis on preventative child care work rather than child protection

Refugee a person whose application for asylum has been granted

Remedy law deals with a situation by providing a remedy, e.g. compensation

Responsible medical officer (RMO) The doctor in hospital (mental health) with particular responsibility for the patient

Restricted patient a patient subject to a restriction order made by the Crown Court when a hospital order is made in respect of an offender

Revision of statutes, a process of updating law

Royal Assent a bill becomes an Act when it receives Royal assent

School Attendance Orders an order issued by the LEA where it is not satisfied that a child is receiving a suitable education either by regular attendance at school or otherwise

Section 8 orders a range of orders provided for in section 8 of the Children Act 1989 which deal with aspects of the exercise of parental responsibility, namely, residence, contact, specific issue and prohibited steps orders

Shared Residence Arrangements following parental separation a child spends more or less equal time with each parent and a residence order may be made in favour of both parents

Solicitors members of the legal profession (in addition to barristers). Solicitors provide legal advice and undertake advocacy (mainly in the lower courts)

Special guardians person(s) appointed under a Special Guardianship Order (introduced by the Adoption and Children Act 2002) to have parental responsibility for a child

Special measures measures introduced by the Youth Justice and Criminal Evidence Act 1999 to assist vulnerable witnesses in court, e.g. giving evidence by video link

Standard of proof the level to which a case must be proven. In Criminal Matters it is beyond reasonable doubt, in civil matters it is on a balance of probabilities

Statement of truth a formal sworn statement of evidence (formerly known as an affidavit)

Statutory instrument secondary legislation in the form of rules and regulations made alongside an Act and often providing additional detail

Supervised discharge or 'after care under supervision' is an arrangement made where after care with requirements (e.g. where a patient lives) for people who have been detained under the Mental Health Act 1983

Sub nom also named. For example the case, Re H (Minors) (Sexual Abuse: Standard of Proof) [1996] 2 WLR 8, *sub nom* (or also known as) Re H and R (Child Sexual Abuse: Standard of Proof) [1996] 1 FLR 80, HL

Tariff the minimum sentence period that must be served before consideration for early release

Tort the law of civil wrongs, including tresspass to the person, negligence, defamation and harassment

Twin track an approach which incorporates concurrent planning for adoption and rehabilitation to birth parents where foster carers are also approved as adopters should attempts at rehabilitation fail

Ultra vires outside the powers given to the body in question, i.e. unlawful action

White paper a command paper presented to Parliament, contains an authoritative statement of Government policy (may follow a green paper)

Witness summons an order which calls a person to attend court as a witness (previously called a *subpoena*)

Youth justice plans an annual plan prepared by the local authority in consultation with other bodies which sets out how youth justice services are to be provided in the area

Youth justice services a range of services to be provided by local authorities and probation stipulated in s. 38(4) Crime and Disorder Act 1998, e.g. provision of appropriate adults, support for juveniles awaiting trial, provision of court reports

Youth offender teams multi disciplinary teams which coordinate provision of youth justice services

Index